Prisoner Reentry in the 21st Century

This groundbreaking edited volume evaluates prisoner reentry using a critical approach to demonstrate how the many issues surrounding reentry do not merely intersect but are in fact reinforcing and interdependent. The number of former incarcerated persons with a felony conviction living in the United States has grown significantly in the last decade, reaching into the millions. When men and women are released from prison, their journey encompasses a range of challenges that are unique to each individual, including physical and mental illnesses, substance abuse, gender identity, complicated family dynamics, the denial of rights, and the inability to voice their experiences about returning home.

Although scholars focus on the obstacles former prisoners encounter and how to reduce recidivism rates, the main challenge of prisoner reentry is how multiple interdependent issues overlap in complex ways. By examining prisoner reentry from various critical perspectives, this volume depicts how the carceral continuum, from incarceration to reentry, negatively impacts individuals, families, and communities; how the criminal justice system extends different forms of social control that break social networks; and how the shifting nature of prisoner reentry has created new and complicated obstacles to those affected by the criminal justice system. This volume explores these realities with respect to a range of social, community, political, and policy issues that former incarcerated persons must navigate to successfully reenter society.

A springboard for future critical research and policy discussions, this book will be of interest to U.S. and international researchers and practitioners interested in the topic of prisoner reentry, as well as graduate and upper-level undergraduate students concerned with contemporary issues in corrections, community-based corrections, critical issues in criminal justice, criminal justice policies, and reentry.

Keesha M. Middlemass, Ph.D., is an associate professor of public policy in the Department of Political Science at Howard University in Washington, D.C. She specializes in studying race, reentry, food insecurity, and public policies using interdisciplinary frameworks to integrate knowledge from different disciplines and across multiple data sources, including participant observations, in-depth interviews, focus groups, policy analysis, and archival research. Her most recent book, *Convicted & Condemned: The Politics and Policies of Prisoner Reentry*, won the W.E.B. DuBois Distinguished Book Award in 2018. Her research is also published in *Public Health Nutrition, International Journal of Eating Disorders, Aggressive Behavior, Criminal Justice & Behavior, The Prison Journal*, and *Punishment & Society*. Dr. Middlemass is a member of the Racial Democracy, Crime and Justice Network, a former Andrew Mellon Post-Doctoral Fellow on Race, Crime, and Justice at the Vera Institute of Justice in New York City, and a former American Political Science Association Congressional Fellow. Dr. Middlemass earned her Ph.D. in public policy, American politics, and public administration from The School of Public & International Affairs at the University of Georgia.

CalvinJohn Smiley, Ph.D., is an assistant professor of sociology in the Department of Sociology at Hunter College-City of New York (CUNY). He specializes in studying race, reentry, and citizenship. His work is published in numerous peer-reviewed journals such as: *The Prison Journal, Race Ethnicity and Education, Punishment & Society, Deviant Behavior, Journal of Human Behavior in the Social Environment*, and *Contemporary Justice Review*. He is currently working on a book manuscript based on his research on reentry that explores the various ways men and women navigate the reentry process with diminished legal rights and amplified social stigmas. His future work will investigate the role of human and nonhuman interactions, particularly in carceral settings (e.g., prison-based animal therapy programs). Dr. Smiley is a member of the American Sociological Association, American Society of Criminology, and Kappa Alpha Psi Inc. He is the Vice-President of the Board of Trustees of the New Jersey Association on Corrections. Dr. Smiley earned his Ph.D. in Sociology from the CUNY Graduate Center.

Routledge Innovations in Corrections

An emphasis on innovation is evident in the field of corrections. While changes in policies and public opinion regarding sentencing philosophies such as mass incarceration bump up against the reality that budgets continue to be tightened and the division of these revenues is more competitive, innovative strategies become all the more valuable. The premise behind innovation is effecting improvements without sacrificing the overall safety and security of the institution. Through research and evaluation, we seek to identify what works and what does not work.

1. Hallett, *The Angola Prison Seminary: Effects of Faith-Based Ministry on Identity Transformation, Desistance, and Rehabilitation*
2. Shah, *The Role of Rehabilitation within California's Correctional System and its Impact on Parole*
3. Pealer, *Correctional Rehabilitation and Therapeutic Communities: Reducing Recidivism Through Behavior Change*
4. Ward, *Rural Jail Re-entry: Offender Needs and Challenges*
5. Pedlar, *Community Re-Entry: Uncertain Futures for Women Leaving Prison*
6. Cross, *Juvenile Justice and Expressive Arts: Creative Disruptions through Art Programs for and with Teens in a Correctional Institution*
7. Roush, *Recalibrating Juvenile Detention: Lessons Learned from the Court-Ordered Reform of the Cook County Juvenile Temporary Detention Center*
8. Middlemass and Smiley, *Prisoner Reentry in the 21st Century: Critical Perspectives of Returning Home*

Prisoner Reentry in the 21st Century

Critical Perspectives of Returning Home

Edited by
Keesha M. Middlemass
and CalvinJohn Smiley

NEW YORK AND LONDON

First published 2020
by Routledge
52 Vanderbilt Avenue, New York, NY 10017

and by Routledge
2 Park Square, Milton Park, Abingdon, Oxon, OX14 4RN

Routledge is an imprint of the Taylor & Francis Group, an informa business

© 2020 Taylor & Francis

The right of Keesha M. Middlemass and CalvinJohn Smiley to be identified as the authors of the editorial material, and of the authors for their individual chapters, has been asserted in accordance with sections 77 and 78 of the Copyright, Designs and Patents Act 1988.

All rights reserved. No part of this book may be reprinted or reproduced or utilized in any form or by any electronic, mechanical, or other means, now known or hereafter invented, including photocopying and recording, or in any information storage or retrieval system, without permission in writing from the publishers.

Trademark notice: Product or corporate names may be trademarks or registered trademarks, and are used only for identification and explanation without intent to infringe.

Library of Congress Cataloging-in-Publication Data
A catalog record for this book has been requested

ISBN: 978-0-8153-5275-4 (hbk)
ISBN: 978-1-351-13824-6 (ebk)

Typeset in Bembo
by Apex CoVantage, LLC

Jerome "Wali" Young

"Wali Barr with the Double R"

November 8, 1952 – September 5, 2015

Contents

List of Tables	xi
List of Contributors	xii

Introduction: Critical Reentry in the 21st Century   1
KEESHA M. MIDDLEMASS AND CALVINJOHN SMILEY

SECTION I
Institutions, Community, and Reentry   11

1 Halfway Home: The Thin Line Between Abstinence
and the Drug Crisis   15
LIAM MARTIN

2 Triaging Rehabilitation: The Retreat of
State-Funded Prison Programming   26
ALLISON GORGA

3 The State's Accomplices? Organizations and the
Penal State   39
NICOLE KAUFMAN

4 Idaho: A Case Study in Rural Reentry   53
DEIRDRE CAPUTO-LEVINE

5 Life Courses of Sex and Violent Offenders After
Prison Release: The Interaction Between Individual-
and Community-Related Factors   66
GUNDA WOESSNER, KIRA-SOPHIE GAUDER, AND DAVID
CZUDNOCHOWSKI

viii Contents

SECTION II
Health, Embodiment, and Reentry 79

6 Mothers Returning Home: A Critical Intersectional
  Approach to Reentry 83
  REBECCA REVIERE, VERNETTA D. YOUNG, AND AKIV DAWSON

7 Release From Long-Term Restrictive Housing 96
  LINDA CARSON

8 Resilient Roads and the Non-Prison Model
  for Women 107
  L. SUSAN WILLIAMS, EDWARD L. W. GREEN, AND KATRINA M. LEWIS

9 Alcohol Use Disorder: Programs and Treatment for
  Offenders Reentering the Community 120
  SARA BUCK DOUDE AND JESSICA J. SPARKS

10 Carceral Calisthenics: (Body) Building a Resilient
   Self and Transformative Reentry Movement 129
   ALBERT DE LA TIERRA

SECTION III
Gender, Criminality, and Reentry 141

11 Black Women Excluded From Protection and
   Criminalized for Their Existence 145
   KEESHA M. MIDDLEMASS

12 The Gendered Challenges of Prisoner Reentry 157
   HALEY ZETTLER

13 An Intersectional Criminology Analysis of Black
   Women's Collective Resistance 172
   NISHAUN T. BATTLE AND JASON M. WILLIAMS

14 Gender Differences in Programmatic Needs for Juveniles 190
   LAURIN PARKER AND KYLIE PARROTTA

15 Prison Is a Place to Teach Us the Things We've
   Never Learned in Life 203
   BREEA WILLINGHAM

Contents ix

SECTION IV
Access, Rights, and Reentry 215

16 "...Except Sex Offenders": Registering Sexual
Harm in the Age of #MeToo 219
DAVID BOOTH

17 Reentry in the Inland Empire: The Prison to
College Pipeline With Project Rebound 232
ANNIKA YVETTE ANDERSON, PAUL ANDREW JONES, AND
CAROLYN ANNE MCALLISTER

18 The Politics of Restoring Voting Rights After
Incarceration 247
TANEISHA N. MEANS AND ALEXANDRA HATCH

19 Restoration of Voting Rights: Returning Citizens
and the Florida Electorate 259
KENESHIA GRANT

20 Perpetual Punishment: One Man's Journey
Post-Incarceration 275
TOMAS R. MONTALVO AND JENNIFER MARIE ORTIZ

SECTION V
Voices, Agency, and Reentry 289

21 Thoughts, Concerns, and the Reality of
Incarcerated Women 293
CALVINJOHN SMILEY, KEESHA M. MIDDLEMASS, AND
INCARCERATED WOMEN

22 Reflections on Reentry: Voices From the ID13
Prison Literacy Project 305
HALLE M. NEIDERMAN, CHRISTOPHER P. DUM, AND THE ID13
PRISON LITERACY PROJECT

23 Being Held at Rikers, Waiting to Go Upstate 320
MARQUES M.

24 Reentry, From My Perspective 322
ABDUL-HALIM N. SHAHID

x Contents

25 The Journey of a Black Man Enveloped in Poverty   325
STEVEN PACHECO

26 My First 24 Hours After Being Released   329
JOSE LUMBRERAS

SECTION VI
Activism, Liberation, and Reentry   341

27 Money for Freedom: Cash Bail, Incarceration, and
Reentry   345
CALVINJOHN SMILEY

28 Agents of Change in Healing Our Communities   357
LIZA CHOWDHURY, JASON DAVIS, AND DEDRIC "BELOVED"
HAMMOND

29 Rehabilitation Is Reentry: Breathing Space,
a Product of Inmate Dreams   368
ROBERT GAROT

30 Making Good One Semester at a Time: Formerly
Incarcerated Students (and Their Professor)
Consider the Redemptive Power of Inclusive
Education   382
JAMES M. BINNALL, IRENE SOTELO, ADRIAN VASQUEZ, AND
JOE LOUIS HERNANDEZ

31 "I Can't Depend on No Reentry Program!":
Street-Identified Black Men's Critical Reflections
on Prison Reentry   396
YASSER ARAFAT PAYNE, TARA MARIE BROWN, AND
CORRY WRIGHT

Conclusion: What's Next for Critical Reentry   409
CALVINJOHN SMILEY AND KEESHA M. MIDDLEMASS

Index   415

Tables

3.1	Nongovernmental Organizations (NGOs) by Type of Relationship	44
17.1	Demographic Characteristics	238
17.2	Criminal History	239
17.3	Participation in Campus Programs by Project Rebound Clients	239
17.4	Participants' Perceptions of Program Strengths	240
17.5	Participants' Perceptions of Improvements to Project Rebound	241
18.1	The Voting Rights Restoration Processes and Requirements in the 12 States that Permit Post-Sentence Restrictions	253
19.1	Potential Registration Among Returning Citizens	267
19.2	Potential Turnout Among Returning Citizens	267
19.3	2018 U.S. Senate Estimate, with Returning Citizens	268
19.4	2018 Gubernatorial Estimate, with Returning Citizens	269

Contributors

Annika Yvette Anderson, Ph.D., is an assistant professor in the Department of Sociology at California State University, San Bernardino. Her research interests are in social stratification, sexuality, social psychology, and race and ethnic relations. She is the director of Project Rebound, a campus-reentry program modeled after San Francisco State's Project Rebound, which helps formerly incarcerated students apply to, enroll in, and graduate with degrees from CSU-SB. She received her M.A. and Ph.D. in sociology from Washington State University.

Nishaun T. Battle, Ph.D., is an assistant professor of criminal justice at Virginia State University. She is a scholar-artist-activist whose research explores lived and historical experiences of Black girls, community activism, and state-sanctioned violence. Her published research examines the role of Black girls as producers of criminological epistemological thought and intellectual activists to promote social and legal community justice. She is a co-investigator for a Department of Justice grant to identify solutions to promote social justice in schools.

James M. Binnall, Ph.D., is an assistant professor of law, criminology, and criminal justice at California State University, Long Beach. He is also a practicing California attorney and a convicted felon. Dr. Binnall has worked with formerly incarcerated and system-impacted students for over ten years. His research centers on the statutory exclusion of convicted felons from jury service and his law practice focuses on the pro bono representation of formerly incarcerated and system-impacted people in their efforts to gain professional licensure from the State Bar of California.

David Booth, Founder of the Sex Law & Policy (SLAP) Center, a nonprofit organization working to radically shift the use of punishment-expanding efforts to community-centered approaches to end sexual harm, especially for gender and sexual minorities. Mr. Booth is a social justice advocate dedicated to prison abolition and sex offense policy reform movements.

He volunteers at the National LGBT/HIV Criminal Justice Working Group, which advocates for currently and formerly incarcerated queer and trans folk.

Tara Marie Brown, Ph.D., is an assistant professor of education at the University of Maryland, College Park. Her research focuses on the experiences of low-income adolescents and young adults of color attending or formerly served by urban public schools, and specializes in qualitative, community-based, participatory, and action research methodologies. Her work is published in *Journal of Social Issues*, *Urban Education*, and *Youth & Society*. She received her doctorate in education from Harvard University.

Deirdre Caputo-Levine, Ph.D., is an assistant professor in the Department of Sociology, Social Work and Criminology at Idaho State University. Her research focuses on questions related to prisoner reentry, punishment, critical criminology, race and ethnicity, and social theory. Her work has been published in *Ethnography*, *Dialectical Anthropology*, *Berkeley Journal of Sociology*, and *Sociological Forum*. She received her Ph.D. in sociology from the State University of New York at Stony Brook.

Linda Carson, M.S.W., L.M.S.W., is an assistant professor at Lander University, a forensic social worker, and a former correctional officer. She is currently volunteering with a supermax step-down program that focuses on looking at social problems through a sociological lens to help men envision ways they can address personal and societal challenges using a new perspective.

Liza Chowdhury, Ph.D., is an activist scholar, teaches at Borough of Manhattan Community College (City University of New York) in the Department of Social Science, Human Services, & Criminal Justice, and is co-founder of the nonprofit organization, Reimagining Justice, which advocates for creating healing centered justice responses – justice reinvestment, safe havens for youth, educational support to support the socio-emotional needs of children, and culturally appropriate mental health programs. Dr. Chowdhury is a former Probation Officer.

David Czudnochowski, M.A., is a researcher in the Department of Criminology at the Max Planck Institute for Foreign and International Criminal Law in Freiburg, Germany; his main research interests are employment and crime, inequality, life courses, and medical sociology. He is a specialized palliative care provider and studied sociology at the Albert Ludwigs University in Freiburg, Germany. His master's thesis explores the connection between employment, violent offenders, and reentry.

Jason Davis, Co-Founder of Reimagining Justice, is an African-American author, peace advocate, poet, gang specialist, mental health advocate, inspirational speaker, and father. As an adolescent, Mr. Davis was drawn to xiv Contributors

a life of drugs and gangs, and is a former high-ranking Harlem Original Gangster (O.G.) Blood Gang leader. In 2005, he began to make amends for his past transgressions through youth advocacy activities, and currently works as Family Engagement Specialist for the Living Redemption Hub in Harlem.

Akiv Dawson, M.A., is a doctoral student in the Department of Sociology & Criminology at Howard University. Her research interests include the study of discourse on police violence, police behavior, and the development of hip-hop in the American South. She is a student advisory editor for *Social Problems*, the official publication of the Society for the Study of Social Problems (SSSP).

Albert de la Tierra, Ph.D., is an assistant professor in criminal justice studies, School of Public Affairs & Civic Engagement, San Francisco State University. As a critical ethnographer, he explores how lived experiences and cultural formations are involved with power relations. His dissertation, *Strength in the Hood*, examines how "street workouts" counter racialized surveillance and discursive criminalization. His work is published in *Feminist Criminology* and *Critical Issues in Justice and Politics*.

Sara Buck Doude, Ph.D., is an associate professor of criminal justice at Georgia College and State University. Her research focuses on radical criminological theory, gender and racial biases within the criminal justice system, drug abuse and treatments, and interpersonal violence within marginalized groups. Her work has appeared in the *Getting Real about Race: Hoodies, Mascots, and Model Minorities* (2017, 2014), the *Encyclopedia of Women and Crime (2008, 2017)* and the *Encyclopedia of Theoretical Criminology* (2010).

Christopher P. Dum, Ph.D., is an assistant professor in the Department of Sociology at Kent State University. Professor Dum is a co-founder of ID13, and his research focuses on inequality, criminal justice policy, and homelessness. His research has been published in *Justice Quarterly*, *Criminology & Public Policy*, and *Critical Criminology*. He is the author of the award-winning book, *Exiled in America: Life on the Margins in a Residential Motel*, available from Columbia University Press.

Robert Garot, Ph.D., is an associate professor in the Department of Sociology at John Jay College of Criminal Justice. His book, *Who You Claim: Performing Gang Identity in School and on the Streets* (NYU Press, 2010), received Honorable Mention for the Robert E. Park Award from the Community and Urban Sociology Section of the American Sociological Association.

Kira-Sophie Gauder, Ph.D., is a researcher at the Institute of Criminology at Eberhard Karls University of Tübingen in Tübingen,

Baden-Württemberg, Germany. Her main research interests include life course criminology, desistance research, and qualitative research methods. She is a former doctoral student in the Department of Criminology at the Max Planck Institute for Foreign and International Criminal Law focusing on the qualitative analysis of life courses of sex offenders after prison release.

Allison Gorga, Ph.D., is an assistant professor of sociology & criminal justice at Edgewood College, in Madison, WI. Her research interests include women and criminal offending, incarceration, and gendered organizations. She researches homophobia in sororities, gender hierarchies among women prisoners, and how organizational actors negotiate the terms of punishment and their ideologies (e.g., gender, social control, and care). She received her Ph.D. in Sociology from the University of Iowa.

Keneshia Grant, Ph.D., is an assistant professor of political science at Howard University in Washington, DC. Her first book, *The Great Migration and the Democratic Party: Black Voters and the Realignment of American Politics in the 20th Century (Forthcoming, Temple University Press)*, describes the political impact of the Great Migration on party politics in three cities from 1915–1965. Originally from Lauderhill, Florida, Grant is also a proud graduate of Florida A&M University. Grant earned her Ph.D. in political science and public administration from the Maxwell School of Citizenship and Public Affairs at Syracuse University.

Edward L. W. Green, Ph.D., is an assistant professor in the Department of Criminal Justice at Roosevelt University in Chicago. Dr. Green focuses on the sociology of punishment, criminological theory, corrections, qualitative prison research, and race, class, and gender consequences of mass incarceration. Dr. Green has studied prisons across Scandinavia and presented his research internationally, including at the British Society of Criminology in Birmingham, England.

Dedric "Beloved" Hammond, Board Member for Reimagining Justice, transformed himself after serving a prison sentence; he went from being a crew leader of Money and Murder (a gang) to motivational speaker, mentor, youth advocate, violence interrupter, and father. Mr. Hammond is a cure violence specialist and outreach supervisor at Living Redemption Youth Opportunity Hub in Central Harlem, where he works to mentor at-risk youth on the consequences of gang involvement. He starred in the documentary, "Triggering Wounds," in 2014.

Alexandra Hatch is a junior at Vassar College in Poughkeepsie, New York, and will graduate in 2020. She is a political science and drama double major. Her research interests are mass incarceration and reentry. After graduation, she intends to help reduce recidivism rates by working with community organizations and plans to attend law school to become a public defender.

Joe Louis Hernandez, M.A., is a graduate of California State University, Long Beach, with a Master's in counseling and student development in higher education. Mr. Hernandez is also a returning citizen and co-founder of Rising Scholars who works at Rio Hondo College as a counselor in the student equity office helping to develop programing for formerly incarcerated students. His goal is to earn his Ph.D. and return to higher education as an administrator or a professor.

ID13 Prison Literacy Project is a collaborative effort between Halle M. Neiderman and Christopher P. Dum at Kent State University and incarcerated individuals at the privately-run Lake Erie Correctional Institution (LaECI) in Conneaut, Ohio. *ID13 – We are Human. We Write.* Additional information about the ID13 Prison Literacy Project is available at: www. id13project.com or www.facebook.com/ID13project.

Paul Andrew Jones, M.A. (social work), is a graduate of Project Rebound at California State University, San Bernardino. After leaving prison on parole, he started his college career at Rio Hondo Community College in Whittier, California. While there, he was awarded Co-student of the Year. Mr. Jones is a certified addictions treatment counselor III (CATC III), and works with individuals suffering from addiction.

Nicole Kaufman, Ph.D., is an assistant professor of sociology at Ohio University. Her research examines citizenship, punishment, the civic sector, and institutional arrangements that socially exclude people with criminal records. Her research has been funded by the National Science Foundation Dissertation Improvement Grant in Law and Social Science and a Mellon-Wisconsin Fellowship. She received her Ph.D. in Sociology from the University of Wisconsin-Madison.

Katrina M. Lewis, M.A., teaches design studio classes in the U.S., China, Afghanistan, and Bangladesh. In her scholarly work, she is passionate about design and social justice, and encourages her students to "think outside the box" to consider the social implications of their careers as designers. Ms. Lewis has a B.A. in interior architecture and product design and a Master's in regional and community planning from Kansas State University.

Jose Lumbreras, M.A., is a former prisoner in California; he was released in 2014. Since, he has worked for a nonprofit organization working with transitional age youth in the Bay Area, and received his Master's from the College of Ethnic Studies at San Francisco State University. He was a 2018 Summer Fellow at Renewing Communities at The Opportunity Institute in Berkeley, California; it promotes social mobility and equity through education. In August 2018, he began his doctoral degree in history at UC San Diego.

Marques M., is a New York City resident, who is currently serving time in state prison. His accounts are from his time awaiting trial and sentencing in New York City's Riker's Island Jail.

Liam Martin, Ph.D., is a lecturer at the Institute of Criminology at Victoria University of Wellington, Australia. His research centers on issues of imprisonment and prisoner reentry. Professor Martin's research focuses on the causes and consequences of large-scale incarceration, prison growth and race and class inequalities, global transfers of punitive crime control policy, the broad impact of prisons on families and communities, and alternative ways of addressing harm.

Carolyn Anne McAllister, Ph.D., is an associate professor at the School of Social Work at California State University, San Bernardino where she directs the Bachelor of Arts in Social Work and teaches courses in micro social work practice and social work research. Her research interests are in the areas of program evaluation, higher education, and disability studies. She received her Ph.D. in social work from Michigan State University.

Taneisha N. Means, Ph.D. is an assistant professor of political science at Vassar College. She specializes in judicial politics, race and ethnicity, and politics. She is the 2014–2016 Pre-doctoral Fellow at the Carter G. Woodson Institute for African-American and African Studies (University of Virginia). Her work has been published in numerous journals and edited volumes. She is finishing a book manuscript on Black state court judges' identities and decision-making. She received her M.A. and Ph.D. from Duke University.

Keesha M. Middlemass, Ph.D., is an associate professor of public policy in the Department of Political Science at Howard University in Washington, D.C. She specializes in studying race, reentry, food insecurity, and public policies using interdisciplinary frameworks to integrate knowledge from different disciplines and across multiple data sources, including participant observations, in-depth interviews, focus groups, policy analysis, and archival research. Her most recent book, *Convicted & Condemned: The Politics and Policies of Prisoner Reentry*, won the W.E.B. DuBois Distinguished Book Award in 2018. Her research is also published in *Public Health Nutrition, International Journal of Eating Disorders, Aggressive Behavior, Criminal Justice & Behavior, The Prison Journal*, and *Punishment & Society*. Dr. Middlemass is a member of the Racial Democracy, Crime and Justice Network, a former Andrew Mellon Post-Doctoral Fellow on Race, Crime, and Justice at the Vera Institute of Justice in New York City, and a former American Political Science Association Congressional Fellow.

xviii Contributors

Dr. Middlemass earned her Ph.D. in public policy, American politics, and public administration from The School of Public & International Affairs at the University of Georgia.

Tomas R. Montalvo is a returning citizen. He battled substance addiction and served a total of seven years in New York and Pennsylvania, exiting prison for the last time in 2009. He has been sober for nearly a decade and shares his story at universities and academic conferences around the country. He currently works as shop supervisor at a commercial carpentry business. Tomas is married to his co-author, Jennifer Marie Ortiz, and is the proud father of three children.

Halle M. Neiderman, M.A., is a doctoral candidate studying rhetoric and composition in the Department of English at Kent State University. She has studied and taught courses in literacy and writing programs across Ohio. Ms. Neiderman helped co-found ID13 with Christopher P. Dum. Her research focuses on institutional critique, education legislation, and prison literacy.

Jennifer Marie Ortiz, Ph.D., is an assistant professor of criminology & criminal justice at Indiana University Southeast. Her research focuses on punishment within the criminal justice system with a focus on individual experiences reentering society. Her work is inspired by her husband's experiences. Dr. Ortiz received her Ph.D. in criminal justice from John Jay College of Criminal Justice.

Steven Pacheco is the inaugural Vera Institute of Justice Opportunity Fellow, the inaugural David Rockefeller Fund Fellow, an inaugural Ron Moelis Social Innovation Fellow, and an inaugural Gun Control Advocacy Fellow. He was elected Vice President and President of Student Government at John Jay College of Criminal Justice and went on to win Echoing Green's NYC Future of Work Social Innovation Challenge. Mr. Pacheco is also a former prisoner.

Laurin Parker, Ph.D., is an associate professor in the Department of Sociology & Criminal Justice at Delaware State University. Her research examines offender rehabilitation and adult and juvenile reentry, the effectiveness of reentry programming in correctional institutions, and the intersection of race, class, and gender in law enforcement recruitment and judicial system processes. She works on initiatives to strengthen juvenile justice training and research at HBCUs. She earned her Ph.D. from the University of Delaware

Kylie Parrotta, Ph.D., is an assistant professor in the Department of Social Sciences at the California Polytechnic State University in San Luis Obispo, California. Her research concentrates on inequality (e.g., race, class, gender, and sexuality), social psychology, and deviance. She has published her work in *Criminal Justice Studies, Journal of Contemporary Ethnography, Sociological Perspectives*, and *Teaching Sociology*. She earned her doctorate in Sociology from North Carolina State University.

Yasser Arafat Payne, Ph.D., is an associate professor in the Department of Sociology and Criminal Justice at the University of Delaware. Dr. Payne's research focuses on street ethnography and identity, resilience in street identified Black populations, and he uses street participatory action research methods (e.g., the process of involving members of street-identified Black populations in research-activism projects). His work has been funded by the National Institute of Drug Abuse (NIH-NIDA).

Rebecca Reviere, Ph.D., is a professor and associate chair in the Department of Sociology & Criminology at Howard University. She is a co-founder of the Women's Studies Program, and her research interests include the physical and mental health of women in prison, representations of women in the media, and attitudes of college students toward relationships.

Abdul-Halim N. Shahid, returning citizen and former resident of Newark, New Jersey, spent 30 consecutive years in New Jersey state prisons. He was released in 2014. He and his wife currently reside in the American south where he works and enjoys spending time with his grandchildren.

CalvinJohn Smiley, Ph.D., is an assistant professor of sociology in the Department of Sociology at Hunter College-City of New York (CUNY). He specializes in studying race, reentry, and citizenship. His work is published in numerous peer-reviewed journals such as: *The Prison Journal, Race Ethnicity and Education, Punishment & Society, Deviant Behavior, Journal of Human Behavior in the Social Environment*, and *Contemporary Justice Review*. He is currently working on a book based on his research on reentry that explores the various ways men and women navigate the reentry process with diminished legal rights and amplified social stigmas. His future work will investigate the role of human and nonhuman interactions, particularly in carceral settings (e.g., prison-based animal therapy programs). Dr. Smiley is a member of the American Sociological Association, American Society of Criminology, and Kappa Alpha Psi Inc. He is the Vice-President of the Board of Trustees of the New Jersey Association on Corrections. Dr. Smiley earned his Ph.D. in Sociology from the CUNY Graduate Center.

Irene Sotelo, B.A. (sociology, minor criminal justice, 2018), is a graduate student at California State University, Long Beach, co-founder of Rising Scholars, a returning citizen, and working on her Master's in social work. Her goal is to work with former offenders and help them accomplish their educational goals. Irene is also the Project Rebound Liaison xx Contributors

at California State University, Long Beach; in this role, Ms. Sotelo travels statewide and nationally to call attention to the importance of higher education for those who have fallen prey to the criminal justice system.

Jessica J. Sparks, J.D., is a graduate student in criminal justice at Georgia College and State University. Her efforts supporting criminal and social justice reform focus on alternatives to incarceration and enhanced legal representation through application of ethical standards for those with substance abuse-related behavioral issues.

Adrian Vasquez, B.A. (sociology, 2018), is a recent graduate of California State University, Long Beach and former treasurer of Rising Scholars. In February 2014, Mr. Vasquez was released from prison after serving 20 years. Since his release, he has worked for the nonprofit organization, Anti-Recidivism Coalition, as an intake specialist and job developer; he assists men and women reentering society by providing them with housing, employment, mentoring, and counseling support services. His goal is to one day become a lawyer and work in the field of criminal justice.

Jason M. Williams, Ph.D., is an assistant professor of justice studies at Montclair State University. His work examines race and the administration of justice, policing and race, Black males and the criminal justice system, and critical criminology. His published work has appeared in the *Journal of Offender Rehabilitation*, and the *Ralph Bunche Journal of Public Affairs*. He is co-editor of *Contemporary Ethical Issues in the Criminal Justice System: A Textbook Reader* and *Critical Analysis of Race and the Administration of Justice*.

L. Susan Williams, Ph.D., is a Professor of Sociology at Kansas State University. She specializes in prisons, gender, and inequality with an emphasis on place. Dr. Williams' research has been supported by the National Science Foundation, National Institute of Justice, the W.T. Grant Foundation, and the Office of Juvenile Justice and Delinquency Prevention. She works with state and local corrections and law enforcement agencies and serves in leadership positions in several professional organizations.

Breea Willingham, Ph.D., is an associate professor of criminal justice at SUNY Plattsburgh. Her research interests include women's pathways to incarceration, Black women's prison writings, the impact of incarceration on families, higher education in prison, and race and crime in the media. Dr. Willingham has presented her research at national and international conferences, lectured at universities in the U.S. and U.K., and led workshops for women and men in prisons. Her research has been published in numerous academic journals and edited collections.

Gunda Woessner, Ph.D., is a senior researcher at the Max Planck Institute for Foreign and International Criminal Law, Department of Criminology, in Freiburg, Germany. Her research activities focus on correctional treatment, recidivism, rehabilitation and reentry processes of sex and violent offenders, electronic monitoring, and alternative measures, such as restorative justice in cases of sexual violence. She has published her research results in various national and international journals and volumes.

Corry Wright, M.A., is a program specialist for Delaware's leading reentry nonprofit organization, Delaware Center for Justice. In this role, Mr. Wright advocates for criminal justice and reentry policy reform. Mr. Wright is a returning citizen as well as a member of the Wilmington Street Participatory Action Research Family.

Vernetta D. Young, Ph.D., is a professor in the Department of Sociology & Criminology at Howard University. Her research interests include race, gender, and crime, the history of juvenile justice, and victimization. Her Ph.D. is in criminal justice from the State University of New York.

Haley Zettler, Ph.D., is an assistant professor in the Department of Criminology and Criminal Justice at the University of Memphis. Dr. Zettler is a former adult probation officer. Her primary research interests focus on corrections, substance abuse and mental health, and recidivism. Some of her recent publications can be found in *Criminal Justice & Behavior, Crime & Delinquency*, and *Youth Violence and Juvenile Justice*.

Introduction
Critical Reentry in the 21st Century

Keesha M. Middlemass and CalvinJohn Smiley

The United States crossed an alarming threshold of mass incarceration in 2007, when the adult population under correctional supervision reached its peak of over 7.3 million people at yearend 2013 (i.e., incarcerated, parole, probation, community supervision; Kaeble, Glaze, Tsoutis, & Minton, 2016). Although the size of the correctional population at the state and federal levels has decreased by an average of 1% each year since its peak in 2007, with a slight increase 2013, there are still over two million people under some form of correctional control in the United States (Bronson & Carson, 2019). As these falling numbers are celebrated in the press by the likes of the *Washington Post* and the *New York Times*, the fact that in 2011 there were more state prisoner releases than prisoners admitted was largely ignored (Carson & Golinelli, 2014; Carson, 2015). The release of prisoners, however, is the norm; 95% of all prisoners are eventually released (Travis, 2005), which means that as the prison population goes up and down, reentry is constant and has reached its own critical juncture.

Being released from jail or prison after being convicted of a felony is a day to celebrate, but it is also a day that brings with it a lot of unease and anxiety as the culture of punishment continues post-incarceration; individuals are released from one correctional institution to a different form of correctional supervision (e.g., parole and probation), are largely expected to reenter society on their own (Middlemass, 2017), and the number of returning citizens is alarming, and only going up. In 1980, 157,604 state and federal prisoners were released, and every year since that number has increased (Carson & Golinelli, 2014). In 2000, 635,094 were released, and in 2010, 708,677 state and federal prisoners were released; that is nearly a 20% increase in ten years (Guerino, Harrison, & Sabol, 2012). More recent figures indicate that 622,400 state and federal prisoners were released in 2017 (Bronson & Carson, 2019). These figures are shocking; in 1980, approximately 3,030 adults returned to the community, and almost 35 years later, approximately 12,000 people are returning home every week. Those numbers are likely to go up as men and women, who were sentenced to long sentences in the 1970s, 1980s and 1990s under policies linked to punitive policies and the War on Drugs come home; communities and individuals are ill prepared for this population movement from prisons and jails back to society.

Three-quarters of individuals who are released from prison are rearrested within five years (Durose, Cooper, & Snyder, 2014). This number has barely changed in the last thirty years, and today's high recidivism rate, which hovers around 67%, is intimately connected to reentry, is seen as a problem that must be addressed because of the numerous consequences to individuals, families, communities, prison populations, reentry organizations, parole and probation, and state budgets. Recidivism and reentry are aligned because when one fails to reenter society successfully, they recidivate and return to prison; the return to prison is disruptive and can be traumatizing for the individual, family, and the community.

Recidivism and the failure to reenter mean different things to different scholars and practitioners; according to Beck (2001), this is because recidivism is a "fruit salad concept" because of the dissimilar numbers used to capture recidivism, and also because it is defined differently by organizations and state and federal agencies. In many instances, recidivism is measured as a person who has been released from prison or jail and is re-arrested, reconvicted or returned to prison during some time period following release (see Beck, 2001). Despite these generally agreed upon parameters, recidivism can include technical parole or probation violations (e.g., failing a drug test) that results in re-incarceration, re-arrest for a new crime but without a new conviction, or re-incarceration for a new crime resulting in a new sentence. In essence, recidivism is not consistent owing to how recidivism is measured, the time frame that is measured (e.g., two, three, five years or longer), and the type of data collected (Beck, 2001; James, 2015; Bronson & Carson, 2019).

Despite the different measures and notions of reentry and recidivism, reentry is a complex process for individuals, families, communities, organizations, and government institutions. Transitioning from prison to the community has profound implications for the individual based on family support, reentry initiatives and programs, neighborhood context, type of criminal conviction, and the geographic and political jurisdiction's collateral consequences. The transition from prison back to the community has always been laden with a number of challenges, but in recent years, despite some initial efforts by elected officials changing criminal justice policies on the edges (e.g., President George W. Bush, Second Chance Act, 2007; President Barack Obama, Fair Sentencing Act, 2010; President Trump, First Step Act, 2019), the general political culture of not fully funding these national laws and being "tough on crime" continues. Criminal justice policy is slow to change because of politicians' fear of being labelled "soft on crime" (Middlemass, 2017), because of the economic incentives that private prisons and prison guard unions have in supporting the system, and because of the clear economic stake in terms of jobs some local communities have in maintaining

Introduction 3

correctional facilities in their rural districts (Kelly, 2015). As a result, despite a national decline in crime rates and a slowly declining prison population, invisible punishments (Travis, 2005) remain in place as politicians enact a new generation of sanctions that impose restrictions on a felons' ability to reenter successfully (Middlemass, 2017).

The criminal justice system is now a paramount government institution in the lives of many urban and rural residents. The penal system is filled with individuals from the bottom half of the social hierarchy, which means that incarceration and prisoner reentry is a pervasive event in the lives of individuals, families, and communities that are under resourced, and experiencing institutional abandonment, social disorder, and high levels of poverty (Lynch & Sabol, 2001; Marcuse, 1985; Fullilove & Fullilove, 2005). Prisoner reentry occurs in largely urban poor communities at a disproportionate rate, however, studies about rural reentry are now expanding because of different challenges under resourced returning citizens have when living in rural areas. The location of where prisoners return means that prisoner reentry can be conceptualized spatially and also means that the challenge of prisoner reentry continues to be concentrated in communities lacking resources.

In order to understand why reentry is so difficult, scholars assess the characteristics of reentry from multiple perspectives to provide a broad overview of what it means to reenter society. This research focuses on the multiple barriers former prisoners face, which include barriers to employment, housing, education and vocation programs, health care, mental health treatment, substance abuse programs, family unification, and a number of other issues that hamper men and women from being able to leave prison and remain out (Middlemass, 2017; Pager, 2003; Travis, 2005; Clear, 2009; Gottschalk, 2015; Petersilia, 2003). Despite the vast knowledge about why men and women fail to reenter successfully, former prisoners continue to recidivate for parole or probation violations, but also because they commit new crimes and are unable to reenter because of the numerous collateral consequences that restrict them from accessing citizenship rights and social benefits (Middlemass, 2017; Travis, 2005).

Prisoner reentry is constantly changing because of new laws being implemented, such as early release programs, changes in parole and probation, the re-establishment of "good time credits" used by state Departments of Corrections, over-crowding, and also because of the increased number of reentry nonprofit organizations and religious institutions that have attempted to fill in the gap left by state budget cuts. But reentry has also changed in terms of the longer time people have been incarcerated, their poor health status when they exit prison, and the diminished levels of family support to help former prisoners acclimate to society. Returning citizens experience a particular disquiet because of the numerous after-effects of incarceration and the collateral consequences of a felony conviction, which all former prisoners must contend with; they cannot ignore this reality but rather must contend with how society has changed since they were initially incarcerated. As a result of changes in reentry and increased knowledge about the harm of incarceration, we argue, it is time to critically assess and reassess reentry in all of its complicated realities.

Critical Reentry

Critical reentry research offers a new way of thinking about prisoner reentry. The term "critical" has a broad set of meanings and is used across the social sciences and a variety of intellectual disciplines, and is mainly used to signify a radical stance on contemporary society; the goal of being "critical" is to challenge expected norms (Foucault, 1972). Critical scholars focus on understanding power relationships, language, social practices and norms, and systems that marginalize, oppress, or complicate relationships between the state and individuals.

Just as critical legal studies (CLS) emerged in the mid-1970s to purposely link various intellectual projects to explore legal doctrine and practices that buttress a pervasive system of oppression and unequal relationships, critical reentry studies should do the same in the field of prisoner reentry. CLS explores the politics of power within the law, legal principles, and its impact on traditionally oppressed groups, and although focused on the law, is interdisciplinary, as it incorporates race, literary theory, sociology, economics, politics, philosophy, and history alongside the law; at times, CLS may appear as a collection of "eclectic intellectual projects" (Minda, 1995, p. 108). However, CLS is primarily about pointing out fundamental contradictions in the law, and it is critical because it consciously tackles how legal principles, doctrines, and rules create advantage for some while disadvantaging others based on race, class, gender, and "otherness."

With an interest in critical reentry, this co-edited book introduces a variety of critical takes on reentry that are designed to promote new questions, engage readers to rethink what they know about reentry, and to promote a new prisoner reentry discourse. Critical reentry makes an effort to understand and explain that there is no politically neutral way to apply the law because it is inherently contradictory, and these contradictions are imbedded within its doctrines and systems; when this reality is ignored, the existence of race, gender, class, and "otherness" is diminished or completely ignored as it pertains to reentry. Here, we elevate the experiences of race, gender, class, and otherness as it applies to coming home after serving time in prison.

The word "reentry" tends to be an uncontested term; it means the transition of people from state or federal prisons or jails back to the community. However, the term can include all of the activities and programs that prepare prisoners to return to society, including programs inside prison, programs focused on the immediate release period, and long-term programs that provide former prisoners with different types of support and/or supervision as

Introduction 5

they reintegrate. Reentry programs differ widely in terms of time period, scope, and focus, and the "what works" literature suggests different treatments and programs depending on the type and length of program, who participates (e.g., men or women, LGBTQ), how long participants served in prison, if the individual has an untreated mental illness or drug or alcohol addiction, and the type of supervision the person experiences (e.g., suspended sentence/no prison time, community supervision, probation, parole, or unconditional release, i.e., maxing out their entire sentence in a state or federal prison).Yet programs, in practice, are rarely tailored to an individual. Just as the law has been used to create and re-create who are legitimate actors in American society and who is not, reentry programs are offered in a "one size fits all" paradigm.This co-edited volume offers an opportunity to understand how "one size fits all" systems actually work to undermine reentry efforts.

Taking a critical approach to prisoner reentry is an attempt to challenge the dogmatic tendencies of reentry scholars who focus on the individual as failing rather than examining the multiple systems that contribute to an individuals' failure to reenter successfully (e.g., Petersilia, 2003).Additionally, quantitative research tends to be given priority over post-positivist or critical approaches because it can provide "acceptable" analyses (Kitchin, 2015). Yet there is a need for a critical ethos to problematize reentry and challenge the type of data that saturates current scholarship. Data is varied, and in all of its arrangements it is informed by specific dominant histories, ideologies, and philosophies (Kitchin, 2015), and "formal identities, thematic continuities, translations of concepts, and polemical interchanges may be deployed" (Foucault, 1972, p. 127).

In this instance, "critical" means that contributing scholars are re-assessing reentry practices and rethinking the assumptions built into reentry scholarship and research. Critical means that they are taking into consideration the social and political assemblages that operate in different reentry spaces. Building on the insights drawn from their own research, contributors offer frameworks and perspectives that tackle the complexity of reentry from different theoretical and practical approaches to shed light on a number of emerging and analytical insights about reentry. Contributors rely heavily on first-person accounts, qualitative data, and historical analysis.We choose this approach purposely; narratives are a powerful way to share experiences, and also make reentry personal and a felt experience.

Prisoner reentry is constantly changing and yet remains the same; in part, this arises from the fact that reentry continues to be difficult for individuals but the sociopolitical problems have not been addressed. In order to move forward, work must analyze how social institutions foster social injustice and inequalities, discrimination, and different forms of oppression via an extension of punishing methods, most notably prison, but also herald programs and institutions that uplift and assist returning citizens (e.g., Project

Rebound and Rising Scholars, both of which are examined in this volume). "Critical" indicates an unapologetic take on current practices and policies, and offers something of value since it reminds readers about how reentry practices and institutions can be a form of social control but also contribute to individuals failing to reenter successfully.

What's New?

Contributors tackle and focus on what it means to reenter society from a range of perspectives, including community organizations and the absence of government, how substance abuse and limited access to health care persist in prison and upon reentry, and also how multiple identities intersect – race, gender, drug user, poorly educated, and prisoner – and complicate reentry experiences. Although traditional policy areas are covered, such as education, the chapters that look at education examine it from the perspective of former prisoners taking classes inside prison and their experiences in creating networks and spaces for returning citizens on university campuses.

Second, this volume addresses the intersection of race and gender, and also includes chapters that examine the reentry life courses of sexual offenders and violent offenders. In particular, how do people convicted of a sex crime think about reentry? One chapter takes on this subject in a straightforward manner that raises important questions about who is "allowed" to reenter and what purpose policies serve if they contribute to a failure to reenter successfully.

Third, we purposely include chapters exploring rural reentry and how nonprofit organizations have become complicit in implementing the state's agenda. Individuals reentering to rural communities have similar but different challenges than adults reentering to an urban community, which is mainly related to resource allocation, the distance one must travel to access resources, and the limited transportation options. The new and emerging field of rural reentry is considered because it is a growing concern for states, families, and individuals who have, incorrectly, thought that crime and punishment was an urban problem for states with large and diverse populations.

The race to incarcerate spans decades of punitive policies and the fear of "Blackness" (Middlemass, 2017). Political calculations have arrived at the conclusion that prison is the best way to deal with hard to solve and intractable social issues, such as poverty, homelessness, mental illness, and addiction. As a result of these political calculations, policies have been passed to incarcerate the less fortunate (Alexander, 2010), which have manifested in a criminal justice system and returning processes that are steeped in different forms of inequality, and these inequalities manifest in the reentry process. Individuals are coming home, and contributors do not focus on "what happened" and "how did we get here;" instead, contributors detail, analyze, and describe the current state of how multiple issues – trauma, mental health, addiction, for instance – and how these personal complications hamper individual reentry efforts, but also how they complicate institutional responses in how individuals are treated while they are incarcerated. Contributors offer a rare glimpse inside the minds of current and former prisoners, as well as institutional complications, as it relates to reentry.

The co-editors have pulled together a set of issues that need to be discussed comprehensively to highlight the interdependence and intersections of reentry because the variety of social experiences and institutions that are intertwined are vast. This volume addresses reentry to highlight that returning citizens do not have it easy and their path to success is not simple; rather, the system is complicated. This volume does not offer a "feel good" account of reentry; instead, because of the shifting nature of reentry, contributors take a critical approach using a variety of theoretical approaches to expand the conversation beyond the traditional measure of reentry (e.g., a dichotomous variable, 1 for success and 0 for failure to reenter). Contributors do not tell readers why men and women fail to reenter; contributors show them through data, analysis, and first-person narratives.

The chapters, collectively, show that reentry is interdependent on a lot of different actors and institutions, and the interdisciplinary approach adds to the conversation and discourse about reentry. Moreover, the contributors offer different perspectives about reentry and the range of what is possible. For instance, the chapters in Section VI: Activism, Liberation, & Reentry, offer different forms of how returning citizens can reenter and become agents of change instead of agents of destruction. These different approaches provide examples of how returning citizens are not passive actors in their own reentry.

Lastly, the co-editors, Middlemass and Smiley, purposely set out to create a space for scholars to engage in what we consider "silenced voices," who include current and former prisoners, who contribute to many of the chapters in this volume, and also the voices of emerging scholars who are in graduate school or are Assistant Professors; in several instances, contributors are both returning citizens and working in various capacities on university campuses. We also recruited Black women scholars, progressive scholars, and scholars willing to challenge traditional norms and ideas about reentry.

Limitations

Despite covering a range of topics, this volume could realistically cover every topic related to reentry and it does not offer solutions. Although many topics are raised in individual chapters and across sections, such as gender, there is not a macro perspective that is easily transferable to each state or community experiencing reentry. The chapters do not offer an assessment of the community context or how communities' may impact prisoners' reentry experiences (see Morenoff & Harding, 2014, for a review of the literature on communities and reentry). One topic that is not included is policing. Although police practices are the usual first contact individuals have with the criminal justice system, police also play a role in the reentry process; however, policing was beyond the scope of this volume. Moreover, police practices are viewed as an extension of the criminal justice system, which includes surveillance and compliance with the rules, which has a long and problematic history for populations deemed "other," and police practices designed to monitor returning citizens have proven to be ineffective and increase the number of technical parole and probation violations (Haldipur, 2018; McGarrell, Zimmerman, Hipple, Corsaro, & Perez, 2004).

Additionally, as the issue of private prisons, immigration, deportation, and Immigration & Customs Enforcement (ICE) raids increase, the intersection of immigrant status and reentry will become more important. As states and local communities resist ICE and declare that they will not help federal agents as it pertains to implementing immigration laws, these intersecting institutions need to be examined; however, immigration status is a federal issue and most state and federal prisoners who are immigrants (legal or undocumented), upon completing their prison sentence, are detained by ICE and deported to their home country. Therefore, reentry for them does not occur in the United States, and is far more complicated when considering culture, language, and immigrant status in their "home country" (e.g., Dominican Republic or Haiti; see Brotherton & Barrios, 2011). Immigration is beyond the scope of our book; for readers interested in this topic, we encourage them to read the full length edited volume entitled, *Outside Justice: Immigration and the Criminalizing Impact of Changing Policy and Practice* edited by Brotherton, Stageman, and Leyro (2013).

Concluding Thoughts

The purpose of this book, *Prisoner Reentry in the 21st Century: Critical Perspectives of Returning Home*, is to add to the criminological literature that focuses on prisoner reentry. Specifically, the contributors in this co-edited volume provide a new way of thinking about some of the issues facing men and women returning home from prison. It focuses on the institutional barriers they face when they return, but also how these barriers make reentry more difficult. Often, research concerning returning citizens describes why men and women fail to reenter; here, we take the approach of critically evaluating the programs, the spatial arrangements, incarceration practices, and race, gender, class, and felony status to offer a critical perspective to show and *explain why* men and women fail.

The contributors identify some of the most significant challenges to reenter society, and how those challenges are complicated by personal trauma and state institutions. This co-edited volume provides a range of research topics that we hope serve as a springboard for discussions about potential policy changes, future research topics, and what needs to happen to make reentry success the norm instead of an anomaly. The critical perspectives included in this book on reentry complement reentry scholarship, and the chapters offer multiple perspectives, including an assessment of nonprofit organizations and their relationship to the state, race, gender, and class, acknowledgement of the harms prison imposes on individuals, as well as the lived experiences of current and former prisoners. The new and emerging scholars included in this volume provide an assessment of what is missing from conversations about prisoner reentry in an effort to rethink the harms inflicted by the criminal justice system and how its focus on punishment negatively impacts reentry efforts. The contributions are informed by a broad spectrum of scholarly insights and research expertise, and first-person experiences are also included, to offer a coherent intellectual project that critically engages the issue of reentry to fill in glaring gaps and biases in the literature.

References

Alexander, M. (2010). *The new Jim Crow: Mass incarceration in the age of colorblindness*. New York: The New Press.

Beck, A. R. (2001). *Recidivism: A fruit salad concept in the criminal justice world*. Kansas City, MO: Justice Concepts, Inc. Retrieved from www.justiceconcepts.com/recidivism.htm

Bronson, J., & Carson, E. A. (2019). *Prisoners in 2017*. NCJ 252156. Washington, DC: U.S. Department of Justice, Bureau of Justice Statistics.

Brotherton, D. C., & Barrios, L. (2011). *Banished to the homeland: Dominican deportees and their stories of exile*. New York: Columbia University Press.

Brotherton, D. C., Stageman, D. L., & Leyro, S. P. (2013). *Outside justice: Immigration and the criminalizing impact of changing policy and practice*. New York: Springer-Verlag.

Carson, E. A. (2015). *Prisoners in 2014*. NCJ 248955. Washington, DC: U.S. Department of Justice, Bureau of Justice Statistics.

Carson, E. A., & Golinelli, D. (2014). *Prisoners in 2012: Trends in admissions and releases, 1991–2012*. NCJ 243920. Washington, DC: U.S. Department of Justice, Bureau of Justice Statistics.

Clear, T. (2009). *Imprisoning communities: How mass incarceration makes disadvantaged neighborhoods worse*. New York: Oxford University Press.

Durose, M. R., Cooper, A. D., & Snyder, H. N. (2014). *Recidivism of prisoners released in 30 states in 2005: Patterns from 2005 to 2010*. NCJ 244205. Washington, DC: U.S. Department of Justice, Bureau of Justice Statistics.

Foucault, M. (1972). *The archeology of knowledge & the discourse on language*. New York: Pantheon Books.

Fullilove, R. E., & Fullilove, M. T. (2005). HIV/AIDS in the African American community: The legacy of urban abandonment. *Harvard Journal of African American Public Policy*, *11*, 33–41.

Gottschalk, M. (2015). *Caught: The prison state and the lockdown of American politics*. Princeton, NJ: Princeton University Press.

Guerino, P., Harrison, P. M., & Sabol, W. J. (2012). *Prisoners in 2010*. NCJ 236096. Washington, DC: U.S. Department of Justice, Bureau of Justice Statistics.

Haldipur, J. (2018). *No place on the corner: The costs of aggressive policing*. New York: New York University Press.

James, N. (2015). *Offender reentry: Correctional statistics, reintegration into the community, and recidivism*. Washington, DC: Congressional Research Service. Retrieved from https://fas.org/sgp/crs/misc/RL34287.pdf

Kaeble, D., Glaze, L., Tsoutis, A., & Minton, T. (2016). *Correctional populations in the United States, 2014*. NCJ 249513. Washington, DC: U.S. Department of Justice, Bureau of Justice Statistics.

Kelly, W. R. (2015). *Criminal justice at the crossroads: Transforming crime and punishment*. New York: Columbia University Press.

Kitchin, R. (2015). Big data, new epistemologies and paradigm shifts. *Big Data & Society*, *1*(1), 1–12.

Lynch, J. P., & Sabol, W. J. (2001). *Prisoner reentry in perspective*. Washington, DC: The Urban Institute.

Marcuse, P. (1985). Gentrification, abandonment, and displacement: Connections, causes, and policy responses in New York City. *Washington University Urban Journal: Urban & Contemporary Law*, *28*, 195–124.

McGarrell, E. F., Zimmerman, C. R., Hipple, N. K., Corsaro, N., & Perez, H. (2004). *The roles of the police in the offender reentry process*. Washington, DC: Working Paper, Reentry Roundtable, Urban Institute. Retrieved from www.urban.org/sites/default/files/publication/58346/900743-Prisoner-Reentry-and-Community-Policing.PDF

Middlemass, K. (2017). *Convicted and condemned: The politics and policies of prisoner reentry*. New York: New York University Press.

Minda, G. (1995). *Postmodern legal movements: Law and jurisprudence at century's end*. New York: New York University Press.

Morenoff, J. D., & Harding, D. J. (2014). Incarceration, prisoner reentry, and communities. *Annual Review of Sociology*, *40*, 411–429.

Pager, D. (2003). The mark of a criminal record. *American Journal of Sociology*, *108*(5), 937–975.

Petersilia, J. (2003). *When prisoners come home: Parole and prisoner reentry*. New York: Oxford University Press.

Travis, J. (2005). *But they all come back: Facing the challenges of prisoner reentry*. Washington, DC: The Urban Institute.

Section I

Institutions, Community, and Reentry

Reentry is a process and not a onetime event, and it takes place across the country in urban, suburban, and rural communities, and embedded in the communities that people return to are a range of institutions that work with formerly incarcerated adults. Scholars often explore the challenges of returning to the community after incarceration to examine the barriers and challenges that occur at the community level; a common finding is that for everyone released from prison, there are limited resources available for those reentering society (Middlemass, 2017; Bobo & Thompson, 2010; Clear, 2009; Petersilia, 2003; Travis, 2005).

With this context, the authors in this section explore community and state institutions as they relate to reentry in different settings. Liam Martin, in "Halfway Home," examines the blurred boundaries between the halfway house, its residents, and the neighborhood. Through an ethnographic study, Martin explores the concept of liminality and its application to a halfway house and reentry; as the halfway house provides programming for residents in an effort to combat their respective addictions, residents find themselves connected to the street and drug culture through a combination of physical proximity and social relationships. Martin's critical examination of halfway houses demonstrates that despite residents' best efforts to adhere to a strict abstinence policy and remain sober, they are confronted by the realities of the illegal drug trade and the neighborhood street scene.

Halfway houses are only one kind of institution that is involved in reentry; in reality, there are dozens of state institutions and agencies, as well as nonprofit organizations that provide a variety of programming and services to men and women returning home. Allison Gorga, in her chapter, "Triaging Rehabilitation," explores how the rehabilitative ideologies promoted by service providers come in conflict with the cost-saving frames used by correctional staff and politicians. Drawing on interview data from prison staff, volunteers, and advocacy workers in Iowa, Gorga analyzes the ways that prison workers interpret and implement evidence-based practices; the responses result in a triaged system of rehabilitation, where programs are sorted and funds are allocated based on evidence that improves the state's return on investment. As government's cut their reentry budgets, nongovernmental organizations, such as nonprofits, fill in the gaps.

State budget cuts have a devastating impact on reentry because community organizations are trying to fill in the gaps and provide educational, vocational, and treatment services for the men and women reentering society. Kaufman, in her chapter, "The State's Accomplices? Organizations and the Penal State," looks at the role of nongovernmental organizations (NGOs) who operate in "reentry spaces." The relationship of NGOs to the penal state is still evolving, but what is known is that the relationship between NGOs, the penal state, and returning citizens shows us that nonprofit organizations, in many ways, have become an extension of the penal state, and are complicit in implementing state policy goals (see LaVigne, Davies, Palmer, & Halberstadt, 2008; Mellow & Dickinson, 2006). In many instances, as Kaufman shows, nonprofit organizations are dependent on state funding, which places them in an uncompromising position.

As the state and federal governments retrench from their respective roles in providing social services and traditional welfare to the poor, retrenchment has taken many forms, including in the creation of a tenacious carceral state that operates in the shadows of mass imprisonment and reaches far beyond the prison gate; the carceral state now imposes real and formidable challenges (Gottschalk, 2015) that formerly incarcerated individuals have to overcome, largely, on their own (Middlemass, 2017). In a case-study about rural reentry, Caputo-Levine, in her chapter, "Idaho: A Case Study in Rural Reentry," explores Idaho and its justice reinvestment plans within rural communities, who are experiencing increased levels of returning citizens. Caputo-Levine shows that participants are reliant on services provided by Idaho's Department of Corrections because the few institutions that do provide reentry services in the state are located in areas that are not easily accessible because of the rural nature of the state, and places returning citizens at risk of violating parole.

As the state and reentry organizations provide a range of services for returning citizens, some organizations focus on hard to treat groups, such as sexual offenders. In their chapter, "Life Courses of Sex and Violent Offenders After Prison Release," Woessner and colleagues explore the social reality of male sex and violent offenders' reentry experiences, how they cope with community related characteristics, and how their experiences interact with the dynamic nature of the reentry process. Woessner and colleagues explore the interplay between structural and psychological dynamics to assess the factors related to recidivism and desistance, and is particularly interesting for two reasons. First, their study is based on interview data from returning citizens living in Germany; Germany's penal institutions and culture is grounded in an integrative and rehabilitative model for all of its prisoners, a vastly different approach than the punitive system the United States imposes.

Second, Woessner and colleagues study the social situations and conditions of sex offenders and violent offenders.

Each chapter in Part I, Institutions, Community, and Reentry, offers a different and critical view of reentry, its related state and nonprofit institutions, and how they interact with returning citizens in the community. It is important, we believe, to take a critical approach to examine reentry practices, institutions, and different returning citizen groups, such as sex offenders and violent offenders, because without their inclusion this volume would be incomplete. Reentry is complicated; until an earnest discourse develops around the institutional limitations that exist and the realities of who is coming home, even if those people make us uncomfortable, is necessary to ensure that real reforms and policy changes are made to improve reentry outcomes for all returning citizens.

References

Bobo, L., & Thompson, V. (2010). Racialized mass incarceration: African Americans and the criminal justice system. In H. Markus & P. Moya (Eds.), *Doing race: 21 essays for the 21st century* (pp. 322–355). New York: Norton.

Clear, T. (2009). *Imprisoning communities: How mass incarceration makes disadvantaged neighborhoods worse.* New York: Oxford University Press.

Gottschalk, M. (2015). *Caught: The prison state and the lockdown of American politics.* Princeton, NJ: Princeton University Press.

LaVigne, N., Davies, E., Palmer, T., & Halberstadt, R. (2008). *Release planning for successful reentry: A guide for corrections, service providers, and community groups.* Washington, DC: Urban Institute.

Mellow, J., & Dickinson, J. (2006). The role of prerelease handbooks for prisoner reentry. *Federal Probation, 70*(1), 70–76.

Middlemass, K. (2017). *Convicted and condemned: The politics and policies of prisoner reentry.* New York: New York University Press.

Petersilia, J. (2003). *When prisoners come home: Parole and prisoner reentry.* New York: Oxford University Press.

Travis, J. (2005). *But they all come back: Facing the challenges of prisoner reentry.* Washington, DC: The Urban Institute.

Chapter 1

Halfway Home
The Thin Line Between Abstinence and the Drug Crisis

Liam Martin

Prologue

Ross Whitaker bursts into my bedroom at the Greater Boston halfway house where I live as an ethnographer.[1] "Yo, I need your help man. My son's mother just called. He got in a fight and he's all fucked up. She wants me to go down there. Can you give me a ride?"

We speed through the dark city streets while Bill Morris, another program resident, tries to get details about what to expect. Ross talks in circles about his son being drunk and having a fight with someone who owed him money. We park under the orange glow of a street lamp. The car goes quiet.

Ross' son, Keith, appears from the darkness partially supported by his mother, Chanelle, one hand on a brick wall topped with barbed wire. They bundle into the backseat of the car and the smell of booze wafts through it.

"What you doin man? Why you even out here?" Ross asks angrily.

"I been out here. I been in the street," Keith responds, slurring.

"What you mean in the street?"

"Come on, I been out here for like the last year."

The conversation goes nowhere on the short drive to Chanelle's apartment. It seems the wrong time for a productive father–son talk about misbehavior. The three disappear inside while I smoke a cigarette and Bill leans against the car.

Ross returns to say the problem is heroin. Keith was on the street dealing, and when the police came after a fight, he swallowed a fistful of small bags to avoid detection. Four of the small bags came up with fingers down his throat, but half a dozen of the bags of heroin remain in his stomach. Keith is only a heroin seller not a user, so has no built up tolerance to the drug, and a leak could be deadly.

Ross says they "poured half a bottle of shampoo down his throat" and he has been drinking glass after glass of water. I offer to drive him to the hospital, but Ross worries it would mean "catching a case" as Ross and Bill debate the meaning of the legal term "intent to distribute." Ross argues that if they pump his stomach and find the individually wrapped bags, it

16   Liam Martin

will be evidence of intent. Bill says he only needs to claim he was trying to commit suicide. Each invokes their own history facing drug charges as a source of expertise. "I been arrested for distribution right on this street!" Ross exclaims, before disappearing back inside.

Bill says all this balloon swallowing and shampoo drinking is "jail shit," and if a rich person's kid had heroin in their stomach, they would have already been to the hospital. He says it's crazy to be selling heroin when media have been reporting a spate of overdose deaths in the city – he could be dealing the lethal concoction. Bill estimates Keith would have made about $30 selling the ten small bags of heroin on behalf of someone else.

Ross and Chanelle return, asking for a ride to CVS to buy a magnesium laxative. We run several red lights on the way. Chanelle calmly announces that she is reaching a limit: "I'm about to have a nervous breakdown," she says. "If this don't work, I'm calling an ambulance. I don't care about no charge. He can hate me later, but I'm not having my son die over this."

It is almost midnight back at the apartment. Ross is worried about continuing to break halfway house curfew, but decides to wait 15 minutes for the laxative to take effect. He emerges 20 minutes later, with the bags still in Keith's stomach. Ross says his goodbyes standing in the apartment doorway: "Call me all right. Keep drinking water, man."

Stone-cold sober, Ross Whitaker watches his son flirt with death over a fistful of heroin-filled balloons, while Ross is on a mission to "get clean." He chooses to be at the halfway house, not as a parole or probation condition, but because it provides shelter and support for addiction recovery. He embraces the program message of abstinence from alcohol and other drugs. Yet he remains wedded to the drug crisis socially and geographically.

Introduction

I lived at the halfway house for nine months across three spells of fieldwork between 2012 and 2014. The husband and wife team who ran the program (while living off-site) tried to create a family atmosphere by bringing together former prisoners and outside community members. Each weeknight the kitchen, which was ringed by wooden cabinets and dark marble counter tops, filled with volunteers from local churches who arrived with bowls of garden salad and silver trays of spare ribs and chicken drumsticks. These charity-minded professionals held hands with residents to say a prayer before sharing a meal around a boardroom table donated by a university or in the lounge, where there were plastic flowers in glass vases and a framed photo of the program director's family dog. There was wireless internet. The house did not look at all prison-like: with no razor wire, high fences or other barriers to exit, it blended in with other homes on a residential street in the formerly working-class neighborhood of Clearview Crossing.[2] Clearview Crossing had been hit hard by deindustrialization. Now, where factories once stood, people can walk for miles past discarded red-brick buildings with long rows of smashed out windows and plywood covered holes and craters filled with weeds.

Despite the desolate surroundings, residents upheld impeccable standards of abstinence, and sobriety was a central cultural value. There were no after work beers or glasses of wine at the dinner table. Not once did I see drug paraphernalia, like pipes or syringes. Yet this was a strange world where strict abstinence was coupled with an intimate connection to the most destructive patterns of street-level drug dependency, and the drug crisis unfolded openly in public spaces. Residents stopped to chat on the sidewalk with emaciated sex workers while heroin users nodded sleepily on concrete stoops. Never mind that many residents had long histories of heavy drug use, experience in the neighborhood street scene, and were experiencing immense stress and uncertainty. Many residents also had friends and family who were still "out there."

The boundary between the abstinence-based halfway house and the street was blurred by physical proximity and social connections. These are structural properties shared by many reentry organizations. Even as these programs aim to assist released prisoners build new lives outside, they institutionalize ongoing connection to the street histories they ask their clients to leave behind.

Liminality in the Halfway House as a Rite of Passage

The anthropologist Arnold van Gennep (1909) noted that all societies use ritual to mark changes in social position and movements between groups. He gave these rituals a common name: "rites of passage." Consider the rites that are ubiquitous in contemporary American society – even among those who are secular and outwardly skeptical of ritual – exchanging vows and rings at weddings; hazing rituals to initiate newcomers into college fraternities, gangs, and military groups; celebrating the end of high school and university with graduation ceremonies; and marking births with baby showers, aging with birthdays, and death with funerals.

The halfway house is its own rite of passage, marking one form of transition during reentry. It is based on the notion that the movement from confinement to freedom is not a natural outcome of physical release, but one that must be socially accomplished. To borrow a phrase from Rose (1999): the halfway house assumes people leaving prison must be "made free." The reformers who developed this idea believed that there were destructive lasting impacts from imprisonment that left the released prisoner susceptible to further offending. Prisoners may have been contaminated by the prison as a "crime school," isolated from family or other sources of support, and have difficulty finding work and legitimate income. A halfway house would not only provide shelter but train residents to establish law abiding and independent lives outside prison.

As a reintegration ritual, a halfway house shares the three-part structure van Gennep (1909) found underlying all rites of passage. Drawing on the Latin root for threshold (limen), he argued that rites move through pre-liminal, liminal, and postliminal stages (that is, before the threshold, on the threshold, and after the threshold). To take one example, young boys in male initiation ceremonies are: (1) physically separated from a village and their mothers; (2) taken to a cordoned-off place to suffer ordeals and receive sacred knowledge; and (3) returned to the village to assume the role of adult men. Similarly, freshly released prisoners in a halfway house are: (1) placed apart from other members of the public; (2) subject to carceral surveillance while being trained and reformed; and (3) released to take up roles as responsible members of mainstream society.

Conceptualizing the halfway house as a rite of passage locates residents in a state of liminality (Turner, 1967) halfway between being inside prison and in society. Halfway house residents are liminaries at the intersection of different positions in the legal and social structure as they have finished their prison terms but remain in a carceral setting, are marked by criminal records, monitored by parole and/or probation, and are part of a community of former prisoners living together outside prison. They often get called "ex-offenders," which presents them as being separate from their criminal status while simultaneously being related to it.

The program pushed addiction recovery as the pathway to reintegration, but rather than providing counseling or drug treatment directly, it outsourced recovery by requiring that residents to attend four meetings each week of either Alcoholics or Narcotics Anonymous. Abstinence was enforced by drug testing and the threat of eviction. The house operations manager, a former resident employed part-time, administered breathalyzer and urine tests based on suspicious behavior. Many of the rules were up for negotiation based on personal circumstances, but when it came to drugs and alcohol, there was no negotiation and the boundary was drawn sharply; anyone who crossed it was evicted from the house and the program.

In the 12 step meetings I attended with residents, I found recovery taught as a process of individual transformation. The men were encouraged to identify as addicts and learn a body of practical wisdom for responsibly governing their lives. The program was at one level pragmatic or even mundane. But the work of habit formation was animated by a language of spiritual awakening (Valverde, 1998), including references to the transcendent (i.e., residents should surrender to a Higher Power), public readings from sacred texts (i.e., the Big Book), and rituals with religious undertones (i.e., recitation of the Serenity Prayer). Doude and Sparks, later in this volume, expound upon alcohol use disorder programs, how they apply to the reentering community, and how the 12 step programs offer people one path to redemption.

Despite the emphasis on individual change and personal responsibility, recovery was also an intensely social experience. The men living in the shared space of the halfway house and participating in the program were instructed to "build a network" in recovery. They were paired with "sponsors" who provided mentoring, and over time some residents became sponsors themselves. The halfway house was ostensibly designed to promote reintegration to mainstream society, but the relationships the men formed were mostly with people like them: former prisoners at the house and others who participated in the 12 step programs who had their own histories of street-level drug dependency. Whether in recovery or on the street, people living around and in close proximity to the residents were not only similar in background and demographics, but sometimes were the same individuals. Therefore, the core ritual of attending regular face-to-face meetings made participation in the neighborhood recovery scene central to recovery as the men were immersed in a set of social relationships crisscrossing the 12 step meetings and the other houses and programs in Clearview Crossing. "Getting clean" was less about upward mobility than redefining a static social position. Residents not only found themselves at an uncertain middle-point of their own reintegration ritual – halfway between inside and outside prison – but in a liminal border zone between an abstinence program and the drug crisis.

Getting Clean in the Shadow of the Drug Crisis

Before arriving at the halfway house, I read widely about the social construction of drugs and addiction. From Alexander's (2010) book, *The New Jim Crow*, I learned that laws ostensibly designed to control drug use were also instruments for reasserting White supremacy, and re-excluding large numbers of African-Americans from the social body through felony convictions for low-level drug offences. My intellectual reference points were critical and sociological. They revealed that misinformation and sensationalized imagery about drug users fueled punitive legislation and the rise of mass imprisonment. I began my fieldwork with a good grasp of structural processes that lead to some people being criminalized for drug use, whereas others consume their substances of choice with impunity. But I was ignorant of the crisis of substance abuse unfolding on the ground.

I spent much of my first summer in the house doing life history interviews with former prisoners in a downtown public park and observing neighborhood residents. It was a crash course in destructive drug use. On one of my first walks, I found a blonde woman in black track pants on all fours, half lying in the road. A man with an ice cream stick in his mouth beckoned me over to help. We each put a forearm under an armpit and carried her home. She was sheet white and had a large bruise on her chin, but refused an ambulance. "I don't usually do this," she said. "I've just been depressed this week."

Louie Bell was a friend of a halfway house resident. He showed up to the interview wasted and belligerent, and when he tried to spit, it got caught on his lip. "I can't believe I'm 57 and still alive," he said repeatedly. My plan was to let him talk and see where it went. Louie would say a couple of sentences at a time, go quiet, then rest his head in his hands. At one point he closed his eyes and slipped into a heroin nod before resuming talking. He said he hurt the woman who loves him, and then started crying quietly before telling himself off: "Stop fuckin crying, you fuckin faggot. You fuckin punk." After 15 minutes of this, I drove him to a detox center. Participants told me one vivid story of drug-related suffering after another. In my original interview guide, I included no questions about drugs, though that did not stop participants talking constantly about "running the streets" in suicidal bouts of substance abuse.

In addition to street drugs, the neighborhood was flooded with mass-produced pharmaceutical drugs. When I was approached by street dealers, they didn't offer crack cocaine or heroin, but Suboxone or OxyContin. Sure, my race and class positioned me in relation to local drug markets, as these were the kinds of substances a White college-type looking man would likely be looking for in the neighborhood. It was also indicative of the plethora of pharmaceutical drugs circulating in the underground economy, including Percocet, Fentanyl, Ativan, and Klonopin.

The intertwined surges in legal and illegal opiate use have created what the Center for Disease Control and Prevention calls "the worst overdose epidemic in US history" (Kolodny et al., 2015, p. 560). In 2016, around 60,000 Americans died of drug overdoses, substantially more than the number killed by either motor vehicle accidents or gun violence (Katz, 2017). The rise of overdose mortality, which has more than tripled since 2000, emerged in three reinforcing waves centered on different kinds of opiates (Ciccarone, 2017). First came the rapid increase in deaths from prescription opiates like OxyContin from the 1990s, then the escalation in heroin mortality from 2010, and finally, from around 2013, a wave of overdoses related to high-potency synthetic opiates like Fentanyl, which is designed for pain relief in palliative care. Nationwide, drug overdose is the leading cause of death for Americans under the age of 50.

Halfway house residents belonged to perhaps the most vulnerable category of drug-related deaths, reentering prisoners. A report by the Massachusetts Department of Public Health (2016) tracking people released from state prison between 2013 and 2014 found that they were *56 times more likely* to die from an opiate overdose than members of the general public. One explanation for these extraordinary rates is their drug tolerance dropping during prison terms when drug access is limited, and upon release the former prisoners use what would previously have been a normal dose, which is now enough to kill them. The increased rates are also indicative of the deep social dislocation involved in reentry, as people are suddenly shunted

Halfway Home   21

between different worlds, removed from the prison community and pushed into another facing extreme social exclusion (Middlemass, 2017).

The drug crisis is among the most immediate and brutal facts shaping the experience of halfway house residents. Analytically, it is best considered a symptom of deeper dynamics of marginality and alienation. But in that house, it was a very real and life-threatening feature of everyday life. Most residents had friends and family among the dead and had come close to overdosing themselves. It was hard to argue when they said that the choice was between recovery and death.

"The Noontime" and the Blurred Boundaries of Recovery

As I watch the Boston Celtics with Matt Carmine in his halfway house bedroom, he pulls from the drawer an article from a local newspaper. It shows a large photo of Matt sitting arms folded across the top of a backwards chair and an American flag hanging on the wall in the background. He gets me to read out loud the article, which is a profile of his success: Of 300 participants in a community corrections program, Matt was one of only two who completed it in the three-month minimum. In white space on the second page, scrawled in big felt pen lettering, he had written: "Living the Dream."

Central to Matt's identity as a changed man is his dedication to the 12 steps, and he has almost three years of "clean time." He invites me to a gathering of Narcotics Anonymous. "I wanna take you to a real meeting," he says. "Not like some of these meetings in the suburbs, like 'ooohh, I'm addicted to sex,' or 'ooohhh, I ate another packet of doughnuts last night and feel guilty.' The people at this meeting are, well, not bottom of the barrel, but come straight from the streets and alleys."

Halfway house residents call the meeting "the noontime" for the hour it takes place every weekday. It is a central site in the daily rounds of their recovery, and the physical location of "the noontime" is important: The Lutheran Church is one block from an open-air drug market, which operates on the main street of Clearview Crossing and the one-and-a-half mile walk from the halfway house to the Lutheran Church takes residents through the heart of the street-level drug economy.

At the next meeting, Matt and I sit around a table at the back of the Lutheran church basement. Exposed pipes cross and clutter a low-hanging ceiling. The air is thick with heat and sweat forms on my forehead, but before the meeting even starts, a young man with white shoes and a shaved head sobs quietly in the seat next to mine, tissue gripped in one hand. The word "Live" is tattooed on his neck, and on his wrist a friendship bracelet says, "Fight the Addiction."

Matt says the meeting chair, James, is 31 years "clean." James opens the meeting with a reading about the tenth tradition of Narcotics Anonymous, and then starts calling people to the front of the room to collect medallions celebrating clean time. The starting point for a medallion is low, but the most important: anyone can receive a "24 hour coin" as it represents the starting point of recovery. The young man next to me sobs louder, then rises slowly and walks forward. Matt leans over and whispers how embarrassing it is to collect a token showing you are using. On the way to the front, a broad-shouldered man embraces him in a hug that lasts half a minute. While walking back to his chair, he gets stopped and hugged another four times.

James opens the floor for reflections from people in attendance at the meeting. The young man speaks first and chokes back tears. After being kicked out of a program, he overdosed on heroin, woke up in a hospital on life support, and he did not know where he was. Now he is homeless. His story is followed by a stream of other painful stories about the misery of life in the street. As the whir of a rickety old fan sometimes makes it hard to hear, people saunter in and out throughout. Some chat right through the confessions. It is just another day at "the noontime."

There are no state representatives or outside experts at "the noontime." Participation may be court-ordered or forced as a program condition, but members organize the space, ensure meetings run on time, make announcements, and share knowledge. The model is one of mutual and freely given support. Organizing work is carried out collectively in ways that encourage relationship building, and taking part in "the noontime" connects men with others in the neighborhood recovery scene.

In the official literature, Narcotics Anonymous promotes strict abstinence, which means avoiding "any mood-changing, mind altering substance" (NA World Services, 2008, p. xxv), which is a prohibition so impossibly broad it would seem to include food. Yet there are contradictions. At "the noontime," the "drugs" of choice are caffeine and nicotine, which are not only allowed but closely integrated into the gatherings with free coffee and members gathering in the parking lot outside to debrief and smoke cigarettes. A range of pharmaceutical drugs, which powerfully alter consciousness, are acceptable when prescribed by doctors, and may include stimulants like Adderall, anti-depressants like Lithium, and anti-anxiety medications like Diazepam. The contradictions are rarely questioned.

The common-sense division between "clean" and "dirty" also collapses on close inspection of social relationships. The only criteria for joining Narcotics Anonymous is "a desire to stop using" (NA World Services, 2008, p. 9), and in practice, anyone can walk into "the noontime" meeting. Many participants come, as Matt Carmine puts it, "straight from the streets and alleys." New arrivals usually know others in the room from shared histories in the drug trade, although the peer networks blur together with the networks of the street-level drug economy. Despite the ambiguities, progress is given a precise quantitative measure called "clean time." Members note the specific date that they stopped using drugs and/or alcohol and count the time since, reciting the days and months and years to demonstrate success. Personal milestones are celebrated in meetings with commemorative tokens, applause, and sometimes even a party.

Old timers like James, the chair at "the noontime," embody the recovery ideal of individual triumph over addiction. At a gathering filled with stories of suffering, his presence is living proof that anyone can escape addiction if they work the program. Yet James' escape is a personal transformation and not a change in his social location; after 31 years clean, he still attends "the noontime." Twelve step principles state that the recovering addict must always attend meetings, and there is no point in time when a person can leave the program. The routines of a committed member will forever include close contact with small groups of people grappling with addiction.

The halfway house treats recovery as the primary pathway to reintegration, but recovery is a perpetual process. Recovery does not mean becoming normal, but learning to live with dysfunction as peacefully as possible. A former prisoner successfully embodies recovery when they admit their deficiencies and submit to being a lifelong work in progress. The 12 steps actively teach an addict that they will always be an addict, which means a permanent liminality is at the core of the program.

Recovery as Transition and Trap

In Clearview Crossing, the old manufacturing district runs parallel to the East, and lunchtime factory whistles once brought throngs of workers onto the main streets. The city's industrial past revolved around making things, such as shoes, envelopes, looms, wires, and corsets. Today, it is eerily empty, and where the halfway house resides. It is a tough setting for a reentry organization tasked with reintegrating former prisoners. The working-class jobs requiring little formal education have largely disappeared. The manual work still available is short-term, underpaid, and a poor foundation for social integration. Residents carry criminal records that create further obstacles to employment, such as legal barriers that interact with and reinforce other markers of race and class disadvantage (Middlemass, 2017).

As a result of this reality, the halfway house did not construct a path to reintegration through the labor market. It did not run resume workshops or soft skills trainings, or even make searching for employment a requirement of living at the house. The focus was addiction recovery. Unable to deal with the larger structural issues at play, such as deindustrialization, retrenchment, and racialized criminal stigma, the program aimed to transform the inner lives of the individuals who walked through their doors. This shifted responsibility from the institution to the men who were expected to abstain from drugs and alcohol or be evicted.

Residents were pushed into 12 step networks operating at arms-length from the program. In these meetings, participants found a forum for going straight despite the bleak prospects in the formal economy. They got clean and embarked on projects of self-transformation, collecting medallions and reciting clean time as a measure of progress, but their social integration was incomplete.

The anthropology of ritual treats liminality as a transitional state or a temporary period on the way from one structural position to another (Turner, 1967, 1977). Yet reintegration by recovery is less about changing social locations and more about changing the substances one puts in their body. A person can successfully abstain from alcohol and other drugs, going from "dirty" to "clean," with little change in social circumstances. Even when participants made a shift in the recovery scene, becoming counselors and program staff, their employment tied them to the same circuits of drug dependency that they had personally left behind. In the reentry programs of postindustrial America, recovery is less a transition than a trap.

Notes

1. All names of the people in this chapter are pseudonyms.
2. The name, "Clearview Crossing," is a pseudonym given to a real neighborhood in Boston.

References

Alexander, M. (2010). *The new Jim Crow: Mass incarceration in the age of colorblindness*. New York: The New Press.

Ciccarone, D. H. (2017). Fentanyl in the US heroin supply: A rapidly changing risk environment. *The International Journal of Drug Policy, 46*, 107–111.

Katz, J. (2017). Drug deaths in America are rising faster than ever. *New York Times*, June 5. Retrieved from https://www.nytimes.com/interactive/2017/06/05/upshot/opioid-epidemic-drug-overdose-deaths-are-rising-faster-than-ever.html

Kolodny, A., Courtwright, D.T., Hwang, C. S., Kreiner, P., Eadie, J. L., Clark, T.W., & Alexander, G. C. (2015). The prescription opioid and heroin crisis: A public health approach to an epidemic of addiction. *Annual Review of Public Health, 36*, 559–574. doi:10.1146/annurev-publhealth-031914-122957

Narcotics Anonymous World Services. (2008). *Narcotics anonymous* (6th ed.). Chatsworth, CA: Narcotics Anonymous World Services.

Rose, N. (1999). *Powers of freedom: Reframing political thought*. Cambridge: Cambridge University Press.

Massachusetts Department of Public Health. (2016). *An assessment of opioid-related deaths in Massachusetts (2013–2014)*. Retrieved from www.mass.gov/files/documents/2017/08/31/chapter-55-opioid-overdose-study-data-brief-9-15-2016.pdf

Middlemass, K. (2017). *Convicted and condemned: The politics and policies of prisoner reentry*. New York: New York University Press.

Turner, V. (1967). *The forest of symbols: Aspects of Ndembu ritual*. Ithaca, NY: Cornell University Press.

Turner, V. (1977). Variations on a theme of liminality. In S. F. Moore & B. G. Myerhoff (Ed.), *Secular Ritual* (pp. 36–52). Amsterdam: Van Gorcum.

Valverde, M. (1998). *Diseases of the will: Alcohol and the dilemmas of freedom*. Cambridge: Cambridge University Press.

van Gennep, A. (1909). *Les rites de passage* [The rites of passage]. Paris, France: Émile Nourry.

Chapter 2

Triaging Rehabilitation
The Retreat of State-Funded Prison Programming

Allison Gorga

The financial crisis of 2008 provided policy makers an opportunity to engage in a new discourse about cost and frugality; these rhetorical frames have infiltrated nearly every public policy realm, including corrections, where the experiment in mass incarceration has been identified as fiscally unsustainable. As a result, fiscally conscious language has become commonplace in criminal justice reform (Aviram, 2015). Many criminal justice reformers and practitioners have turned to "evidence-based practices" to achieve fiscal goals, which is a shift from being "tough on crime" to being "smart on crime" (Cullen & Gendreau, 2001).

Evidence-based practices, in the context of corrections, typically refer to the implementation of programming that has been demonstrated to reduce recidivism through scientific methods (Latessa, Cullen, & Gendreau, 2002). The logic behind evidence-based practices to reduce overall criminal justice spending is the belief that a reduction in recidivism rates will reduce court and processing costs, the cost of re-incarcerating a person, parole and probation expenses, and the related personal costs and property damage when recidivists commit new crimes (Cullen, Myer, & Latessa, 2009). It is believed that evidence-based practices, such as cognitive behavioral therapy and trauma-informed treatment, risk assessments to determine the appropriate level of supervision, as well as vocational and educational opportunities (Latessa et al., 2002), will reduce the use of tax dollars on corrections.

Aviram (2015) argues that criminal justice reform discourse has taken the form of "humonetarianism." This term distinguishes truly humanitarian ideologies evoked to reduce mass incarceration from fiscally-centered ideologies that encourage the use of certain penal models for cost-saving purposes. Though humonetarian concerns often align with humanitarian issues, Aviram states that humonetarianism is neither a critical assessment of punishment nor an embrace of human rights. Aviram contends that cost–benefit analyses and neoliberal rhetoric are particularly polarizing; by framing corrections policies based on economic efficiency, policy makers are able to make significant policy changes without thinking about the consequences of those decisions. Humonetarianism is a depoliticized approach to criminal justice reform that avoids confronting the moral consequences of punishment.

When correctional administrators and staff in Iowa employ "evidence-based practices" as a decision-making tool, they almost always do so in conjunction with ideologies of fiscal responsibility or concerns over how tax dollars are spent. By engaging in humonetarian interpretations of evidence-based practices to manage corrections and decrease dogmatic conflict, prison administrators in Iowa engage in practices that shape the management of the states' prisons in fundamental ways, including diminished correctional treatment and programs for many female prisoners.

Methods

The main site for the current study was the Iowa Correctional Institution for Women (ICIW), which opened in 1981 in Mitchellville, Iowa. ICIW is the only adult correctional facility for women in Iowa, and currently houses 712 prisoners at all security levels (e.g., minimum, medium, and maximum). The prison is overseen by the state's centralized correctional agency, the Iowa Department of Corrections (IDOC). The IDOC exerts control over state prisons, community-based correctional facilities (CBCs), and probation and parole through its power to approve policy changes and state appropriations. When state funds are allocated, the IDOC, utilizing its own team of accountants, dictates to prisons, judicial districts, and CBCs what they can do with the appropriated funds, which can include staffing lines or program changes.

In order to understand how prison staff interpreted and implemented "evidence-based practices" in Iowa's only correctional institution for women, I conducted participant observations at the Department of Corrections' Board of Corrections (BOC) meetings, which met monthly from August 2016 to August 2017 and are open to the public. These meetings, overseen by a governor-appointed board, begin with a statement from the Director of the IDOC followed by presentations from IDOC and prison employees. To supplement BOC meetings, I conducted 38 interviews with current and former ICIW staff and volunteers, IDOC staff, and activists and advocacy workers. Interviews lasted between 50 minutes and 2 hours. Respondents were recruited through ICIW staff and volunteer email list-servs, on-site recruitment at ICIW, and referrals. Corrections staff are often hesitant to speak with outsiders, which makes this a convenient set of respondents contacted through snowball sampling, which is a useful tool for overcoming resistance and barriers (Britton, 2003). All respondents agreed to have their interviews recorded, and names and identifying information were omitted. Respondents were asked questions about how they became involved in correctional work, job training, challenges and successes with implementing programs, what kinds of needs female prisoners have, and how they believe correctional practices might be improved.

28 Allison Gorga

Of the 38 respondents, two thirds of them were women (25 women, 13 men), middle class, and middle aged. Thirty-five identified as White and three identified as African American. Most had at least a Bachelor's degree (n = 18), whereas two had a high school diploma, and 18 had a variety of advanced and professional degrees. Seven respondents were ICIW staff members, including three correctional officers (COs), one health care provider, one administrator, one counselor, and one miscellaneous service provider. Three respondents were current IDOC employees, including a parole officer and counselors in community-based corrections for women offenders. One respondent was formerly employed at the IDOC central office providing services at ICIW and at Iowa's men's institutions. Twenty-three respondents were prison volunteers responsible for providing recreational and fine arts classes, religious services, treatment and reentry assistance, educational and vocational curricula, and family-oriented programs. Four respondents did activist or advocacy work for prisoners in Iowa but did not necessarily interact with prisoners directly.

Interviews were transcribed verbatim and observational notes were typed up immediately after observing meetings. Constructivist grounded theory was used (Charmaz, 1995) during analysis to capture emergent processes by different stakeholders negotiating the terms of punishment. The constructivist approach is derived from symbolic interactionism by focusing on how respondents engage in meaning making. The coding process involved coding for logics and decision-making arguments used to justify or argue against a policy change in the penal system. A multistage coding process was used, beginning with open coding for relevant themes and concepts. The second stage involved a more systematic distillation of themes, and allowed me to assess complexities in how the codes related to one another (Parker & Roffey, 1997). I was concerned with which arguments or frames held cultural weight or were considered "valid." In doing so, respondents revealed two patterns of behavior: First, they were constantly negotiating between providing rehabilitation services and being fiscally conscious, and second, how stakeholders managed conflict between these two cultural frames and responded to the discord by reconfiguring the operation of ICIW.

Results

Early in the research process, it was discovered that the IDOC actively promoted a culture of evidence-based practices. During BOC meetings, IDOC officials frequently referred to "research" and research methodologies when describing their decision-making practices. However, roughly two-thirds of all references to evidence-based practices, research, or science in BOC meetings were used alongside references to fiscal needs, concerns for taxpayer dollars, and limited monetary resources. The increasing fiscal constraints faced by the IDOC drove prison administrators to use evidence-based practices in innovative ways that directly impacted the quality of correctional care received by female prisoners.

Program Reclassification

IDOC employees, especially during BOC meetings, used evidence-based practices alongside cost-benefit analyses, or cost-cutting frames, to identify policy changes, staffing, and resource allocation. The IDOC engaged in weaving the terms "evidence-based practices" and "fiscal issues" in a number of ways that shaped the kinds of programming offered, the kinds of offenders who could access that programming, and the way prisoners were managed and organized. One example of this was how IDOC restructured prison programming:

> *April 2017 BOC Meeting, Dr. Beth Skinner (DOC researcher):* We went to every institution and put their programs in bins. There's A programs – these are programs that are proven effective, and promising, and B programs are essential programming, things like education, apprenticeships, mental health services. Programs in groups A and B are using up staff resources. C programs are a low priority. We want those to be moved to all volunteer-led or offender-led programs. This is an evidence-based decision. . . . Then if there is going to be a new program at a prison, it has to be run through the core team – the decision will be evidence-based and based on resources and needs. It's a model for how to run our prisons.

Dr. Skinner notes that the decision is based on both evidence and "resources and needs;" however, a closer look at this program classification indicates that it is only partially based upon "evidence-based" practices for recidivism reduction. Programs in the "A" group are fully funded by IDOC via state appropriations and are said to reduce recidivism. These programs include cognitive-based treatment and "core correctional practices." Cognitive behavioral therapy is the main rehabilitative treatment for high- and medium-risk offenders, and the use of such practices is part of an ongoing trend in corrections to employ non-counseling staff to do counseling work (Dvoskin & Spiers, 2004). "Core correctional practices" are not treatment, per se, but instead utilize all staff interactions with prisoners as opportunities to assist, counsel, and direct prisoners in certain directions; such moments are intended to supplement cognitive behavioral therapy. In order to implement "core correctional practices," IDOC planned to train all staff, including janitors and maintenance staff, in such practices, like motivational interviewing, effective use of reinforcement, and modeling problem-solving skills.

"B" programs are those that are required by state and federal law, and include many recidivism-reducing programs, such as mental health treatment, basic adult education, literacy classes, GED courses, and apprenticeship programs, all of which can utilize state resources; however, only treatment for serious mental illness and some adult basic education courses are fully funded and staffed by IDOC. Other educational programs, like GED and HiSET courses and testing, are outsourced to local community colleges at a reduced fee via inside-out classes. Apprenticeship programs are mostly funded by the profits made from prisoners' telephone costs while the programs are run by volunteers associated with or with experience related to the apprenticeship skill.

"C" programs are those that are volunteer-supported and funded by volunteers' own monies, grants, or donations. Despite clear evidence of the recidivism-reducing effects of prison education programs, some argue that the recidivism-reducing effects of prison education is strongest for only those who obtain post-secondary degrees (Duwe & Clark, 2014); regardless, prison education is one of the most robust findings in rehabilitation scholarship (Esperian, 2010; Ellison, Szifris, Horan, & Fox, 2017). Yet college education in Iowa's prisons is exclusively provided on a volunteer basis. Other "C" programs include recreational programs, fine arts programs, PTSD treatment, religious programs, reentry programs, parenting and family-related programs, and alcoholics anonymous (AA) and narcotics anonymous (NA), to name a few; most of these programs have a demonstrated negative impact on recidivism (Latessa et al., 2002; Ellison et al., 2017). Earlier in this section, Martin, and later in Section II, Doude and Sparks, both explore different aspects of AA and NA programs; each of whom came to some interesting findings on how such programs are not the singular solution to treating alcohol and drug addiction and may not reduce recidivism based on how the program is structured.

To identify programs to cut or implement, IDOC does not rely on recidivism rates exclusively. Instead, IDOC utilized the clearinghouse "Results First" from the PEW Foundation to identify programs that used rigorous research designs to demonstrate a significant reduction in recidivism rates. "Results First" also provides state correctional agencies with guidelines on how to calculate returns on investment (ROI), which takes into account court and processing costs for prison returnees; harm and damage done to victims, property, and the community; and costs of incarceration. On the basis of "Results First," IDOC began cutting programs that either did not show a significant recidivism reduction rate based on an experimental design or meta-analysis, the gold standard of research, or were costly to run.

Triaging Care: Focusing on High-Risk Offenders

One of IDOC's approaches to fuse evidence-based practices with fiscal needs was to focus on offenders with a high-risk of re-offending, which I call "triaging rehabilitative care." Empirical evidence on risk assessments demonstrates that low-risk offenders do not need as much supervision post-release, and that, in some cases, more state involvement with low-risk offenders can actually increase their recidivism rates; this is the case because state involvement and supervision can lead to stigma and distrust in state institutions (Andrews, Bonta, & Hoge, 1990; Andrews & Bonta, 2010). IDOC administrators frequently explained during BOC meetings that when faced with budget cuts that focusing on high-risk offenders was the best (fiscal) approach.

Although reserving more intensive supervision for high-risk offenders is consistent with common evidence-based practices, there were some problems with IDOC's strategy. Namely, criminological research indicates that although low-risk offenders should have less intensive levels of supervision from parole and probations counselors, they should *not* have less access to prison programming (Andrews & Bonta, 2010). Several advocacy workers explained how IDOC's approach to triaging rehabilitation meant low-risk offenders received little or no programming while incarcerated, and medium- and low-risk offenders were deprioritized for access even when court-ordered programs mandated that a prisoner. During a BOC meeting, one woman whose son was in prison explained the difficulty that her son had getting into programs. First, the Parole Board would not release him until he took a certain drug abuse course, but because he was a low-risk offender his treatment and ability to take a parole-mandated course was not prioritized by prison staff.

> *BOC Meeting, April 2017, Public Comments:* My son has a mandatory minimum. He is supposed to be up for parole in June. He needs a substance abuse treatment course as part of his case management, but there are not enough counselors to teach the course. The staff were helpful, but they simply don't have enough people. There are 300 people on the waiting list, 56 people get through every four months, and you're probably adding another 80 people during that time who come into prison and also need that treatment, so the wait list grows exponentially. . . . At this rate, it will take 25 years to get them all through it. It's just not realistic.

The same was largely true for female prisoners needing drug treatment programs. In response to this public comment, Nick, a Newton Correctional Facility Employee, provided an update about the waiting lists:

> There have been some updates on the waiting list. We are using high-risk identifiers, so 65 people got diverted to [a] shorter substance abuse treatment. A few counselors have been in training. They had to shadow other courses for a certain amount of time, but now they're able to teach their own. That will start in one month.

Despite parole mandating a particular course for release, IDOC was limited in what it could do because of constrained state funds; instead of appealing to state legislators to increase the budget for substance abuse courses, IDOC's solution was to use risk assessments to identify offenders who could receive a shorter version of the substance abuse program. Respondents claimed that these programming strategies were part of a "numbers game" (Tanya, White woman advocacy worker). The goal of IDOC, as many respondents asserted, was to get more offenders out of prison quickly rather than delivering quality correctional care.

After cutting programs and focusing on high-risk offenders, state prisons in Iowa became dependent upon volunteer services, grant funds for programs, and connections with community-based agencies and organizations. At the time of data collection, there were 337 registered volunteers at ICIW, most of whom provided religious services. Many other volunteers provided essential "B" programs, such as Adult Basic Education and GED tutoring, and volunteers also taught and provided "C" programs, such as college courses, PTSD treatment courses, vocational programming, family reunification, mental health treatment, and reentry programming. In the wake of funding cuts and elimination of state-funded programming for medium- and low-risk offenders, volunteers claimed that they were doing IDOC's job for them. Teri, an educational volunteer, explained:

> We received no money from the [Iowa] Department of Corrections and were running a huge number of programs for them, which is ridiculous. . . . They have outsourced so many vital programs out to volunteer programs, and they don't have to pay for it then, and um, you know, the volunteers are intrinsically motivated to keep doing it, but then when you have volunteers who leave. Those programs just fall apart. And there's no continuation. . . . A number of, like, the NA and AA classes have been outsourced and those are done by volunteers. So education certainly, yeah, the trauma programming is all done by volunteers, or by staff that are from other agencies and are not paid by the DOC to do that. There's a number of re-entry programming that has been outsourced and relies upon, really heavily upon volunteers.
>
> (Interviewed February 2017)

Dustin, a White man who provided a reentry program at ICIW, similarly explained how his program was one of a few reentry programs in the prison, and that ICIW did not offer a program funded by the state:

> That's why we did this re-entry course, to try to get them to put in a re-entry curriculum and we tried to model it, and we're staffing it as a volunteer. We're doing their job for them, but we're trying to do it right,

and we're trying to model the way to do it right in the hopes that they'll take it over and put some resources with it and make it more comprehensive and required.

(Interviewed May 2016)

Although some volunteers do not teach a specific program, they did take short shifts of supervising prisoners, which enabled prisoners to use designated spaces without correctional staff supervision or resources. Carmen, who was one of many volunteers in the prison library at ICIW, explained how this posed a problem for prisoners:

I wish I had more time to give them. Their library is not open enough. Obviously, I think their craft room needs to be opened. I don't have enough hours to give 'em and that's frustrating to me. . . . The hours are what we give 'em, so if we're not there, there's no library hours. So like, last week I was on vacation. They didn't get library on that day. So any time I'm gone on my day, there's no library. There's not a sub or anything to go in.

(Interviewed October 2016)

IDOC prison staff and administrators were aware of their dependency on volunteers and outside agencies to provide programming, and yet, IDOC officials increased their dependency by developing additional connections with organizations in the community. During several BOC meetings, Director Bartruff explained how he attempted to foster these connections:

BOC Meeting, February 2017, Director Bartruff: On January 28, I met with the Urbandale Methodist Church to talk about corrections – they have people there who have been part of the re-entry teams. The whole idea is to expand the capacity of community involvement like that. [. . .] We want to bring together corrections folks in an area, and have community services – substance abuse, re-entry, and so on. The point is to increase community connections. We want to develop a resource guide for our staff and offenders.

By triaging rehabilitation in the face of fiscal needs, prisons in Iowa became dependent upon agencies and volunteers who are not compensated by the state for their work. As a result, access to these resources and programs is unpredictable, and such uncertainty may contribute to prisoners' chronic stress (Sugie & Turney, 2017). Additionally, volunteer programs sometimes exclude prisoners based on religious affiliation. For example, the only comprehensive reentry program at ICIW is associated with a Christian church, and program leaders discourage prisoners from participating who might be averse to faith-based reentry programs, even though the program

34 Allison Gorga

is considered nondenominational. Dustin, a White male volunteer who provided services for this reentry program, explained:

> [The program leader] is pretty clear on – "This is a faith-based program. You don't have to like it. If you don't like it, don't come." And so we'll pray and talk about God, and talk about religious stuff. You know, don't sign up for the program if you don't want religious stuff.
>
> (Interviewed May 2016)

The lack of state funding and overreliance on volunteers contributes to the process of triaging rehabilitation programs; non-religious prisoners, or those whose religion is not represented among volunteers, these prisoners had diminished access to essential services.

Prison Reorganization

With the continued funding cuts, IDOC made several changes to reduce and reorganize staff. IDOC began conducting "staffing analyses" to identify positions that could be cut or moved to other institutions based on prisoner risk levels. For instance, IDOC reclassified Mount Pleasant Correctional Facility from a medium-security facility to a minimum-security facility, which allowed for a reduction in staff levels. At North Central Correctional Facility and Fort Dodge Correctional Facility, IDOC created "shared positions;" one individual served as the warden for both prisons. Statewide, IDOC closed access to every minimum live-out (MLO) facility (except for a unit at ICIW, Unit Y) in the spring of 2017; MLOs are housing units for low-risk offenders preparing for gradual release and are extensions of higher security correctional facilities that exist outside of the prison. Prisoners have more freedom of movement in an MLO, and can work and attend job training classes or other reentry related programs, such as completing community service hours or renewing their driver's license. MLO prisoners, however, do not have access to some of the programming or resources offered within prison. By restricting access to MLOs throughout the state, IDOC was able to cut staffing levels, as fewer staff were needed to supervise prisoners in the unit and transport them to and from off-site reentry activities. The reduction in staff also allowed the state to relocate prisoners; in many cases, low-risk prisoners living in an MLO were sent back to a medium- or maximum-security prison. These changes consolidated more prisoners into smaller confined spaces, left prisons with reduced staffing levels, and as a result IDOC disrupted reentry opportunities for many low-risk offenders.

Although the MLO in Unit Y at ICIW did not close, prisoners in this work-release unit received little programming or resources and had limited staff assistance; several respondents claimed that prisoners in Unit Y were "just twiddling their thumbs." Prisoners in Unit Y were not allowed to access programming inside the main prison because of fewer correctional staff; no one was available to move prisoners between Unit Y and the main prison.

Prisoners also suffered a lack of programming and services because of overcrowding; ICIW's population increased from 560 to 808 prisoners in 2015, but staffing levels remained the same, fluctuating between 108 and 122 guards. The prison, renovated in 2015, was designed with more space allocated for programming, but understaffing and budget cuts, as many respondents claimed, limited the prisons' capacity to deliver the programming levels promised by the new design. Nina, a White woman who worked part-time at ICIW, explains:

> There are buildings that were part of the [2015 renovation] plan that aren't open because of staffing. . . . The new prison was built for 888 women. We have less than that on the Census, but in the spaces that are open there are more women in a space than were intended. . . . So all that is frustrating and kinda disappointing. Some of the things that were expected to happen, couldn't happen because of the way the funding came through at the end of the day.
>
> (Interviewed August 2016)

Several respondents described ICIW as a "ghost town" because of the lack of officer presence. Ron, a White man who was a correctional officer, described how staff were stretched thin under these conditions:

> They [IDOC] expect more with the same amount of staff. There's times where you need an officer to help unlock a classroom, and there's nobody available. You have officers doing escorts, you have officers stuck in R&D [Receiving and Discharge] with a new trip, or doing orientation with a new trip. You have other officers getting breaks, 'cause you know we're supposed to get breaks as well, so you could have everybody tied up and there ain't nobody available. And they [prisoners] just gotta wait. Or if you need somebody in reception, 'cause we pulled the reception officers, so there's nobody sitting in reception desk.
>
> (Interviewed July 2016)

Volunteers frequently discussed the lack of a security presence at ICIW. Very few volunteers interacted with COs, who were rarely, if ever, capable of being present for volunteer programming. Most volunteers claimed that they never felt unsafe when they were surrounded by prisoners, but there were a few occasions where they preferred a greater security presence.

Rebecca, a White woman, who provided fine arts services to offenders and occasionally did so with large numbers of offenders present and no guards, was at times uncomfortable:

> If there was something happening, right then, that you had someone violent, I don't have a guard in the room. I'm way up by myself in a

classroom.... I look at the way it started out when I started there. There was a guard in the gym while I did my group. They had more staff then at the time.... Then over time, ... I was the only one there, as a volunteer with a hundred inmates in the gym.... I would have preferred a guard in the room.

(Interviewed July 2016)

In other situations, volunteers were expected to do the work of COs. Many volunteers described de-escalating fights and informally disciplining prisoners for minor infractions. Guards were stretched so thin that the circumstances further exacerbated IDOC's reliance on volunteers for basic operational needs, prisoner management, and the delivery of treatment, which often fell to people without formal training in these areas. In spite of the increased professionalization of corrections (Garland, 2012), fewer prisoners in Iowa receive direct care from trained professionals under the state's fiscal focus.

Conclusion

Concerns about fiscal responsibility and statewide funding cuts are undoubtedly implicated in how Iowa's correctional stakeholders interpreted evidence-based practices to reconfigure the structure and operation of prisons, which produced a unique set of consequences for the delivery of prison programming. Administrators interpreted evidence-based practices through a cost-saving lens as they developed a new program classification, determined which programs to cut, and assessed which prisoners would receive treatment. These stakeholders' interpretation of what constitutes "evidence-based practices" is a far cry from what most criminologists suggest; they argue that evidence more often suggests that additional and different kinds of programs are the best approach to reducing reoffending (Latessa et al., 2002; Andrews & Bonta, 2010; Lowenkamp, Holsinger, Robinson, & Cullen, 2012).

A side effect of Iowa's DOC's approach to evidence-based practices is that it reinforces inequalities. By relying on community organizations and volunteers to provide prison programming, state legislators and IDOC pass the work to concerned volunteer-citizens or nonprofit groups who are free to exclude participants they deemed inappropriate. Most volunteers claimed that they excluded prisoners from participating in their programs for a variety of reasons, such as prisoners who had a different religious or world view, who had a disciplinary infraction or certain conviction (e.g., sex offenders), or who volunteers simply disliked. Additionally, volunteers are not held to the same level of transparency and public oversight as state employees and state-funded programs. With the growing trend of public favor for reduced correctional spending (Aviram, 2015), the overreliance on volunteers and the inequalities that can accompany this strategy of delivering programs are likely to worsen in Iowa.

Although the concept of "evidence-based practices" is appealing, policy scholars argue that states should tread with care (Lowenkamp et al., 2012; Parkhurst, 2017). IDOC's approach to evidence-based practices is humonetarian, which has led to a reduction in state expenditures on corrections and prison services and farmed out rehabilitative and other programs to concerned volunteers rather than trained professionals. In spite of IDOC's "culture shift" toward evidence-based practices, fiscal constraints have led to fewer on-the-ground practices that are actually based on empirical evidence for recidivism reduction.

References

Andrews, D. A., & Bonta, J. (2010). Rehabilitating criminal justice policy and practice. *Psychology, Public Policy, and Law, 16*(1), 39–55.

Andrews, D. A., Bonta, J., & Hoge, R. D. (1990). Classification for effective rehabilitation: Rediscovering psychology. *Criminal Justice and Behavior, 17*(1), 19–52.

Aviram, H. (2015). *Cheap on crime: Recession-era politics and the transformation of American punishment.* Oakland: University of California Press.

Britton, D. (2003). *At work in the iron cage: The prison as gendered organization.* New York: New York University Press.

Charmaz, K. (1995). *Constructing grounded theory* (1st ed.). Thousand Oaks, CA: Sage Publications, Inc.

Cullen, F. T., & Gendreau, P. (2001). From nothing works to what works: Changing professional ideology in the 21st century. *The Prison Journal, 81*(3), 313–338.

Cullen, F. T., Myer, A. J., & Latessa, E. J. (2009). Eight lessons from Moneyball: The high cost of ignoring evidence-based corrections. *Victims and Offenders, 4*(2), 197–213.

Dvoskin, J. A., & Spiers, E. M. (2004). On the role of correctional officers in prison mental health. *Psychiatric Quarterly, 75*(1), 41–59.

Duwe, G., & Clark, V. (2014). The effects of prison-based educational programming on recidivism and employment. *The Prison Journal, 94*(4), 454–478.

Ellison, M., Szifris, K., Horan, R., & Fox, C. (2017). A rapid evidence assessment of the effectiveness of prison education in reducing recidivism and increasing employment. *Probation Journal, 64*(2), 108–128.

Esperian, J. H. (2010). The effect of prison education programs on recidivism. *Journal of Correctional Education, 61*(4), 316–334.

Garland, D. (2012). *Punishment and modern society: A study in social theory.* Chicago: University of Chicago Press.

Latessa, E. J., Cullen, F. T., & Gendreau, P. (2002). Beyond correctional quackery-Professionalism and the possibility of effective treatment. *Federal Probation, 66*(2), 43–49.

Lowenkamp, C. T., Holsinger, A. M., Robinson, C. R., & Cullen, F. T. (2012). When a person isn't a data point: Making evidence-based practice work. *Federal Probation, 76*(3), 11–21.

Parker, L., & Roffey, B. (1997). Methodological themes. *Accounting, Auditing & Accountability Journal, 10*(2), 212–247.

Parkhurst, J. (2017). *The politics of evidence: From evidence-based policy to the good governance of evidence.* New York: Routledge/Taylor & Francis Group.

Sugie, N. F., & Turney, K. (2017). Beyond incarceration: Criminal justice contact and mental health. *American Sociological Review, 82*(4), 719–743.

Chapter 3

The State's Accomplices? Organizations and the Penal State[1]

Nicole Kaufman

Nongovernmental organizations (NGOs) focused on work with formerly incarcerated people in the United States commonly offer case management and programs covering topics ranging from soft skills to substance use to legal rights.[2] The "reentry sector" has become attractive to policy-makers, who observe that NGOs can "enable enduring transformations" and build skills among formerly incarcerated people (Tomczak & Albertson, 2016, p. 58) while costing the state little to nothing. Policy-makers have focused on communities and tasked NGOs with the responsibility for managing criminalized people, even while making limited public funds available for privatized services. Whether or not NGOs receive public funds, this arrangement has them providing services that the state did not previously administer (e.g., spiritual guidance) or providing services decimated through the expansion of penal institutions and/or the thinning of the welfare state.

Increasingly, critics have labeled this field of service provision the "prisoner reentry industry," the "prisoner reintegration industry," or "Reentry, Inc." (Carlen & Tombs, 2006; Shaylor & Meiners, 2013; Thompkins, 2010). Critical scholars have studied the limited ability or will of NGOs working with formerly incarcerated people to address the conditions of mass punishment, penal state surveillance, neoliberalism, economic exclusion, racism, male gender domination, and political disenfranchisement. Critics also observe that funding streams earmarked for post-release services permit the power of the penal state to extend into NGOs' programs and divert their goals (Bumiller, 2013; Haney, 2010). Haney (2010) describes NGOs as "satellite states" who are dependent on the state for survival whereas Kilty and Devellis (2010) describe concerns about "seepage" or the absorption of an increasing number of NGOs into alliances with the penal state. Yet some critical work points to contemporary NGOs who mobilize to protect the rights and dignity of formerly incarcerated people (e.g., Flores & Cossyleon, 2016; Kilroy, Barton, Quixley, George, & Russell, 2013; Owens, 2014).

What is the nature of the relationship between the penal state and NGOs? To what extent are NGOs accurately characterized as the states' accomplices, and under what circumstances do NGOs resist being "tools

40   Nicole Kaufman

of the state" (Cohen, 1985, p. 164)? This chapter investigates these questions by considering two properties of organizations: (1) *hierarchy*, the degree to which NGOs are subordinates of penal state agencies; and (2) *closeness*, the degree to which NGOs view the state as an interlocutor (participant in a conversation) or a target for advocacy. Based on the confluence of these two properties, a four-part typology of NGOs is introduced: *satellite states*, which are located close to and in hierarchical relationships with penal state actors; *satellite-seeking NGOs*, which maintain distant relationships with penal state actors and aspire to receive funding that would place them in a hierarchical relationship; *interlocutors and advocates*, which treat the state as a conversant and/or a target for advocacy on policy and curricular issues; and *NGOs opposing state involvement*, which are located in less hierarchical and more distant relationships with penal state actors. Of these, the latter three types are not well conceptualized in the literature; here, empirical examples are provided using data collected between 2009 and 2013 from 18 NGOs working with former prisoners in Dane and Milwaukee Counties, Wisconsin. The focus was on NGOs that worked with women; therefore, interviews, documents, and observations of programs, community meetings, and legislative hearings were collected from organizations working with formerly incarcerated women, either alone or alongside men. The data provides the basis for cross-type comparisons and allows for an understanding about the dynamics of the NGO sector and recognition of the ways in which NGOs' responses to the penal state range from accommodation to the state's preferences, to resistance to and distancing from state agencies.

Conceptualizing NGO–State Relationships

Amidst mass incarceration, the hollowing of the welfare state, and the devolution of services for criminalized people, examining linkages between NGOs and the penal state is a challenging but crucial task. The penal state is "the punishing arm of the government, consisting of corrections departments, courts, law enforcement, and legislatures," and its boundaries are increasingly ambiguous (Kaufman, Kaiser, & Rumpf, 2018, p. 470; Haney, 2010). Working with, beyond, inside, and outside these institutions are nongovernmental providers of services for criminalized people, which have enlarged their presence and power since the 1960s (Cohen, 1985). Their professional guidelines and accreditation standards mean that these service providers are "not directly or necessarily acting in the best interest of the state" and are not "tools of the state" (Cohen, 1985, p. 164). Instead, Cohen argues that these "elites and self-seeking" professionals enjoy "functional autonomy" and "advance their own interests" (1985, p. 163). However, in the decades since this proclamation, mass incarceration has exploded and arrangements between the penal state and civil society have shifted. Service providers may

Organizations and the Penal State 41

experience political pressure, resource scarcity, and competition not captured in Cohen's work in the 1980s.

As record numbers of incarcerated people have been released to communities, states have sought to meet their needs by relying on NGOs, typically composed of professional staff and volunteers but no government employees. These transformations have changed the tenor of critical penology. As many NGOs are dependent on the penal state for survival, a growing number of contemporary critics (e.g., Thompkins, 2010) are skeptical that they could achieve autonomy from the state's surveillance and control goals. Byrd (2016) raised concerns that as formerly incarcerated people "become objects in the social service industry . . . reentry will simply exacerbate the surveillance aspects of penal control by wrapping them in a cost-effective veneer" (13). Similarly, Shaylor and Meiners cautioned that NGOs are seemingly non-carceral sites that can "render more diffuse, or even mask, carceral practices" (2013, pp. 189–190). The penal state's co-optation of providers' goals, budgetary priorities, programming, and staffing decisions may dampen the prospects for NGOs to operate independently (Haney, 2010); thus, organizations are pulled into the "political vortex" of the state as a pretext to intervene into the lives of criminalized people in stigmatizing and punitive ways (Maidment, 2006a, p. 18). Others have observed that few organizations working with formerly incarcerated people have mobilized to resist conditions of mass incarceration (Bumiller, 2013; Shaylor & Meiners, 2013). NGOs with little interest beyond their own growth are deemed unlikely to challenge the penal state's treatment of formerly incarcerated people (Bumiller, 2013; Corcoran & Fox, 2013; Thompkins, 2010; Shaylor & Meiners, 2013). As a result, the state maintains its dominance over NGOs.

This dominance is related to the property of *hierarchy*, the degree to which penal state actors hold NGOs accountable as subordinates. When relationships are more hierarchical, the penal state as funder steers NGOs' agendas and activities, requires them to report to and be accountable to the state, and expects that NGOs will rely on law enforcement or mirror the controlled prison environment.[3] NGOs in less hierarchical relationships lack the obligation to report to the penal state that accompanies governmental funding.

Critical penological research tends to depict NGOs in very hierarchical relationships with governmental bodies, such that the state has lured NGOs into performing as accomplices. Discussions of co-optation highlight organizations' acceptance of state funding (Shaylor & Meiners, 2013; Thompkins, 2010; Thompkins, Curtis, & Wendel, 2010), which can diminish NGOs' autonomy, encourage convergence between NGOs and the penal state (Kaufman, 2015), pressure NGOs to conform their agendas to policy goals (Maidment, 2006b), and draw organizations closer to law enforcement (Bumiller, 2013; Haney, 2010; Kilty & Devellis, 2010; Shantz, Kilty, & Frignon, 2009). Additionally, state funding impacts organizational activities by requiring NGOs to provide specific programs and measures to assess risk and success (Kilroy et al., 2013). Although the empirical record for NGOs that receive no public funding is thin, the shape of such relationships may hinge on other factors besides funding.

Hierarchy is important in explaining such relationships, but just as crucial is a second property called *closeness*, which is the degree to which NGOs view the state as a vehicle of policy change or as an interlocutor in discussions about curriculum design or services. NGOs are free to participate in or avoid such discussions or be in close or distant relationships with penal state agencies beyond the scope of contracts. Advocacy provides one vehicle to closeness and occurs when NGOs lobby officials to restore rights to people with criminal records, protest against carceral and police actions, pursue criminal justice reform (Flores & Cossyleon, 2016; Katzenstein, 2005; Owens, 2014), and promote policies that accelerate decarceration or abolish prisons (Byrd, 2016; Kilroy et al., 2013). Closeness can also take the form of discussions about developing curricula or broader service issues outside the terms of a contract. For instance, NGOs can participate in a county-wide Reentry Task Force or testify before a legislative committee on criminal justice (Kaufman, 2015); however, acting in an oppositional manner may jeopardize potential standing with future contracts. Alternatively, in a distant relationship, an NGO would regard engaging with penal state agencies around curricular or policy issues as fruitless.

Although hierarchy and closeness are related, disaggregating these dimensions permits an examination of resistance to the state's co-optation, a task modeled with NGOs in other sectors. For example, Thomas and colleagues observed that as governmental drug policies increasingly ask the community to govern drug users organizations may resist or perpetuate the state's power (Thomas, Bull, Dioso-Villa, & Smith, 2016). Similarly, Matthews (1995) found that in the development of rape crisis centers, some organizations accommodated to pressures to accept state funds and became bureaucratized, whereas others took an oppositional stance. Inspired by this research, four types of NGOs that operate based on the co-occurrence of hierarchy and closeness are identified.

First, there are "satellite institutions" or "satellite states," which are NGOs located outside the confines of state structures but "hover around the centralized 'mother ship,'" and rely on the state for material, survival, legitimacy, and authority (Haney, 2010, p. 16). The NGOs I conceptualize as *satellite states* are in close and hierarchical relationships with penal state agencies that provide earmarked "reentry" funds (e.g., Ready4Work). Their proximity to the state via funding may facilitate additional types of conversations around policy and curriculum.

Second, *satellite-seeking* NGOs association with government agencies is more distant because they do not enter arenas where they would critique the penal state or converse with officials about interventions. Yet these NGOs are eager to establish a hierarchical relationship through earmarked "reentry" funding for which they may have applied. This orientation is not well represented in critical penological literature, which has focused on state-funded NGOs.

Third, *interlocutors and advocates* do not receive earmarked "reentry" funds; rather, a core aspect of these NGOs is their financial independence. Their interactions with the state are based on approaching officials as targets of advocacy and/or engaging in conversations unrelated to the fulfillment of a contract. There is less concern about alienating the state as an ally because the organization is not navigating a funding agreement or applying for support.

Finally, *NGOs opposed to state involvement* are in non-hierarchical and distant relationships with penal state actors, and do not seek governmental "reentry" funding. Staff view participating in community–government task forces, testifying, and sharing curricular ideas with correctional administrators as counterproductive to organizational goals, and therefore do not participate in such dialogues. Studying such NGOs will tell us about the capacity of organizations to resist the pull of the penal state beyond traditional activism. The following section presents data on the latter three types of NGOs, which are not well understood.

Data and Methods

Between 2009 and 2013, I collected data in Madison, located in Dane County, and Milwaukee, Milwaukee County, two of Wisconsin's highest reentry counties. All 18 organizations where data was collected work with formerly incarcerated women, and nearly all of them also work with men. To understand how the organizations operated, I interviewed at least one staff member at each organization about the organization's goals, services, and funding, and collected mission statements and descriptions of services from staff, the State of Wisconsin, social service directories, and the archives of the Wisconsin Historical Society. I also observed interactions between NGOs and penal state agencies by attending routine programs at a subsample of seven NGOs.[4] I observed state legislative hearings related to parole and attended community meetings on post-release issues hosted by umbrella organizations in Madison and Milwaukee. Although capturing limited data on NGOs' interactions with law enforcement agencies, the research design did reveal NGO interactions with the Wisconsin Department of Corrections (DOC). I have anonymized all names of individuals and organizations.

Based on the collected data, NGOs in hierarchical relationships were operationalized by the presence of several indicators: the receipt of funding earmarked for "reentry" through the Wisconsin DOC, the U.S. Bureau of Prisons, and the U.S. Department of Labor, which establish criteria for programming and reporting by the NGOs they fund; registration on VendorNet, the purchasing site for the State of Wisconsin, which indicates NGOs' openness to a hierarchical funding/reporting relationship; and the submission of

44   Nicole Kaufman

Table 3.1 Nongovernmental Organizations (NGOs) by Type of Relationship

		Degree of Hierarchy in Relationship with Penal State	
		More Hierarchical	*Less Hierarchical*
Degree of Closeness of Penal State Officials	Closer	Satellite States (n = 6) Community Treatment for Offenders Onward Upward City Support Center Clinics in Wisconsin Ministry of St. Peter Community Environment for Women	Interlocutors and Advocates (n = 2) Heart to Heart Mary Magdalene
	Farther	Satellite-Seeking NGOs (n = 5) All Our Sisters Social Justice, Inc. Healing Our Sisters and Brothers Journey to Stable Work Growing Our Garden	NGOs Opposed to State Involvement (n = 5) St. Matthew House God's Love, Inc. Good Word Bible Study Dinner with Luke Eastern Wisconsin Evangelical Mission

applications for state "reentry" funds.[5] NGOs in closer relationships with penal state agencies were based on several indicators: testifying in the state legislature, protesting officials, and approaching DOC personnel as interlocutors. The most common type of NGO identified was satellite states (six organizations); five satellite-seeking NGOs, two interlocutors and advocates, and five NGOs opposed to state involvement were identified (see Table 3.1).

Closeness and Hierarchy in Action

Satellite-Seeking NGOs

Five NGOs were in or aspired to be in hierarchical relationships with penal state agencies but maintained a distant relationship with them. Many of these NGOs appeared to be less competitive for state funds than satellite states. Growing Our Garden (GOG) illustrates this relationship. GOG is a community-based arts program run by Reverend Liz Smith in connection with a jail ministry, and promotes itself as "a safe place for women who are recreating their lives after incarceration to develop their artistic skills." Such an organization will have a difficult time measuring client interactions and "success" as it pertains to funding prospects.

Reverend Smith identified obtaining financial support as difficult and a source of frustration. Until about 2000, she was able to raise approximately $15,000 from the governing organization of her church, which paid for her and her fellow leaders' time. Yet she observed that other funds from this and other religious sources began to decrease in the early 2000s, and now the money was "going elsewhere within churches" or was "drying up."[6] Further, Reverend Smith said GOG was competing for funds alongside other women-related organizations, such as the area's rape crisis and domestic violence centers. When I asked Reverend Smith if she had considered a private funder (e.g., United Way), she replied that GOG would not be able to compete for foundation grants because the jail ministry is too religious. The remaining funds for which GOG was competitive would not cover salaries, only supplies; Reverend Smith framed herself and her co-leader as volunteers.

The religiosity of GOG might make it eligible for funds through federal faith-based reentry initiatives; indeed, a GOG board member researched whether such funding was possible for GOG. However, Reverend Smith concluded that this money would not be available for "groups like them" because "the accountability and follow-up required is not something we do." DOC contracts require rigorous record-keeping, including the documentation of a program's goals, clients' attendance, referrals, and effectiveness at reducing recidivism, and generating and storing these records would be difficult for GOG, which lacks space to house records and has limited capacity for intake and case management.

GOG's competitiveness for funding is not only limited by record-keeping; GOG's approach to substance use and measures of success conflict with those used by the DOC. Whereas DOC awards are based on a model of "zero-tolerance" of substance use, GOG holds an alternative view of sobriety. Reverend Smith said the group's co-leaders are "loving people" who are "respectful and confidential," so they "accept where people are at" and expect sobriety when participants are present in programs. During our interview, she asked:

> How would you measure the success for someone who repeatedly tries and fails, and each time learns something new about herself? Each time she comes in sober and gets what she needs for the day. She calls the reverend because she knows I worry. . . . I could rescue them left and right, [and say] here's the plan, but they will feel better when they decide [on their own] and ask, "Could you help with this or that piece?"

She described her job as saying to women, "I have confidence you can do this." This view of success is incompatible with "zero-tolerance," which requires removing women from the program who relapse, thereby compromising the organization's core ethos.

46 Nicole Kaufman

Many satellite-seeking NGOs are eager to receive earmarked "reentry" funds, at least in principle, and have submitted unsuccessful funding applications. Several reasons for the denial are possible in the DOC's competitive procurement process. For instance, applications from NGOs with no record of managing a government award could have received a low score because they could not convincingly demonstrate their capacity to do the work. Second, when awards are determined using low-cost bidding, applications that request less money are evaluated favorably, and unsuccessful NGOs could be disadvantaged by asking for a higher dollar amount. Like GOG, some of these NGOs would have a hard time being competitive for funds against well-known satellite state NGOs, even if they could reconcile DOC requirements and core aspects of their work.

Interlocutors and Advocates

Two NGOs maintained close ties with penal state actors while avoiding a hierarchical relationship. The relative infrequency of this type of NGO suggests how difficult or unappealing it is for organizations to sustain interactions with the penal state in the absence of funding relationships. One of these NGOs, Mary Magdalene (MM), seeks to facilitate criminalized women's recovery from the physical, sexual, and emotional traumas spanning their lives. MM is notable for its leaders' disinterest in receiving funding from the DOC and its targeting of county officials on behalf of incarcerated women.

MM leaders frame their work as part of a community of feminist advocates for criminalized women. In an interview with the executive director, Barbara, and program director, Doreen, they listed among their achievements pressuring officials to provide more resources for women in the local jail system.[7] MM took the unusual step of ending its funding relationship with the DOC by not extending its recent contract for work with women on extended post-prison release supervision nor submitting new funding applications to the DOC. Barbara explained that the contract had required staff to physically separate post-prison release women from other clients. This arrangement created logistical difficulties, as one staff person was required to remain in the room with the women supported by DOC funds. Further, Barbara described "frustration" because she believed the women could benefit from "learning to live from or in the community, not being segregated out;" she stressed that MM is designed to "encourage social and community experiences," like cooking together.

As at GOG, MM encountered an inflexible system of correctional funding: DOC funds would not support their kinds of intervention. The DOC was, as the directors put it, "rigid about curriculum." For instance, MM had implemented Moving On, a gender-specific, cognitive behavioral program for women, as an alternative to Criminal Thinking, the "zero-tolerance" approach that was supported by the DOC. Barbara said the staff loves Moving

Organizations and the Penal State 47

On and that the women responded well to the program. In contrast, discussing Criminal Thinking, the directors said, "it's awful," because it is used as a "confrontational therapeutic community" seeking to break someone down, and "harm reduction is not part of that vocabulary." Barbara said the DOC would not fund Moving On, which provided an additional reason to discontinue its funding relationship.

MM and GOG encountered parallel frustrations based on their location in a field structured by a funding system that rewards large NGOs that resemble DOC. Indeed, both directors depicted the DOC as preferring to fund NGOs that run zero-tolerance programs and generate records like minibureaucracies. Yet there are key differences between the two types of NGOs they represent; for instance, interlocutors and advocates like MM do not seek a hierarchical reporting relationship with the penal state, whereas satellite-seeking NGOs like GOG maintain more distant relationships. There are more satellite-seeking NGOs than interlocutors and advocates, indicating that organizations recognize the potential advantages for those that participate in the state's competitive funding process.

NGOs Opposing State Involvement

Five NGOs avoided the state in its funding/accountability function *and* in its role as policy-maker. One of these NGOs with limited contact with penal state agencies is St. Matthew House (SMH).[8] Founded by a man who experienced addiction, this nondenominational Christian mission operates a residence for adults struggling with drugs and alcohol. According to its mission, SMH is part of a "movement" in which people who are "devastated by drugs and alcohol" and "who have long been a burden on the city's resources" are freed through "the healing power of Jesus Christ." Many of the staff and volunteers belong to one evangelical Christian church.

SMH specializes in housing people with drug and alcohol issues, and although some residents transfer from rehab facilities, doing so is not required; instead, residents can enter the house from anywhere and can elect to detox at SMH. Jake and another staff member reported using DOC agents to recruit clients because they said it "works better" and is more efficient to have agents identify potential residents than to have SMH commit years to "walking with" or spiritually mentoring people before and after their release from prison, like other ministries do. SMH staff also presented prison officials with information about their program. Otherwise, SMH has minimal involvement with the DOC.

The nominal role of the state at SMH is remarkable, given its specialization, so I expected to find staff members with medical or mental health degrees. However, independence from the government was essential to SMH's ethos, and this was especially apparent in the refusal to use public funds to support its operations and services. Jake stressed this point in a

48 Nicole Kaufman

newsletter: "We receive *no government funds* and while members here do pay a fee to participate in our ministry, we still have to raise about 55% of our budget from local foundations and individual contributors" (emphasis in the original). As Jake further explained during an interview, he and the board view SMH's funding arrangements as allowing them freedom in hiring.[9] He said that receiving governmental funding would require them to hire certain applicants – in his example, a "gay Muslim." As he explained, "of course we would not have a problem hiring [them, but] it's an issue of, could they teach all the classes." In this view, this applicant's beliefs and identity could limit their ability to perform some job functions (i.e., lead a class promoting conservative views of Christian marriage).

Jake's concerns about hiring may be unfounded, although not entirely. Title VII of the 1964 Civil Rights Act exempts certain religious organizations from parts of the federal ban on employment discrimination, allowing preferential hiring within an organization's own religion (U.S. EEOC, 2019). According to a representative request for proposals from the DOC, religious organizations awarded contracts retain this religious exemption. However, awardees generally cannot discriminate among job applicants based on sexuality, among other criteria (Wisconsin Department of Administration, 2008). Yet Jake's point was not only about this fictional applicant, but rather about the dangers of surrendering autonomy over how to implement SMH's core conservative Christian values if SMH were compelled to meet what he seemed to view as the state's secular, liberal interests. Further, DOC funds require organizations meet various conditions related to certification, education, insurance, record retention, intake, discharge, scheduling, and the posting of rules. These requirements and other state regulations do not apply to SMH because of its independence from the state, which is deliberately minimal.

Accomplices and Everyone Else

The empirical variation shown here demonstrates that the post-release service NGO sector in southern Wisconsin is *not* completely co-opted by the penal state. Instead, NGOs' relationship with the state is more nuanced in how NGOs respond to pressures in order to survive while being true to their missions than the penological literature suggests. Despite the relatively low numbers of each alternative type of NGO, their empirical presence is important. Interlocutors and advocates and NGOs opposed to state involvement provide a strong argument that NGOs can resist the penal state by both staying close and being distant. Satellite-seeking NGOs in this sample demonstrate that they appear ready to be swept into the penal state's orbit; however, as long as they continue working with formerly incarcerated people in ways that the state is unlikely to fund, they are unlikely to be subsumed by the state and have minimal contact with penal state agencies. Although it is less overt than protesting, NGOs adherence to their own principles can be seen as resistance to state control.

What complicates the arguments by critical penologists is the finding that the penal state does not pull all organizations into its orbit. Consistent with Flores and Cossyleon (2016), Kilroy et al. (2013), and Owens (2014), I find NGOs doing more than merely serving as pawns of the state. Results on NGOs opposing state involvement and creating distance from governmental agencies provide an exception to the argument about satellite states and "seepage." Further, expressions of resistance to the penal state's power occur in satellite-seeking NGOs, which have distant connections with the penal state, whereas interlocutors and advocates maintain less hierarchical relationships with the penal state. Although these findings qualify arguments about the impact of the penal state, they do not invalidate them; even if only a small number of NGOs are recognizable as "satellite states," governmental influence on the civic sector is still significant.

The influence of the penal state extends widely. As the directors of GOG, MM, and SMH communicated, NGOs are concerned that state funding would require them to change how they view their program participants, make staffing decisions, retain information on clients, and deliver programs. Certainly, the carceral state structures this field by setting policy goals and establishing rules and criteria to which organizations must conform to receive funding. Yet even the NGOs in less hierarchical relationships (n = 7) experience an inherent imbalance in the distribution of power. The influence of the penal state on NGOs occurs in an array of additional ways not measured or widely captured here, including in the adoption of punitive logics and discourses, attribution of life outcomes to individual choices rather than social structures, provision of services that are aligned with the state's goals, and formation of ties with law enforcement agencies.

By observing closeness in a way that is separate from funding, I identify more potential for deviation from the carceral state than is widely recognized in critical research. I observed not only NGOs' challenge to the state's power, but also NGOs' reluctance to initiate or maintain contact with governmental agencies. The latter NGO behavior is often ignored by critical penological scholars; some NGOs opposed to state involvement may do this in part because organizations like SMH may refuse or resist the authority of medical and behavioral experts in addition to avoiding being subject to governmental authority. These results justify further inquiry into the significance of organizational culture and embeddedness in religious networks (especially evangelical groups) for shaping NGO–state relationships.

The framework introduced here raises additional questions for future scholarship seeking to understand the complicated engagements between NGOs working with formerly incarcerated people and the state. First, comparative research that uses and tests this typology could elucidate which properties of NGOs are unique to this policy context and which reflect

50 Nicole Kaufman

neoliberal policies more broadly. Comparisons of states with differing ideologies would extend the analysis beyond Wisconsin. Second, research using financial records alongside interviews and other data could provide information about how organizations survive over time and how decisions are made between adopting practices preferred by penal state agencies and the available funding and when they are committed to remaining independent from the penal state while maintaining the core aspects of their missions.

Notes

1. The following people provided research support: Santhia Brandt, Carla Carballo, Natalie Feldman, Marie Keller, Cassie Miller, Kristina Nailen, and Chelsea Rolfzen.
2. I refer to "post-release service organizations" and "work with formerly incarcerated people" in lieu of "reentry organizations" and "reentry work;" in many ways, reentry is a misleading term. It is rare that people returning from prison were meaningfully included in communities prior to incarceration; further, organizations are poorly situated to repair the extensive social inequalities that face previously incarcerated people (Gottschalk, 2015; Kaufman, 2015; Shantz, Kilty, & Frignon, 2009).
3. An aspect not examined here is how NGOs employ staff in fields that the state regulates, like mental health and substance abuse, who may find themselves in more hierarchical relationships.
4. I observed routine programs at one satellite state NGO (Onward Upward), two satellite-seeking NGOs (Social Justice, Inc., and Growing Our Garden), one interlocutor and advocate NGO (Heart to Heart), and three NGOs opposed to state involvement (St. Matthew House, Good Word Bible Study, and Dinner with Luke).
5. A small number of awards to NGOs for work inside prisons are excluded from the analysis.
6. Interview in Madison on April 18, 2012.
7. Interview in Milwaukee on March 17, 2011.
8. Intra-type variations add richness to the findings, though space is limited to discuss them. While the NGOs in this type appear ideologically similar based on my interactions with staff and observations at select programs, I had the most contact with SMH and present results on this organization here.
9. Interview in Milwaukee on February 28, 2012.

References

Bumiller, K. (2013). Incarceration, welfare state and labor market nexus: The increasing significance of gender in the prison system. In B. Carlton & M. Segrave (Eds.), *Women exiting prison: Critical essays on gender, post-release support and survival* (pp. 13–33). Abingdon, UK: Routledge.

Byrd, R. (2016). "Punishment's twin": Theorizing prisoner reentry for a politics of abolition. *Social Justice, 43*(1), 1–22.

Carlen, P., & Tombs, J. (2006). Reconfigurations of penalty: The ongoing case of the women's imprisonment and reintegration industries. *Theoretical Criminology, 10*(3), 337–360.

Cohen, S. (1985). *Visions of social control: Crime, punishment, and classification.* New York: Polity Press.

Organizations and the Penal State 51

Corcoran, M., & Fox, C. (2013). A bit neo-liberal, a bit Fabian: Interventionist narratives in a diversionary programme for women. In B. Carlton & M. Segrave (Eds.), *Women exiting prison: Critical essays on gender, post-release support and survival* (pp. 136–155). Abingdon, UK: Routledge.

Flores, E., & Cossyleon, J. (2016). "I went through it so you don't have to": Faith-based community organizing for the formerly incarcerated. *Journal for the Scientific Study of Religion, 55*(4), 662–676.

Gottschalk, M. (2015). *Caught: The prison state and the lockdown of American politics.* Princeton, NJ: Princeton University Press.

Haney, L. (2010). *Offending women: Power, punishment, and the regulation of desire.* Berkeley, CA: University of California Press.

Katzenstein, M. (2005). Rights without citizenship: Activist politics and prison reform. In D. S. Meyer, V. Jenness, & H. Ingram (Eds.), *Routing the opposition: Social movements, public policy, and democracy* (pp. 236–258). Minneapolis: University of Minnesota Press.

Kaufman, N. (2015). Prisoner incorporation: The work of the state and non-governmental organizations. *Theoretical Criminology, 19,* 534–553.

Kaufman, N., Kaiser, J., & Rumpf, C. (2018). Beyond punishment: Dynamic dimensions of penal control through interventionist, covert and negligent involvement. *Law & Social Inquiry, 43*(2), 468–495.

Kilroy, D., Barton, P., Quixley, S., George, A., & Russell, E. (2013). Decentring the prison: Abolitionist approaches to working with criminalized women. In B. Carleton & M. Seagrave (Eds.), *Women exiting prison: Critical essays on gender, post-release support, and survival* (pp. 156–180). London: Routledge.

Kilty, J., & DeVellis, L. (2010). Transcarceration and the production of "grey space": How frontline workers exercise spatial practices in a halfway house for women. In V. Strimelle & F. Vanhamme (Eds.), *Rights and voice: Criminology at the university of Ottawa* (pp. 137–158). Ottawa, ON: University of Ottawa Press.

Maidment, M. R. (2006a). *Doing time on the outside: Deconstructing the benevolent community.* Toronto, ON: University of Toronto Press.

Maidment, M. R. (2006b). Passing the buck: Transcarceral regulating of criminalized women. In G. Balfour & E. Comack (Eds.), *Criminalizing women: Gender and (in)justice in neo-liberal times* (pp. 267–281). Halifax, NS: Fernwood.

Matthews, N. (1995). Feminist clashes with the state: Tactical choices by state-funded rape crisis centers. In M. M. Ferree & P. Martin (Eds.), *Feminist organizations: Harvest of the new women's movement* (pp. 291–305). Philadelphia: Temple University Press.

Owens, M. L. (2014). Ex-felons' organization-based political work for carceral reforms. *The ANNALS of the American Academy of Political and Social Science, 651*(1), 256–265.

Shantz, L., Kilty, J., & Frignon, S. (2009). Echoes of imprisonment: Women's experiences of "successful (re)integration." *Canadian Journal of Law and Society, 24*(1), 85–106.

Shaylor, C., & Meiners, E. (2013). Resisting gendered carceral landscapes. In B. Carleton & M. Seagrave (Eds.), *Women exiting prison: Critical essays on gender, post-release support, and survival* (pp. 181–199). New York: Routledge.

Thomas, N., Bull, M., Dioso-Villa, R., & Smith, C. (2016). Governing drug use through partnerships: Towards a genealogy of government/non-government relations in drug policy. *International Journal of Drug Policy, 28,* 34–42.

Thompkins, D. E. (2010). The expanding prisoner reentry industry. *Dialectical Anthropology, 34*(4), 589–604.

Thompkins, D. E., Curtis, R., & Wendel, T. (2010). Forum: The prison reentry industry. *Dialectical Anthropology, 34*(4), 427–429.

Tomczak, P., & Albertson, K. (2016). Prisoner relationships with voluntary sector practitioners. *Howard Journal of Crime and Justice, 55*(1–2), 57–72.

United States Equal Employment Opportunity Commission. (2019). *Title VII of the civil rights act of 1964.* Retrieved from www.eeoc.gov/laws/statutes/titlevii.cfm

Wisconsin Department of Administration. (2008). *Request for bid DJB 1062F: Secular transitional living program services for female offenders in Milwaukee, WI.* Madison, WI: Wisconsin Department of Administration.

Chapter 4

Idaho

A Case Study in Rural Reentry

Deirdre Caputo-Levine

Scholars of mass incarceration and prisoner reentry often view reentry as a phenomenon in urban communities. However, mass incarceration and the associated problems of reentry and reintegration also shape the lives of people in rural communities (Wodahl, 2006). This chapter is a case study of prisoner reentry in Idaho, and includes observations of events sponsored by community organizations and the Idaho Department of Corrections (IDOC). Research participants' reentry experiences in Idaho are compared to participants in New York metro area (Caputo-Levine, 2013, 2015, 2018). The comparison is based on the structures that shape reentry experiences in rural and urban areas, and is used to elucidate the processes and differences of prisoner reentry and reintegration in a rural context.

Prisoner Reentry in the Rural Context

Prisoner reentry and reintegration within rural communities is an understudied phenomenon (Ward, 2015; Wodahl, 2006). As a result, key differences between the experiences of formerly incarcerated individuals in rural and urban areas have largely been left unexplored despite significant structural and cultural differences that exist between urban and rural contexts. It is important that these differences are taken into account as they may cause policies and programs developed for urban areas to lead to unexpected results when implemented in rural communities. In Idaho, based on the Census Bureau's definition of rural communities, all Idaho counties, even Boise County, where the state capital is located, have large swathes of rural areas (Ratcliffe, Burd, Holder, & Fields, 2016).[1]

Studies have found that formerly incarcerated individuals living in disadvantaged communities are more likely to recidivate (Mears, Wang, Hay, & Bales, 2008; Morenoff & Harding, 2014; Sabol, 2007). Difficulty securing employment is a common theme in the literature surrounding reentry (Decker, Spohn, Ortiz, & Hedberg, 2014; Pager, 2007; Pager & Western, 2015), and restricted employment opportunities lead to higher levels of unemployment and lower wages in rural areas (Weisheit, Falcone, & Wells,

2006), particularly because median incomes are lower and poverty rates higher in nonmetropolitan counties (USDA ERS, 2018). Yet the problems of employment and income are exacerbated in rural communities because there are fewer employment opportunities and they are more likely to be dependent on a single industry (Blank, 2005). The combination of higher levels of poverty and unemployment make it harder for formerly incarcerated persons to secure employment, which increases the likelihood of violating the conditions of probation or parole and potentially raises the risk of them committing new offenses.

There are issues particular to rural areas that complicate both successful negotiation of the requirements of parole and probation and job searches. Rural communities generally have higher levels of acquaintanceship density. Acquaintanceship density is the degree to which residents of a community interact with each other on a personal basis and see each other in a wide range of settings and roles (Flora & Flora, 1993). Acquaintanceship density in Idaho means that participants are under constant surveillance. Allie reported that she felt as if she was constantly under observation.

> It was the judge's friends. He is Mormon so like people that are in his ward just like pick faces out. He would have eyes all over town watching people and telling on us so we would get caught like constantly. . . . The judge and the diversionary court team – all like their friends . . . everybody was like looking out for us. There were eyes and ears everywhere. I didn't feel I could hide from probation anywhere.

Under such circumstances, it is difficult to hide discrediting information in rural areas so leaving a conviction off of an application or attempting to present the conviction using a face-saving script may not be viable options, even for positions, such as dishwasher or day laborer, where employers may not conduct background checks. Small businesses dominate rural employment networks and are less likely to hire formerly incarcerated individuals; this further narrows employment options in rural communities (Wodahl, 2006).

Rural communities tend to have fewer social services, including those offered by the state and not-for-profit organizations, than urban communities (Wodahl, 2006; Garland et al., 2011). The lack of services creates significant difficulties, such as the ones Brett, a formerly incarcerated man, encountered in finding temporary housing. There is only one homeless shelter that accepts single men (who were not veterans) in the five counties that make up southeast Idaho. Expanding the homeless shelter has met with resistance and is on hold (Harris, 2018a).

The first time I called the shelter, staff said that the shelter was full. The second time, I learned that there were two spaces for men. However, Brett told me that he had a serious conflict with one of the residents of the shelter (they were recently in jail together) and did not feel safe staying there. The only other place he could potentially stay was a warming room at a local church, but the church did not have enough people to staff the warming room. The other homeless shelter was 50 miles away; a prohibitive distance given Brett had had to work in the morning and did not have a car. There was a transitional housing service, like Big Mama's House, intended for people who are homeless or formerly incarcerated, but it has been unable to find a location within Pocatello, the largest city in Bannock County, in the southeastern part of the state (Harris, 2018b). The Idaho Housing and Finance Association estimates that there are 4,831 persons "affected by homelessness" (Idaho Housing and Finance, 2018). Homelessness has a negative effect on reentry outcomes. Walker, Hempel, Unnithan, and Pogrebin (2014) found that parolees released to homeless shelters had more difficulties developing social capital, securing employment, and meeting the conditions of their parole.

Housing stress is exacerbated in rural areas because of the unique characteristics that make homelessness among formerly incarcerated persons more likely (Brown & Swanson, 2003; Wodahl, 2006). Securing permanent housing during the reentry process may be more significant in rural locales because housing tends to owner-occupied (Census Bureau, 2017). Fewer rental opportunities are available, and the rents are less likely to be affordable (Wodahl, 2006).

An issue that is related to the availability of housing is transportation. Sparse transportation networks in rural communities make securing housing and employment a challenge. In rural counties, public transportation is limited to areas with higher populations, such as the county seat. More lucrative job opportunities tend to be limited to these communities as well, and this exacerbates unemployment – you need a job to get a car, but you need a car to get a job (Alexander, 1995). It is also more difficult to access community services and parole or probation offices without access to transportation.

A shortage of behavioral health care services presents an additional challenge for formerly incarcerated individuals (Ward & Merlo, 2015). The relative lack of alternative services means that people going through the reentry process in Idaho must rely on services that they access through the IDOC's Bureau of Probation and Parole. To do so can be problematic, particularly when it involves counseling and seeking treatment for substance abuse disorders. Andi reported that his probation officer violated him after he sought assistance from his probation-affiliated counselor for a prescription opioid addiction.

Terrance has Bipolar Disorder and PTSD as a result of childhood abuse and being attacked while he was incarcerated. As a result, when he is able to work, he has difficulty maintaining a job. When Terrance was interviewed, he was over $400 behind on paying his probation supervision costs, and his probation officer had informed him that he would be returned to prison to complete his sentence if he reached $500 in arrears.

> I'll have to get another job too. I'm back on my COS (cost-of-supervision). $480. They said if I go to $500 then they're going to top me off.[2] I haven't topped out yet. 'Cause if you can't make your payments, it's an automatic go back.

Urban areas, such as New York City, tend to have a range of not-for-profit organizations, such as the Fortune Society, the Osborne Association, the Women's Prison Association, and Ready, Willing and Able. These agencies provide a variety of services, including counseling, parenting classes, transitional housing, job development, job search preparation classes, and clothing for interviews.

In Idaho, the not-for-profit infrastructure is in its infancy for returning citizens. Religious entities, such as the Church of Jesus Christ of Latter-day Saints (LDS) and St. Vincent de Paul, offer many of the services that exist. Deseret Industries, which offers employment services and job training, requires a referral from an LDS Bishop for an interview (Deseret Industries, 2018). St. Vincent de Paul of Southwest Idaho (2019) also offers services, a radio show, and advocacy through Systemic Change of Idaho in Canyon and Ada Counties, the most populous of Idaho's counties (Systemic Change of Idaho, 2016). The Idaho Maximum Security Institution (IMSI) Hope Community Phase II (2018), a program developed as part of an experiment in a maximum-security prison, works in conjunction with Victory Over Sin, a Christian support group, St. Vincent de Paul, and Provenance Housing. IMSI Hope Community Phase II provides housing and other services; however, these support services are limited to residents of Canyon and Ada Counties and are located up to a four-hour drive from other parts of the state.

Secular alternatives for services, such as drug treatment, are available through the newly constructed network of eight Recovery Community Centers. However, these centers are competing for a smaller number of state and federal grants (Dutton, 2018) and secular options for prisoner reentry programming outside of those offered by the IDOC do not seem to exist. Only two participants reported accessing services, and those were limited to support groups and volunteer opportunities at a local Recovery Community Center.

Prisoner Reentry and Reintegration in Idaho

The Idaho Department of Corrections

The Idaho Department of Corrections (IDOC) is the key institution that shapes prison, prisoner reentry, and reintegration in the state. The prison population is divided into three categories: Termers, Riders, and Parole Violators. Termers are individuals sentenced to more than a year in prison. Riders are people the court retained jurisdiction over and sentenced to a term of incarceration in an IDOC facility. They are incarcerated in a state facility for a term of three to six months, during which they are required to participate in cognitive behavioral therapy programs and released on probation. Parole violators have violated the requirements of their supervision, such as committing a new offense.

Idaho exemplifies the decoupling of incarceration and crime rates noted by Garland (2001). Historically, Idaho has had a high incarceration rate, relative to other states, while having one of the lowest crime rates (CSG Justice Center, 2014). Between 1996 and 2014, Idaho experienced a rapid rise in the prison population by approximately 84% (Prison Policy Initiative, 2017). The growth of the prison and community supervision populations was not accompanied by a similar growth in the corrections infrastructure. Poor prison conditions, including insufficient medical and behavioral health care, and dry celling[3] have been significant issues since the 1980s. In fact, IDOC is under the supervision of a special master (*Balla v. Idaho State Board of Corrections, 1984*; Clarke, 2016; Boone, 2017). Overcrowding is also a problem, and is because longer than average prison sentences for nonviolent and violent offenders and significant issues with community supervision; more than 40% of the incarcerated population was remanded for violation of conditions of supervision (CSG Justice Center, 2014). All of this has translated into a rise in the number of people reentering. In an attempt to decrease prison overcrowding, the Idaho legislature passed the Justice Reinvestment Act in 2014.

The Justice Reinvestment Initiative

The Justice Reinvestment Initiative (JRI) is a "data-driven reform" intended to help states reduce incarceration (Austin et al., 2013). In Idaho, the JRI is a top-down initiative imposed by the state legislature and IDOC administration. The policy framework focuses on community supervision to reduce recidivism and emphasizes three key areas: improvement of supervision practices; the use of risk assessments and tailored sanctions in the parole process; and increased data collection and quality assessment of programs (CSG Justice Center, 2014, p. 2). Some scholars have criticized JRI programs in other states as having a short-term focus, failing to connect structural disincentives to community-level innovations, and directing funds strictly to law enforcement and corrections agencies (Austin et al., 2013; Clear & Frost, 2014; Gottschalk, 2015). Clear and Frost (2014) argue that the focus on recidivism reduction through reentry programs is flawed.

As a result of the JRI, the IDOC has made changes to community corrections practices that include hiring new parole and probation officers, engaging in training, starting a limited supervision unit, and increasing funding

58 Deirdre Caputo-Levine

for substance use disorder treatment. Community services, including in-house rehabilitation specialists and community clinicians, received funding for behavioral health and substance abuse treatment. Increased priority was given to gathering victim restitution in an attempt to make the legislation more palatable (IDOC, 2018a). The IDOC validated the Level of Service Inventory – Revised (LSI-R)[4] to improve the assessment of risk levels and related services needed. Also, the IDOC has implemented a community mentoring program, Free2Succeed, which matches people on parole and probation with community members who serve as role models that provide support and social capital (Idaho Department of Corrections, n.d.). Formerly incarcerated individuals have served as mentors within the program, and in one of the Probation and Parole districts, a formerly incarcerated individual serves as coordinator for the program.

The JRI has not yet yielded significant changes in the composition of the prison population in Idaho. The prison population has increased by 4.4% since February 2017, and this increase was largely driven by Termers and Riders (IDOC, 2018b). The percentage of the population incarcerated in Idaho state prisons that had their parole revoked has decreased by 4.1% (28 individuals) over the past 12 months. However, there has been an increase in county jail populations. County jails throughout Idaho are often over-crowded, and Sheriff's departments are concerned about the extent to which parole violators are contributing to the overcrowding (Boydston, 2018). Policy changes connected to JRI are at risk because of the conflict between county officials, IDOC, and state legislators. The IDOC has begun to try to alleviate overcrowding by sending "up to 620 male inmates" to the Eagle Pass Correctional Facility in Texas, which is run by the GEO Group (IDOC, 2018b; Katz, 2018).

How Race Has Shaped Reentry in Idaho

The "Prison Movement"

The roots of the "prison movement" lie in the Civil Rights, Black Power, and New Left Movements (Berger, 2014). For African American activists, the prison was a site within which activists were able to make connections and share strategies to create a "school of liberation" that functioned as a metaphor for the Black freedom struggle and enabled prisoners to envision themselves as "part of a collective force strong enough to challenge the totalizing authority of the prison" (Berger, 2014, pp. 7–8). A significant amount of activism occurs within prisons, and the development of "the prison movement," which began in the 1960s as a human rights movement, entailed actions taken by activists within and outside of prison. Between 1968 and 1972, there were uprisings in prisons across the United States, which led to "crises of prison legitimacy" (Berger & Losier, 2018). Prisoners, with assistance from the ACLU and National Lawyers Guild, filed lawsuits in an attempt to improve conditions inside prisons. In addition to uprisings, incarcerated persons in a number of state prisons throughout the country began to form prisoner unions, such as The United Prisoners' Union (Berger & Losier, 2018; Falkof, 1979; Zonn, 1978). Union chapters inside and outside of prison advocated for changes to prison administration and criminal justice policies (Berger & Losier, 2018).

Although the power of the "prison movement" as a political force decreased with the onset of mass incarceration, the organizations that remained facilitated the development of community social movements (Corrigan, 2016). In New York, members of the Resurrection and Conciencia study groups from Green Haven Correctional Facility formed the Center for NuLeadership on Urban Solutions, a policy think tank, which engages in advocacy and community organizing in Brooklyn (Fine, 2018). The Center for NuLeadership exists alongside other organizations, such as the Fortune Society and Citizens Against Recidivism, that offer services, employ formerly incarcerated persons, and participate in political advocacy at the local, state, and federal levels. Organizations such as these have been found to increase community engagement and influence currently and formerly incarcerated people (Owens, 2014). Owens (2014, p. 258) argues that organizations can assist people with felony convictions to build capacity and to "mobilize felons and ex-felons and their families to rehabilitate (or habilitate) citizenship in the communities."

The Lack of a Prison Movement

Idaho does not have a history of prisoners participating in prisoner social movements, and there has not been an analogous structure to prisoner unions within or outside of the prison in the state. The development of social movements requires a critical mass of individuals who not only desire change but are politically conscious (Oliver & Marwell, 1988) and have a sense of collective identity (Polletta & Jasper, 2001). Collective identity requires a "perception of a shared status or relation" and "carries with it positive feelings for other members of the group" (Polletta & Jasper, 2001, p. 285). The "prisoner movement" required a critical mass of prisoners for whom their status as prisoners intersected with an understanding that their position in prison was part of oppressive state policies. Berger and Loiser argue that the "prisoner movement" emerged in states that had "vibrant leftist movements concentrated in Black communities" (2018, p. 75).

When interviewing formerly incarcerated participants, they did not refer to or understand themselves as a class. In Idaho, incarceration is an individual experience. The activism that does occur seems to be limited to filing lawsuits, the most well-known of which is *Balla v. Idaho State Board of Corrections* (1984). When I interviewed Telly, who did time in the 1980s and 1990s, he described mentoring, but it was directed toward personal improvement and did not have a political component. Telly pointed to the activism of one individual, a jailhouse lawyer, who was instrumental in continuing the legal work related to *Balla v. Idaho State Board of Corrections*.

In Idaho, the majority of prisoners (74.3%) are White and 15.6% are Latino (IDOC, 2018b). Male participants described the prison population as being divided between White, Latino, and Native American gangs. The women did not report gangs, but they did describe a situation in which White, Latina, and Native American female prisoners tended to socialize with their own racial or ethnic group. These group dynamics are rooted in survival inside prison and controlling limited resources in the carceral space; the lack of a narrative of struggle and solidarity is not related to being incarcerated. Whereas for Black prisoners during the prison movement "the White-controlled space of criminality and incarceration was transformed into a public arena for Black justice and freedom" (Baker, 1994, pp. 18–19), White prisoners in rural Idaho have little to no incentive to participate in a prisoner movement. Incarcerated Whites are largely drawn from a population with a liminal status of being "White trash." "White trash" is a term commonly used to refer to poor Whites as a means of differentiating them from White middle and upper classes (Linneman & Wall, 2013). Although Whiteness in prison and reentry is a spoiled identity (Goffman, 1963; Gowan, 2002), Whiteness is "salvageable" (Webster, 2008, p. 297). In a context in which there is little assistance for people reentering society who are dependent on goodwill from their communities, there is a significant and negative cost to the lack of social movement organization in prison for Whites.

The absence of prison social movements in Idaho has translated to differences in reentry infrastructures. Without a core group of formerly incarcerated individuals and advocates, it is difficult to develop independent prisoner reentry programs. There have been critiques of reentry programs (Nixon et al., 2008; Thompkins, 2010; Wacquant, 2010), but the lack of available alternatives leads to an increased reliance on services offered by the IDOC or the Bureau of Probation and Parole, which opens individuals up to increased scrutiny and potential revocation. Prisoner reentry organizations can also function as key "resource-rich" social capital centers (Hattery & Smith, 2010, p. 89). For instance, staff members at Second Chance provided a range of services, including social support, job development, and job advice (Caputo-Levine, 2013, 2018). Clients would drop by, hang out, discuss common problems, and strategize with each other on best ways to overcome their individual and collective challenges. Second Chance was also a place where young adults interfaced with older men and women who served as role models. These forms of social capital are difficult to access in correctional institutions, such as the Bureau of Probation and Parole.

Although JRI has had mixed effects in Idaho, the loss of support for reentry services would have a negative impact on people reentering. A side

Idaho 61

effect of the lack of independent prisoner reentry organizations in Idaho is that formerly incarcerated adults may not develop the political power necessary to ensure that positive reforms continue. Owens (2014) notes the importance of "ex-felon organizations" in enabling communities to build human capital. This is a key step to developing and utilizing political capital. In New York, formerly incarcerated individuals and their families were critical in the "Drop the Rock Campaign" (vanden Heuvel, 2009), while Owens (2014) documented the work of Open Door, a Rhode Island community-based organization successful in overturning state felon disenfranchisement laws.

Prisoner reentry is often understood as a unitary phenomenon. However, a number of factors specific to a state influence the institutional context of reentry and reintegration. These factors can include geography, social class, race and ethnicity, and the local history of social movements that can impact the institutions that structure prisoner reentry. Given Kang-Brown and Subramanian's recent finding that rural jail populations are a key component of mass incarceration (2017), understanding the differences that exist between reentry in urban and rural populations are pertinent to critically analyzing reentry in different geographical contexts.

Notes

1. The Office of Management and Budget defines only five of the 44 Idaho counties as urban.
2. Sentences in Idaho are indeterminate (i.e., 5–15 years). Topping out means that one serves their full sentence and is also referred to as "maxing out."
3. Dry cells do not have running water, and the toilet is a hole in the floor. Prisoners are placed in a dry cell while wearing a turtle suit (suicide prevention outfit) and left in solitary confinement (Prentice, 2015).
4. LSI-R is an actuarial risk management and assessment tool used in corrections. Significant concerns around the applicability of the LSI-R to female populations and to racial and ethnic minority populations have been raised (Fass, Heilbrun, Dematteo, & Fretz, 2008; Smith, Cullen, & Latessa, 2009). One review found that the predictive validity of LSI-R scores "ranged from poor to good" and that the total scores "perform slightly better for men than for women" (Desmarais & Singh, 2013, pp. 32–33).

References

Alexander, S. (1995). The need for rural public transportation. *Race, Poverty & the Environment, 6*(1), 31–32.

Association Idaho Housing and Finance. (2018). *Helping Idaho's homeless: Idaho homelessness community report*. Boise, ID. Retrieved from https://issuu.com/idahohousing/docs/idaho__homeless_community_report_20?e=18210154/57018231.

Austin, J., Cadora, E., Clear, T. R., Dansky, K., Judith, G., Gupta, V., & Young, M. C. (2013). *Ending mass incarceration charting a new justice reinvestment*. Washington, DC: The Sentencing Project. Retrieved from www.sentencingproject.org/wp-content/uploads/2015/12/Ending-Mass-Incarceration-Charting-a-New-Justice-Reinvestment.pdf

62 Deirdre Caputo-Levine

Baker, H. A. (1994). Critical memory and the black public sphere. *Public Culture, 7*(1), 3–33.

Balla v. Idaho State Board of Corrections, 595 F.C.F.R. (1984).

Berger, D. (2014). *Captive nation: Black prison organizing in the civil rights era.* Chapel Hill, NC: University of North Carolina Press.

Berger, D., & Losier, T. (2018). *Rethinking the American prison movement* (H. A. Thompson Ed.). New York: Routledge.

Blank, R. M. (2005). Poverty, policy, and place: How poverty and policies to alleviate poverty are shaped by local characteristics. *International Regional Science Review, 28*(4), 441–464.

Boone, R. (2017). Idaho inmates: Prison violations led to amputations, death. *The Spokesman-Review.* Retrieved from www.spokesman.com/stories/2017/mar/25/idaho-inmates-prison-violations-led-to-amputations/

Boydston, M. (2018). *7 investigates: Criminal justice reform being blamed for jail overcrowding.* Boise, ID. Retrieved from www.ktvb.com/article/news/investigations/7-investigates/7-investigates-criminal-justice-reform-being-blamed-for-jail-overcrowding/277–524257492

Brown, D. L., & Swanson, L. E. (2003). *Challenges for rural America in the twenty-first century.* University Park, PA: Pennsylvania State University Press.

Caputo-Levine, D. (2013). The yard face: The contributions of inmate interpersonal violence to the carceral habitus. *Ethnography, 14*(2), 165–185.

Caputo-Levine, D. (2015). *Removing the yard face: The impact of the carceral habitus on reentry and reintegration* (PhD), State University of New York at Stony Brook, Ann Arbor, MI, (3714459).

Caputo-Levine, D. (2018). Learning to be a 'safe' ex-con: Race, symbolic violence and discipline in prisoner re-entry. *Contemporary Justice Review, 21*(3), 233–253.

Census Bureau, U. S. C. (2017). *Quick fact: Idaho.* Washington, DC. Retrieved from www.census.gov/quickfacts/ID

Clarke, M. (2016). Federal judge sanctions Idaho DOC for misleading special master in *Balla* Case. *Prison Legal News,* 44.

Clear, T. R., & Frost, N. A. (2014). *The punishment imperative: The rise and failure of mass incarceration in America.* New York: New York University Press.

Council of State Governments Justice Center. (2014). *Idaho's justice reinvestment approach: Strengthening probation and parole, structuring parole decision making, and measuring recidivism-reduction efforts.* New York. Retrieved from https://csgjusticecenter.org/wp-content/uploads/2014/09/Idaho-JR-Approach.pdf

Corrigan, L. M. (2016). *Prison power: How prison influenced the movement for Black Liberation.* Jackson, MS: University Press of Mississippi.

Decker, S. H., Spohn, C., Ortiz, N. R., & Hedberg, E. (2014). *Criminal stigma, race, gender and employment: An expanded assessment of the consequences of imprisonment for employment.* Retrieved from www.ncjrs.gov/pdffiles1/nij/grants/244756.pdf

Deseret Industries. (2018). *Deseret industries-join us!* Retrieved from www.deseretindustries.org/careers

Desmarais, S. L., & Singh, J. P. (2013). *Risk assessment instruments validated and implemented in correctional settings in the United States.* New York: Council of State Governments Justice Center. Retrieved from https://csgjusticecenter.org/wp-content/uploads/2014/07/Risk-Assessment-Instruments-Validated-and-Implemented-in-Correctional-Settings-in-the-United-States.pdf

Dutton, A. (2018). Idaho slashes substance abuse treatment, surprised by 'extreme budget shortfall'. *Idaho Statesman*. Retrieved from www.idahostatesman.com/news/politics-government/state-politics/article195103734.html

Falkof, B. B. (1979). Prisoner representative organizations, prison reform, and *Jones v. North Carolina Prisoners' labor union*: An argument for increased court intervention in prison administration. *Journal of Criminal Law and Criminology, 70*(1), 42–56.

Fass, T. L., Heilbrun, K., Dematteo, D., & Fretz, R. (2008). The LSI_R and the COMPAS: Validation data on two-risk-needs tools. *Criminal Justice and Behavior, 35*(9), 1095–1108.

Fine, M. (2018). *Just research in contentious times*. New York: Teachers College Press.

Flora, C. B., & Flora, J. L. (1993). Entrepreneurial social infrastructure: A necessary ingredient. *The ANNALS of the American Academy of Political and Social Science, 529*(1), 48–58.

Garland, B. E. A. (2011). Prisoner reentry in a small metropolitan community: Obstacles and policy recommendations. *Criminal Justice Policy Review, 22*(1), 90–110.

Garland, D. (Ed.). (2001). *Mass imprisonment: Social causes and consequences*. Thousand Oaks, CA: Sage Publications.

Goffman, E. (1963). *Stigma: Notes on the management of spoiled identity*. New York: Simon & Schuster, Inc.

Gottschalk, M. (2015). *Caught: The prison state and the lockdown of American politics*. Princeton, NJ: Princeton University Press.

Gowan, T. (2002). The nexus: Homelessness and incarceration in two American cities. *Ethnography, 3*(4), 500–534.

Harris, S. (2018a, December 17). No home for homeless: Another proposed homeless housing facility proving divisive in Pocatello. *Idaho State Journal*. Retrieved from www.idahostatejournal.com/news/local/no-home-for-homeless-another-proposed-home-less-housing-facility-proving/article_e5a71ed1-d143–5414-b9aa-d173fee00472.html

Harris, S. (2018b, December 22). City council again denies location for Big Momma's House. *Idaho State Journal*. Retrieved from www.idahostatejournal.com/news/local/city-council-again-denies-location-for-big-momma-s-house/article_e698a5a7-d149–58f7–9b20-b235d2cf7989.html

Hattery, A., & Smith, E. (2010). *Prisoner reentry and social capital: The long road to reintegration*. New York: Lexington Book.

Idaho Department of Corrections. (n.d.). *Free2Succeed community mentor program*. Boise, ID: Idaho Department of Correction.

Idaho Department of Corrections. (2018a). *Justice reinvestment in Idaho: Impact on the state*. Boise, ID. Retrieved from www.idoc.idaho.gov/content/document/2018_jri_impact_report

Idaho Department of Corrections. (2018b). *Population Snapshot: February 2018*. Boise, ID. Retrieved from www.idoc.idaho.gov/content/document/february_2018_population_snapshot

Idaho Maximum Security Institution (IMSI) Hope Community Phase II. (2018). Retrieved from http://imsihopecommunityphaseii.com

Kang-Brown, J., & Subramanian, R. (2017). *Out of sight: The growth of jails in rural America*. New York: Vera Institute of Justice. Retrieved from https://vera-web-assets.storage.googleapis.com/downloads/Publications/out-of-sight-growth-of-jails-rural-america/legacy_downloads/out-of-sight-growth-of-jails-rural-america.pdf

Katz, M. (2018). Idaho's prisons have run out of beds. So hundreds of inmates are being sent to Texas. *Idaho Statesman*. Retrieved from www.idahostatesman.com/news/local/article199193734.html

64 Deirdre Caputo-Levine

Linnemann, T., & Wall, T. (2013). "This is your face on meth:" The punitive spectacle of "white trash" in the rural war on drugs. *Theoretical Criminology, 17*(3), 315–334.

Mears, D. P., Wang, X., Hay, C., & Bales, W. D. (2008). Social ecology and recidivism: Implications for prisoner reentry. *Criminology, 46*(2), 301–340.

Morenoff, J. D., & Harding, D. J. (2014). Incarceration, prisoner reentry, and communities. *Annual Review of Sociology, 40*, 411–429. Retrieved from www.annualreviews.org/doi/full/10.1146/annurev-soc-071811-145511?casa_token=qGNyb77VnxMAAAAA:S phx6WGDGA4ocSNILPClY2XJrZxUYY_y7ZlPe5-7vfq7Gj2790l5JYQ2tVVa4cz C8x4BpvmQKtE

Nixon, V., Ticento Clough, P., Staples, D., Johnson Peterkins, Y., Zimmerman, P., Voight, C., & Pica Clear, S. (2008). Life capacity beyond reentry: A critical examination of racism and prisoner reentry reform in the U.S. *Race/Ethnicity: Multidisciplinary Global Contexts, 2*(1), 21–43.

Oliver, P. E., & Marwell, G. (1988). The paradox of group size in collective action: A theory of the critical mass. *American Sociological Review, 53*(1), 1–8.

Owens, M. L. (2014). Ex-felons' organization-based political work for carceral reforms. *The ANNALS of the American Academy of Political and Social Science, 651*, 256–265.

Pager, D. (2007). *Marked: Race, crime, and finding work in an era of mass incarceration.* Chicago: University of Chicago Press.

Pager, D., & Western, B. (2015). *Investigating prisoner reentry: The impact of conviction status on the employment prospects of young men.* Rochester, NY: The Scholars Choice.

Polletta, F., & Jasper, J. M. (2001). Collective identity and social movements. *Annual Review of Sociology, 27*, 283–305.

Prentice, G. (2015). Officials ban use of "barbaric" dry cells. *Boise Weekly.* Retrieved from www.boiseweekly.com/boise/in-stunning-reversal-idaho-prison-officials-ban-use-of-barbaric-dry-cells/Content?oid=3579503

Prison Policy Initiative. (2017). *Idaho profile.* Retrieved from www.prisonpolicy.org/profiles/ID.html

Ratcliffe, M., Burd, C., Holder, K., & Fields, A. (2016). *Defining rural at the U.S. Census Bureau: American community survey and geography brief.* Washington, DC: US Census Bureau. Retrieved from https://www2.census.gov/geo/pdfs/reference/ua/Defining_Rural.pdf

Sabol, W. J. (2007). Local labor-market conditions and post-prison employment experiences of offenders released from Ohio state prisons. In S. Bushway, M. A. Stoll, & D. F. Weiman (Eds.), *Barriers to reentry? The labor market for released prisoners in post-industrial America* (pp. 257–303). New York: Russell Sage Foundation.

Smith, P., Cullen, F. T., & Latessa, E. J. (2009). Can 14,737 women be wrong? A meta analysis of the LSI-R and recidivism for female offenders. *Criminology & Public Policy, 8*(1), 183–208.

St. Vincent de Paul of Southwest Idaho. (2019). *Reentry programs – overview.* Retrieved from www.svdpid.org/reentry-programs-overview/

Systemic Change of Idaho. (2016). *Systemic change of Idaho.* Retrieved from www.systemicchangeofid.com/

Thompkins, D. E. (2010). The expanding prisoner reentry industry. *Dialectical Anthropology, 34*, 589–604.

United States Department of Agriculture Economic Research Service. (2018). *Rural American at a Glance, 2017 edition.* Washington, DC: United States Department of Agriculture Economic Research Service. Retrieved from www.ers.usda.gov/publications/pub-details/?pubid=85739

vanden Heuvel, K. (2009). Drop the rock. *The Nation*. Retrieved from www.thenation.com/article/drop-rock/

Wacquant, L. (2010). Prisoner reentry as myth and ceremony. *Dialectal Anthropology, 34*, 377–389.

Walker, A., Hempel, L., Unnithan, N. P., & Pogrebin, M. R. (2014). Parole reentry and social capital: The centrality of homelessness. *Journal of Poverty, 18*(3), 315–334.

Ward, K. C., & Merlo, A.V. (2015). Rural jail reentry and mental health. *The Prison Journal*, 1–26. Retrieved from http://tpj.sagepub.com/content/early/2015/09/16/0032885515605473

Webster, C. (2008). Marginalized white ethnicity, race and crime. *Theoretical Criminology, 12*(3), 1362–4806.

Weisheit, R. A., Falcone, D., & Wells, L. E. (2006). *Crime and policing in rural and small-town America* (3rd ed.). Long Grove, IL: Waveland Press, Inc.

Wodahl, E. J. (2006). The challenges of prisoner reentry from a rural perspective. *Western Criminology Review*, 7(2), 32–47.

Zonn, S. (1978). Inmate unions: An appraisal of prisoner rights and labor implications. *University of Miami Law Review, 32*(3), 613–635.

Chapter 5

Life Courses of Sex and Violent Offenders After Prison Release

The Interaction Between Individual- and Community-Related Factors[1]

Gunda Woessner, Kira-Sophie Gauder, and David Czudnochowski

Although there is a vast body of literature on recidivism rates and the rehabilitation of serious and violent offenders, primarily sex offenders, few scholars have explored the question of how the lives of serious offenders actually look post-incarceration. Literature on the reentry process shows that released offenders face various obstacles (Middlemass, 2017; Petersilia, 2003; Travis, 2005; Visher, La Vigne, & Travis, 2004). For example, it is challenging for former inmates because of an unstable employment history and the view that they are a hard-to-employ population (Middlemass, 2017; Pager, 2007; Petersilia, 2003; Uggen, Wakefield, & Western, 2005). These difficulties result from the stigma of a criminal conviction (Holzer, Raphael, & Stoll, 2003; Visher, Debus, & Yahner, 2008) and/or a lack of education (Vacca, 2004). Housing options for released offenders, especially in countries with housing restrictions for serious offenders, is also limited, thereby increasing the risk of homelessness (Roman & Travis, 2006). In addition, former prisoners experience financial constraints and debts, which are exacerbated because they are unable to make a sufficient living (Petersilia, 2003; Visher, 2007), which negatively impact housing and accommodation opportunities (Helfgott, 1997), whereas limited social resources and social capital make it difficult to achieve successful reentry and desistance (Farrall, 2002). Although a prison sentence negatively affects social bonds, relatives and close friends play a pivotal role in the reintegration process of released offenders: They provide help to find a job or housing (Berg & Huebner, 2011; Visher et al., 2004) and may indirectly increase commitment and perform the role of informal social control (Laub & Sampson, 2003; Sampson & Laub, 1993). In sum, the process of reentry is influenced by a multitude of challenges (Petersilia, 2003).

Though numerous studies have identified different barriers in the lives of released offenders, and there is a growing number of scholars exploring how former inmates cope with these obstacles, including Martin's chapter on halfway houses in this volume, scholars are taking into consideration how individual- and community-related factors interact with each other during the critical phase of returning to the outside world (see Leverentz, 2014; Martin, 2017; Middlemass, 2017). Understanding the interplay between structural constraints and intra-psychic dynamics is important to consider how they contribute to successful or failed reentry. According to Davis, Bahr, and Ward (2013), it is not only the presence of external social support that increases motivation to desist, but also a released offender's ability to make use of this support. Phillips and Lindsay (2011) found a link between how releasees cope with post-incarceration problems and recidivism, whereas others suggest agency can exhibit a stabilizing effect on one's life course after release (Maruna, 2001). However, agency is influenced by social structures and how the acting person "creatively and selectively draws on elements of the environment" (Giordano, Cernkovich, & Rudolph, 2002, p. 1003); because "agency is always exercised within the context of social structures" that either "enable" or "constrain" human agency (Farrall, Bottoms, & Shapland, 2010, p. 547), this interplay determines former inmates' narratives and their "self-concept" (Maruna, 2001; Rajah, Kramer, & Sung, 2014).

The Current Study

This present study seeks to improve our understanding of the complex interaction that exists between subjective factors and structural challenges during the reentry process. Drawing on data from a longitudinal study (2003–2017) evaluating treatment outcomes for sex and violent offenders and assessing factors that correlate with recidivism and desistance, offenders' perspectives are taken into account to "understand how individuals make sense of social forces" (Harding, Dobson, Wyse, & Morenoff, 2017, p. 1). A deeper insight into these processes can be obtained by comparing different offender groups, so this study focuses on two different subgroups: sex offenders and violent offenders. The social situations and conditions of sex and violent offenders after prison release is described, then the interplay between experiences and the released prisoners' reactions that contribute to their social reality (see Gukenbiehl, 2016) is examined. Finally, we analyze the strategies released offenders apply to reintegrate into the community, and examine both stabilizing and destabilizing dynamics.

Originally, 403 male German offenders volunteered to participate and were interviewed at the beginning of their incarceration (wave 1, n = 403).[2] Teplin, Abram, McClelland, Dulcan, &, Mericle (2002) argue that the vast majority of the prison population grew up in detrimental environments, and this was true of the participants; according to wave 1 biographical interviews, 46% experienced family violence as a child, 30% reported child sexual abuse, and 40% reported parental alcohol problems. Additionally, 60% reported school absenteeism, 50% suffered concentration problems during school, which led to disruptive behavior in school, 30% ran away from home, and 50% were regularly involved in fights. Prison inmates face adversarial conditions with regard to low education levels, lack of work experience, and poor professional skills prior to incarceration (Matt, 2014; Middlemass, 2017). The associated developmental deficits influence a person throughout their lives and can lead to substance use disorders, emotion regulation deficits, and maladaptive coping (Zeman & Dallaire, 2017).

Shortly before their release from prison, participants were interviewed again (wave 2, n = 277). The third wave of semi-structured interviews were conducted, on average, 1.5 years after each participant was released from prison (wave 3, n = 144).[3] Included with the wave 3 interview data are self-reported delinquency reports and official crime records. The wave 3 interviews were conducted in meeting facilities of hotels, at parole offices, or inside a prison in those cases where the participants had been re-arrested.

A sub-sample of 37 interviews were analyzed: 24 sex offenders (child sexual abuse, n = 15, 41% and rape, n = 9, 24%), and 13 violent offenders (n = 13; 35%).[4] This choice was deliberate; after reading all of the interview transcripts, and in order to guarantee a maximum variation and contrast with regard to the present research focus (Corbin & Strauss, 2008), we identified interviews that differed in length, quality, structure, and case-specific features, such as age and type of offense (i.e., rape, child sexual abuse), offenders with or without correctional treatment, and treatment dropouts. We stopped the selection process when saturation and representativeness of the different sampling features were achieved.

The average age of the sample was 40 at the time of the interview and ranged from 22 to 76 (SD = 13.2). The participants were incarcerated for the index offense for an average of 5.3 years (SD = 3.2; [1; 15 years]) and exhibited a mean of three prior convictions (SD = 3.0) ranging from zero to 12 prior convictions. Nineteen subjects (n = 51%) had been incarcerated for the first time (13 sex offenders, 6 violent offenders).

Each third wave interview began with an open narration impulse (Kruse, 2015) that is used to "yield spontaneous, rich descriptions" of what the interviewees associate "as the main aspects of the phenomenon investigated" (Kvale, 2009, p. 60). Each interview started with the prompt, "Lives can be very different from each other. For one person, transition from prison to community is easy. Another person has to deal with various difficulties. I would ask you to tell me how you have experienced the past time since release from prison." Each participant was asked to provide a dense narrative. The interview protocol covered the post-release development of the subject's social situation (e.g., employment status, housing, leisure time, family/relationships, impact parole supervision has on conduct). The data provided broad insights about subjects' most important concerns.

To understand the social reality of the participants, we analyzed how they coped with challenges and assessed the strategies that they developed to reenter and adapt. Strategies are conscious or unconscious methods used to achieve a desired goal or solve a problem (Greve & Leipold, 2012). Common findings on coping were incorporated (Hobfoll, 1989; Lazarus & Folkman, 2006). This approach allowed us to carve out explicit and implicit meanings from the interview data.[5]

Results

Across the sub-sample of 37 interviews, we compare and contrast the prevailing common patterns described by sex and violent offenders. Then, specific findings associated with each offender group are highlighted. Selected interview quotations are provided.

Both offender groups faced a multitude of challenges after prison release. The social situation was characterized by financial problems, job-related difficulties, stigmatization, disrupted social situation, and substance abuse problems. Study subjects lacked financial resources,[6] and the vast majority of them were in debt when they were released; their debts included legal costs, and pre-prison debts for installment purchases and mobile phone contracts. Thus, a prevailing post-release task was to make a living. However, efforts to gain legal employment were hampered by a number of difficulties. Because of their criminal past, the chances to enter the job market were limited. Frequently, participants exhibited a lack of knowledge, education, or professional training that – in most cases – existed prior to incarceration. The social-financial situation characterizing participants' post-prison experiences included long-term unemployment, perilous job arrangements, short-term employment, and a series of vocational measures aimed at occupational integration and building qualifications. As a result, participants' lives were marked by setbacks in their job search and remained largely dependent on welfare benefits. This reliance on welfare further restricted their social mobility and lifestyle opportunities.

Both offender groups faced job-related challenges that they traced to the fact that they had been incarcerated and thus felt stigmatized. Rene, a violent offender, emphasized: "Most of the employers ask for a professional job application with CV and everything; and oh, yes, [my] CV, from 1984, escape, prison, foreign legion, escape, prison, you can forget it [getting a job]." Sex offenders were particularly burdened by the stigmatization of their crime: "[W]ith my offense you'll probably never be accepted in the community."

Post-prison stigmatization affected employment reintegration and social rehabilitation. Numerous sex offenders reported having almost no contact with the outside world: Oscar stated that, "Everyone only thinks of himself and his own safety." Patrick felt like "living out here, you are no more than a number." Both were isolated, which resulted in boredom, and left some with an inner emptiness.

Feelings of alienation lead to risky behavior. Herbert, who was desperately looking for social contacts, which seemed to be extraordinarily important for his self-concept of belonging, said: "I always wanted to liven my place up," which is why he "slipped into new crimes" (which remained undetected). Among both offender groups, the fear and expectation of being stigmatized stood in stark contrast to real discrimination while stigmatization was a rare event. Participants described a cycle that was not the result of actual stigmatization but often one that was fueled by their fear of being stigmatized and their individual personality traits. It must be emphasized, however, that a minority of sex offender participants reported being stigmatized.

Although there is no equivalent to a sex offender registry in Germany, people did find out about participants' offenses. Luis reported that neighbors damaged his property and Oscar encountered a photograph of himself taped to the door of a local bank issuing the warning, "child molester." Oscar was so concerned that he placed his own obituary in the local press; he feared that a former inmate would find him and threaten him.

For a subgroup of violent offenders, stigmatization (perceived or actual) did not play a role; this was because they were still deeply rooted in a criminal milieu. When asked about the experience of stigmatization after prison, John emphasized: "Not at all. No prejudices, nothing. No." He lived with his parents and his siblings who were engaged in criminal activities. Talking about one of his younger sisters, John stated: "She is worse than I am, criminal." He met up his old friends, "first, we had a beer or two, from beer to drugs [. . .] and then this continued." Likewise, Marvin was not afraid of being stigmatized. He provided helpful tips for friends' future prison terms: "Whenever I meet someone, whom I know has to go to prison, then I provide one, two tips or try to take away their fear."

A closer look at participants' narratives revealed the socially disruptive situation in which they found themselves. In many cases, imprisonment resulted in a relationship breakdown, separation from a spouse/partner, and the inability to stay in touch with their children because of loss of contact with their children's mother. Consequently, participants' social supports were reduced to family. Families, and for the majority of participants their mother, provided initial accommodations, financial support, and help with completing welfare claims or job applications. Almost all participants were confronted with the same challenges, which resulted in the development of a variety of coping skills and strategies.

Although drug and alcohol problems played a major role in most of the violent offenders' narratives, sex offender participants could be divided into a subgroup with and a subgroup without substance use problems. For a considerable proportion of participants, substance use disorders were an integral part of their post-prison life, which proved to be destabilizing to their precarious social situation. However, this pattern was not necessarily linked to criminal recidivism. Although Marko revolved in and out of prison, John did not reoffend, making abstinence from drugs and alcohol a major stabilizing factor.

Despite these challenges, among the most prominent reintegration strategies was an effort to (re)establish social ties and networks to access social capital and emotional support; such supports facilitated access to housing and in some cases a job. Social bonds were important, but at times were associated with negative and destabilizing effects. This was true if a relationship was conflict-torn and the participant lacked social and emotional skills to address the problem.

Many violent offenders stayed in touch with former prisoners, enabling them to compensate for other severed bonds and feelings of marginalization. "Most of the people I hang around with have already spent some time in prison, too," Lars said. Interestingly, violent offenders were most at risk of meeting former prisoners while working on construction sites. Nurturing these relationships was risky as they involved milieu-specific destabilizing behavioral patterns, such as drug abuse or illegal activities. Lars elaborated: "Even the boss himself was imprisoned. He managed everything during day-release, you know? . . . and all the people who worked for him, they were all criminals. Well, everyone spent time in prison and all of them had been taking drugs." Referring to "a good working atmosphere," Dirk said, "we are all very similar, who spent their time, and – yes – every now and then cause trouble." Despite some constraints, relying on family and friends had a generally stabilizing effect: "If it was not for the family, it would have gone downhill right away," is a representative quotation.

Participants who were willing to accept help benefited from the resources, whereas those who declined help did so because it conflicted with their self-concept as an autonomous person. Thus, their strategy was to be independent, which was a destabilizing factor. Participants stressing their self-efficacy simultaneously severed social bonds, and these participants evaded informal social control. By refusing help and being unwilling to adapt to social norms, participants stressed their autonomy, which became a normative legitimation of self. Often, participants who overemphasized their independence failed to reach their goals, resulting in frustration, passiveness, and avoidance. This dynamic was destabilizing even though the subjects conveyed an agentic narrative.

A particularly interesting facet seen in both offender groups was the belief that a romantic relationship was a crucial building block for desistance. There were three patterns. First, some participants, mainly sex offenders, clung to the idea that "a girlfriend will get me on the right track." Hence, some were desperately looking for a partner whereas others already in a relationship were quick to overemphasize its importance. "She left, and it was all crap. . . . Without her, you could have put me back into jail again," Dirk said.

Second, it was striking how fast some participants started a new relationship. The accelerated process was accompanied by a certain arbitrariness and exchangeability of girlfriends, which can be further differentiated: some relationships were reciprocal and affectionate whereas others were transactional. Rene, for instance, stated, "Well, the problem is, I can't just dump her. First of all, we share an apartment. I can't leave overnight. Where could I go? Live on the streets." Jorge works in his girlfriend's promotion agency. "It turned out rather well," he said "and I am financially well cushioned," whereas later in the interview, he stated that "there are enough chicks out there." Some participants seemed to perceive a relationship as a fundamental unit of society and used it as a hook for reintegration without a noticeable emotional commitment. Others had emotionally unstable girlfriends (e.g., a psychiatric disorder or history of sexual abuse), which allowed a certain offender group to maintain a powerful and agentic self in the relationship. Alwin, for instance, whose girlfriend was diagnosed with an autism spectrum disorder stated: "I got used to it, sometimes people actually admire me for bearing this. . . . If I didn't want to do all that, I would have dumped her long ago." Similarly, Carl emphasized that his girlfriend "went through all that [sexual abuse] as well . . . and her son, too. And that's, of course, why it is particularly difficult. But we fight."

Third, some participants, with a reciprocal understanding, stressed that they wanted to be a good partner and father, did not want to disappoint their families, and were committed to the family. For instance, Bodo summarized his successful efforts to find and complete job training: "To get the family out of unemployment benefit, that's the purpose." Reiner centered on the restoration of his status as a father and breadwinner: "I am daddy, I have a special responsibility," and as a violent offender, he emphasized, "I wanna support my wife, I mean, it was not easy for her." Benjamin, a young sex offender, talked about how stabilizing his relationship with his girlfriend was for him, to the point that he sought help from a psychologist to solve relationship problems. For some sex offenders, a relationship meant dealing with being stigmatized: "You have to open up and then you cannot exclude this topic."

Concerning released child abusers, the findings are ambivalent if a relationship could be stabilizing or destabilizing. Most of the participants had court-imposed orders to have no contact with children, whereas some revealed intimacy and attachment deficits. Patrick, for example, repeatedly stressed that he is not interested in a relationship. "I am considered a misogynist," he explained. "I was repeatedly abused by women during my time in the orphanage." Paul had three relationships in 18 months and emphasized, "I cannot imagine living with a partner, or so, to corset myself." Oscar stated that he was intimidated by women and feared disgracing himself in a relationship. Frank had problems at work "because there are female colleagues and I am so shy," and dating was difficult because he was scared "to say the wrong thing." But even among violent offenders, relationships were perceived as criminogenic: Marvin tried to stay away from women because he "had some complaints in the past because of domestic violence."

Having an intimate relationship was not, per se, beneficial. For former child abusers, it was difficult to evaluate whether a relationship with a mother of minors was stabilizing or destabilizing. Irrespective of offense, some relationships were destabilizing. For instance, Lars' relationship had – at the beginning – a highly stabilizing effect. Without his girlfriend, he would not have managed to cope with administrative issues and "she was the only person who never lost hope." At some point, things got difficult and he coped with "the stress with her" by gambling and substance use. This shows how subjective dispositions can foil the stabilizing effect of ostensibly beneficial environmental structures.

For some, substance abuse covered their entire life, and they had grown up with family members addicted to drugs or alcohol. Especially for violent offenders, former addiction problems became a dysfunctional coping strategy. For many participants, they sought former peer contacts and turned to alcohol or drugs, and for some, this resulted in their exclusion from rehabilitative work opportunities and they were unable to break the cycle of addiction. Substance use problems were closely related to the issue of impulse control, and a strategy for quick tension reduction and immediate relief from frustrating situations. Poor impulse control also affected participants in other areas: those who found it difficult to meet stressful work requirements or when things got complicated, they quit their job. Marvin, who had a history of domestic violence, quit his job because it had been difficult for him to motivate himself every morning. "I had difficulties getting up on time in the morning which in the end led to the termination of the contract," he said.

The choices participants made and the behaviors they exhibited were not only an expression of impulse control but of avoidance. Because of lack of functional coping skills, negating challenges became a maladaptive strategy and was a prevailing strategy for participants and their debts. Most subjects only talked about their debts if they were asked directly. They evaded their problems, and in many cases, were not able to name the sum of their liabilities, names of their creditors, or the number of debts. Frequently, participants talked about not paying back their debts by not declaring their real income or pretending they had paid rent when they had an arrangement with a family member. For most participants, personal bankruptcy was the only solution.

As long as participants benefited from social welfare, they were willing to conform. However, as soon as they feared having their benefits cut, many did not comply; this is linked to an intrapsychic dynamic. The majority of offenders legitimated their attitude with a narrative of disadvantage. Rene stressed, "You're released with a mountain of debts. . . . Everything else is impounded." Thomas emphasized how badly his job paid. He felt "taunted and . . . exploited." Similarly, subjects spoke about not being adequately supported by social welfare: Daniel said, "We are already prepared for the next offense again." Violent offenders emphasized how they were disadvantaged by the welfare system. They stressed that "they keep putting spokes in your wheels." This attitude served as a rationale for why some "threw everything away," took a passive approach to life waiting for "something to come about." This disadvantaged attitude was apparent in participants' narratives who self-reported re-offending behavior.

The similar dynamic of being disadvantaged and stigmatized played out during participants' job search, which proved to be an unconscious strategy of avoiding responsibility. Officially registered work was perceived as too stressful or poorly paid, and it was easier to engage in better-paid illicit work. Daniel, who we interviewed in prison after he was reconvicted for robbery, reported that at some point he "was fed up with working. . . . I made my money with crystal [meth]." Whereas most sex offenders were frugal, "I am trying to cut down my expenses," the desire to make fast money was apparent in a subgroup of violent offenders. Consequently, they were more frequently involved in illegal activities, such as drug trafficking, than sex offenders, which enabled them to live a high-profile lifestyle. Being involved in illegal activities had a destabilizing effect. Thus, avoidance and impulse control issues, in combination with self-stigmatization and disadvantage, prevailed over participants' willingness to assimilate and thwarted their efforts, both with external agencies and individual efforts, to develop and maintain stable employment.

Those subjects who maintained a job – even though it was still associated with stress or financial constraints – displayed an intrinsic motivation and a willingness to assimilate. "I couldn't do the job I desperately wanted to do. But then, you have to be flexible." Intrinsic motivation was key to adapt to challenges. "I wanted to show the employer, now, watch this, I work my way up. I am useful. You cannot do without me. And that has worked out until today." The hope for a certain job or vocational training also proved to be stabilizing for those able to delay gratification and whose impulse control deficits were minimal. Marius, unemployed at the time of the interview, developed a stable future perspective because of "the job training. . . . That's the only ray of hope, because I am dependent on social welfare and I never wanted to depend on the authorities."

Contrary to the tendency of many participants to avoid problems, there were subjects who appeared to be motivated to learn problem-solving skills and wanted to pay back their debts, even paying a small amount regularly despite their limited income. After his release, Reiner spent half a year in a rehab-center before working as a trainee with an automotive supplier. Reiner's life-course after prison shows how various motivational aspects are intertwined: He was motivated when he restored his status as a breadwinner and father, and remained motivated based on his new identity as a working person.

Despite some participants being motivated, there were some who felt disadvantaged or reported a one-time nonconforming activity (e.g., getting into a fight). Some participants presented initial success through their job; however, they ultimately fell back into criminal behavior – this pattern applied, above all, to rapists and violent offenders, and in isolated cases to child abusers. For instance, Sam was highly motivated to reintegrate himself into the labor market and emphasized that he succeeded in getting work, he was in a semi-stabilizing (not destabilizing) relationship, but he was reconvicted of rape and sentenced to five years.

Finally, it is essential to look at post-release supervision of conduct and parole. In Germany, parole refers to community measures for those who are granted a conditional release from prison, and includes meetings with a parole officer, whereas supervision of conduct are restrictive measures for certain offenders who served their complete sentence. Supervision plays a pivotal role in the lives of released offenders who have committed a serious crime. A number of subjects benefited from aftercare interventions and parole measures. This was true for sex offenders who had few social contacts; meetings with parole represented one of the few opportunities to talk to someone and to ask for advice.

In assessing whether aftercare measures proved to be stabilizing or destabilizing, the interplay between the parties involved and the subjects' attitudes and skills was examined. Benjamin rejected post-release supervision of conduct, but he benefited from psychotherapy, which he framed as being voluntary. In general, participants complied with supervision based on the quality of the relationship between the participant and the parole officer or therapist.

Supervision of conduct was a prominent topic for sex offenders. Participants, like Sascha, perceived court-imposed orders as detrimental to his wish to (re)establish social and intimate bonds. Thus, even though many child abusers were adaptive and, on occasion, over-adaptive, which may facilitate acceptance of parole measures and contribute to desistance, others tried to circumnavigate rules about not having contact with children. Interestingly, the participants who tended to over-adapt did not recidivate; however, Sascha was re-convicted of child pornography and bodily injury.

For violent offenders, supervision of conduct was a highly relevant topic. Marvin belonged to a group of violent offenders who lacked any motivation to lead a norm-complying and self-supporting life. He was content to live on welfare and rejected supervision of conduct. In the end, his inability to adapt resulted in numerous new criminal records. Marvin's experience may be because of released prisoners mingling with each other where probation and therapeutic services are provided. Marlon captures this succinctly: "You know exactly whose interested in what and who provides you access to which kind of porn."

Conclusion

The social situation of released sex and violent offenders is paved with many challenges. Although participants generally wished to desist, find a job, and have a family, few succeeded. Confrontation with community barriers, such as employment, financial hardship, stigmatization, and isolation, resulted in stress and disappointment that fueled dysfunctional coping patterns. A stable post-incarceration life course is not only determined by employment or a stable relationship, just as an unstable trajectory is not caused by psychological deficits alone (Fox, 2014). If a released prisoner perceives himself as stigmatized and rejected, he will desist (LeBel, Burnett, Maruna, & Bushway, 2008, p. 137).

Our results reveal that a sense of self-efficacy is not stabilizing in terms of desistance. In some cases, agency might have a stabilizing effect on one's self-worth but at the same time be detrimental for one's life course. Involvement in illegal activities not only betters the individual's financial situation but also their self-esteem resulting in feelings of self-efficacy. In order for disaffected persons to develop functional agency, they must be given the opportunity to use their internal control systems. King (2013, p. 329) emphasizes how easy it is to revert to routines and habitual actions to achieve certain goals; this is applicable to participants: Released offenders who feel they can actually achieve their goals are more likely to exhibit intrinsic motivation to desist and adapt to a norm-complying lifestyle. This requires some kind of hook, such as human capital or social bonds (see Farrall, 2002), but also depends on subjective factors and structural obstacles, which are a substantial burden when reentering society. This study has contributed to a broader understanding of the social reality of prisoners reentering the community and the subtle interaction of external and internal factors. Further research on the aforementioned interplay between community and individual factors will no doubt help improve reintegration measures for certain types of offenders.

Notes

1. The authors thank Dr. Chris Murphy for his editorial assistance.
2. Offense type leading to incarceration qualified subjects to participate in the project.
3. With each point of data collection, we lost some subjects, which is a common phenomenon in longitudinal studies.
4. Participants classified as violent offenders were prisoners incarcerated for assault causing bodily harm, (armed) robbery, murder, manslaughter, or wrongful deprivation of liberty.
5. Pseudonyms are used to ensure anonymity for all of the participants.
6. In five circumstances, participants had savings to draw on, and they were withdrawn at the time of the interview (4 were convicted of child abuse, one for murder).

References

Berg, M.T., & Huebner, B. M. (2011). Reentry and the ties that bind: An examination of social ties, employment, and recidivism. *Justice Quarterly, 28*(2), 382–410.

Corbin, J., & Strauss, A. (2008). *Basics of qualitative research* (3rd ed.). Thousand Oaks, CA: Sage.

Davis, C., Bahr, S. J., & Ward, C. (2013). The process of offender reintegration: Perceptions of what helps prisoners reenter society. *Criminology & Criminal Justice, 13*(4), 446–469.

Farrall, S. (2002). *Rethinking what works with offenders: Probation, social context and desistance from crime.* Cullompton: Willan.

Farrall, S., Bottoms, A., & Shapland, J. (2010). Social structures and desistance from crime. *European Journal of Criminology, 7*(6), 546–570.

Fox, K. J. (2014). Restoring the social: Offender reintegration in a risky world. *International Journal of Comparative and Applied Criminal Justice, 38*(3), 235–256.

Giordano, P., Cernkovich, S., & Rudolph, J. (2002). Gender, crime, and desistance: Toward a theory of cognitive transformation. *American Journal of Sociology, 107*(2), 990–1064.

Gukenbiehl, H. L. (2016). Soziologie als Wissenschaft: Warum Begriffe lernen (Sociology as science: Why learning concepts)? In H. Korte & B. Schäfers (Eds.), *Einführung in Hauptbegriffe der Soziologie (Introduction to key concepts of sociology)* (pp. 11–22). Wiesbaden: Springer.

Greve, W., & Leipold, B. (2012). Problembewältigung und intentionale Selbstentwicklung (Problem-solving and intentional self-development). In W. Schneider & U. Lindenberger (Eds.), *Entwicklungspsychologie (Developmental psychology)* (pp. 563–578). Weinheim, Basel: Beltz Verlag.

Harding, D. J., Dobson, C. C., Wyse, J. J. B., & Morenoff, J. D. (2017). Narrative change, narrative stability, and structural constraint: The case of prisoner reentry narratives. *American Journal of Cultural Sociology, 5*(1), 261–304.

Helfgott, J. (1997). Ex-offender needs versus community opportunity in Seattle, Washington. *Federal Probation, 61*(2), 12–24.

Hobfoll, S. E. (1989). Conservation of resources: A new attempt at conceptualizing stress. *American Psychologist, 44*(3), 513–524.

Holzer, H. J., Raphael, S., & Stoll, M. A. (2003). *Employment barriers facing ex-offenders: Reentry Roundtable.* Washington, DC: The Urban Institute.

King, S. (2013). Transformative agency and desistance from crime. *Criminal Justice, 13*(3), 317–335.

Kruse, J. (2015). *Qualitative Interviewforschung. Ein integrativer Ansatz (Qualitative interview research: An integrative approach)* (2nd Auflage). Weinheim und Basel: Beltz Juventa.

Kvale, S. (2009). *Doing interviews.* London: Sage.

Laub, J., & Sampson, R. (2003). *Shared beginnings, divergent lives: Delinquent boys to age 70.* Cambridge, MA: Harvard University Press.

Lazarus, R. S., & Folkman, S. (2006). *Stress, appraisal, and coping.* New York: Springer.

LeBel, T. P., Burnett, R., Maruna, S., & Bushway, S. (2008). The 'chicken and egg' of subjective and social factors in desistance from crime. *European Journal of Criminology, 5*(2), 131–159.

Leverentz, A. (2014). *The ex-prisoner's dilemma: How women negotiate competing narratives of reentry and desistance.* New Brunswick, NJ: Rutgers University Press.

Martin, L. (2017). "Free but still walking the yard:" Prisonization and the problems of reentry. *Journal of Contemporary Ethnography, 47*(5), 671–694.

Maruna, S. (2001). *Making good: How ex-convicts reform and rebuild their lives.* Washington, DC: American Psychological Association.

Matt, E. (2014). *Übergangsmanagement und der Ausstieg aus Straffälligkeit: Wiedereingliederung als gemeinschaftliche Aufgabe (Transition management and withdrawal from delinquency: Reintegration as a community task).* Freiburg: Centaurus Verlag & Media UG.

Middlemass, K. (2017). *Convicted and condemned: The politics and policies of prisoner reentry.* New York: New York University Press.

Pager, D. (2007). *Marked: Race, crime and finding work in an era of mass incarceration.* Chicago: University of Chicago Press.

Petersilia, J. (2003). *When prisoners come home: Parole and prisoner reentry.* Oxford: Oxford University Press.

Phillips, L. A., & Lindsay, M. (2011). Prison to society: A mixed methods analysis of coping with reentry. *International Journal of Offender Therapy and Comparative Criminology, 55*(1), 136–154.

Rajah, V., Kramer, R., & Sung, H-E. (2014). Changing narrative accounts: How young men tell different stories when arrested, enduring jail time and navigating community reentry. *Punishment & Society, 16*(3), 285–304.

Roman, C. G., & Travis, J. (2006). Where will I sleep tomorrow? Housing, homelessness, and the returning prisoner. *Housing Policy Debate, 17*(2), 389–418.

Sampson, R. J., & Laub, J. H. (1993). *Crime in the making: Pathways and turning points through life.* Cambridge, MA: Harvard University Press.

Teplin, L. A., Abram, K. M., McClelland, G. M., Dulcan, M. K., & Mericle, A. A. (2002). Psychiatric disorders in youth in juvenile detention. *Archives of General Psychiatry, 59,* 1133–1143.

Travis, J. (2005). *But they all come back: Facing the challenges of prisoner reentry.* Washington, DC: Urban Institute Press.

Uggen, C., Wakefield, S., & Western, B. (2005). Work and family perspectives on reentry. In C. A. Visher & J. Travis (Eds.), *Prisoner reentry and crime in America* (pp. 209–243). Cambridge: Cambridge University Press.

Vacca, J. (2004). Educated prisoners are less likely to return to prison. *Journal of Correctional Education, 55*(4), 297–305.

Visher, C. A. (2007). Returning home: Emerging findings and policy lessons about prisoner reentry. *Federal Sentencing Reporter, 20*(1), 93–102.

Visher, C. A., Debus, S., & Yahner, J. (2008). *Employment after prison: A longitudinal study of releases in three states.* Washington, DC: Urban Institute, Justice Policy Center. Retrieved from www.urban.org/UploadedPDF/411778_employment_ after_prison.pdf

Visher, C. A., La Vigne, N., & Travis, J. (2004). *Returning home: Understanding the challenges of prisoner reentry: Maryland pilot study: Findings from Baltimore.* Washington, DC: The Urban Institute.

Zeman, J., & Dallaire, D. (2017). Children's and adolescents' emotion regulation in the context of parental incarceration. In C. A. Essau, S. Leblanc, & T. H. Ollendick (Eds.), *Emotion regulation and psychopathology in children and adolescents* (pp. 351–373). Oxford, UK: Oxford University Press.

Section II

Health, Embodiment, and Reentry

Recently, scholars, activists, and returning citizens have raised concerns and increased social awareness about trauma, substance abuse, physical well-being, and mental health issues as it relates to the criminal justice system in the United States. The changing nature and concern about health and embodiment as it relates to reentry is the shifting nature of drug consumption in the U.S. During the 1980s and 1990s, illicit drug consumers were usually depicted as urban, low-income, undereducated people of color, and on the other hand, drug dealers were characterized as dangerous Black youth involved in crime who were "super predators" (Marable, Middlemass, & Steinberg, 2007). However, as drug users and addicts are just as likely to be White, suburban, middle-class men and women, today's politicians and others have distanced themselves from the demonizing racialized language and no longer characterize "addicts" as morally deficient and criminal. As White drug consumption has sky-rocketed, the terminology related to fighting a "war on drugs" has been replaced with terms like the "opioid crisis" and a public health epidemic related to changes in social and economic patterns. The new language is shifting from a narrative that drug users are criminals to one that makes these "new" drug users victims and that their drug addiction is because of economic circumstances and not their moral failings.

Additionally, as states continue to pass legislation making the growing and selling of marijuana legal, there is a glaring contradiction amidst this seemingly progressive shift in public policy over a drug that had previously been cited as a "gateway" drug that led to a moral panic in the 1930s known as "reefer madness." Now, White business owners are profiting from the sale of a former illegal substance; prior to the legalization of marijuana, the criminal justice system sent hundreds of thousands of urban Black and Brown men and women to prison for being in possession of drug paraphernalia, possession, manufacturing, and distribution. In fact, Alexander (2010) points out that because of various drug policies, individuals with a drug felony conviction are barred from entering the legal marijuana business, which disproportionately impacts people of color.

The current trends and policies surrounding substance use, trauma, and mental health highlight some of the continued racial and economic disparities attached to crime policies and incarceration rates. The following chapters address various aspects of health, embodiment, and substance use as it relates to incarceration and reentry. Here, the authors illustrate how trauma, substance abuse, and mental illness impact reentry experiences. The authors highlight the many ways that trauma, mental health, and substance abuse persist while men and women are incarcerated and beyond the tangible barriers of prison cells.

Reviere, Young, and Dawson, in their chapter, "Mothers Returning Home," offer a critical intersectional analysis of mothers who are incarcerated. Most mothers suffer trauma and high rates of abuse and drug addiction prior to being incarcerated. As a result, they are economically marginalized and suffer the consequences of past decisions while incarcerated and upon returning home. Reviere and colleagues argue that most mothers return to their families and communities, but one factor that complicates their reentry efforts is their relationship with their children; to improve the relationship between mothers and their children, mothers need resources and programs to improve their overall health and mental wellness so that they can be better moms when they return home.

Linda Carson, in her chapter, "Release from Long-Term Restrictive Housing," reviews the literature on the different types of long-term restrictive housing units, such as solitary confinement, which deny prisoners social, emotional, verbal, and physical contact with other people. Carson's literature review shows how the use of restrictive housing units in supermax prisons causes mental anguish for prisoners. Beyond the mental health issues that arise, living in inadequate space can also initiate physical health aliments and other harms. Carson describes some of the harms faced by individuals who are put in restrictive housing, and offers a broad overview on restrictive housing and its connection to mental health; however, despite the fact that Carson's chapter is not necessarily critical of the institutional policies that put individuals into a restrictive housing unit nor does she analyze the use of restrictive housing and its relationship to reentry, her chapter is important. Carson raises important questions, such as, how are prisoners treated? Should prisoners be housed in restrictive housing for short, long or any period of time? If so, under what circumstances should correctional officers and prison administrators use restrictive housing? Which government agency should monitor the use of restrictive housing? Carson also raises important questions about how prisoners should receive treatment as they transition from restrictive housing to the general prison population and then reenter society: What types of treatment should be required? Medical attention? Mental health counseling? Other types of services? If so, who should offer those services, and how should those services be implemented?

Taking into consideration the physical restrictions that prisons pose, Williams, Green, and Lewis, in their chapter, "Resilient Roads and the Non-Prison Model for Women," argue that because women are not simply smaller men, and because they suffer from abuse, trauma, and mental illness prior to incarceration, prisons should be redesigned for incarcerated women and spatial arrangements need to acknowledge the unique needs women face while incarcerated. If the prison spaces are redesigned, Williams and colleagues argue that reentry outcomes will improve for formerly incarcerated women.

Doude and Sparks, in their chapter, "Alcohol Use Disorder: Programs and Treatment for Offenders Reentering the Community," offer a summary of the type of alcohol treatment programs offered in state and federal prisons. This description of the types of programs is important because although the sale and consumption of alcohol is legal and socially acceptable, it is still an addictive substance; alcohol is implicated in the incarceration of 56.5% of all U.S. prisoners. Doude and Sparks conclude that in-prison treatment programs for alcohol use and abuse offer a false sense of abstinence and recovery as alcohol consumption inside prison is not allowed or comes in the form of "prison hooch," pruno, or prison wine, which is a known cause of botulism. Doude and Sparks call for a change in the programs that are available, but do not address some of the underlying substance abuse issues as they relate to criminality and do not connect alcohol use disorder to reentry. However, Doude and Sparks raise important questions about the types of alcohol use disorder programs and treatments that are offered, and whether or not those programs are sufficient. Moreover, Doude and Sparks advance the idea that for those dealing with alcohol addiction, recovery should start inside prison and the programs that are offered need to be studied using advanced methods to see which ones work and for whom. Traditional AA programs do not work for everyone, so what should be offered to prisoners and men and women reentering society?

De la Tierra, in his chapter, "Carceral Calisthenics," hones in on the physical health of male prisoners. Unlike the previous chapters in this section, de la Tierra does not focus on physical harm but instead looks at physical well-being by exploring how previously incarcerated men combat the prison environment through carceral calisthenics; carceral calisthenics are a way that individuals shape their body and mind through specific exercises using their own body weight. Carceral calisthenics provide individual men an acceptable way to set goals, resist prison politics, maintain their peace of mind, and emerge from prison with a routine that they can continue upon reentering society. More specifically, these exercises are allowed within the prison environment and do not require permission from prison administrators or special equipment. De la Tierra examines the exercise routines some men have developed in prison and then continued when they are back in the community, and what it means in terms of resilience and resistance to carceral settings and challenges when reentering society.

82 Health, Embodiment, and Reentry

Together, these chapters in Part II, "Health, Embodiment, and Reentry," contribute to the many concerns raised by critical criminological research in the areas of substance use and abuse, physical and mental health, and trauma as they relate to the criminal justice system and reentry.

References

Alexander, M. (2010). *The new Jim Crow: Mass incarceration in the age of colorblindness*. New York: The New Press.

Marable, M., Middlemass, K., & Steinberg, I. (2007). *Racializing justice, disenfranchising lives: The racism, criminal justice, and law reader*. New York: Palgrave Macmillan.

Chapter 6

Mothers Returning Home
A Critical Intersectional Approach to Reentry

Rebecca Reviere, Vernetta D. Young, and Akiv Dawson

Introduction: Where Have the Mothers Gone?

In the *New Jim Crow*, Alexander (2010) critiques President Barack Obama for asking, "Where have all the fathers gone?" implying that the answer is obvious, they are locked up. However, given the current trend in female incarceration, the appropriate question is, "Where have all the mothers gone?" Currently, the United States incarcerates 219,000 women in jails and prisons across the country (Kajstura, 2018). The female incarceration rate has grown, and research continues to show that women, overwhelmingly, are casualties of the War on Drugs and its castigatory sentencing requirements (Parsons & Warner-Robbins, 2002; Kellet & Willging, 2011). Poor, Black, and Latina women have been swept into the incarceration dragnet (Lipsitz, 2012). Yet scholars continue to focus extensively on men's experiences in the criminal justice system.

A bourgeoning body of literature has identified several ways that women's experiences with mass incarceration differ from men (Nowotny, Masters, & Boardman, 2016). Additionally, scholars argue that policymakers fail to acknowledge that women's needs differ from men's needs (Santo, 2017). Many women offenders have life histories of trauma, such as sexual abuse, drug use, and severe mental health issues (Travis, Western, & Redburn, 2014). Yet prisons and jails rarely have the resources to provide necessary treatment options (Dumont, Brockmann, Dickman, Alexander, & Rich, 2012). Prison administrations have historically ignored women's reproductive and biological needs (Roth, 2010).

The prison label compounds issues of class, ethno-racial, and gender discrimination for minority women (Lipsitz, 2012), who are disproportionately incarcerated (The Sentencing Project, 2019). Furthermore, these women tend to come from poorer socioeconomic backgrounds and have low educational attainment. Another major difference from men is that the majority of incarcerated women are the primary caregivers to minor children (Sawyer, 2018). Thus, it appears the new Jim Crow is both a racial and gendered caste system that further subjugates women, especially mothers. Still, we fail to ask, "Where have all the mothers gone?" and "What will it take to bring them home?"

Despite being an important part of many incarcerated women's social identities, *motherhood* has not garnered as much attention in comparison to race and class. We argue that policymakers and stakeholders must consider the needs of the mothers who will be returning home and the barriers mothers face to successfully reenter. The barriers faced by mothers are the topic of this chapter. We ask, (1) Who are the mothers? (2) Where have all the mothers gone? (3) What do the mothers need? and (4) How can mothers achieve successful reentry? To answer these questions, we examine the impact laws and criminal justice policies have on marginalized groups; how the criminalization of mothers makes them powerless; and the interconnectedness of structures of power.

This work is guided by a critical intersectional approach to understanding reentry. Critical intersectionality draws on elements of extant criminological and sociological theories including conflict theory, critical race theory, and intersectionality. These elements form a theoretical framework for understanding individual characteristics, such as race, class, and gender, and the structural barriers that formerly-incarcerated mothers face when returning home.

Why Did Mothers Go?

Mothers have always gone to prison, but the current wave of mothers coming home from it is relatively new. Women, particularly women of color, were disproportionately impacted by legislative changes in the 1980s and 1990s, such as truth in sentencing practices, mandatory minimums, and the War on Drugs (Parsons & Warner-Robbins, 2002; Kellet & Willging, 2011; National Women's Law Center, 2010; Aiello, 2016). As a result, the female prison population expanded by more than 700% between 1980 and 2014 and continues to outpace male incarceration rates (Sawyer, 2018; The Sentencing Project, 2019). We discuss three main factors that have contributed to the rise in female incarceration: gendered stereotypes, the War on Drugs, and the criminalization of poverty.

Bloom and Chesney-Lind (2003) suggest that the rise in female incarceration is a result of vengeful equity and the idea that men and women should receive equal punishments. Ideas about femininity have always been a part of the justice system's response to female criminals (Wilson, 2003). Traditionally, crime has been thought of as a male issue. Black female offenders violate Eurocentric and patriarchal conceptualizations of femininity, as discussed in Middlemass' chapter later in this volume. Thus, female offenders are not viewed as women and mothers who commit crime and are incarcerated and regarded as bad (Gurusami, 2019).

Black women exist at the nexus of many social identities and at the intersection of social institutions, especially the criminal justice and public welfare systems (Middlemass, 2015). Policy prescriptions have had severe implications for women; the War on Drugs led to the widespread criminalization of poor women. Enforcement strategies designed to punish drug dealers had gendered and racialized consequences. For example, the 1988 revision to the Anti-drug Abuse Act of 1986 added civil penalties for drug offenses and made drug offenses grounds for disqualification from public housing. The 1988 law introduced mandatory minimum sentencing for drug offenses (Alexander, 2010) and was particularly punitive to poor women; they rely on public housing and are overrepresented among drug users. Furthermore, the civil penalties for drug offenses ensure that poor women who cannot afford to pay the fines are incarcerated (Alexander, 2010). Economic hardship is a primary reason that many women are incarcerated and mandatory minimum sentences for drug offenses ensured that women spend years in prison.

The passage of the Personal Responsibility and Work Opportunity Act of 1996 is perhaps the most significant merger of the criminal justice and public welfare systems. The Act's "one-strike rule" mandated the eviction of HUD tenants who are convicted of drug offenses (Middlemass, 2017). Furthermore, the Act enacted a lifetime ban on SNAP benefits for drug convictions (Bloom & Chesney-Lind, 2003), severely limiting women's access to financial assistance (Middlemass, 2017; McCarty, Falk, Aussenberg, & Carpenter, 2016). Although many state legislatures opted out or modified the ban (Brown, 2010), the problem remains for those mothers who are barred from assistance and have no steady source of income. Policies, coupled with widespread residential segregation, pushed women and their families towards criminogenic communities, spaces with dilapidated housing, few employment opportunities, high crime, low collective efficacy, concentrated poverty, and pervasive police surveillance (Lipsitz, 2012). These factors produced the perfect storm for the rise in female incarceration.

Who Are the Mothers?

Incarcerated women tend to be economically marginalized, and are likely to not own household assets prior to incarceration (Turney & Schneider, 2016). Women of color are overrepresented as offenders in local, state, and federal correctional institutions and most are incarcerated for nonviolent property or drug offenses (National Center on Justice Involved Women, 2016). However, women of color receive harsher charges and longer sentences than their White counterparts for similar crimes (Foster, 2018). According to the National Center on Justice Involved Women (2016), "in 2014, the imprisonment rate for African American women was still more than 2 times the rate of imprisonment for White women. For Hispanic women incarceration rates were 1.2 times the rate of White women."

Incarcerated women are more likely than their male counterparts to have histories of physical, mental, and sexual abuse (Travis et al., 2014); as well as mental health, substance use, or co-occurring disorders (Houser & Belenko, 2015). The majority of women in prison have been physically, sexually, and/ or emotionally abused as children and witnessed such episodes in their families of origin. This early abuse is often echoed in later episodes of domestic violence. For example, incarcerated women have experienced elevated rates of sexual victimization, which are estimated to be 50–66% for child sexual abuse, 28–68% for adult sexual abuse, and 56–82% for lifetime sexual assault. Some suggest that a background of sexual abuse is so common among women in prison that it should be considered part of the pathway to prison (Karlsson & Zielinski, 2018). Being battered and abused, either as a child or as an adult, increases the risk for poor health outcomes, including returning to a violent relationship upon reentry or putting their children's health at risk (Felitti & Anda, 2009; Shin & Miller, 2012).

Additionally, the disparities in class, race, and gender are compounded by motherhood. In 2018, an estimated 62% of women in state prisons had minor children and were the children's primary caretaker (Sawyer, 2018). Motherhood is not evenly distributed: Poor women and women of color tend to have more kids on average than middle- or upper-class women and White women, and have children at earlier ages (Edin & Kefalas, 2011). Therefore, families of color are disproportionately disrupted by parental incarceration.

Most mothers will return to their families and communities, but how well they manage reentry with their children depends on many factors, including what their lives were like before they were incarcerated, what happened to them behind bars, and their post-prison opportunities. In addition, mothers' experiences after prison are shaped by the lives of their children and who their children's caregivers were while they were away. A critical intersectional approach provides a lens to focus on the trajectories of their lives and on the need to mitigate harm while they are behind bars. The extent of that mitigation is constrained by criminal justice policies and programs that do not prioritize the importance of mothers to their families and their communities.

These psychosocial issues and the social dimensions of health aren't adequately addressed in correctional settings and are visible when examining health disparities; incarcerated women report poorer physical and mental health and higher substance usage than women in the community and men in prison (Young & Reviere, 2006). Mothers do not enter prison as physically healthy women; they have faced lifetimes of poor diets, lack of exercise opportunities, low education, and inadequate health care. By the time women enter prison, 57% in state and 52% in federal prisons reported having a current medical problem, such as arthritis, asthma, and hypertension. Additionally, HIV rates are relatively high for incarcerated mothers (Sacks et al., 2008).

Almost 75% of women in state and 61% of women in federal prisons report mental health problems (James & Glaze, 2006), particularly depression and post-traumatic stress disorder (Baranyi, Cassidy, Fazel, Priebe, & Mundt, 2018). Women with mental illnesses are more likely to be homeless before arrest, to have experienced physical or sexual abuse, and to have a parent who abused drugs or alcohol (James & Glaze, 2006). These problems are especially acute in second-generation prisoners who witnessed domestic violence as children (Will, Loper, & Jackson, 2016). Substance abuse and addiction problems are common among women in prison; some women use drugs to self-medicate and as a coping mechanism related to their past trauma (Borja, Nurius, & Eddy, 2015). According to the National Institute on Drug Abuse (2019, more than 80% of incarcerated women abused some type of drug within 30 days of her incarceration, with many abusing multiple types of drugs.

What Do Mothers Need During Incarceration?

Mothers carry their mental health problems into prison, and an added source of distress is the pain of separation from their children (Thompson & Harm, 2000). Many mothers experience anxiety, depression, regret, loss, and fear about how their relationship with their children will be affected. When mothers go to prison, someone assumes responsibility for their children; fathers take custody of their children for only 37% of incarcerated mothers (Glaze & Maruschak, 2010). As a result, mothers must find suitable alternatives, such as grandparents, particularly maternal grandmothers (45%), other relatives (23%), foster homes or other state agencies (11%), and friends (8%) Baker, McHale, Strozier, & Cecil, 2010). Children of White mothers are more likely to be placed in foster care or with their fathers, whereas the children of Black mothers tend to be placed with female relatives, including grandmothers, sisters, aunts, or cousins (Collins, 2000). Many of these caretakers are poor and the added responsibility of an additional child or children is not easy, even with government assistance for which many are ineligible (Baker et al., 2010).

Most mothers returning from prison hope to return to their parenting roles (Gurusami, 2019). However, reunification with children can be difficult because it requires that formerly incarcerated women be able to navigate a very complex legal system (Gurusami, 2019). Incarcerated mothers are more likely than incarcerated fathers to have their parental rights terminated by the courts (Garcia, 2016). The 1997 Adoption and Safe Families Act authorized the termination of parental rights when a child has been in foster care for 15 of the last 22 months. Consequently, the parents of these children risk losing custody of their children (Russell-Brown, 2015). State prison sentences average 22 months and federal sentences average 60 months, so the odds for reunification with minor children are greatly reduced for incarcerated mothers.

The development and maintenance of healthy, respectful, and open relationships between mothers, children, and caregivers are crucial for reunification. These relationships dictate how involved the mothers are allowed to be in the raising of her children. Discord may result in behaviors from the caregiver limiting the mother's involvement; according to Loper and Tuerk (2011), disagreements between mothers and caregivers can reduce the caregiver's incentive for continuing contact. Conflict with the children's caregiver can have detrimental consequences for the mother and the child; a study on mother–grandmother parenting dyads found that in "families with better functioning dyads, children had fewer problems related to attention, hyperactivity, defiance, and aggression," (Baker et al., 2010, p. 176). Foster and Hagan (2009, p. 180) found that there are negative "intergenerational collateral consequences" and that "mass incarceration is disproportionately concentrated among disadvantaged groups [so] prisoner reentry cross-cut race and ethnicity as well as gender."

Correctional settings are used as dumping grounds for women suffering from substance abuse and mental health issues, and attendance in substance abuse programs is often mandated as a part of sentencing for drug offenses (National Institute of Drug Abuse, 2019). Drug relapse is linked to recidivism, and anti-recidivism efforts often include drug treatment programs (Kissman, 2004; Cobbina & Bender, 2012; Beichner & Rabe-Hemp, 2014). Ironically, women are more likely to complete drug treatment programs in prison than in community settings (Kissman, 2004). Many female inmates reported that their children were the most important factor in their decision to get clean and sober. For this reason, many drug rehabilitation programs in female prisons and jails also emphasize parenting skills.

Women's relationships with their children are important for reentry (Baker et al., 2010). Unfortunately, few women's state and federal prisons are within 100 miles of their homes (Margolies & Kraft-Stolar, 2006); as a result, more than half of all incarcerated mothers' children do not visit (Frost, Greene, & Pranis, 2006). Considering that most prisoners come from poor families, the costs and logistics of visiting family members means that the majority of mothers' children do not visit (Halperin & Harris, 2004; Russell-Brown, 2015).

Research shows that children of incarcerated parents suffer from behavioral, emotional, and/or psychological problems, experience difficulties in school, embarrassment, stigmatization, abandonment issues, loneliness, stress, and delinquency (Maruschak, Glaze, & Mumola, 2010; Kjellstrand, Cearley, Eddy, Foney, & Martinez, 2012; Turney, 2014; Sparks, 2015). Mothers' worries are mitigated, to some extent, by contact with their children and good relationships with their children's caretakers. But without intervention in preparation for release and the transition home, many incarcerated mothers

Mothers Returning Home   89

are unlikely to have the emotional and parenting skills necessary to facilitate successful parent–child reunification (Snyder, Carlo, & Coats-Mullins, 2001).

Programs that teach mothers effective parenting practices, communication, behavior, and emotional management skills and encourage parent–child bonding, can alleviate some of the stressors of separation and smooth reunification for both mothers and their children (Bruns, 2006; Kissman, 2004; Loper & Tuerk, 2011). Organizations may provide support for children, such as transportation to prison facilities, one-to-one mentoring, and reading to children (Russell-Brown, 2015). These programs help mothers cope with the depression, anxiety, and even their shame associated with incarceration and being separated from their children (Bruns, 2006; Aiello, 2016). Despite the challenges, many formerly incarcerated mothers plan to and do reunite with their children and resume their roles as mothers when they are released (Beichner & Rabe-Hemp, 2014).

What Are the Barriers to Mothers' Successful Reentry?

The available prison programs are not focused on creating sturdy family, community, and formal support systems, so incarcerated mothers' chances of successful reentry are limited.Very few programs support the reunification of mothers and their children, and few address the emotional health of families during the transition home (Purvis, 2013). Additionally, most women leave prison with only the clothes on their backs and are responsible for their own reentry success (Middlemass, 2017; Kellet & Willging, 2011). As a result, the problems range from securing housing and financial support (Arditti & Few, 2008) to coping with addictions and other traumas experienced before and during incarceration; there are limited substance abuse and mental health services (Cobbina, 2010; Kellet & Willging, 2011).

Mothers need housing for themselves and their children for successful reentry, but finding affordable housing is difficult and for those with a criminal record it can be next to impossible (Middlemass, 2017). The regulations regarding public housing deny housing assistance to those convicted of drug offenses but also place family members in jeopardy if they open their homes to family who have been arrested or convicted of a drug offense (Middlemass, 2017). Subsequently, many formerly incarcerated mothers do not live with their children and other family members, cannot find private housing, and are not able to reunite with their children in a safe housing environment. Many formerly incarcerated women face high rates of homelessness (Couloute, 2018).

Housing is connected to employment (Middlemass, 2017), and it is difficult to secure employment without an address. Stable employment is one of the most important aspects of successful reentry and confident mothering, but most returning prisoners face tremendous obstacles in finding and keeping a living wage job (see Middlemass, 2017). It usually takes several months, if ever, to find gainful employment (Middlemass, 2017). Part of the challenge in finding gainful employment post-prison: Studies find that incarcerated women receive educational and vocational training that are not easily transferrable to the job market (Harris, 2018). Other barriers, such as childcare, training, and homelessness, are difficult challenges facing women returning home; "childcare assistance is the least frequently provided reentry service" (Scroggins & Malley, 2010, p. 149), and women cannot afford childcare. These barriers are compounded for Black and Hispanic women because of institutional discrimination while their criminal status reduces their employment chances even more (Couloute & Kopf, 2018).

Formerly incarcerated women return to communities without adequate mental health services to assist with reentry stressors. Accumulated stressors can be particularly dangerous for women dealing with substance abuse or mental health problems. Mental health care for returning mothers is particularly important; women with histories of psychiatric problems are at higher risk for failure in the community (Begun, Early, & Hodge, 2016). Women rarely received help for alcohol and drug addiction, and access to these services were dramatically reduced after incarceration (Kellet & Willging, 2011). As discussed by several authors in this edited volume, alcohol and substance abuse programs are insufficient and inadequate, and individuals who have completed drug and alcohol treatment programs face temptations and lack alternative coping strategies when they return (Begun et al., 2016).

When post-release drug treatment services are available, they enable women to adjust to community life and avoid recidivism (Young & Reviere, 2006; Luther, Reichert, Holloway, Roth, & Aalsma, 2011). The absence of these services has severe implications for reentry, especially family reunification. Without the proper help to address addiction and mental health issues, formerly incarcerated mothers will not be able to adequately parent their children.

The red tape and bureaucracy associated with state child care agencies can prove to be a major barrier for women seeking custody of their minor children (Garcia, 2016). Many mothers regarded their children as the major reason and motivation to achieve post-incarceration success (Cobbina & Bender, 2012; Garcia, 2016). Despite their motivation and desire to be a better parent to their children, many women will not receive the help they need (Cobbina, 2010).

Conclusion: How to Keep Mothers in the Community?

Too often, women's experiences with mass incarceration are overlooked; this is problematic because it leads to the development of programs and passage of policies that do not consider their needs. A critical intersectional lens allows us to focus on mothers who enter and exit prisons. The interlocking oppressions at the crossroads of gender, mothering, poverty, and race are situated in communities with few opportunities and many disadvantages. Formerly incarcerated mothers are perceived as bad mothers and elicit little sympathy. Their prison experience and criminal stigma are compounded by issues of race and culture, especially for women of color, who face discrimination based on gender and race (Garcia, 2016).

Until society acts to eradicate the fundamental inequities and interlocking oppressions that make so many mothers susceptible to incarceration, their families, children, and communities will continue to suffer. Programs that provide adequate mental health and substance abuse services to women inside and outside of prison are needed. Further, resources that offer pathways to quality education and other post-release services are required. Policymakers need to acknowledge the importance of motherhood and consider it in policy prescriptions regarding incarceration and reentry, which requires recognizing incarceration and reentry as an intersectional process involving interconnected experiences, policies, and social institutions.

References

Aiello, B. (2016). Making mothers: Paring classes in a women's jail. *Contemporary Justice Review, 19*(4), 445–461.

Alexander, M. (2010). *The New Jim Crow: Mass incarceration in the age of colorblindness.* New York: The New Press.

Arditti, J., & Few, A. (2008). Maternal distress and women's reentry into family and community life. *Family Process, 47*, 303–321.

Baker, J., McHale, J., Strozier, A., & Cecil, D. (2010). Mother-grandmother coparenting relationships in families with incarcerated mothers: A pilot investigation. *Family Process, 49*(2), 165–184. doi:10.1037/a0026407.

Baranyi, G., Cassidy, M., Fazel, S., Priebe, S., & Mundt, A. P. (2018). Prevalence of posttraumatic stress disorder in prisoners. *Epidemiologic Reviews, 40*(1), 134–145. doi:10.1093/epirev/mxx015.

Beichner, D., & Rabe-Hemp, C. (2014). "I don't want to go back to that town:" Incarcerated mothers and their return home to rural communities. *Critical Criminology, 22,* 527–543.

Begun, A. L., Early, T. J., & Hodge, A. (2016). Mental health and substance abuse service engagement by men and women during community reentry following incarceration. *Administration and Policy in Mental Health and Mental Health Services Research, 43*(2), 207–218.

Bloom, B., & Chesney-Lind, M. (2003). Women in prison. In R. Muraskin (Ed.), *Its a crime: Women and justice* (pp. 175–195). Upper Saddle River: Prentice Hall.

Borja, S., Nurius, P., & Eddy, J. M. (2015). Adversity across the life course of incarcerated parents: Gender differences. *Journal of Forensic Social Work, 5*(1–3), 167–185.

Brown, G. (2010). *The intersectionality of race, gender, and reentry: Challenges for African-American women.* American Constitution Society for Law and Policy: Issue Brief. Washington, DC: American Constitution Society. Retrieved from https://www.prisonlegalnews.

org/media/publications/american_constitution_society_brown_brief_on_intersectionality_of_race_gender_and_reentry_for_african_american_women_2010.pdf

Bruns, D. A. (2006). Promoting mother-child relationships for incarcerated women and their children. *Infants & Young Children, 19*(4), 308–322.

Cobbina, J. E. (2010). Reintegration success and failure: Factors impacting reintegration among incarcerated and formerly incarcerated women. *Journal of Offender Rehabilitation, 49,* 210–232.

Cobbina, J. E., & Bender, K. (2012). Predicting the future: Incarcerated women's views of reentry success. *Journal of Offender Rehabilitation, 51,* 275–294.

Collins, P. H. (2000). Gender, Black feminism, and Black political economy. *The ANNALS of the American Academy of Political and Social Science, 568*(1), 41–53.

Couloute, L. (2018). *Nowhere to go: Homelessness among formerly incarcerated people.* Easthampton: Prison Policy Initiative. Retrieved from www.prisonpolicy.org/reports/housing.html

Couloute, L., & Kopf, D. (2018). *Out of prison & out of work.* Easthampton: Prison Policy Initiative. Retrieved from www.prisonpolicy.org/reports/outofwork.html

Dumont, D. M., Brockmann, B., Dickman, S., Alexander, N., & Rich, J. D. (2012). Public health and the epidemic of incarceration. *Annual Review of Public Health, 33,* 325–339.

Edin, K., & Kefalas, M. (2011). *Promises I can keep: Why poor women put motherhood before marriage, with a new preface* (3rd ed.). Oakland: University of California Press.

Felitti, V., & Anda, R. (2009). The relationship of adverse childhood experiences to adult medical disease, psychiatric disorders, and sexual behavior: Implications for healthcare. In R. Lanius, E. Vermetten, & C. Pain (Eds.), *The impact of early life trauma on health and disease: The hidden epidemic* (pp. 77–87). Cambridge: Cambridge University Press.

Foster, A. (2018). Unfinished uniformity in systematic sentencing: Oppressive treatment and disproportionate punishment outcomes for Black women in federal prisons. *Indiana Journal of Law and Social Equality, 6*(2), 267–282.

Foster, H., & Hagan, J. (2009). The mass incarceration of parents in America: Issues of race/ ethnicity, collateral damage to children, and prisoner reentry. *The ANNALS of the American Academy of Political and Social Science, 623,* 179–194.

Frost, N. A., Greene, J., & Pranis, K. (2006). *HARD HIT: The growth in the imprisonment of women, 1977–2004,* Institute on Women & Criminal Justice. New York: Women's Prison Association.

Garcia, J. (2016). Understanding the lives of mothers after incarceration: Moving beyond socially constructed definitions of motherhood. *Sociology Compass, 10*(1), 3–11.

Glaze, L., & Maruschak, L. (2010). *Parents in prison and their minor children.* Washington, DC: Bureau of Justice Statistics. Retrieved from https://www.bjs.gov/content/pub/pdf/pptmc.pdf

Gurusami, S. (2019). Motherwork under the state: The maternal labor of formerly incarcerated Black women. *Social Problems, 66*(1), 128–143. doi:10.1093/socpro/spx045.

Halperin, R., & Harris, J. (2004). Parental rights of incarcerated mothers with children in foster care: A policy vacuum. *Feminist Studies, 30*(2), The Prison Issue, 339–352.

Harris, A. (2018, April 30). Women in prison take home economics, while men take carpentry. *The Atlantic.* Retrieved from www.theatlantic.com/education/archive/2018/04/the-continuing-disparity-in-womens-prison-education/559274/

Houser, K., & Belenko, S. (2015). Disciplinary responses to misconduct among female prison inmates with mental illness, substance use disorders, and co-occurring disorders. *Psychiatric Rehabilitation Journal, 38*(1), 24–34.

James, D., & Glaze, L. (2006). *Special report: Mental health problems of prison and Jail Inmates.* Washington, DC: Department of Justice, Bureau of Justice Statistics. Retrieved from http://bjs.ojp.usdoj.gov/content/pub/pdf/mhppji.pdf

Kajstura, A. (2018). *Women's mass incarceration: The whole pie 2018.* Easthampton: Prison Policy Initiative.

Karlsson, M. E., & Zielinski, M. J. (2018). Sexual victimization and mental illness prevalence rates among incarcerated women: A literature review. *Trauma, Violence, & Abuse.* doi:10.1177/1524838018767933

Kellet, N. C., & Willging, C. E. (2011). Pedagogy of individual choice and female inmate reentry in the U.S. south. *International Journal of Law and Psychiatry, 256–263.*

Kissman, K. (2004). Incarcerated mothers: Mutual support groups aimed at reducing substance abuse relapse and recidivism. *Contemporary Family Therapy, 26*(2), 217–228.

Kjellstrand, J., Cearley, J., Eddy, J. M., Foney, D., & Martinez, C. (2012). Characteristics of incarcerated fathers and mothers: Implications for preventive interventions targeting children and families. *Child Youth Services Review, 34*(12), 2409–2415. doi:10.1016/j.childyouth.2012.08.008

Lipsitz, G. (2012). In an avalanche every snowflake pleads not guilty: The collateral consequences of mass incarceration and impediments to women's fair housing rights. *UCLA Law Review, 59,* 1746–1809.

Loper, A. B., & Tuerk, E. H. (2011). Improving the emotional adjustment and communication patterns of incarcerated mothers: Effectiveness of parenting intervention. *Journal of Child and Family Studies, 20*(1), 89–101.

Luther, J. B., Reichert, E. S., Holloway, E. D., Roth, A. M., & Aalsma, M. C. (2011). An exploration of community reentry needs and services for prisoners: A focus on care to limit return to high-risk behavior. *AIDS Patient Care STDS, 25*(8), 475–481.

Margolies, J., & Kraft-Stolar, T. (2006). *When "free" means losing your mother, A report of the women in prison project of correctional association of New York.* New York: Correctional Association of New York. Retrieved from file:///C:/Users/Keesha/Downloads/When_Free_Rpt_Feb_2006.pdf

Maruschak, L., Glaze, L., & Mumola, C. (2010). Incarcerated parents and their children: Findings from the Bureau of Justice Statistics. *Children of incarcerated parents: A handbook for researchers and practitioners* (pp. 33–51). Washington, DC: The Urban Institute Press.

McCarty, M., Falk, G., Aussenberg, R. A., & Carpenter, D. H. (2016). *Drug testing and crime related restrictions in TANF, SNAP, and housing assistance.* Washington, DC: Congressional Research Service. Retrieved from https://fas.org/sgp/crs/misc/R42394.pdf

Middlemass, K. (2015). War as metaphor: The convergence of the war on poverty & the war on drugs. In K. Farmby (Ed.), *The war on poverty* (pp. 85–104). Lanham, MD: Lexington Books.

Middlemass, K. (2017). *Convicted and condemned: The politics and policies of prisoner reentry.* New York: New York University Press.

National Institute of Drug Abuse. (2019). *Drug facts: Criminal justice.* National Institute of Drug Abuse. Retrieved from https://d14rmgtrwzf5a.cloudfront.net/sites/default/files/drugfacts-criminal-justice.pdf

National Resource Center on Justice Involved Women. (2016). *Fact sheet on justice involved women in 2016.* Washington, DC: National Resource Center on Justice Involved Women.

National Women's Law Center. (2010). *Mothers behind bars: A state-by-state report card and analysis of federal policies on conditions of confinement for pregnant and parenting women and the effect on their children.* Washington, DC: The Rebecca Project for Human Rights. Retrieved from www.nwlc.org/sites/default/files/pdfs/mothersbehindbars2010.pdf

Nowotny, K., Masters, R., & Boardman, J. (2016). The relationship between education and health among incarcerated men and women in the United States. *BMC Public Health, 16*(916), 1–8. doi:10.1186/s12889-016-3555-2

Parsons, M., & Warner-Robbins, C. (2002). Factors that support women's successful transition to the community following jail/prison. *Health Care for Women International, 23,* 6–18.

Purvis, M. (2013). Paternal incarceration and parenting programs in prison: A review paper. *Psychiatry, Psychology and Law, 20*(1), 9–28.

Roth, R. (2010). Obstructing justice: Prisons as barriers to medical care for pregnant women. *UCLA Women's Law Journal, 18*(1), 79–105.

Russell-Brown, K. (2015). *Children of the incarcerated: Collateral victim of crime, a resource guide.* Gainesville, FL: UF Levin College of Law, Center for the Study of Race and Race Relations. Retrieved from https://www.law.ufl.edu/law/wp-content/uploads/2016/10/children-with-incarcerated-parents.pdf

Sacks, J. Y., Sacks, S., Mckendrick, K., Banks, S., Schoeneberger, M., Hamilton, Z., . . . Shoemaker, J. (2008). Prison therapeutic community treatment for female offenders: Profiles and preliminary findings for mental health and other variables (crime, substance use and HIV risk). *Journal of Offender Rehabilitation, 3–4,* 233–261.

Santo, A. (2017). *What is prison like for women and girls?* New York: The Marshall Project. Retrieved from www.themarshallproject.org/2017/10/10/what-is-prison-like-for-women-and-girls

Sawyer, W. (2018). *The gender divide: Tracking women's state prison growth.* Easthampton: Prison Policy Initiative. Retrieved from www.prisonpolicy.org/reports/women_over-time.html

Scroggins, J. R., & Malley, S. (2010). Reentry and the (unmet) needs of women. *Journal of Offender Rehabilitation, 49,* 146–163.

The Sentencing Project. (2019). *Incarcerated women and girls.* Retrieved from https://www.sentencingproject.org/publications/incarcerated-women-and-girls/

Shin, S., & Miller, D. (2012). A longitudinal examination of childhood maltreatment and adolescent obesity: Results from the National Longitudinal Study of Adolescent Health (AddHealth) study. *Child Abuse & Neglect, 36*(2), 84–94.

Snyder, Z. K., Carlo, T. A., & Coats-Mullins, M. M. (2001). Parenting from prison: An examination of a children's visitation program at a women's correctional facility. *Marriage and Family Review, 32*(3–4), 33–61.

Sparks, S. D. (2015, February 24). Parents' incarceration takes toll on children, studies say. *Education Week.* Retrieved from www.edweek.org/ew/articles/2015/02/25/parents-incarceration-takes-toll-on-children-studies.html

Thompson, P. J., & Harm, N. J. (2000). Parenting from prison: Helping children and mothers. *Issues in Comprehensive Pediatric Nursing, 23*(2), 61–81.

Travis, J., Western, B., & Redburn, F. S. (2014). *The growth of incarceration in the United States: Exploring causes and consequences.* New York: John Jay College.

Turney, K. (2014). Stress proliferation across generations? Examining the relationship between parental incarceration and childhood health. *Journal of Forensic Social Work, 5*(1–3), 167–185. doi:10.1080/1936928X.2015.1093992

Turney, K., & Schneider, D. (2016). Incarceration and household asset ownership. *Demography, 53,* 2075–2103.

Will, J., Loper, A., & Jackson, S. (2016). Second-generation. *Journal of Interpersonal Violence*, *31*(1), 100–121. doi:10.1177/0886260514555127

Wilson, N. K. (2003). Taming women and nature: The criminal justice system and the creation of crime in Salem Village. In R. Muraskin (Ed.), *It's a crime: Women and justice* (pp. 3–11). Upper Saddle River: Prentice Hall.

Young, V. D., & Reviere, R. (2006). *Women behind bars: Gender and race in US prisons*. Boulder, CO: Lynne Rienner Publishers.

Chapter 7

Release From Long-Term Restrictive Housing

Linda Carson

Introduction

The philosophy on rehabilitation changed in federal and state prison systems during the mid-1970s, moving toward retribution, deterrence, and incapacitation. Popular phrases, such as "nothing works" and "just deserts" cultivated harsher narratives surrounding punishment (Bennion, 2015; MacKenzie, 2008). In 1981, the Reagan administration initiated policy changes that advocated more punitive procedures in law enforcement and corrections. In 1994, The Violent Crime Control and Law Enforcement Act was passed under the Clinton administration along with other punitive policies, such as "three strike laws," the elimination of Pell grants, and the denial of public benefits for formerly incarcerated individuals (Pizarro, Zgoba, & Haugebrook, 2014; Mears, Mancini, Beaver, & Gertz, 2013; Nally, Lockwood, Knutson, & Ho, 2012; Mears & Watson, 2006; Pogorzelski, Wolff, Pan, & Blitz, 2005; Mauer, 2005). These policies, and many others, assisted in increasing state and federal prison populations across the nation and led to changes in how inmates were housed in correctional facilities. Two of those changes were the use of restrictive housing and the emergence of super-maximum, or supermax, prisons.

There are three main types of restrictive housing. One type, protective segregation housing, is for individuals who would not be safe in the general population because of their fragility, their previous or pending court testimony, or their career before incarceration. A second type, disciplinary segregation housing, is for inmates who have violated institutional policies. The third type, administrative segregation, is reserved for individuals with known gang affiliation, documented escape attempt(s), a long history of rule violations, or have exhibited violent behaviors towards other inmates or correctional personnel.

In the 1980s, "get tough on crime" rhetoric assisted in the construction of new facilities known as supermax prisons, or rather "prisons within prisons;" supermax prisons are designed for the worst of the worst, such as violent or disruptive prisoners, and represent the most secure level of correctional custody. In a supermax prison, prisoners are housed in single-cell sound-proof units, and the rules are strict and punitive: there is zero contact and no stimulation[1] for prisoners incarcerated in a supermax prison (Resnik et al., 2016; Shames, Wilcox, & Subramanian, 2015). In supermax facilities, individuals remain in their cells for 22 to 23 hours per day, visitations are limited and often occur via video monitor, basic hygiene supplies are regulated, communication with correction officers is kept to the bare minimum, and any movement out of the cell is done in shackles (Resnik et al., 2016; Pizarro & Stenius, 2004). Additionally, inmates in restrictive housing are not allowed to attend any type of program available to other prisoners and are not allowed to have a job in the institution; release from supermax solely depends on an administrative decision, and often prisoners originally housed in a supermax are there indefinitely (Valera & Kates-Benman, 2016; Frost & Monteiro, 2016; Shalev, 2011; Ross, 2007). Furthermore, based on responses from 47 jurisdictions about their corrections' population, 5.5% of inmates spent three to six years in restrictive housing, and 5.4% spent more than six years in restrictive housing (Resnik et al., 2016). Finally, Black and Hispanic prisoners reside in restrictive housing at higher rates than Whites (Resnik et al., 2016).

Issues for Individuals in Restrictive Housing

Many individuals enter the prison system with mental health diagnoses and substance abuse issues, diminished intelligence quotient (IQ), lacking a high school diploma, and have seldom and limited contact with their family (Resnik et al., 2016; Nally et al., 2012; Loper, Carlson, Levitt, & Scheffel, 2009; Herman-Stahl, Kan, & McKay, 2008; Shalev, 2008). These individual shortfalls and family relations complicate living in long-term restrictive housing and reentry through a myriad of ways.

Mental Health

According to the Bureau of Justice Statistics, an estimated 56% of incarcerated individuals have some form of mental illness (James & Glaze, 2006); the number of people incarcerated with a mental illness is the result of policies that started to be passed in the 1970s. Beginning in 1971, state mental health facilities were deinstitutionalized based on the belief that an individual would receive better support in their community (Bachrach, 1978). However, this decision was not partnered with a financial commitment from local communities to increase their mental health services; as a result, the criminal justice system filled that void. Individuals with mental illness receive sentences that are approximately five months longer than an individual without a mental illness and serve four months longer on their sentence (James &

98 Linda Carson

Glaze, 2006). From 1971 to 1996, the incarceration of individuals with mental illnesses grew from 28% to 86% (Harcourt, 2011).

Often times, inmates with mental illness are unable to adhere to the mandated structured and rule-heavy environment of a prison; as a result, they are moved into restrictive housing for rule violations or assaultive behaviors (Frost & Monteiro, 2016). While in restrictive housing, the prisoner, he or she, is exposed to extreme isolation and reduced environmental stimulation. Researchers have documented the negative psychological effects of human deprivation seen and experienced within long-term restrictive housing. When prisoners are released from restrictive housing, they experience hypersensitivity to stimuli, confusion, memory loss, anger, aggression, hallucinations, and panic attacks (Frost & Monteiro, 2016; Hafemeister & George, 2012; Grassian, 2006; Shalev, 2008). Other researchers have found that individuals in long-term restrictive housing did not develop additional mental health disorders, or their current mental health did not worsen over time (Cochran, Toman, Mears, & Bales, 2018; Bulman, Garcia, & Hernon, 2012; O'Keefe, Kliebe, Stucker, Sturm, & Leggett, 2011). The debate regarding the psychological consequences of long-term restrictive housing persists, and the controversial aspects surrounding the use of long-term restrictive housing have resulted in numerous lawsuits.

In 1995, in *Madrid v. Gomez*, a class-action lawsuit brought by prisoners incarcerated at Pelican Bay State Prison, a maximum-security prison, challenged the conditions and practices that affected almost every aspect of prison life. In particular, the lawsuit challenged the inhumane conditions imposed by the Security Housing Unit, commonly referred to as the SHU. Prisoners argued that the correctional officers used undue force without justification, that the SHU was used excessively, and that prisoners were fetally restrained on dozens of occasions.[2] Additionally, the investigation of practices at Pelican Bay found that inmates who were evaluated suffered severe psychiatric disturbances (Grassian, 2006). The court recognized, "[m]ental health, just as much as physical health, is a mainstay of life" (The Psychology of Cruelty: Recognizing Grave Mental Harm in American Prisons, 2015, p. 1262). Furthermore, the court stated, "As the Supreme Court has made quite clear, we cannot, consistent with contemporary notions of humanity and decency, forcibly incarcerate prisoners under conditions that will, or very likely will, make them seriously physically ill . . . [and] these same standards will not tolerate conditions that are likely to make inmates seriously mentally ill" (*Madrid v. Gomez*, 1995, p. 1261). This case resulted in government monitoring of conditions inside Pelican Bay State Prison in an effort to improve its conditions.

In *Ruiz v. Johnson* (1999), state prisoners sued the Texas Department of Corrections' (TDC) prisons for unconstitutional practices. The court found that it was impossible to convey the pernicious conditions and the pain and degradation which ordinary inmates suffered within TDC prisons (*Ruiz v.*

Johnson, 1999, p. 860). Although the final ruling acknowledged that deprivations found in administrative segregation units could be considered cruel and unusual punishment, the court found that solitary confinement was not unconstitutional (Fettig, 2016).

In *Jones'El v. Berge* (2001), prisoners housed at Wisconsin's supermax correctional institution in Boscobel, Wisconsin, argued that the conditions within the restrictive housing units constituted cruel and unusual punishment. The court found that "most inmates have a difficult time handling these conditions of extreme social isolation and sensory deprivation, but for seriously mentally ill inmates, the conditions can be devastating" (*Jones'El v. Berge*, 2001, p. 1098). The decision in *Jones'El v. Berge* resulted in the immediate removal of seven individuals with severe mental illness from restrictive housing units, and the state was mandated to create protocols that identified specific mental health diagnoses in prisoners; if a specific mental illness was identified, that prisoner was restricted from being placed in a long-term restrictive housing unit (Fathi, 2004). Since the *Ruiz v. Johnson* (1999) and *Jones'El v. Berge* (2001) decisions, incarcerated individuals from numerous states have filed lawsuits under the 8th Amendment, challenging the use of restrictive housing units and their impact on prisoners' mental health.

Stigma and Labeling

Stigmas and labels associated with restrictive housing have a double-impact on individuals with mental illness who are not only considered "violent," but are also labeled "crazy." Often times, these labels become the "master status" of the individual and dictate the way correctional officers identify and view these stigmatized individuals (Callahan, 2004). Individuals in restrictive housing may not hear these labels directly, but scholars have documented that they do feel stigmatized (LeBel, 2012). Without proper training, correctional officers working with the restrictive housing population tend to write an increased number of disciplinary charges against them for behaviors directly related to the individual's mental health diagnosis (Callahan, 2004).

Education & Programming

Individuals that are in restrictive housing do not have access to educational or therapeutic programs and are not allowed to work at a prison job (e.g., working in the prison kitchen, laundry, cleaning, or maintenance). Additionally, many institutions do not allow individuals in restrictive housing to have reading materials. Yet basic education classes, such as the General Equivalency Development (GED), high school courses, and vocational programs are present in most correctional facilities (MacKenzie, 2008), and research has shown that educational programs inside have a positive impact on the prison population.

Jiang and Winfree (2006) found educational programming reduced rule violations in the general population. Moreover, there are many benefits of obtaining education while incarcerated, which can assist in reducing recidivism rates and increasing employment opportunities upon release (Frost & Monteiro, 2016; Lockwood, Nally, Ho, & Knutson, 2012; Bazos & Hausman, 2004). According to Nally et al. (2012), individuals that participated in educational programming while incarcerated earned a higher income than those individuals that did not participate in educational programming. Further, as Willingham demonstrates in her chapter in this volume, education inside prison has a positive impact on prisoners' self-esteem and increases their ability to reenter successfully. MacKenzie (2008) identified the most effective programmings as being cognitive skills development and programs that addressed individuals' behavior; however, most educational programming inside prison is focused on vocational training or skills training (MacKenzie, 2008).

Family

The research dealing with family and children tends to focus on the general incarcerated population but not the restricted housing population. Research suggests family support is a key component in addressing recidivism, particularly face-to-face visitation, telephone calls, building close ties with children, and co-parenting, all of which decreases prison rules violations (Herman-Stahl et al., 2008; Jiang & Winfree, 2006). Administrators of prison facilities have the legal right to restrict visitation, media access, and researchers (Zoukis, 2011). Visitation is considered a privilege and individuals in long-term restrictive housing have no privileges (Resnik et al., 2016). When an individual is in restrictive housing, visitation is restricted along with telephone calls, while attendance in educational programming to improve parenting skills or focus on family reunification is *not* available (Resnik et al., 2016). These combined issues further diminish an individuals' success after release from prison.

Economics of Long-Term Restrictive Housing

Supermax housing units, like the SHU at Pelican Bay State Prison, and supermax prisons, such as United States Penitentiary Administrative Maximum Facility, Florence, also known as the Alcatraz of the Rockies, are the most costly prisons to build and operate (United States Government Accountability Office, 2013). Most of these prisons are built in rural areas. Federal and state governmental officials determine locations for prison facilities and many are constructed in rural areas, and for several reasons: (1) The land is less costly; (2) Job creation in areas impacted by globalization and diminished manufacturing jobs is a political win for rural legislators; and (3) Incarcerated residents inflate these communities' populations, which impacts census data for funding and voting districts (Levine, 2018).

In 2012, the cost to house almost 2000 inmates in federal special management, or administrative maximum-security housing units was $87 million; the same number of inmates in medium-security facilities cost $42 million and in high-security facilities the cost was $50 million (Frost & Monteiro, 2016). At the state-level, for instance, Ohio's costs for incarceration at the supermax level was $149 a day, $101 a day for maximum-security, and $63 a day for the general population (Browne, Cambier, & Agha, 2011). Criminal corrections spending at the federal level has increased more than any other federal budget area (Bennion, 2015).

Movement Beyond Long-Term Restrictive Housing

In 2015, President Obama requested that the U.S. Department of Justice review the use of restrictive housing in corrections and recommended limited use (Fact Sheet: Department of Justice Review of Solitary Confinement, n.d.). The report identified 50 guiding principles for adoption, and these principles became "Best Practices" for current implementation of policies in the federal correctional system and many state correctional systems.

Moving to Less Restrictive Housing

An individual is moved to less restrictive housing when the facility administration lowers their classification risk. One of the recommendations is to mandate hearings where an inmate's behavior over the past 90 days would be reviewed so that the prisoner would have a chance to have their classification risk changed so that the prisoner can live in a less restrictive housing unit, or even with the general prison population (Smith, 2016). When an individual is moved to less restrictive housing there are new challenges in acclimating back to being in the general prison population and its social setting. All of the environmental deprivations experienced in the restrictive housing unit become challenging to overcome; the challenges include everyday events, such as interacting with other inmates, correctional officers, and others inside the prison, like administrators or instructors. When an individual is moved from restrictive housing to the general prison population, there must be an adjustment period for the inmates' best interest and for the interest of others inside prison.

Numerous state correctional facilities have begun to provide "step-down" programming for individuals who have been in long-term restrictive housing (Vera Institute of Justice, n.d.). These programs may involve: giving a prisoner access to a television or radio during certain times of the day to assist inmates in reacclimating to noise; allowing a prisoner to communicate with family members via phone or a controlled visit; having the prisoner attend educational programs or start a prison job; and having the prisoner attend skills group training (Schmitt & Galloway, 2013, Vera Institute of Justice, n.d.).

Parole & Reentry

Parole has the responsibility of determining an individual's ability to be successful in the community and uses a range of variables to determine if someone should be released from prison "early," such as age, ethnicity, participation in correctional programming, disciplinary reports, employment, evidence of a place to live, and recommendations from correctional staff about their determination if someone should be released from prison into the community on parole; this risk assessment and analysis is designed to protect the community from future criminal behavior by the individual (Mooney & Daffern, 2014; Hill, 2010; Huebner & Bynum, 2008). A mental health diagnosis, or a dual diagnosis, which includes substance abuse addiction or another mental illness, may or may not influence the parole board's decision (Matejkowski, Draine, Solomon, & Salzer, 2011). Reentry is challenging (Middlemass, 2017), and for those who get a release date, are on parole, and are dealing with a mental illness that has been exacerbated by spending time in a restrictive housing unit, reentry is difficult. Individuals with mental health issues have multiple and additional barriers that must be addressed to prevent returning to prison. Leaving spaces of restrictive housing units and then being released from prison creates multiple shocks for those reentering, and these struggles will impact a person's ability to desist from crime.

Conclusion

States need to implement more rehabilitation programs inside prison that assist individuals who have been in supermax and restrictive housing units and then enter the general prison population. Another program is required for those who have been in restrictive housing units and then reenter society. A major part of criminal justice reform should refocus on offender's rehabilitation needs, and do so with a holistic approach, which would include educational opportunities and marketable job skills to increase employability and family reunification as well as having access to mental health professionals. Offenders would benefit from coping skills training, anger management, counseling, family therapy, and other holistic approaches that are designed to increase their ability to address stressors or triggers in their lives. Beyond mental health, physical health issues need to also be addressed including medical, dental, and substance abuse education to develop a treatment plan prior to release. Finally, for those who have spent time in a restrictive housing unit and reenter society, it would be beneficial for the community and the individual if a mentorship program was established that would provide assistance to an individual returning to the community; this final aspect would create a restorative justice framework and allow the community and individual to come full-circle.

Notes

1. Individuals housed in supermax units have no exposure to televisions or radios and sometimes reading material is prohibited.
2. A fetal restraint is when a prisoners' hands are handcuffed at the front of their body, their legs are placed in leg irons, and then a chain is drawn between the handcuffed hands and legs until only a few inches separate the bound wrists and ankles. At times, it has been documented that officers will use the same restraints but have the prisoner handcuffed in the back, so that the prisoners' arms are behind their back and their ankles were close to their wrists. The fetal restraint is painful, and in *Madrid v. Gomez*, there were no experts at trial that defended the use of fetal restraints; rather, correctional officials did state that there were no security reasons to justify the fetal restraint; its usage, the court determined, was to punish and inflict pain. One correctional officer, at trial, stated that they used fetal restraints "because we can do it" (*Madrid v. Gomez*, 1995, p. 1169).

References

Bachrach, L. A. (1978). A conceptual approach to deinstitutionalization. *Psychiatric Services, 29*(9), 573–578.

Bazos, A., & Hausman, J. (2004). *Correctional education as a crime control program.* Los Angeles, CA: UCLA, School of Public Policy and Social Research, Department of Policy Studies.

Bennion, E. (2015). Banning the bing: Why extreme solitary confinement is cruel and far too usual punishment. *Indiana Law Journal, 90*(2), 741–782.

Browne, A., Cambier, A., & Agha, S. (2011). Prisons within prisons: The use of segregation in the United States. *Federal Sentencing Reporter, 24*(1), 46–49.

Bulman, P., Garcia, M., & Hernon, J. (2012). Study raises questions about psychological effects of solitary confinement. *National Institute of Justice Journal, 269*, 4–7.

Callahan, L. (2004). Correctional officer attitudes toward inmates with mental disorders. *International Journal of Forensic Mental Health, 3*, 37–54.

Cochran, J. C., Toman, E. L., Mears, D. P., Bales, W. D. (2017). Solitary confinement as punishment: Examining in-prison sanctioning disparities. *Justice Quarterly, 35*(3), 381–411.

Fact Sheet: Department of Justice Review of Solitary Confinement. (n.d.). Retrieved from https://obamawhitehouse.archives.gov/the-press-office/2016/01/25/fact-sheet-department-justice-review-solitary-confinement

Fathi, D. C. (2004). The common law of supermax litigation. *Pace Law Review, 24*, 675–690.

Fettig, A. (2016). What is driving solitary confinement reform? *Correctional Law Reporter, 28*(3), 33–46.

Frost, N. A., & Monteiro, C. E. (2016). *Administrative segregation in U.S. Prisons* (Contract No. 2010F_10097, NCJ 249749). Washington, DC: National Institute of Justice, Office of Justice Programs, U.S. Department of Justice.

Grassian, S. (2006). Psychiatric effects of solitary confinement. *Washington Journal of Law & Social Policy, 22*, 325–383.

Hafemeister, T. L., & George, J. (2012). The ninth circle of hell: An eighth amendment analysis of imposing prolonged supermax solitary confinement on inmates with a mental illness. *Denver University Law Review, 90*, 1–54.

Harcourt, B. E. (2011). An institutionalization effect: The impact of mental hospitalization and imprisonment on homicide in the United States, 1934–2001. *The Journal of Legal Studies, 40*(1), 39–83.

Herman-Stahl, M., Kan, M. L., & McKay, T. (2008). *Incarceration and the family: A review of research and promising approaches for serving fathers and families.* US Department of Health and Human Services, Office of the Assistant Secretary for Planning and Evaluation Administration for Children and Families/Office of Family Assistance.

Hill, A. (2010, July 19). Inside the Parole Board: How freedom is granted or denied for prisoners. *The Guardian.* Retrieved June 18, 2019, from www.theguardian.com/law/2010/jul/19/parole-board-members-speak

Huebner, B. M., & Bynum, T. S. (2008). The role of race and ethnicity in parole decisions. *Criminology, 46*(4), 907–938.

James, D. J., & Glaze, L. E. (2006). *Mental health problems of prison and jail inmates* (NCJ 213600). Washington, DC: US Department of Justice, Office of Justice Programs, Bureau of Justice Statistics.

Jiang, S., & Winfree Jr., L. T. (2006). Social support, gender, and inmate adjustment to prison life: Insights from a national sample. *The Prison Journal, 86*(1), 32–55.

Jones 'El v. Berge, 164 F. Supp. 2d 1096, 1098 (W.D. Wis. 2001).

LeBel, T. P. (2012). Invisible stripes? Formerly incarcerated persons' perceptions of stigma. *Deviant Behavior, 33*(2), 89–107.

Levine, S. (2018, February 8). 2020 census will continue to count prisoners where they are incarcerated. *The Huffington Post.* Retrieved June 18, 2019, from www.huffingtonpost.com/entry/2020-census-prison-population_us_5a7cb966e4b044b3821b0507

Lockwood, S., Nally, J. M., Ho, T., & Knutson, K. (2012). The effect of correctional education on postrelease employment and recidivism: A 5-year follow-up study in the state of Indiana. *Crime & Delinquency, 58*(3), 380–396.

Loper, A. B., Carlson, L. W., Levitt, L., & Scheffel, K. (2009). Parenting stress, alliance, child contact, and adjustment of imprisoned mothers and fathers. *Journal of Offender Rehabilitation, 48*(6), 483–503.

MacKenzie, D. L. (2008). *Structure and components of successful educational programs.* Reentry Roundtable on Education, John Jay College of Criminal Justice, New York, March, 31.

Madrid v. Gomez, 889F. Supp. 1146 (N.D. Cal. 1995).

Matejkowski, J., Draine, J., Solomon, P., & Salzer, M. S. (2011). Mental illness, criminal risk factors and parole release decisions. *Behavioral Sciences & the Law, 29*(4), 528–553.

Mauer, M. (2005). Thinking about prison and its impact in the twenty-first century. Walter C. Reckless Memorial Lecture. *Ohio State Journal of Criminal Law, 2*, 607–618.

Mears, D. P., Mancini, C., Beaver, K. M., & Gertz, M. (2013). Housing for the "worst of the worst" inmates: Public support for supermax prisons. *Crime & Delinquency, 59*(4), 587–615.

Mears, D. P., & Watson, J. (2006). Towards a fair and balanced assessment of supermax prisons. *Justice Quarterly, 23*(2), 232–270.

Middlemass, K. (2017). *Convicted and condemned: The politics and policies of prisoner reentry.* New York: New York University Press.

Mooney, J. L., & Daffern, M. (2014). Elucidating the factors that influence parole decision-making and violent offenders' performance on parole. *Psychiatry, Psychology and Law, 21*(3), 385–405.

Nally, J., Lockwood, S., Knutson, K., & Ho, T. (2012). An evaluation of the effect of correctional education programs on post-release recidivism and employment: An empirical study in Indiana. *Journal of Correctional Education, 63*(1), 69–89.

O'Keefe, M. L., Kliebe, K. J., Stucker, A., Sturm, K., & Leggett, W. (2011). *One year longitudinal study of the psychological effects of administrative segregation.* Colorado Springs: Colorado Department of Corrections, Office of Planning and Analysis.

Pizarro, J. M., & Stenius, V. M. (2004). Supermax prisons: Their rise, current practices, and effect on inmates. *The Prison Journal, 84*(2), 248–264.

Pizarro, J. M., Zgoba, K. M., & Haugebrook, S. (2014). Supermax and recidivism: An examination of the recidivism covariates among a sample of Supermax ex-inmates. *The Prison Journal, 94*(2), 180–197.

Pogorzelski, W., Wolff, N., Pan, K-Y., & Blitz, C. L. (2005). Public health consequences of imprisonment. *American Journal of Public Health, 95*(10), 1718–1724.

The Psychology of Cruelty: Recognizing Grave Mental Harm in American Prisons. (2015). *Harvard Law Review, 128*(4), 1250–1271.

Resnik, J., VanCleave, A., Bell, K., Boykin, O., Guilmette, C., Hudson, T., . . . Purcell, J. (2016). *Aiming to reduce time-in-cell: Reports from correctional systems on the numbers of prisoners in restricted housing and on the potential of policy changes to bring about reforms.* Yale Law School, Public Research Paper No. 597. https://doi.org/10.2139/ssrn.2874492

Ross, J. I. (2007). Supermax prisons: Social science and public policy. *Transaction Social Science and Modern Society, 44*(3), 60–64.

Ruiz v. Johnson, 37 F. Supp. 2d 855 (S.D. Tex. 1999).

Schmitt, T. J., & Galloway, E. H. (2013). The challenges of behavioral health services for special housing unit: Inmates at the U.S. disciplinary barracks. *Corrections Today, 75*(2), 56–59.

Shalev, S. (2008). *A sourcebook on solitary confinement.* London: Mannheim Centre for Criminology.

Shalev, S. (2011). Solitary confinement and supermax prisons: A human rights and ethical analysis. *Journal of Forensic Psychology Practice, 11*(2–3), 151–183.

Shames, A., Wilcox, J., & Subramanian, R. (2015). *Solitary confinement: Common misconceptions and emerging safe alternatives.* New York: Vera Institute of Justice.

Smith, P. (2016). Toward an understanding of "what works" in segregation: Implementing correctional programming and reentry-focused services in restrictive housing units. In N. Rodriquez (Ed.), *Restrictive housing in the US: Issues, challenges, and future directions* (pp. 331–366). Washington, DC: US Department of Justice, Office of Justice Programs. Retrieved from https://www.ncjrs.gov/pdffiles1/nij/250315.pdf

United States Government Accountability Office. (2013). *Improvements needed in bureau of prisons' monitoring and evaluation of impact of segregated housing.* Washington, DC: United States Government Accountability Office.

Valera, P., & Kates-Benman, C. L. (2016). Exploring the use of special housing units by men released from New York correctional facilities: A small mixed-methods study. *American Journal of Men's Health, 10*(6), 466–473.

Vera Institute of Justice. (n.d.). *Safe alternatives to segregation initiative: Promising practices*. Retrieved from www.safealternativestosegregation.org/promising-practices/

Zoukis, C. (2011). *Education behind bars: A win-win strategy for maximum security*. Boiling Springs, PA: Sunbury Press, Inc.

Chapter 8

Resilient Roads and the Non-Prison Model for Women

L. Susan Williams, Edward L. W. Green, and Katrina M. Lewis

Of the 200,000 incarcerated women in the U.S., 6% to 10% are pregnant (Dorwart, 2018). Imagine a woman is handcuffed to a bed, knees bent, feet in shackles, her face contorted in anguish; this was Josie's reality. Josie, a 22-year-old American citizen of Mexican heritage with no criminal history, was convicted of check fraud and sentenced to nine years in prison. At the time of her sentencing, she was three months pregnant and gave birth in prison. Medical experts call the practice of shackling during childbirth demeaning and unnecessary, agreeing that it is not only physically damaging but also psychologically traumatizing (American College of Obstetricians & Gynecologists, 2011). This is only the most blatant example of how gender shapes practices within U.S. prisons.

As Dimon (2014, p. 1) states, "Women are not just small men." Yet the corrections industry ignores distinct pathways that push women into prison and discount their unique needs while incarcerated. Women represent the fastest growing segment of the U.S. mass incarceration binge, with an increase of over 700% in the past four decades, twice that of men; the growth is because of the widening net for women offenders, policy changes regarding low-level drug offenses, law enforcement policies, and post-conviction barriers to reentry (National Resource Centeron Justice Involved Women, 2016).

Women prisoners are more likely than men to have suffered past abuse, trauma, and sexual assault (McCorkel, 2013; Pollock, 2012), report exceptionally high rates of post-traumatic stress disorder (PTSD), mental illness, and drug dependence (Belknap, 2001), and they face particularly high rates of sexual violence from prison staff (James & Glaze, 2006). Women are more likely than men to be sentenced for nonviolent crimes (55% versus 35%) and are the custodial parent (62% versus 36%), but are afforded less access to treatment than their male counterparts (National Research Council, 2014). Upon release, women face discrimination and financial hardship, not only as ex-felons, but often with the added stigma of being a *fallen woman* and a blameworthy mother (Cobbina, 2010; Spjeldnes & Goodkind, 2009). Public discussions have largely ignored these added burdens placed upon formerly incarcerated women (Moshenberg, 2014).

O'Brien (2014, p. 1) boldly claims, "We should stop putting women in jail. For anything." A conundrum facing feminist criminologists is the seeming impasse between choosing abolition or reform. Other scholars, reflecting a growing move toward abolition (Gilmore & Kilgore, 2019), join O'Brien, who argues that "efforts to make prison 'work' for women have only perpetuated growth of the prison industrial complex" (p. 3). On the other hand, decarceration proponents work to reduce the prison population incrementally, arguing that its effects are more immediate, incites less public resistance, and offer a more practical range of opportunities (Garland et al., 2014).

It is at this carceral moment that the feminist agenda calls for collective efforts to alleviate re-traumatization of women in prison, and this makes reform and abolition intertwined, not mutually exclusive (Lawston & Meiners, 2014). Here, at the intersection of intervention, defiance, and change-oriented discourses, gendering processes become a tool for resistance (Williams, Green, & Williams, 2018). In this chapter, we draw urgent attention to *place* and how gendered geographies may facilitate personal growth for incarcerated women by calling attention to "built" environments constructed for male-gendered prisoners. We advocate, instead, for a spatial arrangement and design that will aid in healing for women and their families that acknowledges the unique needs of women while preventing further harm. It is with this dual purpose – to incorporate women's experiences and to consider prison design as space for transformation – that we argue for "revolutionary reform" (Faith, 2000) that connects incremental change to broader social movements.

This study leans on work by Dorothy Smith (1987), specifically her conception of standpoint theory and institutional ethnography (IE). Standpoint theory refers to inclusion of a woman's world perspective, largely omitted from scholarly assumptions and political processes. Smith argues that to ignore the duality of women's lives – between home and work, family and colleagues, personal and political – results in duplicity and deceit about how the world works. Related, IE is a method of inquiry that explores social relations structuring everyday lives (Smith, 2005). IE incorporates two concepts important to this study: ruling relations, which "coordinate the everyday work of administration and the lives of those subject to administrative regimes" (DeVault, 2007, p. 1) and bifurcation of consciousness, a separation of women's identity into local and universal, which is a division unaccommodated within institutions (Smith, 1987). This chapter incorporates experiences of incarcerated women while recognizing impasses and frustrations of working within an androcentric correctional industry.

Gendered Prisons and Policies

Much of the growth of women in the justice system (and its outcomes) can be attributed to two ideologies that control women's lives while ignoring their realities. The first is the culture of punishment, which promotes the idea of deterrence through retribution. Such an ideology has produced a formidable "carceral habitus" (Schept, 2015) in the U.S., and supports a ubiquitous use of violence and coercive state control. Much less is written about how the culture of punishment is gendered, and in particular, rooted in patriarchal power. Carlen (1983) was one of the first to point out that prisons promoted "regimes of femininity," and that women prisoners were routinely "infantalised, denied agency and choice, and required to follow outmoded and unrealistic forms of feminine behaviour" (Bosworth & Kaufman, 2012, p. 189).

Within a correctional environment, routine disciplinary actions result in isolation from others, a punishment even more significant for women who "turn to each other for support and basic survival in ways that men don't" (Talvi, 2007, p. 126). Similarly, Smoyer (2014) identifies feeding relationships in prison as a central part of women's social networks, yet it is a practice often condemned and punished. Labotka's (2014) work on hair conventions in women's prisons documents a "walk of shame" and segregation for violations of personal appearance. None of these practices considers the circumstances of trauma, abuse, and self-defense that surround women's criminalization (Williams & Green, 2018), or that "women's ways of knowing" is deeply intertwined with self-concept (Belenky, Clinchy, Goldberger, & Tarule, 1986).

The second ideological hurdle, known as "equality with a vengeance," refers to punitiveness associated with the backlash to women's drive for equality (Dragiewicz, 2011). The position argues that women should be held to the *exact* same standards as men, despite differences in power, situation, or circumstance. Arrests, convictions, and sentencing practices have almost totally disregarded circumstances that bring women to correctional attention. For example, determinate sentencing has removed many considerations relevant to women offenders, such as childcare, family violence, and their actual role in the commission of a crime (Brown & Chesney-Lind, 2018). Coupled with the war on drugs, women are often placed in frontline situations – selling or carrying drugs on the street, prostitution – leaving them more vulnerable to arrest than male counterparts (United Nations, 2014). Past and ongoing abuse are not considered when women fight back (Kruttschnitt, 2010), and statutes related to self-defense rarely acknowledge ongoing violence and isolation (MacKinnon, 2007).

Facing a growing population of female offenders, the National Institute of Corrections (NIC) began initiatives in 1999 to improve strategies for dealing with gender-sensitive risk and need factors. In reality, practices vary widely, and some argue that such initiatives propagate the myth of individual choice, ignoring structural inequalities, especially the overrepresentation of women of color (Carlton & Segrave, 2013). Others, including activist Angela Davis (2005), contend that the rhetoric of equality actually renders the carceral state more powerful.

In Faith's (2000) proposal of revolutionary reform, she distinguishes between a "reformist reform," designed to improve prison conditions, and strategies with potential for revolutionary reform. One growing trend is known as progressive prison design, which is based on the basic principle that spaces affect inhabitants in certain ways, good and bad. However, as Moran and Jewkes (2014, p. 350) point out, it is "clear that prison design is almost always assumed to impinge upon the lives of those inhabiting carceral space in harmful rather than therapeutic ways." If the ideology of punishment is set aside, even for a moment, one can imagine, instead, a goal of restoration and recovery, one in which

> prison architects and designers should actively address ways in which architecture and design might be mobilized in order to promote higher rates of successful rehabilitation of offenders.
>
> (Hancock & Jewkes, 2011, p. 620)

Reexamining prison design is essential when considering women's recovery. Through personal narratives, we highlight some of the environmental challenges and needs of women prisoners. Then, by reviewing two progressive prisons, we are able to showcase design features that acknowledge the unique needs of women, help to prevent further psychological deterioration, and encourage healthy interactions – a non-prison model.

Prison Tales

Interviews were conducted in a state prison for women in the U.S. Midwest. The facility is a hodgepodge of buildings and architecture, housing all security levels, with an average population of around 900. All names are pseudonyms.

The research team first entered Winslow Correctional Facility early on a cold morning in January, 2013. By then, we were trouper prison researchers, excited and eager, but with the distinct clang of the gate behind us, miles of razor wire in sight, and massive gray buildings, the air became decidedly different; we knew we couldn't leave without permission. Women in denim blue move from one building to another; just beyond is the "I-Cell," the maximum-security unit with long, stacked rows of cells flooded with harsh fluorescent lights. The yard holds exercise cages, and ironically, a children's playground. We set up in a series of individual rooms; the study participants, preselected, were brought to us one-by-one. Excerpts offered here represent a sampling of their stories, organized into three themes: Dead Time, Degradation, and Isolation.

Dead Time

The excerpts from interviews with inmates demonstrate a state of liminality (Green, 2016), a limbo-like existence that represents dissolution of their former self without a firm sense of its stand-in (see Middlemass & Smiley, 2016, for further evidence of "lost time"). Janelle struggles to explain this "dead time."

> Doin' time like I'm stuck in a, in like a timeless era. Kind of, you know what I mean? It's time away from everything. I feel like everything stopped right now.
> Similarly, Karen struggled to describe her state of being:
> I'm at the time where I'm pretty just . . . I'm just here. I don't even, it's like, I don't know how to describe myself. I'm just existing. I'm on pause.

Perhaps most eloquently, Betsy, a high-performing attorney in her previous life, chronicled how she struggles with her transition to Prisoner 10210:

> I'm in a place where people live, but many don't stay. I'm passing time, but it's standing still. I'm a mother, but not. An attorney, but not. Living, but not.

The liminal process and loss of self engenders a state of constant disquiet, which, coupled with the daily impasses of incarceration, creates a cognitive disequilibrium that exacerbates trauma and cripples recovery (DeVeaux, 2013); prison is one of the most degrading experiences a human might endure (Clemmer, 1940). As Denise stated, "I'm pretty pissed off. I don't understand it. I have no understanding." Such circumstances hardly propagate an environment conducive to healing.

Degradation

From the moment of sentencing, every step feels like a drawn-out degradation ceremony. Stripped of any sign of civility, the women are issued a number and a jumpsuit (for effects of condemnation, see Middlemass, 2017). The woman's body is examined and probed, a spectacle. Following even a welcomed visit, stark reminders solidify the aim of punishment. Martha explains:

> You have to be herded to strip search after you have a visit. It's terrifying 'cause, you know, they strip you down, push you in the shower, then you get into these clothes – you don't know where they've been. It's scary. And, the whole process is just really demeaning in a way. . . . It takes part of your soul.

Kirsten explained the degradation of anonymity:

> All they can do is look on a computer and see your picture and what they've charged you with. They don't see me, they don't know anything

about how you got here or if you was [sic] just associated with somebody, or anything like that.

Sarah described the sense of doubt and anxiety that permeates their lives. "Yeah, there's always this fear of retaliation. They can use it for any ammunition they need it for." Sharon recounted daily "small cuts" of humiliation: "She (mom) doesn't understand that you have to ask for toilet paper. It's like tryin' to explain to her that this is a whole other world." Finally, Belinda expressed frustration associated with the permanence of the label felon, a prisoner, a criminal:

> You know, at 25 years, I'm wondering, when is it ever over, have you atoned for a life. How do you say that? I get it. But there comes a time when I've maxed out on all the programs, I've done everything that I can possibly do to atone for my wrongs. I don't know what else to do at this point.

These brief personal narratives are just a sampling, and barely signify the larger point: Incarceration deepens the damage brought upon these women in a thousand ways.

Isolation

By far, the most prevalent theme emerges around the expanse of loneliness and isolation (also see Middlemass & Smiley, 2016). Separation from family tops the list, together with missed birthdays, holidays, births, and weddings. As Jennifer expressed, "Life just keeps on going, and I'm standing still." Marilyn explained, "I need to help my youngest boy with a learning disability. What am I supposed to do with that?"

Josephine discloses how loneliness is prevalent in a community of 900 women:

> Because you're not . . . okay. We don't know each other from the streets. They don't know my history. They don't know my family. So, we can talk about our children but there's no deep history there.

Eventually, isolation gives way to self-doubt and a loss of perspective. Ellen explains:

> For a long time, I punished myself. So, I did, I got in serious trouble, you know, I lived in seg[regation] a lot. That was when I felt extreme guilt and just overwhelming like I just didn't feel like even prison was good enough for me.

Eventually, repetition and boredom set in, and the women become resolved to days of mediocrity, as described by Theresa:

> It took me a minute. I still know that I'm here, but now I know that I'm doin' man's time. And, now when I wake up and go to sleep, I know where I'm at, I know where I'm gonna sleep at, I know where I'm wakin' up at, I know how my day's gonna be, how it's gonna end. I'm just here.

Personal narratives reveal that when women are thrust into a situation or environment that assumes male bodies and experiences, they grapple with incongruities between woman and prisoner, often resulting in what Smith refers to as a bifurcated consciousness; prison negates a holistic identity. In this critical transition from everyday woman to prisoner and property of the state – based on assumptions of male experiences – women struggle with their identity and sense of self in ways that are different from men. Such an alienating environment deters women's ability to recover in a holistic, healthy way.

Progressive Prison Design, Gendered

According to Linda Bernauer, chair of the American Institute of Architects' Academy of Architecture for Justice,

> Architects are sort of the psychiatrists of the system. We have to listen to everyone, and victims and perpetrators don't generally have much of a voice. ... The intent is to talk about how therapeutic spaces can provide better outcomes and have architects be the leaders as opposed to just being hired to do what we're told
>
> (Romney, 2014, p. 2).

Because of gendered disparities, this proactive role is even more critical in designing women's prisons. A growing number of architectural initiatives engage women inmates and prison staff to provide perspective, moving stakeholders from "objects" of design to participants. The two case studies that follow demonstrate progressive gendered prison design in action.

Norway's Halden Fengsel prison, known as the Rolls Royce of corrections, is described as the "world's most humane maximum-security prison" (Benko, 2015, p. 1); its philosophy focuses on human rights and respect. Halden Prison, which houses men, stands as one of the first in an international movement away from stark utilitarian prisons, and toward the use of natural light, space, and color (Hancock & Jewkes, 2011). The recidivism rate of Halden prisoners is one-third of that in the U.S. (Dreisinger, 2018). However, much less is known about gender design. Two recent prisons constructed in the U.S. represent a stark contrast to the harsh physical settings of most U.S. prisons, and exemplify structures designed specifically for women. Both are located in California; the Las Colinas Detention and Reentry Facility is in San Diego, and the Women's Brig addition to the Naval Consolidated Facility is in Miramar.

Las Colinas Detention and Reentry Facility

The Las Colinas facility was designed holistically as "a healing environment to promote well-being and prevent further psychological deterioration in inmates" (Krueger & Macallister, 2015, para 8). Inspired by university campus design, the prisons' grounds include smartly landscaped areas that encourage social interaction: lawns, hedges, pedestrian pathways, meeting areas, and an amphitheater are included. Women are housed in small community clusters, and two-story buildings with many windows, skylights, and outdoor spaces that allow for natural light. Large nature-scene murals appear throughout Las Colinas, creating areas for mindful reflection. Las Colinas' strategic design encourages inmates to take control of their choices within their environment. "The idea is that if you treat inmates as autonomous and responsible human beings (albeit within a controlled and managed environment), they will be more likely to act accordingly" (Krueger & Macallister, 2015, para. 5). Mutual respect is a commonly expressed need from a prisoner's standpoint.

Designers of Las Colinas applied "scientifically-proven research on how light, color, materials, texture, air quality, acoustics, and access to nature affect mental and physical well- being to inform design decisions throughout" (Krueger & Macallister, 2015, para. 3). They used soft furniture and natural materials to create a "normalized environment" (Norix Furniture, 2017, para. 4) that takes into account that women inmates are less likely to damage their surroundings than men (Corwin, 2014). In a traditional prison, inmates "live amongst a constant cacophony of steel doors echoing against cinderblock – sounds that can trigger stress reactions for trauma survivors" (Corwin, 2014, para. 10). As a result, wooden (rather than metal) doors were installed to reduce noise.

Research demonstrates that women are less violent than men and "tend to be more sensitive and . . . more responsive to a normative environment" (Argyle, Association of State Correctional Administrators, 2011, para. 19). Las Colinas designers considered concerns specific to women, so it features a visitation area where inmates can interact with their children in a "normal" way, complete with child-height meeting tables, colorful floors, bright walls, and alcoves for privacy (Krueger & Macallister, 2015). This type of environment reduces trauma to both mothers and children, encourages family visits, and ultimately reduces estrangement between an incarcerated woman and her family.

Miramar Women's Brig, Naval Consolidated Facility

The Women's Brig addition to the Naval Consolidated Brig in Miramar, California, includes many of the same features attributed to Las Colinas, especially in terms of space, color, and light. It was designed according to ideas of normalization and direct supervision, but with a consistent eye to interaction. According to Bill Bashore, evaluator and co-coordinator on the Miramar addition, "Women prisoners are defined a lot by the relationships they make in an institute, so we tried to design the facility to give them the ability to form relationships and interact with staff" (Argyle, Association of State Correctional Administrators, 2011, para. 6).

The Miramar Women's Brig layout is single-story rectangular (rather than two-story triangular design typical of male prisons) and consists of smaller housing units to create a stronger sense of community among inmates, officers, and administrators. The units feature partial-height glazed walls that provide some privacy while promoting interaction, which are features standing in stark contrast to cell-lined corridors; the combination of such elements is critical: "[Female] offenders respond to the environment in different ways and are easier to manage if they have the ability to socialize and get away if they need to" (Argyle, Association of State Correctional Administrators, 2011, para. 12).

Other gender-based considerations include privacy panels near toilets and showers, as well as access to laundry areas, which allows for privacy around menstruation (Argyle, Association of State Correctional Administrators, 2011). A pantry was added to the housing units in order to meet nutritional needs of pregnant mothers (Argyle, Association of State Correctional Administrators, 2011), a population ignored in traditional prison design (Dimon, 2014); only nine states have prison nursery programs in operation or under development (Kravitz, 2010). As a mere sampling, these gender-sensitive issues raise even larger questions for architects, designers, and planners with regard to women inmates, their situations, and interacting with their families.

Conclusion

Recently there has been much to say about the monetary cost of prison. Certainly, design issues brought to bear will invigorate debate around investing in what some will call "country club" prisons. But a more complex, less visible, and increasingly critical cost of mass incarceration lies before us. The rising rate of female incarceration exacerbates strain on already disadvantaged populations, the price tag is magnified exponentially when one considers the splaying effect on families and children, and the damage is expanded again when women fail to reenter successfully. Three million U.S. children have a parent in prison. Children of incarcerated mothers (60% have children removed from the home compared to 16% of fathers) have been identified as arguably the most vulnerable population in the U.S. (Coutts & Greenberg, 2015; Sandifer, 2017). Children with parents in prison are at higher risk for poor school performance, maladjustment, and internalizing behavior problems (Trice & Brewster, 2004); as adults, they have elevated risk for antisocial behavior, criminality, and poor physical and mental health (Dallaire, Zeman, & Thrash, 2015). Outcomes for African American children are more dire; one San Francisco study found that while Black women represent 7% of the population, nearly 60% of Black mothers had parental rights terminated (Coutts & Greenberg, 2015).

Perhaps the best-designed women's prison is no prison at all. We propose that progressive prison design can be morphed into a holistic setting that acknowledges the unique needs for women while preventing further psychological deterioration and simultaneously promoting well-being and encouraging healthy interactions. What if Martha could look forward to visiting with her children without dreading the strip search? What if even one staff person knew Kristen's name? What if Ellen could relieve her guilt through happy interactions with others? What if these women – strong, courageous, but often broken and in pain – could live in small communities instead of behind a long row of metal, windowless doors? Do color and natural light and rounded corners really matter? Research suggests that the answer to all of these is resoundingly affirmative.

More important, strengthening relationships remains the most critical of human experience and is critical for successful reentry. We situate this study within the revolutionary reform camp to argue for initiatives that march toward a non-prison model for restoring women caught in the justice system. Revolutionary reform demands that we dismantle false claims of ideologies such as the culture of punishment and attacks on equality, while also diminishing pains of imprisonment. The dawning of designs that encourage healthy interaction while delegitimizing the political economy of mass incarceration provides a good start.

References

American College of Obstetricians & Gynecologists. (2011). *Health care for pregnant and postpartum incarcerated women and adolescent females*. Retrieved from www.acog.org/Clinical-Guidance-and-Publications/Committee-Opinions/Committee-on-Health-Care-for-Underserved-Women/Health-Care-for-Pregnant-and-Postpartum-Incarcerated-Women-and-Adolescent-Females

Argyle, Association of State Correctional Administrators. (2011, December 15). A model for female correctional design. *Correctional News*. Retrieved from http://correctional-news.com/2011/12/14/model-female-correctional-design/

Belenky, M. F., Clinchy, B. M., Goldberger, N. R., & Tarule, J. M. (1986). *Women's ways of knowing: The development of self, voice, and mind*. New York: Basic Books.

Belknap, J. (2001). *The invisible woman: Gender, crime, and justice.* Belmont, CA: Wadsworth.

Benko, J. (2015, August 1). The big read: The most humane prison in the world. *Irish Examiner.* Retrieved from www.irishexaminer.com/lifestyle/features/the-big-read-the-most-humane-prison-in-the-world-345677.html

Bosworth, M., & Kaufman, E. (2012). Gender and punishment. In J. Simon & R. Sparks (Eds.), *Handbook of punishment and society* (pp. 186–204). London: Sage.

Brown, M. M., & Chesney-Lind, M. (2018). Women's incarceration in the United States: Continuity and change. In O. H. Griffin III & V. H. Woodward (Eds.), *Routledge Handbook of Corrections in the United States* (pp. 127–134). New York: Routledge.

Carlen, P. (1983). *Women's imprisonment: A study in social control.* London: Rutledge & Kegan Paul.

Carlton, B., & Segrave, M. (Eds.). (2013). *Women exiting prison: Critical essays on gender, post-release support and survival.* New York: Routledge.

Clemmer, D. (1940). *The prison community.* New York: Rinehart.

Cobbina, J. E. (2010). Reintegration success and failure: Factors impacting reintegration among incarcerated and formerly incarcerated women. *Journal of Offender Rehabilitation, 49,* 210–232.

Corwin, E. (2014, June 5). Trauma statistics inform new women's prison design. *New Hampshire Public Radio.* Retrieved from http://nhpr.org/post/trauma-statistics-inform-new-womens-prison-design#stream/0

Coutts, S., & Greenberg, Z. (2015). "No hope for me": Women stripped of parental rights after minor crimes. *Rewire.News.* Retrieved from https://rewire.news/article/2015/04/02/hope-women-stripped-parental-rights-minor-crimes/

Dallaire, D. H., Zeman, J. L., & Thrash, T. M. (2015). Children's experiences of maternal incarceration-specific risks: Predictions to psychological maladaptation. *Journal of Clinical Child & Adolescent Psychology, 44,* 109–122.

Davis, A. Y. (2005). *Abolition democracy: Beyond prison, torture, and empire.* New York: Seven Stories Press.

DeVault, M. L. (2007). Ruling relations. In G. Ritzer (Ed.), *Blackwell encyclopedia of sociology.* doi:10.1111/b.9781405124331.2007.x

DeVeaux, M. (2013). The trauma of the incarceration experience. *Harvard Civil Rights-Civil Liberties Law Review, 48,* 257–277.

Dimon, L. (2014, April 30). What women have to go through in prison leaves zero doubt our system is broken." *Slay.* Retrieved from https://mic.com/articles/88445/what-women-have-to-go-through-in-prison-leaves-zero-doubt-our-system-is-broken

Dorwart, L. (2018). Giving birth in jail can traumatize women for decades. *Tonic.* Retrieved from https://tonic.vice.com/en_us/article/kznxav/giving-birth-in-jail-can-traumatize-women-for-decades

Dragiewicz, M. (2011). *Equality with a vengeance: Men's rights groups, battered women, and antifeminist backlash.* Boston: Northeastern University Press.

Dreisinger, B. (2018, July 29). I toured prisons around the world. *Business Insider.* Retrieved from www.businessinsider.com/norways-prisons-are-better-than-the-american-prisons-2018-6

Faith, K. (2000). Reflections on inside/out organizing. *Social Justice, 27,* 158–167.

Garland, B., Hogan, N., Wodahl, E., Hass, A., Stohr, M. K., & Lambert, E. (2014). Decarceration and its possible effects on inmates, staff, and communities. *Punishment & Society, 15,* 448–473.

Gilmore, R. W., & Kilgore, J. (2019). *The case for abolition*. New York: The Marshall Project. Retrieved from https://www.themarshallproject.org/2019/06/19/the-case-for-abolition

Green, E. L. W. (2016). *The weight of the gavel: Prison as a rite of passage* (Doctoral Dissertation), Manhattan, KS: Kansas State University.

Hancock, P., & Jewkes, Y. (2011). Architectures of incarceration: The spatial pains of imprisonment. *Punishment & Society, 13*, 611–629.

James, D. J., & Glaze, L. E. (2006). Mental health problems of prison and jail inmates. *Bureau of Justice Statistics Special Report*. Retrieved from www.bjs.gov/content/pub/pdf/mhppji.pdf

Kravitz, R. (2010, April 5). Women in prisons. *The Corrections Connections*. Retrieved from www.corrections.com/news/article/23873-women-in-prisons

Krueger, J., & Macallister, J. (2015, April 30). How to design a prison that actually comforts and rehabilitates inmates. *Fast Company*. Retrieved from www.fastcompany.com/3044758/how-to-design-a-prison-that-actually-comforts-and-rehabilitates-inmates

Kruttschnitt, C. (2010). The paradox of women's imprisonment. *Daedalus, 139*, 32–42.

Labotka, L. (2014). *Healthy, beautiful hair: Cultivating the self in a women's prison* (Doctoral Dissertation), Tucson, AZ: University of Arizona.

Lawston, J. M., & Meiners, E. R. (2014). Ending our expertise: Feminists, scholarship, and prison abolition. *Feminist Formations, 25*, 1–25.

MacKinnon, C. A. (2007). *Women's lives, men's laws*. Boston: Belknap Press.

McCorkel, J. A. (2013). *Breaking women: Gender, race, and the new politics of imprisonment*. New York: New York University Press.

Middlemass, K. M. (2017). *Convicted and condemned: The politics and policies of prisoner reentry*. New York: New York University.

Middlemass, K. M., & Smiley, C. (2016). Doing a bid: The construction of time as punishment. *The Prison Journal, 96*(6), 793–813.

Moran, D., & Jewkes, Y. (2014). "Green" prisons: Rethinking the "sustainability" of the carceral state. *Geographica Helvetica, 69*, 345–353.

Moshenberg, D. (2014). The growth of women's incarceration in the United States. *Women in and beyond the global*. Retrieved from www.womeninandbeyond.org/?p=13371

National Resource Center on Justice Involved Women. (2016). *Fact sheet on justice involved women in 2016*. Retrieved from http://cjinvolvedwomen.org/wp-content/uploads/2016/06/Fact-Sheet.pdf

National Research Council. (2014). *The growth of incarceration in the United States: Exploring causes and consequences*. In J. Travis, B. Western, & S. Redburn (Eds.), *Committee on causes and consequences of high rates of incarceration*. Washington, DC: National Academies Press.

Norix Furniture. (2017). Norix Furniture collaborates with project team to humanize correctional facility. Retrieved from www.norix.com/san-diego-womens-detention.asp

O'Brien, P. (2014, November 6). We should stop putting women in jail. For anything. *Washington Post*. Retrieved from www.washingtonpost.com/posteverything/wp/2014/11/06/we-should-stop-putting-women-in-jail-for-anything/?utm_term=.bd3063646c5b

Pollock, J. (2012). *Prisons and prison life: Costs and consequences* (2nd ed.). New York: Oxford University Press.

Romney, L. (2014, August 18). What kind of prison might the inmates design? *Los Angeles Times*. Retrieved from www.latimes.com/local/great-reads/la-me-c1-restorative-justice-design-20140818-story.html

Sandifer, J. L. (2017). Impact of maternal incarceration on children. *Wiley Online Library.* Doi.org/10.1002/9781118845387.wbeoc115

Schept, J. (2015). *Progressive punishment: Job loss, jail growth, and the neoliberal logic of carceral expansion.* New York: New York University Press.

Smith, D. E. (1987). *The everyday world as problematic: A feminist sociology.* Boston: Northeastern University Press.

Smith, D. E. (2005). *Institutional ethnography: A sociology for people.* New York: AltaMira Press.

Smoyer, A. B. (2014). Feeding relationships: Foodways and social networks in a women's prison. *Affilia: Journal of Women and Social Work,* 1–14.

Spjeldnes, S., & Goodkind, S. (2009). Gender differences and offender reentry: A review of the literature. *Journal of Offender Rehabilitation, 48,* 314–335.

Talvi, S. (2007). *Women behind bars: The crisis of women in the U.S. prison system.* Emeryville, CA: Seal Press.

Trice, A. D., & Brewster, J. (2004). Effects of maternal incarceration on adolescent children. *Journal of Police and Criminal Psychology, 19,* 27–35.

United Nations. (2014, July). *A gender perspective on the impact of drug use, the drug trade, and drug control regimes.* U.N. Women Policy Brief. Retrieved from www.unodc.org/documents/ungass2016/Contributions/UN/Gender_and_Drugs_-_UN_Women_Policy_Brief.pdf

Williams, L. S., & Green, E. L. W. (2018). When women are captive: Women's prisons and culture within. In O. Hayden III & V. H. Woodward (Eds.), *Routledge handbook of corrections in the United States.* New York: Routledge.

Williams, L. S., Green, E. L. W., & Williams, K. R. (2018). Trying on gender is the new black: From female to felon. In S. Jackson & L. Gordy (Eds.), *Caged women: Incarceration, representation, & media.* New York: Routledge.

Chapter 9

Alcohol Use Disorder

Programs and Treatment for Offenders Reentering the Community

Sara Buck Doude and Jessica J. Sparks

Introduction

Alcohol use is implicated in the incarceration of 56.6% of all U.S. prisoners and more than 88,000 deaths annually, which cost the United States $249 billion in 2010 (National Institute on Alcohol Abuse and Alcoholism, 2018; National Center on Addiction and Substance Abuse at Columbia University, 2010). The alcohol culture in the United States encourages pervasive consumption that affects and impairs an individual's emotional, cognitive, and physical control. Substantial evidence indicates that alcohol-desistance programs, treatment support for alcohol use avoidance, and behavior control are essential for rehabilitation and reentry success for those with alcohol abuse issues (James, 2015; Miller, Miller, & Tillyer, 2014). Yet insufficient funding and inconsistent policies deprive prisoners of these opportunities during and after incarceration (National Center on Addiction and Substance Abuse at Columbia University, 2010). Further challenges include the recognized high comorbidity of alcohol use disorder (AUD) with other mental disorders and poor physical health (Grant et al., 2015; Hartzler, Donovan, & Huang, 2011).

Alcohol Use Disorder (AUD)

Alcohol falls within the drug classification that includes opioids, stimulants, cannabis, and caffeine (American Psychiatric Association, 2013, p. 481). Comorbidity of AUD with other mental and physical disorders compounds the challenges of identifying effective AUD programs and treatments for prisoners and those reentering (Grant et al., 2015; Rinaldi, Steindler, Wilford, & Goodwin, 1988; Room, 2011; Substance Abuse and Mental Health Services Administration, 2016; National Institute on Alcohol Abuse and Alcoholism, 2004). Recovery from AUD tends to focus on treatment of a chronic psychological obsession with alcohol and finding help from others with substance abuse issues to create a social and spiritual network to address addiction.

Theories, content, and implementation methodologies for AUD differentiate "program" and "treatment." The former is an educational effort for participants that does not include direct intervention by a health care professional. The latter is a service provided by a licensed professional health care provider. Both approaches encourage individuals to cease or dramatically reduce their alcohol consumption. AUD programs and treatment reflect the understanding that psychological, physiological, biological, and cognitive interactions relate to a person's actions, learning, and interpretation of their life experience as it relates to their addiction (Bloom, Engelhart, Furst, Hill, & Krathwohl, 1956; Glenn & Raine, 2014; Kolb, 1984). The following section briefly discusses and summarizes several program and treatment modalities commonly used in treating AUD.

AUD Programs & Treatment

Mutual-Help Groups (MHGs)

The most common source of help for those with AUD includes group discussions providing peer support and education (Kelly & Yeterian, 2011). Prison and reentry inpatient or outpatient settings heavily utilize MHGs, such as Alcoholics Anonymous (AA) and related 12-step Programs (Alcoholics Anonymous World Services, Inc., 2017, 1981). During the reentry period, MHGs provide support, including on nights and weekends when relapse risk tends to be higher (Huebner & Kantor, 2011). AUD recovery and desistance from crime have been positively associated with MHGs' foundational processes of building social relationships within a community (Albertson, Irving, & Best, 2015). The anonymity associated with MHGs, however, challenges research efforts to ascertain or compare MHG success rates with those of health professional-provided treatments (National Institute on Alcohol Abuse and Alcoholism, 2014).

Therapeutic Communities (TC)

This program model for substance abuse considers the community a positive healing change agent in addressing social problems associated with substance abuse (National Institute on Drug Abuse, 2002; De Leon, 2000). TC programs incorporate group meetings with an overall focus on positive individual–community relationships while modifying individuals' attitudes, behaviors, and social skills (De Leon, 2000). Studies have highlighted that post-release participant outcomes have significantly lower reincarceration rates (Prendergast, Hall, Wexler, Melnick, & Cao, 2003).

Restorative Justice (RJ)

An approach to justice in which those who caused harm make amends to those harmed to repair and restore community accord (Maruna, 2016),

RJ programs hold offenders accountable without excluding them from the community but rather welcomes the offender to participate in the RJ process (Alcoholics Anonymous World Services, Inc., 1981; Fallon, 2014). Imbedded within RJ are restorative circles (RC), which are programs where volunteers create a supportive "circle" around the offender to support self-discovery and positive attitude changes (Petrich, 2016).

Cognitive Behavioral Therapy (CBT)

Psychotherapy is purposed toward helping modify a person's thinking patterns, emotions, and behaviors and its variants are considered effective in treatments for AUD and other mental disorders (Wenzel, Brown, & Karlin, 2011; Longabaugh & Morgenstern, 1999; Witkiewitz, Marlatt, & Walker, 2005). The methodology and goals of changing alcohol-related behaviors through CBT is to replace prior responses with positive behaviors through application of social learning theories. Increasing self-efficacy, a belief in one's personal ability to abstain from alcohol use, is a CBT goal for relapse prevention (Huebner & Kantor, 2011).

Pharmaceuticals

AUD treatments may include medication-assisted treatment (MAT) by prescribed medications shown to help reduce alcohol use, avoid relapse, or achieve and maintain abstinence from alcohol when used in conjunction with other treatments and programs (National Institute on Drug Abuse, 2016; Anton et al., 2006; Pettinati, Anton, & Willenbring, 2006; Huebner & Kantor, 2011).

AUD Programs and Treatments in Prison

Prison programs and treatments for AUD incorporate various methodologies adapted to the unique challenges of the prison environment (National Research Council, 2014). AUD programs are far more commonly provided to prisoners than medical-based treatments, in part because prisons lack the qualified physicians required to supervise prisoners' use of medications, with about 20% of federal prisoners and 25% of state prisoners participating in low-cost treatments (Chandler, Fletcher, & Volkow, 2009).

AUD and the Federal Bureau of Prisons

The substance abuse treatment strategy of the Federal Bureau of Prisons supports various programs that are designed to reduce recidivism, criminality, relapse, and offender misconduct (Federal Bureau of Prisons, 2017; Miller, 2013). Drug abuse educational programs offer a series of courses and

Alcohol Use Disorder 123

classes that are intended to educate offenders about substance abuse and its effects (Federal Bureau of Prisons, 2016, p. 11). The purpose is to motivate offenders to participate in substance abuse treatment by providing information about the nexus between substance use and crime as well as the negative consequences of continued substance abuse.

A cognitive behavioral therapy (CBT) program known as the Challenge Program is offered inside federal prisons and provides interactive group meetings focused on the criminal mind set, criminality, and criminal thinking. The goal is to examine these mindsets in conjunction with the non-criminal mind set to figure out the "errors" in how they think. The Challenge Program has a particular focus on antisocial peer associations, self-control, developing prosocial behaviors, and violence control (Federal Bureau of Prisons, 2016, p. 10).

Another CBT model program for offenders with an alcohol or drug abuse history are residential drug abuse programs. Residential drug abuse programs are located inside a prison, and offenders live in a unit separate from the general prison population (Federal Bureau of Prisons, 2016, p. 14). The programming offers offenders with substance abuse problems co-occurring with mental illness and/or medical problems, which may include addressing antisocial attitudes, pro-social behavior, and interpersonal skills, the criminal mind, as well as interventions and relapse prevention.

Federal prisoners with histories of low-level substance abuse are able to access non-residential drug abuse treatment programs. This CBT treatment program consists of weekly group treatment sessions that address criminal lifestyle, and how to improve skills in rational thinking, communication, and adjustment to institutional and community settings (Federal Bureau of Prisons, 2016, p. 13).

The federal prison system offers transitional programs to offenders who are returning to the community (Federal Bureau of Prisons, 2016, pp. 1–2). The three major reentry program categories are education and vocation, psychology services, and chaplaincy services. One example is the Community Treatment Services (CTS), which is a reentry program that supports offenders who are in Residential Reentry Centers or home confinement, and is designed to prevent criminal behavior and/or relapse into substance abuse.

AUD and State Prisons

Alcohol programs and treatments for imprisoned state offenders vary among the states. The Residential Substance Abuse Treatment (RSAT) program provides federal monies to support state and local governments' substance abuse treatment programs (Bureau of Justice Assistance, 2005, p. 1). Every state and territory are eligible to receive RSAT grants for MAT programs. The most common program implemented inside state prisons and local jails are AA programs. AA programs in correctional facilities are longstanding and widespread and have been determined to rehabilitate and benefit offenders. However, state prisons cannot mandate prisoners attend AA programs.

Conclusion

Reentry to communities presents special challenges to offenders with respect to alcohol use. Paroled offenders may be ordered to abstain from alcohol and monitored or tested for compliance. However, the craving for alcohol – or other addictive substances – may be stronger upon release (Chandler et al., 2009). Prison provides a false sense of abstinence and "recovery," and can mislead offenders into thinking they are "clean," which means they are vulnerable to relapsing (Chandler et al., 2009).

Regardless of the effectiveness of programs inside prison, studies have shown the importance of continuing programs and treatments as offenders reenter the community. Individuals receiving extended assistance are seven times more likely to be drug free and three times less likely to be arrested for criminal behavior than those not receiving help (Chandler et al., 2009, paragraph 8, citing Butzin, O'Connell, Martin, & Inciardi, 2006; Martin, Butzin, Saum, & Inciardi, 1999).Yet no single treatment is effective for all persons with AUD (University of Connecticut, 2017; Huebner & Kantor, 2011).

AUD recovery has been identified as the primary desired outcome of programs and treatments, but has different meanings for researchers, physicians, and persons in recovery (Kaskutas et al., 2014). In the past, recovery was an ongoing self-improvement process requiring abstinence from alcohol use (Laudet, 2007, p. 243). Conversely, a current trend considers recovery a process that includes reduced and/or controlled drinking. Dodge, Krantz, & Kenny (2010) describe recovery as a continuum: the greater a person improves over time, the greater the recovery, identified by physical, biomarker, psychological, psychiatric, chemical dependency, family/social, and spiritual indicators. Huebnor and Kantor similarly consider recovery from alcohol dependence within a range from "partial remission to full abstinence" (2011, p. 296).

Recovery as a process parallels reentry as both are related to transformation and have triggers. The stressors of reentry include poverty, food insecurity, homelessness, lack of employment, rejection by family and friends, lack of education, and comorbidity (Moore, Hacker, Oberleitner, & McKee, 2018). Research indicates that these challenges are very difficult because 50–75% of former inmates recidivate within three years (Alper, Durose, & Markman, 2018; Durose, Cooper, & Snyder, 2014; Langan & Levin, 2002). Ultimately, it is important to support AUD programs and treatments in prison and reentry. However, participating in programs and treatments alone cannot assure reentry success and individuals must have the motivation and self-efficacy to attend programs, take treatments,

Alcohol Use Disorder 125

and accept personal responsibility for maintaining sobriety. Finally, further research should be directed toward identifying the factors associated with reentry success for those with AUD. Despite a lack of agreement as to whether AUD recovery means total abstinence or substantially reduced alcohol intake, total abstinence appears to be the better choice, but may not be possible for everyone.

References

Albertson, K., Irving, J., & Best, D. (2015). A social capital approach to assisting veterans through recovery and desistance: Transitions in civilian life. *The Howard Journal of Criminal Justice, 54,* 384–396.

Alcoholics Anonymous World Services, Inc. (1981). *Twelve steps and twelve traditions.* New York: Alcoholics Anonymous World Services, Inc. Retrieved from www.aa.org/pages/en_US/twelve-s-and-twelve-traditions

Alcoholics Anonymous World Services, Inc. (2017). *Estimated worldwide A.A. individual and group membership.* Service Material from the General Service Office. New York: Alcoholics Anonymous World Services, Inc. Retrieved from www.aa.org/assets/en_US/smf-132_en.pdf

Alper, M., Durose, M., & Markman, J. (2018). 2018 Update on prisoner recidivism: A 9 year follow-up period (2005–2014). Bureau of Justice Statistics. Retrieved from www.bjs.gov/content/pub/pdf/18upr9yfup0514.pdf

American Psychiatric Association. (2013). *Diagnostic and statistical manual of mental disorders* (5th ed.). Arlington, VA: American Psychiatric Publishing.

Anton, R. F., O'Malley, S. S., Ciraulo, D. A., Cisler, R. A., Couper, D., Donovan, D. M., & Zweben, A. (2006). Combined pharmacotherapies and behavioral interventions for alcohol dependence: The COMBINE study: A randomized controlled trial. *JAMA, 295*(17), 2003–2017.

Bloom, B. S., Engelhart, M. D., Furst, E. J., Hill, W. H., & Krathwohl, D. R. (1956). *Taxonomy of educational objectives. Handbook I: The cognitive domain.* New York: David McKay Company, Inc.

Bureau of Justice Assistance. (2005). *Residential substance abuse treatment for state prisoners (RSAT) program.* NCJ 206269. Washington, DC: U.S. Department of Justice, Office of Justice Programs. Retrieved from www.ncjrs.gov/pdffiles1/bja/206269.pdf

Butzin, C. A., O'Connell, D. J., Martin, S. S., & Inciardi, J. A. (2006). Effect of drug treatment during work release on new arrests and incarcerations. *Journal of Criminal Justice, 34,* (5), 557–565.

Chandler, R. K., Fletcher, B. W., & Volkow, N. D. (2009). Treating drug abuse and addiction in the criminal justice system: Improving public health and safety. *JAMA, 301*(2), 183–190.

De Leon, G. (2000). *The therapeutic community: Theory, model, and method.* New York: Springer.

Dodge, K., Krantz, B., & Kenny, P. J. (2010). How can we begin to measure recovery? *Substance Abuse Treatment, Prevention, and Policy, 5*(1), 31–38.

Durose, M. R., Cooper, A. D., & Snyder, H. N. (2014). *Recidivism of prisoners released in 30 states in 2005: Patterns from 2005 to 2010.* Washington, DC: Bureau of Justice Statistics. Retrieved from www.bjs.gov/content/pub/pdf/rprts05p0510.pdf

Fallon, A. (2014). Anonymously restored: The natural partnership and mutual instruction of Alcoholics Anonymous and restorative justice. *Contemporary Justice Review, 17*(1), 104–123.

Federal Bureau of Prisons. (2016). *Directory of national programs.* Washington, DC: Federal Bureau of Prisons. Retrieved from www.bop.gov/inmates/custody_and_care/docs/BOPNationalProgramCatalog.pdf

Federal Bureau of Prisons. (2017). *Substance abuse treatment. Custody & care.* Retrieved from www.bop.gov/inmates/custody_and_care/substance_abuse_treatment.jsp

Glenn, A. L., & Raine, A. (2014). Neurocriminology: Implications for the punishment, prediction and prevention of criminal behaviour. *Nature Reviews Neuroscience, 15,* 54–63.

Grant, B. F., Goldstein, R. B., Saha, T. D., Chou, S. P., Jung, J., Zhang, H., . . . Hasin, D. S. (2015). Epidemiology of DSM-5 alcohol use disorder: Results from the national epidemiologic survey on alcohol and related conditions III. *JAMA Psychiatry, 72*(8), 757–766.

Hartzler, B., Donovan, D. M., & Huang, Z. (2011). Rates and influences of alcohol use disorder comorbidity among primary stimulant misusing treatment-seekers: Meta-analytic findings across either NIDA CTN trials. *American Journal of Drug and Alcohol Abuse, 37,* 460–471.

Huebner, R. B., & Kantor, L. W. (2011). Advances in alcoholism treatment. *Alcohol Res Health, 33*(4), 295–299.

James, N. (2015). *Offender reentry: Correctional statistics, reintegration into the community, and recidivism.* Congressional Research Service. CRS report prepared for members and committees of Congress, 7–5700. RL34287, Congressional Research Service, Washington, DC. Retrieved from https://fas.org/sgp/crs/misc/RL34287.pdf

Kaskutas, L. A., Borkman, T. J., Laudet, A., Ritter, L. A., Witbrodt, J., Subbaraman, M. S., . . . Bond, J. (2014). Elements that define recovery: The experiential perspective. *Journal of Studies on Alcohol and Drugs, 75*(6), 999–1010.

Kelly, J. F., & Yeterian, J. D. (2011). The role of mutual-help groups in extending the framework of treatment. *Alcohol Research Health, 33*(4), 350–355. Retrieved from www.semanticscholar.org

Kolb, D. A. (1984). *Experiential learning: Experience as the source of learning and development.* Englewood Cliffs, NJ: Prentice-Hall.

Langan, P. A., & Levin, D. J. (2002). *Recidivism of prisoners released in 1994* (NCJ 193427). Washington, DC: US Department of Justice, Office of Justice Programs. Retrieved from http://www.aci-adc.com/images/Recidivism/RecidivismofPrisonersReleased1994.pdf

Laudet, A. B. (2007). What does recovery mean to you? Lessons from the recovery experience for research and practice. *Journal of Substance Abuse Treatment, 33*(3), 243–256.

Longabaugh, R., & Morgenstern, J. (1999). Coping-skills therapy for alcohol dependence: Current status and future directions. *Alcohol Research & Health, 23*(2), 78–85.

Martin, S. S., Butzin, C. A., Saum, C. A., & Inciardi, J. A. (1999). Three-year outcomes of therapeutic community treatment for drug-involved offenders in Delaware: From prison to work release to aftercare. *Prison Journal, 79*(3), 294–320.

Maruna, S. (2016). Desistance and restorative justice: It's now or never. Editorial. *Restorative Justice, 4*(3), 289–301.

Miller, J. M., Miller, H. V., & Tillyer, R. (2014). *Effect of prison-based alcohol treatment: A multi-site process and outcome evaluation.* Research report submitted to the U.S. Department

Alcohol Use Disorder 127

of Justice, Office of Justice Programs; not published by the U.S. Department of Justice. Document 246125. Retrieved from https://cor.mt.gov/Portals/104/Resources/Reports/PrisonBasedAlcoholTreatmentEval.pdf

Miller, N. (2013). *RSAT training tool: Medication assisted treatment (MAT) for offender populations*. National Institute of Justice, U.S. Department of Justice, Office of Justice Programs. Residential Substance Abuse Treatment (RSAT) Grant No. 2010-RT-BX-K001. Retrieved from www.rsat-tta.com/Files/Trainings/FinalMAT

Moore, K. E., Hacker, R. L., Oberleitner, L., & McKee, S. A. (2018). Reentry interventions to address substance use: A systematic Review. *Psychological Services*. Advance online publication. http://dx.doi.org/10.1037/ser0000293

National Center on Addiction and Substance Abuse at Columbia University. (2010). *Behind bars II: Substance abuse and America's prison population*. New York: National Center on Addiction and Substance Abuse at Columbia University. Retrieved from www.centeronaddiction.org/addiction-research/reports/behind-bars-ii-substance-abuse-and-america%E2%80%99s-prison-population

National Institute on Alcohol Abuse and Alcoholism. (2004). NIAAA council approves definition of binge drinking. *NIAAA Newsletter* (3) (Winter). U.S. Department of Health and Human Services, National Institutes of Health. Retrieved from http://pubs.niaaa.nih.gov/publications/Newsletter/winter2004/Newsletter_Number3.pdf

National Institute on Alcohol Abuse and Alcoholism. (2019). *Treatment for alcohol problems: Finding and getting help*. NIH publication 14–7974. U.S. Department of Health and Human Services, National Institutes of Health. Retrieved from https://pubs.niaaa.nih.gov/publications/treatment/treatment.htm#chapter02

National Institute on Alcohol Abuse and Alcoholism. (2018). *Alcohol facts and statistics*. Washington, DC: U.S. Department of Health and Human Services, National Institutes of Health. Bethesda, MD: National Institute of Alcohol Abuse and Alcoholism. Retrieved from www.niaaa.nih.gov/alcohol-health/overview-alcohol-consumption/alcohol-facts-land-statistics

National Institute on Drug Abuse. (2002). *Therapeutic community*. NIDA Research Report Series. NIH publication 02–4877. Washington, DC: U.S. Department of Health and Human Services, National Institutes of Health. Retrieved from www.amityfdn.org/wp-content/uploads/2016/07/RRTherapeutic.pdf

National Institute on Drug Abuse. (2016). *Understanding drug use and addiction*. Washington, DC: U.S. Department of Health and Human Services, National Institutes of Health. Retrieved from www.drugabuse.gov/publications/drugfacts/understanding-drug-use-addiction

National Research Council. (2014). The experience of imprisonment. In J. Travis, B. Western, & S. Redburn (Eds.), *The growth of incarceration in the United States: Exploring causes and consequence*. Chapter 6 (pp. 157–201). Washington, DC: The National Academies Press.

Petrich, D. M. (2016). Theorising desistance-promotion in circle processes: The role of community in identity transformation. *Restorative Justice*, *4*(3), 388–409.

Pettinati, H. M., Anton, R. F., & Willenbring, M. L. (2006). The COMBINE study: An overview of the largest pharmacotherapy study to date for treating alcohol dependence. *Psychiatry*, *3*(10), 36–39.

Prendergast, M. L., Hall, E. A., Wexler, H. K., Melnick, G., & Cao, Y. (2003). Amity prison-based therapeutic community: 5-year outcomes. *The Prison Journal*, *84*(1), 36–60.

Rinaldi, R. C., Steindler, E. M., Wilford, B. B., & Goodwin, D. (1988). Clarification and standardization of substance abuse terminology. *JAMA*, *259*(4), 555–557.

Room, R. (2011). Substance use disorders – A conceptual and terminological muddle. Commentary. *Addiction, 106*, 879–882.

Substance Abuse and Mental Health Services Administration. (2016). *Binge drinking: Terminology and patterns of use*. Rockville, MD: Substance Abuse and Mental Health Services Administration. Retrieved from www.samhsa.gov/capt/tools-learning-resources/binge-drinking-terminology-patterns

University of Connecticut. (2017). *Project MATCH: Matching alcoholism treatments to client heterogeneity: A multistate clinical trial of alcohol treatment*. University of Connecticut School of Medicine, Community Medicine and Health Care, UCONN Health. Retrieved from www.commed.uchc.edu/programs/health_services/match/index.html

Wenzel, A., Brown, G. K., & Karlin, B. E. (2011). *Cognitive behavioral therapy for depression in veterans and military servicemembers: Therapist manual*. Washington, DC: U.S. Department of Veterans Affairs. Retrieved from www.mirecc.va.gov/docs/cbt-d_manual_depression.pdf

Witkiewitz, K., Marlatt, G. A., & Walker, D. (2005). Mindfulness-based relapse prevention for alcohol and substance use disorders. *Journal of Cognitive Psychotherapy, 19*(3), 211–228.

Chapter 10

Carceral Calisthenics
(Body) Building a Resilient Self and Transformative Reentry Movement[1]

Albert de la Tierra

Taken-for-granted aspects of daily life – including safe housing, gainful employment, and reliable transportation – are often major challenges for formerly incarcerated men (Garland, Wodahl, & Hershberger, 2011; Urban Institute, 2006; Wodahl, 2006). Conventional reentry scholarship attends to the problems involved with reintegration by encouraging program development and policy reform (Seiter & Kadela, 2003; Travis & Petersilia, 2001; Visher, 2007). Such programs and policies contribute toward progressive incremental social change insofar as they address the immediate needs of individuals confronted with undue and excessive obstacles to a dignified life. However, the conventional approach does little to challenge the status quo functioning of the U.S. criminal justice system.

Critical reentry scholarship looks beyond immediate needs and incremental changes to shed light on how prisoner reentry is related to broader carceral problems. Reentry is a system that extends the prison industrial complex's political-economic relations (Thompkins, 2010), bolsters the penal order and co-opts abolitionist critiques (Byrd, 2016), and intensifies population racism that maintains the intersecting sociohistorical underpinnings of mass incarceration (Nixon et al., 2008). Suffice it to say, critical reentry scholarship challenges this status quo and the functioning of the U.S. criminal justice system by demonstrating how prisoner reentry is a part of deeper radical social justice concerns.

Despite their differing foci, conventional and critical reentry scholarship complement each other. The former is concerned with individuals' immediate needs and aims to develop programmatic services and reforms. The latter is focused on how the challenges related to reentry in the 21st century are more immense, and aims to advance a transformative reentry movement.[2] Taken together, these approaches provide a multilayered understanding of the difficulties involved with returning home from prison, and as former prisoners' needs have changed, social structures need to be restructured accordingly; however, both approaches risk leaving the deficiency framework intact.

The "deficiency framework" is akin to what social workers refer to as the "problem-oriented approach" (Weick, Rapp, Sullivan, & Kisthardt, 1989). This lens views former prisoners as characteristically *lacking in* some or many areas of their life or personality, and *in need of* services or intervention (Andrews, Bonta, & Hoge, 1990). For example, a myopic focus emphasizes the facts that a large proportion of former prisoners do not have strong bonds with their receiving communities; are missing the educational attainment requisite for legal employment; have inadequate interpersonal communication skills; carry with them a marker of disrepute (e.g., a felony conviction or the physical mark of imprisonment); all of which risks framing former prisoners as fundamentally impotent and reliant on others. These deficiencies certainly limit an individuals' life chances in a host of social settings, but within the deficiency framework, former prisoners' redeeming qualities and individual capabilities – their "reservoirs of mental, physical, emotional, social, and spiritual abilities" (Weick et al., 1989, p. 352) – are left untapped. Ignoring former prisoners' reservoirs of capabilities should be of concern to conventional and critical reentry scholars alike.

By focusing on the possibilities of service provision via reentry nonprofit organizations and reentry agencies, conventional reentry scholarship often subscribes to the deficiency framework. By focusing on broader issues, such as those related to history and political economy, critical reentry scholarship often leaves the deficiency framework unscathed and lacking a critical assessment. Leaving the deficiency framework intact amounts to missed opportunities for collaboration (e.g., improving programmatic services) and empowerment and agency (e.g., expanding former prisoners' role in building a transformative reentry movement). There is a need for a framework capable of recognizing former prisoners' strengths and their potential for contributing to and advancing various reentry goals.

A growing number of reentry scholars are calling for a shift away from the deficiency framework toward one that is capable of recognizing capacity or "strengths" (Burnett & Maruna, 2006; Hunter, Lanza, Lawlor, Dyson, & Gordon, 2016; Maruna & LeBel, 2003; Miller, 2006; Schlager, 2013; Van Wormer, 1999; Ward & Stewart, 2003; Woods, Lanza, Dyson, & Gordon, 2013). Drawing inspiration from social work scholars and practitioners, the "strengths-based" framework places the "focus on strengths, empowerment, and capacity building" (McMillen, Morris, & Sherraden, 2004, p. 317). This means appreciating the often-overlooked potential that many former prisoners exhibit.

Saleebey (1992; quoted in Schlager, 2013, p. 250) outlines the strength-based framework's key assertions, which are that all people: possess strengths that are identifiable and can be used to improve the quality of their lives; can be motivated to achieve goals based upon the strengths they possess or believe they possess; can discover their own strengths with the assistance of professionals; can focus their attention on their strengths to the exclusion of their deficits, which encourages a forward-looking approach; and that all people live in an environment that contains resources. Taken together, these assertions produce a framework that enables reentry scholars to acknowledge and foreground former prisoners' strengths.

Based on recognizing the capacity or "strengths" of former prisoners, I introduce and analyze the concept of "carceral calisthenics," a body project set within the context of penal institutions, which is a strength-building practice that cultivates a resilient sense of self. The data for this chapter is drawn from an ongoing ethnographic study titled, *Strength in the Hood* (de la Tierra, 2019); this project put me in direct contact with many formerly incarcerated men. Over the past three years, I regularly interacted with formerly incarcerated men, as well as men with no criminal records, as they performed calisthenics in public spaces in neighborhoods putatively and locally regarded as "the 'hood." Conversations and semi-structured interviews form the basis of the analysis below. Pseudonyms for participants are used throughout.

Carceral Calisthenics

The prison experience is characterized by total control (Goffman, 1961). The social relation of power between prisoners and institutional arrangements includes the denial of autonomy and self-determination. Prisoners are subjected daily to schedules and disciplining routines (Foucault, 1977/1995). Taken-for-granted aspects of daily life – when to wake and sleep, what and how to eat, with whom and for how long to interact, where and when to physically move, and so on – are determined for prisoners by prison guards and administrators. Prisoners' autonomy is stripped and their individuality is denied; therefore, a prisoner's sense of self risks being completely determined from without, except for calisthenics.

Calisthenics are exercise movements that consist of using one's bodyweight to work out, and consist of things such as pushups, pullups, triceps dips, squats, and various abdominal exercises. In the popular imagination, carceral settings are closely associated with calisthenics. For example, movie scenes, television shows, music lyrics, and other popular cultural artifacts perpetuate the truism that prisoners spend a lot of time working out and doing calisthenics in their cells or on the yard. When asked, formerly incarcerated men confirm that calisthenics figure prominently in their daily routine when living behind bars.

Ed, one of my interlocutors, is a Black man from Brooklyn, N.Y. He is 6'2", weighs around 250 pounds, and often displays his muscular physique by working out shirtless in the neighborhood park. During a conversational interview, I asked him how he developed the muscle endurance to be able to perform 200 pushups without rest.

Albert: How're you able to do so many pushups in a set?
Ed: From being upstate.
Albert: What do you mean?
Ed: I was doing thousands of pushups and thousands of pullups every day when I was in prison. It was the only thing I had to spend my time on.

Ed attributes his physical strength to the exercise regimen he kept during his incarceration. Also, his response reveals calisthenics' central role in some incarcerated men's lives. For Ed, calisthenics occupied a great deal of his time because he felt it was the only worthwhile activity available to him. Others have documented similar explanations of calisthenics' role in prison life.

In a publicly available interview, David discusses how he used calisthenics to manage his own time while imprisoned (Checo & "David", 2017 [Interview audio-visual file]):

> To keep it real, [calisthenics is] basically what got me through my time [inside prison]. If it wasn't for that I probably would have got into trouble easily. You know, got into the mix in there and found myself sitting in the hole with more time to go. . . . It took up my time while I was inside the cell. And when I went out to the yard, instead of running around and talking about the same ol' stuff with gang members, I applied [my time] to the bars.

Similar to Ed, David spent a great deal of his incarcerated time performing calisthenics. Many of my interlocutors made similar statements. But in addition to using calisthenics as a way to pass time while incarcerated, the men were also providing a deeper understanding of what carceral calisthenics means to them beyond simply as a way to pass time.

David's account, for example, reveals more than his exercise regimen. In practical terms, carceral calisthenics was a way for him to avoid participating in prison politics, which often result in extended and intense conversations. But also, David suggests that carceral calisthenics allowed him to not only avoid but also *distinguish himself* from gang members; by participating in carceral calisthenics, David and other formerly incarcerated men – like most people in late-modern society – use their bodies to construct an identity (Frank, 1991; Turner, 1991). Thus, carceral calisthenics emerges as more than physical exercise, and can be viewed as a "reflexive project of the self" (Giddens, 1991).

Calisthenics within a penal setting unfolds at a site where the "tightening relationship" between the body and identity is hard to deny (Shilling, 2003, p. 6).

The implications for the cultivation of self is the primary locus, so it is important to situate calisthenics within the penal settings from which it emerges, with particular attention to the physical and mental traumas associated with incarceration.

Sites of Resilience

Resilience is an individual choice to resist personal suffering and distress; for example, working out enables a person to employ their body to get through mental and emotional angst, but working out does not necessarily challenge the carceral regime.[3] To be resilient is to be able to withstand or recover quickly from difficult conditions. In his review and critique of traditional resilience scholarship, Payne (2008, 2011) offers a "sites of resilience" theory that appreciates how iniquitous social contexts give rise to creative forms of resiliency and resilient outcomes. He explains that the notion of sites of resilience is a:

> conceptualization [that] takes into account . . . personal and subjective construction of resiliency and resilience; examines it in relation to issues of race, gender, and social class; and identifies psychological and/ or physical spaces or "sites" for evaluating more relevantly the ways in which [individuals] cope and become resilient
>
> (2011, p. 429).[4]

With this in mind, carceral calisthenics can be viewed as a site of resilience. Carceral calisthenics is a creative practice for achieving mental and physical well-being that requires disciplined and regimented strategies of implementation. Formerly incarcerated men recall their participation in calisthenics as a strategy for withstanding the difficult conditions involved with confinement and explain that daily participation in carceral calisthenics promotes a sense of well-being that mitigates the adverse and traumatizing conditions in which they were held.

Carceral settings make ontological security nearly impossible to achieve. Prison culture, minimally a result of institutional and administrative arrangements (DiIulio, 1987; Huebner, 2003; Reisig, 2002), makes daily living a taxing endeavor. For example, one of the core problems of life in a penal institution is the incessant threat of violence. In "The Trauma of the Incarceration Experience," DeVeaux (2013) explains:

> I found the prison experience traumatic because of the assaults and murders I witnessed while incarcerated, because of the constant threat of violence, because of the number of suicides that took place, and because I felt utterly helpless about the degree to which I could protect myself. I found the experience extremely stressful – during my incarceration,

I was tense and always on guard because the threat of violence was real and ever present

(p. 264–265).

The carceral setting, particularly in men's prisons, is an environment replete with threats to inmates' physical security and mental health. This amounts to a daily life characterized by ongoing traumas, particularly those related to mental health and well-being (Haney, 2001, 2006); studies have shown that captivity gives rise to new, as well as exacerbates preexisting, physical and mental health problems (Amour, 2012). These traumas often have adverse effects on the reentry process (Schnittker, 2014; Schnittker & John, 2007). Thus, it would behoove individuals concerned with reentry and reentry outcomes to anticipate ameliorating post-incarceration mental health problems that stem from the experience of being held in captivity. The strengths-based framework is one way, as it foregrounds the healthy coping strategies current and former prisoners already possess. Moreover, the strengths-based framework focuses on building upon assets individuals already hold.

Carceral calisthenics is a strategy that imprisoned men employ for managing and coping with the traumas involved with incarceration. Xavier, one my interlocutors, is a Latino man from the Bronx. He is 5'9", weighs around 175 pounds, and served over ten years in prison. During a semi-structured interview, I asked Xavier to reflect on his experiences while incarcerated, and when he mentioned it, I asked him to elaborate on his interest in exercise:

Albert: Give me a sense of what it's like in there.

Xavier: First of all, Rikers is fucking chaos. Have you ever read Lord of the Flies . . . ? It's like that. . . . What makes it worse is that you feel like you're in limbo because you're waiting to go to trial and you don't know what's going to happen; it puts everyone on edge. At least once you're upstate you have a [release] date and can prepare for it. . . . My first two years upstate were almost as bad as my time at Rikers. It was crazy up there. So, I had to establish myself by getting into a lot of fights to gain a reputation. That's when I started working out.

Albert: What do you mean?

Xavier: Before I got locked up, I wasn't into exercise. I was partying and ate whatever. I started working out in solitary confinement. And I kept it up once I got back on the yard.

Albert: I still don't understand. What made you start working out?

Xavier: I was listening to Danny Trejo on NPR earlier today, and he put it perfectly: "In prison, you don't have the luxury of getting angry. You go from calm to rage in an instant."[5] You see, it's different in there. Outside, conflict grows little by little. The angrier you get the louder you get, right? Inside, there's a lot at stake when there's conflict. I have to make a decision, and it's one of two extremes: "Am I going to walk away from this guy or am I going to stab him?" There's no space to be emotional about shit. Inside, you can't get mad about shit, and there's no getting sad about shit either. You can't go to the yard and tell guys, "Hey, I cried last night." So, I channeled those feelings and emotions into working out.

Xavier acknowledges that calisthenics, and working out in general, can be much more than the weaponization of one's body in preparation for physical violence.[6] Bodily strength training is often employed as a coping strategy for managing the stresses involved with life in captivity. Feeling unable to express emotions of any kind related to the traumas of confinement, many incarcerated men participate in carceral calisthenics, and exercise in general, because it is beneficial for their mental health and well-being (Battaglia et al., 2015; Buckaloo, Krug, & Nelson, 2009; Cashin, Potter, & Butler, 2008).[7] Carceral calisthenics, in this regard, can be viewed as a site of resilience.

Technology of Self & a Transformative Reentry Movement

All human beings possess unique abilities, and the strengths-based framework encourages reentry scholars to locate and foreground former prisoners' capacities and abilities rather than only focusing on their deficiencies. By introducing carceral calisthenics as a site of resilience, this approach offers a new way to think about men reentering society. More than just physical strength training, carceral calisthenics offers prisoners a practice for coping with the physical and mental traumas associated with the conditions of confinement, and upon reentering offers men a way to manage their reentry experiences and feelings. My analysis of carceral calisthenics has implications for both conventional and critical approaches to reentry.

All prisoners who return home have endured traumas associated with captivity; thus, all former prisoners are trauma survivors. Although this chapter focuses on carceral calisthenics as a site of resilience, there are likely many others; future reentry scholarship should examine the prison library, chapel, or classroom as potential sites of resilience (in this volume, see Willingham's chapter about the role of education as a potential site of resilience and Williams, Green, & Lewis' chapter about how different spatial arrangements inside prison can impact women's ability to become resilient). Locating new sources of resilience and building upon former prisoners' resilience and available assets promises to assist conventionally minded reentry scholars and organizations in helping to move individuals toward successful reintegration.

136 Albert de la Tierra

For example, reentry service providers who are aware of an individual's survival and creative coping skills inside prison can assist those same individuals in translating their skills into specific areas of their life. A focus on individuals' strengths can also be used to recalibrate reentry programs. Focusing on individuals' strengths not only will change the nature of the services provided and get them to shift, but also the foregrounding of service recipients' (i.e., former prisoners') unique capacities might transform the organizational logic. That is, whereas the deficiency framework results in a hierarchical social relation between programs and service recipients, the strengths-based framework can result in collaboration and partnership. Seen as a group of assets and resources, former prisoners can then be included in program development, implementation, and evaluation.

Carceral calisthenics can also be viewed as, what Foucault (1988) calls, a "technology of the self." Technologies of the self:

> permit individuals to effect by their own means or with the help of others a certain number of operations on their own bodies and souls, thoughts, conduct, and way of being, so as to transform themselves in order to attain a certain state of happiness, purity, wisdom, perfection, or immortality
>
> (p. 18).

By offering a brief analysis of how carceral calisthenics speaks to deeper and further-reaching questions of societal transformation, reentry scholars and activists can start to consider its role in personal transformation. Carceral calisthenics also calls into question the prison's total control of and dominance over subject formation. Through daily physical strength-training, prisoners engage in self-discipline and self-regimentation that allows them to develop a sense of self not determined by the prison regime (Middlemass & Smiley, 2016).

Conclusion

The strengths-based framework has implications for critically minded reentry scholars and organizations. First, undoing the essentialism that constructs formerly incarcerated men as fundamentally deficient is akin to removing the sutures that bind marginalized groups to crime (Byrd, 2016; Davis, 1998). Second, including former prisoners in the decision-making processes of the institutions and organizations that hold great influence over their life trajectories, but that have historically been closed off to their input, will likely lead to getting institutions to transform their organizational missions and goals. Changing how former prisoners are seen and how they are related to would be transformative.

Can carceral calisthenics be viewed as a technology of self? Is it a practice of resilience? Of liberation? Do its practitioners strive for freedom? Answering these questions goes beyond the scope of this chapter, but these questions can certainly be asked of former prisoners, which would allow them to tell us how they have reclaimed control of their selves by structuring their time and activity around bodily exercise (for examples about the broader research project and sport and exercise as a technology of self, see Chapman, 1997; Johns & Johns, 2000; Markula, 2004).

While living inside prison, participants demonstrated their ability to retake some control over their identity beyond physical strength alone. In this case, carceral calisthenics is viewed as a strategy for coping with and overcoming the stresses involved with life in captivity. However, rather than stop at resilience, it is important to push toward more robust understandings of the profundity of strength (Guo & Tsui, 2010), which is important because in social contexts defined by powerlessness, the implications of strength are more far-reaching than strong muscles.

Notes

1. I am grateful to CalvinJohn Smiley and Keesha M. Middlemass for their editorial brilliance and leadership. I also want to extend my appreciation to the members of the Crime, Law, Deviance, and Policy Workshop at the CUNY Graduate Center. Without these colleagues' critical feedback on earlier versions, this chapter would not have been possible. Thank you.
2. Or, as Byrd (2016) puts it, "it is necessary to ground reentry work in a politics of abolition that is attentive to the inherent violence of the state and the imbrication of the prison with neoliberal globalization, heteronormativity, gendered relations of ruling, and longer histories of enslavement and colonialism" (p. 7).
3. I recognize that the nature and practice of "resistance" is an ongoing debate, and here I purposely keep the concept of resistance and resilience separate and distinct. Traditionally, practices of resistance openly challenge carceral regimes and attempt to force those regimes to respond in some form; the regimes' response may make life more difficult or worse for prisoners. Practices of resilience, on the other hand, enable one to survive and endure a punitive environment without challenging the regime's imposition of punitive rules and structures.
4. Payne (2011) builds his theory from the experiences of street life-oriented Black men. I have removed the specificity of this identifier because his theory is also valuable for understanding individuals and groups that are outside of his research focus.
5. See Saman and Chaloner (2018).
6. I do not refute that brute strength is an integral part of prison culture and surviving a prison term. However, interlocutors explained that on the occasions when personal conflicts between prisoners become physically violent, the violence more often than not came through a surprise attack with bladed weapons. Straight on hand-to-hand combat (e.g., a fist fight) was rare. Thus, because attackers are more likely to ambush others rather than confront them face-to-face, muscular physique and physical strength becomes less relevant for understanding violence in male carceral settings.
7. Exercise is especially effective at reducing insomnia in prisoners (Elger, 2009); insomnia has been found to be significantly related to suicidality (Carli et al., 2011).

References

Amour, C. (2012). Mental health in prison: A trauma perspective on importation and deprivation. *International Journal of Criminology and Sociological Theory, 5*(2), 886–894.

Andrews, D. A., Bonta, J., & Hoge, R. D. (1990). Classification for effective rehabilitation: Rediscovering psychology. *Criminal Justice and Behavior, 17,* 19–52.

Battaglia, C., Di Cagno, A., Fiorilli, G., Giombini, A., Borrione, P., Baralla, F., . . . Pigozzi, F. (2015). Participation in a 9-month selected physical exercise programme enhances psychological well-being in a prison population. *Criminal Behavior and Mental Health, 25,* 343–354.

Buckaloo, B. A., Krug, K. S., & Nelson, K. B. (2009). Exercise and the low-security inmate: Changes in depression, stress, and anxiety. *The Prison Journal, 89,* 328–343.

Burnett, R., & Maruna, S. (2006). The kindness of prisoners: Strengths-based resettlement in theory and in action. *Criminology & Criminal Justice, 6,* 83–106.

Byrd, R. M. (2016). "Punishment's twin": Theorizing prisoner reentry for a politics of abolition. *Social Justice, 43,* 1–22.

Carli, V., Roy, A., Bevilacqua, L., Maggi, S., Cesaro, C., & Sarchiapone, M. (2011). Insomnia and suicidal behavior in prisoners. *Psychiatry Research, 185,* 141–144.

Cashin, A., Potter, E., & Butler, T. (2008). The relationship between exercise and hopelessness in prison. *Journal of Psychiatric and Mental Health Nursing, 15,* 66–71.

Chapman, G. (1997). Making weight: Lightweight rowing, technologies of power, and technologies of self. *Sociology of Sport Journal, 14,* 205–223.

Checo, E. (Interviewer), & "David" (Interviewee). (2017). *Actual PRISON Workout (Raw Footage!)* [Interview audio-visual file]. Retrieved from OfficialBarstarzz YouTube channel: www.youtube.com/watch?v=UTbRcZYlb2Q

Davis, A. Y. (1998). Race and criminalization: Black Americans and the punishment industry. In J. James (Ed.), *The Angela Y. Davis reader.* Malden, MA: Blackwell Publishing.

de la Tierra, A. (2019). *Strength in the hood* (unpublished doctoral dissertation). The Graduate Center, City University of New York.

DeVeaux, M. (2013). The trauma of the incarceration experience. *Harvard Civil Rights-Civil Liberties Law Review, 48*(2), 257–277.

DiIulio, J. J. (1987). *Governing prisons: A comparative study of correctional management.* New York: Free Press.

Elger, B. S. (2009). Prison life: Television, sports, work, stress and insomnia in a remand prison. *International Journal of Law and Psychiatry, 32,* 74–83.

Frank, A. (1991). For a sociology of the body: An analytic review. In M. Featherstone, M. Hepworth, & B. Turner (Eds.), *The body: Social process and cultural theory* (pp. 36–102). London: Sage.

Foucault, M. (1977/1995). *Discipline and punish: The birth of the prison.* New York: Vintage Books.

Foucault, M. (1988). Technologies of self. In L. H. Martin, H. Gutman, & P. H. Hutton (Eds.), *Technologies of the self: A seminar with Michel Foucault* (pp. 16–49). Amherst, MA: University of Massachusetts Press.

Garland, B., Wodahl, E., & Hershberger, J. (2011). Prisoner reentry in a small metropolitan community: Obstacles and policy recommendations. *Criminal Justice Policy Review, 22,* 90–110.

Giddens, A. (1991). *Modernity and self-identity: Self and society in the late modern age.* Cambridge: Polity Press.

Goffman, E. (1961). *Asylums: Essays on the social situation of mental patients and other inmates.* New York: Anchor Books.

Guo, W., & Tsui, M. (2010). From resilience to resistance: A reconstruction of the strengths perspective in social work practice. *International Social Work, 53,* 233–245.

Haney, C. (2001, January 30–31). *The psychological impact of incarceration: Implications for post-prison adjustment.* Working paper prepared for the From Prison to Home Conference, U.S. Department of Health and Human Services. Retrieved from http://webarchive. urban.org/UploadedPDF/410624_PyschologicalImpact.pdf

Haney, C. (2006). *Reforming punishment: Psychological limits to the pains of imprisonment.* Washington, DC: American Psychological Association.

Huebner, B. M. (2003). Administrative determinants of inmate violence: A multilevel analysis. *Journal of Criminal Justice, 31,* 107–117.

Hunter, B. A., Lanza, A. S., Lawlor, M., Dyson, W., & Gordon, D. M. (2016). A strengths-based approach to prisoner reentry: The fresh start prisoner reentry program. *International Journal of Offender Therapy and Comparative Criminology, 60,* 1298–1314.

Johns, D. P., & Johns, J. S. (2000). Surveillance, subjectivism and technologies of power: An analysis of the discursive practice of high-performance sport. *International Review for the Sociology of Sport, 35,* 219–234.

Markula, P. (2004). "Turning into one's self:" Foucault's technologies of the self and mindful fitness. *Sociology of Sport Journal, 21,* 302–321.

Maruna, S., & LeBel, T. P. (2003). Welcome home? Examining the "reentry court" concept from a strengths-based perspective. *Western Criminology Review, 4,* 91–107.

McMillen, J. C., Morris, L., & Sherraden, M. (2004). Ending social work's grudge match: Problems versus strengths. *Families in Society, 85,* 317–325.

Middlemass, K. M., & Smiley, C. (2016). Doing a bid: The construction of time as punishment. *The Prison Journal, 96*(6), 793–813. doi:10.1177/0032885516671872

Miller, H. A. (2006). A dynamic assessment of offender risk, needs and strengths in a sample of pre-release general offenders. *Behavioral Sciences & the Law, 24,* 767–782.

Nixon, V., Clough, P. C., Staples, D., Peterkin, Y. J., Zimmerman, P., Voight, C., & Pica, S. (2008). Life capacity beyond reentry: A critical examination of racism and prisoner reentry reform in the U.S. *Race/Ethnicity: Multidisciplinary Global Contexts, 2,* 21–43.

Payne, Y. A. (2011). Site of resilience: A reconceptualization of resiliency and resilience in street life-oriented black men. *Journal of Black Psychology, 37,* 426–451.

Payne, Y. A. (2008). "Street life" as a site of resiliency: How street life-oriented black men frame opportunity in the United States. *Journal of Black Psychology, 34,* 3–31.

Reisig, M. D. (2002). Administrative control and inmate homicide. *Homicide Studies, 6,* 84–103.

Saman, H., & Chaloner, T. (Producers). (2018, March 14). *Fresh Air* [podcast]. Retrieved from www.npr.org/2018/03/14/593446805/danny-trejo-on-acting-addiction-and-playing-the-mean-chicano-dude

Schlager, M. (2013). *Rethinking the reentry paradigm: A blueprint for action.* Durham, NC: Carolina Academic Press.

Schnittker, J. (2014). The psychological dimensions and social consequences of incarceration. *The ANNALS of the American Academy of Political and Social Science, 651,* 122–138.

Schnittker, J., & John, A. (2007). Enduring stigma: The long-term effects of incarceration on health. *Journal of Health and Social Behavior, 48,* 115–130.

Seiter, R. P., & Kadela, K. R. (2003). Prisoner reentry: What works, what does not, and what is promising. *Crime & Delinquency, 49,* 360–388.

Shilling, C. (2003). *The body and social theory* (2nd ed.). London: Sage.

Thompkins, D. E. (Ed.). (2010). The prison reentry industry [Special issue]. *Dialectical Anthropology, 34*(4), 589–604.

Travis, J., & Petersilia, J. (2001). Reentry reconsidered: A new look at an old question. *Crime & Delinquency, 47,* 291–313.

Turner, B. (1991). The discourse of diet. In M. Featherstone, M. Hepworth, & B. Turner (Eds.), *The body: Social process and cultural theory* (pp. 1–35). London: Sage.

Urban Institute. (2006). *Understanding the challenges of prisoner reentry: Research findings from the Urban Institute's prisoner reentry portfolio.* Washington, DC: Urban Institute.

Van Wormer, K. (1999). The strengths perspective: A paradigm for correctional counseling. *Federal Probation, 63*(1), 51–58.

Visher, C. A. (2007). Returning home: Emerging findings and policy lessons about prisoner reentry. *Federal Sentencing Reporter, 20,* 93–102.

Ward, T., & Stewart, C. (2003). Criminogenic needs and human needs: A theoretical model. *Psychology, Crime & Law, 9,* 125–143.

Weick, A., Rapp, C., Sullivan, P., & Kisthardt, W. (1989). A strengths perspective for social work practice. *Social Work, 34,* 350–354.

Wodahl, E. J. (2006). The challenges of prisoner reentry from a rural perspective. *Western Criminology Review, 7,* 32–47.

Woods, L. N., Lanza, A. S., Dyson, W., & Gordon, D. M. (2013). The role of prevention in promoting continuity of health care in prisoner reentry initiatives. *American Journal of Public Health, 103,* 830–838.

Section III

Gender, Criminality, and Reentry

Women reentering society after being convicted of a felony have different challenges because of their gender and criminal status. The incarceration rate of women has increased 31% from 2000 to 2012 (Minton, 2013). Women's unique experiences mean that they face different challenges then men when reentering society, and these challenges are exacerbated owing to the fact that most reentry organizations and programs are male-centered and fail to consider women's needs or do not integrate their perspectives into reentry programs and services (Koski & Bantley, 2013).

Women commit less crime than men in every criminal category except prostitution (Belknap, 2007), and a small but growing literature examines intersectionality of gender and race on offending (Potter, 2015; Haynie & Armstrong, 2006; Krivo & Peterson, 2000; Katz, 2000) and offending as it relates to gender and race in the early life course (Bell, 2013; Jones, 2010). In terms of exiting the criminal justice system, it is well known that men and women experience different barriers to reentering society after prison (Spjeldnes & Goodkind, 2009), that women utilize a different set of coping mechanisms and strategies as they reintegrate (Koski & Bantley, 2013), and that reentry is a gendered phenomenon (Cobbina, 2010).

Traditionally, when women's reentry experiences are explored, an emphasis is placed on understanding social and familial relationships (Leverentz, 2014; see Cobbina, 2010) and how women reentering society have co-occurring needs and challenges (Richie, 2012, 2001), but this research leaves unanswered questions about the process of reentering society that have gendered dimensions. Additionally, racial disparities in the criminal justice system are well documented and persist amongst all racial minorities, but Black women and men are disproportionately incarcerated and overrepresented in the criminal justice system (Alexander, 2010; Bobo & Thompson, 2010). The historical residue of race is embedded in today's criminal justice policies that determine who is policed, arrested, convicted, incarcerated, and reenter (Middlemass, 2017).

The combination of gender, race, policies, and society's hostility towards female felons, and Black women felons in particular, means that a conviction

142 Gender, Criminality, and Reentry

becomes a self-sustaining petite penal institution that serves no purpose except to punish (Middlemass, 2014, 2017; Willingham, 2011; Russell & Milovanovic, 2001). Women reentering society tend to have multilayered issues that can be explored through an intersectional framework. The authors in this section explore gender, criminality, reentry, and criminal justice responses to gender.

In her chapter, "Black Women Excluded from Protection & Criminalized for their Existence," Middlemass explores how Black women have been marginalized and excluded from the protection of the law. This exclusion is because of historical patterns in the law, and how the law interacts with race, gender, and the criminal justice system. The oppression and criminalization of Black women, Middlemass argues, follows almost a straight line from when they were enslaved to contemporary times vis-à-vis the state.

Zettler, in her chapter, "The Gendered Challenges of Prisoner Reentry," reviews the literature on gendered reentry challenges, including those faced by transgender offenders. Based on work from feminist criminologists, Zettler describes some of the risk factors for women's criminal offending and why they recidivate. Zettler reviews several programs and finds that, despite the increasing number of women reentering society, their needs are not being met by reentry programs. She offers an assessment of gender-responsive strategies and programs and argues that these programs would help women and transgender persons returning home after serving time in prison.

In an intersectional analysis about Black women and their resistance against the police and criminal justice tactics, Battle and Williams, in their chapter, "An Intersectional Criminology Analysis of Black Women's Collective Resistance," explore how Black women have been punished and harmed by various forms of state violence. By exploring both historical and contemporary "sheros," the authors elucidate how Black women have been impacted by the criminal justice system and other forms of criminal supervision. Battle and Williams examine historical and contemporary cases of Black women and state violence to showcase acts of state violence; the individuals discussed come from activist backgrounds who fight for social justice in different ways by opposing the state.

In their chapter, "Gender Differences in Programmatic Needs for Juveniles," Parker and Parrotta study gendered differences between juvenile girls and boys who are incarcerated in program-based transitional programs. Based on interviews with juvenile offenders, both boys and girls, as well as correctional staff, they found that there are gendered differences in the types of support and services participants were offered, what they desired, and their perceptions of what would be beneficial to their reentry. Further, Parker and Parrotta demonstrate through their original data that correctional staff was inclined to reinforce gendered perceptions of which programs would be most effective for residents. Parker and Parrotta argue that reentry programs

Gender, Criminality, and Reentry   143

for juveniles must be aligned with gendered needs and expectations to be effective.

Willingham, in her chapter, "Prison Is a Place to Teach Us the Things We've Never Learned in Life," examines how higher education inside women's prisons is an effective strategy that improves reentry outcomes. Moreover, Willingham, using interview data from women who were formerly incarcerated, shows how higher education reconcile the various traumas in their lives, but also that education is an important component for women's self-esteem. Through first person accounts, participants in Willingham's study show that education has a profound and positive impact on women's lives inside and outside of prison.

The chapters in Part III, Gender, Criminality, & Reentry, provide different perspectives about the intersection of gender, race, criminality, and reentry. The critical approaches show that women face multiple challenges when reentering society and how some of those challenges are because of ineffective programming that does not take into consideration gendered needs.

References

Alexander, M. (2010). *The new Jim Crow: Mass incarceration in the age of colorblindness.* New York: The New Press.

Belknap, J. (2007). *The invisible woman: Gender, crime, and justice.* New York: Thomson/ Wadsworth.

Bell, K. E. (2013). Young adult offending: Intersectionality of gender and race. *Critical Criminology, 21,* 103–121.

Bobo, L. D., & Thompson, V. R. (2010). Racialized mass incarceration: African Americans and the criminal justice system. In H. Markus and P. Moya (Eds), *Doing race: 21 essays for the 21st century* (pp. 322–355). New York: W. W. Norton & Company.

Cobbina, J. (2010). Reintegration success and failure: Factors impacting reintegration among incarcerated and formerly incarcerated women. *Journal of Offender Rehabilitation, 49,* 210–232.

Haynie, D. L., & Armstrong, D. P. (2006). Race- and gender-disaggregated homicide offending rates. *Homicide Studies, 10,* 3–32.

Jones, N. (2010). *Between good and ghetto: African American girls and inner city violence.* New Brunswick, NJ: Rutgers University Press.

Katz, R. S. (2000). Explaining girls' and women's crime and desistance in the context of their victimization experiences. *Violence Against Women, 6,* 633–660.

Koski, S., & Bantley, K. (2013). Coping with reentry barriers: Strategies used by women offenders. *InSight, 9*(1), 1–17.

Krivo, L. J., & Peterson, R. D. (2000). The structural context of homicide: Accounting for racial differences in process. *American Sociological Review, 65,* 547–559.

Leverentz, A. (2014). *The ex-prisoner's dilemma: How women negotiate competing narratives of reentry and desistance.* New Brunswick, NJ: Rutgers University Press.

Middlemass, K. (2014). War as metaphor: The convergence of the war on poverty & the war on drugs. In K. Farmbry (Ed.), *The war on poverty: A retrospective* (pp. 85–104). Lanham, MD: Lexington Books.

144 Gender, Criminality, and Reentry

Middlemass, K. (2017). *Convicted and condemned: The politics and policies of prisoner reentry.* New York: New York University Press.

Minton, T. (2013). *Jail inmates at midyear 2012 – statistical tables* (NCJ 241264). Washington, DC: United States Department of Justice. Retrieved from www.bjs.gov/content/pub/pdf/jim12st.pdf

Richie, B. (2001). Challenges incarcerated women face as they return to their communities: Findings from life history interviews. *Crime & Delinquency, 47*(3), 368–389.

Richie, B. (2012). *Compelled to crime: The gender entrapment of battered Black women.* New York: Taylor & Francis.

Russell, K., & Milovanovic, D. (2001). *Petit apartheid in the U.S. criminal justice system: The dark figure of racism.* Durham, NC: Carolina Academic Press.

Spjeldnes, S., & Goodkind, S. (2009). Gender differences and offender reentry: A review of the literature. *Journal of Offender Rehabilitation, 48*(4), 314–335.

Willingham, B. (2011). Black women's prison narratives and the intersection of race, gender, and sexuality in U.S. prisons. *Critical Survey, 23*(3), 55–66.

Chapter 11

Black Women Excluded From Protection and Criminalized for Their Existence

Keesha M. Middlemass

Introduction

The social position of Black women in the United States reaches back to the 18th and 19th centuries when Black women played a critical role in the formation of criminal laws. Although they were nonparticipants, Black women were in the minds of White legislators as evidenced by the language embedded in criminal laws that established a disciplinary matrix, forced gendered hierarchies and practices, and sanctioned racial differences (see Ainsworth, 2012). Statutes provided the necessary language to discriminate, police, and survey Black women in an effort to protect White supremacy and White gendered norms (Cameron, 2006). This chapter examines Black women as social actors using the epistemological framework of intersectionality, specifically examining institutional and structural racism and racialized and gendered norms through a legal and sociohistorical lens. The focus is on how Black women were targeted through the use of select criminal laws that connected race, gender, social positions, and legal statutes with the goal of oppressing them. This oppression, and how it was constituted, is central to understand Black women's position in historic and contemporary society vis-à-vis the role of the state (see Battle and Williams chapter, "An Intersectional Criminology Analysis of Black Women's Collective Resistance," in this volume, for examples of Black women's relationship with the state).

Laws tend to be valued by society because they are thought to protect each member, and the criminal code is no different; it is the written embodiment of society's ethical and moral standards, racial hierarchy, and gendered positions. An important feature of the law is how it establishes who matters and who does not while simultaneously empowering some while making "others" invisible. For example, slavery created and perpetuated racialized and gendered stereotypes about Black women while elevating and promoting social behaviors of White women as "customary." Black women's oppression came from different sets of social standards; although Black men and women were assumed to be "criminal" based on their skin color, Black women did not fit into the racial and gendered norms of the criminal justice system.

Black women were deemed aberrant because of their race and deviant because they could not meet society's expectations of White women's gendered standards. As a result, the law marginalized Black women by implicitly and explicitly leaving them outside of the laws' protection because of the powerful social marker of race and their subservient gendered position.

In order to understand the marginalization of Black women by the law and their exclusion from the law, the complex historical, social, and legal associations between race, gender, and the criminal justice system are examined. Further, examining multiple converging issues offers a deeper understanding of the role Black women have played in the development of criminal laws, provides insights about how legal oppression is constituted based on Black women as constrained social actors, sheds light on how they were excluded from societal protection and punished for their existence, and how the oppression of Black women follows almost a straight line from when they were enslaved to contemporary times vis-à-vis the state.

Contextualizing Intersectionality & the Development of Law

The law is gendered and racist, which necessitates an exploration of the intersecting nuances that produce different experiences and outcomes (Brown, 2012). Excluding Black women from the protection of the law was not a historical accident; rather, social, political, economic, and legal institutions purposely omitted them. Ignoring Black women in the law was fundamental to elevating the legal status of White women, but by eliminating Black women from consideration the assumption was that all women are White, but when gender is *not* considered then all Blacks are men (hooks, 1981; Haley, 2013). Yet because Black women "stand at the intersection of race and gender" (Grillo, 2013, p. 18), they were placed in a unique social and legal position.

Historically, Black women's humanity went unrecognized (Haley, 2013) and they became examples of "what a human being was *not*" (Spillers, 1984, p. 78). Such intersecting patterns of race and gender demonstrate the set of "layered oppressions" foisted upon Black women via multiple and converging systems (Shields, 2008) and demonstrates how their intersecting social identities operate and continue to be used for legal and policy purposes (Middlemass, 2015). This understanding of Black women provides the foundation with which to study how Black women's race *and* gender shaped the development of criminal laws.

Intersectionality places Black women at the center of the analysis by integrating diverse social contexts where Black women are situated, and their social position produces and reproduces social inequalities (Crenshaw, 1991, 1989; Collins, 1990; Brah & Phoenix, 2004). Black women's identities differ from White women, and as a result their intersecting identities confer a minority status that is unescapable (Crenshaw, 1989). For instance, negative racial stereotypes about Black women are sustained through the embeddedness of race in the language of the law, which are used to reinforce racial and gendered exclusion, while the role of the state is pervasive in exacerbating racial inequalities (Lieberman, 1998; Hancock, 2007).

The systemic bias that encourages the exclusion of whole groups from the protection of the law forms the basis to create more discriminatory laws that limit the ability of Black women to access social and legal rights and public benefits (Brown, 2012; Middlemass, 2018). Discriminatory laws have put Black women into a marginalized status within dominant society (Crenshaw, 1991), and their legal options are limited because they "fall into the void between concerns about women's issues and concerns about racism" (Crenshaw, 1991, p. 1282). Furthermore, Black women are burdened by the consequences of race and gender when their gendered performances are gauged based on White standards of womanhood, which have been promoted as "natural" while concurrently sustaining White supremacy.

Black Enslaved Women & White Womanhood

The enslavement of Africans and their descendants was a structurally and ideologically institutionalized form of social control that bolstered White supremacy, but in order to transition from a "society with slaves" to a "slave society," Whites had to justify the oppression and enslavement of an entire group of people (Berlin, 1998). This was possible through the creation of artificial distinctions based on race and gender using distorted biblical interpretations and "scientific racism" (Berlin, 1998). By socially and legally problematizing Africans and their descendants as "other," the door was opened for the institutionalization of slavery and its supporting social practices (Middlemass, 2017; Lieberman, 1998, 2005).

For instance, as early as 1662, Virginia passed a law that determined social status as free or slave based on the condition of the mother, which legally recognized slavery as a hereditary and lifelong condition; children born to Black slave mothers and fathered by White men were automatically enslaved (Hening, 1823, p. 170; Roberts, 1993). Such a policy demonstrated the hypocrisy of White patriarchy as it violated the central tenant of patriarchy that mandated a child's status follow its father, except when the child had a Black mother (Omolade, 1987, p. 244; Roberts, 1993). "The intimate intertwining of race and gender in the very structure of slavery makes it practically impossible to speak of one without the other" and demonstrated that White patriarchy owed nothing to Black female slaves (Roberts, 1993, p. 7). The enslavement of Black people served multiple goals, including solidifying economic, political, and social power in the hands of Whites; sustaining White patriarchy by separating White women from Black women to make it possible to portray White women as "pure" and to mark Black women as "corrupt" and "deviant;" and controlling Black women and their bodies through distinct forms of oppression (White, 1999).

Within these interconnected systems – race, gender, economics, slavery, and the law – the subjugation of Black women was done by comparing their gendered public performance to White normative female behaviors. White women were expected to personify the ideal of "true womanhood," which emphasized purity, submissiveness, and traditional gender roles (O'Sullivan, 2016). In exchange for being "pure" and maintaining the color line, White women enjoyed the benefits of the law, were customarily protected from sexual violence, and supported the oppression of Black women (Dent, 2003). In this regard, White women needed Black women in order to achieve the concept of "pure" White womanhood and maintain their position in society. The White trope of "true womanhood" obscures the role that Black women played in maintaining this trope.

White women had the luxury to presume that White men, societal norms, and the law would protect them and guard them from the most severe penalties and criminal punishment. The legal subordination of Black women, on the other hand, was deemed necessary to reinforce racialized gendered norms and ensure that Black women were viewed in direct opposition of White women. Black women were unable to perform White womanhood and could not claim any societal benefits based on their gender, while their race left them vulnerable (Haley, 2013) to laws that ensured Black women stayed in their "place" and "normalized" legal violence against Black women (Butterfield, 1996).

The Master–Slave Dyad

The relationship between slave owners and slaves were shaped by the meaning of property, racial and gendered hierarchies, and plantation politics that buttressed and sustained White wealth (Penningroth, 2007). The maintenance of slavery required the "perpetual exercise" of inequality, degrading submissions, and unremitting despotism by masters (Jefferson, 1781). Through the degrading submission that forced the enslavement of Blacks by Whites, two dyads emerged.[1] The first dyad designated Blacks as property in legal and practical terms, which created the master–slave association; slaves belonged to a master and as property could not be *in* society nor play a role in society (Penningroth, 2007). This propertied connection allowed White supremacy to flourish and ideas about Black racial inferiority to also blossom (Williams, Lavizzo-Mourey, & Warren, 1994) and justify White ideology that Blacks without White slave masters would become cold-blooded savages (Middlemass, 2017, p. 42).

The second dyad revolved around the sexual interactions between the White master and other White men and enslaved Black women. Although White society was preoccupied over the sexual activities of White women, and various systems regulated the sexual activities between slaves for the production of more slaves and outlawed interracial sexual relations, the law was markedly silent on the sexual activities of Black women (Getman, 1984). This was because the law allowed White men complete independence, including sexual autonomy, over their slaves (Higginbotham, 1978). The illicit sexual dyad between White men and enslaved Black women commodified the intimate relations of Black women to serve their slave owners' interests (Getman, 1984; Roberts, 1997); the consequences of the law and White male sexual proclivities encouraged "rape for profit" (Higginbotham, 1996). White men raped, sexually abused, and exploited Black women, and their brutal treatment of Black women rarely, if ever, was contested. These illicit relationships were a form of gendered supremacy and sexualized control, which was supported by the law and social systems (Jacobs, 2017; Getman, 1984). It was critical for Whites to control enslaved Black women's bodies to maintain the color line, safeguard against their gendered existence, which theoretically might imperil White womanhood, and preserve Black women's integral position in the political economy. Enslaved Black women bodies were considered public space available for sexual violation, and they were raped and forced to bear children for the profit of slave owners (Hutchinson, 2014). The law protected White men from any claims of inheritance by the children produced by enslaved Black women (Jacobs, 2017).

Enslaved Black women were forced to breed, and any child(ren) produced was owned by the slave master (Berry, 2007). When an enslaved Black woman birthed a child as a result of being raped, the slave master would enslave his own progeny, which made him into a breeder of slaves (Higginbotham, 1978) while strengthening his own wealth; illicit transgressions resulting in a child were acceptable because it supported the self-reproduction of the enslaved population (Getman, 1984).

Yet such behavior reinforced the negative social construction of Black women as Jezebels, which supported the stereotype that they were "less than" White women (White, 1999). Enslaved Black women's sexual exploitation and repression was reinforced via laws that made them and their children property while having no control over their reproductive rights, sexual choices, or the right to mother their own children (White, 1999). White men suffered no criminal, legal, or social repercussions, and Black women were silenced because of their legal status (White, 1999; Hutchinson, 2014).

Black Women as a "Social Problem"

Based on their race and gender, Black women have been problematized as a "social problem," yet were *not* initially deemed to be able to be a victim of crime because of their slave status. For instance, the rape and violation of Black women was not acknowledged in American law as a crime: "For most of American history, the crime of rape of a Black woman did not exist"

(Roberts, 1997, p. 31; Broussard, 2013). White society failed to "see" Black women as "rapeable" or as victims of sexual or other types of violence; raping a Black woman was considered an oxymoron (Hutchinson, 2014). In many states, original rape laws only referred to the rape of White women (Klein & Kress, 1976).

Race and gender have influenced how certain crimes are defined and who is targeted to be sentenced while the racial status of an offender and the victim contribute to determining the degree of punishment (Middlemass, 2017; see Lieberman, 2005). Therefore, offenses and methods of punishment were designed for and targeted White and Black men and Black women; as long as White women adhered to gendered cultural expectations of "true womanhood," they were largely shielded from punishment (White, 1999).[2] As such, White women rarely experienced structural violence, whereas Black women experienced it regularly at the hands of White women and men alike and were continuously reminded of their vulnerability as victims of violence (Getman, 1984; Roberts, 1997). The criminalization of Black women's bodies created racial inequalities, gendered violence, and structural disparities; because they were purposefully excluded from the law's protection, the historical residue is visible in how Black women are punished for crimes that violate the concept of "true womanhood."

Black Women & the Law

Negative stereotypes about Black women are used to blame them for a host of public problems because of their perceived sexual promiscuity, criminal tendencies, alleged drug use, the decline of two-parent Black families, and for being poor (Greenbaum, 2013); these characterizations are used to support the passage of laws purposely designed to control their behaviors and social choices (Hancock, 2004). Moynihan's 1965 report, *The Negro Family: The Case for National Action*, reinforced racist beliefs, prosecuted Black culture, and sowed the seed of what became known as a "tangle of pathology" that was unique to Black "matriarchal dominance" (Greenbaum, 2013, p. 3). All of the "so called" flaws of the Black family, so-called experts have argued, were rooted in an internal defect of Black cultural norms and Black women (Greenbaum, 2013). For instance, when the birth of "crack babies" was splashed across major news outlets in connection with the violence associated with crack cocaine and its open-air drug markets, the crack epidemic solidified society's belief that race and drugs were synonymous and an acute inner-city problem; in response, elected officials appeared to be "tough on crime" by passing draconian drug laws related to *who* was using crack cocaine while ignoring White powder cocaine users (Middlemass, 2017, pp. 4–5).

Wacquant (2010) argues that the criminalization of Black women and revanchist public welfare policies have merged to create interlocking control mechanisms fueled by the stereotype of welfare queens and perceptions about the dysfunctional Black family (Greenbaum, 2013; Hancock, 2004; Middlemass, 2015). The criminal justice and welfare systems are now relentless in punishing criminals and those living in poverty (Middlemass, 2015); Black women are viewed as subjects for harsh treatment because they do not perform as suitable societal actors (Roberts, 1997; Davis, 1998). This was evident during the welfare reform efforts in 1997, which focused on controlling the sexual and reproductive decisions of poor, primarily Black, mothers (Roberts, 2014; Hancock, 2004). Similar efforts continue today as politicians attempt to revamp the welfare system into a work program with the goal of forcing behavior modification programs onto a distinct subpopulation. The misplaced culpability guiding policy decisions tighten social control mechanisms over Black women, particularly poor Black women, who are blamed for their own poverty and attacked for their failure to adhere to White "true womanhood" norms (O'Sullivan, 2016; see Roberts, 1993, 2014; Greenbaum, 2013).

Because of the increased presence of the state in the lives of Black women (i.e., child protective services, foster care, welfare, and the criminal justice system), they are more likely to be under the state's surveillance (Roberts, 2014). The concentration of state supervision directed at Black women and their children is another example of the state's effort to control Black women's bodies. Has the master in the master–slave dyad been replaced by the state while the expectations of Black women have been inverted? For instance, enslaved Black women were prized for having a baby every year though they had no rights to mother and raise their own children (White, 1999).

Today, Black women continue to be targeted with the "welfare queen" stereotype, which demonizes Black women who have several children, particularly if the children have different fathers (Middlemass, 2015; Hancock, 2004). Punitive policies and the "culture of poverty" have figured prominently in the creation of criminal laws (Kohler-Hausmann, 2007). Black women tend not to be thought of as an added value in a capitalist society, so policies attempt to restrict their reproductive rights and choices (see Roberts, 1993, 2014). For instance, White women tend to be praised for staying at home to mother her offspring, while Black women continue to fight for the right to conceive, be pregnant, and mother their own children (Roberts, 2014). Black women are expected to work in exchange for benefits provided under the Temporary Assistance for Needy Families (TANF) program, which makes it harder for them to mother.

The over policing of Black women's bodies also extends into the area of drug laws, which has resulted in the subjective nature of policing, particularly as it relates to mental impairment (Gur, 2010; Dai, Frank, & Sun, 2011). Although state laws vary in how women are treated when they are arrested, co-occurring health problems, such as drug use and mental illness, increase the likelihood of arrest (Fisher et al., 2014). Mental illness and its related symptoms can be exacerbated during interactions with police, which has resulted in high rates of individuals with mental illness being detained, charged, and incarcerated (Jacobs, 2017); scholars have documented high rates of mental illness and associated mental problems in the general prison population (Gray & Saum, 2005; Jacobs, 2017). Physical signs of addiction tend to mimic some mental health-related behaviors, such as screaming, impulsivity, hostility, disrespectful conduct, aggression, disorganized thoughts, confusion, kicking, hitting, and spitting, all of which are also associated with addiction (see Gur, 2010; Dai et al., 2011).

Although Black women do not use drugs at higher rates than White women, they are arrested and incarcerated at more than twice the rate of White women (109 per 100,000 to 53 per 100,000; Sentencing Project, 2015). Some scholars have found that Black women are not granted the same leniency that is extended to White women as it relates to drugs (Crawford, 2000), and they are more likely to be incarcerated because of being poor and unable to access appropriate mental health care resources (Beckett, Nyrop, & Pfingst, 2006).

Tammy Jackson, who was mentally ill and pregnant, was put in an isolation cell in a Florida detention center in April 2019; after complaining about contractions and needing assistance, the guards ignored her. Ms. Jackson was forced to have her baby alone in an isolation cell, and had to wait several hours before medical assistance arrived. Such blatant disregard for a Black woman is now, unfortunately, commonplace, and Black women are continuing to experience violence at the hands of law enforcement (Jacobs, 2017). The #SayHerName campaign is attempting to bring Black women's stories into public discourses to increase the amount of attention given to Black women who are harmed at the hands of the state.

Conclusion

Black women have always had a complicated, long-standing, and specific history as it relates to the state, and that experience is marked by violence (Jacobs, 2017). Black women are "the most socially and economically marginalized group in America" (hooks, 1981, pp. 70–83), and this is the result of the foundational years that created cultural and racist stereotypes that have extended beyond slavery. Moreover, Black women have been deemed unworthy to be brought within the bounds of the protection of the law. The lack of legal protection extended by the state has allowed for the criminalization of Black women who are unable to adhere to recognized "acceptable" social norms; as a result, they are "problematized" by the law and arrested for failing to achieve "true womanhood."

The creation and maintenance of the concept of "true womanhood" established a bifurcated system, one for White women and one for Black women.

Black Women Excluded and Criminalized   153

The historic residue of race excluded Black women from the law, and the construction of boundaries through gender created a hierarchical gendered system. The omission of Black women from legal protection allowed racial proponents to continue to use Black women's race and gender against them to impose criminal justice standards on Black women's behavior (Middlemass, 2018). The social position of Black women has largely been based on their relationship to White women, but this analysis also demonstrates that the position of Black women is in relationship to White male-centric social, legal, and economic systems. The state chose to control the Black community, and in particular Black women, via the law. The state adopted paternalistic policies that are fundamentally based on Black women's racialized and gendered position.

The relationship between race, gender, and the *lack* of legal protection extended to Black women demonstrates that they are integral to understanding racialized and gendered forms of social control, especially as it pertains to the criminal justice system. By focusing on Black women, it shows how they influence the law, which has been detrimental to their well-being. As Black women are excluded from the law's protection, it validates how the law perpetuates social inequality and their social position. The law represents a form of state power, and the absence of Black women from the law's protections shows how the law is gendered and racist.

By exploring the intersection of race and gender from a historical perspective, a troubling relationship is revealed about how historical practices exist today about the racial and gender differences that are visible in the 21st century. By examining the connection between slavery and the creation of White "womanhood," I've demonstrated three important roles Black women have played in influencing the creation of laws. First, Black women are key instigators behind the development of Black structural oppression; second, Black women are at the heart of structural, legal, and other societal issues related to how systems of oppression are created and maintained; and third, they are at the epicenter of the law's development, evidenced in how the intersection of race and gender subjugate Black women in the 21st century.

Notes

1. Dyad, in classical Greek philosophy, refers to the concept of twoness, and is used to describe the combination of two elements by force. A dyad, in its most basic social form, is the interaction between two people and this interaction determines the locus of both individuals. The behaviors and circumstances within the dyad are best understood as being directly influenced and shaped by the environment and experiences of the people in the dyad.
2. White upper-class women were far more protected from the law than lower class White women, who were not able to fulfill the concept of "true womanhood" because they worked, contradicting traditional White gender roles. When White women of any

154 Keesha M. Middlemass

class broke gendered expectations, such as infanticide or adultery, they tended to be punished more harshly than White men for comparable criminal acts (White, 1999). When poor White women were found guilty of committing a criminal offense, she was labeled an offender and found to be morally suspect.

References

Ainsworth, J. (2012). The performance of gender as reflected in American evidence rules: Language, power, and the legal construction of liability. *Gender & Language, 6*(1), 181–195.

Beckett, K., Nyrop, K., & Pfingst, L. (2006). Race, drugs, and policing: Understanding disparities in drug delivery arrests. *Criminology, 44*(1), 105–137.

Berlin, I. (1998). *Many thousands gone: The first two centuries of slavery in North America.* Cambridge, MA: Belknap Press of Harvard University Press.

Berry, D. R. (2007). *Swing the sickle for the harvest is ripe: Gender and slavery in antebellum Georgia.* Urbana and Chicago: University of Illinois Press.

Brah, A., & Phoenix, A. (2004). Ain't I a woman? Revisiting intersectionality. *Journal of International Women's Studies, 5*(3), 75–86.

Broussard, P.A. (2013). Black women's post-slavery silence syndrome: A twenty-first century remnant of slavery, Jim crow, and systemic racism – who will tell her stories? *Journal of Gender, Race & Justice, 16*, 373–421.

Brown, G. (2012). Ain't I a victim? The intersectionality of race, class and gender in domestic violence and the courtroom. *Cardozo Journal of Law & Gender, 19*, 147–183.

Butterfield, F. (1996). *All God's children: The Bosket family and the American tradition of violence.* New York: First Vintage Books.

Cameron, D. (2006). *On language and sexual politics.* New York: Routledge.

Collins, P. H. (1990). *Black feminist thought: Knowledge, consciousness, and the politics of empowerment.* Boston: Unwin Hyman.

Crawford, C. (2000). Gender, race, and habitual offender sentencing in Florida. *Criminology, 38*, 263–280.

Crenshaw, K. (1989). Demarginalizing the intersection of race and sex: A black feminist critique of antidiscrimination doctrine, feminist theory and antiracist politics. *University of Chicago Legal Forum*, 139–167.

Crenshaw, K. (1991). Mapping the margins: Intersectionality, identity politics, and violence against women of color. *Stanford Law Review, 43*(6), 1241–1299.

Dai, M., Frank, J., & Sun, I. (2011). Procedural justice during police-citizen encounters: The effects of process-based policing on citizen compliance and demeanor. *Journal of Criminal Justice, 39*, 159–168.

Davis, A. J. (1998). Prosecution and race: The power and privilege of discretion. *Fordham Law Review, 67*, 13–67.

Dent, Jr., G. W. (2003). Traditional marriage: Still worth defending. *Brigham Young University Journal of Public Law, 18*(2), 419–447.

Fisher, W., Clark, R., Baxter, J., Barton, B., O'Connell, E., & Aweh, G. (2014). Co-Occurring risk factors for arrest among persons with opioid abuse and dependence: Implications for developing interventions to limit criminal justice involvement. *Journal of Substance Abuse Treatment, 473*, 197–201.

Getman, K. A. (1984). Sexual control in the slaveholding south: The implementation and maintenance of a racial caste system, *Harvard Women's Law Journal, 7*, 115–152.

Black Women Excluded and Criminalized   155

Gray, A., & Saum, C. (2005). Mental health, gender and drug court completion. *American Journal of Criminal Justice, 30*(1), 55–69.

Greenbaum, S. D. (2013). *Blaming the poor: The long shadow of the Moynihan Report on cruel images about poverty.* New Brunswick, NJ: Rutgers University Press.

Grillo, T. (2013). Anti-essentialism and intersectionality: Tools to dismantle the master's house. *Berkeley Journal of Gender, Law & Justice, 10*(1), 16–30.

Gur, O. (2010). Persons with mental illness in the criminal justice system: Police interventions to prevent violence and criminalization. *Journal of Police Crisis Negotiations, 10,* 220–240.

Haley, S. (2013). 'Like I was a man': Chain gangs, gender, and the domestic carceral sphere in Jim Crow Georgia. *Signs: Journal of Women in Culture and Society, 39*(1), 53–77.

Hancock, A. (2004). *The politics of disgust and the public identity of the "Welfare Queen."* New York: New York University Press.

Hancock, A. (2007). When multiplication doesn't equal quick addition: Examining intersectionality as a research paradigm. *Perspectives on Politics, 5,* 63–78.

Hening, W. W. (1823). *The statutes at large; being a collection of all the laws of Virginia from the first session of the legislature, in the Year 1619.* New York: R. & W. & G. Bartow. Retrieved from www.encyclopediavirginia.org/_Negro_womens_children_to_serve_according_to_the_condition_of_the_mother_1662

Higginbotham, Jr., A. L. (1978). *In the Matter of Color: Race and the American legal process: The Colonial period.* New York: Oxford University Press.

Higginbotham, Jr., A. L. (1996). The ten precepts of American slavery jurisprudence: Chief Justice Roger Taney's defense and Justice Thurgood Marshall's condemnation of the precept of Black inferiority. *Cardozo Law Review, 17,* 1695.

hooks, bell. (1981). *Ain't I a woman.* Boston: South End Press.

Hutchinson, S. (2014). White picket fences, white innocence. *Journal of Religious Ethics, 42*(4), 612–639.

Jacobs, M. S. (2017). The violent state: Black women's invisible struggle against police violence. *William & Mary Journal of Women and the Law, 24,* 39–100.

Jefferson, T. (1781). Notes on the state of Virginia. *Query, XVIII.*

Klein, D., & Kress, J. (1976). Any woman's blues: A critical overview of women, crime and the criminal justice system. *Crime & Social Justice, 5*(Spring–Summer), 34–49.

Kohler-Hausmann, J. (2007). 'The crime of survival': Fraud prosecutions, community surveillance, and the original 'Welfare Queen.' *Journal of Social History, 41*(2), 329–354.

Lieberman, R. C. (1998). *Shifting the color line: Race and the American welfare state.* Cambridge, MA: Harvard University Press.

Lieberman, R. C. (2005). *Shaping race policy: The United States in comparative perspective.* Princeton, NJ: Princeton University Press.

Middlemass, K. (2015). War as metaphor: The convergence of the war on poverty & the war on drugs. In K. Farmby (Ed.), *The war on poverty* (pp. 85–104). Lanham, MD: Lexington Books.

Middlemass, K. (2017). *Convicted and condemned: The politics and policies of prisoner reentry.* New York: New York University Press.

Middlemass, K. (2018). Hiding in plain sight: Black women felons reentering society." In J. Jordan-Zachery & N. Alexander-Floyd (Eds.), *Black women in politics* (pp. 69–96). Albany, NY: SUNY Press.

Omolade, B. (1987). The unbroken circle: A historical study of Black single mothers and their families." *Wisconsin Women's Law Journal, 3,* 239–274.

O'Sullivan, S. (2016). Who is always already criminalized? An intersectional analysis of criminality on *Orange Is the New Black*. *The Journal of American Culture, 39*(4), 401–412.

Penningroth, D. C. (2007). The claims of slaves and ex-slaves to family and property: A transatlantic comparison. *The American Historical Review, 112*(4), 1039–1069.

Potter, H. (2015). *Intersectionality and Criminology: Disrupting and Revolutionizing Studies of Crime.* New York: Routledge.

Roberts, D. (1993). Racism and patriarchy in the meaning of motherhood. *Journal of Gender & the Law, 1*(1), 1–38.

Roberts, D. (1997). *Killing the Black body: Race, reproduction, and the meaning of liberty.* New York: First Vintage Books.

Roberts, D. (2014). Complicating the triangle of race, class and state: The insights of Black feminists. *Ethnic and Racial Studies, 37*(10), 1776–1782.

The Sentencing Project. (2015). *Fact sheet: Incarcerated women and girls.* Washington, DC. Retrieved from www.sentencingproject.org/wp-content/uploads/2016/02/Incarcerated-Women-and-Girls.pdf

Shields, S. (2008). Gender: An intersectionality perspective. *Sex Roles, 59,* 301–311.

Spillers, H. J. (1984). Interstices: A small drama of words. In C. S. Vance (Ed.), *Pleasure and danger: Exploring female sexuality* (pp. 73–100). Boston: Routledge & Kegan Paul.

Wacquant, L. (2010). Class, race & hyperincarceration in revanchist America. *Dædalus, 139*(3), 74–90.

White, D. G. (1999). *Ar'n't I a woman? Female slaves in the plantation south.* New York: Norton.

Williams, D., Lavizzo-Mourey, R., & Warren, R. (1994). The concept of race and health status in America. *Public Health Reports, 109*(1), 26–41.

Chapter 12

The Gendered Challenges of Prisoner Reentry

Haley Zettler

The female incarceration rate has dramatically increased since the 1980s, outpacing male incarceration rates by over 50% (Carson & Golinelii, 2013; Kelly, 2015). As a result, a larger number of female inmates are now reentering society compared to the past. Research on reentry finds that there are collective challenges to reentry that affect both males and females returning to society. However, there is additional evidence that there are important differences in reentry risk and needs for men, women, and transgendered former inmates.

Before discussing the gendered challenges to prisoner reentry, it is necessary to consider universal challenges to reentry. The research on reentry identifies an array of barriers that released prisoners face, including but not limited to, employment, substance use, mental and physical health, family and community stabilization, civil disenfranchisement, and housing (Middlemass, 2017; Travis, 2005; Clear, Rose, Waring, & Scully, 2003; Fashey, Roberts, & Engel, 2006; Petersilia, 2001; Visher, LaVigne, & Travis, 2004). These challenges are related to post-release recidivism, and the negative effects hold across gender. One study of inmates released from prisons in Ohio found that education, employment, and residential mobility were significantly related to recidivism for both female and male releasees (Makarios, Steiner, & Travis, 2010). Despite the number of shared difficulties reentering, empirical efforts suggest that challenges to reentry may vary across gender (Johnson, 2015).

The majority of reentry programs have focused primarily on the criminogenic risk factors of males, largely neglecting the potentially unique needs of female offenders (Holtfreter & Wattanaporn, 2014). The recognition of gender differences in post-release risk factors can help to develop gender-specific reentry programs and promote successful reentry (Lattimore & Visher, 2009). A large body of literature has documented that female parolees have greater educational, employment, and health care needs than men, which can subsequently increase post-release recidivism (Bloom, Owen, & Covington, 2003; Lattimore & Visher, 2009; Visher & Travis, 2001). These characteristics may contribute to recidivism; Benda (2005) notes that "childhood and recent sexual and physical abuse, adverse feelings, living with a criminal partner, and drug use are particularly powerful of women's recidivism" (p. 337). In order to understand the distinctive challenges that females face upon reentry, a brief overview of the gendered pathways to crime is necessary.

Gender Differences in Offending and Incarceration

A large body of work from feminist criminology focuses on the gendered pathways to crime, which seeks to understand the relationship between childhood and adult experiences in offending, arguing that males and females may possess different risk factors that are associated with offending behavior (Daly, 1992; see Belknap, 2015). Feminist criminology centers on the idea that women's criminal offending, and recidivism, are based on factors that are: (a) not usually seen in men, (b) usually seen in men but in higher rates in women, or (c) seen in relatively equal frequency, but have unique effects for women (Belknap, 2015; Chesney-Lind & Pasko, 2013; DeHart, Lynch, Belknap, Dass-Brailsford, & Green, 2014; Gehring, 2018; Taylor, 2015; Wattanaporn & Holtfreter, 2014). In her seminal work, Daly (1992) identified five distinct pathways for female offenders: (a) the street woman, (b) the battered woman, (c) the harmed and harming woman, (d) the drug connected-woman, and (e) the "other" woman. More recently, Gehring (2018) examined a sample of women pretrial defendants in order to identify pathways to criminality. Her analysis found that a pathway including childhood abuse, through its indirect effects on mental health and substance use, predicted pretrial failure for women only.

Scholars have found consistent support that women have specific life histories that contribute to gendered offending behavior, such as physical and sexual abuse, poverty, mental illness, and substance abuse (Belknap, 2015; DeHart et al., 2014; Gehring, 2018; Jung et al., 2017). Whereas men are more likely to be incarcerated for violent crimes, a higher percentage of women are incarcerated for a drug-related crime (Carson, 2018). Further, there is evidence that although incarceration increases the likelihood of both drug and property recidivism for males and females, women are more likely to recidivate based on a property crime (Mears, Cochran, & Bales, 2012). As there are distinct characteristics of female offending behavior that are associated with incarceration and recidivism, these factors must be considered when discussing the gendered challenges of prisoner reentry.

Gender-Specific Challenges of Prisoner Reentry

Research on incarcerated women has found that female offenders are more likely to experience prior victimization (Staton-Tindall, Duvall,

Leukefeld, & Oser, 2007) and have higher rates of trauma in their lifetime compared to women in the general population (Grella, Lovinger, & Warda, 2013). In a survey of more than 2 million male inmates and 190,000 female inmates in correctional facilities in the United States, females were over seven times more likely to experience sexual abuse and four times more likely to report experiencing physical abuse prior to incarceration as compared to males (Center on Addiction and Substance Abuse [CASA], 2010). For instance, James (2004) found that more than 50% of female prisoners had a history of sexual abuse as compared to 10% of male prisoners. Female inmates have extensive victimization histories that are not only related to offending behavior, but have a compounding impact on other significant hurdles to successful reentry, such as mental health, substance use, and limited job opportunities (Chesney-Lind, 2000; Fedock, Fries, & Kubiak, 2013; van Wormer & Bartollas, 2007). James (2004) also found that inmates who had experienced prior abuse were three times more likely to have mental health problems than inmates without abuse histories. Thus, if prior trauma and victimization are not properly addressed during incarceration, they can exacerbate existing substance abuse problems that have been linked to failing parole (Huebner, DeJong, & Cobbina, 2010).

Although all groups of offenders are more likely to have mental health problems than the general population (Steadman, Osher, Robbins, Case, & Samuels, 2009), there is evidence that female offenders have higher rates of mental health problems than their male counterparts (Binswanger et al., 2010; Constantine et al., 2010). In a random sample of 491 women incarcerated in jails, 43% of the respondents met the criteria for a serious mental illness, and 32% met the criteria in the past 12 months (Lynch et al., 2014). Regarding substance use, Bronson and colleagues (2017) found that female prisoners in state facilities met DSM-IV criteria for substance dependence or abuse at a higher rate than male prisoners (69% versus 57%). Specifically, Bronson, Stroop, Zimmer, and Berzofsky (2017) found that among state prisoners, females were more likely to have reported drug use in the month prior to their arrest than males as well as more likely to have reported being under the influence of drugs at the time of their arrest (Bronson et al., 2017). In a sample of female prison releases, Huebner and colleagues (2010) found that women who were drug dependent, had less than a high school education, and more extensive criminal histories were more likely to recidivate while on parole and during the eight year follow-up period.

Female offenders are also more likely to suffer from co-morbid disorders, such as mental health and substance abuse (Bloom et al., 2003; Zlotnick et al., 2008). These comorbid disorders present an increased risk of homelessness, which may negatively impact desistance from offending (Morgan, Fisher, Duan, Mandracchia, & Murray, 2010; Osher, 2013), thus increasing the risk of recidivism upon release (Messina, Burdon, Hagopian, & Prendergast, 2006). In a multisite evaluation of the Serious and Violent Offender

Reentry Initiative (SVORI) by Lattimore and colleagues (2010), adult female offenders compared with males were significantly more likely to report needing mental health treatment (50% versus 25%) and substance use treatment (about two-thirds versus 40%) upon reentry, respectively.

A particular issue relevant to women is pregnancy; among female prisoners, an estimated 4% of state prisoners are pregnant at the time of their incarceration (Maruschak, 2008). Pregnancy in prison provides a myriad of challenges during incarceration, as prior to confinement many women do not receive adequate prenatal care, education, or psychosocial support to prepare them for separation from their infant (Ferszt & Clarke, 2012). A number of pregnant inmates have high-risk pregnancies because of their social conditions, such as living in poverty, having a lack of education, inability to access health care, and substance abuse that contributed to their incarceration (Hotelling, 2008). As there is no national policy regarding infant separation, the majority of children born to incarcerated mothers are immediately separated from their mothers (Women's Prison Association, 2009). Thus, pregnant women must also face the stress and worry about separation from their child after giving birth in prison.

Beyond pregnant inmates, the concern over children is prevalent among the larger population of incarcerated mothers. Although a large number of both male and female inmates are parents of minor children, research finds that a larger proportion of female inmates lived with their children prior to incarceration. Mumola (2000) found that of state prisoners, 65% of women compared to 55% of men lived with their children prior to incarceration. Similarly, in a sample of Texas prisoners, Foster and Hagan (2009) found that when mothers are compared to fathers, mothers were more likely to have been living with their children prior to incarceration and expect to live with their children after incarceration (76% and 58% vs. 56% and 38%). In addition to living with their children, parenting duties are a common concern expressed by female inmates (Kazura, 2001). Female prisoners report being stressed about their children while they are incarcerated, as well as reporting that they worry about their ability to provide for their children upon release (Greene, Haney, & Hurtado, 2000; Wright, Salisbury, & Van Voorhis, 2009). In a sample of 155 reentry programs in ten of the largest metropolitan areas, Scroggins and Malley (2010) found that childcare was the least frequently provided reentry service in every metropolitan area included in the study.

Gender-Specific Programming

In order for released women to effectively reintegrate back into society, programs for females while incarcerated should simultaneously address the multiple barriers to successful reentry. One way to achieve this goal is the use of risk assessments that identify which needs are the most important to treat during incarceration (Wright, Van Voorhis, Salisbury, & Bauman, 2012).

The Gendered Challenges of Prisoner Reentry 161

There is a growing body of evidence that indicates that gender-specific risk assessments and programming are more effective in reducing recidivism for female offenders as opposed to gender-neutral approaches (Chesney-Lin & Pasko, 2013;Van Voorhis, Wright, Salisbury, & Bauman, 2010).

In order to accurately identify the criminogenic needs of females during incarceration, gender-specific risk/needs assessments should be employed to deliver programming that will promote successful reentry. Although the use of risk assessments is commonplace, such instruments have historically been developed for and validated on male populations (Geraghty & Woodhams, 2015). Gender-specific instruments can be helpful in identifying more appropriate programming for female offenders. For example, Reisig and colleagues (2006) examined the effectiveness of the Level of Service Inventory-Revised (LSI-R), a commonly used risk/needs assessment, and found that the LSI-R did not accurately predict the risk and needs related to recidivism for female offenders (Reisig, Holtfreter, & Morash, 2006). Similarly, Heilbrun and colleagues (2008) compared female and male offenders who had been released from prison and received a risk/needs assessment. The authors compared several domains of the LSI-R and the Level of Service/Case Management-I (LS-CMI) measuring employment, companions, and financial measures (Heilbrun et al., 2008). The results demonstrated that females had significantly higher deficits in both companion and financial domains (Heilbrun et al., 2008), thus suggesting gendered differences in risk/needs.

With growing concerns about the appropriateness of gender-neutral risk/ needs assessments, several gender-specific assessments have been developed. Gender-responsive approaches consider the differences in the offending pathways and experiences of males and females by identifying correctional policies and practices to address these differences (Gobeil, Blanchette, & Stewart, 2016;Van Voorhis et al., 2010).Van Voorhis and colleagues (2008) note that gender-specific assessments should (a) be used across all correctional populations, (b) lend themselves to gender-responsive programming, (c) involve subjective judgment, and (d) view gender-neutral risks and needs from a gendered framework. In an examination of one such assessment,Van Voorhis et al. (2010) found that in six of eight samples, the use of gender-responsive variables offered distinct and statistical significance in predicting risk as compared to the use of a gender-neutral instrument.The use of gender-specific risk/needs assessments can provide important information to identify criminogenic needs specific to female inmates (e.g., prior trauma), which are often neglected from gender-neutral approaches (Van Voorhis et al., 2010). In a recent meta-analysis of gender-specific interventions for women offenders, Gobeil et al. (2016) found that gender-responsive programs were more likely to be associated with reductions in recidivism than those that were gender-neutral.

Utilizing gender-specific assessments would provide correctional staff with responsive treatment recommendations, which would assist in creating a comprehensive and integrated gendered program approach. For instance, as there is a well-established relationship between prior trauma, substance use, mental illness, and subsequent offending, several gender-responsive prison and community-based programs have been developed for female offenders. One such program is Helping Women Recover (Covington, 1999), which is a 17-session treatment program that integrates three theories: a theory of addiction, women's psychological development, and trauma. Another trauma specific program, Beyond Trauma, integrates the relationship between trauma and substance use throughout its curriculum (Covington & Bloom, 2007). There is evidence that integrated, gender-responsive programs are effective in reducing recidivism following release. In an experimental pilot study of post-release outcomes of women who participated in prison-based substance abuse treatment, Messina and colleagues (2010) found that participation in gender-responsive treatment programs (Helping Women and Beyond Trauma) led to greater reductions in drug use, longer time spent in residential aftercare, and a decreased likelihood of reincarceration 12 months after parole.

Seeking Safety, a focused therapy designed to help women with comorbid PTSD and substance use disorders, simultaneously addresses trauma histories as well as substance dependence (Najavits, 2002; Najavits, Weiss, Shaw, & Muenz, 1998). Evaluations of Seeking Safety, including a meta-analysis about its effectiveness (Lenz, Henesy, & Callender, 2016), found that participants reported fewer PTSD symptoms and reduced use of substances after participation, and that recidivism rates three months after participation were reduced compared to women in traditional treatment programs (Hien, Cohen, Miele, Litt, & Capstick, 2004; Najavits et al., 1998; Wolff, Frueh, Shi, & Schumann, 2012; Zlotnick, Najavits, Rohsenow, & Johnson, 2003).

As trauma and substance use are closely related to mental health problems, one community-based trauma-focused treatment, Trauma Recovery and Empowerment Model (TREM), targets women with trauma histories that also suffer from serious mental health and substance use disorders (Harris & Anglin, 1998). TREM focuses on the long-term cognitive, emotional, and interpersonal consequences of physical and sexual abuse, while emphasizing supportive skill-building to enhance participants' strengths (Harris & Anglin, 1998). In a quasi-experimental evaluation of TREM, Fallot and colleagues (2011) found that TREM participants reported greater reductions in their alcohol and drug composite scores from the Addiction Severity Index (ASI), decreased anxiety symptoms, and showed greater increases in perceived personal safety (i.e., how often they felt unsafe in general or in their home in the past six months) than those receiving standard services.

Although gender-specific programming efforts have identified some of the considerations specific to female offenders, research has largely neglected the needs of transgender inmates reentering society. Transgender individuals not only face barriers to reentry that impact both males and females, but also present distinct characteristics that may be related to post-release outcomes.

Moving Beyond the Binary: Reentry Challenges of Transgender Offenders

Historically, correctional populations have segregated sexes using a binary definition of biological male and female (Jenness & Fenstermaker, 2014; Sevelius & Jenness, 2017; Sumner & Jenness, 2014). There is a growing awareness of the presence and experiences of transgender inmates. Although the total population of transgender inmates is unknown, there is evidence that transgender persons are overrepresented in prison populations as compared to the general population (Grant et al., 2011; Meerwijk & Sevelius, 2017; Reisner, Bailey, & Sevelius, 2014). Using data from the National Transgender Discrimination survey, 19.3% of respondents reported being incarcerated (Reisner et al., 2014). As the body of research on transgender inmates continues to grow, there have been efforts to understand the demographic characteristics of this population. In a sample of 315 transgender female inmates in California,[1] transgender inmates were incarcerated at disproportionately higher rates for property crimes, classified at higher risk levels as gang members, and reported mental health problems (Sexton, Jenness, & Sumner, 2010). Additionally, the authors found that transgender inmates have disproportionately higher rates of prior drug use, mental illness, HIV, and homelessness (Sexton et al., 2010). More recently, scholars have identified several distinct challenges transgender individuals are faced with when encountering the criminal justice system (Brennan et al., 2012; Jenness, 2015; Routh et al., 2017).

As there is little consensus on how to define the term transgender in the correctional system, there is variation in how prisons identify transgender individuals in custody and knowledge and training on transgender populations is often lacking (Jenness, 2015). Further, the historical use of assigning inmates to prisons based on their sex at birth creates difficulties in establishing and maintaining the gender identity of transgender inmates (Cassaidy & Lim, 2016; Jenness & Fenstermaker, 2014; Lydon, Carrington, Low, Miller, & Yazdy, 2015). In a survey of LBTQ inmates, 76% of transgender respondents reported experiencing emotional pain from hiding their gender identity while they were incarcerated (Lydon et al., 2015). Sumner and Sexton (2016) conducted a series of focus groups with male prisoners and staff and found that transgender inmates were also spoken about in negative ways by fellow inmates and correctional staff. Jenness and Fenstermaker (2014) found that transgender prisoners expressed a desire to secure standing as a "real girl" or the "best girl" while incarcerated. Taken together, research demonstrates that transgender individuals experience difficulties displaying their gender identities while they are incarcerated.

During incarceration, transgender inmates experience higher rates of sexual and/or physical victimization (Jenness & Fenstermaker, 2016; Jenness, Maxson, Matsuda, & Sumner, 2007; Reisner et al., 2014; Sexton et al., 2010). Additionally, transgender women are differentially vulnerable to both sexual assault and other unwanted sexual acts, such as engaging in prostitution in order to avoid being harmed in other ways by fellow inmates (Jenness & Fenstermaker, 2016). The psychological effects of sexual victimization may follow inmates post-release and differentially effect minority transgender women (Reisner et al., 2014).

There is evidence that transgender individuals with a history of incarceration are more likely to have negative health outcomes, including being HIV-positive (Harawa, Amani, Bowers, Sayles, & Cunningham, 2017; Reisner et al., 2014). In a series of interviews of HIV-positive individuals, the authors found that individuals who were currently or formerly incarcerated reported difficulty accessing care and maintaining HIV treatment during and after incarceration (Harawa et al., 2017). Although most states have recognized the condition and diagnosis of gender identity disorder and gender dysphoria as a medical need that may require treatment, there is difficulty getting prison medical staff to properly diagnose and provide adequate care (Cleary, 2015). In a sample of 20 correctional health care providers (e.g., physicians, social workers, psychologists, and counselors), the majority of the respondents stated that transgender inmates do not consistently or sufficiently receive gender-affirming treatment during incarceration (Hughto et al., 2017). Respondents stated that the lack of care was because of structural factors (e.g., lack of training, restrictive policies, budget), interpersonal factors (e.g., staff bias), and individual factors (e.g., lack of cultural competence and training for staff). Many prisons claim that they protect transgender inmates by housing them in long-term segregation; however, this practice has been found to have a negative impact on mental health (Cleary, 2015; Kaba et al., 2014).

Based on these findings, transgender females are faced with significant challenges surrounding physical and mental health inside prison and upon reentry (Jenness & Fenstermaker, 2016; Reisner et al., 2014). As there is wide variation in medical care policies for transgender inmates, it is important that states adopt screening processes as well as provide training for both custody and health care staff (Routh et al., 2017). Prisons should consider policies that take into consideration how best to provide safe housing; adequately training correctional staff; and making HIV and gender-affirming healthcare available (Cassaidy & Lim, 2016; Sevelius & Jenness, 2017). Being incarcerated has also been associated with low self-esteem, substance use, victimization, and intimate partner violence of transgender individuals upon release (Brennan et al., 2012; Grant et al., 2011). Therefore, reentry programs should provide appropriate programming to address the effects of victimization during incarceration.

The Need to Consider Gender in Reentry

Despite the increasing number of women returning to society following incarceration, the specific needs of women have largely been ignored in reentry programming (Holtfreter & Wattanaporn, 2014), particularly as it relates to transgendered individuals. Effective programming during incarceration should prepare women and transgender individuals for reentry, as the pre-release stage is a critical component of success in terms of identifying the needs and providing continuity of care in the reentry process (Angell, Matthews, Barrenger, Watson, & Draine, 2014; Hunter, Lanza, Lawlor, Dyson, & Gordon, 2016; Miller, 2014). As most therapeutic treatment programs were designed for male offenders, it is important that reentry programs employ gender-responsive programs that are specifically designed to target the unique needs of females (Smith & Manchak, 2015). Gender-responsive treatment programs, such as Seeking Safety and TREM, have been found to be effective in treating trauma and substance use in both community and incarcerated samples (Lenz et al., 2016; Fallot, McHugo, Harris, & Xie, 2011), and may also be successful in reentry populations. Correctional agencies should consider adopting gender-specific treatment programs in order to improve post-release outcomes.

As females face distinct barriers to reentry, it is important that gender-specific reentry programs focus on a multipronged approach to treating trauma, mental health, and substance use during incarceration and post-release (Gobeil et al., 2016). Reentry programs should include clearly defined female-specific components in order to increase the likelihood of success among females returning from incarceration (Miller, Miller, & Barnes, 2016). One example is providing wraparound services.

As there are a variety of challenges that female inmates face upon reentry, the need for wide-reaching, coordinated services in the community is crucial for their success. As Covington and Bloom (2007) clarify, these coordinated efforts should draw from existing community organizations that provide services to women who are reentering society and provide a holistic approach needed for successful reintegration. For example, this would include mental and other health care services, substance use programs, and trauma survivor programs; family service agencies; emergency shelter, food, transportation, and financial assistance programs; educational, vocational, and employment programs; welfare system; and self-help groups, faith-based organizations, and community service nonprofit organizations.

The vast majority of prisoners returning to society face a significant number of barriers when they reenter. However, if correctional administrators and workers only focus on common challenges to reentry, they are neglecting the challenges that differentially impact males, females, and transgender populations. Thus, it is necessary that corrections take a gender-responsive approach to identifying and responding to inmates during incarceration and upon reentry. By taking such an approach, programming can help to reduce recidivism and help facilitate successful reintegration. As the area of research on reentry of transgender persons grows, there is a critical need for more research to evaluate the services and programming that is provided to transgender inmates, especially post-release. Future research should examine whether transgender individuals are more likely to recidivate, and what types of responsive programming is needed for these offenders.

Note

1. Transgender inmates were defined as an inmate in a men's prison who: (1) self-identifies as transgender (or something analogous); (2) presents as female, transgender, or feminine in prison or outside of prison; (3) receives any kind of medical treatment for something related to how she presents herself in terms of gender; or (4) participates in groups for transgender inmates (Sexton, Jenness, & Sumner, 2010).

References

Angell, B., Matthews, E., Barrenger, S., Watson, A. C., & Draine, J. (2014). Engagement processes in model programs for community reentry from prison for people with serious mental illness. *International journal of law and psychiatry, 37*(5), 490–500.

Belknap, J. (2015). *The invisible woman: Gender, crime, and justice* (4th ed.). Stanford, CT: Cengage Learning.

Benda, B. B. (2005). Gender differences in life-course theory of recidivism: A survival analysis. *International Journal of Offender Therapy and Comparative Criminology, 49*, 325–342.

Binswanger, I. A., Merrill, J. O., Krueger, P. M., White, M. C., Booth, R. E., & Elmore, J. G. (2010). Gender differences in chronic medical, psychiatric, and substance-dependence disorders among jail inmates. *American Journal of Public Health, 100*(3), 476–482.

Bloom, B., Owen, B., & Covington, S. (2003). *Gender-responsive strategies: Research, practice, and guiding principles for women offenders.* Washington, DC: U.S. Department of Justice.

Brennan, J., Kuhns, L. M., Johnson, A. K., Belzer, M., Wilson, E. C., Garofalo, R., & Adolescent Medicine Trials Network for HIV/AIDS Interventions. (2012). Syndemic theory and HIV-related risk among young transgender women: The role of multiple, co-occurring health problems and social marginalization. *American Journal of Public Health, 102*(9), 1751–1757.

Bronson, J., Stroop, J., Zimmer, S., & Berzofsky, M. (2017). *Drug use, dependence, and abuse among state prisoners and jail inmates, 2007–2009.* Washington, DC: U.S. Department of Justice: Bureau of Justice Statistics.

Carson, E. A. (2018). *Prisoners in 2016.* Washington, DC: U.S. Department of Justice: Bureau of Justice Statistics.

Carson, E. A., & Golinelii, D. (2013). *Prisoners in 2012 – Advance counts.* Washington, DC: Bureau of Justice Statistics.

Cassaidy, M., & Lim, L. (2016, May). *The rights of transgender people in prisons.* Auckland, NZ: Equal Justice Project Symposium of University of Auckland.

Center on Addiction and Substance Abuse. (2010). *Behind bars II: Substance abuse and America's prison population* (pp. 1–120). New York: Center on Addiction.

Retrieved from https://www.centeronaddiction.org/addiction-research/reports/behind-bars-ii-substance-abuse-and-america%E2%80%99s-prison-population

Chesney-Lind, M. (2000). What to do about girls? Thinking about programs for young women. In M. W. McMahon (Ed.), *Assessment to assistance: Programs for women in community corrections* (pp. 139–170). Lanham, MD: American Correctional Association.

Chesney-Lind, M., & Pasko, L. (2013). *The female offender: Girls, women, and crime.* Thousand Oaks, CA: Sage.

Clear, T. R., Rose, D. R., Waring, E., & Scully, K. (2003). Coercive mobility and crime: A preliminary examination of concentrated incarceration and social disorganization. *Justice Quarterly, 20*, 33–64.

Cleary, P. (2015). Transgender and behind Bars. *Nev. Law, 23*, 8.

Constantine, R., Andel, R., Petrila, J., Becker, M., Robst, J., Teague, G., . . . Howe, A. (2010). Characteristics and experiences of adults with a serious mental illness who were involved in the criminal justice system. *Psychiatric Services, 61*(5), 451–457.

Covington, S. (1999). *Helping women recover: A program for treating addiction* (with a special edition for the criminal justice system). San Francisco: Jossey-Bass.

Covington, S. S., & Bloom, B. E. (2007). Gender-responsive treatment and services in correctional settings. *Women and Therapy, 29*, 9–33.

Daly, K. (1992). *Gender, crime, and punishment.* New Haven, CT: Yale University Press.

DeHart, D., Lynch, S., Belknap, J., Dass-Brailsford, P., & Green, B. (2014). Life history models of female offending: The roles of serious mental illness and trauma in women's pathways to jail. *Psychology of Women Quarterly, 38*(1), 138–151.

Fallot, R. D., McHugo, G. J., Harris, M., & Xie, H. (2011). The trauma recovery and empowerment model: A quasi-experimental effectiveness study. *Journal of Dual Diagnosis, 7*, 74–89.

Fashey, J., Roberts, C., & Engel, L. (2006). *Employment of ex-offenders: Employer perspectives.* Boston: Massachusetts Executive Office of Public Safety: Crime & Justice Institute.

Fedock, G., Fries, L., & Kubiak, S. (2013). Service needs for incarcerated adults: Exploring gender differences. *Journal of Offender Rehabilitation, 52*, 493–508.

Ferszt, G. G., & Clarke, J. G. (2012). Health care of pregnant women in US state prisons. *Journal of Health Care for the Poor and Underserved, 23*(2), 557–569.

Foster, H., & Hagan, J. (2009). The mass incarceration of parents in America: Issues of race/ethnicity, collateral damage to children, and prisoner reentry. *The Annals of the American Academy, 623*, 179–194.

Gehring, K. S. (2018). A direct test of pathways theory. *Feminist Criminology, 13*(2), 115–137.

Geraghty, K. A., & Woodhams, J. (2015). The predictive validity of risk assessment tools for female offenders: A systematic review. *Aggression and Violent Behavior, 21*, 25–38.

Gobeil, R., Blanchette, K., & Stewart, L. (2016). A meta-analytic review of correctional interventions for women offenders: Gender-neutral versus gender-informed approaches. *Criminal Justice and Behavior, 43*(3), 301–322.

Grant, J. M., Mottet, L., Tanis, J. E., Harrison, J., Herman, J., & Keisling, M. (2011). *Injustice at every turn: A report of the national transgender discrimination survey.* Washington, DC: National Center for Transgender Equality. Retrieved from https://www.transequality.org/sites/default/files/docs/resources/NTDS_Report.pdf

Greene, S., Haney, C., & Hurtado, A. (2000). Cycles of pain: Risk factors in the lives of incarcerated mothers and their children. *The Prison Journal, 80*, 3–23.

Grella, C. E., Lovinger, K., & Warda, U. (2013). Relationships among trauma exposure, familial characteristics, and PTSD: A case control study of women in prison and in the general population. *Women & Criminal Justice, 23*, 63–79.

Harawa, N. T., Amani, B., Bowers, J. R., Sayles, J. N., & Cunningham, W. (2017). Understanding interactions of formerly incarcerated HIV-positive men and transgender women with substance use treatment, medical, and criminal justice systems. *International Journal of Drug Policy, 48*, 63–71.

Harris, M., & Anglin, J. (1998). *Trauma recovery and empowerment: A clinician's guide for working with women in groups*. New York: The Free Press.

Heilbrun, K., Dematteo, D., Fretz, R., Erickson, J., Yasuhara, K., & Anumba, N. (2008). How "specific" are gender-specific rehabilitation needs? *Criminal Justice and Behavior, 35*, 1382–1397.

Hien, D., Cohen, L., Miele, G., Litt, L., & Capstick, C. (2004). Promising treatments for women with comorbid PTSD and substance use disorders. *American Journal of Psychiatry, 161*, 1426–1432.

Holtfreter, K., & Wattanaporn, K. A. (2014). The transition from prison to community initiative: An examination of gender responsiveness for female offender reentry. *Criminal Justice and Behavior, 41*(1), 41–57.

Hotelling, B. A. (2008). Perinatal needs of pregnant, incarcerated women. *The Journal of Perinatal Education, 17*, 37.

Huebner, B. M., DeJong, C., & Cobbina, J. (2010). Women coming home: Long-term patterns of recidivism. *Justice Quarterly, 27*, 225–254.

Hughto, J. M. W., Clark, K. A., Altice, F. L., Reisner, S. L., Kershaw, T. S., & Pachankis, J. E. (2017). Improving correctional healthcare providers' ability to care for transgender patients: Development and evaluation of a theory-driven cultural and clinical competence intervention. *Social Science & Medicine, 195*, 159–169.

Hunter, B. A., Lanza, A. S., Lawlor, M., Dyson, W., & Gordon, D. M. (2016). A strengths-based approach to prisoner reentry: The fresh start prisoner reentry program. *International Journal of Offender Therapy and Comparative Criminology, 60*(11).

James, D. J. (2004). *Profile of jail inmates, 2002* (NCJ No. 201932). Washington, DC: Bureau of Justice Statistics.

Jenness, V. (2015). Gender and sexuality as methodological confounds in the study of transgender prisoners. In *Envisioning criminology* (pp. 65–75). Cham: Springer.

Jenness, V., & Fenstermaker, S. (2014). Agnes goes to prison: Gender authenticity, transgender inmates in prisons for men, and the pursuit of "the real deal." *Gender & Society, 28*(1), 5–31.

Jenness, V., & Fenstermaker, S. (2016). Forty years after Brownmiller: Prisons for men, transgender inmates, and the rape of the feminine. *Gender & Society, 30*(1), 14–29.

Jenness, V., Maxson, C. L., Matsuda, K. N., & Sumner, J. M. (2007). Violence in California correctional facilities: An empirical examination of sexual assault. *Bulletin, 2*(2), 1–4.

Johnson, I. M. (2015). Women parolees' perceptions of parole experiences and parole officers. *American Journal of Criminal Justice, 40*, 785–810.

Jung, H., Herrenkohl, T. I., Lee, J. O., Hemphill, S. A., Heerde, J. A., & Skinner, M. L. (2017). Gendered pathways from child abuse to adult crime through internalizing and externalizing behaviors in childhood and adolescence. *Journal of Interpersonal Violence, 32*(18), 2724–2750.

Kaba, F., Lewis, A., Glowa-Kollisch, S., Hadler, J., Lee, D., Alper, H., . . . Venters, H. (2014). Solitary confinement and risk of self-harm among jail inmates. *American Journal of Public Health, 104*(3), 442–447.

Kazura, K. (2001). Family programming for incarcerated parents: A needs assessment among inmates. *Journal of Offender Rehabilitation, 32*, 67–83.

Kelly, P. (2015). Mass incarceration. *Public Health Nursing, 32*, 1–2.

Lattimore, P. K., Steffey, D. M., & Visher, C. A. (2010). Prisoner reentry in the first decade of the twenty-first century. *Victims and Offenders, 5*, 253–267.

Lattimore, P. K., & Visher, C. (2009). *The multi-site evaluation of SVORI: Summary and synthesis*. Washington, DC: U.S. Department of Justice.

Lenz, A. S., Henesy, R., & Callender, K. (2016). Effectiveness of seeking safety for co-occurring posttraumatic stress disorder and substance use. *Journal of Counseling & Development, 94*(1), 51–61.

Lydon, J., Carrington, K., Low, H., Miller, R., & Yazdy, M. (2015). Coming out of concrete closets a report on black and pink's national LGBTQ prisoner survey. *Black & Pink*. Retrieved January 12, 2019, from www.blackandpink.org

Lynch, S. M., DeHart, D. D., Belknap, J. E., Green, B. L., Dass-Brailsford, P., Johnson, K. A., & Whalley, E. (2014). A multisite study of the prevalence of serious mental illness, PTSD, and substance use disorders of women in jail. *Psychiatric Services, 65*(5), 670–674.

Makarios, M., Steiner, B., & Travis, L. F. (2010). Examining the predictors of recidivism among men and women released from prison in Ohio. *Criminal Justice and Behavior, 37*, 1377–1391.

Maruschak, L. M. (2008). *Medical problems of prisoners*. Washington, DC: U.S. Department of Justice Office, Bureau of Justice Statistics.

Mears, D. P., Cochran, J., & Bales, W. (2012). Gender differences in the effects of prison on recidivism. *Journal of Criminal Justice, 40*, 370–378.

Meerwijk, E. L., & Sevelius, J. M. (2017). Transgender population size in the United States: A meta-regression of population-based probability samples. *American Journal of Public Health, 107*(2), e1–e8.

Messina, N., Burdon, W., Hagopian, G., & Prendergast, M. (2006). Predictors of prison-based treatment outcomes: A comparison of men and women participants. *American Journal of Drug and Alcohol Abuse, 32*, 7–28.

Messina, N., Grella, C. E., Cartier, J., & Torres, S. (2010). A randomized experimental study of gender-responsive substance abuse treatment for women in prison. *Journal of Substance Abuse Treatment, 38*, 97–107.

Middlemass, K. (2017). *Convicted and condemned: The politics and policies of prisoner reentry*. New York: New York University Press.

Miller, H.V., Miller, J. M., & Barnes, J. C. (2016). Reentry programming for opioid and opiate involved female offenders: Findings from a mixed methods evaluation. *Journal of Criminal Justice, 46*, 129–136.

Miller, J. M. (2014). Identifying collateral effects of offender reentry programming through evaluative fieldwork. *American Journal of Criminal Justice, 39*(1), 41–58.

Morgan, R. D., Fisher, W. H., Duan, N., Mandracchia, J. T., & Murray, D. (2010). Prevalence of criminal thinking among state prison inmates with serious mental illness. *Law and Human Behavior, 34*, 324–336.

Mumola, C. J. (2000). *Incarcerated parents and their children*. Washington, DC: Bureau of Justice Statistics.

Najavits, L. M. (2002). *Seeking Safety: A treatment manual for PTSD and substance abuse*. New York: Guilford Press.

Najavits, L. M., Weiss, R. D., Shaw, S. R., & Muenz, L. R. (1998). "Seeking safety": Outcome of a new cognitive-behavioral psychotherapy for women with posttraumatic stress disorder and substance dependence. *Journal of Traumatic Stress, 11*, 437–456.

Osher, F. C. (2013). *Integrating mental health and substance abuse services for justice-involved persons with co-occurring disorders.* Retrieved from http://gainscenter.samsha.gov

Petersilia, J. (2001). Prisoner reentry: Public safety and reintegration challenges. *The Prison Journal, 81*(3), 360–375.

Reisig, M. D., Holtfreter, K., & Morash, M. (2006). Assessing recidivism risk across female pathways to crime. *Justice Quarterly, 23,* 384–405.

Reisner, S. L., Bailey, Z., & Sevelius, J. (2014). Racial/ethnic disparities in history of incarceration, experiences of victimization, and associated health indicators among transgender women in the U.S. *Women & Health, 54,* 750–767.

Routh, D., Abess, G., Makin, D., Stohr, M. K., Hemmens, C., & Yoo, J. (2017). Transgender inmates in prisons: A review of applicable statutes and policies. *International Journal of Offender Therapy and Comparative Criminology, 61*(6), 645–666.

Scroggins, J. R., & Malley, S. (2010). Reentry and the (unmet) needs of women. *Journal of Offender Rehabilitation, 49,* 146–163.

Sevelius, J., & Jenness, V. (2017). Challenges and opportunities for gender-affirming healthcare for transgender women in prison. *International Journal of Prisoner Health, 13*(1), 32–40.

Sexton, L., Jenness, V., & Sumner, J. M. (2010). Where the margins meet: A demographic assessment of transgender inmates in men's prisons. *Justice Quarterly, 27*(6), 835–866.

Smith, P., & Manchak, S. M. (2015). A gendered theory of offender rehabilitation. In F. Cullen, F. Adler, P. Wilcox, J. Lux, & C. L. Johson (Eds). *Sisters in Crime Revisited: Bringing Gender into Criminology* (pp. 371–395). New York: Oxford University Press.

Staton-Tindall, M., Duvall, J. L., Leukefeld, C., & Oser, C. B. (2007). Health, mental health, substance use, and service utilization among rural and urban incarcerated women. *Women's Health Issues, 17,* 183–192.

Steadman, H. J., Osher, F. C., Robbins, P. C., Case, B., & Samuels, S. (2009). Prevalence of serious mental illness among jail inmates. *Psychiatry Services, 60,* 761–765.

Sumner, J., & Jenness, V. (2014). Gender integration in sex-segregated U.S. prisons: The paradox of transgender correctional policy. In D. Peterson & V. Panfil (Eds), *Handbook of LGBT Communities, Crime and Justice* (pp. 229–259). New York: Springer.

Sumner, J., & Sexton, L. (2016). Same difference: The "dilemma of difference" and the incarceration of transgender prisoners. *Law & Social Inquiry, 41*(3), 616–642.

Taylor, C. J. (2015). Gendered pathways to recidivism: Differential effects of family support by gender. *Women & Criminal Justice, 25*(3), 169–183.

Travis, J. (2005). *But they all come back: Facing the challenges of prisoner reentry.* Washington, DC: The Urban Institute.

Van Voorhis, P., Salisbury, E., Wright, E. M., & Bauman, A. (2008). *Achieving accurate pictures of risk and identifying gender responsive needs.* Washington, DC: National Institute of Corrections, U.S. Department of Justice.

Van Voorhis, P., Wright, E. M., Salisbury, E., & Bauman, A. (2010). Women's risk factors and their contribution to existing risk/needs assessment: The current status of a gender-responsive supplement. *Criminal Justice & Behavior, 37,* 261–288.

Van Wormer, K. S., & Bartollas, C. (2007). *Women and the criminal justice system* (2nd ed.). Boston: Pearson Education.

Visher, C. A., LaVigne, N., & Travis, J. (2004). *Returning Home: Understanding the challenges of prisoner reentry.* Washington, DC: Urban Institute.

Visher, C. A., & Travis, J. (2001). Life on the outside: Returning home after incarceration. *The Prison Journal, 9,* 1025–1195.

Wattanaporn, K. A., & Holtfreter, K. (2014). The impact of feminist pathways research on gender-responsive policy and practice. *Feminist Criminology, 9*(3), 191–207.

Wolff, N., Frueh, B. C., Shi, J., & Schumann, B. E. (2012). Effectiveness of cognitive-behavioral trauma treatment for incarcerated women with mental illnesses and substance abuse disorders. *Journal of Anxiety Disorders, 26,* 703–710.

Women's Prison Association. (2009). *Mothers, infants and imprisonment: A national look at prison nurseries and community-based alternatives.* Retrieved from www.wpaonline.org

Wright, E. M., Salisbury, E. J., & Van Voorhis, P. (2009). Predicting the prison misconducts of women offenders: The importance of gender-responsive needs. *Journal of Contemporary Criminal Justice, 23,* 310–340.

Wright, E. M., Van Voorhis, P., Salisbury, E. J., & Bauman, A. (2012). Gender-responsive lessons learned and policy implications for women in prison: A review. *Criminal Justice and Behavior, 39*(12), 1612–1632.

Zlotnick, C., Clarke, J. G., Friedmann, P. D., Roberts, M. B., Sacks, S., & Melnick, G. (2008). Gender differences in comorbid disorders among offenders in prison substance abuse treatment programs. *Behavioral Sciences & the Law, 26,* 403–412.

Zlotnick, C., Najavits, L. M., Rohsenow, D. J., & Johnson, D. M. (2003). A cognitive-behavioral treatment for incarcerated women with substance abuse disorder and post-traumatic stress disorder: Findings from a pilot study. *Journal of Substance Abuse Treatment, 25,* 99–105.

Chapter 13

An Intersectional Criminology Analysis of Black Women's Collective Resistance

Nishaun T. Battle and Jason M. Williams

Historically, the State served as an instrument for the colonizing ruling class that possesses a self-serving interest designed to promote and reproduce social control through repression, oppression, and violence (Middlemass, 2017). Within the past decade, research on State-sanctioned violence has examined the relationship between the United States political and socioeconomic systems and repressive State policies (Willingham, 2018; Ritchie, 2017; Smith, 2016). This peculiar relationship between capitalism and socially constructed identities, designed and created through the exploitation of labor, has also created a criminal identity of those who make the choice to challenge these repressive policies (Muhammad, 2011). A critical analysis of race, class, and gendered politics emanating from both individual acts of resistance and within a network of radical organizations, with one common goal among Black women, illustrates the importance of Black women within the civil rights movement. Further, this examination extends into an economic analysis found at the intersection of State-sanctioned violence, the criminal legal system, and socially constructed identities (Gore, 2011).

What remains understudied in the field of critical criminology is the relationship between intersectionality, activism, and State-sanctioned violence. The purpose of this chapter is to illustrate the ways in which the State continues to construct and identify individuals and organizations as social threats, while engaging in repressive acts and State violence against Black bodies to maintain a fascist regime. This chapter examines historical themes and patterns of punishment faced by Black women radicals involved in activist networks, in particular, the Black Panther Party, which was a target of State violence, and present-day Black women who found themselves enmeshed within the criminal legal system for individual acts considered nonconforming to State authority. This chapter also advances an economic analysis of punishment by underscoring the importance of contextualizing punishment with an economic ideology and material conditions.

The purpose of utilizing intersectional criminology is to deconstruct the intricate complexities of the material, gendered, and oppressive social conditions faced by Black women in the Black community, which they fought to empower. Based on case studies, we underscore the historical and contemporary plight of Black women regarding their interactions with the State to argue that there is a direct connection between the oppressive tradition of punishing Black women based on their intersectional identities and the police-State that members of the Black Panther Party sought to eliminate. Specifically, we investigate the treatment of Black women activists by the State and the legal system and cases of Black women who were victims of State-sanctioned violence and considered dissident by the government.

The activism and rebellious acts of Angela Davis, Ericka Huggins, Assata Shakur, Sandra Bland, Jasmine Richards, and Korryn Gaines are included; these Black women vocalized their discontent with the State and the consequences resulted in their incarceration, death, or both (Spencer & Perlow, 2018). These women explicitly criticized the State's economic policies, its racialized laws that disproportionately impacted poor people of color and economically marginalized communities of all races, and its affiliation with radical interests of the State.

Intersectionality and Criminology

Potter's (2015) groundbreaking book on contextualizing intersectionality within the field of criminology draws from tenets of critical race theory and Black feminist thought (Collins, 1990). Potter's analysis centers the narratives of women and other socially constructed identities while highlighting the political and theoretical implications they encompass. Potter defines intersectional criminology as "a perspective that incorporates the intersectional or intersectionality concept into criminological research and theory and into the evaluation of crime or crime-related policies and laws and the governmental administration of justice" (Potter, 2015, p. 3). Burch (2013) examines how contemporary policies are harsh relics of punishment undergirded by political participation, arguing that a heightened form of punishment overpowered by the penal State hinders the political involvement of communities. Murakawa (2014) explores the rise in legalized punishment in the form of imprisonment that stems from the interplay between resistance and uprisings, and how law and order policies become more punitive based on actions considered dissident by the State.

Advancing a materialist analysis, Katz-Fishman, Gomes, and Scott (2007) argue that the effectiveness of the United States both historically and contemporarily is predicated upon: maintaining an exploitative labor relationship; reproducing inequity through a repressive social construction between the economy and social institutions; and fostering racial and gender oppression through racialized privileges created to maintain a monopoly of White-male-capitalist patriarchy (also see, hooks, 2000). On a systemic level, a materialist analysis suggests that the relationship between the capitalist economy and social institutions are solely designed to advance a White supremacist economic ideology. A materialist interface is supplanted by creating an unfair economic environment, which for many marginalized community members creates a pathway into the prison system, whereby the ruling class regime creates and reproduces a criminal class for their economic interests (Gonzalez & Katz-Fishman, 2010). Haley (2016) uncovers the brutality faced by Black women in the late nineteenth and early twentieth centuries by highlighting how structures of economic exploitation created and maintained a legalized system of convict labor grounded in supporting racial and gender ideologies and practices of capitalism (see also Middlemass' chapter earlier in this volume). State-created mechanisms of social control are designed to create fear and submissiveness in the masses, which operates as a symbolic warning to individuals and organizations considered rebellious and nonconforming.

Individuals may be aware of how their labor is used to maximize profits for the ruling class, but the dominant ideology has been so indelibly etched into the consciousness of the masses that they often believe that there is no alternative or equitable system (Katz-Fishman, Brewer, & Albrecht, 2007; Okazawa-Rey, 2018). Meanwhile, the poor are caught in an economic trap created by the ruling class, and some enter the incarcerating system, designed to police Black bodies physically and mentally in order to create what Marx calls, the "State-sanctioned man" (Reiman & Leighton, 2017; Gabbidon, 2007–2010). This form of policing poor bodies is designed as an apparatus of the State to control and repress efforts of social movement and mobilization.

One official group that was instrumental in initiating transformative sociopolitical and economic change was the Black Panther Party, which advocated for self-determination both economically and socially through the creation of social and economic programs (Spencer, 2016). These programs were needed to respond to the structural inequalities relegated primarily to poor, Black, and Brown communities. The State produced and reproduced oppressive laws and policies, a remnant of a period in which State oppression was legalized and extant (Alexander, 2010; Muhammad, 2011; Middlemass, 2017).

The Coming of the Black Panther Party (BPP)

Activism emerging out of the 1960s and 1970s in the United States was in response to a growing call for social and economic transformation based upon political, social, and cultural changes by groups considered marginalized (Thompson, 2009). Growing economic inequities and racial challenges led scores of young and emerging activists to subscribe to the ideology of Black Power and an advanced political understanding of the inherent socioeconomic contradictions immersed within the fabric of the country (see Van Deburg, 1992). The Black Power movement was viewed as an emerging effort to not only highlight injustices, such as dilapidated social institutions, poor housing infrastructures, mass unemployment, gun violence, drugs, a lack of necessary resources in school systems for Black people, but to also create solutions that would foster social justice for all people, in which both poor Black and White Americans would have a vested interest (McCartney, 1992).

During the mid-1960s, Black Americans were not afforded equal protection of the law and were often subjects of police brutality (Austin, 2006). Furthermore, the basic humanitarian goal of the BPP for the Black community was its ten-point program calling for freedom and self-determination, and included:

> obtain full employment, decent housing, education exposing the true nature of American society, exemption from military service for Black men, an immediate end to police brutality, freedom for all Black men in prisons and jails, to be tried in front of a court in front of their own peers, and the distribution and development of land, bread, housing, education, clothing, justice, and peace

> (Newton, 2009, pp. 4–5).

Within two years of its founding, the Black Panther Party grew into a national organization with chapters across the United States (Jones, 1988).

As Spencer (2016) argues, the BPP operated as a vehicle in which self-determination could be actualized through both theory and praxis by building alliances, engaging in direct activism, and developing a political ideology that would influence the masses that were politically oppressed. Bloom and Martin (2013) coined the term "strategic genealogy" to explain how the BPP developed a specific blueprint, including planning, organizing, and mobilizing against global capitalism. The BPP recognized the relationship between the base economy and the superstructures that colluded with each other to create and maintain socioeconomic oppression, and envisioned a society where social and economic freedom for Black and all oppressed communities was the norm, rather than the exception.

The role of Black women in the BPP did not differ from men in many ways according to Elaine Brown (1992) and included being armed for self-defense. Self-defense, an integral component of the Party designed to address police brutality by the State, was necessary for survival, because of the sanctioning of violence against poor, Black, and all oppressed people, which historically has been upheld by the courts in the United States (Smith, 2016). Several women were not only drawn to the militancy of the Black Panther Party, but were trained for tactical self-defense, which included women like Assata Shakur, Kathleen Cleaver, and women in the Black Liberation Army (see Perkins, 2000); others were drawn to the service programs geared towards the sustainability of the Black community. Brown noted that there were gendered expectations; Black women were assigned gendered roles, including cooking and cleaning, but Black women were also asked to use their bodies as weapons if a situation called for it. This included both the expectation of producing children to be future revolutionaries and enticing men who were considered the enemy into sexual encounters ending in their murder.

Black women were instrumental and necessary in the mobilization and organization of the BPP. Assata Shakur (1987) described the strategic planning of women in the BPP as including coordinated political objectives and armed and unarmed resistance aboveground that were aligned with organizing underground, all with the intention of supporting "actions that Black people would clearly understand and support" (p. 243).

As noted by Collier-Thomas and Franklin (2001), once Black women in the Party stepped outside of traditional gendered roles, the racist and sexist government agencies responded to them as they would their Black male comrades. As maintained by Eldridge Cleaver, Black women in or associated with the BPP were victims of the same State violence and repression experienced by their male counterparts, including police brutality, racial profiling, and excessive punishment in the criminal legal system; in the case of Ericka Huggins, law enforcement considered revolutionary women to be just as much a threat as men in the Party (Abu-Jamal, 2004). Black political activists involved in social movements conducting revolutionary actions, including massive Black rebellions, was a response to the extended history of social, material, and economic inequities and conditions (Churchill & Vander Wall, 1990).

State Repression and COINTELPRO

The ideas and activism of the Black Panther Party were not well-received by the State, and in response, the State resorted to extreme tactics to dismantle the organization and disempower its known and emerging leaders (Churchill & Vander Wall, 2002; Perkus, 1975). A specific ruling class initiative by the FBI was derived from a COunter INTELligence PROgram, called COINTELPRO; created by J. Edgar Hoover in 1956, the covert and at times illegal activities were designed to dismantle political groups who challenged the position of the United States government (Heynen, 2009). Specifically, the underlying motive of COINTELPRO operation was meant to "expose, disrupt, misdirect, discredit, or otherwise neutralize the activities of Black nationalist, hate-type organizations and groupings, their leadership, spokesmen, membership, and supports" (Perkus, 1975, p. 33).

The organizational structure and ideology entrenched in Hoover's FBI initiative were racist, and reflected the ideology of the State in terms of racialized terror directed at a small sector of society that the ruling class believed needed to be controlled (Haas, 2011; Shakur, 1987; Brown, 1992). According to O'Reilly, "The director and the men around him had a private conference for segregation within their own bureaucracy, and an institutional interest in letting it alone in those areas of the country where separate but equal ruled" (1989, p. 355). "J. Edgar Hoover and his proto-FBI organization, in kind with White vigilante formations, seem to have seen one of their primary missions as keeping Blacks 'in their place' by whatever repressive means were available" (Churchill & Vander Wall, 1990, p. 91).

Any Black power organization that adhered to the militant ideology of Malcolm X automatically became a COINTELPRO target (Drabble, 2008). Some of the organizations included the Black Liberation Army, the U.S. Movement by Ron Karenga, and the MOVE organization. By 1969, the Black Panther Party was a primary focus of government surveillance and was the target of 233 out of 295 authorized Black nationalist COINTELPRO operations (Day & Whitehorn, 2001). The FBI preferred COINTELPRO tactics included using covert human sources as a means to infiltrate targeted Black activist organizations to gather information on radical activists (Garrow, 1988); wiretapping, mail tampering, assassinations, and fabricating correspondence to create dissension among Black activist organizations (Churchill & Vander Wall, 1990); and targeting and arresting members of Black organizations were never viewed by the perpetrators as criminal activity. Instead, the FBI's activities were sanctioned by the State, resulted in numerous killings and false arrests leading to the imprisonment of several innocent Black women and men, and dismantled several radical organizations, including the Black Panther Party, the American Indian Movement, the Young Lords, the Brown Berets, the Lawyers Guild, and the Universal Negro Improvement Association (Churchill & Vander Wall, 1990; Perkus, 1975).

Analyzing State-Sanctioned Violence Against Black Activist Women: Six Case Studies

The Black women activists explored in this chapter illuminate an alarming pattern of State violence towards Black women who actively engaged or who vocalized discontent against imperialism, fascism, and State violence targeting Black communities, and include Angela Y. Davis, Ericka Huggins, Assata Shakur, Sandra Bland, Jasmine Richards, and Korryn Gaines. Their understanding of State violence, engagement with radical politics, and their political consciousness of social injustices exacerbated by racism, sexism, and classism led to their engagement in the dissemination of knowledge through activism. The case studies demonstrate that the Black women did not hold the same political views or advocacy tactics. Rather, their lived experiences reveal the ongoing legacy of State violence against Black female bodies. State violence, as contextualized here, is not only physical brutality by State agents, but intentional structural inequities that include poor health care, educational, legal, and community institutions. The Black women examined here prove that when Black women fight for the economically marginalized and against State sanctioned violence, the protection of the Black female body from the State is an afterthought (Crenshaw & Ritchie, 2015).

Angela Y. Davis, Assata Shakur, & Ericka Huggins

Angela Y. Davis was instrumental in the organization and strategic efforts of the Los Angeles chapter of the Student Non-Violent Coordinating Committee (SNCC), Ericka Huggins was active in the Los Angeles Chapter of the Black Panther Party, in addition to starting a chapter in New Haven, Connecticut, and Assata Shakur was active in both the Black Panther Party and the Black Liberation Army. These three Black radical women activists, as members or associates of the Black Panther Party, were targets of State violence and repression for fighting against systemic inequities and social injustices within the communities they sought to educate and empower. Using intersectional criminology as an analytic tool allows for the assessment of activism of a select few Black Panther Party women to juxtapose their implied definition of socioeconomic justice with that of the State.

Ture and Hamilton (2016) maintain that "colonial subjects have their political decisions made for them by the colonial masters, and those decisions are handed down directly or through a process of indirect rule" (2016, p. 6). This dialectical reproduction of social inequity was what Black women activists advocated against. Cleaver described, "our colonized status was the basis on which we organized for liberation; therefore, all members of the Black Panther Party were drawn from the colonized community" (Cleaver, 2005, p. 51).

Angela Y. Davis – Black Panther Party Affiliate/ Communist Party (Former)

Angela Y. Davis was one of the FBI's ten most wanted criminals and was subjected to anti-Panther counterintelligence operations by the FBI, which included State actors orchestrating the murder and attempted murder of BPP members and the States' attempts to deny funding for BPP legal defense efforts (Churchill & Vander Wall, 1990, 2002).

A prison fight at California's maximum-security Soledad Prison erupted between Black and White prisoners on the recreation yard; in response, and without a warning shot, Opie G. Miller, a correctional officer, shot and killed three Black prisoners and injured one White inmate, who lost a testicle after being shot in the groin. Several weeks after the incident, a prisoner died, and three prisoners, George Lester Jackson, Fleeta Drumgo, and John Wesley Clutchette, were indicted for first-degree murder for the death of fellow prisoner John V. Mills. In response to the indictment, a Soledad Brothers

Defense Committee was created to defend Jackson, Drumgo, and Clutchette; Angela Davis supported the men's defense efforts and became leader of the movement.

Jackson, Drumgo, and Clutchette went on trial in Marin County in August 1970, and during the trial Jackson's younger brother, Jonathon, held up the courtroom and took the judge, deputy district attorney, and three jury members hostage to secure the release of the "Soledad Brothers." In the melee, the judge, Jonathon, and two other prisoners on trial were killed. Angela Davis played an integral role; she purchased the guns used by Jonathon Jackson.

Davis was charged with first-degree murder, aggravated kidnapping, and criminal conspiracy, and a warrant was issued. On August 18, 1970, four days after the warrant was issued, Davis was listed on the FBI's Ten Most Wanted Fugitive List. She fled California and became a fugitive; in October, Davis was captured in a New York hotel by FBI agents, arrested, and sent back to the Marin County Superior Court for trial, where she faced the death penalty (Davis, 1988). Davis was initially represented by John Abt, general counsel at the time for the Communist Party, USA, and was held for a time in an isolation cell, in the city's Women's House of Corrections without bond (Churchill & Vander Wall, 1988, p. 96). During her trial, the guns she purchased and had registered in her name were used in an effort to make Davis an accessory to the conspiracy charge of murdering State agents (James, 1999). However, the State's efforts were insufficient; an all-White jury found Davis not guilty of all charges.

Davis faced imprisonment and the loss of her faculty position at UCLA based on her political and ideological beliefs and activism, which were deemed as threatening by the State. The policing of her body in a carceral space and punitive institutional measures based upon her freedom of speech highlights the State's violent practices against Black female activists through the criminal legal system (Ritchie, 2017).

Ericka Huggins – Black Panther Party

Ericka Huggins was born in Washington D.C. and married John Huggins, a Black Panther captain for the Southern California Black Panther Party chapter. Erika became a leader in the Los Angeles Black Panther chapter and lost her husband at the age of 23; John was killed during a shoot-out between the BPP and the U.S. Movement, another Black national collective, at an event held at UCLA on January 17, 1969 (Brown, 1992). Shortly after the assassination of John Huggins and Alprentice "Bunchy" Carter, Ericka, along with three other women, were ambushed in a massive raid by the Los Angeles Police Department (Churchill & Vander Wall, 1988). During the raid, a police officer placed a gun to the head of Huggins six-month-old baby and threatened to kill her baby (Churchill & Vander Wall, 1990).

Huggins and four other women were detained by law enforcement, who believed that they were part of a conspiracy planning to violently overthrow the U.S. Movement, whom COINTELPRO specifically targeted to create dissension between the two groups (Churchill & Vander Wall, 1990). Ericka was released on bail (Brown, 1992) and shortly thereafter moved to New Haven, Connecticut, to be closer to her husband's family.

Huggins began a Black Panther Party chapter in New Haven, started teaching a political education class for the Connecticut Panthers, and opened an experimental school in New Haven (Freed, 1973, pp. 300–301). Then, she was arrested on conspiracy charges, alongside Bobby Seale, for the killing of Black Panther Alex Rackley (Freed, 1973). Because of her previous actions, Huggins was in grave danger of being sentenced to death by the electric chair (Black Panther Party, 1971a, 1971b). Even though eight other members of the BPP were arrested on murder charges related to the death of Rackley, only Ericka Huggins and Bobby Seale were singled out in the media, which included mug shots and headlines targeting them (Freed, 1973). As she awaited trial, Huggins spent two years in isolation (Freed, 1973).

During the trial, the State placed Huggins at the scene of the crime and accused her of being an accessory to murder; she was described as being complicit in watching several pots of boiling water used to scald the victim. Yet on the sixth day of the trial, on May 24, 1971, it was announced that the jury "cannot reach a verdict in either case on any of the charges" (Freed, 1973, p. 329). Huggins and Seale were freed.

After the trial, Huggins moved back to Oakland, California, and resumed her social justice activism (Gore, Theoharis, & Woodard, 2009). Huggins was instrumental in the development and functioning of the Oakland Community School; in 1973, she became its director (Gore et al., 2009). The school, in particular, is one aspect of Huggins' relentless pursuit of justice in the face of oppression. The students and staff were racially diverse, and their pedagogical approach focused on the whole child, including dialectical training and modeling justice in the community. This genealogical pathway to freedom was borrowed by the women of the BPP, and provides a model of what a transformative society should look like (Gore et al., 2009).

As a result of years of service to the community and adherence to the BPP's ten-point platform, in 1976, Huggins was appointed as the first Black person and woman to serve on the Alameda County Board of Education (Gore, 2011). Despite Huggins serving her community unremittingly, she was viewed as an internal threat to the United States government; as a result, she was subjected to COINTELPRO's covert and repressive actions (Churchill & Vander Wall, 1988; Freed, 1973). Huggins' body was policed through the State's efforts, and was an example of racialized and gendered punishment of Black women, which has historically been cruel and rooted in racism in the criminal legal system. This form of racialized State violence against Black women is based on their resistance to the State's oppression (Battle, 2016).

Assata Shakur – Black Panther Party/Black Liberation Army

Assata Shakur joined the Black Panther Party in 1970 out of a dire need to determine the destiny of Black people (Shakur, 1987; Cleaver, 2005). Shakur fought for justice in her community, and her efforts included participating in the BPP's free breakfast program, health care, and the ongoing political education of community members. Despite her good works, Shakur was indicted ten times and had seven different criminal trials between 1973 and 1977. During this time, police alleged that she committed armed robbery, bank robbery, kidnapped a drug dealer, murdered a drug dealer, and attempted to murder police officers during an ambush; the cases were dismissed or Shakur was acquitted on all charges, except for one (Shakur, 1987).

In each case, Shakur served as her own co-defense counsel, and as a member of the Black Liberation Army (BLA), she stated during one of her trials:

> The idea of a Black Liberation Army emerged from conditions in Black communities: conditions of poverty, indecent housing, massive unemployment, poor medical care, and inferior education. The idea came about because Black people are not free or equal in this country. Because ninety percent of the men and women in this country's prisons are Black and Third world
>
> (Shakur, 1987, p. 169).

Shakur's notion of social justice addressed systemic complexities including social, economic, and political conditions (Shakur, 1987). In 1972, Shakur, as a target of COINTELPRO, was the subject of a nationwide manhunt for allegedly murdering a number of New York City police officers and being the de facto leader of the BLA. The police and FBI tried to connect Shakur to every suspected BLA action.

In 1973, while driving on the New Jersey Turnpike, the car Shakur was traveling in was pulled over by State Trooper James Harper, who was backed up by Trooper Werner Foerster in a second car. While the driver, Sundiata Acoli, was questioned by Harper, there was a confrontation; during the struggle, Shakur and Harper were wounded, Foerster was killed, and Zayd Shakur, the third person in the car with Assata, was fatally wounded. Acoli, Assata Shakur, and Zayd Shakur fled the scene, but were eventually caught. Zayd was dead from his bullet wounds and Assata was arrested and treated for gunshot wounds in her arms and shoulder; while shackled to her hospital bed, police punched and kicked her, and threatened several times to murder her (Shakur, 1987; Gore et al., 2009). This specific brutal treatment of a Black female body is a remnant of abuse from slavery (Davis, 2016).

The Turnpike shootout took place on May 2, 1973, and while waiting to go to trial she was in custody for four years. In the first trial, there was a mistrial declared by the prosecution because Shakur was pregnant. She gave birth while imprisoned, and the retrial took place in 1977. In March, Shakur was convicted on all eight counts, including for the murder of fellow BLA member, Zayd Shakur, and New Jersey Trooper Werner Foerster (Battle & Brown, 2014). Shakur was sentenced to 26 to 33 years in state prison. In 1979, a group of BLA members began to plan Shakur's escape; with the help of three BLA members who came to visit her at the Clinton Correctional Facility for Women in New Jersey, they were able to commandeer a van and escape. By 1984, Shakur was in Cuba, where she was granted political asylum, and continues to live in exile (Shakur, 1987).

#SayHerName/#BlackLivesMatter

Current Black women activists who are not officially members of a collective organization, but whose ideas align with the overarching Black power movement, Black Lives Matter, have been victims of State violence. Black women who have been victims of State violence have found a national platform of support situated within the Say Her Name movement (Crenshaw & Ritchie, 2015). The cases of Sandra Bland, Jasmine Richards, and Korryn Gaines are contextualized within the discussion of State violence against Black female bodies.

Sandra Bland – #SayHerName/#BlackLivesMatter

Sandra Bland had a substantial social media following and based on her viral videos was an activist in her own immediate community space; she spoke out against police brutality and social injustices on a platform she named #SandySpeaks (Nathan, 2016). In July 10, 2015, Bland was pulled over for a traffic violation and was questioned by the police, not for her violation of the law but based on her perceived verbal disrespect of a law enforcement officer (Spencer & Perlow, 2018). The confrontation was caught on videotape; the stop by a White police officer was deeply antagonistic and confrontational; his behavior and language demonstrated that he believed that he had the right to demand that Bland put her cigarette out.

Bland, while seated in her car, stated, "I am in my car. Why do I have to put out my cigarette?" Officer Encinia replied, "You can step on out now," indicating that Bland had to get out of her car. Bland remained calm and seated in her car. Encinia responded by manhandling Bland out of her car, which led to her arrest and detainment (Cevallos, 2015).

While detained, Bland was alleged to commit suicide in the county jail in Waller County, Texas. Her alleged suicide was suspicious and the police were not forthcoming with information about what took place while Bland was in police custody (Nathan, 2016). Unfortunately, this is not an unusual experience for Black women; how Black women are treated by law enforcement is a blatant disregard of their humanity and is the dire opposite of how White women are treated by law enforcement (O'Sullivan, 2016). Black women "stand at the intersection of race and gender" (Grillo, 2013, p. 18), which places them in a unique social position where their humanity often goes unrecognized (Haley, 2013). The opposing ways in which law enforcement treat Black women sends a warning message to Black girls, Black women, and the Black community in general.

Jasmine Richards – #BlackLivesMatter

Jasmine Richards, a Black Lives Matter organizer, is the founder of the Pasadena, California chapter of Black Lives Matter (Kolhatkar, 2016). As a Queer identified activist, who actively engaged in youth justice by organizing youth-based programs, Richards described growing up fearful of police violence being inflicted upon her body and her community. As her political consciousness grew, she organized around issues of State violence in an effort to promote social change to end police brutality (Garcia, 2016).

Her activism centered on police brutality; she joined a freedom caravan traveling from Pasadena, California, to Ferguson, Missouri, to protest against the killing of Mike Brown (Garcia, 2016) and protested against police brutality when Kendrec McDade, a Black teenager, was killed by police, in 2012. As Richards was returning home from a peaceful protest in commemoration of Kendrec McDade on August 29, 2015, a restaurant owner called the police and accused an unidentified Black woman of allegedly not paying for her meal. When the police arrived on the scene, they arrested a woman; a video showed Richards and additional Black Lives Matter activists running to aid and protect the woman from any potential police brutality. As a result of her actions, Richards was arrested two days later under a California law called a "felony lynching" (Gyamfi & Abdullah, 2016). Richards was initially charged with "inciting a riot, child endangerment, delaying and obstructing peace officers, and felony lynching" (Massie, 2016). However, most of those charges were dismissed, and the only charge remaining was felony lynching; originally, when the law was established in 1933, it was designed to protect Black and Latino populations from racist lynch mobs (Garcia, 2016). Richards was the first African American to be charged under the 1933 law.

Richards was convicted by an all non-Black jury and faced up to four years in prison. Richards' attorney, Nana Gyamfi, argued that the arrest and sentencing of Richards was a deliberate act of State oppression against Black activists and was designed to thwart any efforts at organizing and mobilizing the masses around issues of State violence (Garcia, 2016). In the end, Richards was sentenced to 90 days in jail minus time served, three years' probation, and was ordered to take 53 courses in anger management (Kolhatkar, 2016). As a Queer activist and organizer, the prosecution asked the judge, as a part of her sentencing, to order Richards away from a park where her youth programs were based. This did not occur, but was a possibility.

Korryn Gaines – #SayHerName

Based on a historical and gendered ideology that devalues and renders Black women invisible based on their socially constructed identities, punishment is often harsher for Black women than for White women (Williams & Battle, 2017; Battle, 2016). Korryn Gaines was considered a nonconforming person critical of the State. The performative neo-lynching of Gaines ended in a standoff between her and the Baltimore police, which resulted in her untimely death while holding her five-year-old son. Many celebrated her death and believed it was justified based on her unwillingness to acquiesce to law enforcement authoritarian orders (Spencer & Perlow, 2018).

The specific details leading to the death of Gaines and the preceding events are still unclear, and since Gaines is no longer living, she is unable to provide her account of the fatalistic event or the predicating events. What is known, however, is that she maintained her innocence and attempted to document the State's violence against her. In that documentation, she maintained her innocence against the larger system of structural and State violence.

Gaines recorded her own words, and said:

> I'm muthafucking tired, but the devil at my door, and he's refusing to leave. I'm at peace. I'm in my home. I ain't trying to hurt nobody. . . . They been quiet a while so they plotting to come in here and disturb the peace. . . . I am not a criminal
> (Knezevich & Rector, 2016).

The fact that Gaines used the specific language explicitly demanding to be seen as a valued woman and not a constructed criminal, speaks volumes to the ways in which punishment varies based on intersectional identities, insofar as a Black woman's identity. Gaines felt the need to defend her honor and record her thoughts, as if she knew that the White, male, supremacist, patriarchal regime at her door would not believe her.

Conclusion: Relevance of Intersectional Criminology

The reproduction of State violence and targeted initiatives against Black power movements were designed to dismantle individuals and organizations that were and are effective at raising the consciousness of the masses to social injustices, and there is a recurring theme; Black women continue to be under-protected by the State and policed harshly (Ritchie, 2017). In considering the role that intersectionality plays in the criminal legal system, the experiences of Black women in or affiliated with Black power movements illustrates the powerful presence of the State during their revolutionary activism, and Black women are an integral part of the Black power struggle. Bobby Seale conducted a survey of BPP membership in 1969, and responses revealed that two-thirds of the Party's members were women (Cleaver, 1998). The Black Lives Matter movement was started by activist Black, Queer-identified women, who saw a repeated pattern of abuse by law enforcement sanctioned by the State; these Black Queer-activist women organized and mobilized around the central issue of social justice.

A revolutionary criminological approach can advance analyses regarding State patterns of abuse against oppressed people in the United States (Williams & Battle, 2017), such as those patterns against Bland and Gaines, while intersectional criminology argues for the merging of theory and praxis that centers the voices of those who work in collaboration for social change as a social science methodological foundation (Potter, 2015). At the core of these troubling patterns is how the State constructs structural inequalities and punishes activists for attempting to transform an exploitative system. A component of intersectional criminology maintains that activism by Black women during the Black Power movement and contemporary social justice movements addresses the needs of the entire Black community. Black women activists played multiple roles both within and on the front lines of the movement for social justice, to prepare and create a world embodying equality and fairness.

As illustrated by J. Edgar Hoover's program, technically ending on April 28, 1971, the FBI used tactics, such as violence and deceit, disguised under the notion of State justice, to suppress the democratic rights afforded to every citizen. As maintained by Allen (2005), "Blacks were under control of a criminal justice system in which they had no power" (p. 3). Davis and Huggins were victorious against State repression, and eventually were set free. Although Korryn Gaines and Sandra Bland were not known to be members of a specific social justice organization, what is known is that they were fierce advocates against State-sanctioned violence.

State-sanctioned violence is an increasing phenomena, especially against Black bodies, and in response the literature examining State-sanctioned violence is growing (Hill, 2016; Lowery, 2016). These works are critical to our understanding of State-sanctioned violence, and when the narratives and lives of Black women are center, intersectional criminology makes Black women an integral part of the analysis of punishment, activism, and State violence. Such an approach allows for the examination of the treatment of Black women by the State in America and exposes the historical tenets of State repression and power inequities. Intersectional criminology provides insights that will benefit current and future scholar-activists who examine historical and contemporary events, and stands on the traditions of Black feminist theoretical analysis. Lastly, intersectional criminology offers a new way to conduct historical analysis of the material conditions of society and Black women's experience.

References

Abu-Jamal, M. (2004). *We want freedom*. Cambridge, MA: South End Press. Retrieved from https://act.colorofchange.org/sign/freejasmine-no-jail-time-black-lives-matter-activist-accused-lynching/?

Alexander, M. (2010). *The new Jim Crow: Mass incarceration in the age of colorblindness*. New York: The New Press.

Allen, R. L. (2005). Reassessing the internal (neo) colonialism theory. *The Black Scholar, 35*(1), 2–11.

Austin, C. J. (2006). *Up against the wall: Violence in the making and unmaking of the Black Panther Party*. Fayetteville: The University of Arkansas Press.

Battle, N. (2016). From slavery to Jane Crow to Say Her Name: An intersectional examination of Black women and punishment. *Meridians: Feminism, Race, Transnationalism, 15*(1), 109–136.

The Black Panther. (1970, Saturday December 26). To the Concerned People of New York.

The Black Panther. (1971a, Saturday March 6). Bobby's and Ericka's struggle is our struggle.

The Black Panther. (1971b, Saturday March 6). The trial of Bobby Seale and Ericka Huggins.

Bloom, J., & Martin, W. (2013). *Black against empire: The history and politics of the Black Panther Party*. Berkley, CA: University of California Press.

Brown, E. (1992). *A taste of power: A Black woman's story*. New York: First Anchor Books.

Burch, T. (2013). *Trading democracy for justice: Criminal convictions and the decline of neighborhood political participation*. Chicago, IL: University of Chicago Press.

Cevallos, D. (2015). *Was the Sandra Bland traffic stop legal – and fair?* Retrieved from www.cnn.com/2015/07/23/opinions/cevallos-sandra-bland-traffic-stop/index.html

Churchill, W., & Vander Wall, J. (1988). *Agents of repression: The FBI's secret wars against the Black Panther Party and the American Indian movement*. Cambridge, MA: South End Press Classics.

Churchill, W., & Vander Wall, J. (1990). *The cointelpro papers: Documents from the FBI's secret wars against dissent in the United States*. Cambridge, MA: South End Press Classics.

Churchill, W., & Vander Wall, J. (2002). *The cointelpro papers: Documents from the FBI's secret wars against dissent in the United States* (2nd ed.). Cambridge, MA: South End Press Classics.

Cleaver, K. (1971, April 3). Reply to the article. *Free Kathleen*.

Cleaver, K. (2005). The fugitive. *Essence Magazine*. Former Black Panther Assata Shakur-a mother, grandmother, painter and poet-has been living in exile in Cuba for decades. So why has the FBI now placed a million-dollar bounty on her head?

Cleaver, K. N. (1998). Women, power, and revolution. In C. Jones (Ed.), *The Black Panther Party reconsidered*. Baltimore, MD: Black Class Press.

Collier-Thomas, B., & Franklin, V. P. (2001). *Sisters in the struggle: African American women in the civil rights-Black power movement*. New York: New York University Press.

Collins, P. (1990). *Black feminist thought: Knowledge, consciousness, and the politics of empowerment*. New York: Routledge.

Crenshaw, K., & Ritchie, A. J. (2015). *Say her name: Resisting police brutality against Black women*. New York: The African American Policy Forum. Retrieved from http://aapf.org/sayhernamereport

Davis, A. (1988). *An autobiography*. New York: International Publishers.

Davis, A. (2016). *Freedom is a constant struggle: Ferguson, Palestine, and the foundations of a movement*. Chicago, IL: Haymarket Books.

Day, S., & Whitehorn, L. (2001). Human rights in the United States: The unfinished story of political prisoners and COINTELPRO. *New Political Science, 23*(2), 285–297.

Drabble, J. (2008). Fighting Black power-new left coalitions: Covert FBI media campaigns and American cultural discourse, 1967–1971. *European Journal of American Culture, 27*(2).

Freed, D. (1973). *Agony in New Haven: The trial of Bobby Seale, Ericka Huggins & the Black Panther Party*. Los Angeles, CA: Figueroa Press.

Gabbidon, S. L. (2007–2010). *Criminological perspectives on race and crime* (2nd ed.). New York: Routledge.

Garcia, F. (2016). *California Black lives matter activist convicted of 'felony lynching'*. Retrieved from www.independent.co.uk/news/world/americas/jasmine-richards-felony-lynching-black-lives-matter-california-a7064726.html

Garrow, D. J. (1988). FBI political harassment and FBI historiography: Analyzing informants and measuring the effects. *The Public Historian, 10*(4).

Gonzalez, B., & Katz-Fishman, W. (2010). New openings for movement and consciousness in the U.S. *Interface: A Journal For and About Social Movements, 2*(1), 232–242.

Gore, D. F. (2011). *Radicalism at the crossroads: African American women activists in the cold war*. New York and London: New York University Press.

Gore, D. F., Theoharis, J., & Woodard, K. (2009). *Want to start a revolution? Radical women in the Black freedom struggle*. New York and London: New York University Press.

Grillo, T. (2013). Anti-essentialism and intersectionality: Tools to dismantle the master's house. *Berkeley Journal of Gender, Law & Justice, 10*(1), 16–30.

Gyamfi, N., & Abdullah, M. (2016). *Black lives matter activist convicted of "Felony Lynching": "It's more than ironic, it's disgusting"*. Retrieved from www.democracynow.org/2016/6/2/black_lives_matter_activist_convicted_of

Haas, J. (2011). *The assassination of Fred Hampton: How the FBI and the Chicago Police murdered a Black Panther*. Chicago, IL: Lawrence Hill Books/Chicago Review Press.

Haley, S. (2013). 'Like I was a man': Chain gangs, gender, and the domestic carceral sphere in Jim Crow Georgia. *Signs: Journal of Women in Culture and Society, 39*(1), 53–77.

Haley, S. (2016). *No mercy here: Gender, punishment, and the making of Jim Crow modernity*. Chapel Hill, NC: University of North Carolina Press.

Heynen, N. (2009). Bending the bars of empire from every ghetto for survival: The Black Panther Party's radical antihunger politics of social reproduction and scale. *Annals of the Association of American Geographers, 99*(2), 406–422.

Hill, M. L. (2016). *Nobody: Casualities of America's war on the vulnerable, from Ferguson to flint & beyond*. New York: Atria Books.

hooks, bell. (2000). *Feminism is for everybody: Passionate politics*. New York: Routledge.

James, J. (1999). *Shadowboxing: Representation of Black feminist politics*. New York: St. Martin's Press.

Jones, C. (1988). The political repression of the Black panther party 1966–1971: The case of the Oakland Bay area. *Journal of Black Studies, 18*(4), 415–434.

Katz-Fishman, W., Brewer, R., & Albrecht, L. (2007). *The critical classroom: Education for liberation and movement building.* Atlanta: Project South.

Katz-Fishman, W., Gomes, R., & Scott, J. (2007). Materialism. In G. Ritzer (Ed.), *Blackwell encyclopedia of sociology* (Vol. VI). Oxford, England and New York: Blackwell Publishing.

Knezevich, A., & Rector, K. (2016). *Investigative files provide new insights into Korryn Gaines' 6-hour standoff with Baltimore County police.* Retrieved from www.baltimoresun.com/news/maryland/investigations/bs-md-co-korryn-gaines-timeline-20161103-story.html

Kolhatkar, S. (2016). *Partial victory for Black lives matter activist Jasmine Richards.* Retrieved from www.commondreams.org/views/2016/06/10/partial-victory-black-lives-matter-activist-jasmine-richards

Lowery, W. (2016). *They can't kill us all: Ferguson, Baltimore, and a New Era in America's racial justice movement.* New York: Little, Brown, & Company.

Massie, V. (2016). *What activist Jasmine Richards's "lynching" conviction means for the Black lives matter movement.* Retrieved from www.vox.com/2016/6/6/11839620/jasmine-richards-black-lives-matter-lynching

McCartney, J. T. (1992). *Black power ideologies: An essay in African American political thought.* Philadelphia, PA: Temple University Press.

Middlemass, K. (2017). *Convicted and condemned: The politics and policies of prisoner reentry.* New York: New York University Press.

Muhammad, K. (2011). *The condemnation of Blackness: Race, crime, and the making of modern Urban America.* Cambridge, MA: Harvard University Press.

Murakawa, N. (2014). *The first civil right: How liberals built Prison America.* New York: Oxford University Press.

Nathan, D. (2016). *What happened to Sandra Bland?* Retrieved from www.thenation.com/article/what-happened-to-sandra-bland/

Newton, H. (2009). *To die for the people: The writings of Huey P. Newton.* New York: Random House. Retrieved from www.nydailynews.com/news/national/jasmine-richards-prisoner-black-lives-matter-article-1.2659110

Okazawa-Rey, M. (2018). No freedom without connection. In C. T. Mohanty & L. E. Carty (Eds.), *Feminist freedom warriors: Genealogies, justice, politics, and hope.* Chicago, IL: Haymarket Books.

O'Reilly, K. (1989). *Racial matters: The FBI's secret file on Black America.* New York: The Free Press, A Division of Macmillan, Inc.

O'Sullivan, S. (2016). Who is always already criminalized? An intersectional analysis of criminality on *orange is the new Black. The Journal of American Culture, 39*(4), 401–412.

Perkins, M. V. (2000). *Autobiography as activism: Three Black women of the sixties.* Jackson: University Press of Mississippi.

Perkus, P. (1975). *Cointelpro: The FBI's secret war on political freedom.* New York: Monad Press.

Potter, H. (2015). *Intersectionality and criminology: Disrupting and revolutionizing studies of crime (New Directions in Critical Criminology).* London and New York: Routledge.

Reiman, J., & Leighton, P. (2017). *The rich get richer and the poor get prison: Ideology, class, and criminal justice.* New York: Routledge. Retrieved form www.cnn.com/2016/09/15/us/sandra-bland-wrongful-death-settlement/

Ritchie, A. J. (2017). *Invisible no more: Police violence against Black women and women of color.* Boston, MA: Beacon Press.

Shakur, A. (1987). *Assata: An autobiography*. Chicago, IL: Lawrence Hill Books, Chicago Review Press.

Smith, A. L. (2016). Black women matter: Neo-capital punishment ideology in the wake of state violence. *The Journal of Negro Education, 85*(3), 261–273.

Spencer, R. (2016). *The revolution has come: Black power, gender, and the Black Panther Party in Oakland*. Durham, NC: Duke University Press.

Spencer, Z., & Perlow, O. (2018). Sassy mouths, unfettered spirits, and the neo-lynching of Korryn Gaines and Sandra Bland: Conceptualizing Post Traumatic Slave Master Syndrome (PTSMS) and the familiar "Policing" of Black women's resistance in 21st century America. *Meridians, 17*(1), 163–183.

Thompson, H. (2009). *Speaking out: Activism and protest in the 1960s and 1970s*. New York: Routledge.

Ture, K., & Hamilton, C. V. (2016). *Black power: The politics of liberation in America*. New York: Vintage Books.

Van Deburg, W. L. (1992). *New day in Babylon: The Black power movement and American culture, 1965–1975*. Chicago and London: The University of Chicago Press.

Williams, J., & Battle, N. (2017). African Americans and punishment for crime: A critique of mainstream and neoliberal discourses. *Journal of Offender Rehabilitation, 56*(8), 552–566.

Willingham, B. C. (2018). Black women and state-sanctioned violence: A history of victimization and exclusion. *Canadian Review of American Studies, 48*(1), 77–94.

Chapter 14

Gender Differences in Programmatic Needs for Juveniles

Laurin Parker and Kylie Parrotta

Gender Differences in Programmatic Needs for Juveniles

Juvenile programing is designed to assist adolescent offenders with their transition to adulthood, and for programming to be successful, it must be tailored towards the needs of specific offenders. The existing reentry programming or transitional services for juveniles are frequently divided between "what works" and gender-specific treatment. The "what works" services highlight empirically tested programs with clearly defined treatment goals. For instance, some programing includes structured mentoring with built-in group planning and counseling sessions (Bouffard & Bergseth, 2008) and educational and job placement programing (Inderbitzin, 2005). Gender-specific programming tends to focus on issues likely to affect juvenile females, such as risk and resiliency. Gender-responsive programs are considered to be effective primarily because of their attention to how social contexts shape teen girls' lives, the factors leading to their delinquency, and are grounded in understanding characteristics that shape female offending (Hubbard & Matthews, 2007, pp. 230–231). Hubbard and Matthews (2007) conclude that both types of programming – "what works" and gender-specific programs – have value for juvenile females.

Other gender-specific programming research focuses on explicit risk factors, gendered needs of juveniles, and available programming options. In their study of pre-adjudicated and adjudicated girls, Belknap and Cady (2008) find girls have fewer placement options and programs with specific attention to their needs when compared to boys. Foley (2008) argues that programming for young women offenders requires more focus on the risk factors in comparison to program for young men. For instance, having a history of victimization (Miller, 2001; Belknap, 2007; Dougherty, 2008; Belknap & Holsinger, 2008), experiencing family disruption (American Bar Association and National Bar Association, 2001; Miller, 2001; Chesney-Lind & Shelden, 1998), and lacking a sufficient level of education and legitimate employment (Snyder & Sickmund, 2006) are some of the characteristics associated with female juvenile offending. Chesney-Lind (2008) found that fewer than 8% of reentry-based programs provided services for girls between the ages of 9 and 15, which misses the "at risk" years. Chesney-Lind argues programming should focus on overlapping issues girls are likely to encounter, such as providing treatment and therapy to young parents, rather than focusing on single issues, such as teen pregnancy or mothering. Programs for young women tend to be reactive rather than preventive (Chesney-Lind, 2008, p. 264).

Regardless of gender, most residential programs incorporate developmental perspectives and employ a "continuity of care" approach as young offenders age (Altschuler & Brash 2004 Chung, Little, & Steinberg, 2005). Programs rooted in corrections-community partnerships and that follow a continuity of care approach show effective results for juvenile offenders with substance abuse problems (Henderson, Young, Jainchill, Hawke, Farkas, & Davis, 2007). Despite substance abuse programing being frequently offered to juvenile offenders who use alcohol and drugs, the scope of programs varies (Young, Dembo, & Henderson, 2007). Treatment for substance-abusing adolescents typically falls on a continuum of treatment interventions ranging from minimal outpatient contacts to long-term residential treatment (Center for Substance Abuse Treatment, 1999).

Reentry programming provides a foundation for understanding what types of support girls require while under correctional supervision, but scholars rarely consider the perspective of the girls themselves. Garcia and Lane (2010) offer an exception by interviewing adult women who had previous involvement with the justice system as juvenile offenders. Their respondents wanted prevention programming and grief counseling, which challenges the claim that juvenile offenders just want vocational programming. Moreover, differences emerge when male and female offenders are asked about programming needs.

Gender-specific programming recognizes that male and female juvenile offenders have different needs prior to and upon their release from correctional supervision. Research findings, however, indicate that there exists a need for programs to respond to the specific needs of female juvenile offenders. Based on survey research, Fields and Abrams (2010) find female juvenile offenders had greater concerns about housing situations and were more receptive to therapeutic counseling. Sedlak and McPherson (2010) found a lukewarm relationship between the staff and youth in custody. In their study, 49% of youth described staff as friendly, 47% thought staff was helpful, and 40% considered staff difficult to get along with (Sedlak & McPherson, 2010). In contrast, Marsh and Evans (2004) find that a good rapport between staff members and offenders is related to juveniles' perception of success. For instance, when there is a balance in coping strategies and closeness between the staff members and juvenile offenders, the offenders will perceive that reentry success is possible. Youth residing in community-based treatment facilities and residential treatment programs reported the most positive relationship with the staff members. Therefore, juvenile offenders' relationship with staff members can be an important consideration in not only understanding the climate in juvenile facilities but also gaining insight in the role that staff members can play in the reentry success of juvenile offenders.

Although not all juvenile offenders in residential facilities take full advantage of the programming available to them, the goal here is to answer key questions related to whether or not juveniles who do participate in the offered programs benefit and if they see the programming as useful. Specifically, are programs meeting the needs of young men and women and addressing their reentry concerns? Do staff members think that programs are working and what do they think should be improved? To answer these questions, young men and women offenders' perceptions of services and supports they receive in residential program-based transitional facilities prior to their release are examined. Correctional staff members were also interviewed to see how they perceive the type of programming and services offered to residents in their custody in comparison to the types of programming staff members consider important for the successful reentry of juvenile residents.

Setting & Method

In order to protect the anonymity of the correctional institutions, participating programs, juvenile offenders, and staff members, pseudonyms are used throughout this chapter. Access to juvenile residents and staff members was facilitated by the superintendent of the residential programs, program managers, and staff members. As residents were juveniles, recruitment letters were sent to program managers, who then forwarded them, by mail or in-person, to parents and/or guardians. The recruitment letter provided information about the study, inquired about their child's potential interest in participating in this study, and asked for consent. In cases when a parent or guardian was unavailable or did not respond, consent was obtained from the state, as the state acts as the legal guardian (*parens patriae*) of residents under age 18.

From August 2011 to May 2012, 21 interviews were conducted with female residents at Delta Residence Program, ten interviews were conducted with males at Community Betterment or the Foundation School, and six interviews were conducted with staff members. All of the interviews with the juvenile residents occurred on-site at one of the three residential program facilities, which serviced either male or female juvenile offenders who were nearing release from correctional supervision. With the exception of one staff interview, the staff interviews took place at the residential facilities.

The Delta Residence Program was for female offenders typically between the ages of 16 and 17 years of age with unstable home lives and poor school records. The second site, Community Betterment, was a residential treatment program for juvenile males between the ages of 16 and 17 who faced difficulties related to academic challenges, unstable home lives, or with community-based services; they typically stayed for 90 days. The third site, the Foundation School, housed adjudicated juvenile males, typically for six months prior to their release back into the community. Foundation School residents were characterized as serious or chronic offenders and considered to be a public risk. Residents were required to attend educational classes and credits could be applied towards high school diplomas or GEDs. Residents could receive home passes and attend outside counseling services during their time at the facility.

All participants completed a subject demographic form. Of the 21 young women interviewed, 38% (8) identified as African-American or Black, 19% (4) as Caucasian or White, 14% (3) as Hispanic or Latino, and 29% (6) as multiracial. Three participants were currently pregnant and two were mothers. Of the ten male offenders interviewed, 40% (4) identified as African-American or Black, 30% (3) as Caucasian or White, and 30% (3) as multiracial. Juvenile respondents ranged in age from 13–17, and 13 women and five men reported being in relationships. The majority of participants had prior arrest records accompanied by previous stays in detention facilities; therefore, participants in this study are uniquely positioned to criticize the system.

The six staff members who were interviewed included three women and three men; they held titles of male youth rehabilitative counselor, male treatment specialist supervisor, family crisis therapist, treatment specialist, and youth rehabilitation and treatment specialist. Five staff members identified as African-American or Black and one as White. The staff members who were interviewed had at least a high school diploma and two had Master's degrees.

Juvenile Residents' on Juvenile Programming

Juvenile participants responded favorably to individual and family counseling sessions; individual sessions were provided by either licensed therapists or residential program staff. Five of the young women and two of the young men valued individual sessions that allowed them to express their feelings while concentrating on their own personal issues. Another 11 respondents reported family counseling sessions as being the most beneficial.

DeVaughn (17, African-American) was a repeat resident of the Foundation School whose criminal history included robbery. During a previous stint at a residential program, DeVaughn was involved in two physical altercations with other residents; he had to be physically restrained by staff members. Yet he still perceived staff as being invested in his personal rehabilitation. In particular, he was fond of the one-on-one interactions with staff that enabled him to better control his emotions and behavior during negative encounters.

Similarly, Chris (17, White), whose delinquent history included property crime, robbery, drug use, and probation violations, said individual counseling sessions helped him gauge his temper and other emotions. He said:

> I always keep things bottled up and you don't wanna keep things bottled up cause if you do, one day you're just gonna, you know, pop. And that's not good so it's good to have one-on-one and have a therapist and a shrink. . . . I know where my emotions stand at.

Individual counseling sessions facilitated the young men's emotional growth and helped them to better control their emotions. DeVaughn focused on how various staff members helped him control how he responded to confrontations whereas Chris spoke of his time with professionals as helping him manage his emotions. These respondents' experiences are representative of other young men in the sample.

Young women also reported that individual counseling session were beneficial. Kristin (17, White), a repeat resident, had a history of petty theft. Kristin explained her strained relationship with her mother, a recurring theme for women in this sample, and relied on her grandmother for emotional support. Kristen said counseling helped address personal issues she was uncomfortable discussing with others. Kristin found comfort in therapy, and remarked:

> My mom would judge me for what I tell her and friends would judge me because they don't really care. Like here, you sit down with staff and the therapist that works here. She sits down and talks about what you're thinking about, what's going on. She'll like help you through it and stuff.

Participants found the family counseling sessions helpful, as they entailed parents or guardians being involved in sessions with the resident. Eleven respondents, only one of which was a male juvenile, thought these sessions were good, and that counselors provided a "safe space" to discuss trauma, abuse, and delinquency with their family members.

Maria (18, Latina), whose charges include terroristic threatening, had cycled through foster care families but planned to live with her biological mother after release, and was especially anxious about reentry. During family counseling sessions, Maria and her mother talked through the challenges, like not violating probation and learning to live at home. Two currently pregnant residents expressed that family counseling sessions were helpful for repairing their relationships with their mothers, which was especially important to them since they were about to have their own children. Alongside ten women, Mr. Chandler (Staff, African-American), a Youth Rehabilitative Counselor, reported that family counseling was beneficial, as such sessions helped understand family dynamics, especially with step-family members.

Youth respondents viewed positively the substance abuse and relapse prevention programs. Fifteen participants had taken part in such programming led by staff members, but it was not always a substance abuse specialist who would run the program. However, one benefit reported by several respondents was learning how drugs and alcohol affected their bodies alongside drug-refusal skills. While on probation, Judy (16, Multiracial) tested positive for prescription painkillers, which led to her current detainment. Judy's immediate family members used drugs and her mother had been imprisoned for possession. Judy relied on her mother and grandmother for emotional support and spoke positively of the substance abuse treatment program. She said it was useful and explained, "We learn about the drugs that you use and why you shouldn't use them and the effects that it has on your body."

Other residents said the programs encouraged them to recognize their problems with substance and alcohol abuse. DeVaughn had problems with marijuana and alcohol, and claimed that most of his friends sold drugs. He found lessons on resisting peer temptation beneficial; however, he maintained that he would continue to associate with his friends after release, suggesting the program only had a temporal effect. Whitney (15, White) struggled with using marijuana, prescription pills, hallucinogens, liquor, and abusing cold medicine for three years; he acknowledged that the substance abuse treatment program offered in her facility helps her maintain her sobriety. She said,

> I know it's going to be hard when I have to go back out and stay away from it, but I believe that I can do that. Yeah. It's kept me sober for a while. It's gonna keep me sober for a while so I mean I can actually have straight thinking now.

Like DeVaughn, Whitney knew her friends' drug and alcohol use had a negative influence on her. They both acknowledged avoiding drugs would be difficult after transitioning out of their respective facility.

The self-reflection process was difficult for Tasha (17, Latina), who did not understand the severity of her alcohol addiction: "I guess no one ever really told me my drinking was bad until I got here and I went through withdrawal and everything." Tasha was required to participate in and complete a highly structured substance abuse treatment program for adolescents that included group therapy, family therapy, individual counseling, and 12-step self-help groups.

On the other hand, Maurice (16, African-American), who had assault and drug charges, claimed he did not benefit from the substance abuse treatment or relapse prevention programs, but planned to cut ties with his friends and to secure a job prior to his release. He stated, "I rather work there then be on the street with Tyrna sellin' drugs." Despite saying these programs were beneficial, participants admittedly will likely struggle with drugs and alcohol after release, strongly suggesting the residential substance abuse programs are effective in a controlled environment and only offer juveniles some transferable skills that they can use upon reentering society.

Ideal Services

There were marked gender differences in the programs and services young men and women wished to receive while they were confined. Although some of the programs that respondents wanted existed at residential programs, these programs were offered inconsistently and were not always available during the window of their confinement. Two young women wanted programs on pregnancy prevention, and the mothers and pregnant respondents wanted programming permitting more time with their children. Aliyah (16, African-American), whose charges include assault and robbery, enjoyed the parenting classes offered, but was concerned about inadequate time to form and maintain a bond with her son. Similarly, Erica (17, African-American), who was detained for a probation violation and an assault charge, wanted to be released so she could spend quality time with her daughter. She explained, "I want to go home for a day with her [daughter] and spend a lot of time with her and stuff and still have her come in twice a week." Aliyah and Erica desired more time with their children and shared fears that their absence during detainment would negatively impact their children. Autumn, whose father was incarcerated most of her life, was motivated to reconnect with him after she was released. She thought programming for restoring relationships between parents and residents was essential. Despite the same treatment and services offered in the juvenile male facilities, the young women expressed greater concern about relationships with their families, friends, and partners after release over securing a job or going to school.

Male participants wanted more information on how to find a job. While all residential programs assisted youth who were of age with completing applications and finding a job, some respondents sought additional practical and skills-based services. For instance, two men wanted to learn a trade to enhance employment prospects. Chris stated, "You know, a trade like electric maybe or some type of thing, plumbing, cooking, you know." Two men wanted to secure their driver's licenses, two simply wanted more freedom and opportunities to go home, and others were primarily concerned with serving their time and getting out, and not on programs or services.

Staff Members on Juvenile Programming

Six staff members previously worked with both male and female offenders; based on their experiences, staff members felt juvenile offenders had different programmatic needs based on "behavioral" differences rooted in gender

Gender and Programmatic Needs for Juveniles 197

ideology. As a result, staff responses to residents' opinions on the types of reentry services offenders wanted and required reflected stereotypical conceptions of teen boys and girls. For example, Ms. Reynolds (African-American), a Youth Rehabilitation Treatment Specialist for Residential Program Delta, painted female residents as requiring emotional energy:

> I think males, by their nature, tend to hold more things in and I think that it's okay for females to be more needy and it's not okay for males to. As soon as they're needy, they're sissies and so I think that program wise, the difference with that is the girls are going to just require more. The boys are easier to work with because they don't require as much of your emotional energy as the girls do.

When asked why boys and girls require different services, Ms. Smith (African-American), a Treatment Specialist at Residential Program Delta currently working with teen girls, stated:

> You don't deal with the neediness. With boys, they can let stuff go quicker than the girls, especially when it comes to their peer altercations that they bump heads. Two boys will get into a disagreement and then they'll be like, "Ok guys, it's over, you know." With girls, they let it linger. They do that silent bullying.

Both staff respondents describe young women as needier than young men and stress that young women's emotions complicate their interactions with other residents and staff. On the other hand, staff members were less likely to engage young men in conversations on their emotional well-being because they often said they were "fine."

Male staff echoed these gendered explanations for residents' behaviors. For example, Mr. Martin (African-American), a Youth Rehabilitation Counselor, quipped, "I mean females are little bit more catty . . . needier. They get more frustrated and irritated just with the situation at hand. I mean, they're more 'attitudey' all day long from start to finish." Similarly, Mr. Riley (African-American), a Treatment Specialist Supervisor, said, "You know with females, they are more dealing with insecurities. . . . I think males are more dealing with the whole macho aspect of not being looked at as a pushover or a softie."

Male staff stressed the importance of exposing detained girls to law-abiding women, so to address girls' perceived low self-esteem and neediness, staff often brought in guest speakers to serve as role models, promoted empowerment strategies, and coordinated field trips involving interactions with professional women. Mr. Riley was supportive of a fieldtrip to a women's conference: "It was pretty huge and it was kinda like talking about girl power, really rejuvenating yourself, standing tall, having a backbone, not allowing people to run all over you." However, when asked about trade skills and program development, Mr. Riley promoted a cosmetology program for young women while he wanted young men to focus on enhancing job skills and establishing a trade, such as becoming a barber. Mr. Riley also suggested creating athletic programs where, "They can build on skills like speed, strength, agility, and health as far as their food intake."

Programmatic needs for young men were framed by traditional notions of masculinity, such as becoming a "man" and being a breadwinner. Ms. Brenner (White), a Family Crisis Therapist at Residential Program Delta, sympathized with young men who didn't want to work a fast food job for minimum wage when they could hustle, but wanted programs to address legitimate job skills. Likewise, Ms. Reynolds (African-American) stressed teaching personal responsibility and finding legitimate means of making a living. She went on to explain what she called "manhood training," where boys would learn how to be "tough," "grow into responsible young men," "not abuse power," and "get money the proper way." She thought young men needed role models to emulate. These same thoughts were not expressed by male staff during interviews. When discussing programmatic needs for male and female residents, male and female staff members consistently drew on and reinforced gendered expectations for juvenile offenders' employment after release.

Consistent with Garcia and Lane's (2010) research, staff believed programs for young women needed to be focused on improving deficient self-esteem and employment programs that emphasized the beauty industry, whereas programs for young men should be centered on learning a trade or developing technical skills that could be useful in finding a job upon reentry. Yet young men encountered self-esteem and confidence issues and required similar educational and health awareness classes (i.e., HIV awareness, pregnancy prevention) as young women, but staff respondents all stressed that learning a trade was essential for successful reentry for young men.

Discussion: Is Gender-Specific Programming Necessary?

Regardless of gender, juvenile participants shared their concerns about life after release. Both young women and men feared confronting risky situations and were primarily concerned about the difficulty of avoiding delinquent peers. The value of substance abuse programs did not vary by gender, but both young men and women in the sample worried about relapsing if the opportunity arose. Some young women, especially the mothers and soon-to-be mothers, expressed interest in repairing strained relationships whereas others were anxious about their relationships with existing children; they found various counseling options helpful. Although some young women

Gender and Programmatic Needs for Juveniles 199

wanted to pursue their educations further, most were not career oriented, even those who enjoyed the beauty courses. Young women also discussed needing to avoid unhealthy relationships with "boys," which would be a reentry challenge. The young men, on the other hand, were concerned with job training and learning technical skills that would make them employable upon release. Most of them focused on gaining practical job skills that would facilitate their employment opportunities and their independence post-release.

Although both groups worried about confronting risky situations with delinquent peer groups after release and relapsing, they also worried they wouldn't have the same level of support on the outside. Some respondents shared positive relationships with staff, which included high levels of trust and a willingness to express vulnerabilities, and knew that in order to reenter successfully they had a need for continued services as they acclimated back into their families and society. Although individual (and family) counseling were accessible for residents, continued access to such services after release was not guaranteed.

Although juvenile offenders evaluated some gender-specific programming positively and we acknowledge that there are some gendered needs (i.e., pregnancy), we are concerned that programming reinforces gendered expectations on the residents and restricts their options to reenter. For example, several of the men who were detained were also fathers, but they were not given opportunities to benefit from parenting classes. Similarly, while young women were exposed to career training, it was limited to cosmetology. Interviews with staff members at the three residential youth programs, who worked with juvenile offenders nearing release from correctional supervision, revealed that they believed detained teens had different requirements and needs based on gender; as a result, residential programs that were offered reflected these ideas.

The transitional facilities are also shaped by their missions and philosophies, which influence gender-specific programing, but gender-specific programing is more likely to exist in facilities where staff members perceive that young men and women need different things to succeed after release. For instance, staff overwhelmingly depicted teen girls as requiring more emotional and social support compared to their male counterparts, which aligns with the gendered assumptions suggesting young women are more difficult to work with than young men (Baines & Adler, 1996; Britton, 2000). Much like Belknap, Holsinger, and Dunn (1997), staff portrayed young women as often outwardly expressing their emotions, having them linger, and then spill into later interactions, whereas young men kept their emotional problems bottled up; if they did lash out it was a temporary incident. As a result of these perceptions and experiences, staff members believed it was easier to deal with male residents than female residents because they weren't as emotionally "needy."

Staff members' assessment of detained juveniles was based on their experiences working at male and female facilities and rooted in their own sexist conceptions of gendered emotions; staff members' perceptions of teens' emotional states shaped how they interacted with juvenile residents and these observations crossed over into programmatic offerings as it related to employment and reentry services. Staff routinely endorsed the residential programs in their facilities, and routinely emphasized the importance of gendered programs for incarcerated young men or women. For example, if staff members highlighted the utility of their programs and failed to make other programs available that are not associated with gender stereotypes, it is likely that juvenile residents will request only the programs offered at the facility that subscribe to gendered stereotypes. Staff emphasis was evident in how participants viewed their reentry needs.

Gendered differences can also reflect how juveniles already subscribe to traditional gender role expectations in society; the programs that both male and female juveniles desire to receive parallel the available programs offered in schools and organizations outside of the correctional setting, which also follow gendered assumptions. However, programming responsive to gender-specific needs can simultaneously challenge and reproduce gender expectations. For instance, young fathers could benefit from parenting classes and young women could learn money management and trade skills to work towards economic independence. Although young women were more interested in completing their high school degrees, young men should be encouraged in following academic pursuits, especially as young men were more worried about reoffending.

By including young women juveniles in this study, it was possible to learn what types of programs and services they perceive to be most helpful and to provide a space for them to voice their concerns about reentry. This study contributes to understanding the needs of juvenile delinquents, residential facility programming, and reentry concerns. By interviewing staff and detained teens at program-based residential facilities, it was possible to explore the types of challenges youth believed they would face upon release.

These findings contribute to expanding our understanding of different gendered needs of confined juveniles prior to release, offers a glimpse of what they worry about prior to reentering, and suggests how juveniles view some of their reentry challenges. Illuminating the first-person perspective of participants can assist policymakers to craft better policies and programs. For instance, there is the Second Chance Act, which provides funding for various reentry initiatives; greater emphasis should be placed on redesigning programing to respond to the needs of juveniles, especially repeat offenders. In 2011, approximately one million juveniles were arrested for various types of crimes that often resulted in confinement in a juvenile facility (US Department of Justice, Federal Bureau of Investigation: Crime in the United States, 2010). Interviews with detained juvenile offenders revealed a number of prerelease services that youth want to facilitate their reentry process, but also what they need as bridge services as juveniles transition home. Future researchers should conduct long-term studies of female and male juvenile offenders and residential facilities to determine whether or not the programs offered are applicable to successful reentry for juvenile offenders, and then follow them after release to see which in-house programs were helpful in managing real-time barriers youth face upon reentry. These ideas can turn into legitimate transitional programs that can be funded by the Second Chance Act.

References

Altschuler, D. M., & Brash, R. (2004). Adolescent and teenage offenders confronting the challenges and opportunities of reentry. *Youth Violence and Juvenile Justice, 2*(1), 72–87.

American Bar Association and the National Bar Association. (2001, May 1). *Justice by gender: The lack of appropriate prevention, diversion and treatment programs for girls in the justice system.* Retrieved from www.americanbar.org/

Baines, M., & Adler, C. (1996). Are girls more difficult to work with? Youth workers' perspectives in juvenile justice and related areas. *Crime & Delinquency, 42*(3), 467–485.

Belknap, J. (2007). *The invisible woman: Gender, crime, and justice.* Belmont, CA: Thomson Wadsworth Publishing Company.

Belknap, J., & Cady, B. (2008). Pre-adjudicated and adjudicated girls' reports on their lives before and during detention and incarceration. In R. T. Zaplin (Ed.), *Female offenders: Critical perspectives and effective interventions* (pp. 251–281). Washington, DC: Jones and Bartlett Publishers.

Belknap, J., & Holsinger, K. (2008). An overview of delinquent girls: How theory and practice have failed and the need for innovative changes. In R. T. Zaplin (Ed.), *Female offenders: Critical perspectives and effective interventions* (pp. 3–43). Washington, DC: Jones and Bartlett Publishers.

Belknap, J., Holsinger, K., & Dunn, M. (1997). Understanding incarcerated girls: The results of a focus group study. *The Prison Journal, 77,* 381–404.

Bouffard, J. A., & Bergseth, K. J. (2008). The impact of reentry services on juvenile offenders' recidivism. *Youth Violence and Juvenile Justice, 6,* 295–318.

Britton, D. M. (2000). Feminism in criminology: Engendering the outlaw. *Annals of the American Academy of Political and Social Science, 571,* 57–76.

Center for Substance Abuse Treatment/SAMHSA. (1999). *Tailoring treatment to the adolescent's problem. In Treatment of Improvement Protocol (TIP) Series, No 32.* Rockville, MD: Center for Substance Abuse Treatment. Retrieved from www.ncbi.nlm.nih.gov/books/NBK64344/

Chesney-Lind, M. (2008). Innovative programs for girl offenders. In R. G. Sheldon & D. Macallair (Eds.), *Juvenile justice in America: Problems and prospects* (pp. 261–276). Long Grove, IL: Waveland Press, Inc.

Chesney-Lind, M., & Shelden, R. G. (1998). *Girls, delinquency, and juvenile justice.* Belmont, CA: West Wadsworth.

Chung, H. L., Little, M., & Steinberg, L. (2005). The transition to adulthood for adolescents in the juvenile justice system: A developmental perspective. In D. W. Osgood, E.

M. Foster, C. Flanagan, & G. R. Ruth (Eds.), *The John D. and Catherine T. MacArthur Foundation Research Network on Transition to Adulthood. On your own without a net: The transition to adulthood for vulnerable populations* (pp. 68–91). Chicago, IL: University of Chicago Press.

Dougherty, J. (2008). Female offenders and child maltreatment: Understanding the connection. In R. T. Zaplin (Ed.), *Female offenders: Critical perspectives and effective interventions* (pp. 349–369). Washington, DC: Jones and Bartlett Publishers.

Foley, A. (2008). The current state of gender-specific delinquency programming. *Journal of Criminal Justice, 36*, 262–269.

Fields, D., & Abrams, L. S. (2010). Gender differences in the perceived needs and barriers of youth offenders preparing for community reentry. *Child & Youth Care Forum, 39*, 253–269.

Garcia, C. A., & Lane, J. (2010). Looking in the rearview mirror: What incarcerated women think girls need from the system. *Feminist Criminology, 5*(3), 227–243.

Henderson, C. E., Young, D. W., Jainchill, N., Hawke, J., Farkas, S., & Davis, R. M. (2007). Program use of effective drug abuse treatment practices for juvenile offenders. *Journal of Substance Abuse Treatment, 32*(3), 279–290.

Hubbard, D. J., & Matthews, B. (2007). Reconciling the difference between the 'gender responsive' and the 'what works' literatures to improve services for girls. *Crime and Delinquency, 54*, 225–258.

Inderbitzin, M. (2005). Growing up behind bars: An ethnographic study of 192 adolescent inmates in a cottage for violent offenders. *Journal of Offender Rehabilitation, 42*, 1–22.

Marsh, S. C., & Evans, W. P. (2004). Youth perspectives on the relationships with staff in juvenile correctional settings and perceived likelihood of success on release. *Youth Violence and Juvenile Justice, 7*, 46–67.

Miller, J. (2001). *One of the guys: Girls, gangs, and gender.* New York: Oxford University Press.

Sedlak, A. J., & McPherson, K. S. (2010, May). Conditions of confinement: Findings from the survey of youth in residential placement. In *Office of juvenile justice and delinquency prevention.* Retrieved from www.ncjrs.gov/

Snyder, H. N., & Sickmund, M. (2006, March). *Juvenile offenders and victim: 2006 national report.* Office of Juvenile Justice and Delinquency Prevention. Retrieved from www.ojjdp.gov/

U.S Department of Justice-Federal Bureau of Investigation: Crime in the United States. (2010). Retrieved from https://ucr.fbi.gov/crime-in-the-u.s/2010/crime-in-the-u.s.-2010

Young, D. W., Dembo, R., & Henderson, C. E. (2007). A national survey of substance abuse treatment for juvenile offenders. *Journal of Substance Abuse Treatment, 32*(3), 255–266.

Chapter 15

Prison Is a Place to Teach Us the Things We've Never Learned in Life

Breea Willingham

Introduction

Higher education for incarcerated women and men is a pathway to successful reentry, including being able to become gainfully employed. Yet higher education in prison is not a given; men and women struggle to access accredited educational programs inside (Middlemass, 2017). Most incarcerated people have low educational levels when they enter the criminal justice system; they often have had negative educational experiences and have reservations about taking a college course because they doubt their ability to succeed. While incarcerated, they often spend their time without access to appropriate educational programs that will decrease their likelihood of returning to prison after they are released.

The lack of certified and accredited educational programs inside prison becomes a chronic and serious deficit for women and men attempting to reenter society. Educational exclusion raises the unemployment rates for formerly incarcerated people, making it "nearly impossible" for them to find employment in an increasingly demanding job market (Couloute, 2019). Research has consistently proved that a college education improves reentry outcomes for people returning home. A RAND meta-analysis found that people who participated in any type of prison education program were 28 percent less likely to recidivate than their counterparts who did not participate in an education program (Bozick, Steele, Davis, & Turner, 2018). The recidivism rate for people who participated in college programs in prison was more than 50 percent lower than that for those who did not participate in these programs (Davis, 2016).

In addition, rehabilitative programming has more positive effects when it incorporates educational goals (Cullen & Gendreau, 2000; Castellano et al., 1993). It is especially important that incarcerated people, regardless of their crime and sentence, are able to access programs that will assist in their personal development and growth and improve their employment chances. In June 2019, the Andrew W. Mellon Foundation awarded $3.3 million in grants to support four prison education and reentry programs across the country.

To illustrate the impact higher education has on formerly incarcerated people, this chapter focuses on the narratives of women who have taken college courses in prison and are continuing their educational pursuits as they reenter society. College education for incarcerated women is particularly important because women report experiencing multiple kinds of traumas prior to incarceration, including but not limited to, physical abuse, drug addiction, family dysfunction, mental illness, and lack of access to health care. These traumas are exacerbated by the degrading and disempowering context of prison and being separated from their children (see Reviere, Young, and Dawson's chapter in this volume for more about trauma experienced by incarcerated women).

Kristi Fraga, one of the participants in this study, stated "By the time we get to prison, we've already had some pretty messed up core beliefs about women and about ourselves. I think that prison reinforces those core beliefs, demeans and degrades [us]." Prison becomes part of women's lived experiences with trauma, and as a result, they view their relationship with the criminal justice system as traumatizing. Ironically, it is not until they get to prison and have the opportunity to take college courses that the women experience the power of learning, understand how liberating education can be, and why it is crucial to their recovery and reentry. They gain confidence, realize their potential and purpose, and begin to envision a life that is not limited to the confines of imprisonment – whether physical walls or psychological limitations.

Data and Methods

The women in this chapter are part of a larger study I am conducting about higher education in women's prisons; five interviews of formerly incarcerated women are included in this chapter. I solicited participants by posting a query on the Higher Ed in Prison listserv and on Facebook, Twitter, and Instagram, explaining that I am interested in interviewing women who took college courses in prison, and how that education helped them during and after their incarceration.

In each interview, the women talked about their experiences with higher education before, during, and after their incarceration. I conducted the interviews via phone during February, March, and April 2018; each lasted between 45 minutes to an hour. The women were given the option of using pseudonyms; only one woman chose to use a pseudonym. The women range in age from 31 to 56 and have served time in state and federal prisons in Michigan, Washington State, Minnesota, and California, and the length of their sentences ranges from 10 months to 10 years. The crimes for which they served time include fraud, forgery, first-degree attempted murder, and selling drugs. Although some of the women chose to give details of their crime, I did not ask them to do so. The stigma of being a formerly incarcerated woman carries enough judgement, and my study is not about crime, guilt, or innocence.

Challenges of Taking College Courses Inside

Taking classes in prison can be challenging for women. They must contend with multiple institutional factors, such as the number of instructors that are allowed to teach inside prison, and when security-related incidents put the prison on lockdown, classes are cancelled (Middlemass, 2017). Women prisoners also must deal with their own personal issues, have a willingness to learn, and a desire to better themselves. This is not always easy, as illustrated by the story of Kristi, a 43-year-old woman who served nearly six years in prison in Michigan. During our phone interview, Kristi told me that she had developed a "pretty fierce drug addiction" by the age of 33 following the death of her husband and mother.

> I didn't have good coping skills; I was abused as a child and was basically fed medications to make me complacent from the time I was 11. So, a lack of coping skills and just a perfect storm of events. Once I didn't know how to better myself or think that I deserved it, I ended up picking up a needle after my husband died and I walked in the hospital and saw my mother dead. I had been hanging out with my old crowd from high school who had progressed into heroin and pills and needles, and that was about it for me. I went from being a controlled, functional addict to I did not care, and I started shooting up.

Despite her addiction, Kristi completed her practical nursing degree, but admits nursing is not a field for someone with an addiction. Kristi's drug abuse, stemming from her unresolved traumas, including an abusive relationship, contributed to her incarceration. On the day she shot her boyfriend, Kristi said she believes she had a "psychotic break" and every beating and rape she had ever experienced "just came out in a rage." After the shooting, Kristi said she was so "whacked out on drugs" that she drove around thinking she had killed her boyfriend; after deciding she was going to kill herself, she engaged the police in a high-speed chase, "trying to get them to shoot me."

Kristi's narrative and life experiences are not unusual; rather, her story is an exemplar of what it means to be in a trauma-induced relationship within the criminal justice system. Trauma becomes a pipeline to prison for many women while education becomes the funnel with which women can learn skills, live life beyond surviving, and think about reentering society and doing so successfully. Yet for drug addicted women to think about reentering society and doing so successfully, they must be drug free. However, as Gorga noted earlier in this volume, drug and alcohol addiction programs are not always available inside prison whereas Martin demonstrates the challenges of coming home and living in a halfway house that is in close proximity to street drugs.

For Kristi, she knew she had to get clean in order to move forward.

> I went to prison absolutely convinced I could never use drugs again because that would be a slap in the face to my family, to him, to his family. I had to change. I went to prison with the mindset that I was going to get help. I remember the judge saying at my sentencing – the only thing I really remember from my sentencing besides apologizing profusely – was the judge saying the purpose of your incarceration is for punishment, but also rehabilitation. I thought I was going to get rehabilitated. I didn't think I was going to have to fight for every benefit that I received. It was very disenchanting and disappointing.

Historically, educational programming at women's prisons has always paled in comparison to that in men's facilities. For instance, in its 1980 Report to the Congress, the Government Accountability Office noted the inequitable treatment in women's prisons, stating, "Women in correctional institutions are not provided comparable services, educational programs, or facilities as men prisoners."

As Kristi described:

> I was like auto mechanics? Building trades? I'm not a genius, but I'm pretty sure mechanics and building trades, custodial maintenance technician and horticulture – so we're talking about being a mechanic, a carpenter, a janitor, or a landscaper. How many women work in those fields? So, I was like well now . . . I just been abused my whole life and a drug addict, and then you're gonna send me to voc[ational] class to go work with a bunch of men, if I can even get a job? It didn't make sense to me.

To add insult to injury, Kristi could not get into any substance abuse group meetings for six months because they were full. There were waiting lists for programs and fights over chairs in the dayroom; having a chair was important and required to attend the meetings because women were not allowed to stand in the dayroom, where meetings were held, because in prison terms, guards viewed prisoners standing together as "congregating." Congregating is not allowed because that is generally how fights start. To avoid fighting with other women over chairs, Kristi said she stayed in her cell. Despite wanting to get clean, the prison was not a conducive environment to doing so. Kristi told me someone offered her cocaine just three days after she was incarcerated. She did not accept the drugs, despite the temptation because "the horror [of being so high] was still fresh in my mind . . . but then I looked around me and thought well this is not a fun place to even be tweaking."

Kristi started taking classes through the Jackson College Prison Education Initiative, but she said she was "still broken, angry, [and] had low self-esteem." Instead of focusing on improving herself, she would write letters to men in other prisons and talked to random men on the phone. She was in a self-described "co-dependent, unhealthy state of mind" that was perpetuated by the prison environment. Kristi did not believe she was smart enough for college, and even after receiving a 4.0 grade point average, she doubted herself.

> I thought, well maybe they're dumbing it down [the classes taught inside prison]. I guess I didn't know because I didn't have a lot of belief in myself. Like my nursing school, I made it through on crystal meth. I thought that crystal meth got me through nursing school. I did not believe I had any intellectual capacity of my own.

For Mariah Wilberg, who served a year and a half in the Minnesota Correctional Facility in Shakopee, the state's only women's prison, simply trying to survive prison was hard enough. She had multiple personal challenges, and could not concentrate on taking classes. She told me:

> It was hard when I got to prison. I found out that my HIV maybe had progressed to AIDS because I had not been taking my medications for four years and that's probably scarier than the original diagnosis. And I naturally wanted to reach out and have comfort and I ended up confiding in people who broke my confidentiality. So, I did have a hard time as ladies were gossiping about my status, but the librarian was wonderful. She found books specifically with stories of people living with HIV that were not available in the library and myself and another person living with HIV did an anonymous interview with our prison newspaper reporter who wrote about what it was like to live with HIV, so that went out in our prison to try to address some of the stigma.

Josanne English, convicted of accessing a device to commit fraud (e.g., using a laptop or other device to illegally transfer money), spent 11 months at the Federal Correctional Institute in Dublin, California. Josanne had taken some community college courses prior to her incarceration. As a tutor in prison, Josanne experienced some unique challenges related to the learning environment in prison, which included making it difficult for some women to ask for help.

> [In prison,] it's different in that you have to appear that you are strong and you know what you're doing, but [to learn, you have to be] vulnerable enough to say, "hey, I need to take this class to better myself."

[In class,] there were a lot of times where it was very brave for someone to raise their hand and ask a question and say, "hey, I don't understand this, can you help me?" That took a lot of courage just to even do. Then there's also the women who were really super tough and gangster like, and, you know, for them to be there [in class they are saying], "hey, I want to better myself," and that took a lot of strength, too. [As a tutor,] I had to balance myself in that I didn't want to appear as "a know it all" or that I know everything because I'm not, I don't know it all.

Part of the learning experience must include being comfortable to be vulnerable, and that requires trust between the teacher and student and between each student. No one wants to be made fun of for what they don't know, and Josanne found it hard to create a learning environment where students trusted her and felt safe to learn new things.

I never judged anybody and I just really was genuine and sincere in wanting to help people. I think that that was reflected in my actions and when you're in there, in prison, people can tell when you're fake. I think that that helped out a lot. I didn't have too much trouble when I was in there because I just kept it real.

From her experience as a tutor, Josanne told me that she was able to witness how empowering education is for incarcerated women. "If you don't have a lot going on, once you get out, this is the one thing that she can have under her belt to say, 'you know, I did this in the worst situation. I was able to do that.' And it's so inspiring for others."

When I spoke to Josanne in February 2018, she told me she had another baby and is working for the Otis Elevator Company: "I'm super happy to finally have a job with benefits. Everything is peachy keen and I'm finally living the life I was supposed to live." However, Josanne explained her path to reentry was challenging and paved with "more steps backwards" before she was able to get to where she is now.

The reentry was difficult because it feels like your probation officers against you, they're trying to make things very difficult in regards to scheduling, and it still feels like your business is all out there. Nobody wants to hire you. You know, having a criminal background is terrible and I had to start from the very bottom. It's taken me 10 years to get here and it can happen, but it was super hard.

Even after finding a good job and stability, Josanne said she still has hurdles to overcome.

I'm trying to get my pharmacy tech license right now and even that I have to jump through hoops, spend 10 years to find all kinds of court records and court documents. I'm just like, man! I'm just trying to move into a different direction in my life and it's just like dragging me down.

Taking Those Classes in Prison Relit My Passion for Education

Despite the challenges of taking college credit courses inside prison, it was a life-changing experience for many of the women I interviewed, especially as it reminded them of a time prior to being incarcerated. Mariah, whose story I introduced earlier in the chapter, had always excelled in school. As a straight-A student, she graduated high school a year early, but did not go to college right away because "I was experiencing some instabilities." Mariah enrolled in the dental hygiene program at Argosy University when she was 20 but dropped out after one semester.

> I happened to find out that I was living with HIV the same day I was taking my entrance tests. I did still take my placement exams and I enrolled for that initial semester, but I was pregnant, I was in an abusive relationship and then just finding out my HIV status. . . . So, I ended up dropping out after that first semester. I did complete the semester, but I failed one class. I was on academic probation, but it was just too much on my plate to go back.

After leaving Argosy, Mariah said her life consisted of "more instability, crime, drug use, homelessness, sex work – all the way up until my incarceration at the age of 25" in 2012. Incarcerated for drug sales, Mariah spent the next year and a half in the Minnesota Correctional Facility in Shakopee; while incarcerated, Mariah was reintroduced to educational opportunities, and fell back in love with education. During our interview, Mariah described the two education opportunities that were important to her during her incarceration. The first was a traditional office support certificate program in which she learned Microsoft Office, and took classes in business English and math. While inside, she earned 16 college credits that were fully transferable to Minnesota's state college system upon reentering.

Mariah's other prison education experience was more personal.

> It was really having the library being a haven for me because they do have a lot of books that can help you learn about yourself and your emotions. So, I tried to piece together why I had landed in prison and what I could change about myself to make sure that didn't happen again. But I also learned more about like the social context of why I ended up in prison. I didn't realize that yes, I made a lot of bad choices, but there is also a lot of missed opportunities for intervention right before I went to prison.

Mariah said she left prison "changed" in July 2013 and started college the following month. She graduated from Metropolitan State University in May 2017 with her bachelor's and in January 2018, started working towards a master's degree in public and nonprofit administration at Metropolitan State University.

> I think taking those classes in prison really relit the fire and passion I had for education. All of the instability in my life and failing out of college when I first tried had made it seem like college wasn't an option for me. Having these teachers and librarians supporting me and learning new things, getting excited about it, and knowing that I'm taking a good step for my future, when I went home it really inspired me.

Despite her academic achievements and family support, Mariah's reentry was not easy.

> I wouldn't say it was seamless. It was difficult, but I had a lot in favor that made it easier for me. I had a family member to live with. I am White, so people are more likely to view my crime as a mistake I recovered from instead of something indicative of character. I grew up middle class so I have a lot of privilege, but there was still difficulty. It was really hard for me to get a job with my record, even though it was just a drug crime. I had 96 hours of community service to do, so I found an organization doing HIV education and took a training with them so I can be on the speaker's bureau, and that turned into a job for me.

As Mariah's narrative highlights, race and privilege play a significant role in how successful some women's reentry may be over others. Homelessness, unemployment, and poverty are some factors that inhibit Black women's reentry (Middlemass, 2019). Mariah shared with me how she saw this first hand.

> My best friend, she's mixed [race]. We met in prison. We got out within a few months of each other. We have a very similar resume as both of us working at call centers. We were charged with the same drug crime, the same severity level. I've seen her struggle more than me. And granted I did get into a very niche field with the nonprofit work focused on HIV and it helped that I am living with HIV and that I was really into telling my story, but that can't explain the entire difference. People are willing to give me that chance whereas I don't see people as willing to extend that grace to all of the other people who might not have the same privilege.

School and Prison Saved My Life

Education in prison also saves some women's lives. Like Kristi, Patsy Murphy's pathway to prison was paved by trauma and her drug addiction. About 20 years ago, Patsy said she witnessed her apartment manager shoot and kill her boyfriend. Patsy told me she started drinking to cope with the trauma, which became the gateway to her meth addiction that lasted about 20 years and has shaped her relationship with the criminal justice system.

"I ended up in prison over the meth most of time," Patsy said. The first time, she served ten months in 1999. Patsy admitted she was not ready to change her life the first time she entered and exited prison; upon reentering, she returned to the same place, interacted with the same people, and resumed her drug use. "I had nowhere else to go."

In 2005, Patsy was sentenced to six years in Washington State, but only had to serve two years. It was during her second time in prison that she decided that she was "sick and tired of this life" and wanted something new. While incarcerated, she enrolled in several information technology classes offered by Tacoma Community College and completed domestic violence and drug treatment programs.

Patsy lived in a homeless shelter for a year after her release from prison. While there, she interned at a drug treatment program and decided to return to school to complete her associate's degree. She registered for writing and math classes at Highline Community College in Des Moines, Washington, and pursued her goal of becoming a drug counselor. Patsy ultimately received her master's degree in 2017, and now lives in Seattle and works for King County as a substance abuse care authorizer. She authorizes funds for and handles in-patient substance use placements for people in the county.

Patsy said her successful reentry the second time is because of the courses she was able to take inside prison. Prison saved her life, and without college, she said:

> I would have been right back to the same people, places and things. I know I would've went back to drugs. I probably wouldn't be alive today or I'd either be dead or back in prison. I think that school is my saving grace and the prison was my saving grace and you know, while I was in prison, my whole attitude changed because of that. I delved into school and I delved into my work. School is what made me who I am today and surrounded me with people who were positive and like-minded and I wouldn't be where I am today without it.

Education for incarcerated women is more than courses and credits. As Mariah explained to me, education provides a "lifeline" for women.

> The vast majority of women who are in prison are mothers. Many of them are going back to the role of being the primary caretaker and if

you're keeping people incarcerated, but you're not giving them the tools and skills they need to have a different life when they go home, nothing is going to change. . . . A lot of prisons have the goal of rehabilitation, at least on paper, but if you're not backing that with education and opportunities, all you're doing is locking people up and keeping them out of society and throwing them back into the same situation that brought them to prison in the first place.

Felisa Bryant, who was incarcerated from October 2008 to December 2012 in Washington State for forgery and identity theft thought that any chance she had to be "good" on the outside was lost because she had committed a crime against a person, and such crimes usually restrict former prisoners from accessing a range of jobs, especially working with vulnerable populations. Because of this reality, Felisa knew that she had to make the best of her time inside so she could prepare herself for life on the outside. The prison's horticulture program became her saving grace; she learned about landscaping, gardening, and identifying flowers. Another component of the program includes floriculture and it was during this program that Felisa discovered she had a hidden talent for floral design. Felisa was so good at designing flower arraignments that after she completed the program, she became a teaching assistant.

The floriculture program provided Felisa hope about her future, boosted her self-esteem, and allowed her to start thinking about a career versus just finding a job after prison. Felisa was able to get a job with the vendor that supplied the flowers to the prison's horticulture program after her release. She worked there for a year before getting hired as a floral manager for a local grocery store, where she worked for three years. Felisa told me she was determined to make a way for myself some way, somehow, and credits the classes in prison for setting the foundation for where she is today – working on her doctorate in psychology at Grand Canyon University (online) and as a case manager for the Urban League; she still does floral arrangements on the side.

Conclusion

Education for women in prison is important because they go inside broken, having little or no hope, and are lacking in self-esteem. Education not only provides incarcerated women an opportunity to learn about themselves, but also improves their self-esteem and allows them to think about life in a different way, which improves their reentry chances. As Josanne told me:

> What better way to end recidivism than through educating those that are incarcerated to give them a better opportunity for life that they won't have to go back to the habits and the life that they knew that led

them there. It's like one plus one equals two. The best way to spend tax dollars is to do that and a true form of rehabilitation is through education rather than building more prisons.

Additionally, Kristi, who graduated with her associate's degree in General Studies from Jackson College in May 2018 and was nominated for macroeconomics student of the year, described the powerful impact college has had on her life.

Higher education in prison was not just a program, it was a life-changing intervention that gave me options besides poverty or crime. This is so much more motivating than the minimum-wage career and dependence on a man or state assistance that would have resulted otherwise, if not worse.

As the narratives of the women in this study illustrate, education makes a profound difference on the lives of women reentering society. Approximately 95 percent of people incarcerated in state prisons will return to society at some point. Not only will a college education reduce their chances of recidivism, research has consistently proven that people who receive an education while incarcerated have a better chance of finding employment post-release.

Additionally, providing an education to incarcerated people is an investment in their future and that of their communities, and should not be viewed as a reward for "good" behavior. The shortsightedness of taxpayers, politicians, and others who vehemently oppose supporting college-in-prison programs is symptomatic of our country's obsession with incarcerating its citizens instead of educating them. Although higher education programs challenge the use of prison as an institution of social control, it should not be something that happens in spite of the criminal justice system; education should be a legitimate objective of reforming the system and those it incarcerates. There is something inherently nefarious about controlling institutions of the state that exercise power on the powerless, especially in women's prisons, where their experiences with trauma are exacerbated. Higher education for incarcerated women destabilizes and undercuts the strength of their sexual abuse, traumas, and the gendered oppressions they routinely experience and are subjected to; by allowing incarcerated women the opportunity to take college courses, it provides them a chance to reclaim their self-efficacy in a racist and sexist punishment system and society. However, despite the women in this study obtaining some measure of reentry success after serving time in prison, they still face difficulties with reentry. Thus, although providing incarcerated women with a higher education is important and necessary to help with a successful reentry, it is not the sole solution.

References

Bozick, R., Steele, J., Davis, L., & Turner, S. (2018). Does providing inmates with education improve postrelease outcomes? A meta-analysis of correctional education programs in the United States. *Journal of Experimental Criminology, 14*(3), 389–428.

Castellano, T., Cowles, E. L., McDermott, J., Cowles, E. B., Espie, N., Ringle, C., . . . Tongsookdee, R. (1993). *The implementation of Illinois' PreStart program: An initial assessment.* Chicago, IL: Illinois Criminal Justice Information Authority.

Couloute, L. (2019). *Getting back on course: Educational exclusion and attainment among formerly incarcerated people.* [online] Prisonpolicy.org. Retrieved from www.prisonpolicy.org/reports/education.html

Cullen, F. T., & Gendreau, P. (2000). Assessing correctional rehabilitation: Policy, practice, and prospects. In J. Horney (Ed.), *Criminal justice 2000: Policies, processes, and decisions of the criminal justice system* (Vol. 3, pp. 109–176). Washington, DC: U.S. Department of Justice.

Davis, L. (2016). *The pendulum swings back: Support for postsecondary education in prison.* [online] Rand.org. Retrieved from www.rand.org/blog/2016/12/the-pendulum-swings-back-support-for-postsecondary.html

Middlemass, K. (2017). *Convicted and condemned: The politics and policies of prisoner reentry.* New York: New York University Press.

Middlemass, K. (2019). Hiding in plain sight: Black women felons reentering society. In J. Jordan-Zachery & N. Alexander-Floyd (Eds.), *Black women in politics: Demanding citizenship, challenging power, and seeking justice* (pp. 69–95). Albany: SUNY Press.

Section IV

Access, Rights, and Reentry

One of the biggest controversies within reentry discourse is the ability of returning citizens to access services and rights. Persons who are justice-affected often lose some aspect of formal, as well as informal, rights and privileges. The loss of rights and privileges highlights the notion of perpetual punishment post-imprisonment; state legislators add a number of statutory restrictions directed at former prisoners, who are continually reprimanded beyond their original legal criminal sentence by "secret sentences" (Chin & Holmes, 2002) and civil disabilities that are collectively known as the collateral consequences of a felony conviction (Love, 2011; Travis, 2005). The loss of access to rights and privileges makes reentry harder than it needs to be (Middlemass, 2017). Having a felony conviction that is accessible via public records undermines various legal, political, economic, and social rights.

In many states, individuals are banned from various aspects of society, such as receiving social welfare benefits and Pell grants, and denied access to housing and employment opportunities (Middlemass, 2017). These sanctions are designed on the principle that returning citizens are morally corrupt and consequently are not worthy of social benefits. This section offers a variety of perspectives about different groups of returning citizens and their experiences accessing rights as they reenter society. These groups include individuals convicted of sexual crimes, returning citizens attending university, voting rights – the politics of voting rights for former prisoners and how the 2018 restoration process of voting rights in Florida unfolded – and one man's journey to become free after serving time. The following chapters take a critical approach in order to unpack the costs of losing one's rights during the reentry process.

David Booth, in his chapter, "' . . . Except Sex Offenders:' Registering Sexual Harm in the Age of #MeToo," tackles a taboo aspect within reentry by exploring the various restraints and restrictions for individuals who have been convicted of sex crimes. Booth elucidates how this population, in addition to the "normal" collateral consequences of a felony conviction, faces "extra" restrictions related to their specific crime, such as having to adhere to sex offender registration and notification (SORN) requirements, and individuals convicted of sex crimes are often excluded from reentry programs and services offered by nonprofit organizations. As a result of the "extra" restrictions and community notification rules, sex offenders must announce their crimes through various government channels and are not able to access resources that could address sexual harm.

Booth's chapter may make some readers uncomfortable, but if society is going to start to take reentry challenges and criminal justice reform seriously, in all its various forms of ugliness, then it is necessary to address those things that make us uncomfortable. Although the majority of people incarcerated in state prisons are considered perpetrators of a violent crime, and the system incarcerates a lot of people society considers "bad," in reality, to create a more just system, it is necessary to hear from all voices to start a critical conversation about what should be done and what can be done. Booth raises complex questions about who should be able to access treatment programs, who should be restricted from treatment programs, and why, and what should society do with certain groups of returning citizens. Policies create different classes of returning citizens, and sexual offenders, as current policies are configured, are at the bottom of the criminal caste system.

In their chapter, "Reentry in the Inland Empire," Anderson, Jones, and McAllister examine an educational program entitled Project Rebound. The three authors are all affiliated with California State University, San Bernardino, and implement and support Project Rebound in a variety of ways. Project Rebound is specifically designed to assist formerly incarcerated individuals apply for and access higher educational programs at CSU–San Bernardino. Education is considered a beneficial tool for returning citizens that assists in successful reentry. Project Rebound assists returning citizens in accessing four-year university programs at CSU–San Bernardino, including providing referrals for on- and off-campus resources, educational materials, psychosocial support, and career development, to name a few. Anderson, Jones, and McAllister describe the various ways that Project Rebound seeks to make justice-affected students feel included within the college environment and provides different forms of help to ensure academic completion by Project Rebound participants.

The following two chapters explore different aspects of voter disenfranchisement; unlike previous work on voting rights and returning citizens, these authors look beyond disenfranchisement in several ways. In "The Politics of Restoring Voting Rights After Incarceration," Means and Hatch focus on the politics of restoring voting rights post-incarceration in Iowa and Virginia to highlight the onerous process to have one's voting rights restored. Taking a comparative approach, they highlight the different methods used to deter returning citizens from pursuing their right to restore their voting rights. Today, because of the grueling administrative requirements to restore one's voting rights, felon disenfranchisement laws have become the de facto form of banning voters, a large percentage of whom are Black. Voting rights are not critical to reentry like safe and secure housing and employment are; however, voting is an important key to gaining one's citizenship rights to participate in the democratic process and becoming part of civil society.

In Grant's chapter, "Restoration of Voting Rights: Returning Citizens and the Florida Electorate," she examines the restoration of voting rights in the state of Florida. Florida has become a flashpoint in electoral politics since the 2000 presidential election, when George W. Bush was elected president of the United States by the Supreme Court after the court ruled in favor of Bush in the famous case known as *Bush v. Gore*. In sum, there was a political dispute surrounding Florida's ballot design and how certain ballots were counted. The recount created a new lexicon for elections, such as hanging chads, voter purges, and felon disenfranchisement. A latent consequence of this controversial election was Florida's use of voter purges based on a felony conviction, barring felons from voting. Historically, voting in the United States has racial implications as voting rights were a staple point of contention in the post-Civil War era in preventing Blacks from voting. Grant reaffirms that the racial impact continues into the 21st century; through her analysis, she demonstrates that individuals who are disenfranchised in Florida are overwhelmingly people of color, disadvantaged economically, and most likely to vote for the Democratic Party. As a result, Florida election results are skewed because of the sheer number of individuals with a felony conviction who were disenfranchised from voting.

In 2018, through the efforts of activists and their support of a citizens' initiative, known as Amendment 4, Florida has re-enfranchised its returning citizens. Grant, through an in-depth case study, describes how voting rights were restored and provides an analysis of the potential political ramifications of Amendment 4 in future elections, theoretically indicating that felon disenfranchisement influences and undermines the democratic process (see Uggen, Manza, & Thompson, 2006). Grant concludes her chapter by offering suggestions on how Amendment 4 should be implemented to ensure equity and parity, but to also ensure people with a criminal record understand that they can now access their voting rights without going through an arduous administrative review process.

Although voting is only one example where formerly incarcerated individuals are barred, Michelle Alexander argues in her seminal book, *The New Jim Crow: Mass Incarceration in the Age of Colorblindness*, that the United States has essentially created a new caste system of people who were incarcerated and can no longer participate fully in society. In "Perpetual Punishment: One Man's Journey Post-Incarceration," Montalvo and Ortiz provide a detailed account of one man's journey reentering society. Montalvo, as a returning citizen, provides a first-person account of the substantial obstacles he faced while trying to reintegrate and despite his best efforts, he discusses how the system impeded his efforts, including reconnecting with his children, child support, and the courts.

Montalvo and Ortiz provide a fantastic perspective that engages in academic research, first-person account of a returning citizen, and that returning citizen's wife, Ortiz. The two authors engage in a back-and-forth conversation about how the system impacts returning citizens, and how those interactions can have a negative impact on individuals and families. More specifically, Montalvo and Ortiz offer an understudied area of reentry – child support, reentry, and wage garnishment – and how the combination of having to pay back child support that has accrued while an individual is incarcerated impact's an individual's financial and emotional stability while they attempt to reenter society. The first-hand account offers an insightful and intimate look at how child support payments can be used as a threat to one's freedom. Drawing from personal experiences, this chapter is a critical examination of how the collateral consequences of a felony conviction are a felt experience and more than just a set of inconvenient restrictions, and that these "silent punishments" create different types of hardships that perpetuate the criminal caste system within the reentering population.

References

Chin, G., & Holmes, R. (2002). Effective assistance of counsel and the consequences of guilty pleas. *Cornell Law Review, 87*(3), 697–742.

Love, M. C. (2011). Paying their debt to society: Forgiveness, redemption, and the Uniform Collateral Consequences of Conviction Act. *Howard Law Journal, 54*(3), 753–794.

Middlemass, K. (2017). *Convicted and condemned: The politics and policies of prisoner reentry.* New York: New York University Press.

Travis, J. (2005). *But they all come back: Facing the challenges of prisoner reentry.* Washington, DC: The Urban Institute.

Uggen, C., Manza, J., & Thompson, M. (2006). Citizenship, democracy, and the civic reintegration of criminal offenders. *The Annals of the American Academy, 605*, 281–310.

Chapter 16

"... Except Sex Offenders"
Registering Sexual Harm in the Age of #MeToo

David Booth

Ever since Bill O'Reilly's ignominious departure from Fox in 2017 triggered a wave of allegations against Harvey Weinstein, America's been reckoning with how to address sexual harm and misconduct.[1] Across the country, the social and political narratives around sexual harm and misconduct have spun into a maelstrom, gathering strength with each allegation. Drowning in the chaos, many struggle to understand the details of each allegation and wrestle with the maelstrom. The question remains then, how to reconcile sexual harm and misconduct within the current paradigms that address criminal behavior.

America is perversely fond of locking people in cages. The concept of "justice" is measured by the number of years that an individual is incarcerated, and not by measures of rehabilitation, restoration, or community transformation. Approximately 2.3 million people are incarcerated in the U.S., and another 5 million are under some form of state control, such as probation or parole (Wagner & Sawyer, 2018). In recent years, the number of people imprisoned has slowly dwindled as formerly incarcerated people, community activists, legal professionals, and policymakers have brought significant attention to the harms of the prison industrial complex and modified some laws.

A direct result of these actions has started to shift the punishment paradigm in some jurisdictions, including reforming the bail system, closing jails and prisons, reducing racial disparities, and rethinking the criminalization of women and girls, among other reforms. These reforms have only been palatable because of distinctions drawn around people labeled for so-called nonviolent, violent, or sexual offenses. Reforms have almost exclusively been reserved for people who can safely be labeled as nonthreatening, while leaving out those considered beyond redemption. Even as attitudes about people convicted for violent crimes have begun to shift, people convicted of sex crimes are considered irredeemable (American Civil Liberties Union, 2017).

Over the last 30 years, there's been a marked expansion of draconian policies for people convicted of sex crimes and reentering society. These policies have created a more expansive law enforcement effort, including increasingly

220 David Booth

stringent tracking and monitoring systems and post-conviction barriers to reentry, all of which are unique to people on a sex registry. Certainly, a comparatively small number of registrants have committed particularly egregious crimes, but the label "sex offender" extends to people convicted of less serious offenses. Behaviors prosecuted as registerable sex offenses vary by state, but include public urination, consensual sex between teenagers, sex work, cruising for sex, and non-disclosure of HIV status (Extein & Booth, 2015). Sex offense registries are rapidly expanding and are a popular tool to sustain the carceral system. Understanding the role sex registries play in denying civil rights and the reasons for prioritizing registry reforms requires a critical understanding of their evolution and their use as a tool for social control.

Registering Queerness

America's current sex offender registration and notification (SORN) laws have roots in mid-20th century sex panics, when California parents, concerned about a supposed rise in sex crimes, enacted the first sex offense registry in 1947 (De Orio, 2017a). Initially, the laws targeted people engaging in oral or anal consensual sexual activity and other similar behaviors (De Orio, 2017a). During the 1950s and 1960s, law enforcement officials commonly employed discrete tactics to entrap gay men cruising in parks, restrooms, bars, bathhouses, and other out-of-the-way places (Extein & Booth, 2015).

Even though registries initially targeted queer and trans folk, they were slow to catch on and were riddled with errors; as a result, many registration practices fell out of use. By 1976, only six states – Alabama, Arizona, California, Florida, Nevada, and Ohio – had a sex offense registry (Logan, 2009). In the 1970s and 1980s, gay activists in California fought for and won the removal of public sexual conduct (e.g., acts ranging from cruising for sex in a park to dancing in a gay bar) from the registry (De Orio, 2017a). However, public sex remained a registrable sex offense in many states. Some progressives in the 1970s argued that registering people for morally inappropriate sexual behavior was unconstitutional because it created a criminal underclass of people permanently excluded from the rights and benefits of citizenship (De Orio, 2017b).

These sentiments changed in the mid-1980s with the rise of the AIDS epidemic and a moral sex panic involving daycares across the country (DeYoung, 1998). Around-the-clock media attention on the purported Satanic and sexual abuse of children involving the McMartin Preschool (Fukurai & Butler, 1994; Summit, 1994), Fells Acres Day Care Center (DeYoung, 1998), the wrongful conviction of Bernard Baran (Pollitt, 2000), and the Bronx Five (Berger, 1984), among others, captivated the American public. These events were followed, in quick succession, by a number of high-profile abductions, sexual assaults, and murders of children, including Jacob Wetterling, Megan Kanka, Polly Klaas, and Jimmy Ryce, in the 1990s.

Race, Class, Gender, and SORN Laws

Sex offense registries are disproportionately populated with low-income, people of color, and/or queer and trans folk, unmistakably the most marginalized people within our communities. Men of color are registered for sex crimes at twice the rate of White men (Hoppe, 2016). Gay and bi-sexual men are four times as likely, and lesbian and bi-sexual women are twice as likely to be convicted of a violent sex offense than any other crime as compared to their straight peers (Meyer et al., 2017).

Transwomen of color and queer youth are frequently profiled for engaging in sex work, public lewdness, or other sex offenses and are punished for their behavior (Hanssens, Moodie-Mills, Ritchie, Spade, & Vaid, 2014). Wealthy and powerful people, especially White men, are often protected by institutions of power and privilege. Criminal charges won't be brought against many of them, or the charges will be lenient despite overwhelming evidence (e.g., Jeffrey Epstein). However, people of color, marginalized people, and poor people will continue to be targeted and punished.

Modern Sex Crime Laws

Federal lawmakers responded to the resultant public outrage by rapidly expanding sex offense registries. Most of the SORN requirements that shape the lives of people convicted of a sex offense in the United States are mandated by federal legislation. In 1994, Congress passed the first federal sex offenses registration law, entitled the Jacob Wetterling Crimes Against Children and Sexually Violent Offender Registration Act ("Wetterling Act").

The Wetterling Act encouraged all states to develop and maintain registries for individuals convicted of sexually violent offenses and crimes against children, as well as individuals determined to be sexually violent predators. Under the Wetterling Act, registration information was only available to law enforcement authorities. Public access to the registry was prohibited unless releasing information about a registrant became a matter of public safety. The Wetterling Act allows for states to develop their own rules, which means that the circumstance for public disclosure differs based on jurisdiction, but the basic mechanisms for public notification haven't changed much since the passage of the Wetterling Act. Community notification rules depend on a mix of factors, including whether the state has an offense or risk-based classification system for crimes, and whether that system is statutorily connected to community notification.

In 1996, Congress enacted Megan's Law, amending the Wetterling Act, which attempted to strengthen registration programs and decrease community notification requirements. What began as a list of individuals on a state sex registry quickly mushroomed into lengthy, publicly available dossiers of personally identifiable information for anyone on the sex registry. In 2006, in an effort to standardize and strengthen SORN laws, Congress passed the Adam Walsh Act (AWA). Title I of the AWA, the Sex Offender Registration and Notification Act (SORNA), created stringent national minimum standards aimed at strengthening the national network of registration and notification programs. AWA requires states to categorize sex registrants in one of three tiers based on the offense for which they were convicted. Registerable sex offenses under the AWA include most convictions for sex offenses under federal, military, state, tribal, or local law (e.g., rape, sodomy, sexual abuse, sexual assault, child pornography, indecent exposure, and an unwanted sexual act by force or threat). The AWA requires the registration of anyone convicted of a serious sex crime who is 14 years of age or older. Further, the AWA created a new felony, failure to register: Any person who is required to register and fails to do so, or fails to update any required information, can be re-incarcerated or face hefty fines.

The AWA establishes minimum national standards, but states are allowed to enact stricter requirements for offenses that do not fall under the AWA. Some states, like Texas, require children younger than 14 years of age and convicted of a sex crime to register. Other states, like Mississippi, register adults convicted for consensual sexual activity with other adults. The AWA also grants the U.S. Attorney General discretion to apply the law retroactively, meaning those who were convicted before the law passed can be required to register. Current federal regulations require retroactive application.[2]

As a result, the number of people registered for sex crimes has exploded. The National Center for Missing and Exploited Children (NCMEC) argues that almost a million people are registered for sex crimes based on publicly available information that is incomplete or inaccurate. NCMEC's estimate includes people registered in multiple states and people who are deceased. Their number also excludes people in certain states who are considered low-risk and whose registration information is not publicly available, people who are incarcerated but will need to register, and juveniles in some states.

Modern Sex Crime Laws in Practice

Currently, every state, the District of Columbia, the five principal U.S. territories, and certain Native American tribes have established a sex offense registry. Most states, however, have not established the baseline standards required by the AWA. As of December 2018, 17 states are compliant with the baseline standards (Office of Sex Offender Sentencing, Monitoring, Apprehending, Registering, and Tracking, 2018). Many of the other 32 states find it cost prohibitive to implement the AWA standards, and administer their own SORN laws, even after accounting for the 10% reduction in federal law enforcement funding for failing to comply with baseline standards. The resultant status of SORN laws for people registered for sex crimes can

"...Except Sex Offenders" 223

be confusing, arbitrary, and ineffective; all of them, however, include two provisions, registration and notification.

Registration requires people convicted for sex crimes to "provide valid contact information and other identifying data to law enforcement authorities" (Prescott, 2012, p. 48). The required registration information can be any combination of their home or employment address, or the school they attend. The information can be a U.S. Census block (e.g., the smallest geographic unit), street name, or precise mailing address. Additional information that may be required on a persons' registrant includes the registrant's physical description, current age, date of birth, age at the time of conviction; any email address and other Internet identifiers they use regularly; professional licenses; vehicles driven or titled in their name; and their offense, usually listed as a criminal code. All of this information may be publicly available. Every state determines what information their registrants are required to provide and deadlines for when that information must be uploaded and or updated. Most state SORN laws mandate, at a minimum, a current photograph and current residence.[3]

Community notification requires the release of a registrants' information to the community where the registrant lives. States take wide latitude in deciding who should be notified about a registrants' location, under what circumstances, and which registrants' will have their information made public. If the registrant's information is available publicly, then the primary way to access the information is through an online database maintained by the state police department of the registrant's current state of residence. Each states' SORN law decides whether or not a registrants' information is made publicly available through other means, such as at community meetings, newspaper announcements, or the establishment of toll-free numbers. Every state now has a designated law enforcement office or agency that handles SORN laws, their implementation, and the notification processes. For instance, many states do not provide community notifications, but will allow interested people to subscribe to receive email updates to the state-run sex offense registry.

If a state has passed its own distinct law, then the states' SORN laws dictate registration and dissemination policies. New Jersey registrants must notify their local Megan's Law Unit, usually located at a local police department, of a change in residence ten days prior to moving, but any changes in employment are to be reported within five days. In contrast, Nebraska requires state registrants to notify the office of the sheriff of the county of their residence, in-person, three working days prior to any change of residence, employment, or educational program. Under the AWA, failing to comply with any of these deadlines, among a tangle of other requirements, often results in an additional felony, further incarceration, and/or thousands of dollars in fines.

Upwards of 40 states monitor people convicted for certain sex offenses with a GPS tracking device, sometimes for life. These devices are fraught with technological challenges. Often a charging malfunction, spotty cell reception, or no access to a charging station leads to further incarceration for people wearing these devices (Thompson, 2018). Additionally, some people have to pay for their own monitoring, and are unable to do so, which results in their re-incarceration. Others are never released from prison. Twenty states have enacted laws that allow for people convicted of certain sex crimes to be involuntary and indefinitely held past their sentences in civil commitment programs, and are commonly referred to as Sexually Violent Predator Acts.

SORN Requirements and Civil Death

Standard among the consequences imposed by a felony conviction is unemployment and housing instability, which affects almost anyone with a criminal conviction (Middlemass, 2017). SORN laws and their attendant requirements impose an additional battery of social, personal, and legal consequences on anyone convicted of a sex offense and required to register. SORN laws have not been studied to determine if they are effective at reducing harm nor if there is a relationship between the offense and the additional consequences.

As an expert in the area of SORN laws, I know, for example, people on a registry are also convicted felons, and the registries further isolate them from society by stigmatizing them and restricting their ability to participate in civic and social activities. Tennessee, Florida, and Delaware permanently disenfranchise registrants, even after they have completed their sentence and community supervision. In other states, like Washington, the right to vote is restored after the completion of community supervision. Many registrants, however, are sentenced to lifetime community supervision, which permanently disenfranchises them.

Alabama, Arizona, Florida, and Louisiana are among a number of states that require registrants to obtain specialized identification cards or driver's licenses emblazoned with some variation of "sex offender" in bright red letters. As a result of this unique branding, registrants have reported being denied hotel rooms, scrutinized in grocery check-out lines, and refused service at gas stations. Some states, like Washington, don't mandate specialized identity cards, but registrants are required to reveal their registered status prior to engaging in sexual activity. Passports for registrants are also regulated under the statute, International Megan's Law. As a result, international travel is severely restricted for people on a registry, even though there is no evidence supporting the perceived connection between child sex trafficking and people on a registry (Hamilton-Smith, 2017).

A number of states and localities also legislatively restrict people on the registry from living, working, or loitering within a specified distance from places children may frequently gather (e.g., schools and parks) or from residing near or with other people on a registry. These residency restrictions, despite a lack of evidence about their effectiveness, force people to live on the margins of society (Mustaine, 2014). Registered people have been forced to live under bridges, in Walmart parking lots, cloistered in tent colonies, and away from their families (Cohen & Feige, 2016). Many registered people who are also parents, but are not convicted of harming children, are restricted from taking their kids to parks or even living with their own children (Cohen & Feige, 2016). SORN laws designed to restrict where registrants live or work aren't going to protect individuals from sexual harm and living in any number of communities if the registrant and danger comes from a family member, such as a sibling or an uncle, which is statistically more likely (Center for Sex Offender Management, 2008).

The consequences of SORN laws extend into a registered person's home. Louisiana forbids registrants from giving out gifts to anyone under the age of 18 on any recognized holiday, such as Halloween or Easter. Any person in Louisiana registered for a sex crime that gives a child a gift, even their own children, risks a potential term of re-incarceration ranging from six months to three years. Registered people in a number of states also cannot hand out candy on Halloween despite evidence debunking "stranger danger." Other states forbid registrants from taking prescribed medications while under community supervision or from accessing social media.

The consequences of SORN laws means that someone who is convicted of a violent rape, engaged in sex work, convicted of cruising for consensual sex, convicted for consensual sexual activity between juveniles, such as in Romeo and Juliet cases, or any other registerable offense are treated virtually the same by the law. All of them must register as a sex offender, which effectively relegates them to the margins of society. This is tantamount to a state-sponsored civil death. Opportunities to reintegrate and reenter society are systematically removed, and increasingly the punitive restrictions guarantee that registrants will be involved in the system forever, even after death their name may remain on the registry. The lesson communicated to people registered for sex crimes is that they are a "pariah class of unemployable, uprooted criminal outcasts" (Lancaster, 2017, p. 93).

SORN's Questionable Efficacy

The public overwhelmingly supports sex offense registries, reasoning that their communities and their children are safer from sexual harm and misconduct with the laws' enactment; 94% of Americans support the existence of sex offense registries and the treatment of those registered (Saad, 2005). Further, the judicial system largely fails to recognize the extent of the oppressiveness and lack of due process inherent in SORN laws. In fact, the entire political and judicial systems justify denying social and legal protections to those on sex offense registries by weaponizing a callous disregard for evidence-based information (Center for Sex Offender Management, 2010).

226   David Booth

Together, the political and judicial systems, alongside the mass media, have devised a detailed mythology about sex crimes and the people who commit them. The most consequential of these myths is that people who commit sex crimes are incurable and predatory strangers prone to committing multiple sex crimes, which justifies the increasingly stringent penalties placed on registrants (Yung, 2010). Focusing on this mythology masks the real threat to children, of being sexually harmed by someone close to them, and exaggerates the rare occurrences of children being abducted by a stranger. Statistically, a child is more likely to be struck by lightning than to be abducted, raped, and murdered by a stranger (Lancaster, 2011). Over 90% of sexual harm is caused by someone known to the person harmed, such as a family member, coach, teacher, or friend (Williams, 2009). In addition, over 70% of sexual harm is perpetrated in a private residence, such as in the home of the person harmed or the home of a friend, neighbor, or relative (Colombino, Mercado, & Jeglic, 2009; Duwe, Donnay, & Tewksbury, 2008). Because of who is doing the harm, many people are discouraged from reporting sexual harm fearing repercussions for people they know, love, and trust.

In addition to the reality that sexual harm is more likely to be caused by someone known to the person who is harmed, research casts doubt on the potential for SORN laws to advance public safety. Policymakers argue that SORN laws promote public safety, support law enforcement in investigating sex crimes, reduce sexual re-offense, and deter future sex crimes (Meloy, Curtis, & Boatwright, 2013). While these laws are premised on the idea that society needs protection against a group of dangerous people who pose a "frightening and high" risk of re-offense, research demonstrates otherwise (Ellman & Ellman, 2015; Ewing, 2011; Koon-Magnin, 2015; Mancini, 2014; Tewksbury & Jennings, 2010). According to the majority of the extant research, people convicted of sex crimes have the lowest rate of re-offense than any other class of people with criminal convictions (Przybylski, 2015). Numerous studies indicate that sexual re-offense rates for registrants is around 3.5%, even in studies commissioned by the Department of Justice (Garner, 2008; Langan, Schmitt, & Durose, 2003). An overwhelming number of registrants are registered for their first and only sex offense conviction (Ellman & Ellman, 2015).

Research has also found that SORN legislation has no significant effect on reducing new or additional offenses (Ewing, 2011; Sandler, Freeman, & Socia, 2008; Tewksbury & Jennings, 2010; Zgoba, Witt, Dalessandro, & Veysey, 2008). An evaluation of SORN's efficacy didn't find a reduction in the rates of sex offenses post-SORN legislation implementation; findings indicate that SORN laws do not significantly reduce sex offense recidivism (Agan, 2011). Other research echoes this conclusion, finding no evidence that current policies reduce sexual harm and sexual misconduct (Ackerman, Sacks, & Greenberg, 2012). Furthermore, empirical research doesn't support the belief that legislation is serving a protective function (Koon-Magnin,

"...Except Sex Offenders" 227

2015). However, re-offense rates for non-sex crimes do increase because of the collateral consequences of SORN rendering it impossible for registrants to locate housing, maintain steady employment, and preserve community support systems (Prescott & Rockoff, 2011).

Discussion: Rethinking SORN Laws

Although addressing sexual harm and sexual crimes is critical, SORN laws as a harm-reducing strategy fail. SORN laws define people by their actions with little space for repairing harm, restoring lives, and rebuilding communities. As a result, people who've experienced sexual harm are deprived of their agency, people who've caused harm are punished but remain unaccountable for the harm they inflicted, sexual harm isn't prevented, communities are disempowered, and incredible social, personal, and legal costs are exacted.

What's at stake isn't only the prevention of sexual harm but also how to effectively respond to sexual harm and sex crimes. Repairing harm, restoring lives, and rebuilding safer and stronger communities requires society to challenge SORN laws and their expansion. Instead of relying on the prison industrial complex to fix societal ills, it's important to consider options that support people who've experienced sexual harm and trauma in order to move towards a system of accountability and redemption.

Restorative justice identifies harm as a violation within an interpersonal relationship between a person who is harmed and a person who caused the harm. The goal of restorative justice is to address the needs of the person harmed by empowering them in a supportive environment. This is achieved by having the person harmed voice the harm they experienced, describe its effect, and express what justice and healing means to them. Additionally, restorative justice requires the person who caused harm to be held accountable for their actions by developing an understanding of the harms they caused. People who have damaged others are held accountable for their actions, must accept responsibility for their crimes, and then steps are taken to lower the chance of them committing another offense.

Research for a restorative approach to sex offenses yields some promising results. Circles of Support and Accountability (COSA) is a restorative justice practice implemented in Canada and the U.S. for people who've committed sex crimes. Within a COSA, a member is surrounded by a small group of trained community volunteers as they adjust to life outside of prison. There is an emphasis on humanizing the member. The community volunteers aid the member in navigating social life outside of prison, helping them to learn how to develop healthy relationships, and accepting accountability to their circle, the person they harmed, and their community (Fox, 2013). COSAs have shown significant success in reducing re-offense rates (Höing, Bogaerts, & Vogelvang, 2014). Restorative justice does not provide a

228 David Booth

definitive answer for addressing interpersonal harm caused by sexual offenders, but it is one way that allows for transformative justice. Transformative justice, similar to restorative justice, is a community-centered approach to harmful interpersonal behaviors. Born out of the experiences of women of color, transformative justice advocates for accountability, healing, forgiveness, and safety (Critical Resistance & Incite, 2003; GenerationFive, 2017).

Under our current retributive punishment paradigm, opportunities for restoration and transformation on an individual, let alone a community level, are absent. Restorative and transformative justice practices are working to empower communities by responding holistically to sexual harm rather than using punishment as the sole resolution. Relying on the punishment paradigm instead of exploring alternatives to SORN laws is a testament to society's inability to have open, honest, and thoughtful conversations about what should be done to address sexual harm and misconduct.

The current narrative is that sexual harm and misconduct is perpetrated by a select number of "bad people" who should be punished. This narrative has been repurposed to justify the expansion of SORN practices to punish, surveil, isolate, dehumanize, and banish anyone branded as a "sex offender." The lesson is that if society can neatly identify "sex offenders," then it is possible to prevent sexual harm and misconduct. Efforts to date have done little in the way of prevention, but continue to keep communities from confronting the realities of sexual harm. The focus of SORN laws on individual punishment fails to address systemic causes of sexual harm, which need to be meaningfully addressed if sexual harm is ever to be addressed in a systematic way.

In the age of #MeToo, society is willing to name, shame, and isolate people who've caused harm or engaged in criminal misconduct. Once someone is punished, when are they punished enough? For change to happen, society must start to ask and answer hard questions, such as, is healing and redemption possible? Should people who've caused harm be provided an opportunity to rejoin society? Is our community complicit in the perpetuation of sexual harm if we refuse to consider alternatives to the current punishment paradigm? Here, the conversation has started by acknowledging harm and trying to envision a different future.

Notes

1. In this chapter, someone has experienced sexual harm when they engage in a sexual experience they don't want, or are forced into *any* kind of sexual activity by another person. The intent behind using sexual harm as an umbrella term for sexual abuse, harassment, violence and other forms of misconduct is to capture the broad application of the "sex offender" label and to shift our attention to the systemic issues and behaviors allowing for sexual harm to happen in the first place. "Sexual harm" takes into consideration the spectrum of sexual victimization without making some experiences of sexual harm appear more valid than others. Misconduct includes sexual behaviors that

"... Except Sex Offenders" 229

are not harmful but are still criminalized, such as consensual sexual activity between juveniles.
2. See 28 C.F.R. § 72.3 2018.
3. This information is based on my expertise and work at Sex Law & Policy (SLAP) Center.

References

Ackerman, A., Sacks, M., & Greenberg, D. (2012). Legislation targeting sex offenders: Are recent policies effective in reducing rape? *Justice Quarterly, 29*(6), 858–887.

Agan, A. (2011). Sex offender registries: Fear without function? *Journal of Law and Economics, 54*(1), 207–239.

American Civil Liberties Union. (2017). *Polling on Americans' attitudes on criminal justice.* Washington, DC: Smart Justice Campaign. Retrieved from www.aclu.org/sites/default/files/field_document/aclu_campaign_for_smart_justice_poll_results.pdf

Berger, J. (1984, August 3). 3 seized in child abuse at Bronx Center. *New York Times.*

Center for Sex Offender Management. (2008). *What you need to know about sex offenders [Fact sheet]* (pp. 1–12). Retrieved from www.csom.org/pubs/needtoknow_fs.pdf

Center for Sex Offender Management. (2010). *Exploring public awareness and attitudes about sex offender management: Findings from a national public opinion poll.* Washington, DC: Office of Justice Programs. Retrieved from www.csom.org/pubs/CSOM-Exploring%20Public%20Awareness.pdf

Cohen, R. R. (Producer), & Feige, D. (Director). (2016). *Untouchable* [Motion picture]. United States of America: Blue Lawn Productions.

Colombino, N., Mercado, C., & Jeglic, E. (2009). Situational aspects of sexual offending: Implications for residence restriction laws. *Justice Research and Policy, 11,* 27–43.

Critical Resistance & Incite! (2003). The intersection of ideologies of violence. *Social Justice, 30*(3), 141–150.

De Orio, S. (2017a). Creation of the modern sex offender. In D. Halperin & T. Hoppe (Eds.), *The war on sex* (pp. 247–267). Durham, NC: Duke University Press.

De Orio, S. (2017b). The invention of bad gay sex: Texas and the creation of a criminal underclass of gay people. *Journal of the History of Sexuality, 26*(1), 53–87.

DeYoung, M. (1998). Another look at moral panics: The case of satanic day care centers. *Deviant Behavior, 19*(3), 257–278.

Duwe, G., Donnay, W., & Tewksbury, R. (2008). Does residential proximity matter? A geographic analysis of sex offense recidivism. *Criminal Justice and Behavior, 35*(4), 484–504.

Ellman, I., & Ellman, T. (2015). 'Frightening and high': The Supreme Court's crucial mistake about sex crime statistics. *Constitutional Commentary, 30*(3), 495–508.

Ewing, C. (2011). *Justice perverted.* Oxford, UK: Oxford University Press.

Extein, A., & Booth, D. (2015, April 28). Is queer sex legal? How sex laws have changed (or not) since 1964. *Truthout.* Retrieved from https://truthout.org/articles/is-queer-sex-legal-how-sex-laws-have-changed-or-not-since-1964

Fox, K. (2013). *Circles of support & accountability.* Burlington, VT: State of Vermont Department of Corrections.

Fukurai, H., & Butler, E. W. (1994). Sociologists in action: The McMartin sexual abuse case, litigation, justice, and mass hysteria. *American Sociologist, 25,* 44–71.

Garner, A. (2008). *Recidivism rates compared 2005–2007.* Indianapolis, IN: Indiana Department of Corrections. Retrieved from www.in.gov/idoc/files/05_07RecidivismRpt.pdf

GenerationFIVE. (2017). *Ending child sexual abuse: A transformative justice handbook.* San Francisco, CA: GenerationFIVE. Retrieved from www.generationfive.org/wp-content/uploads/2017/06/Transformative-Justice-Handbook.pdf

Hamilton-Smith, G. (2017, November 9). We're putting sex offender stamps on passports. Here's why it won't curb sex tourism & trafficking. *The Appeal.* Retrieved from https://theappeal.org/were-putting-sex-offender-stamps-on-passports-heres-why-it-wont-curb-sex-tourism-trafficking

Hanssens, C., Moodie-Mills, A., Ritchie, A., Spade, D., & Vaid, U. (2014). *A roadmap for change: Federal policy recommendations for addressing the criminalization of LGBT people and people living with HIV.* New York: Center for Gender & Sexuality Law at Columbia Law School. Retrieved from www.law.columbia.edu/sites/default/files/microsites/gender-sexuality/files/roadmap_for_change_full_report.pdf

Höing, M., Bogaerts, S., & Vogelvang, B. (2014). Circles of support and accountability: How and why they work for sex offenders. *Journal of Forensic Psychology Practice, 13*(4), 267–295.

Hoppe, T. (2016). Punishing sex: Sex offenders and the missing punitive turn in sexuality studies. *Law & Social Inquiry, 41*(3), 573–594.

Koon-Magnin, S. (2015). Perceptions of and support for sex offender policies: Testing Levenson, Brannon, Fortney, and Baker's findings. *Journal of Criminal Justice, 43*(1), 80–88.

Lancaster, R. (2011, August 20). Sex offenders: The last pariahs. *New York Times.* Retrieved from www.nytimes.com/2011/08/21/opinion/sunday/sex-offenders-the-last-pariahs.html

Lancaster, R. (2017). The new pariahs. In D. Halperin & T. Hoppe (Eds.), *The war on sex* (pp. 65–125). Durham, NC: Duke University Press.

Langan, P., Schmitt, E., & Durose, M. (2003). *Recidivism of sex offenders released from prison in 1994.* Washington, DC: Bureau of Justice Statistics. Retrieved from www.bjs.gov/content/pub/pdf/rsorp94.pdf

Logan, W. (2009). *Knowledge as power: Criminal registration and community notification laws in America.* Stanford, CA: Stanford University Press.

Mancini, C. (2014). *Sex crime, offenders, and society.* Durham: NC: Carolina Academic Press.

Meloy, M., Curtis, K., & Boatwright, J. (2013). The sponsors of sex offender bills speak up: Policy makers' perceptions of sex offenders, sex crimes, and sex offender legislation. *Criminal Justice and Behavior, 40*(4), 438–452.

Meyer, I., Flores, A., Stemple, L., Romero, A., Wilson, B., & Herman, J. (2017). Incarceration rates and traits of sexual minorities in the United States: National Inmate Survey, 2011–2012. *American Journal of Public Health, 107*(2), 267–273.

Middlemass, K. (2017). *Convicted and condemned: The politics and policies of prisoner reentry.* New York: New York University Press.

Mustaine, E. (2014). Sex offender residency restrictions: Successful integration or exclusion? *Criminology & Public Policy, 13*(1), 167–177.

National Center for Missing and Exploited Children (NCMEC). Retrieved from www.missingkids.com/

Office of Sex Offender Sentencing, Monitoring, Apprehending, Registering, and Tracking. (2018). *SORNA state and territory implementation progress check.* Retrieved from https://smart.gov/pdfs/SORNA-progress-check.pdf

Pollitt, K. (2000, February 3). Justice for Bernard Baran. *The Nation.* Retrieved from www.thenation.com/article/justice-bernard-baran/

"... Except Sex Offenders" 231

Prescott, J. (2012). Do sex offender registries make us less safe? *Regulation* (2), 48–55.

Prescott, J. J., & Rockoff, J. (2011). Do sex offender registration and notification laws affect criminal behavior? *Journal of Law and Economics, 54*(1), 161–206.

Przybylski, R. (2015). *Recidivism of adult sexual offenders.* Washington, DC: Office of Sex Offender Sentencing, Monitoring, Apprehension, Registering, and Tracking. Retrieved from www.smart.gov/pdfs/RecidivismofAdultSexualOffenders.pdf

Saad, L. (2005, June 9). Sex offender registries are underutilized by the public. *Gallup News Service.* Retrieved from http://news.gallup.com/poll/16705/sex-offender-registries-underutilized-public.aspx

Sandler, J., Freeman, N., & Socia, K. (2008). Does a watched pot boil? A time-series analysis of New York state's sex offender registration and notification law. *Psychology, Public Policy, and Law, 14*(4), 284–302.

Sex Law & Policy (SLAP) Center. Retrieved from www.sexlawandpolicy.org/

Summit, R. C. (1994). The dark tunnels of McMartin. *The Journal of Psychohistory, 21*(4), 397–416.

Tewksbury, R., & Jennings, W. (2010). Assessing the impact of sex offender registration and community notification on sex-offending trajectories. *Criminal Justice and Behavior, 37*(5), 570–582.

Thompson, O. (2018, June 14). Shackled: The realities of home imprisonment. *Equal Justice Under Law.* Retrieved from https://equaljusticeunderlaw.org/thejusticereport/2018/6/12/electronic-monitoring

Wagner, P., & Sawyer, W. (2018). *Mass incarceration: The whole pie 2018.* Northampton, MA: Prison Policy Initiative. Retrieved from www.prisonpolicy.org/reports/pie2018.html

Williams, F. (2009). The problem of sexual assault. In R. Wright (Ed.), *Sex offender laws: Failed policies, new directions* (pp. 17–63). New York: Springer Publishing Company.

Yung, C. R. (2010). The emerging criminal war on sex offenders. *Harvard Civil Rights: Civil Liberties Law Review, 45*, 435–481.

Zgoba, K., Witt, P., Dalessandro, M., & Veysey, B. (2008). *Megan's law: Assessing the practical and monetary efficacy.* Trenton, NJ: New Jersey Department of Corrections. Retrieved from www.ncjrs.gov/pdffiles1/nij/grants/225370.pdf

Chapter 17

Reentry in the Inland Empire
The Prison to College Pipeline With Project Rebound

Annika Yvette Anderson, Paul Andrew Jones, and Carolyn Anne McAllister

Introduction

According to the California Department of Corrections and Rehabilitation (2014), 61% of parolees return to prison within three years of release. These statistics corroborate that many parolees unsuccessfully assimilate back into society (Bahr, Harris, Fish, & Armstrong, 2010; Bowman & Travis, 2012). Some scholars argue that prison-based programs can effectively reduce recidivism rates (Travis, 2005; Visher & Travis, 2003). However, there are mixed results in the literature regarding the effectiveness of reentry programs. Many prison-based programs attempt to improve the work skills or academic standing of prisoners, which is helpful in post-release job attainment (Travis, 2005, p. 169). Recent studies show that prison- and community-based education programs can assist prisoners in the desistance process as well as promote successful reintegration (Cho & Tyler, 2013; Davis, Bozick, Steele, Saunders, & Miles, 2013; Davis et al., 2014; Duwe, 2017; Halkovic et al., 2013).

The incarcerated populations who obtain an education reduce their likelihood of returning to prison, increase their chances of securing employment, reduce their involvement with law enforcement, increase self-efficacy, and improve social mobility (Cho & Tyler, 2013; Davis et al., 2013, Davis et al., 2014; Duwe, 2017; Halkovic et al., 2013; Liem & Sampson, 2016). Meta-analyses by Davis and colleagues demonstrate that receiving education while in prison may reduce recidivism by as much as 43%, with the most significant decrease in recidivism related to programs that focus on postsecondary education (Davis et al., 2013). Earning an education during incarceration may show potential employers the motivation and efforts an offender has taken to change their criminal lifestyle (Zgoba, Haugebrook, & Jenkins, 2008).

Despite California's high recidivism rates (California Department of Corrections and Rehabilitation, CDCR, 2014), the Stanford Criminal Justice Center indicates that there are roughly 4,500 incarcerated men and women participating in face-to-face community college classes as of Fall 2017, which is more than any other state (Mukamal & Silbert, 2018). Taking community college classes is likely to bring participants into contact with prosocial influences. According to Lam (2012), prosocial behavior "usually refers to voluntary actions that are intended to help or benefit another individual or group of individuals," such that the behavior of "the actor is directed toward promoting and sustaining a positive benefit for the help-recipient" (p. 1). Therefore, community-based reentry programs, access to services, and interaction with prosocial individuals may also be consequential in the reentry process (Anderson, Nava, & Cortez, 2018).[1]

Based on the existing literature, we explain the common barriers and conduits to successful reentry for ex-prisoners in San Bernardino. We argue that social bond theory can adequately explain the reentry process. Then, utilizing an intersectional approach, we investigate the difficulties formerly incarcerated individuals face when entering university environments. Specifically, we explore the importance of Project Rebound, a campus-based reentry program for formerly incarcerated individuals that operates within the unique California State University, San Bernardino environment. Based on case files and interviews, we identify which interventions or resources are needed to further develop the program, based on the perceptions of Project Rebound participants. Then, we discuss the study results and its implications for program evaluation and accompanying policy implementations. Finally, we discuss our study limitations and make suggestions for future research.

Literature Review

Reentry Programs

Since the 1960s, there have been several programs at California's public colleges and universities that have provided supportive services for formerly incarcerated students (Mukamal, Silbert, & Taylor, 2015). These programs often follow a model similar to other programs that serve students from special populations (e.g., veterans and foster youth; Mukamal et al., 2015, p. 26). The programs offer a variety of services, including financial support for textbooks, connections to community-based reentry organizations, bridge programs or transitional courses, peer mentorship, and labor market assistance (Mukamal et al., 2015). Although research generally demonstrates the benefits of reentry programs, there is much less research on the specific services offered in these programs (Davis et al., 2014).

Case management services generally are noted to be an important component of successful reentry programs, particularly those using the Risk-Need-Responsivity model of practice (Bonta & Andrew, 2007; Day, Hardcastle, & Birgden, 2012). These program models emphasize identifying the risk of reoffending, the specific reentry needs and concerns of the individual, and individualized interventions, such as academic aid, employment training, and cognitive behavioral therapy (Bouffard & Bergseth, 2008; Day et al., 2012). Consistently, programs that offer models of supervision that include case management interventions demonstrate a lower rate of recidivism when compared to models that focus on intensive supervision only (Aos, Miller, & Drake, 2006; Day et al., 2012; McDonald, 2014; Veysey, Ostermann, & Lanterman, 2014).

Researchers have also determined the importance of familial ties, prosocial institutions (e.g., employment and education), and the need for collaborative efforts among San Bernardino county agencies as key to the reentry process (Anderson et al., 2018). For example, Anderson and colleagues (2018) found that the formerly incarcerated population has intersecting, disadvantaged identities that require referrals to multiple services and agencies. However, few studies have examined the attitudes or perceptions of former prisoners regarding successful reentry into their communities (Middlemass, 2017; Trimbur, 2009). Furthermore, based on a perusal of the literature, few studies have examined campus-based reentry programs, specifically in the Southern California context. This setting is important, given that San Bernardino County has the second largest number of entering parolees with 8%, second only to Los Angeles (Department of Corrections and Rehabilitation, 2013).

Social Bond Theory

Theory emphasizes the role of institutions and social networks in aiding reentry, such as how external stimuli and the influence of others are important, which is a central theme in social bond theory. Hirschi (1969) argues that there are four social bonds in society that prevent juveniles from committing delinquent acts: commitment, attachment, involvement, and belief. Commitment is the element of the bond that reflects an individual's time, energy, and effort in the pursuit of conventional and prosocial activities (e.g., education); attachment is the emotional ties an individual has to others who symbolize conforming society (e.g., parents or teachers); involvement is the amount of time individuals spend participating in conventional activities (e.g., the time spent in school or after school programs); and finally, belief is the bond that reflects the moral validity of the rules (e.g., some delinquents may not believe in the accuracy or legitimacy of the law; Hirschi, 1969). Taken together, juveniles (and similarly adults) are less likely to participate in crime and have a greater likelihood of conformity if they have strong bonds of commitment, attachment, involvement, and belief (Anderson, 2015; Hirschi, 1969).

Social bond theory is one of the theories often used to explain reentry (Bales & Mears, 2008). Frequent contact with their family or friends during incarceration may make offenders more likely to adhere to a conventional lifestyle upon returning to the community. In particular, contact with children (Spjeldnes & Goodkind, 2009), close ties to family, or contact with law-abiding partners strongly reduces recidivism (Bales & Mears, 2008; Berg & Huebner, 2011). Newly formed positive networks and social roles can also serve as social hooks for change after incarceration. Participation in positive social roles, such as being an employee, can aid in successful identity transformation by reaffirming an ex-prisoner's commitment to conformity (Berg & Huebner, 2011). Stakes in conformity (or commitments that keep people from violating prosocial norms; Rocque, 2017) can include parenthood, intimate partner relationships, and preexisting family ties, and can, depending on the quality of the relationships, "contribute to successful reentry" (Liem & Sampson, 2016, p. 206).

One way of expanding social support is to enroll in college, which demonstrates an individual's motivation to change and illustrates Hirschi's (1969) involvement element of social bond theory. Through college enrollment, ex-prisoners engage in the socialization process that takes place on a college campus. This positive engagement can win the approval of a family's support and may increase the level of attachment to family members, which may lower the odds of an individual reoffending (Jones, 2018).

Intersectional Approach

Intersectional paradigms explain the development of social inequalities and the impact of multiple identities on an individual's experience (Collins, 2000). Intersectionality scholars tend to focus on the intersection of race, gender, and class (Acker, 2006). Reentering individuals experience inequities based on their status as being formerly incarcerated and as a convicted felon, but in many cases also may experience inequities based on their ethnicity, socioeconomic status, gender, or having a disability or a substance use disorder diagnosis (Bunn, 2018; Middlemass, 2019). Research highlights higher rates of recidivism based on race/ethnicity (e.g., Black or Native American), age at release (over 40), type of offence (e.g., drug offenders experience the highest level of inequity), and gender (male; CDCR, 2014; Durose, Cooper, & Snyder, 2014; Steinmetz & Henderson, 2015). People with disabilities and substance use disorders are also more likely than other populations to be incarcerated (Bunn, 2018; Bronson, Maruschak, & Berzofsky, 2015). As Parker and Parrotta, Reviere, Young, and Dawson, as well as Zettler in this volume demonstrate, women and girls who are imprisoned have multiple identities that they must navigate when reentering society.

Intersectional research also highlights the impact of identity within higher education. Studies identify the struggles students with multiple identities have in deciding whether to disclose their identities or express their authentic self (Jones, Kim, & Skendall, 2012), whereas programs provide a venue for students and the campus community to understand the need to identify and work with students based on their complex identities (Castro & Cortez, 2017; Levin, Viggiano, Damián, Vasquez, & Wolf, 2017; Suggs & Mitchell, 2011).

Intersectionality can be used to explain the intersection of race, sex, and class in the lives of formerly incarcerated adults, and criminal status should be looked at in addition to other axes of oppression and domination (Bunn, 2018; Willingham, 2011; Middlemass, 2019). The aforementioned factors make it imperative for campus programs designed for reentering populations to focus on the complex identities of each participant, to work collaboratively with other programs (on and off campus) that support college and career success, and to offer advocacy to support participants that may experience a variety of inequalities.

Project Rebound: A Campus Reentry Program

Project Rebound assists formerly incarcerated students to apply, enroll, and graduate with postsecondary degrees and subsequently attain employment. The late Professor John Irwin started Project Rebound in 1967 as an on-campus reentry program for the formerly incarcerated at San Francisco State University (SFSU). Irwin realized that education could lower recidivism rates and began to foster Project Rebound to assist formerly incarcerated individuals register at a four-year university and go beyond a bachelor's degree. Project Rebound's success is evidenced by its 50 years of actively serving formerly incarcerated students. Because of its success, the CSU Chancellor's office supported the development of Project Rebound programs at all CSU campuses. Since 2016, Project Rebound has expanded to several California State Universities, including California State University, San Bernardino. In 2016, Carolyn Eggleston (Professor, Special Education) and Annika Yvette Anderson (Assistant Professor, Sociology) started the program at CSUSB, which is located in Southern California.

San Bernardino County has higher levels of poverty, issues with substance abuse and human trafficking, and arrest rates and greater local incarceration rates than the state of California as a whole (Center on Juvenile and Criminal Justice, CJCJ, 2018; U.S. Census Bureau, 2015). Almost half (45%) of San Bernardino County residents identify as Hispanic or Latino (U.S. Census Bureau, 2015). According to the California State University, San Bernardino (CSUSB) web site, CSUSB hosts the second largest Black and Hispanic student body in all of California's public universities, and is designated as a Hispanic Serving Institution (CSUSB, n.d.; Jones, 2018). In Fall 2017, 81% of the student body was first-generation college students, and almost two-thirds (62%) received a Pell Grant (CSUSB, 2018). San Bernardino County also has a disproportionate number of parolees and adult probationers (CJCJ, 2018), many, if admitted, may be eligible to participate in CSUSB's Project Rebound (Jones, 2018).

Recruitment, Enrollment and Retention Strategies

One full-time coordinator and an intern, both with prior incarceration experiences, staff the program. The program coordinator acts as a liaison and advocate with campus and community programs. Prospective students, whether currently out or incarcerated, complete a questionnaire describing their academic history and interests; with this information, staff determines if an applicant is eligible to enroll. Based on the questionnaire, the coordinator will request to evaluate the applicant's transcripts, advise them whether or not community college preparation classes are needed, and will help the applicant, if ready, to apply to CSUSB.

Project Rebound uses a strength-based and person-in-environment case management system that incorporates client assessment into the evaluation process. Once participants are enrolled, Project Rebound staff reviews their progress each academic term and provides case management services. These services can include financial support for educational materials, information and referral for on-campus resources for academic advising, writing, career development, psychosocial support or services for students with disabilities, and emotional support, as needed. These interventions assist students to remain in good academic standing, enroll in the correct classes for their degree, complete their degree in the timelines determined by the major, graduate, and apply for labor market positions or additional education. Staff also refer students and encourage them to apply for work-study positions, paid internships, job opportunities, and professional conferences. The program also has outreach events on campus, such as the Yotie Talk (similar to a Ted Talk) and annual orientation. However, since the program is still in its infancy at CSUSB, staff continuously seeks feedback from participants to improve the program in an effort to improve successful outcomes.

Data & Methods

The current study utilizes a mixed-methods approach that incorporates intersectionality, case files, and interviews to answer two research questions: (1) What does a successful reentry program look like, and (2) What interventions are most correlated with success? Institutional Review Board approval was gained through CSUSB's School of Social Work. Sociodemographic information was collected from 18 of the 21 current Project Rebound participants (86% participation rate) between September 2017 and February 2018 using preexisting program case files. Additionally, participants were invited to participate in oral interviews with the second author, Paul Andrew Jones, a full-time Project Rebound staff member. Thirteen of the 21 Project Rebound participants completed an interview (62% participation rate). Interview questions focused on the strengths and areas of growth and services used by Project Rebound students at CSUSB. Interviews were audio recorded and transcribed verbatim for analysis. The data was coded for similarities and differences in responses with the frequencies of themes tallied. SPSS was used to complete a frequency analysis for all variables.

Results

Demographic Characteristics

Table 17.1 presents sociodemographic information for current Project Rebound students. Participants ranged in age from 31 to 70 and most identified as male (77.8%). Blacks (38.9%) comprised the largest racial/ethnic group, followed by Hispanics (27.8%), Whites (16.7%), and Native Americans (16.7%). The majority of the participants were not married (61.1%), whereas living with a family member (38.9%) was the most common response for their respective housing situation. The majority of participants worked at the time of the interview (61.1%) and had at least one child (83.3%). In addition to college enrollment, employment, parenthood, and familial ties may represent prosocial influences, such as accountability and motivation to succeed in school, and serve as a deterrent from crime.

Table 17.1 Demographic Characteristics

	Frequency	Percent
Age		
31–40	8	44.4%
41–50	5	27.8%
51–60	3	16.7%
61+	2	11.1%
Gender		
Male	14	77.8%
Female	4	22.2%
Ethnicity		
Black/African American	7	38.9%
Hispanic	5	27.8%
Native American	3	16.7%
White	3	16.7%
Marital Status		
Not Married	11	61.1%
Married	7	38.9%
Housing		
Family	7	38.9%
Rent	5	27.8%
Own	3	16.7%
Communal Living	2	11.1%
Homeless	1	5.6%
Employment Status		
Working	11	61.1%
Not Working	7	38.9%
Children		
At least one child	15	83.3%
No children	3	16.7%

Table 17.2 Criminal History

Variables	Mean	Standard Deviation	Minimum	Maximum
Age at first Arrest	19.9	7.3	11.0	35.0
Number of Arrests	10.4	6.5	1.0	60.0
Number of Violations	1.7	2.2	0.0	7.0
Number of years Incarcerated	5.7	4.6	0.0	15.0

Table 17.3 Participation in Campus Programs by Project Rebound Clients

Variables	Frequency	Percent
Services for Students with Disabilities	5	27.8%
Career Center	5	27.8%
Vocational Rehab	4	22.2%
Student Assistance in Learning (SAIL)	4	22.2%
Psychological Counseling	3	16.7%
First People's Center for Indigenous Students	2	11.1%
The Den (Food Assistance Program)	2	11.1%
Veterans Success Center	2	11.1%
Workability	1	5.6%
Other Programs	1	5.6%

Criminal background data was gathered through case files (Table 17.2). All but one participant reported returning to the community where their crimes had been committed after release from prison. Yet despite their criminal record, to our knowledge, none of our participants have been rearrested or reincarcerated since their enrollment at the university.

Other Program Participation

Data on other programs Project Rebound students participated in was collected through case files (Table 17.3). Of the 18 participants, 16 (88.9%) are affiliated with at least one other campus program. Students are most frequently affiliated with Services for Students with Disabilities and the Career Center; each program was utilized by a little over a quarter of participants (27.8%). Taken together, Tables 17.1–17.3 illustrate the need to take an intersectional approach when looking at reentry. Our sample, mostly male and minority participants, reinforces the need to pay attention to how race and sex reflect the reentering population and their accompanying needs. The use of Services for Students with Disabilities further highlights the need to consider the needs of each student as an individual (see Bunn, 2018).

Table 17.4 Participants' Perceptions of Program Strengths

Variables	Frequency	Percent
Books/Supplies	12	92.3%
Relationships with Project Rebound staff	8	61.5%
Informational Meetings	6	46.2%

Note: Data from interviews of 13 participants

Participant Perceptions of Services

In the interviews (n = 13), participants discussed the strengths of Project Rebound (Table 17.4). The most frequent strength noted by all but one participant (92.3%) was books and supplies. The next most common response, given by 61.5% of participants, was the role of Project Rebound staff. Participants discussed feeling less alone, like they had a mentor, and that there was always someone to talk to on campus. The third most common strength of Project Rebound noted by participants was the type of information provided by on-campus events or at meetings organized by Project Rebound staff (n = 46.2%). Specifically, participants noted they appreciated the information provided during "legal night," when an attorney discussed the processes to expunge records and other pertinent topics for former prisoners.

Participant Perceptions of Program Improvements

During each interview, participants were asked to discuss areas of program improvement (Table 17.5). All but one participant (92.3%) stated the program should have more office space. Three-quarters of participants (76.9%) wanted more programming that allowed for interaction with other Project Rebound participants. Some participants mentioned having support groups (15.3%), whereas others discussed wanting space and time to be with peers on campus so they did not feel so alone (38.5%). Many (69.2%) brought up tangible items they wanted, such as access to computers, parking passes, and reduced fees. Finally, a little more than half of the participants (54.0%) signaled that they wanted to maintain the current private enrollment process; program participation and enrollment is confidential so participants can maintain anonymity on campus, if they choose to do so; participants did not see any need for changes to this aspect of the program.

Program Outcomes

Important measures of program success are defined by program retention, university retention, successful graduation, connection with other programs

Reentry in the Inland Empire   241

Table 17.5 Participants' Perceptions of Improvements to Project Rebound

Variables	Frequency	Percent
Bigger office space	12	92.3%
More interaction with Project Rebound Students	10	76.9%
Benefits towards education (computer use, parking pass, reduced fees)	9	69.2%
Maintaining privacy	7	54.0%

Note: Data from interviews of 13 participants

on campus, positive regard for Project Rebound, and use of Project Rebound case managers and services. Since January 2018, Project Rebound averaged 20.25 office visits per month. Of the 18 research participants, 12 will graduate in Spring 2018, with five earning a bachelor's degree, seven graduating with a master's degree, six continuing their degree programs, three accepted into a graduate program, and zero students dropping out of Project Rebound or CSUSB. These statistics reflect the commitment and involved elements of prosocial bonds; students are actively involved in the program and committed to attaining their post-secondary degrees.

Discussion

This study of Project Rebound was framed using social bond theory and an intersectional approach. Findings supported three of the four aspects of social bond theory: Participants' success in persisting in school (none have left without a degree); degree completion (66.7%); and graduate education (16.7%), which shows participants' strong commitment to their education. The mentoring and support the majority of participants (61.2%) noted receiving from Project Rebound staff demonstrates their attachment to the program. The connections that participants maintain (88.9%) with other programs demonstrates other attachments they have made on campus. Additionally, the time participants committed to being on campus and to successfully progressing towards their degree completion show their commitment and the involvement they have towards these activities. Future research should examine the facets of social bond theory in more detail as it pertains to higher education, particularly in the area of belief. Future research should also study the process participants went through to seek and persist in higher education, and further examine their social support networks off campus.

The study findings highlight the importance of an intersectional approach in working with the returning prison population. All but two of the participants (88.9%) partook in at least one other campus program, many of which are for specialized populations, such as the Services for Students with Disabilities and the Veterans Success Center. This, along with other sociodemographic characteristics (e.g., 83% are persons of color, and 83% also have at least one child), inform us that the Project Rebound population at CSUSB should be thought of through an intersectional lens, and services must take into account the complexity of each student's strengths and challenges. This program should draw from research on other intersectional approaches to college participation and retention, such as by Castro and Cortez (2017), and Levin and colleagues (2017). Future research should also examine participants' perspectives on their intersectional identities. The findings here underscore the importance of the case management approach to further develop relationships between individuals, programs on campus, and in the community to further enhance the success of Project Rebound students.

When Project Rebound came to CSUSB, the goal was to create a culture of empathy, acceptance, and understanding for formerly incarcerated students enrolled in a college reentry program. This study was designed to understand participants' perceptions of what interventions are most correlated with their integration into the university community and their success. Generally, participants had positive perceptions of Project Rebound, and all agreed that because Project Rebound had its own space, it legitimizes them as a group, and some wanted to have more space and visibility on campus. On the other hand, more than half (54%) of the participants did not want to be identified as program participants to the rest of the campus community. It will be important to find a balance between giving participants the ability to remain anonymous on campus and balancing that with increasing the programs' visibility. Perhaps there can be a way to build more social networking opportunities between participants currently in the program, so those that want to build connections with each other are able to, and those that want to use the services with anonymity can continue to do so.

Implications for Future Studies

CSUSB is the first school in the Project Rebound consortium to conduct scholarly research of its participants as they reenter society and join the campus community (Jones, 2018). Although the results of this exploratory study are illuminating, given that we have a small sample of participants, our results are not generalizable to other Project Rebound programs. Future researchers should use a larger sample size that includes all nine Project Rebound sites in California to analyze the perceptions of program participants' experiences at different campuses. Furthermore, future researchers should use more advanced statistical tests to investigate which interventions are correlated with a seamless transition from prison to university, and which variables lead to high graduation rates and low recidivism rates.

Lastly, future research should examine connections with current prisoners and Project Rebound staff. To date, staff has visited several correctional institutions to recruit potential future participants, and have received numerous letters, transcripts, and phone calls from current prisoners. Therefore, future research should investigate how regular visits, phone calls, and mailings from Project Rebound staff during incarceration can lead to higher and earlier enrollment rates among inmates.

Note

1. We acknowledge that not all employment opportunities and personal or familial relationships are positive. For example, hazardous or illegal jobs and family members or significant others engaged in crime would have a negative effect on individuals seeking to desist from crime. Thus, we use the term "prosocial" (as opposed to "antisocial") to refer to individuals or institutions that are generally beneficial to or will have a positive effect on incarcerated or formerly incarcerated individuals.

References

Acker, J. (2006). Inequality regimes: Gender, class, and race in organizations. *Gender and Society, 20*, 441–464.

Anderson, A., Nava, N., & Cortez, P. (2018). The conduits and barriers to reentry for formerly incarcerated individuals in San Bernardino. *Journal of Prison Education and Reentry, 5*, 2–17.

Anderson, A.Y. (2015). *The impact of socio-demographic characteristics and cognitive transformation on desistance from high risk behaviors* (Doctoral dissertation). Retrieved from http://research.wsulibs.wsu.edu/xmlui/handle/2376/6186

Aos, S., Miller, M., & Drake, E. (2006). *Evidence-based adult corrections programs: What works and what does not*. Olympia, WA: Washington State Institute for Public Policy. Retrieved from www.wsipp.wa.gov/ReportFile/924/Wsipp_Evidence-Based-Adult-Corrections-Programs-What-Works-and-What-Does-Not_Preliminary-Report.pdf

Bahr, S., Harris, L., Fish, J., & Armstrong, A. H. (2010). Successful reentry: What differentiates successful and unsuccessful parolees? *International Journal of Offender Therapy and Comparative Criminology, 54*, 667–692.

Bales, W., & Mears, D. (2008). Inmate social ties and the transition to society. *Journal of Research in Crime and Delinquency, 45*, 287–321.

Berg, M.T., & Huebner, B. M. (2011). Reentry and the ties that bind: An examination of social ties, employment, and recidivism. *Justice Quarterly, 28*, 382–410.

Bonta, J., & Andrews, D. A. (2007). *Risk-need-responsivity model for offender assessment and rehabilitation* (User Report 2007–06). Ottawa, ON: Public Safety Canada. Retrieved from www.pbpp.pa.gov/Information/Documents/Research/EBP7.pdf

Bouffard, J.A., & Bergseth, K.J. (2008). The impact of reentry services on juvenile offender's recidivism. *Youth Violence and Juvenile Justice, 6*, 295–318.

Bowman, S. W., & Travis, R. (2012). Prisoner reentry and recidivism according to the formerly incarcerated and reentry service providers: A verbal behavior approach. *The Behavior Analyst Today, 13*(3–4), 9–19.

Bronson, J., Maruschak, L. M., & Berzofsky, M. (2015). *Disabilities among prison and jail inmates, 2011–2012*. Washington, DC: Bureau of Justice Statistics. Retrieved from www.bjs.gov/content/pub/pdf/dpji1112.pdf

Bunn, R. (2018). Intersectional needs and reentry: Re-conceptualizing 'multiple and complex needs' post-release. *Criminology & Criminal Justice*. https://doi.org/10.1177/1748895817751828

California Department of Corrections. (2014). *2013 Outcome evaluation report*. Sacramento: CDC. Retrieved from www.cdcr.ca.gov/Adult_Research_Branch/Research_Documents/ARB_FY_0809_Recidivism_Report_02.10.14.pdf

Castro, E. L., & Cortez, E. (2017). Exploring the lived experiences and intersectionalities of Mexican community college transfer students: Qualitative insights toward expanding a transfer receptive culture. *Community College Journal of Research and Practice, 41*, 77–92.

Center on Juvenile and Criminal Justice. (2018). *San Bernardino county adult correctional statistics*. Retrieved from http://casi.cjcj.org/Adult/San-Bernardino

Cho, R. M., & Tyler, J. H. (2013). Does prison-based adult basic education improve post release outcomes for male prisoners in Florida? *Crime & Delinquency, 59*, 975–1005.

Collins, P. H. (2000). *Black feminist thought: Knowledge, consciousness, and the politics of empowerment* (2nd ed.). New York: Routledge.

CSUSB. (2018). *Facts and stats*. Retrieved from www.csusb.edu/about-csusb/facts-and-stats

CSUSB. (n.d.). *About us*. Retrieved from www.csusb.edu/about-csusb

Davis, L. M., Bozick, R., Steele, J. L., Saunders, J., & Miles, J. N. V. (2013). *Evaluating the effectiveness of correctional education: A meta-analysis of programs that provide education to incarcerated adults*. New York: The Rand Corporation. Retrieved from www.rand.org/content/dam/rand/pubs/research_reports/RR200/RR266/RAND_RR266.sum.pdf

Davis, L. M., Steele, J. L., Bozick, R., Williams, M. V., Turner, S., Miles, J. N. V., . . . Steinberg, P. S. (2014). *How effective is correctional education, and where do we go from here? The results of a comprehensive evaluation*. New York: The Rand Corporation. Retrieved from www.rand.org/pubs/research_reports/RR564.html

Day, A., Hardcastle, L., & Birgden, A. (2012). Case management in community corrections: Current status and future directions. *Journal of Offender Rehabilitation, 51*, 484–495.

Department of Corrections and Rehabilitation (CDCR). (2013). *County and region of parole*. Department of Corrections and Rehabilitation. Retrieved from www.cdcr.ca.gov/Reports_Research/Offender_Information_Services_Branch/Annual/MISC5/MISC5d2012.pdf

Durose, M. R., Cooper, A. D., & Snyder, H. N. (2014). *Recidivism of prisoners released in 30 states in 2005: Patterns from 2005 to 2010*. Office of Justice Programs. Retrieved from www.bjs.gov/content/pub/pdf/rprts05p0510.pdf

Duwe, G. (2017). *The use and impact of correctional programming for inmates on pre- and post-release outcomes*. Washington, DC: U.S Department of Justice. Retrieved from www.ncjrs.gov/pdffiles1/nij/250476.pdf

Halkovic, A., Fine, M., Bae, J., Campbell, L., Evans, D., Gary, C., & Tejawi, A. (2013). *Higher education and reentry: The gifts they bring: Reentry research in the first person*. New York: John Jay College of Criminal Justice. Retrieved from https://files.eric.ed.gov/fulltext/ED558779.pdf

Hirschi, T. (1969). *Causes of delinquency*. Berkeley, CA: University of California Press.

Jones, P. (2018). *What does an effective reentry program look like at a California State University campus?* (Unpublished master's project). California State University San Bernardino, San Bernardino CA.

Jones, S. R., Kim, Y. C., & Skendall, K. C. (2012). (Re-)framing authenticity: Considering multiple social identities using autoethnographic and intersectional approaches. *The Journal of Higher Education, 83*, 698–723.

Lam, C. M. (2012). Prosocial involvement as a positive youth development construct: A conceptual review. *The Scientific World Journal, 2012.* http://dx.doi.org/10.1100/2012/769158

Levin, J. S., Viggiano, T., Damián, A. I. L., Vasquez, E. M., & Wolf, J. (2017). Polymorphic students. *Community College Review, 45*, 119–143.

Liem, M., & Sampson, R. (2016). *After life imprisonment: Reentry in the era of mass incarceration.* New York: New York University Press.

McDonald, D. (2014). The role of intensive case management services in reentry: The Northern Kentucky female offender reentry project. *Women & Criminal Justice, 24*, 229–251.

Middlemass, K. (2017). *Convicted and condemned: The politics and policies of prisoner reentry.* New York: New York University Press.

Middlemass, K. (2019). Hiding in plain sight: Black women felons reentering society. In J. Jordan-Zachery & N. Alexander-Floyd (Eds.), *Black women in politics: Demanding citizenship, challenging power, and seeking justice* (pp. 69–95). Albany: SUNY Press.

Mukamal, D., & Silbert, R. (2018). *Don't stop now: California leads the nation in using public higher education to address mass incarceration: Will we continue?* Berkeley, CA: Renewing Communities. Retrieved from https://correctionstocollegeca.org/resources/dont-stop-now

Mukamal, D., Silbert, R., & Taylor, R. M. (2015). *Degrees of freedom: Expanding college opportunities for currently and formerly incarcerated Californians.* Retrieved from www.law.berkeley.edu/files/DegreesofFreedom2015_FullReport.pdf

Rocque, M. (2017). *Desistance from crime: New advances in theory and research.* New York: Palgrave Macmillan.

Spjeldnes, S., & Goodkind, S. (2009). Gender differences and offender reentry: A review of the literature. *Journal of Offender Rehabilitation, 48*, 314–335.

Steinmetz, K. F., & Henderson, H. (2015). On the precipice of intersectionality: The influence of race, gender, and offense severity interactions on probation outcomes. *Criminal Justice Review, 40*, 361–377.

Suggs, V. L., & Mitchell, S. (2011). The emergence of women's centers at the HBCUs: Centers of influence and the confluence of Black feminist epistemology and liberal education. *Diversity in Higher Education, 8*, 145–162.

Travis, J. (2005). *But they all come back: Facing the challenges of prisoner reentry.* Washington, DC: Urban Institute Press.

Trimbur, L. (2009). Me and the law is not friends: How former prisoners make sense of reentry. *Qualitative Sociology, 32*, 259–277.

U.S. Census Bureau. (2015). *Estimates of San Bernardino county, 2011–2015 American community survey 5-year estimates.* Retrieved from https://factfinder.census.gov/faces/tableservices/jsf/pages/productview.xhtml?src=CF

Veysey, B. M., Ostermann, M., & Lanterman, J. L. (2014). The effectiveness of enhanced parole supervision and community services: New Jersey's serious and violent offender reentry initiative. *The Prison Journal, 94*, 435–453.

Visher, C. A., & Travis, J. (2003). Transitions from prison to community: Understanding individual pathways. *Annual Review of Sociology*, *29*, 89–113.

Willingham, B. (2011). Black women's prison narratives and the intersection of race, gender, and sexuality in US prisons. *Critical Survey*, *23*(3), 55–66.

Zgoba, K. M., Haugebrook, S., & Jenkins, K. (2008). The influence of GED obtainment on inmate release outcome. *Criminal Justice and Behavior*, *35*, 375–387.

Chapter 18

The Politics of Restoring Voting Rights After Incarceration

Taneisha N. Means and Alexandra Hatch

Introduction

In February 2018, a group of formerly incarcerated people whose voting rights had been denied in Florida brought a lawsuit against state Governor Rick Scott. In *James Michael Hand et al vs. Rick Scott et al* (hereafter *Hand et al vs. Scott et al*), U.S. District Court Judge Mark Walker found Governor Scott's voting rights restoration process violated formerly-incarcerated citizens' 1st Amendment rights and Equal Protection Rights under the 14th Amendment.[1] Scott's process required individuals to:

> wait at least five years after completing their sentence, including probation and paying any restitution, before they can apply for rights restoration. The individual must then go before the clemency board, a four-member panel headed by the governor that only meets four times a year. The state gives the governor "unfettered discretion" to grant or deny clemency for any reason
>
> (The Sentencing Report, 2018).

Judge Walker commented that, "In Florida, elected, partisan officials have extraordinary authority to grant or withhold the right to vote from hundreds of thousands of people without any constraints, guidelines, or standards. . . . The question now is whether such a system passes constitutional muster. It does not" (The Sentencing Report, 2018, p. 2). Re-enfranchisement is a contemporary social justice issue, and illustrates how voting rights restoration processes are salient to ongoing discourses on (in)equality, mass incarceration, and reentry (Nave, 2018). Therefore, in the following chapter, Grant provides a detailed analysis of Florida's 2018 re-enfranchisement efforts and how various groups came together to pass Amendment 4, "The Voting Rights Restoration for Felons Initiative."

Most states deny the suffrage rights of persons under correctional supervision. Consequently, more than 6 million voting-age U.S. citizens are currently denied the right to vote (Hull, 2009; López-Guerra, 2014; Manza & Uggen,

2008; Thompson, 2002).[2] Whereas in most states ex-offenders' voting rights are automatically restored upon completion of sentence, 12 states permit post-sentence voting rights restrictions that authorize permanent disenfranchisement for all or at least some people (Brennan Center for Justice, 2018).[3] For these 12 states, some criminal convictions, such as treason, murder, or felony sexual offenses, result in the irremediable denial of voting rights, and simultaneously in many of these states, there are processes and requirements that facilitate re-enfranchisement for other criminal convictions.

Research stemming from think tanks, social justice organizations, and scholars has not fully explored these processes and requirements for re-enfranchisement. Consequently, the politics of re-enfranchisement have received very little scholarly attention (see Jackson, 2017). Here, we discuss post-sentence restrictions and what states require for re-enfranchisement. We argue that re-enfranchisement processes and requirements, which are often incorrectly characterized as race-neutral, are intentionally arbitrary and burdensome and consequently discourage and obstruct ex-offenders' access to the democratic process. We maintain that states purposely make re-enfranchisement challenging because the population implicated is disproportionately comprised of Black and Brown citizens because of the nation's deeply racist criminal justice system. Given what we know about the politics of minority citizens and the histories of racism in the 12 states that permit permanent disenfranchisement, limiting the participation of a significant proportion of these oft-oppressed racial minority groups is not a new phenomenon, but is a continuation of historical efforts that aim to maintain the political and social status quo.

As the United States is a republic and representative democracy, scholars must continue studying and denouncing anti-democratic policies and practices. Moreover, scholars need to consider the interplay of race in re-enfranchisement policies and how these policies are consistent with, and not significantly different from, other policies that have suppressed and silenced the voices of minority citizens (Brewer & Heitzeg, 2008; Crenshaw, 1995; Delgado & Stefancic, 2017). Re-enfranchisement is inherently a civil rights concern, and how former inmates transition from correctional supervision to their communities, and what governments and community organizations can do to assist with that transition, is a burgeoning topic both in and outside of academia (Middlemass, 2017; Petersilia, 2003; Travis, 2005). Re-enfranchisement helps individuals reconnect to their community by affording them opportunities to participate in civic life via voting and serving as jurors. Given the focus on disenfranchisement policies, this chapter complements that work by exploring re-enfranchisement.

Felony Disenfranchisement

Felony disenfranchisement can be traced to the period before the U.S. was founded. Proponents of felony disenfranchisement argued that restricting suffrage of convicted felons did not conflict with the principles of universal suffrage; therefore, it was not unconstitutional (Hull, 2009; Manza & Uggen, 2008). Proponents also argue that, by breaking the social contract, convicted felons gave up their civil rights conferred by the government. Some proponents argue that engaging in criminal activity was an indication of poor judgment and individuals with poor judgment could not be trusted to participate in the democratic process.

Opponents of felony disenfranchisement, however, argue that disenfranchisement inherently conflicts with the principle of universal suffrage – restricting, rescinding, or denying individuals the right to vote was literally the antithesis of universal suffrage (Liles, 2006; Manza & Uggen, 2008). Because these laws target a specific group in society, opponents see such laws as inherently unconstitutional. More recently, opponents have argued that felony disenfranchisement violates the 15th Amendment because Black people are disproportionately represented among those under correctional supervision, and therefore are disproportionately impacted by these laws. Despite strong political opposition, felony disenfranchisement is the current policy for individuals under correctional supervision in most states (Brennan Center for Justice, 2018).

Felony disenfranchisement has long been challenged in the legal arena, and the courts have consistently said felony disenfranchisement is not unconstitutional. In a 6–3 decision in *Richardson v. Ramirez* (1974), the U.S. Supreme Court ruled that barring parolees and convicted felons who completed their sentences from voting did not necessarily violate the Equal Protection Clause of the 14th Amendment. More recently, the primary claim in *Hayden v. Pataki* (2006), a case argued in the U.S. Court of Appeals for the Second Circuit, was that because racial and ethnic minorities are disproportionately represented among those incarcerated and formerly incarcerated owing to policing and prosecutorial practices (Alexander, 2012; Clear, 2009), felony disenfranchisement laws also violated Section 2 of the Voting Rights Act (VRA), which provides that:

> [n]o voting qualification or prerequisite to voting or standard, practice, or procedure shall be imposed or applied by any State . . . in a manner which results in a denial or abridgment of the right of any citizen of the United States to vote on account of race or color.

In an 8–5 decision, Second Circuit judges affirmed *Richardson v. Ramirez*, arguing that the plaintiffs could not challenge New York states' felony disenfranchisement laws under the VRA or the U.S. Constitution because Congress did not specify that the VRA applied to felony disenfranchisement laws. Because the courts have consistently upheld *Richardson* and ruled in favor of felony disenfranchisement laws and other post-sentence restrictions, states continue to restrict the voting rights of felons in and outside of prison (Brennan Center for Justice, 2018).

As of 2019, only two states do not currently have state felony disenfranchisement restrictions – Maine and Vermont. The other 48 states permit some form of voting restriction for individuals who have been convicted of a felony: 14 states restrict felony disenfranchisement to incarcerated individuals only; 4 states restrict both individuals in prison and on parole; 18 states restrict individuals in prison, on parole, and on probation; and 12 states restrict individuals in prison, on parole, on probation, and have post-sentence restrictions. These voting rights restrictions are directly attributed to mass incarceration. The number of disenfranchised individuals was 1.17 million in 1976, and in the last four decades, that number has grown by roughly 421 percent as the total number of incarcerated individuals has increased (The Sentencing Project, 2014, 2016).

Whether the 6 million disenfranchised citizens will ever be re-enfranchised largely depends on the state they reside in; the 12 states that permit post-sentence restrictions have the highest percentage of disenfranchised voters (The Sentencing Project, 2014, 2016). Drawing on (1) the extant literature in law, political science, sociology, and criminal justice, (2) state records, and (3) reports by nonprofit organizations, we highlight what states require ex-offenders to do in order to regain their suffrage rights. This research reveals that, while there are processes to restore voting rights to ex-offenders, they vary significantly across states, appear to be arbitrary and burdensome, and lack transparency and clarity around re-enfranchisement processes. Such laws should be considered wholly undemocratic.

States differ widely when it comes to re-enfranchisement processes and requirements. While 12 out of the 12 states that disenfranchise everyone under correctional supervision and require an application, 10 out of the 12 states permit the perpetual disenfranchisement for some or all individuals with felonies, the other requirements and criteria used by each state varies greatly. Some states require a "thorough" investigation after applications have been submitted. For instance, in Alabama, if an ex-offender meets the criteria and applies for the restoration of their voting rights, the Board of Pardons and Paroles will conduct an investigation and will make a determination if the person can vote.

Six out of the 12 states require fines and restitution be paid before applying for rights to be restored. In addition to fines and restitution, Tennessee requires child support to be paid. Five states require certified documents from a courthouse,[4] which typically means that individuals must travel to obtain the required records. Five states require ex-offenders to wait a specified amount of time that varies depending on the state and sometimes the type of conviction. In Wyoming, for example, most ex-felons were forced to wait five years until they were eligible to register to vote, but this policy was repealed on January 1, 2016. Three states specify that petitioners cannot have any pending charges, and one state counts felonies from other states when it comes to registering to vote. In sum, we find there is very little uniformity when it comes to state re-enfranchisement processes and requirements, and, most importantly, states are often asking a lot of individuals who are already marginalized in society and trying to reenter society.

Bottom line, regardless of the jurisdiction in question, it is quite onerous to go through the process to have one's voting rights restored. To highlight the laboriousness inherent in many states' re-enfranchisement processes, we discuss the voting rights restoration process in two states: Iowa and Virginia. These two states were selected because they differ in terms of geographical location, politics, and racial demographics.

Iowa permanently disenfranchises its citizens with past felony convictions and grants the governor the authority and power to restore voting rights; approval from the governor requires the completion of an Executive Clemency application, which must include proof of payment of fines, fees, and restitution, a criminal history record, other certified documents, and a signed release that authorizes "any and all persons, firms or corporations, to release any and all information or documents they may now have or hereinafter receive concerning me" (Iowa, n.d.). Although roughly 80% of applicants are approved, this is not a welcoming process. Only 17 people applied for rights restoration in the state of Iowa in 2015 (Brennan Center for Justice, 2018). In 2016, just under ten percent of Iowa's Black population was disenfranchised while just over two percent of Iowa's total citizens were disenfranchised (The Sentencing Project, 2016). Iowa's disenfranchisement and re-enfranchisement policies have been revised numerous times through executive orders made by Democratic Governor Vilsack and his Republican successor, Governor Branstad, as a result of legal challenges and political objections. Nonetheless, in January 2019, disenfranchisement is a reality for convicted felons in Iowa, and the state continues to require much of individuals wanting their voting rights restored.

Prior to 2014, individuals in Virginia lost their suffrage rights upon conviction of a felony, and they were only eligible to have their rights restored three years after completing their prison, jail term, parole, and/or probation, and after paying all court mandated fines, restitution, and court costs. To remain eligible, applicants had to have no pending criminal charges, misdemeanor or felony, during the three-year period. If someone was deemed eligible, they could apply to the governor for rights restoration. To apply, the state, like Iowa, required the same items, plus a letter from the most recent probation or parole officer outlining the period of supervision, a copy of the pre-sentence report, if applicable, a certified copy of every sentencing order for each felony conviction on one's record from the Clerk of Court in which one was convicted, certified copies of any court order or other official document modifying any sentence, including probation or parole, a letter of petition, three letters of reference, and a letter addressed to the governor.

Like in Iowa, the voting rights restoration process in Virginia has been challenged and amended through a series of executive orders to address political objections and because of legal challenges, such as the July 2016 ruling in *Howell v. McAuliffe*, which said that re-enfranchisement could only be granted on a case-by-case basis. Since January 2019, while Virginia's state constitution continues to permanently disenfranchise individuals with past felony convictions, the governor vowed to restore voting rights on an individual basis. The requirements are less burdensome: To be eligible for rights restoration, a person needs to be free from correctional supervision, and then the person can contact the Secretary of the Commonwealth to obtain an application, which requires contact information, conviction history, and certification by the ex-offender that they have completed any and all terms of incarceration, parole, and/or probation.

Re-enfranchisement presents an additional challenge to individuals who are already expected to surmount numerous obstacles (Middlemass, 2017; Pager, 2003). As Table 18.1 and the brief summary of restoration processes in Iowa and Virginia demonstrates, re-enfranchisement processes and requirements are arbitrary and onerous, especially for individuals who often lack social, political, and economic resources (Middlemass, 2017). The process is also subject to amendments because of political administrative changes and political objectives. Consequently, while restoration processes are available, they tend to discourage rather than encourage re-enfranchisement. This is supported with the evidence from Iowa: only 17 people applied for rights restoration in 2015 (Brennan Center for Justice, 2018). Iowa is not unique; in most states, re-enfranchisement processes and requirements discourage ex-offenders from applying to have their voting rights restored (Brennan Center for Justice, 2018).

Returning citizens do not apply for re-enfranchisement because procedures are intentionally difficult and highlight the great lengths some states are willing to go to in order to maximize the number of felons within their jurisdictions that are disenfranchised. Disenfranchisement laws further marginalizes racial minorities, who disproportionately comprise the population under correctional supervision. Even with a process to re-enfranchise available to returning citizens, the reality is that certain communities end up with many individuals who experience perpetual felony disenfranchisement because of the burdensome restoration processes.

The Impetus & Implications of Post-Sentence Restrictions & Restoration Processes

Interestingly, the states with the highest rates of incarceration include Alabama, Georgia, Louisiana, Mississippi, and Oklahoma, yet they do not have the highest number of disenfranchised voters (The Sentencing Project, 2016). When states with the highest rates of incarceration, Louisiana and Oklahoma, are compared to states with the lowest rates of incarceration, Maine and Minnesota, we found that there is no substantial difference in

Table 18.1 The Voting Rights Restoration Processes and Requirements in the 12 States that Permit Post-Sentence Restrictions

	DISENFRANCHISEMENT WHILE IN PRISON, AND ON PROBATION AND PAROLE	APPLICATION	THOROUGH INVESTIGATION	CHILD SUPPORT	FINES RESTITUTION PAID	PERPETUAL DISEN-FRANCHISEMENT FOR SOME	CERTIFIED DOCUMENTS	WAIT PERIOD	NO PENDING CHARGES	FELONIES IN OTHER STATES COUNT
ALABAMA	X	X	X		X	X			X	
ARIZONA	X	X**			X	X	X	X		
DELAWARE	X	X				X				
FLORIDA	X					X****				
IOWA	X	X			X	X	X			
KENTUCKY	X	X			X	X			X	
MISSISSIPPI	X*	X				X				
NEBRASKA	X	X**						X		X
NEVADA	X	X**				X	X	X		
TENNESSEE	X	X		X	X	X				
VIRGINIA	X	X								
WYOMING	X	X				X	X	X***		

*   Some individuals in prison can vote
**   Application required by some offenders, but not all (e.g., Nebraska – treason; Nevada – "violent" offenses)
*** No wait time for first time, nonviolent offenders
**** According to the Florida Commission on Offender Review, as of January 15, 2019, no process has been defined to re-enfranchise former felons. Their website says: "With the passage of Amendment 4 in the November 2018 General Election, the Clemency Board will temporarily postpone consideration of pending applications for restoration of civil rights while the new framework required to implement the constitutional changes is defined, which may include the need for implementing legislation in the upcoming legislative session. The Clemency Board will continue to process and hear pending applications for other forms of clemency, including commutations, pardons, restoration of firearm authority, remission of fines or forfeitures, and restoration of alien status." (www.fcor.state.fl.us/index.shtml).

terms of the voting rights restoration process that a state chose to enforce. Some states with high rates of incarceration have the same post-sentence restrictions and voting rights restoration process as states with low rates of incarceration, which suggests that incarceration rates are not the driving force behind voting restrictions and re-enfranchisement processes (The Sentencing Project, 2016).

Some scholars argue that, after one considers a myriad of different variables, the only factor that truly explains policies concerning felony disenfranchisement is race and racism (Bowers & Preuhs, 2009; Preuhs, 2002; Dilts, 2014). Preuhs (2002) argues that felony disenfranchisement policies stem from institutionalized racism and are meant to undermine the voting power of people of color, especially Black and Latinx Americans. His empirical analysis revealed a curvilinear relationship between the severity of voting restrictions and the size of the minority population, indicating that "as the minority population increases, felon disenfranchisement policy will at first increase in severity, and then subsequently become less restrictive" (p. 739). Moreover, he created the Prisoner Parity Ratio (i.e., number of people of color in prison divided by the number of people of color in the population), which was statistically significant as well. According to Preuhs (2002):

No other explanations [are] likely – Government ideology, the level of democratic inclusion, the incarceration rate as a proxy for crime policy, party competition, and socioeconomic indicators all fail to significantly explain the level of severity of voting restrictions. Even the argument that southern states are more apt to impose severe restrictions on felons' voting rights fail to hold in the analysis

(p. 743).

We agree; race and racism are driving post-sentence voting restrictions and voting rights restoration processes (The Sentencing Project, 2016), and our historical analysis revealed a clear pattern; most states with post-sentence restrictions and burdensome voting rights restoration processes (see Table 18.1) have long histories of marginalizing racial minorities. Matos (2017) urges scholars to think critically about geography and the "sociohistorical legacies of localities" (p. 808) to understand immigration policies, and although she focuses on immigration policy, her work inspired us to think more critically about the sociohistorical legacy of racism and exclusion in the states with post-sentence restrictions and how these policies might relate to broader exclusionary and discriminatory racial projects (Omi & Winant, 2015).

In the past, historical policies and practices, such as grandfather clauses, literacy tests, and poll taxes (i.e., voting qualifications), were developed and enacted to keep racial minorities, but especially Black Americans, from voting. Most of these practices were outlawed by the mid-20th century, which

Restoring Voting Rights After Incarceration   255

sent a clear signal that such explicit racial disenfranchisement tactics would not be tolerated in the post-Jim Crow era. Given policing practices and incarceration, it seems many states turned to post-sentence voting rights restrictions and complex re-enfranchisement processes as a way to do the work historical voting qualifications had once done.

According to the Brennan Center for Justice (2018), millions of U.S. citizens are currently barred from voting. While some of these individuals are currently incarcerated or under correctional supervision, many of these individuals have already reentered society but have not had their voting rights restored. When looking more closely at who is disproportionately affected, it is clear that it is concentrated among the Black voting-age population (Brennan Center for Justice, 2018). For instance, more than 20% of Black voters in 4 states – Florida, Kentucky, Tennessee, and Virginia – are disenfranchised because of a felony conviction. Studying who is disenfranchised, temporarily or permanently, in conjunction with re-enfranchisement processes and requirements, reveals the strong connections that exists between felony disenfranchisement and the more explicit and historical disenfranchisement of Black Americans. Not seeing this historical connection may lead to the type of "unsound historical analysis" that Thurgood Marshall critiqued his U.S. Supreme Court Justice brethren of doing in his poignant dissent in *Richardson v. Ramirez* (1974).

Looking at the impetus for why felony disenfranchisement policies in a lot of states have been adopted, it is notable that states with post-sentence restrictions have long histories of voter suppression, marginalization, and terror. This is consistent with what we know about mass incarceration, which should not be seen as a late-20th century racial project but should be recognized as a racial project that has a longer history given the convict-lease system and the policing of Black people in the post-slavery era (Haley, 2016; LeFlouria, 2015). Florida's permanent disenfranchisement policy concerning ex-felons was added to its Constitution in 1868, the same year the 14th Amendment was passed. Felon disenfranchisement laws ensured the political, social, and economic status quos would remain unchanged given the inherent intersection of racism, policing, and the criminal justice system.

When looking at the states that subscribe to post-sentence restrictions, it is important to note that the history of slavery is evident in *all* of the 12 most restrictive states in terms of post-sentence voting rights restrictions *and* re-enfranchisement processes and requirements. Thus, Matos' theory concerning geographies of exclusion can be applied to the study of voting rights restoration processes; it provides an analytic framework to process and make sense of why 12 states from various regions across the continental U.S. have policies that discourage and, in some cases, prevent felons from voting. It is not a coincidence; it is because of their enduring racial projects that are at the core of anti-Black policies and racial inequality.

Conclusion

Widespread suffrage is central to any democracy, especially representative democracies; for 6 million voting-age American citizens to be ineligible to vote because of a felony conviction raises serious questions regarding the health of our democracy. Moreover, because disenfranchisement laws are part of a racial project that is inherently anti-Black, these laws also represent a civil rights and social justice crisis.

If states are unwilling to permit individuals under correctional supervision to vote, they should allow automatic restoration of voting rights upon completion of their entire sentence (i.e., prison, parole, and/or probation). There should be no separate process or burdensome set of requirements because the process and requirements, regardless of what they are, make it extremely unlikely for already-marginalized individuals in society to be re-enfranchised. This is especially true when the stipulations require an applicant to get official court records, pay all fines, court costs, and restitution, be caught up on child support, and any number of other requirements states mandate. The current restoration processes and requirements likely dissuade potentially otherwise-eligible-voters from petitioning to have their rights restored. Moreover, there are numerous lawsuits in states with post-sentence voting rights restrictions because of the fact that flawed felon lists have resulted in legitimate voters being disqualified from voting (Clayworth, 2019).

Scholars are increasingly focusing on the reentry of formerly-incarcerated persons, and this work complements the ongoing discourse concerning what communities and governments can do to better support people reentering society (Middlemass, 2017). Although voting is not as urgent as housing, food, employment, or education, it matters in a democracy, and the processes that grant former offenders access to the electoral booth is critical in order to challenge and change existing laws, processes, and requirements to become re-enfranchised.

In conclusion, it is clear that, without understanding, discussing, and challenging re-enfranchisement processes and requirements, society ignores a major challenge to our democratic principles; allowing a specific group of citizens to be further marginalized and subject to second-class citizenship is unacceptable. How "universal" is universal suffrage when millions of Americans, many Black and Latinx, are prohibited from voting because of a felony conviction? This topic warrants further scholarly inquiry and needs to be included in the common public discourse.

Notes

1. The summary judgment for *Hand et al vs. Scott et al* is available here: www.scribd.com/document/370550182/James-Michael-Hand-v-Gov-Rick-Scott-State-of-Florida
2. Under correctional supervision refers to individuals who are jailed, incarcerated, or on parole or probation.

3. Alabama, Arizona, Delaware, Florida, Iowa, Kentucky, Mississippi, Nebraska, Nevada, Tennessee, Virginia, and Wyoming.
4. These documents most commonly include a Certificate of Absolute Discharge which verifies that all court fines and restitution were paid, charging indictment and judgment information, and probation order documents, if applicable. In Iowa, convicted felons are required to include a signed release that authorizes "any and all persons, firms or corporations, to release any and all information or documents they may now have or hereinafter receive concerning me".

References

Alexander, M. (2012). *The new Jim Crow: Mass incarceration in the age of colorblindness.* New York: The New Press.
Bowers, M., & Preuhs, R. R. (2009). Collateral consequences of a collateral penalty: The negative effect of felon disenfranchisement laws on the political participation of non-felons. *Social Science Quarterly, 90*(3), 722–743.
Brennan Center for Justice. (2018). *Criminal disenfranchisement laws across the United States.* Retrieved from www.brennancenter.org/criminal-disenfranchisement-laws-across-united-states
Brewer, R. M., & Heitzeg, N. A. (2008). The racialization of crime and punishment: Criminal justice, color-blind racism, and the political economy of the prison industrial complex. *American Behavioral Scientist, 51*(5), 625–644.
Clayworth, J. (2019, January 13). 'This is wrong': Iowa's flawed felon list has been disqualifying legitimate voters for years. *Des Moines Register.* Retrieved from www.desmoinesregister.com/story/news/investigations/2019/01/13/iowa-election-felon-voting-rights-ban-voters-polling-place-how-register-vote-state-rejected-votes-ia/2359082002/
Clear, T. R. (2009). *Imprisoning communities: How mass incarceration makes disadvantaged neighborhoods worse.* New York: Oxford University Press.
Crenshaw, K. (1995). *Critical race theory: The key writings that formed the movement.* New York: The New Press.
Delgado, R., & Stefancic, J. (2017). *Critical race theory: An introduction.* New York: New York University Press.
Dilts, A. (2014). *Punishment and inclusion: Race, membership, and the limits of American Liberalism.* New York: Fordham University Press.
Haley, S. (2016). *No mercy here: Gender, punishment, and the making of Jim Crow modernity.* Chapel Hill, NC: University of North Carolina Press Books.
Hull, E. (2009). *The disenfranchisement of ex-felons.* Philadelphia, PA: Temple University Press.
Iowa. (n.d.). *Streamlined application for restoration of citizenship rights.* Retrieved from https://governor.iowa.gov/sites/default/files/documents/Voting%20Application_0.pdf
Jackson, T. A. (2017). Dilution of the Black vote: Revisiting the oppressive methods of voting rights restoration for ex-felons. *University of Miami Race & Social Justice Law Review, 7,* 297.
LeFlouria, T. L. (2015). *Chained in silence: Black women and convict labor in the New South.* Chapel Hill, NC: University of North Carolina Press Books.
Liles, W. W. (2006). Challenges to felony disenfranchisement laws: Past, present, and future. *Alabama Law Review, 58,* 615.

López-Guerra, C. (2014). *Democracy and disenfranchisement: The morality of electoral exclusions*. New York: Oxford University Press.

Manza, J., & Uggen, C. (2008). *Locked out: Felon disenfranchisement and American democracy*. New York: Oxford University Press.

Matos, Y. (2017). Geographies of exclusion: The importance of racial legacies in examining state-level immigration laws. *American Behavioral Scientist, 61*(8), 808–831.

Middlemass, K. M. (2017). *Convicted and condemned: The politics and policies of prisoner reentry*. New York: New York University Press.

Nave, R. L. (2018). Felon voting ban draws another federal lawsuit. *The Mississippi Today*. Retrieved from https://mississippitoday.org/2018/03/27/felon-voting-ban-draws-another-federal-lawsuit/

Omi, M., & Winant, H. (2015). *Racial formation in the United States*. New York: Routledge.

Pager, D. (2003). *Marked: Race, crime, and finding work in an era of mass incarceration*. Chicago, IL: University of Chicago Press.

Petersilia, J. (2003). *When prisoners come home: Parole and prisoner reentry*. New York: Oxford University Press.

Preuhs, R. (2002). Black and Latino representation, institutional position and influence. In *Annual State Politics and Policy Conference, Milwaukee, WI*.

The Sentencing Report. (2014). *Felony disenfranchisement laws in the United States*. Retrieved from www.sentencingproject.org/publications/felony-disenfranchisement-laws-in-the-united-states/

The Sentencing Report. (2016). *6 million lost voters: State-level estimates of felony disenfranchisement, 2016*. Retrieved from www.sentencingproject.org/publications/6-million-lost-voters-state-level-estimates-felony-disenfranchisement-2016/

The Sentencing Report. (2018). Disenfranchisement news: Judge rules Florida's rights restoration process is unconstitutional. Retrieved from www.sentencingproject.org/news/5960/

Thompson, M. E. (2002). Don't do the crime if you ever intend to vote again: Challenging the disenfranchisement of ex-felons as cruel and unusual punishment. *Seton Hall Law Review, 33*, 167.

Travis, J. (2005). *But they all come back: Facing the challenges of prisoner reentry*. Washington, DC: The Urban Institute.

Chapter 19

Restoration of Voting Rights
Returning Citizens and the Florida Electorate

Keneshia Grant

Before November 8, 2018, Florida's constitution denied people with felony criminal convictions the right to vote into perpetuity. Florida was not alone – Kentucky, Iowa, and Virginia had laws that called for a lifetime denial of access to the ballot box for adults convicted of a felony.[1] Other states' positions varied, with some allowing returning citizens' access to the vote at varying points in their reentry process, whereas just two states – Maine and Vermont – place no restriction on individuals voting rights. Before November 2018, Florida had the largest share of people affected by felony disenfranchisement statutes. Approximately one and a half million people were excluded from our nation's democratic process in Florida. These facts changed on November 8, 2018, when Florida voters passed the Voting Rights Restoration for Felons Initiative, popularly referred to as Amendment 4. This chapter explores the restoration process and its political implications for future elections.

Denial of access to the ballot box is a problem for all returning citizens, with 2.47 percent of the potential American electorate locked out of the system (Uggen, Larson, & Shannon, 2016). However, disenfranchising laws disproportionately affect Black voters. Nationally, 7.44percent, or 1 in 13 Black people, are thought to have lost their right to vote because of a criminal conviction (Chung, 2013). The numbers are much worse in Florida, and the cumulative effect for the Black electorate in the state is dramatic. The number of disenfranchised Black Floridians is double the overall rate at 21.35 percent.[2] This means that 1 in 5 Black people in Florida are affected by felony disenfranchisement policies (Uggen et al., 2016). Any denial of access to the democratic system is problematic, but Florida is an especially interesting case because of its historically close electoral margins of victory in national and state-wide elections. For example, during the 2000 presidential election, George W. Bush beat Al Gore by 537 votes (Manza & Uggen, 2008); a few years later, the 2018 gubernatorial race was decided by 32,463 votes in a state with a population of more than 20 million people.

Using the state of Florida as a backdrop, I describe why voting rights are so important, estimate the potential political consequences of extending the franchise to returning citizens, and provide suggestions for state officials who must grapple with the mandate handed down by the citizens via Amendment 4. This chapter describes the importance of the right to vote in a democratic society and highlights the dissonance of ideas inherent in denying returning citizens the right to vote. Next, I detail the history of disenfranchisement in Florida before examining Amendment 4 – the citizen-led constitutional amendment that opened access to the political system for returning citizens. The potential political ramifications of Amendment 4 for future elections is examined, and is followed by suggestions for officials in the state of Florida on how they should implement Amendment 4.

Collateral Consequences as Civil Death

Entities outside of the criminal justice system have erected post-incarceration penalties for returning citizens, that include but are not limited to: denial of the right to vote, inability to access welfare benefits, including subsidized housing, and exclusion from responsible work opportunities (Middlemass, 2017). Together, these punishments amount to a "civil death" for individuals who return to communities after serving their sentences (Ewald, 2002; see Miller & Spillane, 2012).

Over the past few decades, the number of people who have interacted with the criminal justice system – and by extension the number of returning citizens – has grown tremendously (Shannon et al., 2017). As a result, the number of citizens living in a state of civil death has also increased (Middlemass, 2017). Scholars, practitioners, politicians, and observers are questioning whether a civil death makes sense given the explosion in the number of people who interact with the carceral state and the stated goals of those interactions. Experts are questioning the political consequences of civil death for our increasingly competitive electoral environment (Chin, 2012).

The stated aims of the criminal justice system are in conflict with the actions of decision and policy makers. They advertise rehabilitation as the purpose of jails and prisons. The very name of these departments reinforces that notion; it is the Department of "Corrections" that incarcerates people in most states. However, laws are passed and policies are implemented that prevent full reintegration for the 95percent of people who eventually return to their communities (Travis, 2005; Middlemass, 2017). This is problematic for many reasons. First, to bar an individual from the opportunity to participate in the system of government, based on a previous act, is to acknowledge that the criminal justice system does not rehabilitate. Second, to inflict a system of post-punishments on individuals is to punish the individual twice for their original offense. Third, the consequences inflicted on returned citizens are not limited to the returning person. In many instances, their families and communities share the burden of their civil death (Middlemass, 2017). Finally, denying returning citizens the opportunity to reintegrate is problematic for democracy. Our "government by the people, for the people" is supposed to be shaped by the people, yet the system excludes the voices of a large segment of the population.

Access to political participation through voting is a classic example of the problems of this incongruity. The dissonance in ideas about rehabilitation and collateral consequences has more nefarious effects than a simple mismatch in aims. When states deny felons access to the vote, they implicitly promote the idea that the criminal justice system has failed to rehabilitate enough for the former prisoner to make basic choices about the society in which they live. The decision to deny suffrage to returning citizens also unfairly distorts the electorate. Although the largest number of people with criminal convictions are White, Black people account for a disproportionately large percentage of returning citizens (Chang, 2018; Mak, 2018). Felon disenfranchisement policies disproportionately mute the voices of Black people and their communities. Given the very competitive nature of elections today, particularly as it relates to the evenly partisan divided state of Florida, muting the voices of Black returning citizens has real consequences for the outcome of elections and by extension the outcome of public policies.

Felon Disenfranchisement in the State of Florida

Florida's history of felon disenfranchisement is rooted in its historic objective to prevent Black political participation (Manza & Uggen, 2004). Following the Civil War, the state refused to grant voting rights to its Black citizens, but as a requirement for re-admission to the Union, Florida changed its constitution and extended the right to vote to "all free men" in 1868. Yet state officials used various legal strategies to restrict access to the ballot; Florida's 1868 constitution was careful to specify disenfranchisement of individuals with felonies as one method of many to circumvent the 15th Amendment to the U.S. Constitution (Wood, 2016; Lewis, 2018). Article VI, Section 4(a), of Florida's constitution, previously read:

> No person convicted of a felony, or adjudicated in this or any other state to be mentally incompetent, shall be qualified to vote or hold office until restoration of civil rights or removal of disability.

This seemingly race-neutral practice had specific consequences for Black Floridians (Middlemass, 2006; Dugree-Pearson, 2001). Along with other southern states, Florida enacted policies called Black Codes that criminalized Blackness; the crimes listed in the Black Codes were classified as felonies. Consequently, the Black Codes linked Blackness to felonious interaction with the state and linked felonies to loss of one's ability to vote and other rights (Middlemass, 2017).

Although Florida's constitution linked felonies to suffrage, the state's governors varied in their approaches to clemency, reinstatement, and the restoration of civil rights, and the removal of the felony "disability" (see Middlemass, 2017). While governor from 2007–2011, Charlie Crist – a Republican who changed his party identification to Independent while in office – worked to counter the state's Constitution by automatically restoring rights to returning citizens upon completion of their sentences. Crist's Republican successor, Rick Scott (2011–2019), changed the system to severely restrict access to the vote for returning citizens (Wood, 2016). During the Scott administration, returning citizens had to wait a period of five to seven years – depending on their charges – before they could apply for clemency. Further, they were required to appear before the state's Clemency Board.

Florida's Clemency Board was fraught with problems. The body met infrequently and made arbitrary decisions about which people could regain the right to vote. The seemingly haphazard method of decision making was actually a process through which White Republican returning citizens were three times more likely to have their rights restored than their Black Democratic peers (Brennan Center for Justice, 2019). In 2017, Scott's Clemency Board's system drew a legal challenge in the form of a federal class action lawsuit – *Hand et al. v. Scott et al.* – which was brought by the Fair Elections Legal Network and Cohen Milstein Sellers & Toll PLLC on behalf of nine returning citizens. In 2018, the U.S. District Court of the Northern District of Florida heard the case and ruled that Scott's Clemency Board's practice was unconstitutional because it violated the 1st and 14th Amendments of the U.S. Constitution. The state appealed and the case was referred to the 11th U.S. Circuit Court of Appeals.

Amendment 4

In Florida, Article VI, Section 4(a), of Florida's constitution from the 1868 Constitutional Convention stood until Amendment 4 overturned it in 2018, and it took an extraordinary effort by Florida residents to get the Amendment on the ballot. Before the U.S. District Court could force the state of Florida to change its civil rights restoration process, something unprecedented happened. Floridians engaged the state's citizen-led ballot initiative process to put the question of felon disenfranchisement to a vote before the people of the state.

In Florida, citizens can petition the electorate to change the state constitution.[3] For the 2018 election, citizens had to collect 766,200 signatures in order to have the amendment appear on the ballot (Florida Department of State, 2017). Desmond Meade, himself a returning citizen, began collecting signatures for a ballot amendment in 2015. His organization, Floridians for a Fair Democracy, collected 842,796 signatures – far surpassing the requirement. The language for the proposed amendment reads:

> This amendment restores the voting rights of Floridians with felony convictions after they complete all terms of their sentence including parole or probation. The amendment would not apply to those convicted of murder or sexual offenses, who would continue to be permanently barred from voting unless the Governor and Cabinet vote to restore their voting rights on a case by case basis.[4]

Meade found allies among other Floridians returning home and seeking a way to reenter the electorate. Most notably, he was joined in the early stages of the campaign by Neil Volz. Volz was a former staffer in the U.S. House of Representatives who was convicted of a felony as part of a lobbying scandal in 2007 (Volz, 2011). Civil rights organizations – the American Civil Liberties Union (ACLU), The Sentencing Project, and the Sixteen Thirty Fund – were also vocal supporters of Amendment 4, and played a critical role in voter education campaigns in the lead up to the November 2018 election. The Democratic Party, including its nominee for governor, Andrew Gillum, supported Amendment 4. Floridians for a Fair Democracy raised $25.3 million and spent $21.5 million in support of the effort according to campaign finance reports from Florida's Department of State.

Despite the support, Amendment 4 was not without opposition. An organization called Floridians For A Sensible Voting Rights Policy was Amendment 4's primary adversary. Richard Harrison, a lawyer from Tampa, started the organization in 2017 after Floridians for a Fair Democracy collected the required number of signatures to get the initiative on the 2018 ballot. The goal of Harrison's organization, as outlined by the organization's literature, is "honoring the constitutional ban on felon voting while restoring the right to vote to convicted felons who complete their sentences only after a thorough, case by case review" (Floridians for Fair Democracy, n.d.). Amendment 4 was also opposed by the Republican Gubernatorial candidate at the time, Ron DeSantis. Floridians For A Sensible Voting Rights Policy did not report campaign spending with Florida's Department of State.

In spite of the opposition, Amendment 4 earned 5,148,926 votes or 64.5 percent of the vote and passed on November 8, 2018, changing Florida politics and creating one of the largest expansions of the electorate in American history. The support for Amendment 4 was more votes than each of the candidates for governor and U.S. Senate. As a result, Florida's constitution changed to specify the following (the *italicized* text notes the changes in Florida's constitution):

> any disqualification from voting arising from a felony conviction shall terminate and *voting rights shall be restored upon completion of all terms of*

sentence including parole or probation. (b) No person convicted of murder or a felony sexual offense shall be qualified to vote until restoration of civil rights.

Will Returning Citizens Vote?

Whether and how returning citizens will participate in the electorate is an open question. Experts have differing opinions about their potential involvement, and the vast majority of the literature describes the number of returning citizens voting in elections as low (Uggen & Manza, 2002). For context, what follows is an analysis of turnout numbers for the voting eligible population (VEP) of Americans in the 2016 and 2018 elections. Figures for the 2018 midterm elections suggest that about 50 percent of the American VEP turned out to vote. In Florida, the turnout number was a bit higher at 54.9 percent. Turnout numbers are generally higher in presidential elections; in the 2016 presidential election, about 60 percent of the American VEP voted, and in Florida, turnout numbers were higher again, at 65.6 percent (McDonald, 2018).

By comparison, scholarly estimates for potential turnout among returning citizens average about 28 percent. For instance, Uggen and Manza (2002) suggest 35 percent turnout for a presidential election and 24percent for a midterm congressional election. Other scholars have argued that 35 percent is too high and their lower estimates range from 23.7 percent to 5percent (Burch, 2007, 2011; Haselswerdt, 2009; Meredith & Morse, 2014). In fact, Meredith and Morse (2014) suggest that the turnout among returning citizens in Florida for the 2016 midterm elections was just 16 percent for Black voters and 12 percent for White voters. What is unclear is the impact incarceration has on an individual's desire to participate in the political process via voting. Some suggest going to prison reduces the likelihood of voting (Lerman & Weaver, 2014) whereas others argue that incarceration does not impact an individual's future political participation (Gerber, Huber, Meredith, Biggers, & Hendry, 2017).

What Happens if Returning Citizens Do Vote in Florida?

In past studies, returning citizen turnout rates in Florida were lower than those in other states.[5] Burch (2011) considers the 2008 election, which was the first presidential election when felons could vote in Florida under Charlie Crist's clemency system. Burch finds that the overall rate of voting for returning citizens in the state of Florida was lower than that in other states. Although Burch's work provides data points that are helpful to understand how returning citizens may respond in 2019 and beyond, studying the 2008 presidential election presents some generalization problems.

The election occurred very soon after the 2007 clemency rule change, and the rule change was not well publicized in comparison to the educational campaign about Amendment 4. Future elections in the state of Florida will differ because returning citizens have approximately one year to prepare and register for the next presidential election and four years to prepare for the next gubernatorial election. Also different is that Amendment 4 was a watershed moment for electoral history in the United States. Unlike the 2007 rule changes, Amendment 4 was widely reported in local and national media and is likely to be more well-known among returning citizens, their families, and reentry organizations assisting returning citizens than the previous changes.

Notwithstanding the inability to generalize, Burch's work can help us to understand what to expect in future Florida elections. Most interesting among her findings was the information about Black voters. For the 2008 presidential election, she finds that the rate of turnout for Black returning citizens was higher than for their White counterparts; half of the voters in the study identified themselves as Democrats, and Black returning citizens were far more likely to turn out and vote for Democrats. She writes:

> Among registered Black male ex-felons, 71.7 percent in North Carolina and 84.2 percent in Florida are registered Democrats. Among Whites, however, only 35.3 percent and 36.4 percent of ex-felons are registered Democrats in North Carolina and Florida, respectively
> (Burch, 2011, pp. 701–702).

According to research from The Sentencing Project, the estimated percentage of Florida's overall population that is disenfranchised because of a felony conviction is 10.43 percent (Uggen et al., 2016). When we account for race and the number of Black – and by extension likely Democratic – citizens who are disenfranchised because of their status as felons, the percentage increases to 21.35 (Uggen et al., 2016). Yet Florida has its own detailed assumptions about potential participation of returning citizens. A report from the state's Office of Economic and Demographic Research suggests "the initial pool of eligible felons equals 736,375" and that the "potential one-time voter registration pool of felons with records in need of review ranges between 174,090 and 257,095 individuals" (Baker, 2016, p. 12). In the years that follow, the state assumes that with "69,744 total releases [from prison, creating], a potential registration pool of felons with records in need of review would range between 16,529 and 24,410 annually."

Estimates for Voting Among Florida's Returning Citizens

My assumptions about registration and turnout among returning citizens are based on four premises. First, Amendment 4 was very popular in the state and widely publicized. It should follow from this that the lack of political information – one of the biggest barriers to participation among returning citizens – should not have as strong an effect. Second, Florida is a highly competitive state, with very close margins of victory in state-wide contests. Thus, both political parties have a strong incentive to mobilize their respective voters. Third, returning citizens describe voting as an act that brings them closer to full citizenship, and many returning citizens seek to be a positive contribution to society. Voting is a public act that is frequently shared across social networks – including social media – and can be used to foster a positive image of a returning citizen. Finally, evidence already exists that suggests returning citizens in Florida are exercising their right to register in preparation for voting.

In this analysis, I assume the participation numbers for returning citizens in Florida between January 8, 2019, when Amendment 4 was implemented, and the November 2020 presidential election will be higher than initial predictions from experts in the field for at least two reasons. First, the percentage of Florida residents who have turned out to vote has surpassed the national average in every election since the year 2000, except for one.[6] Second, there has been an initial uptick in the number of people who have registered to vote in Florida since Amendment 4 went into effect. In Duval County, for example, 3,700 new registrations were recorded in the first few weeks after Amendment 4 took effect. Although it is too early to determine exactly who these newly registered individuals are, data demonstrates that many of these new registrants are older, Black, male, and Democrat (Taylor, 2019; Pantazi, 2019) Many of these voters live in predominantly Black communities that are home to a higher percentage of returning citizens (Clear, 2009; Lynch & Sabol, 2001). Put simply, many of these new registrants fit the profiles of returning citizens. Third, the level of attention to voting rights for returning citizens reached unprecedented levels in Florida's 2018 election, and this high level of attention and public discourse may lead to greater turnout among the population of returning citizens. For these reasons, it is safe to assume that the rate of registration and voting in Florida will be inconsistent with previous findings (for a detailed analysis see Taylor, 2019). For the rest of this section, I outline an estimate of voter registration and turnout among returning citizens in Florida in future elections.

My estimation begins by reducing the state's assumption of 736,375 eligible returning citizens to 700,000 to account for various factors that would disqualify an individual who seeks to register to vote, regardless of previous criminal status. These factors include, but may not be limited to, leaving the state, moving to a new jurisdiction and not re-registering, inability to establish permanent residence or homelessness, recidivism, or death. The Sentencing Project estimates that approximately 25 percent of returning citizens are Black, leaving 75 percent as non-Black. The non-Black figure includes all other racial distinctions, including White (non-Hispanic) and Hispanic (Uggen et al., 2016). Therefore, the racial breakdown of the estimate used

Restoration of Voting Rights 267

here is that there are approximately 175,000 Black and 525,000 non-Black returning citizens.

Further, it is assumed that returning citizens register to vote at a rate of 40 percent, regardless of race. This would reduce the returning citizen electorate to 280,000 voters, equaling 70,000 potential Black voters and 210,000 potential non-Black voters (see Table 19.1). Following Burch (2011), it is safe to assume that approximately 85 percent of Black voters will align with the Democratic Party, 10 percent with the Republican Party, and 5 percent with no party affiliation. For White returning citizens, approximately 37 percent should align with the Democratic Party, 37 percent with the Republican Party, and 26 percent will have no party affiliation. Given these assumptions, the 280,000 potentially registered returning citizens would be distributed as follows.

The last step to think about is how these numbers translate in terms of turnout. Black returning citizens are more likely to turn out than their White counterparts, and in past studies, they have turned out at varying rates based on the election (i.e., local, state, or national). The high participation estimate for the entire population is around 39 percent and low participation estimates are around five percent. However, turnout varies based on race, with Black returning citizens more likely to vote than non-Black returning citizens. Therefore, I estimate turnout among Black returning citizens at a rate equal to the overall population of voters in Florida; 54.9 percent. I estimate that turnout among White returning citizens will be lower, at 39 percent. Given these estimates, the returning citizen turnout could account for up to 120,330 votes (see Table 19.2).

Table 19.1 Potential Registration Among Returning Citizens

	Black	Non-Black	Total
Democrat	59,500	77,700	137,200
Republican	7,000	77,700	84,700
No Party Affiliation	3,500	54,600	58,100
Registration Totals, by race	70,000	210,000	280,000

Table 19.2 Potential Turnout Among Returning Citizens

	Black	Non-Black	Total
Democrat	32,666	30,303	62,969
Republican	3,843	30,303	34,146
No Party Affiliation	1,922	21,294	23,216
Turnout Totals, by race	38,430	81,900	120,330

268 Keneshia Grant

These estimates raise important questions about whether returning citizens could have made a difference in Florida's 2018 election, which featured very close margins of victory in two of the state-wide races. Assuming that the presence of returning citizens in the electorate would not have dramatically changed the tenor of the election, I applied the estimated returning citizen voters to the overall population. In both instances, Republicans won the election by less than 33,000 votes. Whether the results of the election would have changed based on returning citizen participation is difficult to know with certainty as it requires counterfactual analysis, which is not possible with available data. However, we can use the estimate above to make guesses about what could have happened in the election.

There is disagreement among scholars about how returning citizens would participate if they could. Meredith and Morse – two scholars who have written extensively on this topic – suggest that returning citizen impact would have been minimal, given the lower levels of participation among these voters in the past. Therefore, they argue, the 2018 election results would likely remain the same (Meredith & Morse, 2018). Still, others argue that the shift in the electorate would have changed the outcome of the electorate, though not by much (Bump, 2018).

2018 Senate Race: Nelson v. Scott

Table 19.3 2018 U.S. Senate Estimate, with Returning Citizens

Nelson	4,156,167
Scott	4,136,378
Margin	(19,789)
Outcome	Nelson wins
Nelson Estimate result, with Returning Citizens	
Current Total	4,089,472
RC* Black Dem	33,665
RC Non-Black Dem	33,030
New Total	4,156,167
Scott Estimate result, with Returning Citizens	
Current Total	4,099,505
RC Black GOP	3,843
RC Non-Black GOP	33,030
New Total	4,136,378

* RC refers to Returning Citizen

2018 Florida Gubernatorial Race: Gillum v. DeSantis

Table 19.4 2018 Gubernatorial Estimate, with Returning Citizens

Gillum	4,110,418
Desantis	4,113,041
Margin	2,623
Outcome	DeSantis wins
Gillum Estimate result, with Returning Citizens	
Current Total	4,043,723
RC* Black Dem	33,665
RC Non-Black Dem	33,030
New Total	4,110,418
DeSantis Estimate result, with Returning Citizens	
Current Total	4,076,168
RC Black GOP	3,843
RC Non-Black GOP	33,030
New Total	4,113,041

* RC refers to Returning Citizen

According to the estimates in Tables 19.1 and 19.2, I find that having returning citizens participate in Florida's 2018 midterm elections would have changed the outcome of the U.S. Senate election, but not the race for governor. For the U.S. Senate race (Table 19.3), my estimate of 65,695 additional Democratic votes for Bill Nelson means that he would have earned 18,789 more votes than Scott and retained his seat (see Table 19.3). In the Governor's race, the benefit of additional votes for Andrew Gillum would not have been enough to overcome the existing votes for Ron DeSantis, considering the additional 36,873 vote benefit that would have accrued to the Republican Party (see Table 19.4). Although these estimates suggest that the gubernatorial election would not have changed if returning citizens voted, many of the assumptions in the estimates should be questioned given the heightened interest in Andrew Gillum's historic candidacy as the first Black Democratic Nominee for Governor in the history of Florida.

Implementation Suggestions for Florida Officials

Amendment 4 has the potential to reshape Florida's political environment and will require a period of adjustment for voters and state officials alike, and it is not yet guaranteed that Amendment 4 will be fully implemented. In the weeks following the passage of Amendment 4, government officials across the state began to express concern about how the law would be implemented. For supervisors of elections in Florida counties, there was frustration about a lack of guidance from the state.

For the newly elected Republican governor and the Republican-led state legislature, there were questions about ways they may be able to halt enactment of the amendment (see Austin & Santil, 2019). DeSantis suggested that the legislature should pass "implementing language" before Amendment 4 could take effect (Bennett, 2018). These responses to Amendment 4's passage beg important questions about how the constitutional change could impact the political environment and how it will play out in terms of responses from government officials and groups like Floridians for a Fair Democracy.

There are some steps that Florida can take to ease the transition for voters and elected officials. State officials should continue educating themselves about the ways that citizens return to electorates. In particular, they should look to other states that have undergone similar transitions for "best practices" and potential ideas about how to move forward. One of the greatest lessons from other states is that the restoration of rights process should be automatic or have minimal barriers. Requiring individuals to complete clemency applications decreases the likelihood that they will participate in the electoral process (Meredith & Morse, 2015).

It will also be necessary for the state to behave with intention and dedicate financial resources to ensure returning citizens are incorporated into the electorate. For example, budget expenditures from the former Board of Executive Clemency should be redirected to a newly compromised board that would facilitate, educate, and promote voting among returned citizens, such as through an aggressive voter education program (Haselswerdt, 2009; Meredith & Morse, 2014). If the legislature does act, it should be towards writing administrative regulations to assist counties as they prepare for an uptick in registrations. Also helpful would be legislation specifying that the burden of proof for voter eligibility should be on the state, not on the returning citizen. This could be facilitated with a formally established relationship between the Departments of State and Corrections, who could create a process to automatically determine – in the offices of the supervisor of elections – whether individuals have completed all terms of their sentence. Although many questions about Amendment 4 remain unresolved, state officials should focus on ensuring that the will of the voters is upheld and implemented.

Conclusion

There is sorrow and promise in Florida's history of felon disenfranchisement. The sorrow is that for 150 years Florida was able to mute the voices of people who had already paid their debt to society. That sorrow extends to the communities that are home to currently incarcerated individuals and returning citizens. These communities often receive less than their fair share from the political system because the very same system is structured to disadvantage them as political participants. Equally devastating is many Black Floridians' inability to escape the consequences of the unjust system, even after they survive the state's arrest and incarceration traps. Andrew Gillum is one case-in-point. Unlike many other Black men in Florida, Gillum *was* able to survive his youth in Florida without interacting with the state's carceral system. What Andrew Gillum needed in 2018 – but could not get because of the injustice of felon disenfranchisement laws – was the electoral support from some of the people who would have been most likely to vote for him.

There is a great deal of promise in the passage of Amendment 4. Chief among the things to celebrate is that most of the benefit of this change will likely accrue to the Democratic Party. According to data from Duval County, Florida; "forty-one percent of new voters registered Democratic compared to just 24.5 percent who registered Republican" (Pantazi, 2019). Florida elections are likely to remain competitive and this boost in the number of potential Democratic voters could be what that party needs to achieve success in state-wide and local races.

Andrew Gillum is also a good case-in-point of the promise of Amendment 4. As described above, there are a number of reasons to believe that the assumptions inherent in the estimates presented here may not lead to the best understanding of the 2018 gubernatorial election. First is the dynamism of Andrew Gillum as a candidate. Voters in the state were as excited about Andrew Gillum as they had been about the candidacy of President Obama in 2008. Because of voters' excitement, Gillum increased the overall number of individuals voting for the Democratic Party in traditionally Republican strongholds across the state. Further, the Gillum campaign successfully increased the number of first-time voters entering the electorate by over 500,000 voters! For these reasons, it is highly likely that Gillum and the Democratic Party may be able to harness the potential of returning citizens in ways that reshape political outcomes.

This chapter has focused on the political consequences of returning citizen's votes on state-wide elections. However, these voters' potential to impact municipal and state legislative districts is also very promising and worthy of examination. Because Florida cities – like many across the nation – are segregated, returning citizens are often grouped together in racially homogenous communities that elect individual representatives to city councils and to state legislatures. Those are the elections that will have the most influence on citizens' day-to-day lives. Returning citizens' voices have been missing from those important spaces; they have the potential to change local election outcomes, where the vote spread between the winner and loser is often much smaller. Even if the Democratic Party is unable to win state-wide elections now that Amendment 4 is law, benefits will accrue directly to Black communities who may have a louder voice now that more members of their chorus can sing.

Notes

1. Although Virginia does not automatically restore voting rights, current and immediate past governors of the state have used their discretion to ensure access to the ballot box for returning citizens.
2. The overall percentage of people in Florida – of all races – who are disenfranchised is 10.43 percent.
3. Information about the 2018 process for amending Florida's constitution is on the Florida Department of State website.
4. Summary information about Amendment 4 is available on the Florida Department of State website.
5. Here, I rely heavily on Burch's analysis because it was cited in documents produced by the state of Florida that describe Amendment 4's potential impact on the state.
6. The 2006 election was the exception, when fewer Floridians than the national average turned out to vote. That year, 1.2 percent fewer Floridians cast ballots than the national average McDonald, 2018)

References

Austin, S. W., & Santil, T. (2019, February 4). Should amendment 4 be delayed? *The Gainesville Sun.* Retrieved from www.gainesville.com/opinion/20190204/sharon-d-wright-austin-and-taisha-saintil-should-amendment-4-be-delayed

Baker, A. J. (2016). Voting restoration amendment. In *Financial impact statement* (pp. 14–10). Gainesville, FL: Florida Office of Economic and Demographic Research. Retrieved from http://edr.state.fl.us/Content/constitutional-amendments/2018Ballot/VRATransmit-talLetters.pdf

Bennett, G. (2018, December 12) DeSantis to act quickly on water, supreme court, Broward sheriff. *The Palm Beach Post.* Retrieved from www.palmbeachpost.com/news/20181212/exclusive-desantis-to-act-quickly-on-water-supreme-court-broward-sheriff

Brennan Center for Justice. (2019, April 11). *Voting rights restoration efforts in Florida.* New York: Brennan Center for Justice. Retrieved from www.brennancenter.org/analysis/voting-rights-restoration-efforts-florida

Bump, P. (2018, November 8). Allowing felons to vote likely would have changed the result in Florida's Senate race. *The Washington Post.* Retrieved from www.washington-post.com/politics/2018/11/08/allowing-felons-vote-would-likely-have-changed-result-floridas-senate-race/?noredirect=on&utm_term=.43766d56eed1

Burch, T. (2007). *A study of felon and misdemeanant voter participation in North Carolina.* Washington, DC: The Sentencing Project. Retrieved from www.sentencingproject.org/wp-content/uploads/2016/01/A-Study-of-Felon-and-Misdemeanant-Voter-Participation-in-North-Carolina.pdf

Burch, T. (2011). Turnout and party registration among criminal offenders in the 2008 general election. *Law & Society Review, 45*(3), 699–730.

Chang, A. (2018, November 2). *In Florida, people with past felony convictions can't vote, but that could all change.* National Public Radio. Retrieved from www.npr.org/2018/11/02/663655567/in-florida-people-with-past-felony-convictions-cant-vote-but-that-could-all-chan

Chin, G. J. (2012). The new civil death: Rethinking punishment in the era of mass conviction. *University of Pennsylvania Law Review, 160,* 1789–1833.

Chung, J. (2013). *Felony disenfranchisement: A primer.* Washington, DC: The Sentencing Project. Retrieved from www.sentencingproject.org/doc/publications/fd_Felony%20Disenfranchisement%20Primer.pdf

Restoration of Voting Rights **273**

Clear, T. (2009). *Imprisoning communities: How mass incarceration makes disadvantaged neighborhoods worse.* New York: Oxford University Press.

Dugree-Pearson, T. (2001). Disenfranchisement – A race neutral punishment for felony offenders or a way to diminish the minority vote. *Hamline Journal of Public Law & Policy, 23*, 359.

Ewald, A. C. (2002). Civil death: The ideological paradox of criminal disenfranchisement law in the United States. *Wisconsin Law Review, 5*, 1045–1137.

Florida Department of State. (2017, March 16) *2018 initiative petition handbook.* Gainesville, FL: The Florida Department of State. Retrieved from https://dos.myflorida.com/media/697659/initiative-petition-handbook-2018-election-cycle-eng.pdf

Floridians For A Sensible Voting Rights Policy. (n.d.). Retrieved from www.floridavotingrights.org

Gerber, A. S., Huber, G. A., Meredith, M., Biggers, D. R., & Hendry, D. J. (2017). Does incarceration reduce voting? Evidence about the political consequences of spending time in prison. *The Journal of Politics, 79*(4), 1130–1146.

Hand et al. v. Scott et al. 888 F.3d 1206 (2018, April 25), No. 18–11388-G, U.S. District Court of Appeals, 11th Circuit.

Haselswerdt, M. V. (2009). Con job: An estimate of ex-felon voter turnout using document based data. *Social Science Quarterly, 90*(2), 262–273.

Lewis, S. A. (2018, December 10–14). The disenfranchisement of ex-felons in Florida: A brief history. *ECAN Bulletin*, p. 40.

Lerman, A. E., & Weaver, V. M. (2014). *Arresting citizenship: The democratic consequences of American crime control.* Chicago: University of Chicago Press.

Lynch, J., & Sabol, W. (2001). *Prisoner reentry in perspective* (Crime Policy Report, 3). Washington, DC: The Urban Institute. Retrieved from www.urban.org/ Uploaded-PDF/410213_reentry.PDF

Mak, T. (2018, November 7). Over 1 million Florida felons win right to vote with Amendment 4. National Public Radio. Retrieved from www.npr.org/2018/11/07/665031366/over-a-million-florida-ex-felons-win-right-to-vote-with-amendment-4

Manza, J., & Uggen, C. (2004). Punishment and democracy: Disenfranchisement of non-incarcerated felons in the United States. *Perspectives on Politics, 2*(3), 491–505.

Manza, J., & Uggen, C. (2008). *Locked out: Felon disenfranchisement and American democracy.* New York: Oxford University Press.

McDonald, M. P. (2018). *2018 November general election turnout rates.* United States Elections Project. [Dataset]. Retrieved from www.electproject.org/2018g

Meredith, M., & Morse, M. (2014). Do voting rights notification laws increase ex-felon turnout? *The ANNALS of the American Academy of Political and Social Science, 651*(1), 220–249.

Meredith, M., & Morse, M. (2015). The politics of the restoration of ex-felon voting rights: The case of Iowa. *Quarterly Journal of Political Science, 10*(1), 41–100.

Meredith, M., & Morse, M. (2018, November 2). Why letting ex-felons vote probably won't swing Florida. *Vox.* Retrieved from www.vox.com/the-big-idea/2018/11/2/18049510/felon-voting-rights-amendment-4-florida

Middlemass, K. M. (2006). Rehabilitated but not fit to vote: A comparative racial analysis of disenfranchisement laws. *Souls, 8*(2), 22–39.

Middlemass, K. M. (2017). *Convicted and condemned: The politics and policies of prison reentry.* New York: New York University Press.

Miller, B. L., & Spillane, J. F. (2012). Civil death: An examination of ex-felon disenfranchisement and reintegration. *Punishment & Society, 14*(4), 402–428.

Pantazi, A. (2019, March 4). After amendment 4, thousands registered in Duval County. *Now, will they vote?* Jacksonville, FL: The Florida Times-Union. Retrieved from www.jacksonville.com/news/20190301/after-amendment-4-thousands-registered-in-duval-county-now-will-they-vote

Shannon, S. K., Uggen, C., Schnittker, J., Thompson, M., Wakefield, S., & Massoglia, M. (2017). The growth, scope, and spatial distribution of people with felony records in the United States, 1948–2010. *Demography, 54*(5), 1795–1818.

Taylor, L. (2019). Amendment 4 is already changing Tampa's electorate. *The Tampa Bay Times.* Retrieved from www.tampabay.com/florida-politics/buzz/2019/02/07/amendment-4-is-already-changing-tampas-electorate-heres-how/

Travis, J. (2005). *But they all come back: Facing the challenges of prisoner reentry.* Washington, DC: The Urban Institute.

Uggen, C., Larson, R., & Shannon, S. (2016). *6 million lost voters: State-level estimates of felony disenfranchisement.* Washington, DC: The Sentencing Project.

Uggen, C., & Manza, J. (2002). Democratic contraction? Political consequences of felon disenfranchisement in the United States. *American Sociological Review, 67*(6), 777–803.

Volz, N. (2011). *Into the sun: A memoir.* Bloomington, IN: AuthorHouse.

Wood, E. L. (2016). *Florida: An outlier in denying voting rights.* New York: The Brennan Center for Justice. Retrieved from www.brennancenter.org/sites/default/files/publications/Florida_Voting_Rights_Outlier.pdf

Chapter 20

Perpetual Punishment
One Man's Journey
Post-Incarceration

Tomas R. Montalvo and Jennifer Marie Ortiz

Preface by Jennifer Marie Ortiz

Tomas R. Montalvo was born in Puerto Rico and raised in New York City's South Bronx neighborhood. In his early childhood, he experienced both physical and sexual violence. Beginning at the age of 12, Tomas was addicted to narcotics, including heroin and crack-cocaine. In 1997, Tomas was arrested for the first time; he was 18 years old. Although this arrest was for a first-time nonviolent drug offense, under the draconian Rockefeller Drug Laws he received an incarcerative sentence. He served seven and a half years at the Auburn Correctional Facility, a maximum-security prison in Upstate New York. Following his initial arrest and incarceration, Tomas cycled in and out of the criminal justice system on petty misdemeanor offenses. I first met Tomas on a NYC Subway train in March 2008, when he was homeless and heroin addicted. The following year, Tomas' life would change forever.

Arrest and Incarceration

Academic Prelude: Beginning in the 1970s, the United States waged a war on drugs, which increased sentence lengths for non-violent drug offenses. The result of the War on Drugs is mass incarceration. There are currently 2.2 million individuals incarcerated in the United States. Of the 2.2 million individuals currently incarcerated, over 95% accepted plea bargains rather than risk a lengthy sentence after trial, a concept known as the trial penalty phase (National Association of Criminal Defense Lawyers, 2018). The collateral damage of the War on Drugs are the millions of substance-addicted individuals who entered the correctional system instead of entering drug and alcohol treatment facilities. Fifty-eight percent of prison inmates and over 60% of jail inmates meet the medical standard for drug dependence (Bureau of Justice Statistics, 2017). Most of these individuals receive no substance abuse treatment during their incarceration (Chandler, Fletcher, & Volkow, 2009).

Ortiz:	*In March 2009, Tomas traveled to Pennsylvania to visit family. After an altercation with a family friend, Tomas was arrested and charged with multiple felonies and misdemeanors. Upon arriving at the police station, Tomas was tortured and subsequently incarcerated in an attempt to coerce him to confess to crimes he did not commit. Tomas was incarcerated in Luzerne County, the same county that was home to the infamous Cash for Kids scandal, where two county judges received financial kickbacks for sentencing juveniles to prison sentences. Although he was only visiting for the weekend, it would be six months before Tomas returned to his family in New York City, and six years before he truly experienced freedom. Below is his story told in his own words.*
Montalvo:	My last incarceration was in Luzerne County, PA in 2009. I went to Pennsylvania for a weekend to visit my brothers and ended up getting into a fight at a neighbor's house. I was arrested for that fight and taken to the police station where officers locked me in a cold room. One officer told me to take off all my clothes except my underwear; I did.

The officer proceeded to ask me "why did you break into the house and where is the stuff that you stole?" I told the police officer that I didn't break into anybody's house and I didn't steal anything. I was arrested for a simple fight in the residence, and I thought that I should be charged with simple assault, assault, or something of that nature. The officer said, "Yeah right," and then proceeded to pump up the A/C as he walked out of the room. He left me in there for approximately four to five hours.

I began to experience heroin withdrawal symptoms. I was in pain and sick. Nobody cared. After four to five hours in that room, they took me to the county jail and placed me in the maximum-security wing. I asked the C.O. (Corrections Officer) why I was in the maximum-security wing, and he informed me that it was because I was being charged with multiple felonies. So, I asked what my charges were because I hadn't seen a judge yet. He informed me that the charges were for a home invasion. I had all these trumped up charges of home invasion, robbery, and other stuff that never really happened.

I sat in that maximum-security cell block for five months before I even saw a lawyer. The prosecutor came to see me two times asking me to cop out to a plea deal, which was for ten years. I refused. I guess that's why they took so long to appoint me a lawyer. Once I saw the lawyer, which was 5 ½ months after my arrest, I got a court hearing. After six months in jail, I get my court date, and the court appointed lawyer tells me: "I got you a good deal. I got you a simple assault charge and your sentence will be a year. You'll be released today with six months served and six months on parole."

At the time, I was so frustrated and desperate to get back home that I copped out to the simple assault charge, which is the crime I actually committed. If I knew then what I know now, I would have never taken the deal. If I knew how much hell I would have to go through, I would have served the whole year in jail. But I took the deal and was released five to six hours later.

Release and Parole

Academic Prelude: Criminal records permanently brand the formerly incarcerated as a subgroup of society (Foucault, 1979; Middlemass, 2017). These individuals are systematically excluded from employment (Pager, 2003), creating a cycle of re-incarceration (Martin, 2013). The process of reentering society is complicated by state supervision of the formerly incarcerated. Approximately 80% of individuals who leave state prisons are placed on post-release supervision, like parole (Hughes & Wilson, 2003). Some jurisdictions charge a monthly fee for their own supervision, which serves as an additional barrier to reentry (Diller, Greene, & Jacobs, 2009). The fees often lead to financial instability, and failure to pay may result in a parole revocation (Pogrebin, West-Smith, Walker, & Prabha Unnithan, 2014).

Ortiz: *Following his release from jail, Tomas was placed on parole in Pennsylvania. Unable to meet the financial obligations imposed by parole, Tomas traveled to New York City. His brother helped him return to the construction job he held prior to his incarceration.*

Montalvo: Parole was the worst. I was arrested in a state I did not reside in. I am originally from New York City. Now remember I went to Pennsylvania, to the town of Hazleton, to go spend the weekend with my family. I was paroled to my sister-in-law's house in Pennsylvania, but she tells me I can't stay there because she doesn't want me around her children. I start to get frustrated because I had nothing in Pennsylvania. My job, my kids, and my immediate family were all in New York so I went to see the parole officer on my first visit and asked him if I could transfer my parole to New York City. I had a job lined up there and my wife was waiting for me. The parole officer told me I had to finish my parole in Pennsylvania, pay $100 every month to remain on parole, and not be re-incarcerated.

I tried to go and look for a job, but I couldn't find a job because in every newspaper in the county it said I was arrested for a home invasion and robbery. When jobs did a background check, every single charge that I was arrested for came up on my rap sheet. The problem there is that I pled guilty to simple assault. Why should the fact that I was arrested for home invasion and robbery come up every time that my name is searched? Those charges still come up on my record today.

I started to get frustrated because everything I loved, my wife, my kids, my mom, everything and everyone was in New York City. To top it all off, I couldn't find a job in Pennsylvania. I couldn't pay the parole fees because I didn't have any money. A month after my release, I decided to cross state lines from Pennsylvania to New York to find work. Once a month, I would drive back to Pennsylvania to see my parole officer, so I wouldn't be violated for a parole technicality. I technically violated parole by leaving the state to make money to pay my parole fees so I wouldn't be violated by parole, if that makes sense. I had to leave the state to work, and I had to work because if I didn't pay my parole fees I would be violated and forced to serve another six months, the time I had left on parole. I wasn't going to do that, especially not in the racist county of Luzerne. Parole put me in an impossible situation. I had to choose between a guaranteed loss of freedom for not paying my parole fees or face the potential loss of freedom if my parole officer ever made a surprise home visit. I chose to take the risk and cross state lines. That might not make sense to people but at the time it made perfect sense to me.

Child Support Nightmare

Academic Prelude: During incarceration, many incarcerated individuals accumulate debt (Levingston & Turetsky, 2007). Debt serves as a major barrier to successful reentry because it makes providing for oneself difficult. Courts continue to enforce child support orders throughout one's incarceration leading to large debts, which the formerly incarcerated must pay as a condition of their post-release supervision (Pearson, 2004). Although most non-custodial parents can request a child support adjustment, that right is not often afforded to the incarcerated. Incarcerated individuals must wait until their release to apply for an adjustment hearing; however, at the time of their release many individuals owe thousands in child support. The decision to adjust that child support payment is left to the sole discretion of the family court judge (Pearson, 2004). Failure to make child support payments is a felony in some jurisdictions and can result in a return to prison.

Perpetual Punishment   279

Ortiz:	*Three months after his release from jail, Tomas and I decided to move in together. We moved into a one-bedroom basement apartment in Queens. While we were initially very happy to be together again, during our first month in our new apartment, we learned about his child support debt. The courts, employers, and the mother of his son used this debt as a justification to dehumanize him. This debt would serve as the most significant barrier to his reentry and to our happiness.*
Montalvo:	I have three children. My oldest is Nashalie, who I didn't meet until she was 18 years old. Today, she is 22 years old. I met her mom in Puerto Rico when I was 16 years old. She was older than I was and I lived with her for two years before moving back to New York City. Nashalie's mom never told me she was pregnant. I didn't find out I had another daughter until she was aging out of the foster care system. Since I found out about her, I have been in her life. We speak almost daily.

My second child is my 19-year-old daughter, Keishla. Because of my first incarceration and my drug addiction, I never got to be a father to Keishla. It remains one of my biggest regrets in life. My youngest child is my son Adam. He is 16 years old and I have been in his life since birth.

Prior to my last incarceration, I made child support payments directly to Adam's mother. However, I did not know that she had filed child support paperwork in Family Court a year prior to my arrest. Having worked "off the books" jobs for most of my life, I never had my check garnished, so I didn't know I owed anything. During my six-month incarceration, my debt grew to almost $15,000 in child support. I had no idea that child support keeps accumulating while you're locked up. I came out of jail and I went to New York. I moved in with my wife and I was happy. My first job on the books, I was making $1200 every two weeks after taxes. I was happy because I had a good job and was finally ready to do the right thing.

When I received my first paycheck, I got a paycheck for $600. The other $600 was garnished. I found out from human resources at my job that the garnishment was for child support. The courts garnished half of my pay for child support, which I didn't even know had accrued to such a large amount. The fact that my check was being garnished 50% took a toll on me. I got upset. I got depressed. I didn't even want to work anymore.

To make matters worse, my ex-girlfriend did not allow me to see my son on a consistent basis. I thought that because I was his father and paying child support that I had a right to see him. He was six years old at the time. I wanted to be a father to him. My first bid destroyed my relationship with Keishla. I was determined not to make that same mistake with Adam. His mom had other plans. There were times when I would see him every other weekend but there were times when she would not let me see him for months. When I would see him, he would tell me about the horrible things his mother said about me. She told my son I was nothing but a crackhead and that I didn't love him. She even told my son that I was a deadbeat and wasn't paying child support, even though my check was being garnished. Knowing that she was badmouthing me to my son made me angry, but I knew I couldn't do anything about it. She had the power. I was just the ex-con. I was paying like a father should but I wasn't allowed to be a dad. It was the most frustrating situation to me.

Nevertheless, because I had the support of my wife, I got a second job. I worked in the morning as a sheet rocker and got an "off the books" job at night as a maintenance worker for another construction contractor. I worked ridiculous hours, often getting home at 11pm or midnight and then heading back out the door at 6am, just to make ends meet. I did this so that my child support debt wouldn't take a toll on my wife as all the bills were falling on her shoulders. After nearly two years of breaking my back and making my child support payments on time, plus making additional payments when I could, including having our income tax return ceased by the division of child support, the recession hit the construction market and I got laid off from both of my jobs. I applied for unemployment benefits, so I could survive until I found another job.

When I got on unemployment, half of my unemployment check was garnished. My wife suggested I go to Family Court and try to get my child support payments lowered. Unfortunately, my son's mother works for the New York City Fire Department and has many friends in the court system. On the day of my adjustment hearing, she walked up to the clerk, whispered something, and our case was the first one heard that day. I would later find out that the judge assigned to our case was notorious for railroading fathers he deemed unfit. The judge refused to lower my child support payment, even though I was unemployed and receiving unemployment benefits. I only got $335 per week in unemployment and the court took 50% of that. Because the judge refused to lower my child support payments, the debt I spent two years making payments towards started to increase again. All the progress I made on the $15,000 was gone. That also took a toll on me. I didn't feel like a man because I couldn't provide for my wife.

In one court hearing, the judge threatened to send me back to prison. Because I was no longer able to make the $600 a month payment, the judge gave my son's mother the choice of what would be the outcome of my life. He asked her if she wanted me to go to jail that day or if he should put me on probation. That was the first time that I heard of a judge giving the other party the right to choose what would happen to someone. She decided that the proper punishment would be to put me on probation for a year and that if I stopped paying during that year of probation then I should go to jail for six months. The judge agreed with her, put me on probation, and suspended my driver's license. I felt helpless and scared because I knew that my son's mother controlled my life. I hadn't even committed a crime, but a year and half after completing my parole sentence, I was back on supervision.

Probation entailed having to spend eight hours a day, five days a week at a substance abuse program, even though by that point I was three years sober. In the eyes of the court, I was just a junkie criminal. I would go to this office in Manhattan, just sit there, and work on resumes and take parenting classes. I already had a resume and I knew how to be a father. There was nothing in the program to help me find a job.

For a year, I spent eight hours a day, five days a week sitting in this program that did nothing to help, just so I wouldn't go to jail again. There I was doing the right thing or at least trying to do what I thought was the right thing, working and paying child support. My son's mother still kept him from me in spite of all that I was doing right. I was trying to be what the courts would consider a productive member of society. Yet by doing the right thing, I was still being treated like a criminal. The program director came to the court hearings with me and told the judge I did not belong in the program. The judge didn't care. He asked me why I still didn't have a job. I tried to explain that I couldn't find a job because I had to spend all day at the program. He didn't care. The program director told the judge that not having a driver's license made me ineligible for some jobs. The judge reinstated my license. A year later, they said I had graduated out of the program. I still didn't have a job and the system never offered me help after that day. A year of my life was lost and yet I was in the same position where I started. I was suffering and my son was suffering without a father. Nobody cared.

Perpetual Punishment

Academic Prelude: The formerly incarcerated face substantial barriers to finding gainful employment post-incarceration (Bushway, Stoll, & Weiman, 2007). Although studies indicate that employment reduces recidivism (Uggen, 2000), employment discrimination against the formerly incarcerated is legal (Middlemass, 2017). Employers reject over 90% of applications submitted by felons (Pager, 2003). A recent Prison Policy Initiative study found that the unemployment rate for the formerly incarcerated was higher in 2008 than the national unemployment rate during the Great Depression (Prison Policy Initiative, 2018). Employment discrimination is exacerbated by unrealistic parole conditions including attending unnecessary programming during standard business hours (Thompkins, 2010).

Ortiz:	*For a year, I watched helplessly as the civil court system railroaded my husband. I wanted so badly to tell that judge who my husband really was, but I was not allowed inside of the court hearings because I was not a party to the case. Every court hearing my husband came out looking more defeated. His overall self-esteem and feeling of self-worth was further diminished every time he applied for a job he was qualified for but was denied because of his criminal record. Every day that I walked out of the door and headed to work, I looked at the sadness in his face because he wanted to work but couldn't. At one point, he became so desperate that he worked a 10-hour shift at a Manhattan restaurant for $30. Another time he stood in front of Home Depot trying to get work as a day laborer. That day he worked 8-hours for $60. I wanted to tell the Family Court that he was trying everything, but no one cared, and no one would listen. They had made up their mind about who he was based on mistakes in his past. They did not care that he changed his life.*
Montalvo:	Eventually, my unemployment benefits ended but I still couldn't find a job, well a steady job at least. I would work odds-and-ends jobs. For instance, I knew people around the neighborhood that would introduce me to somebody that needed pictures hung, and I would do that. Someone needed tiles laid and I would do that. But nothing was ever steady. There was never a job that helped me overcome the feeling of drowning in debt. I kept on looking for work and finally found a job at an upholstery company in Long Island City making $10.00 an hour. The NYS Child Support system immediately started garnishing my pay but I understood the garnishment because I owed child support. The problem that I had was that although my pay was being garnished, I received a letter from Family Court for a new hearing for non-payment. I took the letter to my place of employment and the owner informed me that he hadn't sent any payments to child support. For the four months that my check was being garnished, he had not sent one payment. Here I am thinking I am doing the right thing and yet once again I have the fear of being arrested because this business owner decided to screw me over because I had a criminal record. He thought he could get away with it. This same owner would always pay me short and I could never say anything. I didn't want to lose the job, so I just took whatever he gave me, as long as I thought my child support was being paid.

Perpetual Punishment   283

The employer was dehumanizing me. I was an ex-con, so he could do what he wanted to me, and I blame society for giving that employer the right to dehumanize me. Everyone dehumanizes ex-cons. No one cares what happens to us, so the owner knew he could get away with it. He could take advantage of me because to them I'm nothing but an animal. I'm an ex-convict. I'm not even human in their eyes. Who was I going to tell? Who was going to listen to me? Who was going to care?

For years I struggled working dead end jobs and scraping up every little bit of money I could to pay my child support. Whenever I didn't have the money, my wife would decide which bill not to pay so she could pay my child support so I wouldn't go back to jail. She always made sure we sent a payment even if it meant we had to skip meals. She did it because she loved my son like her own. She shouldn't have had to do that because that was my responsibility. That experience puts pressure on a person. I tried my best to stay levelheaded and stay on the right track. At one point, I started traveling to Pennsylvania every week to work for my father-in-law's company in York, a four-hour bus ride from New York City. I would travel there every week and then travel back to New York City on the weekends to see my kids and be with my wife. At one point, my wife convinced Adam's mom and Keishla's mom to let the kids stay in our house every other weekend for a few months. That was the one bright spot in all of this madness but it didn't last long. I traveled back and forth from New York City to Pennsylvania for several months. It took a toll on my marriage and my health. I couldn't do it anymore so I returned to New York City and again started looking for work.

Second Child Support Payment

Ortiz: *Tomas' initial child support case was for his son, Adam. In 2013, the mother of his daughter, Keishla, applied for public assistance, which resulted in a second child support case. Unbeknownst to us at the time, this second child support case would be our saving grace. Tomas lost contact with Keishla in 2004 when her mother moved to Guatemala. We reestablished contact with Keishla through social media. She began visiting us approximately two years after Tomas' release from the Pennsylvania Department of Corrections.*

Montalvo: My luck finally changed when my daughter's mother lost her job and decided to get on public assistance. I received a letter stating that because my daughter was on public assistance, via her mother, the Family Court was opening a child support case against me. Although I was initially scared of more debt and threats, the Family Court combined both child support cases and I finally received a new judge. Because I was unemployed, that judge lowered my child support obligation to $50.00 per month for both children. Bear in mind this occurred over two years after

I was initially laid off in 2011. From 2011 to 2013, the Family Court system continued to charge me $600 per month for my son, even though I was unemployed. It took another child support case and a different judge for me to receive a child support adjustment.

During a two-year period, from 2011 to 2013, the mother of my son harassed me, including showing up at my house, making a scene, and threatening to send me to jail all because the first Family Court judge gave her that power. I couldn't do anything because in the end the cops would believe her, and I would end up in jail again. One time I told her I wanted to see my son after school but I didn't know where he lived. She went to the courts and told the judge that she feared for her life so the court wouldn't give me my son's home address. Mind you, she was the one harassing me and my wife. One time she followed me home from my son's birthday party so she could see where I lived. I got to my house and she got out her car. She started screaming in front of my neighbors that I was nothing but a deadbeat crackhead. I lived on the same street as the precinct so I had to stand there and take it all. I didn't want the cops to show up and arrest me even though she was the one harassing me. Her sister and brother-in-law are officers in the New York City Police Department. Back when we were dating, she broke all of my apartment windows and never faced charges for it, even though I called the police. So, I knew how the system worked. She was untouchable and I had to accept whatever she did to me. All of this took a toll on me, it took a toll on my wife, and we constantly had to move because of my son's mother.

In 2014, my wife confronted my son's mother and made it clear that the harassment had to stop. During that confrontation, my son's mother became aware that my wife was the one making the child support payments; she was the one supporting our son when I couldn't. The mother of my son then decided to go to court and close her child support case because she didn't want my wife's money. At that point, we had only managed to get the debt down to $12,000. But my son's mother signed off on the debt because she never needed the money, and the remaining balance of the debt was gone. The child support court order and the debt were her way of controlling my life. Until this day, she regularly threatens me with court every time I don't give her exactly the amount of money she wants. She has the power because she knows that in the eyes of the courts I am nothing but a loser, a deadbeat, an ex-convict, a criminal.

Finding Freedom

Academic Prelude: Incarceration has a traumatic effect on family members (Braman, 2007), and often weakens already strained relationships between parents and children (Miller, 2006).

Perpetual Punishment 285

	In addition to the various reentry obstacles discussed earlier, formerly incarcerated adults also combat housing discrimination. In recent decades, there has been an increase in the use of criminal background checks to exclude the formerly incarcerated from housing (Thacer, 2008). Although people of color are disproportionately more likely to have criminal records, it is legal to discriminate against the formerly incarcerated.
Ortiz:	*In 2015, Tomas and I decided to leave New York City. After I found employment at Indiana University Southeast, we moved to the Midwest. In Indiana, Tomas has been able to transform his life and has finally found freedom.*
Montalvo:	At the end of all of this drama, my wife and I decided to leave New York City. My wife graduated with her doctorate and went on the job market. She received an offer from Indiana University Southeast, and we ended up moving to Indiana, which is where I reside today. My past would come back to haunt me when I tried to rent a house in Indiana, where it is commonplace to run criminal background checks on potential tenants. I sat in a management office where a woman told me, "You have a lot of felonies on your record." The felonies she was referring to were the arrest charges from that dreadful weekend in Pennsylvania. Luckily for me, I am married to a criminologist who was able to explain to the woman the difference between arrests and convictions. I also had to explain my low credit score caused by the child support debt. Although the debt is now gone, my credit score is low because the child support case will remain on my credit report until 2020, serving as a constant reminder of what I had to endure.

Within a week of moving to Indiana, I had three job interviews that I acquired through a temporary employment agency. Surprisingly, when I moved to southern Indiana they only asked me if I had a felony conviction within the past five years. The Pennsylvania case was a misdemeanor. The only felony conviction I have on my record is the nonviolent drug charge from over 20 years ago so there was no more checking that box for me. Today, I am a shop supervisor at a great company that cares about me as a human being. I've been sober for ten years, and life is good.

Before moving to Indiana, we sat with Adam, Keishla, and their mothers to gather their opinions about us moving. Although both children were okay with us moving, I know it hasn't been easy on them. Shortly after moving to Indiana, we offered Keishla to come live with us. Although she was initially excited, her mother refused to let her move because it would reduce her welfare benefits.

After arguing with Keishla on the phone about her showing up at her mother's house drunk one night, Keishla stopped speaking to me for a year. Keishla recently made me a grandfather and I am doing my best to financially help her with the baby. I contact her regularly to let her know that I love her and am always there for her. Her child support case is active and my check is garnished $100 every two weeks, but her mother keeps that money. Adam and I are close and speak on the phone regularly. However, I still battle with his mother for visitations, even though I am now paying $500/month and provide additional funds for educational and medical expenses. He says he wants to come live with me when he graduates high school in 2020. Now that he's older, he understands everything that happened. I really wish I could have sheltered him from it because no child deserves to witness what he did.

It took a lot to get to where I am right now. A lot of sweat, tears, and many sleepless nights where I would wake up sweating because I thought every noise I heard was the police coming to arrest me. Every time I walked the streets, I had a fear of being arrested because I wasn't doing what society wanted me to do. I am here now and I am happy where I am today. I am working. I am sober. I support my children without a problem. But why did I have to go to hell and back just to do the right thing? Why did I have to jump through so many hoops just to get child support payments lowered? Why was I not treated like every other father who lost his job? Why did my record have any influence over how I was treated in Family Court? Whatever the reasons were, I can say now that the system did not break me. The judge, parole, and my son's mother tried with everything they had but I am here doing the right thing and I am happy. I am finally free.

References

Braman, D. (2007). *Doing time on the outside*. Ann Arbor, MI: University of Michigan.

Bureau of Justice Statistics. (2017, June). *Drug use, dependence, and abuse among state prisoners and jail inmates, 2007–2009* (Publication No. NCJ 250546). Retrieved from www.bjs. gov/content/pub/pdf/dudaspji0709.pdf

Bushway, S. D., Stoll, M. A., & Weiman, D. (2007). *Barriers to reentry? The labor market for released prisoners in post-industrial America*. New York: Russell Sage Foundation.

Chandler, R. K., Fletcher, B. W., & Volkow, N. D. (2009). Treating drug abuse and addiction in the criminal justice system: Improving public health and safety. *Journal of the American Medical Association, 301*(2), 183–190.

Diller, R., Greene, J., & Jacobs, M. (2009). *Maryland's parole supervision fee: A barrier to reentry*. New York: The Brennan Center Retrieved from www.brennancenter.org/sites/ default/files/legacy/publications/MD.Fees.Fines.pdf

Foucault, M. (1979). *Discipline and punish: The birth of the prison*. New York: Random House.

Hughes, T. A., & Wilson, D. J. (2003). *Reentry trends in the United States.* Washington, DC: US Department of Justice, Bureau of Justice Statistics.

Levingston, K. D., & Turetsky, V. (2007). Debtors' prison: Prisoners' accumulation of debt as a barrier to reentry. *Clearinghouse Review Journal of Poverty, Law, and Policy, 41*(2), 188–191.

Martin, L. (2013). Reentry within the carceral: Foucault, race, and prisoner reentry. *Critical Criminology, 23*, 493–508.

Middlemass, K. (2017). *Convicted and condemned: The politics and policies of prisoner reentry.* New York: New York University Press.

Miller, K. M. (2006). The impact of parental incarceration on children: An emerging need for effective interventions. *Child and Adolescent Social Work Journal, 23*(4), 472–486.

National Association of Criminal Defense Attorneys. (2018). *The trial penalty: The sixth amendment right to trial on the verge of extinction and how to save it.* Retrieved from www.nacdl.org/trialpenaltyreport/

Pager, D. (2003). The mark of a criminal record. *American Journal of Sociology, 108*(5), 937–975.

Pearson, J. (2004). Building debt while doing time: Child support and incarceration. *Judges Journal, 43*(1), 4–11.

Pogrebin, M., West-Smith, M., Walker, A., & Prabha Unnithan, N. (2014). Employment isn't enough: Financial obstacles experienced by ex-prisoners during the reentry process. *Criminal Justice Review, 39*(4), 394–410.

Prison Policy Initiative. (2018). *Out of prison & out of work: Unemployment among formerly incarcerated people.* Retrieved from www.prisonpolicy.org/reports/outofwork.html

Thacer, D. (2008). The rise of the criminal background screening in rental housing. *Law & Social Inquiry, 33*(1), 5–30.

Thompkins, D. E. (2010). The expanding prisoner reentry industry. *Dialectical Anthropology, 34*(4), 589–604.

Uggen, C. (2000). Work as a turning point in the life course of criminals: A duration model of age, employment, and recidivism. *American Sociological Review, 65*(4), 529–546.

Section V

Voices, Agency, and Reentry

In order to critically examine reentry and the experiences of returning citizens, Middlemass and Smiley, as co-editors, recruited chapters that purposely included the voices of returning citizens. Section V includes six chapters where the voices of men and women who have been or are still incarcerated offer their insights, thoughts, and concerns about reentry, but also what reentry means to them. This section is particularly important because the personal narratives, voices, and lived experiences of those reentering are vital to understand what works and what does not work, and provides insight and knowledge that may not translate via traditional research studies.

There has been some published research exploring reentry from former prisoners' perspective, the challenges they must navigate in order to establish their life post-prison, and how they deal with each challenge. In order to add to this literature and fill in some of the gaps, Section V presents several first-person accounts of reentry and what returning and potential returning citizens are thinking about as they transition from prison back into society. Voices from individuals who are still incarcerated in some capacity (e.g., prison or halfway facility) and are about to experience reentry are an important part of the reentry conversation. Regardless if this is their first time reentering society or if they have tried and failed at reentering, it is essential to know what they are thinking about as it pertains to reentry. The first-hand accounts also offer a limited view of a pre-release program available inside a women's prison in a northeastern state. The objective of this section is to increase readers' understanding of reentry from the perspective of those who are doing reentry, and that is accomplished by including personal narratives about what actually happens when men and women come home and what it means to them.

In "Thoughts, Concerns, and the Reality of Incarcerated Women," Smiley and Middlemass compile written narratives from women who are currently incarcerated in the same prison in a northeastern state. Smiley and Middlemass detail the challenges of communicating with current prisoners, and because the women were incarcerated at the time they wrote their entries, they were fearful that their words may be used against them by prison administrators or correctional officers; therefore, we went to extra-lengths to ensure their anonymity. The individual women who are represented in this chapter are identified by very few characteristics to ensure their identities remain unknown to each reader. The compilation of writings explores the first day inside, what it is like to be on death row, what some of the participants learned about themselves while incarcerated and how prison has impacted their life. The women also wrote about the reentry unit at their prison, the types of information that is available for those who are in need of resources when they reenter, and what reentry means to them.

In the chapter, "Reflections on Reentry," Neiderman and Dum introduce readers to the ID13 Prison Literacy Project. ID13 is a literary collaboration between Kent State University and a privately-run correctional facility, Lake Erie Correctional Institution, located in Conneaut, Ohio. Professor Dum and doctoral student (at the time of this writing) Halle Neiderman created The ID13 Prison Literacy Project, whose title is inspired by participants' use of their prison identification number (ID) that is used to sign their work combined with the 13th Amendment of the U.S. Constitution, which reads, "Neither slavery nor involuntary servitude, except as a punishment for crime whereof the party shall have been duly convicted, shall exist within the United States, or any place subject to their jurisdiction." The motto of the writing project is *ID13: We are human. We write.* Neiderman and Dum introduce us to the writings of some of their students who are incarcerated and enrolled in ID13; their narratives cover a range of topics about reentry and their thoughts about prison and its impact on them as humans. This conversation about reentry is critically important because of its personal and intimate look at what incarcerated men think about what it means to reenter society, but also about potential policy solutions to the challenges adults encounter when they return to society.

The next four chapters offer insights from men on their journey in prison and coming home. In "Being Held at Rikers, Waiting to Go Upstate," Marques, at the time of this writing, was 18 years old and incarcerated at Rikers Island while waiting to be sentenced; once his sentence was handed down, he would be transferred to an upstate New York prison. Marques was likely to be given a very long prison sentence, and despite this reality and his current circumstances, he was trying to maintain a positive attitude, was already thinking about how to improve himself, and was thinking about what it will mean for him to reenter society sometime in the distant future. We purposely do not share his full name because he is incarcerated.

In his chapter, "Reentry, From My Perspective," Shahid, after serving a 30-year sentence in several New Jersey state prisons, has successfully reentered society. In his chapter, he shares his thoughts about what it means to reenter society and how reentry organizations and programs offer some assistance. For instance, he was able to be a receptionist at a reentry program.

As a receptionist, Shahid's chapter offers us his critical review of how reentry organizations operate, and it is not flattering.

In, "The Journey of a Black Man Enveloped in Poverty," Pacheco shares his experience reentering society as a poor man trying to make a life after serving time in prison. Pacheco spent 2,012 days under correctional supervision, which included prison, parole, and probation. His first-person account tells readers what happens to people who are simultaneously on parole and probation, which is unusual but not unheard of. Pacheco has successfully reentered society because of his perseverance in finding resources that were specifically designed for formerly incarcerated and criminal justice affected people. Despite his success in being an inaugural fellow at four prestigious institutions and organizations, his life is a testimony about how incarcerating human beings is *not* a way to rehabilitate and transform them; rather, his story is about having his freedom and autonomy stripped from him, how he has been traumatized by the experience, and how he was the property of Jefferson County, New York. Pacheco felt helpless and disconnected from family, who lived in the Bronx, an almost six-hour drive away from where he was incarcerated, and as a result he struggled to hold onto his sanity. Pacheco writes about his strong support system, which includes family, mentors, and formerly incarcerated individuals, who are important for his reentry success. Although he has achieved many metrics of success, he continues to grapple with what he has lost, feels a tremendous amount of stress, and is constantly thinking about *not* making a mistake so he won't recidivate, all the while as he learns to navigate the world as a former prisoner.

In, "My First 24 Hours After Being Released," Lumbreras writes about his first 24-hours reentering society in California after being released from a fire camp in California, which is a minimum security prison that is staffed by Department of Corrections officers, but prisoners work with CALFire as firefighters and do everything that firefighters do. Lumbreras describes the challenges he had to overcome and how he managed to overcome them, but what was glaring is how the prison labor used at the prison fire camps serves a vital role in the state, which is plagued with wildfires on an ongoing basis, but that work experience does not translate into a paid job on the outside. Despite the fact that the prison fire camps are promoted as a rehabilitate program, prison firefighters are not hired by CALFire after they serve time; they are deemed unemployable because of their felony conviction. Yes, you read that correctly; while incarcerated, prisoners are authorized to be legal firefighters, but upon reentering society those same people are considered unviable and deemed unacceptable to hire as firefighters. This is one of *many* instances that a rehabilitative program inside prison that has immediate application on the outside, but because of state statutes preventing felons from working for CALFire after release, the training and experience is not transferrable; instead former prisoner firefighters, such as Lumbreras, must find employment opportunities that differ from the real-world skills they learned inside.

References

Braman, D. (2007). *Doing time on the outside*. Ann Arbor, MI: University of Michigan.

Bureau of Justice Statistics. (2017, June). *Drug use, dependence, and abuse among state prisoners and jail inmates, 2007–2009* (Publication No. NCJ 250546). Retrieved from www.bjs. gov/content/pub/pdf/dudaspji0709.pdf

Bushway, S. D., Stoll, M. A., & Weiman, D. (2004). *Barriers to reentry? The labor market for released prisoners in post-industrial America*. New York: Russell Sage Foundation.

Chandler, R. K., Fletcher, B. W., & Volkow, N. D. (2009). Treating drug abuse and addiction in the criminal justice system: Improving public health and safety. *Journal of the American Medical Association, 301*(2), 183–190.

Diller, R., Greene, J., & Jacobs, M. (2009). *Maryland's parole supervision fee: A barrier to reentry*. New York: The Brennan Center Retrieved from www.brennancenter.org/sites/ default/files/legacy/publications/MD.Fees.Fines.pdf

Foucault, M. (1979). *Discipline and punish: The birth of the prison*. New York: Random House.

Levingston, K. D., & Turetsky, V. (2007). Debtors' prison: Prisoners' accumulation of debt as a barrier to reentry. *Clearinghouse Review Journal of Poverty, Law, and Policy, 41*(2), 188–191.

Martin, L. (2013). Reentry within the carceral: Foucault, race, and prisoner reentry. *Critical Criminology, 23*, 493–508.

Middlemass, K. (2017). *Convicted and condemned: The politics and policies of prisoner reentry*. New York: New York University Press.

Miller, K. M. (2006). The impact of parental incarceration on children: An emerging need for effective interventions. *Child and Adolescent Social Work Journal, 23*(4), 472–486.

National Association of Criminal Defense Attorneys. (2018). *The trial penalty: The sixth amendment right to trial on the verge of extinction and how to save it*. Retrieved from www. nacdl.org/trialpenaltyreport/

Pager, D. (2003). The mark of a criminal record. *American Journal of Sociology, 108*(5), 937–975.

Pearson, J. (2004). Building debt while doing time: Child support and incarceration. *Judges Journal, 43*(1), 4–11.

Pogrebin, M., West-Smith, M., Walker, A., & Prabha Unnithan, N. (2014). Employment isn't enough: Financial obstacles experienced by ex-prisoners during the reentry process. *Criminal Justice Review, 39*(4), 394–410.

Prison Policy Initiative. (2018). *Out of prison & out of work: Unemployment among formerly incarcerated people*. Retrieved from www.prisonpolicy.org/reports/outofwork.html

Thacer, D. (2008). The rise of the criminal background screening in rental housing. *Law & Social Inquiry, 33*(1), 5–30.

Thompkins, D. E. (2010). The expanding prisoner reentry industry. *Dialectical Anthropology, 34*(4), 589–604.

Uggen, C. (2000). Work as a turning point in the life course of criminals: A duration model of age, employment, and recidivism. *American Sociological Review, 65*(4), 529–546.

Chapter 21

Thoughts, Concerns, and the Reality of Incarcerated Women

CalvinJohn Smiley, Keesha M. Middlemass, and Incarcerated Women

Gaining first person accounts from current prisoners about their experiences inside and what reentry means to them is challenging, at best, and for many reasons. First, current prisoners do not want to identify themselves for fear of getting in trouble for what they say or write while they are still incarcerated. Getting in trouble with prison administrations can lead to losing hard-earned privileges. Second, prisoners who do not have life terms have a release date, which means that reentering for them is real, even if it is a long time in the future. Thinking about this process can be: demoralizing, as it requires introspection; scary, as it requires taking responsibility for one's past actions; and hopeful, as leaving prison and its horrors is like a dream come true. Third, as Neiderman and Dum refer to in their chapter, the incarcerated do not have the same freedoms as those on the outside. Prisoners are the legal "property" of the state, and therefore, when prisoners write about their experiences, the state has the power and authority to prohibit having their words displayed in public.

Another challenge is how communication takes place between prisoners and those on the outside. Prisons have started to use technology for practical reasons, such as electronic messaging, to ensure that contraband is not smuggled into the prison via the traditional mail. In the prison where the women are incarcerated, there was a state-wide shutdown for security reasons, which necessitated the use of electronic messages (i.e., emails). These systems are set up as a standalone system and offers prisons a new revenue stream (Raher, 2016). In a prison email system, each email costs money. Someone on the outside can send an email to a prisoner via a website; the outside person logs on to a specific webpage (e.g., like logging onto Facebook or Amazon.com), writes an email, and hits send. That email is reviewed by correctional officers, and if approved, is printed and a paper copy of the email is distributed to the recipient (Raher, 2016). If a prisoner wants to respond, there are two options depending on the prisons' technology and system. In a one-way system, the prisoner responds to the email via traditional mail. If a two-way system is available, she can access an "email kiosk" or other available system (e.g., some prisons provide limited-function tablets to prisoners so that they can access their messages on a closed system) that is controlled by the prison, access her email, and then pay a fee to send a response.

Despite these and other challenges, we wanted to include first-person accounts from incarcerated women to better understand their perspective on reentry. In order to share the stories of currently incarcerated women – some of them have a future release date whereas others do not – we reached out to our respective networks and asked if anyone who had access to prisoners would be willing to work with us; this person, our gatekeeper, was promised anonymity, and all of the responding prisoners were promised anonymity, too. The gatekeeper asked female prisoners in her writing group to write about their thoughts and ideas about reentry. Owing to the fact that the women we were communicating with had limited access to email and wanted to remain anonymous from prison administrators, our gatekeeper had prisoners write down their thoughts inside, then the gatekeeper would bring the hard copies out of the prison and either mail them to us or scan them and send them via email. This process was necessary to keep each contributor's written word private and away from prison administrators' eyes.

As a result of their different release dates, length of their respective prison sentences, and different criminal charges, reentry looks different; some women have detailed reentry plans whereas others have abstract and less defined reentry plans. A few of the entries are written by "lifers," women who will never have a release date. Participants wrote what they wanted to and covered topics they found interesting; below, we share their words and reflections on what reentry means to them. Light editing was been done for clarity purposes only, and pseudonyms are used to protect the identity of each prisoner.

The First Day Inside

Kassidy was 16 years old when she arrived in prison to serve a ten to 20 year sentence for murder. These are her thoughts and recollections of her first day in prison.

> One of the experiences I remember the most was the first day I came to [prison]. It was May 10th 2012, and I was 16 and scared senseless. I had a 2.5 hour trip to get to the prison and all I could think about was all the prison movies I had seen and all the horrible things that happened to people in prison. Not to mention what happens to kids in prison. When I arrived I was escorted through the compound to intake. We walked by about 100 inmates and all they did was stare. I remember thinking, "Oh my god what have I got myself into? This is going to be the equivalent to hell," but I also told myself I wouldn't cry. We kept walking and made it to intake. When we got there I was thrown in a cage with six other inmates, and they all turned to stare at me as the door slammed shut

behind me. I sat frozen with my eyes down cast, hoping nobody noticed me and thank god everyone remained the same way.

Kassidy also wrote about how she was stripped, processed, and made into a prisoner. This experience can be jarring and upsetting, as Kassidy testifies of her horror:

> After being taken from the cage, stripped, I had to give a urine sample. I was picked up by a lieutenant, and he escorted me to my new dwelling. We approached a brick building surrounded by razor wire. After we proceeded through the gate, passed 2 locked stainless-steel doors, we reached a concrete corridor. All I could think of was that this was going to be the place where I died. Finally, I could no longer hold it in, and I began to sob. I begged the lieutenant to please not let me die. I didn't want to die, and that I was sorry, just please don't let me die here. He looked at me and chuckled and said, "I promise you won't die here. I'll be back to check on you." His kind words were the first such words I had heard in a long time, and his promise helped me get through the next few months until I could believe in myself and knew that I was going to be okay, or at least as okay someone could get inside prison.

Living Life on Death Row

Before coming to prison, Cheri's life, through her own words, was a train wreck.

> I allowed my past to hold me hostage. I never measured up or felt good enough for my mom. She made me feel less than, and not only [did she] make me feel that way from a young age, but she also told me that she never wanted me. I suppressed my feelings for years and I got high to numb my feelings. I ran away from any kind of feelings. And because I didn't know how to deal with my feelings, I had control issues and developed an eating disorder trying to control the only thing that I could control, what I did or didn't eat. I struggled and sought outside validation and was always an over achiever, but not in a good way. Like I said before, life for me before prison was a train wreck and the worse of it was with relationships because they were all abusive, I have never had a healthy relationship.

Cheri was sentenced to death and as a result was not offered any reentry programming or assistance, but her insights on what happens to someone when they are sentenced to death has important implications for how prisoners are treated.

> I spent 22 years of my life on death row and while I was on death row I had three death warrants signed [by the Governor]. When your death

warrant is signed, you are moved from the area where you were normally housed to a separate area where you are in a cell with a single light on for 24 hours a day and a guard who sits with you 24 hours a day. Everything that you get [or receive in the segregated housing unit for death row inmates] is searched before it is given to you. I was allowed three showers a week and before I could get a shower, I had to be strip searched, then handcuffed with a waist chain and shackles on my ankles to be escorted to the shower. Guards stayed in the shower with you when I showered, and once I was done they would escort me back and strip search me again. It was a lot of strip searching, especially since I was in a cell 24 hours a day that had nothing but a bed and linen, nothing else was allowed in my cell. I went through this three times, [each time my death warrant was signed]. The longest that I was under a death warrant before receiving a stay was 54 days; the other two times was not as long.

Each time Cheri's death warrant was signed, she received a stay from the Governor and was not executed; eventually, her death sentence was commuted to life imprisonment, so she does not have a release date and will never get one in the current political environment; however, that does not mean she is not trying to improve herself. In fact, Cheri is working on a treatment plan to recognize the origins and effects of her cognitive distortions, defense mechanisms, and maladaptive behaviors on all areas of functioning. This may seem like a lot, but inside prison there are many mental health issues and struggles, including PTSD, depression, anxiety, eating disorders, and other undiagnosed mental illnesses. As described by Reviere, Young, & Dawson in their chapter, women in prison tend to have experienced trauma prior to their incarceration, and because of the physical spatial arrangements, as discussed by Williams, Green, & Lewis in their chapter, women experience further trauma. Moreover, Zettler, in this volume, explores the gendered challenges of reentry that are related to women's criminal offending. Cheri's narrative and experiences describe how the criminal justice system provides some assistance and programming that allows women to become more aware of their own histories and how to improve their decision-making skills, which is similar to Willingham's chapter on how higher education inside can improve women's reentry experiences.

Cheri has taken courses to understand her own mental health, but also to address her drug addiction. She takes classes to help herself and to help others. She encourages her fellow prisoners to create:

a list of at least 15 thinking errors and defense mechanisms and how I use them, as well as the ways in which they benefit me in short -term but also kept me sick in my addiction. I had to create a timeline of my life that details both positive and negative memories and experiences

The Reality of Incarcerated Women 297

that I have been through. Next, I had to use that timeline and how those events have shaped who I am emotionally, mentally, in her relationships, as an addict, and as a criminal.

Cheri shared that she was learning a lot about herself and her past addiction. She shared the following poem with us.

I had a best friend, lover, boss, and child, that's what it cost.
I can never be in denial, you made me crawl on my knees, crying please!
You owned me, and sold me, all awhile you stole me.
You stole my body & mind a little at a time.
I cried for you, said I would even die for you, and I even tried for you.
I never wanted it to end, so I just did it again.
Each day sinking deeper & deeper in the abyss, you my love, I could never resist.
You held me tight all through the night, and didn't dare release me in the morning light.
I rode the waves of bliss never wanting to miss the next pill, snort or that sweet spike in my veins knowing instantly there would be no pain.
Hope came one dark night when I cried out, I need help with this fight.
You were the best friend I told my secrets, the lover that said you will always be my wife, the boss that said get on your knees, I didn't think twice, I did it with ease, and you were the little child that said, "oh! no, please, I just wanted candies."
Here you come again, I can see, but this time it won't be me.
I have hope can't you see.
RIP to the addiction in me.

Carol admits she is a work in progress, and the lessons she has learned she can help others face their fears and addictions. She is in the process of completing a mental health program and hopes to help others because "the medical care here is awful and we have doctors that tell you to drink water no matter what your symptoms are."

How Has Prison Impacted You? What Have You Learned?

Critical Self-Reflection

Shona elaborates on the ups and downs of life while locked up: "I have watched verbal and mental abuse of my peers [other prisoners]. I've felt so hopeless because there's nothing I could do to help them." "Life inside prison has its ups and downs. I have my good and bad days. Of course, I miss my family, missed watching my children grow until [they became] responsible adults, and [I've missed] the birth of my granddaughter?"

Julissa, a Black woman, says that she has changed in several ways since she was locked up. "One being I take my freedom more seriously. I think more thoroughly before making rash decisions. This experience shows me that I value my freedom more and would rather not be told when to eat, sleep, move." Julissa's words echo the reality that inside prison the prison environment and guards have total control over prisoners, and as a result, prisoners have a lack of agency and power in making decisions. Julissa also described that since she has been locked up, she has met a lot of women with tons of "potential who will never get the chance to go home or try again at life on the outside. It makes me want to work harder at doing the right thing and using my abilities more accurately."

Roberta, a White woman from a rural community, had been locked up before. However, her mindset had changed since the last time she was incarcerated: "This time here has allowed me to get a grip on my life again. I have lost everyone and everything that was important to me and that allowed me to feel hopeless for a long time. Now I am stronger than I was before and I still have a future. [Since being inside, I now know that] I hold the power to change the outcome of my life."

Sarah knows that prison has affected her in many different ways, and that:

> This time has taught me the value of life, freedom and family. I've learned that family isn't just blood related, but it is also a bond formed from trust and communication. Also, that just because a person is incarcerated that does not make them a bad or evil person. I've come in contact with quite a few strong willed and warm-hearted women while here. They've encouraged and empowered me to push myself to be the woman I know I can be and reach my goals, and for that I thank them.

Cristen has been locked up several times, knows that she must change, and her most recent time being incarcerated has been a time of reflection: "This time [being locked up] has impacted my life [and] it has made me self-reflect on things I have done and the choices I've made. I know now that I want to do something productive with my life. I want to be an amazing mother, a great friend, sister, and wife." Spending time inside has allowed Cristen to think about her life and who she wants to be when she reenters society.

Alecia knows that being incarcerated has had some positive effects on her life.

> This time has affected both myself and my loved ones tremendously. For me personally, I know I needed to sit. Before this, I'd never been to jail, in either state or county. Being locked up has taught me a lot about

myself and I've been able to reflect in a way that I couldn't have otherwise. The support from family, friends, and my boyfriend have been tremendous and I know I'm not the only one doing time. It's taught me to think before I act as well as be more cautious of with whom I surround myself.

Meredith, a 24-year old White woman, reflects on how prison has impacted her life in numerous ways.

This time has impacted my life in more ways than one. It's my first time being in jail, country and state. First, I needed to evaluate my life, friends, and surroundings. Before this time, I was ignorant to life around me, to an extent. The first couple months [being locked up] I was mad. I lost two people that were very dear to me. On the other hand, I'm glad I was locked up. I could be in the ground. Secondly, prison has also affected my family. It has taught me more understanding, better communication and a good perspective on things. As much as I dislike saying it, I needed this.

More importantly, Meredith is a mother, and being locked up has been hard on her three-year-old son, but being incarcerated has been harder for her.

A little over a year I've been away [, and] it's killing me. He's talking, learned his ABCs, [and his numbers] 1, 2, 3's. [He] knows his shapes. I'm happy to hear my son excel. I just loath I'm not the one helping him and showing him. It should be me. After my time [and I get out] it will be me.

Meredith is not the only one to talk about how being incarcerated has affected their role as a mother. Sarah has three daughters:

Being locked up has affected them a great deal with myself and their father both being incarcerated. Their behavior is inexplicable; they lash out on each other, their peers, and those taking care of them in my absence. Their grades are up and down, [and] they're in therapy. Every time I talk to them I can hear in their voices something is wrong and they want to cry.

Men & Women Differ, but Men's Prison Rules Rule

Women make up about ten percent of the adult prison population – state and federal – and because of the gender disparity in incarceration rates women's prisons tend to be ruled by the same regulations as men's prisons.

Although the women did not have a lot of experience dealing with someone who had done time in a men's prison, they did share their thoughts and opinions on what the biggest differences were, and from their perspectives, this is what they had to say:

> In my opinion there are many differences between a male and female prison. I believe that men are seen as more volatile and physically combative whereas women are seen as less physical and less volatile. This makes it difficult because then rules, regulations, and policies are geared towards issues that arise within the male population, but then affect the women's population in significantly different way
>
> [Kassidy].

The perception of women writers is that because of the nature of prison, men differ in that they have to prove themselves inside with other prisoners and how they interact with one another. Although there seems to be less violence between women who are incarcerated, in Julissa's opinion, "women fight for all the wrong things where as the men stand together to get things done." Cristen thought that doing time for women is just "harder cause of hormones, [but also because] us women have a harder time being away from our children cause we have more of an emotional attachment." Sarah touched on the same topic: "Women have issues with sticking together, [and] instead of battling the system for what's right they battle each other over stupid stuff that is irrelevant to their time [being] incarcerated."

Another participant, Roberta, wrote: "I don't really know how the men and women prisoners differ [in terms of how they operate]. I do know that when the men do something wrong, us women deal with their consequences. I don't think that's fair." Roberta is discussing how rules and regulations are made for prisons, and that the rules instituted in the men's prisons tend to then be implemented in the women's prisons, despite the gendered differences in how prisoners respond and interact with one another.

Shona shared her thoughts on prison and mass incarceration, writing:

> I honestly don't think mass incarceration will end. It's a business for one. Secondly, I look at it is modern day slavery. Prices keep going up on commissary [prison store] but yet [our] pay stays the same, 19 to 42 cents an hour. No pay for overtime hours. They are ripping our families off by charging them to send us money, charging them for anything to do with us. You see there are so many victims in a person's crime.

The Reentry Unit

Every prison should have some program or unit that helps prisoners prepare for release and to reenter society. However, the reentry process is

The Reality of Incarcerated Women   301

different depending on where one is incarcerated, where one is released, and the type of hard and soft resources a former prisoner can access immediately upon release (Middlemass, 2017). The resources can include money to purchase weather appropriate clothes and a bus pass, stable housing and a place to stay for an extended period of time (i.e., at least one year), the time needed to transition from a controlled environment to the community, and a number of other needs that *must* be met when individuals return to society if they are to have a chance to successfully reenter. Reentry starts inside prison.

One woman, Stefani, who worked in the reentry unit, described the reentry unit inside the prison where she was incarcerated. She wrote that working in the reentry unit provided lots of opportunities to learn about reentry and what each person had to do.

Shona, who also worked in the reentry unit, appreciated working in the reentry unit because she had the opportunity "to create binders of information for all counties in the state. These binders were full of information about community resources, transitional housing, and other resources related to employment." Before the creation of the reentry unit, the women reported that there was very little information available to prisoners planning their exit from prison and reentry into society. Having these binders full of information is a good starting point for women planning their reentry. Shona took an active role in collecting information. For instance, she would mail requests to counties asking them to send her information about reentry services in the county and any other information that would be helpful for those coming home.

Shona likes helping:

Anything that's allowed of me to be able to help my peers, I'll do. And once outside, I'd love to come back and speak to groups of ladies here [who are locked up] and advocate for them as well. I will never forget this experience or the people I'm gonna soon leave behind.

Despite Shona's efforts, Kassidy did not feel as hopeful about the reentry unit and the information that was available.

For me, I believe reentry has a lot beneficial programs but it's just a matter of people available to inform inmates of these programs. Most of us have no idea the programs that exist for those incarcerated, because there are so few people here talking about it. Personally I feel as though here you have to know and be involved with certain people to obtain knowledge of programs that exist for us. Personally reentry to me is successful [when] combined with education. I believe the more I become educated through classes or experiences the better chance at being successful I have.

Words From Behind the Wall – What Does Reentry Mean to You?

Shona writes:

> Prison has taught me a lot. I believe it's one's state of mind if you learn from this experience or not. For me I now think before I react. I play the whole picture out first. I ask for help. And if there's a problem going on once I'm calmed down I try to solve it, make amends, and not just walk away from it. I'm no longer shot tempered; I'm firm yet open-minded. Prison may or may not work for people. I would look at the circumstances of the situation.

Cheri also wrote about feeling calmer and more in control of her life: "Those difficult times [in my past] fostered in me a strong faith and change on a deep level. Doing that brought a sense of peace, relieving the insecurities I felt, and allowing me to accept the here and now. I like being open to what life brings me."

Sarah, a 29 year old who had been incarcerated for two years when we communicated with her wrote that:

> reentry looks like a reconnection with the real world and my family. [It is] a chance to get my life back on track with better choices on my behalf and further [my] education and [get] a job.

Julissa, who was born in May 1989, wrote that "reentry looks promising for me because it is like a blueprint to being back on track. It tells you about housing, programs for benefits, jobs [and companies] that hire felons, and it helps you with health care issues and to get your paperwork such as birth certificates, ID's, social security cards."

Cristen, who was 33 years old, wrote that: "What does reentry look like for me . . . going home, getting a job, spending time with my children, finding a sober support group, getting a sponsor and going to meetings, and also having a good relationship with my probation officer."

Meredith, who like other women incarcerated in this chapter who struggle with addiction, had been locked up for 14 months, and was due to be released within a year:

> I already set up a sponsor for when I leave. I plan to attend NA [Narcotics Anonymous] meetings. [I've] already started changing people and places. Changing everything is not easy. Here [while I have been incarcerated], I've already started to change myself for the better, and [I now know that] to change it starts with me. I've got great support behind me. If I didn't have the amazing support system behind me it'll be difficult [to reenter].

The Reality of Incarcerated Women   303

Alecia, struggles with substance addiction, said that upon leaving prison, she was going to spend time attending NA meetings and lots of group meetings, as many as possible:

> I know I have to work hard every day, [because] being the kind of person I want to be, [I know] that I won't walk out of these gates cured of all the issues I have with myself. [Those issues still exist, and are what] led me here [to prison]. I plan to surround myself with positive people, do things I love, and live the life I deserve.

Kassidy, who has served nearly a decade of her ten to 20 year sentence, is scheduled for release in June 2021. When she was arrested for murder, she had just completed the ninth grade. When she gets out, Kassidy would like to work with animals, hopefully as a vet tech; she knows she has to go back to school in order to become a vet tech, which is her long-term goal. "However, my short-term goal is get a job, get a driver's license, get an apartment, then go back to school."

Roberta was not sure what was going to happen when she reentered society.

> Re-entry is the unknown for me. I won't be getting released to anything familiar so it's a little scary. I'll be starting my life from scratch with new people, places, and things. I think the resources and reentry programs will highly benefit me for the future. It will point me in the right direction for the help that is available for someone in my position.

When Shona gets out, she is looking forward to becoming reactivated with my family and friends:

> I often think about and have set goals for once I'm released. I'm going to find work as a certified peer support specialist or recovery specialist. Then I'll enroll in college part-time for behavioral health and human services. I think working full-time and school full-time will be a little too much and may overwhelm me. While here in prison, I've received my Certificate Peer Specialty Business Education, and OSHA certificates, as well as many more.

Shona hopes that those certificates will help her find employment and attend college when she gets out, but she is also realistic about how hard reentering society will be.

> My only fear once released is how easy it is to return to prison. You can easily be violated as an accomplice in situations you had nothing to do with or [no] knowledge of [others' peoples crimes]. I see it all the time. I have also lost many rights. I need permission to relocate, go out

of state, go on a family vacation, permission for just about everything. Yes, I have the support of my family, I'm grateful for that, but I'll be returning to my home city but all of my family is now out of state. Plus, to be labeled a felon, I don't think it's necessary. It's just a label, but sadly society judges people by that label without getting to know the true person.

Sarah has a very clear idea of what she needs to reenter society:

> The kind of programs that would help me are parenting [classes] to teach me how to deal with my children's difficult behavior and programs for ex-felons to learn trades to further their education and career choices. I have issues with people pleasing and saying no, so a self-help program would also help me progress further in a healthy lifestyle.

Cristen, a White women born in 1985, knows that she will need a strong support system that includes Alcoholics Anonymous and staying away from old people, places, and things.

Conclusion

The incarcerated women that we communicated with have some ideas of what they need to do and what they need in terms of assistance to reenter, but in many ways the programs that are available inside prison are not sufficient to assist these women reenter society successfully. For instance, the women only had a vague sense of what they would have to do to make their reentry plans a reality. They had a sense of what they needed, but there were no hard details or facts about how to get the education, training, find NA and AA meetings, and a host of other things that they knew they needed. Their reflections, despite the reentry unit inside their prison, demonstrate that reentry is not an integral part of correctional programming inside prison and that when women are released to reenter society, they will likely be unprepared or overwhelmed with what needs to happen in order to reenter successfully.

References

Middlemass, K. (2017). *Convicted and condemned: The politics and policies of prisoner reentry.* New York: New York University Press.

Raher, S. (2016). *You've got mail: The promise of cyber communication in prisons and the need for regulation.* Northampton, MA: Prison Policy Initiative. Retrieved from www.prisonpolicy.org/messaging/report.html

Chapter 22

Reflections on Reentry
Voices From the ID13 Prison Literacy Project

Halle M. Neiderman, Christopher P. Dum, and the ID13 Prison Literacy Project

The pieces included in this chapter give voice to the struggles of the incarcerated and the laws that make it impossible for them to speak for themselves (Gramsci, 1982; Spivak, 1988). All work from ID13 is reviewed by the Ohio Department of Rehabilitation and Correction prior to public display. Because of this, many writers' ID numbers are prohibited from public display. This review policy also requires that some writers shorten their names, use initials only, or adopt pen names for public display. However, each ID13 contributor was asked to create a short biography, and they could include any information about themselves that they wanted to convey. Contributors also had the right to *not* include a biography. We, the co-authors and co-editors, respect their individual choices. Because of the individual nature of each human being that writes, every ID13 contributor had the freedom to write whatever and however they wanted to write about themselves because, *ID13 – We are Human. We Write.*

Placed in tandem with theories on recidivism and literacy, writing by participants from LaECI attempts to forge a dialogue about reentry between those who are incarcerated and readers in the public. We argue this conversation is necessary to begin to construct new language regarding incarcerated individuals, thereby encouraging productive reentry and public policy solutions. We cannot begin a conversation on reentry without the voices, the hopes, and the fears of those reentering.

Each of the ID13 contributors acknowledges the role literacy has in altering the landscape of incarceration and returning to society, not just on the inmate, but on the public, too, if not more. It is important to note that we do not understand literacy as a skill (Ong, 1982), but rather it is a constructed practice engendering knowledge through literate practices of surroundings (Street, 1984). The works contained within this chapter are not present to fetishize the experience of incarceration; rather, they are included here to begin a conversation of what incarceration does and doesn't do to the individual, which the voting public is largely not privy to. In particular, the pieces contribute to this conversation while speaking to many important issues that scholars have touched on over decades of prison research. For instance,

"Fear," "Caged Mentality," and "Returning Home" represent worry. They are testimonials about reentering a society that presents ex-prisoners with a dearth of resources and a wealth of stigma (Western, 2018; Middlemass, 2017). The pains of imprisonment and fears of survival (Toch, 1992) appear in "According to the Movies," which takes on the pop culture rhetoric of prison to tackle many issues, among them the pains of imprisonment (Sykes, 1958) while "The Mind or the Trees" presents concerns regarding the anger of those who are incarcerated.

Despite living through the prison industrial complex,[1] there is hope in the words of some writers, as evidenced by the use of the word "home." Specifically, the piece, "Going Home," speaks of hope for redemption, whereas "Returning Home" reveals hope for the opportunity to help others and make good (Maruna, 2001). Finally, "I Refuse" is a testament to dealing with prison through what Johnson calls "mature coping" (2002, p. 83).

According to the Movies

> By **J. Shrefi**: *I am a 28 year old Black male serving a mandatory 10 year prison term. I am father to two children and am an aspiring fiction writer. My only mission in this life is to be the best father I can be; to show my children that through diligence you can overcome any obstacle set before you. Life is what you make it, not what others will have it to be.*

to the movies, prison is a zoo of brutish, animalistic men. A dog eat dog world where only the strong survive and all others fall victim to their rule. From the outside looking in, every convicted felon is just another blemish upon the creamy smooth complexion of America's face, and the judicial system is the miracle cream that erases them. The penitentiary is depicted as a place of cold steel and busted, dripping pipes, communal showers, makeshift shivs and food trays full of slop.

Allow me to set the record straight.

Well, the food trays are full of slop, but I digress.

The perception of a reality nearly always differs from actuality. Prison is not what you see on TV. Although there is violence, and there are inmates who prey upon the weak, be it mentally, financially, or sexually, what is portrayed of prison [through the media] is an embellishment upon small instances. Assaults, rapes, and extortion are not things that occur daily, nor are they experiences that each person will have. Also, a man's [criminal] charge does not dictate what his life in prison will be. From murderers and rapists to burglars and drug addicts, life in confinement will be what they[, each individual,] make it.

The actual experience of being in prison itself is akin to being an A student who finds himself in detention after having made a boneheaded mistake,

[and] forced to be around the delinquents of the school who threw erasers at the teachers and cyber-bully them online. Imagine those same loud, disruptive kids from back in your high school days as adults, well not adults per say, but of legal age. They've grown beards and developed the musculature of men but their mental ages ceased to mature beyond a grade school level. Imagine being forced to live 24 hours of each and every day surrounded by those men, their relentless raucity pounding into your tender ear drums continually. All you can do is look straight ahead and do your best to drown out the noise and get through your day.

The worst part of prison for me, the greatest punishment, has been being away from my family. If you've ever wondered what it will be like to die, how life would go on without you once you've passed, then prison is your teacher. With conviction and subsequent incarceration, life as you know it ceases to exist and, much like in death, you are abruptly snatched from the roles you play in the lives of your loved ones. No longer are you a husband or father, a son or a brother, but rather, you become a shell of these things, only present in the form of the memories you've left behind. The separation is devastating. Although you are still living, your life is placed on hold while your family's lives must go on as if nothing has changed. You struggle to remain relevant in their hearts and minds while the ebb and flow of the day to day demands their attention. You're forced to sit idly by as your wife struggles to hold it together while having to maintain a career on top of a two child household alone. You miss all of your children's firsts and have to experience them vicariously through the occasional story or picture. As time wanes on, your loved ones grow accustomed to your absence and suddenly all of the frequent letters and accepted phone calls become infrequent, and visits don't come as often. The storm winds of lust batter your wife's levee until it breaks and infidelity floods her heart's shore. Your kids grow older and develop their own personalities and only get on the phone to say they love you and miss you because they've been told to. When you do get your oldest son to carry a conversation, you hear the sadness in his voice because he remembers a life with you before prison and he misses you; unlike his little sister who doesn't know the difference because she was born while you sat in the county jail awaiting sentencing.

You begin to understand that your actions don't only affect just you, [but] that you were responsible for more than just your own well-being. All of these realizations dawn on you and you're ready to get back out there to right your wrongs, and be the man your family needs and deserves. But you can't; because you still have [prison] time ahead of you. It feels as if a rattlesnake eeled its way down your throat and into your chest cavity to sink its teeth into your heart and pump its venomous saliva through your bloodstream, killing you painfully and slowly.

Each time I call home I realize more and more how out of touch I am with society. After nearly seven years of incarceration I am surprisingly behind the times. When I think of returning home, however, I feel little anxiety. I am a former active duty member of our United States Air Force, so I know what it takes to maintain a job, and I don't require much to be happy. Having lived so long with so little I've found enjoyment out of the little things in life, and do not want anything outside of being a family man. I am not swayed by today's social platforms or the influence they have over society, nor do I feel the need to "catch up." My expectations for my return err on the side of servitude, all I want is to be there to show my loved ones the love and support they've given me over these trying years, and [also] help raise my children. So long as I do that I am confident all other aspects of my life will fall into place with time.

Regarding receiving any assistance from the state with my mental preparedness to be released, I am pretty much on my own. After conviction and prior to first entering prison, you are processed through intake and [then] transferred to a parent institution, or permanent prison, [but] you are not designated a mandatory case plan or automatically enrolled into programs deemed beneficial to your "rehabilitation." You don't even see a case manager unless you are up for a security review, where the institutional staff evaluates your behavior, emotions[, and progress in rehabilitative self-improvement programs] to either raise or drop your [security] level, or a reclassification into another institutional job.[2] Instead, you are left to your own devices. There are tools and programs available, but you have to seek them out. Once you do, you find you're not eligible to participate in them because you have too much time [left on your prison sentence as] enrollment is based off of your release date. The classes that you can take are all inmate-led and are not respected by the courts [or outside institutions].

Why is it that the criminal justice system is so proactive in convicting a person, controlling and overseeing their communications, monitoring time spent with family, is so strict with how much property you[, as a prisoner,] are allowed, and so worried about whether your institutionally issued shirt is tucked in, but be so passive when it comes to addressing that person's issues and what landed them in prison to begin with? How they can better that individual? Help them become productive members of society? Is there not an "R" in the state's corrections acronym?[3]

The short answer to these questions is simple; prison is a business and nothing more, because there is no recidivism where there is rehabilitation.[4]

It seems that the goal of the system is to make life in prison as comfortable as possible so you grow complacent and accepting of life in confinement. The inmate population is provided with entertainment in the means of television, multimedia players and video game consoles with updated games. They are fed three times a day, housed, clothed, and medical care is free; all of their basic needs and some of their wants are met. If you're not careful you will find yourself stuck in a routine that has nothing whatsoever to do with addressing your own negative thought patterns or behaviors, [and] things about yourself that should be bettered. Instead, you get lost in the fictitious land of television and pop culture and Xbox, [and] then before you know it your release date arrives and you're thrust back into the deep end of real life with no better knowledge of how to swim with no flotation device. In other words, you are still unfit to function in our society. You find yourself reverting back to what you know, [with] the same knowledge that led you to a jail cell in the first place, because without making a change it is all that's familiar to you. Then one day you look up and find you've become a career criminal.

With that being said, you cannot place all responsibility on the Department of Corrections. Even if it did blatantly outline a rehab plan for you upon arrival, you still have to desire to change if any progress is to be made. That begins with an honest self-assessment and reflection, which is not an easy task. Most people feel as if the way they live is the right way while everyone else does things wrong, even after they have hurt, stolen from, and victimized people. [At some point,] you have to take responsibility for your actions and be accepting of the fact that you need to change. What flashed the bulb for me was seeing my own behavior and flaws in other people. I began to recognize myself in the unfavorable traits and actions that others displayed, and hear my own ugliness in the words that another man spoke. I realized that the man I was seeing and began to identify myself as was not one who could or even should be a father to two precious children or husband to a lovely wife. I was ugly; bitter, angry, and selfish.

I viewed other men as objects to be manipulated and saw women as sexual outlets, rather than the peers and beautiful equals that they are. I wanted to be a man that my children could be proud of and who I was wouldn't have made the cut. A part of me is grateful for this idle time because it has forced me to stare into the looking glass and examine my character and work at correcting my flaws. I don't feel I had to be here for as long a time as I was given but that is another story.

In that regard I feel the judicial system is a federal reserve churning out conviction numbers an impressionable public takes at face value, numbers often unsubstantiated by sufficient evidence. The wording in penal codes is such that one action or crime is subjected to a wide variety of interpretation, a proverbial 31 flavors of law. It will support whatever agenda is necessary for conviction. It is hard to win against it, which is even more reason to steer clear of lady trouble.

When I am released, I will be ready.

Prison is the home wayward teens run away from. A home out of which they seek emancipation.

Caged Mentality

By **Franklin**: *I achieved the rank of Lieutenant Commander, after eight years of service to my country in the Navy. At the time of this writing, I am 60 years old and have been incarcerated in Ohio since 2017. I have experienced bouts of homelessness and at one time, spent 18 months living in a tent. In addition to writing about my own experiences, I love science fiction and the way it makes you wonder what the future holds or will become.*

Picture this;

There is a dog locked in a cage that is not much bigger than itself.

Week after week food and water is provided and sometimes clean newspaper,

But never is the dog allowed to leave its cage.

Years go by and a child sees the dog and wants to play, and so opens the cage to let the dog out.

Reaching out and calling, [the child] waits for the dog to come out, instead the dog cowers in the back of its cage.

Not willing to be touched, but most of all, not wanting or willing to leave its cage.

A man is incarcerated for 30 years for something he did when he was 20 years old. Now 50 years old he is told to get ready to leave, his time [inside prison] is done. The morning he is to be released he sits on his bunk looking at his home for the past 30 years, thinking, "Now what?"

The officer comes and gets him, and after signing the needed paperwork, he was given some money and a bus ticket to his hometown. After getting off the bus, he walks around the town not knowing what to do or how to act. When it's night he takes a large rock and breaks a store's window. Sitting down inside the store, he waits for the police to come get him. When asked why he did this, he said, "I want to go back home."

Fear

By Anonymous

My greatest fear is going back to who I was before. All of the growth, all of the progress, all the reflection, for nothing. A ticking time bomb; only a matter of time before I self-destruct again. Before I ruin everything I touch, hurt everyone who cares about me. Back to jail or an early grave are the only inevitabilities.

Here, I'm depressed and lonely, but at least I'm not destroying anything or hurting anyone. Being in purgatory is damage control.

Going Home

By D.R.

Going home, man what a trip! I wish that I could say that this was the first time I felt like this. This is my second number [second prison sentence and second offender" prison identification number] and I don't ever want to put my family through this again. It's not only them though, it's me. I don't think that I'd survive another ride[, another prison sentence].

As of now though, I'm ninety-five days and a wake away from the door. Ninety-five days away from a new beginning and a new life and more; I can't wait to see my mom to see her face, feel her hugs squeeze me her kisses on my cheeks to hear her thank God for her baby boy will surely make me weak in the knees. I think I've missed mom the most. I've asked God every day to keep her safe and to hold her close. I can't wait to eat real food, take a bath, put on a pair of jeans and the watch that was once my dad's. I can't wait to sleep in a real bed; I doubt that I'll sleep the night before I leave or when I'm rolling up on out if I forget to breathe.

I don't have a ride home as of yet so I'll get on a Greyhound heading west and I'll have a little time to try to clear my head.

Am I scared? Hell yes. I don't let it show and I really don't know what to expect. But this time I'll definitely do my best to build a good life for myself, chase down my dreams, and lay the past to rest.

Returning Home

> By **E.L.**: *I am . . . originally from the cities of the east coast, currently residing in the Ohio judicial system. I started writing as a freshman in high school, a hopeless romantic seeking the approval from women through my poems and influential rap lyrics with my comrades. Even then, while taunted by suicidal thoughts, empty from the lack of love from someone or self, I knew, "He that love not know not God for God is love." It was within this time I realized my passion for writing as well as my true passion for a spiritual connection with Love. So when I write, it's these thoughts that motivate me. I'm not limited to the here and now. These fences don't stop me from connecting with the unseen controller of all things. I connect with the creator you the reader connect with me and we connect eternally for harmonious moments of time. Even during this lonely metaphorical death called incarceration, we still project peace.*

In a cell searching for proper sunlight to sow
Books like mental soil planting seeds to grow.
Ranch style house dreams reaching for sweat underground streams.
Looking beyond the dimensions refracted paradise light beams.
That's kinda what returning home means.
Practically homeless with no ambition
Completed programs just for submission
Clean drug habit now in remission
Seeking my equal in heart and religion

My fear
Its violent sickness filling my brain
Dirt and filth become routine
No family no friends just cocaine.
All seen strangers call me a fein.
Home is my weakness with so much pain.
Free checks from the state with no real gain sad and lonely with no
real change.
But
It's all joy and laughter from my family and friends
All because my jail time ends
But the prison mentality I'm still consumed
I tried to shank my brother when he entered the room.
I ask my Mom to make me a break
And use pieces of a cut up steak
Doggie bags from restaurants when they take me to eat
Everywhere I go I wear crocks on my feet.
Checking the clock fearing the count
My Dad screams what's this all about.
Ceram [saran] wrap in my pocket and I'm saving cereal bags
Cutting up his towels to use them as rags.
I'll miss prison.
Absolutely
And all my friends
The positive lifers that helped me while I was in.
I won't miss the beating even when it was well deserved
The absolute justice when a bloody beating was served
The prison football, basketball, and softball teams
The agony in the late night shower screams
Conveniently controlled by the prison things
I'll miss the structure and the time for dreams
But a free choice of freedom is what returning home means.

Untitled

By E.L.

I write romantic poems to the fantasy, fantasy poems to humanity,
intellectual poems to stupidity and story lines with humility for all
to see.
I am the physical spiritual writer of love and reality.
Read and journey with me to a realm where we are free.

Returning Home

By Nado Jenkins

Dear world,

I would like to talk about what returning home means, but first I would like [to] talk about the experience of prison and the system. I know you've probably read about prison or seen it on the movies and thought wow! Prison is tough, there's people being raped, stabbed, and killed. Then there's the terrible food they eat, or the constant degrading from the officers. Now those things still exist, but prison is much more than just that. It all starts from the corporations. Take CCA, for example, a private institution owned by a billionaire. How much of these billions do you think is invested in our rehabilitation? Maybe 1%, and even if it's more the wardens probably don't stress the rehabilitation and if they do the staff aren't doing their best job. So, when we speak on returning home, most people in prison will return home the same way they left because of the lack of attentiveness they[, the officers and wardens and everyone,] have after we were sentenced.

There are some programs they have for prisoners but if you have a long sentence you can't get in them. Now what difference will 6 months make when I spent 10 years uneducated, lazy, violent and reckless? Slim to none, [and] only if you take the initiative yourself, to be better, to change, and learn from your mistakes and find your purpose, will you be rehabilitated. For me returning home means I have a second chance to be positive, productive, and progressive in my community and in my everyday life.

Returning home can be difficult without a support group, family, friends, etc. . . . I'm blessed to have family who still loves me and that enables me to take my time, be patient, because I have a place to sleep, and food to eat. You must have a plan, preferably a positive one, something to keep you moving forward. Having a plan, setting goals and managing your priorities are all important aspects of returning home. I plan on returning home and applying for a job, something to assist me with my needs. I also want to [go to school and] major in business management and minor in psychology.

I know I can't afford the college tuition so I will apply for financial aid. Getting a job and applying for college will be my biggest priorities when I return home. Those will be short-term goals for me. Returning home is an opportunity for me to build trust with my family, and show them the true love that they deserve. Helping the youth is very important to me as well; in a world so corrupt, I would like to teach them values and resources instead of entertainment. I want to let them know the world will be better if they have love in their hearts and become educated on how to heal the world and make it better in the future. So no I don't fear returning home. I'm excited about the opportunity to return home because I have so much to give to the world and once I return home my voice can be heard. To sum this up, we must make the most out of the situations we're in. If we prepare ourselves for the future (our returning home) we can live good lives [by] taking one step at a time.

The Mind or the Trees

By **Karl Meier**: *I'm 61 yrs old. I have 2 years left on a 5-year sentence. I am disabled and have been in a wheelchair for 2 and 1/2 yrs because of degenerative arthritis in my back and legs. I am a licensed ordained minister and a licensed dog handler. I have done extensive traveling and plan to do more when I get out; England is one of my destinations. I also plan on training a new dog to take into hospital and rehabilitation facilities. My certified comfort dog had to be put to sleep during my incarceration here.*

I love the mind, it takes me to places I've been and places I can't go to physically anymore. As I sit and look out at the trees on the far side of my yard, I can see the train beyond and it takes me back to those times when myself and best friends would hop that train. In our hearts we knew where it would take us, but in our minds it was the world and adventure ahead. When I look at those trees it takes me back, back to my home in the country. Those lazy happy days of summer. To be awaken by a gentle breeze blowing through my bedroom window. The sweet sounds of the early morning birds drifting in that breeze. Watching those leaves swaying in the wind or to change into magnificent colors in the fall just before their death. They take me back to those lazy walks across fields and through wooded paths with my loving dog.

As I sit here and look across my yard to the woods beyond I can still recall all those travels and adventures of days gone by. But those days are only dreams of the past.

As I sit here in my thoughts, my mind begins too clear and my eyes again refuse to focus, my surroundings begin to creep in around me. The metal and brick building again suffocate me. The chain fences and razor wire shred my view. Memories begin to retreat and reality reappears. My head is bowed and heavy my heart, it's a weight in my chest. I see I am no longer alone but surrounded by a moving multitude of blue. My yard is a yard [that] belongs to the State and my home is a cauldron of hate and rage shared with 1800 other strangers. I think I'll go back home to my bunk for the day. So I shift my tired body and begrudgingly turn my chair around. My four wheels click on the cracked blacktop as I head home.

Don't worry my old friends, I'll be back tomorrow. Until then stay safe in my memories. We may meet again soon, I'm sure. There are still adventures and memories to be had, and new ones to make. They can't keep me in here forever, I hope! Can they?

I Refuse

By Karl Meier

I refuse to fall victim of the mentality of this place.
I refuse to let others take or change my oral and spiritual beliefs.
I refuse to become one of the unmoral majority.
I refuse to debase myself by debasing the females of this world by
lowering them to objectivity.
I refuse to let my higher mental functions be forgotten over a mere
word or insult.
I refuse to deface by body just because it's what you do or what's cool.
I refuse to change my spiritual beliefs because they're not cool or the
thing to do.
I refuse to accept that nothing can be changed and all I can do about
it is complain.
I refuse to sit idle and let the injustices done to good men go
unchallenged.
I refuse to lower by standard or change my beliefs for the price of a
couple donuts.
And I refuse to accept that we cannot change and that this is my life.
I just fuckin' refuse.

Conclusion

At every stage of incarceration, the criminal justice system enacts its will
upon human beings. The writings from the ID13 participants illustrate this,
indicating that for many incarcerated men, returning home cannot be separated from the ingrained mentalities of survival and masculinity each of the
incarcerated develops throughout their time. In 2015 and 2016, over 620,000
people were released from the state and federal prison systems (Carson,
2018), and although these numbers (like the numbers assigned to individuals as they enter prison) fail to capture the full picture of human existence
encompassing mass incarceration, the previous narratives attempt to reclaim
some of that humanity for those 620,000 returning home every year. It is
our hope that by sharing the contributions of ID13 participants with those
on the outside, the public will receive a fuller image of the reentry experience while acknowledging the humanity within incarcerated persons.

These brief introspections of self indicate the complex tensions embodied
in the incarcerated. They categorically fall into narratives of survival and critiques of the prison system. Franklin's "Caged Mentality" compares himself
and surrounding inmates to dogs who have developed learned behaviors
to survive only in small spaces and lack the trust of those on the outside.

Likewise, Karl Meier's "I Refuse" traces Meier's stream of conscious as he has to continually tell himself to not fall victim to the lack of humanity he is experiencing while incarcerated. These two narratives illustrate two important aspects of the survival tactics of male inmate narratives: Conditioned aggression, and as addressed earlier, "mature coping" (Johnson, 2002, p. 83).

The contributors of this chapter use their words and experiences to remind readers of the inescapable truths regarding mass incarceration and prisoner reentry. J. Shrefi, in "According to the Movies," reminds us of the great toll that incarceration takes on families and the difficulties of being a father while incarcerated (Arditti, Smock, & Parkman, 2005). He goes on to discuss what he views as a lack of rehabilitation within prison, stressing that its absence does little to prepare him for reentry. However, scholarship demonstrates that visitations may reduce recidivism (Bales & Mears, 2008) and maintaining social ties can have prosocial effects for individuals upon release (Berg & Huebner, 2011). Therefore, the rehabilitative programming that J. Shrefi asks for in his writing could be as simple as maintaining the social ties and family connections that individuals had before going to prison. Such efforts would also benefit the children of incarcerated parents, who undergo stress and trauma because of the separation (Wakefield & Wildeman, 2013).

While J. Shrefi discusses the lack of programming inside prison, or when it is offered, it is led by other prisoners, it is undeniable that successful reentry and successful "returning home" cannot occur without community support. Returning citizens are often dependent upon the willingness of community members as they struggle to find housing (Middlemass, 2017; Metraux & Culhane, 2004), gain employment (Pager, 2003), and establish prosocial networks (Hirschfield & Piquero, 2010). The challenges surrounding these key aspects of reentry can be overwhelming.

Numerous studies demonstrate how the deck seems stacked against returning citizens in their search for employment and housing (Western, 2018; Middlemass, 2017). There is no question that incarcerated individuals are heavily stigmatized, and that the public and society continues to stigmatize returning citizens upon release (Middlemass, 2017). As Franklin alludes to in "Caged Mentality," the prison experience changes individuals so much that in the face of community stigma and little hope for success, retreating back to the "cage" seems inevitable. Therefore, it is little wonder that almost three-quarters of returning citizens will be re-arrested within five years of release (Durose, Cooper, & Snyder, 2014).

What can help encourage community members to reduce the stigma they apply to returning citizens and to embrace the key roles they play in successful reentry? We believe that a key to success lies in changing public perceptions of incarcerated individuals and the reentry process. Research shows that increasing familiarity with stigmatized groups (such as returning citizens) may change people's feelings towards that group (Allport, 1954; Pettigrew & Tropp, 2006; Rade, Desmarais, & Mitchell, 2016; Viki, Fullerton,

Raggett, Tait, & Wiltshire, 2012). Therefore, the written words of incarcerated individuals may have the power to humanize their experiences, and we hope transform public perceptions of what they can add to their communities upon release. As the authors of this chapter remind us throughout their work, the incarceration experience is full of deprivation, introspection, horror, hope, and evolution. These written pieces are reminders of the humanity that exists behind prison walls and tells us the ways in which the complex lives of the incarcerated reflect the imperfections and struggles of those on the outside, too, and prompts us all to recall the challenges we *all* face in our human existence.

Interestingly, and relating to the narrative of survival, participants, though asked to write on "returning home," most of their work omits, glosses over, or admits fear regarding the act. This indicates the writers' understanding that reentry is not just the act of leaving prison, but a part of the entire inmate process. This is a critically important contribution to see emerge from ID13; the public's perception of reentry is focused on the actual event of leaving prison, but participants know it is not a one-time event. As Joan Petersilia points out, reentry is "all activities and programming conducted to prepare ex-convicts to return safely to the community and to live as law-abiding citizens" (2003, p. 3).

Here, the writers of ID13 remind us that thinking about reentry and returning home must acknowledge what occurs, or what doesn't occur inside prison, and how incarceration impacts individuals when they leave. Anonymous' writes "Fear," and he states: "Here, I'm depressed and lonely, but at least I'm not destroying anything or hurting anyone. Being in purgatory is damage control." The notions of depression and loneliness speak to a prison experience devoid of catalysts for change and self-improvement. Meanwhile, D.R.'s "Going Home" ruminates on his lack of prospects for the future, and though he's going home soon, he writes about the lack of family or friends to even meet him. Both of these pieces indicate spaces where the system is failing in its rehabilitation duties, almost proving J. Shrefi's and Jenkins' points that the system is not meant for rehab, but it is set up for inmates to recidivate to maintain the cash crop and money siren for the billionaires. In their eyes, Petersilia's vision of reentry fails to exist.

We hope the consciousness crafted in the above writings serves as a bridge between criminal justice research, individuals at any stage of incarceration, and the public. These writings and the future works composed by inmates through *ID13* serve to scaffold the public's re-imaginings of the roles and realities of incarceration and reentry on the individual. It is important that prison writing programs are not isolated, cathartic processes within the prison, but consumed by the public to reconstruct literacies of incarceration and reentry. In, "From Cell to Society: Who is Returning Home?," Joan Petersilia (2005) acknowledges that this question has no easy answers. Mass incarceration has poisoned so many communities, institutions, and intentions, that those returning home could be any of us. We are human. We write. We are J. Shrefi, Franklin, Anonymous, D.R., E.L., Nado Jenkins, and Karl Meier.

Notes

1. As Angela Davis and Cassandra Shaylor write, many scholars and activists "have deployed the concept of the 'prison industrial complex' to point out that the proliferation of prisons and prisoners is more clearly linked to larger economic and political structures and ideologies than to individual criminal conduct and efforts to curb 'crime.'" (Davis & Shaylor, 2001, p. 2). This is particularly relevant to the Lake Erie Correctional Institution because it is a private prison. Furthermore, a siren goes off at Lake Erie to signal the arrival of new prisoners, and ID13 participants referred to this as "the money siren."
2. The federal government and every state prison system use a classification system that assesses and evaluates each prisoner to determine their risk level in order to house them in the corresponding security level prison (i.e., minimum-, medium-, or maximum-security facility). The classification process is designed to balance the inmates' security risk with the program needs of each prisoner. In practice, however, despite most systems using an elaborate process to assess, evaluate, and classify individuals to develop an in-depth profile of each prisoner, the assessment process tends to simply match a prisoner with an available bed in a prison at their security classification level (Middlemass, 2017).
3. The State of Ohio's corrections acronym is ODRC, which stands for Ohio Department of Rehabilitation and Correction.
4. Here, J. Shrefi is explaining that because the prison system is based on a business profit model, the prison system is not interested in rehabilitating prisoners. If prisons invested in rehabilitation, then there would be increased levels of successful reentry and decreased numbers of prisoners recidivating and returning to prison, which would impinge on the prison business model that relies on having bodies incarcerated in order to make a profit.

References

Allport, G. W. (1954). *The nature of prejudice*. Reading, MA: Addison-Wesley.

Arditti, J. A., Smock, S. A., & Parkman, T. S. (2005). "It's been hard to be a father": A qualitative exploration of incarcerated fatherhood. *Fathering, 3*(3), 267–288.

Bales, W. D., & Mears, D. P. (2008). Inmate social ties and the transition to society: Does visitation reduce recidivism? *Journal of Research in Crime and Delinquency, 45*(3), 287–321.

Berg, M. T., & Huebner, B. M. (2011). Reentry and the ties that bind: An examination of social ties, employment, and recidivism. *Justice Quarterly, 28*(2), 382–410.

Carson, E. A. (2018). *Prisoners in 2016*. Washington, DC: U.S. Department of Justice: Bureau of Justice Statistics. Retrieved from www.bjs.gov/content/pub/pdf/p16.pdf

Davis, A. Y., & Shaylor, C. (2001). Race, gender, and the prison industrial complex: California and beyond. *Meridians, 2*(1), 1–25.

Durose, M. R., Cooper, A. D., & Snyder, H. N. (2014). *Recidivism of prisoners released in 30 states in 2005: Patterns from 2005–2010*. Washington, DC. Retrieved from www.bjs.gov/content/pub/pdf/rprts05p0510.pdf

Gramsci, A. (1982). *Selections from the prison books* (Q. Hoare & G. Nowell-Smith, Trans.). London: Lawrence and Wishart.

Hirschfield, P. J., & Piquero, A. R. (2010). Normalization and legitimation: Modeling stigmatizing attitudes toward ex-offenders. *Criminology, 48*(1), 27–55.

Johnson, R. (2002). *Hard time: Understanding and reforming the prison* (3rd ed.). Belmont: Wadsworth Publishing Company.

Maruna, S. (2001). *Making good: How ex-convicts reform and rebuild their lives.* Washington, DC: American Psychological Association.

Metraux, S., & Culhane, D. P. (2004). Homeless shelter use and reincarceration following prison release. *Criminology & Public Policy, 3*(2), 139–160.

Middlemass, K. (2017). *Convicted and condemned: The politics and policies of prisoner reentry.* New York: New York University Press.

Ong Walter, J. (1982). *Orality and literacy: The technologizing of the word.* New York: Routledge.

Pager, D. (2003). The mark of a criminal record. *American Journal of Sociology, 108*(5), 937–975.

Petersilia, J. (2003). *When prisoners come home: Parole and prisoner reentry.* New York: Oxford University Press.

Petersilia, J. (2005). From cell to society: Who is returning home? In J. Travis & C. Visher (Eds.), *Prisoner reentry and crime in America* (pp. 15–49). New York: Cambridge University Press.

Pettigrew, T. F., & Tropp, L. R. (2006). A meta-analytic test of intergroup contact theory. *Journal of Personality and Social Psychology, 90*(5), 751–783.

Rade, C. B., Desmarais, S. L., & Mitchell, R. E. (2016). A meta-analysis of public attitudes toward ex-offenders. *Criminal Justice and Behavior, 43*(9), 1260–1280.

Spivak, G. C. (1988). Can the subaltern speak? In C. Nelson & L. Grossberg (Eds.), *Marxism and the interpretation of culture* (pp. 271–313). Chicago, IL: University of Illinois Press.

Street, B. V. (1984). *Literacy in theory and practice* (Vol. 9). New York: Cambridge University Press.

Sykes, G. M. (1958). *The society of captives: A study of a maximum security prison.* Princeton, NJ: Princeton University Press.

Toch, H. (1992). *Living in prison: The ecology of survival.* Lawrenceville: American Psychological Association.

Viki, G. T., Fullerton, I., Raggett, H., Tait, F., & Wiltshire, S. (2012). The role of dehumanization in attitudes toward the social exclusion and rehabilitation of sex offenders. *Journal of Applied Social Psychology, 42*(10), 2349–2367.

Wakefield, S., & Wildeman, C. (2013). *Children of the prison boom.* New York: Oxford University Press.

Western, B. (2018). *Homeward: Life in the year after prison.* New York: Russell Sage Foundation.

Chapter 23

Being Held at Rikers, Waiting to Go Upstate

Marques M.

Note: *This entry has been slightly edited for understanding and clarity by the co-editors.*

My name is Marques, and I am a young Black male incarcerated for many felonies I did not commit. While being [in jail], I did not let nothing bring me down even after being two weeks away from freedom and having charges put on me. Being in jail is a mental game; this place could change you for the best or the worst, and no one leaves here the same. There was a point while being here [that] I didn't care about nothing because I was so mad at what was happening to me, and no one could tell me nothing. Then one day it was when I thought I can't let this place change me. I got to know a very wise lady who worked in the jail, and she would always say, "Marques just know who you are, a very smart, kind person and we can't let this place change you." My mother always tells me before it gets better it gets worse. Being here has made me stronger, smarter, and a better person because I let it.

My thoughts on New York City jails are it sucks to be here. COs [corrections officers] are very foul, not all of them, but a lot of them. The CO's should be trying to help better us as people and teach us how not to come back, especially for those of us who put our self out there, ask for help, or simply do something wrong or at the wrong time, CO's should help us, not give us more time and punishment.

Reentry to me means coming home and changing the people, places, and things in my life. I say that because being around people who don't want better for you or even have their own issues is not good. Changing places [means] you won't get to see the negative people who were inside your life. I feel like changing things and your thinking is key to staying home after reentering because things you do will put you right back in jail but when you change your THINKING you would know not to be around certain people, and you also would know never to go to certain places, and you would know not to do things that would bring you back to jail.

Successful reentry to me looks like coming home [and] staying away from all of the negative things and also looking at negative situations different. Also making positive goals and obtaining those goals. Successful reentry is hard [because] you may go to an old hang out spot [and that leads to bad things and then] you might not never see the streets again. Successful reentry also is really liking life [and knowing that] there is more to life than just one block.

I feel shutting Rikers Island [down] isn't the solution to the problem; it is who is in charge of things, and who lets D.O.C. get away with stuff, and what they do, those are the real problems. If they take us off Rikers Island and put us wherever else, what will happen? New place, and the problems will still be the same, the same rules and the same people [will be] in charge, so shutting the place down wouldn't change anything. I know if you change who is in charge and the thing they [are allowed to do then], D.O.C. will stop doing everything.

The criminal justice system is a system that I feel needs a lot of help. I feel it needs help because me, going back and forth, to court I see how corrupt New York's justice system is. This system will put innocent Black men in jail who will have to learn to adapt in jail; probably 8 out of 10 times you will have to fight; you get into trouble with COs for doing nothing but because they are corrupt; and a lot of us sit here, and then your case gets dismissed. If your case doesn't get dismissed, you wait [in jail on Rikers Island], wait to get charged, wait to get sentenced, wait to go upstate [to a state prison], all of this while you are innocent.

This system is built to break you inside of your head. Being inside is crazy because of gangs that have problems with one another for no reason at all so fights happen, then slashings, then new arrests, and you are stuck here.

When you try to do the right thing, like going to school or taking classes, COs will mess with you. This system does not follow the rights of people. I say this because people who get cases don't have money for a paid lawyer so you get a legal aid lawyer who works with the DA and who will feed you lies, never answer your calls, and probably tell you to cop out [take a plea] to something when you probably could have went home. DAs love to give people 6/5 splits, that is 6 months jail time and 5-years probation. When those people go home there is nothing for them, no jobs, no money, and no food. They probably don't have family who cares for them so they get back on the block and try to make money, and go back to jail. When you have felonies on your record employers won't hire you so you gotta survive one way or another and it's just a cycle that won't break unless the system changes.

Chapter 24

Reentry, From My Perspective

Abdul-Halim N. Shahid

Reentry was a system originally designed to assist those individuals returning to society following a period of incarceration. While most programs, I believe, still adhere to this objective without additional requirements, it's been my experience that being released from incarceration isn't the only criteria to be met.

In order to receive assistance from several organizations, you must sign-up for a counseling session, or several of them, in order to receive the benefits of the particular Organization.[1] Miss a few of these meetings and your quest for assistance is terminated. But then, that's kind of understandable, since most of these Organizations operate based upon a series of either Federal or State Grants. That being the case, the Organization has to mold its services to meet the criteria of those Federal or State institutions that provide the grant money. This can, in many instances, impede the Reentry programs' ability to assist those individuals returning to society following a period of incarceration, especially when that period of incarceration has covered a period of decades as opposed to a few years or months. While any time spent in these prison dungeons, euphemistically called "Correctional Facilities," warrants inclusion and acceptance into a reentry program, some individuals need the services more than others.

That aside, my personal experience with the reentry process was as follows: My first exposure to the reentry program system was as a receptionist, while in the half-way house, for a Newark, New Jersey, based Program, which had been in existence for more than a decade, at the time I was reentering. There I would witness, first hand, the system at work. In order for the program to continue functioning and being successful, the request for Grant money to fund this Nonprofit organization had to continuously be shaped, changed, and remolded to fit the criteria set by the Grant providers. Without the Grant, the organization could not function at all; yet, with the Grant money, the organization was limited to what it could actually do because of the restrictions placed by the granters of the Grant.

Program participation in weekly meetings was a requirement, which many of the individuals seeking assistance only adhered to until they received the base assistance, which they needed and required, on a personal level.[2]

Jobs were sought for the recently released individuals, and usually found, although these jobs didn't pay a wage sufficient enough to sustain oneself and/or meet all of the Court imposed fines and sanctions, which oftentimes included child support and arrears, which had not been suspended during incarceration. There was no mandate, or system in place, to ensure that the ex-offender possessed an education sufficient enough to acquire a job which would pay a comparable salary that would enable them to deal with society on society's terms. While the intent was great, the system was flawed; many of the clients of reentry programs that were supposedly designed to assist, actually recidivated (and were sent back to prison for parole violation or committing a new crime because they could not make it by following the rules).

Approximately 20 months later, upon returning to society and dealing with a Federally Funded Reentry program, where training and a level of opportunity to educate oneself was available, I still faced obstacles and [had to jump through] hoops that I felt like I had to overcome in order to receive the needed assistance. After electing to attend tractor-trailer driving school, I was informed that I had to choose 3 potential schools from a list of Trucking Schools and that the cost of the school could not exceed $3,000.00. This $3,000.00 requirement effectively excluded the top named and most reputable truck driving schools in the region, as most of them cost at least $4,500.00 to attend. Adding to this financial restriction was the fact that this proposed list had been highlighted with which 3 schools could be chosen from. That eventually didn't work out well. After 2 weeks of "memorizing" the answers to acquire the CDL [Commercial Driver's License] permit and spending a total of 15 hours on the "driving range," I was scheduled for my road test, which I failed. That was on me, I guess. After inquiring about some other alternative, I was advised that I would have to attend "counseling sessions" in order to qualify for additional assistance. I moved on, as I needed to earn money to assist in providing for my family.

Overall, I still believe the concept of reentry programs is admirable and effective for some, if not most, individuals. It just wasn't for me. While in prison we work for, generally, $1.35 a day [in New Jersey]. Some make more than this and almost all forward-thinking prisoners say, "when I get out I'll work for minimum wage after working for $1.35 a day," but the truth, and reality, sets in when it's seen that minimum wage doesn't suffice when there's rent, child support, food, and all other types of expenditures that minimum wage just won't cover.

If the reentry programs are to be truly successful and reduce recidivism rates, I believe they should include an educational mandate and remove existing restrictions to vocational training at reputable schools and organizations, not just those whom they have some sort of unspoken alliance with. Jobs, job training, and counseling should be based upon the particular needs of the individual former prisoner, where practical, as not everyone has the same needs post-prison or experiences during their periods of incarceration.

Notes

1. Organization, in this instance, refers to nonprofit reentry service organizations that provide services to men and women reentering society. Each nonprofit organization in the reentry space offers different kinds of services, such as GED and resume building classes, group counseling sessions, bus passes, job training and placement, housing assistance, and case management services to assist returning citizens navigate local, state, and federal bureaucracies to obtain benefits, if they are eligible; identification, including state picture identification and Social Security card; and Veteran's Benefits, if eligible.
2. The base assistance that individuals needed could include access to the computer lab, which allowed individuals to get online to learn how to surf the net, set up an email account or Facebook page, learn how to use a software package, like Word, Excel, or PowerPoint, or to apply to jobs.

Chapter 25

The Journey of a Black Man Enveloped in Poverty

Steven Pacheco

By the time these words reach your conscience, I'll be completely free from this criminalization system, colloquially known as the criminal justice system, after being held captive for a concurrent year in jail and prison and then under government supervision (community supervision isn't accurate because the community is formally and traditionally absent in this process) by the city and state for five and one years, respectively. Because of my charges being categorized as nonviolent versus violent, I was released on "good time" for not being charged with any infractions or exhibiting any notable behavioral issues throughout my sentence. I mean, it was better than the potential 15-year maximum that I could have been sentenced to if I was courageous enough to take the case to trial and lose. Despite not having any drugs on my person or within my domain, I was coerced into taking a plea deal by my "public pretender" (the nickname people often call court-appointed lawyers, who are also known as public defenders) because of a pending case similar to this in New York City and the socio-racial dynamics of my being Black in a predominantly White rural small town. I spent a total of 2,012 days of my life stripped of my freedom for low-level drug-related charges that I was not even guilty of – 312 days of incarceration and 1,700 days on parole and probation.

For those who caught the nuance: yes, I was on parole and probation at the same time. Truthfully speaking, I don't even know if it is legal for a person to serve out a parole and probation sentence simultaneously, but it certainly felt unconstitutional. Prior to my incarceration, the majority of my friends and associates shuffled in and out of jail and/or prison as if it were inevitable for mostly Black and Brown men to continuously lose their freedom over the course of their lifetime. I can't recall when I came to the realization that being Black in America was more akin to a handicap than being a full citizen, but I wasn't older than 10 years of age. I write that to say, while I was opposed to the treatment my community was being subjected to, incarceration registered as a matter of fate for us based on the life experiences shared with me and that I witnessed my family and loved ones endure.

I was born in Dallas, Texas, relocated to New York when I was two, and my family and I would end up settling down in the Highbridge section of The Bronx by the time I was seven. If you ask me, people don't consider the impacts associated with frequently changing your place of residence and how it relates to incarceration. Moving from place to place can lead to all sorts of issues for a young person who is seeking a place of belonging. Fortunately, I did not have a hard time making friends, but I did have a tendency to cause disruption in the classroom. Maybe I was looking for acceptance by making a name for myself, maybe it was just a cry for attention. Whatever the reason for my behavior, my teachers' reactions to my actions taught me a lot about how the world would respond to my outbursts. There would be little to no questions about why I was behaving the way I was, but I would be removed from the general classroom as a consequence. Aside from the fact I was coming into my own as a growing person, I was also faced with an absent father and a family greatly damaged by the War on Drugs. This taught me very early that few people, if any, will care about what you're going through as a Black man enveloped in poverty.

On the other hand, my grandmother, my mother, other family members, and extended family – which includes people in my neighborhood – showered me with lots of love. Through all of these people I learned the significance of love as an action – loyalty, integrity, respect, and collective responsibility. And, sometimes my people also showed me quite the opposite, which is a large part of where my uncanny ability to understand and break down nuance comes from. I would come across teachers and school administrators like Ms. Salmon, Mr. Huff, Ms. Cherry, and Brother Ptah who poured so much into me. Not only did they meet their requirements as educators, but they went the extra mile. Ms. Salmon made sure that I took my academics seriously and had a huge hand in making sure I was accepted into the Morry's Camp program (now known as Project Morry) just before graduating from elementary school. Ms. Cherry was the "school mother" who you could always expect to receive a smile and a nice, big bear hug from; Mr. Huff introduced us to classical music by the greats like Mozart and Beethoven during our exams, and he even brought some Michael Jackson and Motown into the mix as well; and Brother Ptah was the intellectual disciplinarian who helped create and run my high school alma mater, the now-defunct Urban Assembly Academy of History and Citizenship, which initiated my journey for knowledge of self.

It's as important to honor the nuances of any given circumstance as it is to speak truth in all regards. With that being said, I've been able to leverage my trauma and misfortunes by targeting opportunities for formerly incarcerated and justice-affected people. I'm the inaugural Vera Opportunity Fellow, the inaugural David Rockefeller Fund Fellow, an inaugural Ron Moelis Social Innovation Fellow, and an inaugural Gun Control Advocacy Fellow. I was elected Vice President and President of Student Government at John

Jay College of Criminal Justice. Then, I went on to win Echoing Green's NYC Future of Work Social Innovation Challenge with two of my peers from the Ron Moelis Social Innovation Fellowship; and I was also one of four U.S. Delegates chosen by a panel of judges for the British Council's 2018 Future Leaders Connect program. All of these accomplishments were amassed between my release from prison on August 4, 2014, and November 1, 2018 – roughly four years.

While I'm sure there are people who are tempted to see my story as a testament to the effectiveness of incarcerating human beings, it is quite the opposite. Having my freedom and autonomy stripped from me has crippled and terminally damaged my humanity is ways seen and unseen. My mental health is in constant limbo as a result of the multilayered violence I faced throughout my incarceration – physical, psychological, and spiritual. It may come as a surprise to you that my only physical altercation throughout my imprisonment was at the hands of correctional officers at the Jefferson County Correctional Facility. This was late into the night after the entire facility was locked down, so that should tell you how unjustified their assault on me was without going through the trouble of further re-traumatizing myself by recounting the specifics of the targeted attack. Ironically, it would be the only time I would be placed in solitary confinement as a form of punishment during my entire time being incarcerated.

Being that I was just another Black man encased in poverty six hours away from New York City, I was practically helpless in the face of this injustice despite doing the little I could to contact my family in efforts to have the facility held accountable for their actions. My mother was single handedly doing her best to maintain the livelihood of my ailing grandmother, two younger sisters, and my niece in my absence. Prior to being snatched off the streets, I was making the ends meet where no one else could. As property of Jefferson County, I was a very expensive, inconvenient expense, and a liability.

What made me feel even more hopeless was that I received a call from my mom stating that my grandmother had passed away about two weeks into my time in solitary. Adding insult to injury, she also informed me that the facility would not be taking me to the wake or the funeral. The reasoning for this I cannot recall, and I'm not sure it was ever even expressed. My guess is that it had to do with the expenses and logistics of transporting me from Watertown, NY to New York City (~300 miles). This was one of the most challenging, disheartening obstacles I had to live with during that period of my life. Holding onto my sanity was such a struggle after this transpired; the most consolation I have yet to receive is from Meek Mill's song entitled, "Trauma" (2018). In that song, Meek Mill raps about his own experiences growing up, going in and out of prison, how guys are trapped in the system, and about the system labeling men as a felon. I totally understand what Meek Mill is rapping about, and how the system makes sure we know we are not equal.

328 Steven Pacheco

Now, as I move through the world with my destiny in my hand, I'm faced with a constant complexity in every endeavor that I take on because of my record of arrests and prosecutions (rap sheet). With all of my hard work, skills, and networking, there will always be a higher set of stakes for me based on the mistakes and unsound decisions I made doing my best to learn how to navigate a world that has always shown me it doesn't want me to be in a position to self-determine what I want for myself. Being the symbolic figure that I am for so many communities – Highbridge, John Jay College, CUNY, Black people, formerly incarcerated people, and the list goes on – the pressure and stress of continuing to prevail and break barriers sends me through a seesaw of emotions, sometimes even battling with suicidal thoughts. Fortunately, I have a strong support system in my mother, my partner, and my extended family, many of whom are not biologically related to me.

What concerns me the most is the countless number of people who aren't as fortunate as I am. People who have served far more time than I have for crimes people consider way more heinous than mine. People who didn't have a resume with adequate work experience before being convicted. People who didn't obtain a high school diploma or the certified equivalent, let alone attend college. Not a day goes by where I don't think about all of my loved ones who have been battered by a judicial system that is supposed to be in place to deliver justice. Even worse is the fact there are roughly 11 million people or so who have been directly impacted by this broken system. And, that's without counting the impact it's had on their loved ones.

One thing for sure is my life will forever be dedicated to righting the wrongs of the powers that be. From incarceration to poverty and everything in between, I will be a living testament to how much better we can do as a society through my personal life, as well as the efforts I contribute to the fight for true justice. If you want to know why, I'll tell you by using one of my favorite quotes of all time, which happens to be by Assata Shakur: "we have nothing to lose but our chains."

Reference

Mill, M. (2018). Trauma. In *Championships*. Miami, FL: Atlantic Records (Maybach Music Group).

Chapter 26

My First 24 Hours After Being Released

Jose Lumbreras

Preface

While serving time at a Conservation Camp in California, prisoners support local, state, and federal government agencies who respond to public emergencies, such as fires, floods, and manmade disasters, as well as being involved in search and rescue efforts. The individual camps are commonly known as fire camps and are minimum-security facilities that are staffed by Department of Corrections officers. Prisoners who have a "minimal custody" status, which means that they are in good standing, conformed to the rules within prison, and have participated in rehabilitative programming, are eligible to volunteer to work at a fire camp; no prisoners are mandated to work at a fire camp (California Department of Corrections & Rehabilitation, 2018).

The California Department of Corrections & Rehabilitation (CDCR) is responsible for the selection, supervision, care, and discipline of inmate firefighters whereas CALFire maintains the camps, supervises the work of inmate fire crews, and "grades" inmates on daily reports (CDCR, 2018). CDCR supervises all firefighting prisoners' 24-hours a day while they are on work projects and assigned to emergencies around the state. When not fighting fires, inmate firefighters engage in conservation and community service projects, such as clearing brush and fallen trees, maintaining state parks, filling sand bags to combat flood damage, and reforestation. All prisoner firefighters receive the same entry-level firefighting training that CALFire's seasonal firefighters receive, in addition to ongoing training from CALFire throughout the time they are at the fire prison camp (CDCR, 2018).

CDCR uses prison labor to serve a vital role in the state, and has done so since 1915, when the first prison road camp was established to build and maintain roads and highways, provide labor to benefit the state economy, and provide an opportunity for prisoners to earn wages through labor (Goodman, 2010). The use of prison labor expanded during World War II, when there were few able-bodied men available to work in the state (CDCR, 2018). Today, there are 43 adult and two juvenile prison fire camps throughout the state of California, which house >4000 men and women. Prison fire camps are promoted as a rehabilitative program (Goodman, 2010).

Waking Up: November 12, 2014, 5am

There was a 10pm curfew at the Conservation Fire Camp, and at that time everyone had to be in bed; the lights got turned off and inmates like me were not allowed to be in the hallways. My time at the Conservation Fire Camp was ending, and I couldn't sleep the night before my release; I was too anxious, so I was left in my bed with my thoughts, and my emotions, interspersed with a few trips to the restroom to walk off the stress. That was it. I lay in my bed with my eyes wide open thinking about walking on the sidewalk, seeing cars drive on the street, and imagining what it would be like once I stepped out of the California Prison System. I recreated images of what my life could be like once I left, and in one of those moments while I was imagining being away from the continuous presence of correctional officers, locked doors, controlled meals, and the constant sound of jangling keys attached to correctional officers' waists as they patrolled the hallways, I fell asleep.

It was only a few hours before I was awake again. The moment I opened my eyes, I smiled. The barracks were still quiet, it was dark, and no one was moving. The hallways were not accessible to walk around and/or visit other people by their bunk until 6am. I got up from my bed, pulled the box with my civilian clothes towards me, which had been handed to me the night before by one of the correctional officers, and started to change out of my prison clothes. While I was changing clothes, a correctional officer that was doing count passed by and told me, "Don't come back." I looked at him and nodded. Right before the first breakfast call, I heard on the intercom, "Lumbreras, get ready, your ride leaves in 15 minutes, unless you want to stay here longer." I packed the letters that I had received over the last two and half years and I grabbed all my blankets to take to the laundry room. As I walked away from my bunk, I hoped it was my last walk in the hallways of the barracks.

Walking Out of the Dorms

As I stepped away from my bunk, one of my crew members yelled, "Don't forget about us!" I joked with him and said in return, "Wait, what was your name again?" We both laughed. Another crew member came up to me and said, "It's been good man, take care." As I continued my walk to the laundry room and out of the dorms, there was a genuine feeling shared amongst us, who for the past eight months I had shared the barracks with. For some, my release meant a checkpoint for their own timeline. One of my good friends came up to me and said, "I was waiting to see you walk out of here, because now I only have two more months left for my day to come." I could not agree more with my friend, I was also waiting for my day to walk out of the

My First 24 Hours After Being Released 331

dorms and into freedom. I was happy to make that walk down the hallway as I waved at my friends.

I knew I was never coming back, and I started counting all the "lasts" as I did them. This would most likely be the last time I would see many of the people that I met at the Conservation Camp. As I walked that walk for the final time out the barracks, I looked back as people made their way to the cafeteria. It was over. I had completed my time.

My walk outside the barracks felt so fresh; I felt brand new as I filled my lungs with fresh "free" air and I had this fresh feeling all over my body, a feeling of being free. I felt a big relief, I held my head up high, wore a big smile on my face, and had a nice rhythm to my walk as I made my way to the main office to receive my gate money,[1] and a check for the hours I worked while I lived at the fire camp.[2] While at the prison fire camp, I served in a regional firefighting group during the summer of 2014, and when I was not fighting fires, I worked Monday through Friday as part of a fire crew run by a CALFire captain who supervised our crew while we worked on local projects. This work resulted in me earning about five hundred dollars. At that time, I thought five hundred dollars was a lot. I felt confident that the money I earned would last me a while once I was released. However, I did not know the cost of things and more importantly I was unaware of my immediate release costs. What would I need in my first 24 hours after being released? I was not sure. I was not thinking about the cost of reserving a hotel room or paying rent, buying a cell phone and food, the cost of transportation, getting another set of clothes, or paying for a California identification card and a new social security card.

After I signed off for my check and gate money, I smiled. I received a 500 dollar check and an additional 200 dollars cash to buy my bus ticket. It felt good to have cash in my pocket and some extra dollars from my check. But, once I left the camp, I was clueless about how to manage and budget the money I had, and my only identification card was my prison identification card that had my name, my prison number (which I doubt I'll ever forget), and a photo of me in my jumpsuit.

These were things I would have to figure out. I got into a pick-up truck with a correctional officer, and he drove me to the local Greyhound station. A few minutes into our drive, the correctional officer asked, "so where are you going?" I froze. I was unsure where home was. This was a question that I had dreamed about, but did not think through to set a plan on where I would go after my imprisonment and who would be my support team in my first 24 hours after being released. I was naive, ignorant, and hurt. I did not want to take my reentry baggage to my parents or friends. I wanted my life back. I wanted to have my independence. So, I decided to head back to the place where I was living before my incarceration, where I lived with my girlfriend and step-son, and that was the Bay Area. It was also the place where I had to report to my parole officer.

The Greyhound Bus Ride

Twenty minutes later, I had finally left the conservation camp and arrived at the Greyhound Station, both of which felt like a victory. The correctional officer walked with me to buy my bus ticket to the Oakland Greyhound station and a few minutes later the bus arrived. My correctional officer did not leave my side until I boarded the bus and then I was free.

After boarding the Greyhound bus, I found a seat next to the window and sat down for the long ride to Oakland. I laid my head back on my seat and gave myself a minute to live in the moment. Doing time was now something in my past. I sat on my seat thinking, "What am I supposed to do now?" I was reentering society after being controlled and under surveillance for the past two and half years. In my mind, I continued to recreate what I was supposed to do once I was released; however, this was my first time ever being released from prison. I did not have a tool kit or a guide that could assist me with what I should do once I got off the Greyhound bus. Not knowing how to survive made me fearful and anxious. Do I put this burden of reentering society on my family? Close relatives? Friends? I was not sure. My thoughts began to go in circles. At one point, I thought that it would be easier to spend another day in prison then spend my first day reentering society. I couldn't push my mind any further, so I just had to live in the moment. I knew I was on a bus and heading to Oakland, but was I heading home? Only time would tell.

The First Greyhound Bus Stop

The Greyhound bus pulled over for a scheduled pit-stop. I got off the bus with the other passengers and stood still on the sidewalk. I looked around and there were few people; I felt like it was just me. I couldn't understand what was happening, except that I knew I was standing free. At one point, I felt so uncomfortable I began to stretch while looking around while not really looking for anything or anyone. I was curious about where I was and trying to understand my experience in that strange moment. After a while, I walked inside the gas station store to make my first purchase – chocolate and a bottle of water. I was taking my first steps away from the fire camp, penitentiary, and county jail. After eating a chocolate bar, the sugar kicked in and I realized I had crossed another checkpoint. It was my first time standing in society as a free individual after two and a half years.

I re-boarded the bus to travel the last stretch to the Oakland Greyhound Station. I was getting closer to my final destination and my nerves kicked in again. Some very practical questions were starting to form in my formerly paralyzed mind: Where will I sleep tonight? Can I re-enroll in school? What will I eat? How long will seven hundred dollars last? When and where will I be able to buy another pair of underwear? Underneath these questions, the questions I was dying to know the answers to but unable to face, let alone answer, were, "Will I survive outside of prison on my own? What happens if I don't? What will my family go through?" The self-doubt, fear, and guilt that I was feeling at that moment was worse than anything I had endured in prison.

Arriving at the Oakland Greyhound Station

Before my incarceration, I lived in Berkeley, California, and life was good. I was working on my PhD at UC Berkeley, I had a job, and I lived with my girlfriend and stepson in in the Bay Area. However, when I arrived at the Greyhound Station in Oakland, the warm feelings of "home" didn't come over me. I had changed too much, and I didn't have anything left to come back to. As a result, making my way out of the Oakland Greyhound Station was probably the most daring walk I've ever taken; every step I took felt like my last step as adrenaline and desperation took ahold of me. I was literally walking into the unknown. I didn't have a plan for my release. You may think that I must have spent two and a half years incarcerated planning my exit, but planning wasn't the right word. Dreaming about it is more accurate, but dreams are not a plan. I didn't call any of my friends in Berkeley to let them know I was getting out and I hadn't called my family in Los Angeles, so they didn't know about my release, either. At some point, probably when the correctional officer helped me buy my bus ticket, I made the unconscious decision that I wasn't going back to Los Angeles to stay with my parents. I think, now, four years removed from making that initial decision to go to Berkeley, it would have been easier for me if I had returned to Los Angeles. But at the time, I did not have a plan. Plus, going to Berkeley was a requirement for my post-incarceration supervision.

When I was in prison, after I was transferred from reception to mainline, I met with my counselor twice, once when I first arrived to mainline and the second time when it was getting close to my release day. In both of my meetings, there was no discussion about planning for my release day, and my counselor did not offer any practical advice, such as transferring my parole to Los Angeles or anywhere else in the state I would like to go. I was assigned to head back to Bay Area where I would report to my parole officer, and that was it.

Looking for a Place to Sleep

That first day out of prison, as I walked out the Oakland Greyhound Station, I knew this to be true: I was no longer enrolled in a PhD program, I didn't have a job, and more importantly, I didn't know where I was going to sleep: Should I just continue walking . . . but where to? Then, I saw a taxi cab and I decided to head to where I used to live. I knew I had to report to parole within 48 hours after my release, so staying in the Bay Area was the right thing to do, but where? With who? What was I supposed to do in my first 24 hours after being released?

The taxi ride to Berkeley was safe as being in a car gave me a sense of security. However, chatting with the taxi driver made me acutely aware and regretful about my lack of planning. I had no idea of what I should have planned for in my first few days, weeks, and months back in society. As a result, I did not do any planning. When I was in prison, everything I dreamed about when I was laying on my bunk did not include details about how the process would be. I thought about the life that I wanted to achieve after being incarcerated, which included the ability to move freely, but I had no clue about the process of achieving my freedom and moving freely. I had been dreaming about being readmitted into school, having a job, getting a place to live, and being independent. I was not aware of the immediate obstacles I was supposed to overcome during my first 24 hours of being released, such as securing my housing, food, and showering.

Once I arrived to downtown Berkeley, I got out of the taxi, and I identified a tangible next step. I needed to call someone. It was around seven in the evening, and I was standing in downtown Berkeley thinking about who to call. No one "felt" right. I was too desperate to call an acquaintance and risk rejection. I started to panic and began asking random people on the street to borrow their cell phone so I could make my first call. One woman said yes, but the call didn't go through. The night continued and I asked someone else if I could borrow their cell phone. My second phone call also did not go through. It was getting darker and later, and I didn't know where I could go and couldn't think of a place to stay besides laying down somewhere on the sidewalk. The sidewalk probably wasn't harder than my bunk at the prison camp, but the sidewalk smelled like piss, so I decided that somewhere near the UC Berkeley campus would be better.

My stomach was growling; I had lost track of time and besides the chocolate bar I'd eaten hours before, I had not eaten. I had already walked for blocks in search of something, but I found nothing. I was walking aimlessly and had no direction. I made a couple more phone calls, but no one answered. By this time, it was close to nine thirty at night when I finally decided to get something to eat. I went into a bar and ordered a prime rib sandwich with a glass of Hennessey on the rocks. Food only helped me stay calm for the first couple of bites; it was ten o'clock at night and I was running out of time as bars and restaurants would start closing. After eating, I went out again to ask people passing by on the sidewalk if I could borrow their cell phone to try calling the two real friends I had that lived in the Bay Area. The thought that I would spend my first night on the street haunted me.

Finally, after a few more calls, my friend finally answered. He was glad to hear my voice, and once I told him that I was in the area, he agreed to pick me up in his car. We went for a late Target run. He was kind enough to buy me a couple of shirts, socks, and boxer shorts to get me started with building my wardrobe, and I was grateful because clothes were on my "must do" list. By the time we left Target, it was about 11:30pm, and when we got in his car he asked me, "Jose, where do you want to go?" I paused. I couldn't ask him if I could stay over at his house. We were friends, but he had a full house with his family. Instead, I asked him to drive me into downtown Berkeley, and as we got closer I began to see people making their beds on the sidewalk. I asked him if I could borrow his cell phone, and I called my other friend that lived in Berkeley. I called and no one picked up. I was lost for words. I had travelled ten plus hours to a place that I didn't have any family or support. I had no more options.

"Jose, you okay? What do you want to do?" my friend asked me. I thanked him for the clothes he bought me and asked him to drop me off near my friend's home address, despite no one answering earlier. I used the address she had provided when we exchanged a few letters while I was incarcerated. I never thought about verifying if she still lived there. I also hadn't tried to contact her ahead of time to see if I could stay at her place for a night or two. I was taking a chance, but my other option was to sleep on the streets.

My friend dropped me off near the address I gave him. When I got out of the car, he wished me good luck and mentioned to give him a call if I needed anything. I grabbed my letters and phone book that I had brought with me from the prison camp and walked away from his car. I began to walk towards my friends' home. As I was getting closer, my body was tensing as I thought to myself, "What if she doesn't live here anymore? How do I know if I will be able to stay at her place for the night? How many nights will I need to stay? What about my meeting with my parole officer tomorrow? I don't have a home address for him, so what was I going to do?" I knocked a few times, but there was no answer. By now it was well past midnight, and although I was trying to avoid it, the moment I feared the most came true at this precise moment. With my friend not answering my phone calls and not answering her door – if she even still lived there – I had no place to go. I sat on the floor next to her front door, curled up, and fell asleep.

A couple of hours later, I got tapped on my shoulder, and it was my friend. She invited me inside her home, and we began to catch up; it had been a few years since we last saw each other. I was able to stay at her place for the rest of the night, and the next morning, she offered to drive me to my first meeting with my new probation officer; I accepted. During the drive, we discussed the possibilities of me staying at her place for a couple of months while I worked on stabilizing my life, which was a fuzzy concept that I was unprepared for.

Looking Back

During the two and a half years that I was incarcerated, I learned from others that I did not have a long prison sentence. In fact, a lot of men, women, and youth serve ten years or more, and many more will be incarcerated for their entire life. Being incarcerated for two and a half years, however, was long enough for me to lose everything that oriented me in life, allowed me to function, and gave me some sense of being part of society at large. I had nothing when I was released, but hope and the phone numbers of two friends. My experience is "normal" for many coming home; they have nothing but hope and a couple of vague connections.

Although there are several nonprofit and religious based organizations in Oakland that I could have contacted for assistance and help during those first few weeks after being released, I was unaware of their existence. As a result of my experiences, I will never take for granted the privilege of having a home, being able to work, going to school, and having the freedom to go to different places in the community, like the grocery store, post office, park, or the library. Only after I'd been home for a few months after my first night back in society, I learned about the program, Building Opportunities for Self Sufficiency, also known as BOSS, which is a reentry assistance program in Oakland.[3]

Now, four years after my release, I have found stability. I understand now how other formerly incarcerated individuals reentering society may not be as lucky as me and end up homeless, on drugs, or back in prison. In retrospect, a pre-exit program that is set up in every prison that lasts at least three months prior to one's release date would be a helpful resource for prisoners prior to entering society. My experiences are not unique; it happens to thousands of formerly incarcerated individuals coming home every single day of the year. Being released from prison is a complicated process – emotionally, physically, and psychologically – and reintegrating back into society can be equally challenging and life altering.

A Kit for Your First 24 Hours After Being Released

Every month there are thousands of individuals exiting correctional facilities across the country, and every one of those prisoners should receive an information kit that helps them during the first 24 hours after release and the necessary steps to achieve successful reentry and reintegration. The kit should be put together up to three months prior to being released, and needs to include information on how to contact several social agents from different institutions that can assist anyone coming home. Prisoners should contact these organizations prior to being released via phone calls, letters, and even face-to-face meetings. The goal should be focused on helping each individual identify their immediate needs upon release and connect them to the best tools and organizations in the community they return to provide for as smooth as possible transition to society. Ultimately, the kit and educational process should be designed to assist individuals to understand reentry and its related challenges so that they can think and focus on becoming self-sufficient during their own reentry process.

The kit must be sensitive to the realities individuals who are incarcerated face. For instance, individuals who finally reach their release date, that is an exciting moment, but it is also very overwhelming because of the realities they must face (Middlemass, 2017). Based on my own personal experiences, below is what I think needs to be included in an informational kit to help prisoners' transition back to society during the first 24 hours they are out of the correctional environment.

As mentioned above, the kit must start prior to an individuals' release date, and the initial kit should focus on role playing and scenarios to answer questions that each individual needs to think about and have to answer prior to their release date and for their own personal reentry process. Here are some important questions that individuals need to think about prior to being released:

1. Do you have a primary person you can contact before you are released that might help you once you are released? Have you been in contact with them? Have you thought about writing them a letter about six weeks prior to your release to let them know you are coming home? Who else have you been in contact with? Have you thought about others, such as immediate and extended family and friends, that may be able to help you?
2. Once you arrive at your destination, do you have someone that would pick you up from the bus station? Help you get toiletries and a change of clothes?
3. Do you know where would you sleep your first night after being released? What do you think are some options? What organizations in your community of release offer housing assistance? Have you thought about writing these organizations a letter prior to your release date so that you have a place to go that first night back in society?
4. Do you have any health issues that should be addressed after being released? If so, are you eligible for Medicaid, Medicare, or a similar state program? Who will help you fill in these forms? Who will help you access any medications you need?
5. Have you thought about finding a support group that can help you once you are released? Who should be in this support group?

A second part of the information kit should include a list of current prices of things, such as how much does a cell phone cost, average price of a taxi, the prices of food, and clothes. A third section needs to include a list of stores and where they are located in the city as it pertains to the main Greyhound station, such as a full-service grocery store, a clothing store (e.g., Target, Walmart), and a place to buy a basic cell phone. A fourth section needs to consist of a list of nonprofit organizations and religious institutions in the area where someone is returning to that provides immediate

338 Jose Lumbreras

assistance, such as temporary or emergency shelter, food banks, and health care. This type of information would serve as an important part of an informational kit that would help individuals prepare for their first 24 hours after being released.

For this kit to work, a key part would be the role of different social agents from different institutions. This can include redefining the role of counselors in the prison system and correctional officers. They have the closest contact with incarcerated individuals and can have a major influence on individuals that are getting close to being released from prison and could assist with making sure individuals have the information they need. Probation and parole officers can also serve in the reentry and reintegration process prior to individuals being released. For instance, probation and parole agencies could send prisons information about organizations that serve the returning prison population so that a paper database could be created inside for those nearing their release date. Also, the role of grassroots, nonprofit organizations, and state services would have a significance influence on the reentry of many formerly incarcerated individuals. The role of social agents from these various organizations and institutions, such as social workers, counselors, case managers, and community members would be important to the reentry process of formerly incarcerated individuals. Although each grassroot organization, nonprofit, and state institution would work from a different framework, the end goal is to assist formerly incarcerated individuals with the collateral consequences of incarceration. The reentry and reintegration success of formerly incarcerated individuals is the responsibility of the entire society, starting from the individual and the community in which they return.

Notes

1. When a prisoner is paroled or discharged from most state prisons, they are entitled to a small amount of money referred to as "gate money." The amount of gate money varies by state. In addition to "gate money," some states provide "dress out clothes," a set of prison-issued civilian clothes, which varies with the seasons and tends to be of low-quality (Middlemass & Smiley, 2016; Smiley & Middlemass, 2016). If a prisoners' family can afford to send civilian clothes, prisoners are able to wear those clothes on their release date.
2. Inmates at fire camps are paid less than minimum wage for the dangerous and potentially deadly work, $1 an hour plus $2 a day. Although the pay is paltry, most first-person accounts of working at the fire camps indicate that the food is better, there is less security, prisoners are able to earn "good time credits," and there is greater relative freedom (within the rules) than in a traditional prison (Goodman, 2010).
3. BOSS is an award-winning organization that helps people who face deep poverty and multiple special needs, such mental illness, substance abuse, HIV/AIDS, and chronic homelessness. BOSS works one-on-one with each individual or family in an effort to help them achieve stable income, permanent affordable housing, and lasting wellness (https://self-sufficiency.org/).

References

California Department of Corrections & Rehabilitation, CDCR. (2018). Retrieved September 10, 2018, from www.cdcr.ca.gov/Conservation_Camps/

Goodman, P. (2010). *A brief history of California's prison camps*. Retrieved September 10, 2018, from www.cdcr.ca.gov/Conservation_Camps/docs/History_of_firecamps.pdf

Middlemass, K. M. (2017). *Convicted and condemned: The politics and policies of prisoner reentry*. New York: New York University Press.

Middlemass, K. M., & Smiley, C. (2016). Jumpsuit to button-down: Clothing used as resistance in prisoner reentry. *Journal of Criminal Justice & Law Review, 5*(1–2), 63–80.

Smiley, C., & Middlemass, K. M. (2016). Clothing makes the man: Impression management and prisoner reentry. *Punishment & Society, 18*(2), 220–243.

Section VI

Activism, Liberation, and Reentry

The proliferation of activism surrounding issues of returning citizens and incarcerated individuals stems from decades of mass incarceration, which has wrought devastation to millions of individuals, families, and communities who have been directly and indirectly impacted by a range of public policies found within the criminal law and civil statutes connected to a felony conviction. Movement building surrounding issues related to mass incarceration and prisoner reentry are not formed in a vacuum but birthed out of existing movements that have helped to create new movements.

Historically, the Civil Rights Era in the United States began to unearth many of the inequalities that people of color, specifically Black Americans, faced because of their treatment as second-class citizens. It is not far-fetched to see a direct connection between the Civil Rights Movement and modern Black Power movements, such as Black Lives Matter (BLM). BLM is in response to the outgrowth of documented police harassment and misconduct, which has largely gone unchecked even as 21st century technology continues to capture pictures and videos of police malfeasance, misconduct, and illegal activities. These pictures and videos are archived and disseminated across multiple media platforms to document police wrongdoing. BLM highlights the ways Black people come into contact with the criminal justice system via the police officers and other law enforcement agents, and the negative impact of those interactions.

When it comes to movement building surrounding the issue of criminal justice there are calls for reforms, which seek to change the laws and the rules of the system in order to create more equity and transparency, which has mainly focused on the police, and includes the use of body cameras and police car camera systems, bias training, community relations, de-escalation tactics and strategies, and holding police officers accountable for their misconduct and illegal actions. Reform also includes addressing correctional spaces by updating older facilities, creating common spaces for classes and training of prisoners, and providing a range of programs, treatments, and classes within carceral spaces. Part of the reform system is to drastically reduce the use of prison as the primary form of punishment and instead advocate for changing the system from one that is retributive to a restorative system that focuses on the principles of humanity and agency, dignity, public safety, shared responsibility, systems collaboration and integration, accountability between the system and individuals, and restoration of rights (Reentry Ready, 2019).

The authors in the last section provide different perspectives on what activism and liberation can mean when it occurs within reentry services and spaces. Smiley, in his chapter, "Money for Freedom," examines cash bail, incarceration, and reentry. Cash bail, which has monetized release from jail based on the ability to pay, targets disadvantaged populations, including socioeconomic hardship combined with the intersection of race and gender. Smiley details how cash bail in the U.S. is directly linked to reentry as it determines whether or not an individual will have the opportunity to return to their family and community prior to adjudication. Smiley's examination of cash bail criticizes cash bail and determines it is a failure and he looks at the growing activism surrounding cash bail. His chapter highlights how the bail system is effectively a class-based apparatus that overwhelmingly incarcerates disadvantaged individuals from lower socioeconomic backgrounds. Smiley's critique concludes that the cash bail system needs to be abolished and social movements must reenvision a justice system that practices restorative justice rather than different types of punitive policies.

In their chapter, "Agents of Change in Healing Our Communities," Chowdhury, Davis, and Hammond discuss community action work in disadvantaged neighborhoods that formerly incarcerated individuals are involved in. Formerly known as "O.G.s" (Original Gangsters), some men have left different prison environments with a wealth of knowledge about the streets, gang culture, and the system. Through grassroots organizations, these men have sought out opportunities to apologize to their community and to utilize restorative justice methods to heal communities. Change agents are taking an active role in healing their communities by interrupting violence, creating social justice frameworks, sharing their stories, and investing in various programs, such as mental and physical health. By chronicling the reentry experiences of two change agents, Chowdhury, Davis, and Hammond show that activism can be liberating in the reentry context.

In his chapter, "Rehabilitation is Reentry," Garot explores a community built by and for returning citizens. Located in a rural area in upstate New York, this commune invites formerly incarcerated individuals to become involved in self-healing and more importantly self-discovery in an environment that is conducive with successful reentry. Garot documents the work of three returning citizens and how they dreamed of reentry while they were incarcerated. While dreaming, they created new programs, worked to implement the programs within carceral spaces, and then upon release, continued to innovate to create Breathing Space, an entrepreneurial project. Garot's chapter demonstrates how liberation from traditional thinking can inspire and change reentry experiences.

Binnall, and three of his students, Sotelo, Vasquez, and Hernandez, write about their experiences at California State University, Long Beach. In their chapter, "Making Good One Semester at a Time," Binnall et al. consider the redemptive power of higher education, and how returning citizens can form supportive social environments on a college campus. The authors discuss the program, Rising Scholars, which was started by three of the authors, and was specifically for justice-affected students. Rising Scholars allowed students to create a formal network of academic and social support, and provided the basis to become active in daily campus life. Rising Scholars allowed students the space to acclimate to college life and the community, while providing returning citizens a sense of identity and place. Current Rising Scholars act as role models for new members who want to pursue higher education.

In the chapter, "I Can't Depend on No Reentry Program!," Payne, Brown, and Wright use an activist framework to study street-identified Black men's reflections on prisoner reentry. Based on an ethnographic analysis and utilizing a street participatory action research framework, Payne et al. demonstrate how street-identified Black men view their reentry experiences, but also how their experiences can be used to improve reentry services and programs. Based in two low-income communities in Wilmington, Delaware, Payne et al. find that, contrary to the dominant notion in reentry literature, Black men understand best what leads them to prison and what they need when they return home. Moreover, Payne et al. find that street-identified Black men cared deeply about other returning citizens, who were often family members, and wanted to help these men reenter successfully.

Reference

Reentry Ready. (2019). *Reentry ready: Improving incarceration's contribution to successful reentry*. Washington, DC: Convergence Center for Policy Resolution. Retrieved from www.convergencepolicy.org/latest-projects/successful-reintegration/

Chapter 27

Money for Freedom
Cash Bail, Incarceration, and Reentry

CalvinJohn Smiley

Introduction

There are currently over 2.3 million people under correctional supervision in the United States because of various punitive policies, and cash bail has helped to inflate this figure. According to the Vera Institute of Justice, between 1970 and 2015 pre-trial detention has risen by 433%: "Approximately two-thirds of the more than 740,000 people held in locally run jails across the United States have not been convicted of a crime – they are presumed innocent and simply waiting for their day in court" (Digard & Swavola, 2019, p. 1). Consequently, cash bail has impacted the lives of thousands of individuals who are unable to afford their bond, creating an unequal system that further criminalizes low-income members of society as well as impacts reentry because the longer an individual is exposed to incapacitation the more strain and collateral consequences manifest.

This chapter examines the growing activism surrounding cash bail – the monetized payment for release. It argues that cash bail undermines democracy because it places a numeric value on freedom that not everyone can afford and has incentivized the creation of entrepreneurial business of bail bond organizations. In order to unpack the movement that challenges the use of cash bail, this chapter examines four critical areas of concern. First, I examine high-profile cases that involve cash bail issues to underscore its failure. Second, a brief historical summary of the cash bail system in the United States is covered, including the intended and unintended consequences of cash bail, particularly in relationship to reentry. Third, I discuss the various efforts designed to dismantle cash bail. Finally, I consider recent reforms that have occurred to theorize where the bail system should go from here.

The Failure of Cash Bail

The name Kalief Browder has become emblazoned in the movement for criminal justice reform and prison abolition. In May 2010, Browder, age 16, was stopped and arrested in the Bronx, New York. He was charged with second-degree robbery, a crime he adamantly denied; his bail was set at $3,000, a cash bond price his family could not afford (Gonnerman, 2014). For three years, Browder resided in New York City's largest jail, Riker's Island, and experienced physical and mental traumas from violent altercations with prison staff and other residents, and emotional turmoil because of spending close to two years in solitary confinement. While waiting for his case to be adjudicated, Browder was offered various plea deals, which he consistently rejected; in response, prosecutors would delay his trial date (Gonnerman, 2014). Finally, in May 2013, all charges against Kalief Browder were dropped. Yet having the charges dropped and being released from Riker's Island did not end Kalief's suffering; just over two years after his release, in June 2015, Kalief Browder took his own life (Gonnerman, 2015).

Browder's arrest, imprisonment, and court proceedings became a rally cry to seek justice for his false incarceration and to thwart discriminatory procedures in the criminal justice system, namely cash bond. According to the City of New York Independent Budget Office (IBO), nearly 78% of all persons detained on Riker's Island in 2016 were in pretrial custody (Lowenstein, 2017).[1] Of this number, 72% were imprisoned because they simply could not post bail at their arraignment (Lowenstein, 2017). According to the IBO, 90% of all pretrial detainees were male and 52% and 33% were Black and Hispanic, respectively. In other words, a disproportionate number of individuals in jail who cannot afford bail are a racial minority who is poor.

In addition to Kalief Browder, Pedro Hernandez became another focal point of the exorbitant costs related to cash bail in New York City. Hernandez, age 17, spent a year on Riker's Island after refusing a plea deal to an armed robbery charge in the Bronx, where his bail was initially set at $250,000 before being reduced to $100,000 (Crane-Newman, Rayman, & Schapiro, 2017). Eventually, the prosecutor had to dismiss the case and charges against Hernandez because of inconsistent and contradictory evidence. In fact, Hernandez's family hired a private investigator to investigate; the private report contends that police falsified their records and at least one officer involved in the case had his badge and gun stripped for various unrelated misconduct issues (Crane-Newman et al., 2017).

The Vera Institute of Justice report highlights that the length of pretrial detention stays have steadily increased, going from roughly 14 days in 1983 to 23 days in 2013, nationally (Subramanian, Delaney, Roberts, Fishman, & McGarry, 2015). New York City's jail stays increased from 40 to 55 days from 2000 to 2015 (Augenstein, 2017). In cases where more serious violent charges are brought against the accused, the stay increased from 89 to 119 days (Augenstein, 2017). Therefore, individuals are missing anywhere from a little over a month to almost four months before seeing their day in court, which impacts such things as housing, employment, education, and familial relationships.

The issue of cash bail extends beyond young men of color in New York City. Sandra Bland, a Black woman in Texas, was driving and stopped by a state trooper for failure to use a turn signal while changing lanes. Upon being given a citation, the officer requested she put out her cigarette. When Bland refused, the police officer escalated the situation, and Bland was arrested for suspicion of assaulting a public servant; bail was set at $5,000, which her family could not immediately pay, so she was detained at the county jail (Appleman, 2016). Three days later, Bland's body was found hanging in her jail cell; her death was ruled a suicide. However, many in the Black Lives Matter (BLM) movement and community-at-large believe Bland's death was not a suicide but something more insidious. Her death sparked the hashtag #SayHerName, which became a pivotal point in the BLM movement highlighting that Black women are also victims of police harassment and cash bail.

Research highlights that the longer someone spends imprisoned the more likely they are to be convicted, which will be discussed in the next section. The next session provides a brief history of the bail system and the intended and unintended consequences of cash bail. I also discuss how cash bail impacts reentry.

A Brief History of Cash Bail

The United States Constitution gives judicial power to the courts to determine and try criminal cases. The Bill of Rights' 8th Amendment states, "*Excessive bail* shall not be required, nor *excessive fines* imposed, nor *cruel and unusual punishments* inflicted" (Browne-Marshall, 2010). Drawn from English law, the intended use of bail for the accused was to establish an incentive for this person to appear in court in order to recoup their money. If they did not return for their court hearings, the person forfeits their bail. The founders of the United States seemingly acknowledged the potential misuse of bail by adding the word "excessive." Yet over time, the courts have left this term to interpretation.

In 1951, the Supreme Court ruled in *Stack v. Boyle* that defendants' 8th Amendment rights were violated. Chief Justice Vinson wrote, "Since the function of bail is limited, the fixing of bail for any individual defendant must be based upon standards relevant to the purpose of assuring the presence of that defendant" (1951). Typically, four factors are considered when setting or revoking bail, which include: seriousness of the crime, the individual's ties to the community, their flight risk, and any possible danger posed by the defendant to the community (Wald, 1964). Despite these basic criteria, other biases have been found in the use of cash bail, such as race, gender, and class discrimination in setting or revoking a bail for a defendant (Sacks & Ackerman, 2014). Furthermore, in 1987, the Supreme Court ruled in *United States v. Salerno* that it was constitutional for federal courts to detain an arrestee when that individual was potentially dangerous to other people in the community, and these actions did not violate the 5th or 8th Amendments (Goldkamp, 1985).

In theory, bail is intended to keep the public safe. Nevertheless, bail has various unintended consequences. For instance, individuals with similar cases will have drastically different bails set by a judge based on the race of the defendant or race of the victim (Jones, 2013). There are also other negative consequences related to pretrial detention. Lowenkamp, VanNostrand, and Holsinger (2013) found that those who have experienced longer pretrial detention are more likely to fail to appear in court if they are released prior to final adjudication. Moreover, those who are pretrial detainees are more likely to be convicted because of several factors. First, those incarcerated have limited contact and access to counsel (Digard & Swavola, 2019). Second, the longer someone is in jail waiting for trial, the more financial burden they accrue (Digard & Swavola, 2019). Finally, prosecutors are incentivized to set a high bail in order to induce a guilty plea; roughly 90% of all criminal cases never go to trial (Alexander, 2012).

The growth of American jails spurred the increase of bail bondsmen, a private contractor who as a third party will agree to pay a defendant's bond, typically with some percentage of the bond being paid directly to the bondsmen as a fee. Additionally, bondsmen typically insure their investment by drawing up a collateral contract. In the case of a collateral contract, if the defendant fails to appear in court and the bondsmen loses their money, they have the assets(s) of the accused family or friend who put up the bond; this could include real property, investment accounts, and jewelry. In the end, the courts and bondsmen are ensured financial security, whereas the defendant is not. Therefore, some have cited that bail bonds have become a predatory lender situation, where the customer might not totally understand the consequences and can be exploited (Rivlin-Nadler, 2014).

Cash bail impacts reentry. While someone is incarcerated, they lose out on various opportunities as well as involuntarily forfeit many of their rights. For instance, in most situations when someone is incarcerated, they are not afforded the right to vote, no matter their conviction status. Additionally, if someone is a pretrial detainee this could impact their employment, education, and housing, which are three pillars to stability and significant for desistance (Freudenberg, Daniels, Crum, Perkins, & Richie, 2005). Furthermore, jails have become the primary institutions for mental health services. Roughly 40% of individuals admitted to Riker's Island come with mental health issues (Winerip & Schwirtz, 2014). Therefore, the incentive should be to get people out of these institutions as quickly as possible versus allowing individuals to languish and experience various forms of violence and trauma (DeVeaux, 2013).

All of this impacts one's return to society and ability to function within society, regardless of conviction status. In other words, jails are chaotic and violent institutions that disrupt the life-course, impact physical and mental

Money for Freedom 349

health, and create obstacles to social and civic engagement. The next section looks at how organizations and individuals have become involved in bail reform to get people out of pretrial detainment.

Bail-Reform, Abolition, and Reentry

This section discusses and briefly describes several organizations that have intervened to combat the cash bail system as well as two individuals from the hip-hop community who have taken on the cash bail system and paid for individuals to be released on bond pending a hearing or trial. Here, these organizations and individuals articulate as well as recognize the connections between race, class, and gender disparities within the criminal justice system.

The Bail Project

The Bail Project (TBP) is a national organization founded by Robin Steinberg. Prior to heading up TBP, Steinberg was the founder of The Bronx Defenders, The Bronx Freedom Fund, and Still She Rises. TBP state on their website, "Cash bail criminalizes poverty, devastating low-income communities and disproportionately affecting women and people of color. Pretrial detention accounts for all jail growth in the U.S. in the past 20 years. We cannot end mass incarceration without addressing our indefensible bail system" (The Bail Project, 2019).

According to the website, TBP is an outgrowth of The Bronx Freedom Fund that in 2007 was the first of its kind revolving bail fund in the United States and their results as follows. First, 96% of individuals who are bailed out return for their court date. Second, when individuals were remanded to jail because they could not afford bail 90% plead guilty. Whereas, when bail was paid 50% of cases were dismissed and <2% received a jail sentence (The Bail Project, 2019). TBP is the national movement to replicate this process and currently has 14 locations throughout the United States.

The mission of TBP states, "The Bail Project is a non-profit organization designed to combat mass incarceration by disrupting the money bail system – one person at a time" (The Bail Project, 2019). In order to achieve this goal, TBP employs persons who have titles such as "bail disruptors" and "client advocates" who are the hands-on-the-ground individuals who grow the network through community-based efforts in securing bail for individuals. In order for this work to happen, TBP has a specific action plan, which is highlighted on their website. TBP outlines what they call, "Our Approach" and "How We Work."[2] The former has four parts, which include context, partners, impact, and vision. Whereas the latter has five parts which establish: connect, pay bail, court reminders, advocacy and support, and stories and data. This approach is two-fold. First, it works to establish local connections with public defenders, community-organizations, and others to identify who is at most need for bail. Second, upon securing an individual's bond, TBP continues to work with that individual to ensure that they are getting assistance. Through this combined initiative of advocacy, justice, and support, TBP looks to continue to expand around the nation by identifying regions and areas in most need for bail reform and cash bail assistance.

National Bail Out

Better known as #FreeBlackMamas, National Bail Out (NBO) is an organization dedicated to securing bail and release of Black mothers. According to their website,[3] "We work with groups all over the country on Mother's Day to bail out as many Black Mamas and caregivers as we can, provide supportive services and fellowship opportunities for those we bail out and organize to end money bail and pretrial detention." NBO has a targeted group, Black women, for whom they focus resources in securing bond.

Black women are marginalized and are a rising incarcerated population (Barnes, 2017). Additionally, Black women are caregivers in the forms of mothers, aunts, grandmothers, and other maternal relationships with children (Roberts, 2011). NBO, by partnering with other organizations, intends to disrupt the bail system by bailing women out, particularly on Mother's Day as a symbolic form of resistance to the system. NBO provides a toolkit, which is a downloadable file on their website,[4] which is a useful guide that assists in educating people about bail, with topics including: creating a bailout plan, fundraising, and beyond bailout. This accessible toolkit is open for public consumption to empower bail abolition.

Additionally, NBO highlights the historical connections of the Black Code systems in the 19th and 20th centuries to 21st century bail. Entitled, "The Black Codes of Bail,[5]" NBO emphases five ways individuals who post bail are still directly impacted and under criminal justice duress, which include: (1) Unreasonable curfew requirements; (2) Loss of Public Defender; (3) Two Year Waiting Periods; (4) Forced Payment for Electronic Monitoring; and (5) Bail Forces People to Plead Guilty.

Finally, NBO has the "Free Black Mama's Fellowship," which is an eight-week paid fellowship for Black women who have been bailed out and includes political education and organization as well as participation in a national conference. NBO sees itself as part of the abolition movement and legacy of combating injustice, particularly forms of injustice that are both racialized and gendered or as Francis Beal stated, Black Women face a "double jeopardy" for being both Black and Female (Beal, 2008).

The Dollar Bail Brigade

The Dollar Bail Brigade (DBB) is a New York City focused collective that concentrates on bailing individuals out of the NYC jail system who are

Money for Freedom 351

being held on bail for one dollar. DBB website explains,[6] "The Dollar Bail Brigade is a coalition of volunteers who pay their fellow New Yorkers' $1 bails in their spare time. The DBB advocates for the *abolition* of money bail, pretrial detention, and the prison-industrial complex" (The Dollar Bail Brigade, 2019, emphasis in original). DBB has brought volunteers together, who are willing to travel to one of the several city jails to sit and wait in order to pay this symbolic bail of one dollar.

According to the DBB website, a dollar bail is often set when a person has two open cases simultaneously. Typically, the more serious charge will have a more traditional bail amount and the lesser charge will be set at $1. Unfortunately, in some cases, families and friends pay the larger bail and are unaware of the $1 bail and the defendant continues to be detained and since paying the bail can be a long process, often times, people detained do not have individuals who can sit and wait to pay the bail amount. DBB's website gives the statistics of how long individuals wait to bail someone out of jail, which consists of freeing 201 people with 815 volunteers. The mean wait time is 7.5 hours and the median wait time is 3 hours. Lastly, the longest wait was 49 hours to bail someone out for a dollar (The Dollar Bail Brigade, 2019).

DBB stresses the importance of volunteers on educating themselves in the task they have signed up to accomplish, which is freeing people from jail being held on cash bail. DBB has a checklist entitled, "How to Pay Bail in NYC," which each volunteer should download, print, and bring with them while they are attempting to bail an individual out. This pertinent information is broken down into three steps, which include: 1. Before You Leave-listing items that you need to bring with you; 2. Find out where to go to post bail and how to get there since NYC has four locations a person could be held in a city jail; and 3. What to do once you arrive, particularly the pertinent information that a volunteer needs to give the Department of Corrections. Once all this is done, the process of release commences.

★★★

Beyond organizations that have established networks in communities, fundraising to expand these projects, and focused advocacy and education surrounding the disproportionate inequality of cash bail and its impact on low-income communities, particularly women, minorities, immigrants, and LGBTQIA communities, there has been work by individuals who have expressed their contempt for the bail system.

Jay-Z and T.I., Hip-Hop musicians, have paid the bail to release individuals being held on cash bail. Jay-Z is vocal in speaking out against inequalities in the criminal justice system. For instance, he penned an op-ed in *The New York Times* in November 2017 about the case of rapper Meek Mill who was remanded back to prison after violating his probation on a charge that was nearly a decade old (Jay-Z, 2017). In addition, Jay-Z was an executive producer for the documentary entitled, *Time: The Kalief Browder Story*. In June 2017, after being inspired by organizations that were bailing mother's out of jail for Mother's Day, Jay-Z donated funds to bail out father's for Father's Day (Carter, 2017; Craighead, 2017). Additionally, Jay-Z's company, Roc Nation, has financially supported an app called "Promise," which is being developed to assist bail reform by setting clients up with a calendar to monitor and assist individual success in reducing recidivism and incarceration (Keck, 2018). Beyond Jay-Z, rapper T.I. has recently joined the struggle for bail reform. In April 2019, T.I. bailed out 23 individuals from jail in his home state of Georgia for Easter Sunday (McKinney, 2019). T.I., alongside the New Birth Missionary Baptist Church's "Bail Out" program, helped secure the release and connected these individuals with mentors for weekly check-ins.

Through both organizational and individual awareness and advocacy bail reform and bail abolition have become a way to tackle mass incarceration. The final section looks at what has already been done in some places to combat cash bail systems and theorizes how these policy changes could be extrapolated nationally. If cash bail could be abolished what is the possibility of abolishing other aspects of a draconian punitive criminal justice system?

Conclusion – Beyond Bail

There is no denying the costly system of cash bail on individuals and their families as well as overwhelming costs on local, state, and national budgets in housing individuals' pre-trial (Wagner & Rabuy, 2017). Placing a monetary value on a person is nothing more than an arbitrary and subjective form of punishment. The history of punishment and state-sanctioned violence has a long precedent of being exacted on poor communities and people of color.

Some places have begun the process of trying to curb or reverse the impacts of cash bail and pretrial detainment. For example, in 2017, New Jersey passed The New Jersey Criminal Justice Reform Act, which has eliminated cash bail and only in cases where a defendant is facing life imprisonment or a prosecutor can convince a judge that a defendant is a threat to the public or flight risk can they be retained. Under this new system, a risk assessment based on a host of factors is computed to determine if a person should or should not be released until trial.

Although there is obviously a space for criticism of the futuristic *Minority Report*[7] style of assessment, the statistics since implementing this policy do not lie. The ACLU reports that there has been a 20.3% decline from 2016 to 2017 in the pretrial jail population, which reduces the overall jail population (ACLU, n.d.). Additionally, under this system individuals are monitored by a system called Pretrial Monitoring Level 3+, which could include home detention or electronic monitoring. To date, fears of a surge of crimes have fallen flat. In fact, recent reports indicate that people released are no more likely to commit a crime than anyone else and the trend of the falling pretrial jail detainee continues to plummet (Pugliese, 2019).

In California, legislation was passed that eliminates all forms of cash bail beginning in October 2019 (Park, 2018). Similar to New Jersey, defendants will go through a risk assessment process before being released. Despite this being seen as a progressive stance, some critics still believe it has not gone far enough. For example, CNN reports, "But the ACLU in California expressed disappointment over the bill, saying it 'is not the model for pretrial justice and racial equity that California should strive for'" (Park, 2018). Finally, New York has made sweeping changes to pretrial evidence by requiring prosecutors to share evidence, known as discovery, in the early stages of a case. According to a report by the Marshall Project, "If a defendant facing felony charges is offered a plea deal, information must be shared at least three days before his deadline to accept" (Schwartzapfel, 2019). Although this does not directly overhaul cash bail, this new process will certainly impact cash bail indirectly as defendants and their attorneys will have knowledge of what evidence the prosecution has against them.

The bail system is an outdated and archaic system that needs to be eliminated nationally. The movement surrounding the abolition of cash bail is growing with more and more organizations and individuals disrupting the system by advocating for the persons impacted by this system. However, activists and others must be cognizant of what and how cash bail could be replaced. These risk assessment systems could retain implicit bias and other factors not taken into consideration that would simply remand low-income, women, LGBTQIA, immigrants, and minorities into pre-trial detention, even without the use of cash bail.

Finally, the abolition movement cannot stop at the end of cash bail, but must continue to look at other practices and policies that should be eliminated. For example, a move to end all forms of solitary confinement must be undertaken. Studies and testimonies by individuals who have experienced this indicate that there are long-term neurological impacts as well as the short-term torture endured (Mualimm-ak, 2013). The elimination and abolition of capital punishment should also be instituted as no other developed nation in the western world uses the death penalty with the exception of the United States. Abolitionists should not stop at the death penalty but also advocate and fight to end life imprisonment. These "life" sentences are misleading as they are simply death sentences without the use of any sort of tool or weapon. The elimination of criminal offender registries, websites, and other systems that can hinder a person's chances of finding housing, employment, and other social aspects of life should also become obsolete. Ultimately, the abolition of jails and prisons in their current design should be eliminated. Society must invest in re-envisioning a justice system that practices restorative qualities rather than punitive punishments that ensure reentry not simply as jargon but a national responsibility for the greater society to not just reprimand but heal and protect all within society. This must be the goal and nothing less.

Notes

1. Pretrial custody refers to being incarcerated in jail prior to the adjudication of one's case. During pretrial custody, each person is determined to be not guilty of all charges.
2. www.bailproject.org/our-work.
3. www.nationalbailout.org.
4. www.nationalbailout.org/untilfreedomcomes.
5. www.nationalbailout.org/blackcodes.
6. www.dollarbailbrigade.com.
7. In the film, crimes such as murder can be predicted before they happen and therefore police arrest individuals prior to committing the crime.

References

ACLU. (n.d.). *Pretrial justice reform: American civil Liberties union*. Retrieved May 25, 2019, from www.aclu-nj.org/theissues/criminaljustice/pretrial-justice-reform

Alexander, M. (2012, March 10). Go to trial: Crash the justice system. *The New York Times*. Retrieved May 25, 2019, from www.nytimes.com/2012/03/11/opinion/sunday/go-to-trial-crash-the-justice-system.html

Appleman, L. I. (2016). Nickel and dimed into incarceration: Cash-register justice in the criminal system. *Boston College Law Review, 57*, 1483–1541.

Augenstein, S. (2017, April 5). *NYC has cut pretrial jail admissions, while increasing length of stay*. Retrieved April 27, 2019, from www.forensicmag.com/news/2017/04/nyc-has-cut-pretrial-jail-admissions-while-increasing-length-stay

The Bail Project. (2019). Why bail? *The Bail Project*. Retrieved May 25, 2019, from https://bailproject.org/why-bail/

Barnes, M. (2017, May 4). Mass incarceration of Black women soaring. *Rolling Out*. Retrieved February 7, 2018, from https://rollingout.com/2017/04/28/mass-incarceration-black-women-soaring/

Beal, F. M. (2008). Double jeopardy: To be Black and female. *Meridians: Feminism, race, transnationalism, 8*(2), 166–176.

Browne-Marshall, G. J. (2010). *The U.S. constitution: An African American context* (2nd ed.). New York: Law and Policy Group Press.

Carter, S. (2017, June 16). Jay Z on politics, criminal justice reform and bail bonds. *Time*. Retrieved February 18, 2018, from http://time.com/4821547/jay-z-racism-bail-bonds/

Craighead, O. (2017, November 10). Jay Z is going to bail out dads for father's day. *The Fader*. Retrieved May 25, 2019, from www.thefader.com/2017/06/16/jay-z-bail-industry-op-ed-fathers-day

Crane-Newman, M., Rayman, G., & Schapiro, R. (2017, September 6). Charges dismissed against Pedro Hernandez, Bronx teen jailed following 2015 shooting. *New York Daily News*. Retrieved February 5, 2019, from www.nydailynews.com/new-york/charges-dismissed-bronx-teen-pedro-hernandez-article-1.3473832

DeVeaux, M. (2013). The trauma of the incarceration experience. *Harvard Civil Rights-Civil Liberties Law Review, 48*, 257–277.

Money for Freedom   355

Digard, L., & Swavola, E. (2019, April). *Justice denied: The harmful and lasting effects of pretrial detention*. New York: Vera Evidence Brief, Vera Institute.

Dollar Bail Brigade. (2019). *Dollar bail brigade*. Retrieved May 25, 2019, from www.dollarbailbrigade.com/

Freudenberg, N., Daniels, J., Crum, M., Perkins, T., & Richie, B. E. (2005). Coming home from jail: The social and health consequences of community reentry for women, male adolescents, and their families and communities. *American Journal of Public Health, 95*(10), 1725–1736.

Goldkamp, J. S. (1985). Danger and detention: A second generation of bail reform. *Journal of Criminal Law & Criminology, 76*, 1–74.

Gonnerman, J. (2015, June). Kalief Browder, 1993–2015. *The New Yorker*. Retrieved May 24, 2019, from www.newyorker.com/news/news-desk/kalief-browder-1993-2015

Gonnerman, J. (2014, September 29). Before the law. *The New Yorker*. Retrieved April 27, 2019, from www.newyorker.com/magazine/2014/10/06/before-the-law

Jay-Z. (2017, November 17). Jay-Z: The criminal justice system stalks black people like meek mill. *The New York Times*. Retrieved February 7, 2018, from www.nytimes.com/2017/11/17/opinion/jay-z-meek-mill-probation.html

Jones, C. E. (2013). Give us free: Addressing racial disparities in bail determinations. *New York University Journal of Legislation & Public Policy, 16*, 919–961.

Keck, C. (2018, March 21). Jay-Z's roc nation backs bail reform startup promise: How it works. *Inverse*. Retrieved February 18, 2019, from www.inverse.com/article/42659-jay-z-s-roc-nation-backs-bail-reform-startup-promise-how-it-works

Lowenkamp, C. T., VanNostrand, M., & Holsinger, A. (2013). *The hidden costs of pretrial detention*. Houston, TX: The Laura & John Arnold Foundation.

Lowenstein, R. (2017, May 16). *The city of New York Independent budget office*. Retrieved from https://ibo.nyc.ny.us/iboreports/pretrial-detention-rates-may-2017.pdf

McKinney, J. (2019, April 22). T.I. Bails 23 nonviolent offenders out of jail for Easter. *Vibe*. Retrieved May 24, 2019, from www.vibe.com/2019/04/t-i-bails-out-23-nonviolent-offenders-easter

Mualimm-ak, F. O. (2013, October 30). Solitary confinement's invisible scars. *Five Omar Mualimm-ak*. Retrieved August 13, 2016, from www.theguardian.com/commentisfree/2013/oct/30/solitary-confinement-invisible-scars

Park, M. (2018, August 29). California eliminates cash bail. *CNN*. Retrieved May 25, 2019, from www.cnn.com/2018/08/28/us/bail-california-bill/index.html

Pugliese, N. (2019, April 2). Did NJ bail reform cause a surge in crime? Court analysis says no. *Northjersey.com*. Retrieved May 22, 2019, from www.northjersey.com/story/news/new-jersey/2019/04/02/nj-bail-reform-no-crime-surge-pretrial-release/3336423002/

Rivlin-Nadler, M. (2014, June 14). Report: NYC's bail bond industry is a $20 million predatory mess. *The Village Voice*. Retrieved May 5, 2019, from www.villagevoice.com/2017/06/14/report-nycs-bail-bond-industry-is-a-20-million-predatory-mess/

Roberts, D. E. (2011). Prison, foster care, and the systemic punishment of black mothers. *UCLA Law Review, 59*, 1474–1500.

Sacks, M., & Ackerman, A. R. (2014). Bail and sentencing: Does pretrial detention lead to harsher punishment? *Criminal Justice Policy Review, 25*(1), 59–77.

Schwartzapfel, B. (2019, April 1). "Blindfold" off: New York overhauls pretrial evidence rules. *The Marshall Project*. Retrieved May 14, 2019, from www.themarshallproject.org/2019/04/01/blindfold-off-new-york-overhauls-pretrial-evidence-rules

Subramanian, R., Delaney, R., Roberts, S., Fishman, N., & McGarry, N. (2015, February). *Incarceration's front door: The misuse of jails in America.* Vera Institute of Justice. Retrieved from https://law.yale.edu/system/files/area/center/liman/document/workshop16_readings_class08.pdf

Vinson, F. M. (2019). *Stack v. Boyle*, 342 U.S. 1 (1951). Retrieved May 24, 2019, from https://supreme.justia.com/cases/federal/us/342/1/

Wagner, P., & Rabuy, B. (2017, January 25). Following the money of mass incarceration. *Prison Policy Initiative.* Retrieved May 24, 2019, from www.prisonpolicy.org/reports/money.html

Wald, P. (1964). Pretrial detention and ultimate freedom: A statistical study. *New York University Law Review, 39*, 631–640.

Winerip, M., & Schwirtz, M. (2014, July 14). Rikers: Where mental illness meets brutality in jail. *The New York Times.* Retrieved May 25, 2019, from www.nytimes.com/2014/07/14/nyregion/rikers-study-finds-prisoners-injured-by-employees.html

Chapter 28

Agents of Change in Healing Our Communities

Liza Chowdhury, Jason Davis, and Dedric "Beloved" Hammond

Introduction

The underlying premise of the United States criminal justice system has been deterrence, retribution, and incapacitation. The "Great Social Control Experiment" has resulted in millions of men and women being incarcerated, and the never-ending collateral consequences for those that have been incapacitated, as well as their loved ones and their communities (Alexander, 2012; Middlemass, 2017). There have been a growing number of discussions about ending "mass incarceration" and criminal justice "reform."(Bradley, 2018; Taylor, 2016); however, there is also a growing movement focusing on a multidiscipline understanding of how to heal communities facing trauma because of the mass imprisonment of men and women of color. This social movement highlights restorative justice, emphasizes the importance of understanding violence as a public health problem, emphasizes educating those that work with communities impacted by mass incarceration, and centers on the impact trauma has on individuals and how it can be used as a path to healing and reconciliation.

At the forefront of this movement are those who have been isolated from mainstream solutions designed to combat crime because of their criminal history, such as Original Gangsters (OGs), drug dealers, gang leaders, and formerly incarcerated peoples. In many communities, these men and women have been facilitating the push to change the narrative that characterizes oppressed and marginalized individuals and communities as incorrigible and unredeemable. The new narrative is one that redefines returned citizens as resilient and credible. OGs become credible messengers and community activists focused on healing communities and mentoring youth in an effort to break the cycle of crime and violence (Wilkinson et al., 2018).

This chapter chronicles the experiences of two OGs, Jason Davis and Dedric "Beloved" Hammond, as they moved from prison to reenter society to become credible messengers for today's youth. The discussion covers their role as violence interrupters, public speakers, and mentors for justice-involved youth, and highlights the trauma, redemption, barriers to reentry, and successes achieved. It is our perspective that criminal justice, social justice, and public and mental health programs need to incorporate returned citizens and their lived experiences into their practices; this approach would lead to real solutions directed at healing communities by those that have "been there and done that." Moreover, former OGs are credible messengers and can be true agents of change in the effort to end mass incarceration.

Restorative Justice

The foundation of restorative justice is rooted in indigenous practices that promote community participation and healing (Zehr, 2015). This is in stark contrast to the present-day assembly-line justice system based on an adversarial process that focuses on punishment. Instead, the restorative justice framework concentrates on relationships between members of the same community and how behaviors harm the community; in order to understand the harm, both sides of the experience must listen to each other so participants understand the needs and motivations of the offender and the fear and anxiety of the victim and/or community (Zehr, 2015). The process requires a mediation model, direct communication between victim and offender, and/or family conferences or programs that include community members, who are the victim (McGarrell & Hipple, 2007). The process highlights the importance of truth and reconciliation, offenders' accepting responsibility for their behavior, and the community addressing ways to reintegrate the offender *and* heal the victim (Zehr, 2015).

When discussing reintegration, scholars, activists, and individuals reentering society seldom discuss how to heal relationships that need repairing before exiting prison and returning home. Traditional criminal justice practices have been unsuccessful with reintegration, which is evident by high recidivism rates (Clear, Reisig, & Cole, 2018). A paradigm shift focusing on restoration can be helpful in strengthening the ties between the formerly incarcerated and their communities. For instance, true reintegration means that those who have been formerly incarcerated are immersed and integrated back into their family so that they can contribute to finding solutions for their communities.

Many communities that suffer from high rates of violence also suffer from high rates of imprisonment and reentry. Once a violent act occurs, the justice system responds by arresting the offender; however, in the instance of gun violence, victims and the community have to endure the impact of multiple traumas (Whitehill et al., 2014). Imprisonment, for instance, provides a temporary solution by taking the perpetrator out of the community (see Travis, 2005), but many gun incidents remain unresolved by the criminal justice system and result in other acts of trauma and/or violence. The criminal justice response, when there is one, does little to address the issues that led to the violent act and does not address how to prevent future violent

Agents of Change in Healing Our Communities 359

acts by the perpetrator. Utilizing credible messengers as healing agents to mediate conflict in their community can help to restore bonds and address the harms associated with violence. Programs, such as Cure Violence, which operates in several cities across the United States, have utilized the influence that credible messengers are equipped with in order to mediate conflict and become peacekeepers in their neighborhoods (Butts, Roman, Bostwick, & Porter, 2015).

Returning citizens often come home to the same neighborhoods they left behind, and those places continue to be plagued by the consequences of poverty and marginalization (Middlemass, 2017). Many returning citizens are under parole supervision and frequently return to prison within the first three years of return because of technical violations or commission of new crimes (Alexander, 2012). Recidivism rates continue to be high for those that have spent years in isolation in a prison system that is ill-equipped to prepare them for success in society (Middlemass, 2017). Overemphasis on surveillance and control inside prison contradicts the idea of reintegration and rehabilitation for reentry. Career opportunities are scarce for those who have a criminal record and many are unable to apply for social services and traditional welfare aid or assistance (Kirk, 2018; Hall, Wooten, & Lundgren, 2016). In addition to limited, if any, financial resources to assist reentry efforts, returning citizens also face the social harm they left behind and must take the responsibility of mending many strained relationships.

Some community programs that focus on reducing gang-related violence have employed returned citizens as credible messengers to younger generations in the community. Programs that utilize credible messengers to prevent violence are grounded in restorative justice principles. Evaluations of these programs support the impact of this form of inclusion and restoration, and include Arches and Next Steps in New York, Homeboy Industries in California, Living Redemption Youth Opportunity Hub in New York, and Cure Violence.

Programs that use credible messengers as an integral part of the solution have yielded positive results (Lynch, Astone, Collazos, Lipman, & Esthappan, 2018). In the traditional restorative justice practices, support circles are implemented to allow stakeholders in the community to come together to heal from harm committed against them. Credible messengers have been utilizing restorative justice principles and putting them into practice in their neighborhoods; restorative justice practices utilize designated safe spaces in schools for young people to mediate conflict and talk about their trauma (Zehr, 2015), but also build relationships with community leaders, youth, and various stakeholders on city corners, parks, and other public places where youth congregate. Facilitating healing circles and having trained restorative justice circle keepers has helped reduce the use of punitive policies that have fueled the school to prison pipeline (Mallett, 2016). Training young people on how to resolve conflicts and heal from the trauma they have experienced while in school can also help to reduce conflicts that may spill over into the community. One particular program, Reimagining Justice Inc., utilizes credible messengers in schools in New Jersey to facilitate healing circles to discuss trauma related to growing up in communities with high rates of violence, incarceration, and reentry. Other schools in California, Maryland, and New York have adopted restorative practices in lieu of traditional zero-tolerance policies.

Violence as a Public Health Issue

Violence has traditionally been a criminal justice problem. However, to fully understand the impact of violence, it is important to examine the consequences of violence from a public health and psychological standpoint to create effective prevention and intervention efforts (Slutkin, Ransford, & Decker, 2015). There are several adverse effects of being exposed to violence, and they can include physical harm, *and* emotional, psychological, and other health issues that increase because of additional violent events.

Homicide is the third leading cause of death among 10 to 24 year olds in the United States, the number one cause of death for African-American and Latino males aged 15 to 24, and has been the leading cause of death for 10 to 24-year-old African-American males and females for decades (David-Ferdon et al., 2016). These numbers demonstrate that violent victimization disproportionately impacts young men of color and Black girls and women. Homicide should be understood as a public health issue and not addressed as a crime problem as violence and victimization are concentrated in specific communities.

Along with the interaction of race, gender, and age as it relates to homicide rates, the same groups also experience high rates of exposure to violence. Socially disorganized neighborhoods have high rates of delinquency and violence because of the lack of economic opportunity and social isolation from mainstream society as well as high rates of victimization, incarceration and reentry. The study that first highlighted the importance of understanding social disorganization was completed in Chicago in the 1940s (Shaw & McKay, 1942). Social learning theory emphasizes that at an early age, youth that reside in a marginalized community are exposed to gun violence, drug addiction, and assault at higher rates (David-Ferdon & Simon, 2014). Exposure to violence increases one's risk of becoming violent, as violence is learned through modeling, observing, imitating, and copying others in the community (Bandura, 1977). It is believed that young people who live in chaotic social environments learn how to survive, and some may adapt by creating subcultures (Rios, 2011; Cloward & Ohlin, 1960). Youth subcultures that support the formation of gangs and cliques may seem like appropriate safe havens for youth who feel unsafe at home and/or in their community (Hagedorn, 2008; Rios, 2011; Van der Kolk, 2015).

Youth gang membership continues to be prevalent in socially isolated neighborhoods, and gang activity and association are often used as a mode of adaptation (Rios, 2011). This is a cause for concern because young gang members are more likely to perpetuate violence than non-gang-involved youth (Li et al., 2002). Despite over a century of gang-related scholarship that exposes the harsh ordeals socially disorganized communities face, policy makers continue to utilize suppression and crime control tactics to address violence (Tita & Papachristos, 2010); however, these mechanisms have been ineffective and costly (Hagedorn, 2008, 2017). Zero-tolerance policing methods can increase distrust between communities of color and law enforcement (Hagedorn, 2008).

Social learning theory (Bandura, 1977) explains how behaviors are learned. Family is the first protective factor for youth. Victimization in the home by a parent or caretaker can encourage a child to accept that aggression is the appropriate way to handle conflict. Children who are victims feel vulnerable and take refuge outside of their home in an effort to seek protection. When the prevailing youth control complex, which encompasses a web of institutions, such as the criminal justice system, families, businesses, residents, media, and the community, criminalizes Black and Brown youth to control them, marginalized youth respond to this criminalization by sometimes engaging in violent crime or utilizing violence to control or regulate the ownership of public spaces and garner respect (Hagedorn, 2008; Rios, 2011).

Although gang and crew members are rarely seen as victims (Rios, 2011; Quinn, Pacella, Dickson-Gomez, & Nydegger, 2017), studies indicate that gang members have experienced a multitude of traumatic events in their lives (Kerig, Chaplo, Bennett, & Modrowski, 2016; Rios, 2011). Youth in communities that have been victimized by structural inequality, familial violence, social isolation, and disorganization create subcultures to survive (Hagedorn, 2008). Past research has uncovered that many gang members initially joined gangs because of early exposure to family conflict and violence at home (Quinn et al., 2017). Gang involvement and the subsequent violence that members may participate in is part of the culture that is developed to address social problems that they have to handle on their own. Gangs form when other formal structures, such as the criminal justice system, schools, and child welfare system, fail to protect youth, who may respond by protecting themselves by forming cliques and gangs. Gang members gravitate towards their pseudo-family for protection, and in return they pledge their love and allegiance (Kerig et al., 2016). Youths in gangs and cliques have high rates of victimization as adolescents (Kerig et al., 2016).

Experiencing violence is a traumatic event. Many people who have been exposed to violence may suffer from post-traumatic stress disorder (PTSD), a mental health problem that some people develop after experiencing or witnessing a life-threatening event, like combat, a natural disaster, a car accident, or sexual assault (Van der Kolk, 2015). Although trauma exposure increases the risk for delinquency, involvement in antisocial behavior also increases the risk for traumatization (Begle et al., 2011). There is a recognized link between exposure to violence, antisocial behavior, disrupted family processes, substance use, and internalizing problems, such as depression, low self-esteem, and suicidal ideation, and externalizing problems including attempted suicide (Li et al., 2002).

Under such circumstances, credible messengers can be effective peace builders and violence interrupters based on their past experiences; they have proven to be effective in the process of engaging youth who have been isolated from mainstream institutions and distrust systems who have failed to protect them. Often, society has labeled our most vulnerable as monsters or super predators (Equal Justice Initiative, 2014). This in turn has allowed the criminal justice system to create policies that have been unduly harsh and punitive for several decades. The result has been the disruption of families and communities, the ongoing victimization of youth that have already had long histories of trauma, and the release of those incarcerated for their crimes that were never truly healed because of their victimization (Rios, 2011). It is time that we understand that gang membership is a form of resiliency for youth living in harsh conditions (Hagedorn, 2008). Instead of demonizing young people who are in gangs, it is imperative to understand their pain and create solutions that incorporate gang culture instead of further isolating them.

Agents of Change the Story of "Sicko" and "Bad News"

The reintegration of those who have been formerly incarcerated is an arduous process (Middlemass, 2017). To involve former prisoners in the collective efficacy efforts designed to address community, family, and individual violence is challenging. Traditional law and order practices continue to be pushed by politicians while the politics of fear challenge the implementation of humanistic approaches to address harm and violence experienced in Black and Brown communities. There are several collateral consequences that those returning home from prison face (Middlemass, 2017; Travis, 2005), and for those interested in working with youth, they are barred from doing so because of felony records (Crutchfield & Weeks, 2015). Despite these challenges, two credible messengers at the forefront of bringing public awareness to the issues plaguing their communities prove that resilience and redemption are possible.

Jason "Sicko" Davis

Jason "Sicko" Davis grew up in the Lincoln Housing Projects in Harlem, New York, during the epitome of the crack epidemic. Throughout his childhood, he witnessed despair in his community because of poverty, unemployment, racism, and substance abuse. Violence was a frequent occurrence, and throughout his formative years he had to navigate adolescence while attempting to survive. Some of his most traumatic experiences happened inside his home. His father was an addict and physically abused his family. Jason developed severe mental health issues as a result, and coped with his pain by harming himself through cutting, burning, and branding. During his teenage years, Jason became increasingly angry and found comradery with a street gang. He began inflicting violence on others and found himself submerged in chaos both in and out of his home. Although he was involved in gang activity, he was also intelligent and continued his education at Delaware State University. However, he found himself socially isolated from other college students.

Davis became a father in college and resorted to illegal activities to support his family financially. He quickly found himself surrounded by violence, death, and destruction. He became a suspect in a violent crime and was on the run for 6 years prior to his capture and incarceration in Delaware. While inside, he began to understand his mental illness and started to transform his life to one of healing instead of violence. He co-authored, *War of the Bloods in My Veins*, discussing the effects of trauma and gang culture on Black youth. The book was a success, and when he was released, he was offered the opportunity to speak around the country about the importance of understanding why young people join gangs and the importance of implementing better mental health services for youth in Black communities.

Davis' experiences growing up during the crack epidemic in Harlem and as a gang leader gave him the credibility to explain to audiences how to work with youth. He became a youth advocate and mentor to youth who were placed in residential treatment centers in New York City. He spent several years as a counselor for young people who were abused and neglected. He co-founded a nonprofit organization entitled, Reimagining Justice, which is designed to use credible messengers to consult, train, and advocate for youth experiencing trauma, mental and health challenges, and exposure to violence. Davis assists families in obtaining resources and engages youth in their own healing process. Reimagining Justice utilizes restorative justice practices and serves as a hub of opportunities for the youth in Harlem.

Davis's lived example proves that a former gang leader is resilient, redeemable, and can successfully reintegrate. Moreover, he has used his experiences to be a credible messenger to youth in an effort to prevent violence and restore communities that have been victims of violence. Davis has become a key figure in fostering peace in his community.

Dedric "Beloved" Hammond

Dedric "Beloved" Hammond was not always beloved in his community. He was known as "Bad News" because of his past criminal activity. Beloved lived in Tennessee, and was used to the slower pace and southern culture, so when he moved to New York City, he was bullied and exposed to aggressive behavior; to survive, he went from being a victim to aggressor, which resulted in being severely disciplined at home. This cycle reaffirmed his belief that violence was acceptable to survive. Hammond formed a crew called Fuck Shit Up (FSU), and it was known for its violent acts and destructive behaviors in the St. Nicholas Housing Projects. Hammond dropped out of high school, turned to criminal activity, and churned in and out of prison. He was twice a victim of gun violence. His violent reputation and behavior subsequently landed him in prison, where he spent a large portion of his twenties.

Upon his release, Hammond relinquished his reputation of "Bad News" and transformed his life to become someone who was beloved by his community for positivity and healing instead of violence and destruction. He did this by volunteering to speak at local youth centers, churches, and schools and mentoring youth in his neighborhood. Hammond was able to use the respect he had as an OG to mediate conflicts. He publicly forgave the man who shot him, and spoke out about gun violence and mental health. Hammond was recruited by the New York City Cure Violence chapter, called S.N.U.G., and became a hospital-response member and violence interrupter. Hammond's credibility as a credible messenger in his community of Harlem allowed him to reduce violent gang retaliations and assist gun violence victims. He continues to discuss the importance of restoration and healing throughout the country.

Currently, Hammond is a supervisor and credible messenger at the Living Redemption Hub in Harlem. He mentors youth and uses his own experience with violence to help youth who have been victims of violence or are considering engaging in a violent act to direct their anger, hurt, and frustration into other activities. Hammond's life is an example of how a credible messenger can act as a healing agent in the same community they plagued with violence. His story is one of resilience and healing that can be modeled by others who are coping with trauma and violence.

Conclusion

The last three decades have impacted the lives of millions of people who have been engulfed by a criminal justice system and crime that disrupts their communities and families. Many victims of mass incarceration have also experienced high rates of exposure to trauma and violence. Traditional criminal justice responses towards gang-related violence have proven to be costly but yield low levels of success in the neighborhoods that are suffering from the trauma of violence (Hagedorn, 2017). Therefore, new responses are needed based on informed research that understands the context of those who have experienced violence (Rios, 2011). For instance, mental health interventions and trauma informed care, coupled with financial opportunities, should be used to address social harms in communities most impacted by mass incarceration.

Because of the stigma associated with gang membership (Rios, 2011), issues of mental health linked with early exposure to trauma are rarely studied, but need to be. Many pass-through institutions, such as school, family court, and correctional systems, are unable to provide the informed level of care gang members need (Cheng, 2017). Youth that feel socially isolated are more likely to engage in gang activities and need better systems of care that are culturally appropriate.

Mass incarceration is not an effective means to address social problems. Instead, investment should go into healing-centered justice approaches that focus on building stronger relationships and communities that can assist in integrating those returning from prison. Programs that encourage the involvement of credible messengers show promise and need to be supported by policy makers to truly restore a history of trauma inflicted by a broken criminal justice process.

References

Alexander, M. (2012). *The new Jim Crow: Mass incarceration in the age of colorblindness*. New York: The New Press.

Bandura, A. (1977). *Social learning theory*. Englewood Cliffs, NJ: Prentice Hall.

Begle, A. M., Hanson, R. F., Danielson, C. K., McCart, M. R., Ruggiero, K. J., Amstadter, A. B., . . . Kilpatrick, D. G. (2011). Longitudinal pathways of victimization, substance use, and delinquency: Findings from the national survey of adolescents. *Addictive Behaviors, 36*(7), 682–689.

Bradley, A. B. (2018). *Ending overcriminalization and mass incarceration: Hope from civil society*. Cambridge: Cambridge University Press.

Butts, J. A., Roman, C. G., Bostwick, L., & Porter, J. R. (2015). Cure violence: A public health model to reduce gun violence. *Annual Review of Public Health, 36*, 39–53.

Cheng, T. (2017). Violence prevention and targeting the elusive gang member. *Law & Society Review, 51*(1), 42–69.

Clear, T. R., Reisig, M. D., & Cole, G. F. (2018). *American corrections*. Boston, MA: Cengage Learning.

Cloward, R., & Ohlin, L. (1960). *Delinquency and opportunity*. New York: The Free Press.

Crutchfield, R. D., & Weeks, G. A. (2015). The effects of mass incarceration on communities of color. *Issues in Science and Technology, 32*(1), 109.

David-Ferdon, C., & Simon, T. R. (2014). *Preventing youth violence: Opportunities for action*. Atlanta, GA: Centers for Disease Control and Prevention.

David-Ferdon, C., Vivolo-Kantor, A. M., Dahlberg, L. L., Marshall, K. J., Rainford, N., & Hall, J. E. (2016). *A comprehensive technical package for the prevention of youth violence and associated risk behaviors*. Atlanta, GA: Centers for Disease Control and Prevention.

Equal Justice Initiative. (2014). The super predator myth, 20 years later. *EJI.org*.

Hagedorn, J. (2008). *A world of gangs: Armed young men and gangsta culture* (Vol. 14). University of Minnesota Press.

Hagedorn, J. M. (2017). Gangs, neighborhoods, and public policy. In *Gangs* (pp. 441–454). New York: Routledge.

Hall, T. L., Wooten, N. R., & Lundgren, L. M. (2016). Postincarceration policies and prisoner reentry: Implications for policies and programs aimed at reducing recidivism and poverty. *Journal of Poverty, 20*(1), 56–72.

Kerig, P. K., Chaplo, S. D., Bennett, D. C., & Modrowski, C. A. (2016). "Harm as harm" gang membership, perpetration trauma, and posttraumatic stress symptoms among youth in the juvenile justice system. *Criminal Justice and Behavior, 43*(5), 635–652.

Kirk, D. S. (2018). The collateral consequences of incarceration for housing. In *Handbook on the consequences of sentencing and punishment decisions* (pp. 73–88). New York: Routledge.

Li, X., Stanton, B., Pack, R., Harris, C., Cottrell, L., & Burns, J. (2002). Risk and protective factors associated with gang involvement among urban African American adolescents. *Youth & Society, 34*(2), 172–194.

Lynch, M., Astone, N. M., Collazos, J., Lipman, M., & Esthappan, S. (2018). *Arches transformative mentoring program.* Washington, DC: Urban Institute.

Mallett, C. A. (2016). The school-to-prison pipeline: From school punishment to rehabilitative inclusion. *Preventing School Failure: Alternative Education for Children and Youth, 60*(4), 296–304.

McGarrell, E. F., & Hipple, N. K. (2007). Family group conferencing and re-offending among first-time juvenile offenders: The Indianapolis experiment. *Justice Quarterly, 24,* 221–246.

Middlemass, K. (2017). *Convicted and condemned: The politics and policies of prisoner reentry.* New York: New York University Press.

Quinn, K., Pacella, M. L., Dickson-Gomez, J., & Nydegger, L. A. (2017). Childhood adversity and the continued exposure to trauma and violence among adolescent gang members. *American Journal of Community Psychology, 59*(1–2), 36–49.

Rios, V. (2011). *Punished: Policing the lives of Black and Latino boys.* New York: New York University Press.

Shaw, C. R., & McKay, H. D. (1942). *Juvenile delinquency and urban areas.* Chicago, IL: University of Chicago Press.

Slutkin, G., Ransford, C., & Decker, R. B. (2015). Cure violence: Treating violence as a contagious disease. In *Envisioning criminology* (pp. 43–56). New York: Springer International Publishing.

Taylor, C. J. (2016). Ending the punishment cycle by reducing sentence length and reconsidering evidence-based reentry practices. *Temple Law Review, 89,* 747.

Tita, G., & Papachristos, A. (2010). The evolution of gang policy: Balancing intervention and suppression. In R. Chaskin (Ed.), *Youth gangs and community intervention: Research, practice and evidence.* New York: Columbia University Press.

Travis, J. (2005). *But they all come back: Facing the challenges of prisoner reentry.* Washington, DC: The Urban Institute.

Van der Kolk, B. A. (2015). *The body keeps the score: Brain, mind, and body in the healing of trauma.* New York: Penguin Books.

Whitehill, J. M., Webster, D. W., Frattaroli, S., & Parker, E. M. (2014). Interrupting violence: How the cease fire program prevents imminent gun violence through conflict mediation. *Journal of Urban Health, 91*(1), 84–95. doi:10.1007/s11524-013-9796-9

Wilkinson, D., Lamarr, F. V., Alsaada, T. F., Ahad, C., Hill, D., & Saunders, Sr., J. (2018). Building an engaged community to prevent and heal from gun violence. *Engaged Scholars*, 6.

Zehr, H. (2015). *The little book of restorative justice: Revised and updated.* New York: Simon and Schuster.

Chapter 29

Rehabilitation Is Reentry

Breathing Space, a Product of Inmate Dreams

Robert Garot

Approximately 700,000 prisoners are released into the community in the United States per annum (Bloom, 2009), and roughly two-thirds will return to prison within a year (Reentry Policy Council, 2008). The basic needs of such individuals have remained constant across time. As Halsey (2010, p. 254) notes,

> The challenges faced by those released from prison have remained fundamentally of the same kind for many years [. . . .]. Each would have to deal with varying levels of stigma and all the problems this poses for those trying to start anew. Each would need shelter, food and a legitimate means of providing for themselves and any dependents. Each would need to be buoyed by occasional or more persistent encouragement from significant others that they can indeed forge a new life for themselves in spite of what they had endured.

Many observers have noted how the current institutional support for such individuals is fundamentally lacking in the capacity to meet these needs (Travis, Solomon, & Waul, 2001). Some have noted that a prison reentry industry has developed, as substantial, well-funded organizations, such as The Fortune Society, The Osborne Association, Strive, and the Exodus Transitional Community, and often provide jobs within their own ranks, creating a cycle of institutional dependency (Thompkins, Curtis, & Wendel, 2010). Fundamental to reentry is the necessity of finding gainful employment, not simply employment within the reentry complex. As Kontos (2010, p. 575) notes, "There is a slim chance of successful reentry without ex-inmates being able to support themselves through legitimate work."

Yet returning citizens[1] do not simply survive through the provision of basic needs. Rather, they survive by following their dreams, but are these dreams nurtured? Many authors have discussed how rehabilitation is integral to reentry programs (Garrett, 2017; Gideon & Sung, 2011), but returned citizens who have successfully reintegrated into society ten years or more after release from prison provide a lens into the long-term effectiveness of

Rehabilitation Is Reentry   369

rehabilitation programs inside prison, which can lead to reentry success. Through in-depth participant observations, face-to-face and phone interviews with returned citizens who founded Breathing Space, it is found that they are now living the embodiment of their dreams cultivated on the inside. Furthermore, such dreams were possible through the nurturing and empowering programs that fostered integrity, autonomy, responsibility, peaceful living, positive energy, and personal success. Many of these programs were developed by inmates. This chapter focuses on the vitality of such programs, how they are viewed by returning citizens, and the urgent need to maintain and expand them.

Breathing Space, founded by returning citizens, is located on 32.5 acres in the Catskills of New York; the founders emphasize that more than a place, Breathing Space is a state of mind. At Breathing Space, returning citizens develop micro-businesses, practice skills with licensed trade people, and center themselves for their own reentry journey. Breathing Space participants have created camp grounds, built chicken coops to produce and sell eggs and poultry, and started a greenhouse project to sell organic produce to local restaurants and residents. Participants have also been demolishing unrecoverable buildings on the property and using the materials to build items, such as picnic tables, which are sold. Breathing Space has produced its own wine from grapes they hand-picked, and has developed two retail food projects, Mikey Likes It Ice Cream[2] and the Red Wagon Barbeque Stand. Additional ideas in the development stage include selling Christmas trees and wood chips, thereby providing for themselves through their own sweat and toil.[3]

I examined Breathing Space by focusing on three facets of the organization; as an example of an entrepreneurial reentry initiative pioneered by returning citizens; how this venture was made possible by rehabilitation programs inside the penitentiary; and how programs inside prison allowed inmates to imagine and then by joining Breathing Space how they were able to enact their future. I studied these three features through a two-pronged approach. First, I conducted a participant observation study of Breathing Space. This involved weekly visits to the site in New York and interviews with all consenting members. I wrote fieldnotes according to the methodology developed by Emerson, Fretz, and Shaw (1995), engaged in analytic induction (Katz, 1983), and constant comparison (Charmaz, 2006) in coding and analyzing the data. These are practices, which I have developed and refined in studies of a Section 8 Housing Office (Garot, 2011), gangs in an inner-city alternative high school (Garot, 2010), and immigrants in Italy (Garot, 2013, 2014). Secondly, I made a short, 10-minute introduction to the program.[4] Although there was some overlap and synergy between the ethnographic and the filmmaking aspects of this project, each project stood alone.

Below, I explore the blossoming of Breathing Space as discussed by three of its primary champions, all men who have served between ten to 30 years

370 Robert Garot

behind bars. First, how the idea of Breathing Space arose from a dream Ray Rios had inside his cell while he was incarcerated at Sing Sing Penitentiary, and the programs and community at Sing Sing that enabled his imagination. Second, the trials of Ray and his partners, John Mandala, founder of Breathing Space Florida, and Angel Ramos, are explored as they exited prison, attempted to find jobs, and worked with their respective parole officers.[5] At the same time, while Rios, Mandala, and Ramos were reentering, they continued their efforts at self-improvement. Lastly, this chapter explores how, through Breathing Space, returned citizens continue to forge new opportunities, both inside and outside prison walls, to enable other returning citizens to succeed.

Prison Dreams

Breathing Space, like most successful entrepreneurial projects, is the product of a dream. The dream was facilitated by a vibrant, Renaissance-like prison culture. Although Angel Ramos was not present at the initial gestation of Breathing Space, when I asked him how it began, he related it to another program:"It's kinda the same as Hudson Link. It started inside. It started with Ray and a couple other guys." Hudson Link, now a $1.5 million program in five New York penitentiaries, was developed by John Mandala, when courses offered through Mercy College were discontinued.[6]

John Mandala (Phone Interview): I went to Bill Webber [the President of New York Theological Seminary (NYTS) and facilitator of the Sing Sing NYTS Master's program, and author of *Led by the Spirit*] and said, "What are you going to do? There's going to be no more Bachelor Degree candidates. So how is the Master's degree going to keep going?" He said to me, "You like to fix things. Fix it." And I wrote a proposal called "CAPE: College Alternative Prison Education." I still have it. People told me I was crazy.

According to John, such thinking was the direct result of an arts programs inside:

John (Phone Interview): And also, I don't know if you've heard of it, do you know what RTA is? Rehabilitation through the Arts?

Robert Garot: Ray mentioned that today.

John (Phone Interview): That was a big thing for me. It allowed me – like this guy said, I like to fix things. It allowed me to be able to do things that

Rehabilitation Is Reentry 371

> nobody had ever been able to do. It gave me the creative spirit in life. That's why when Ray talks about Breathing Space at that time, I was excited about it. I bought into it, I liked it. Because it was about creating. For me, that's the most important thing we can do. Reentry is like that.

This statement encapsulates the point of Breathing Space. Through the Rehabilitation Through the Arts Program,[7] John realized that he liked to fix problems and create programs that were previously unimaginable. That "creative spirit in life" is central for health, resilience, and successful reintegration in society (Rutter, 1987), and often seems to be missing from reentry programs that are managed through performance accountability systems under the auspices of New Public Management (Halushka, 2017). Where is there space for an inmate to develop an exciting program s/ he can buy into in programs that are high on accountability but low on dreams?

For John Mandala, a man who entered the penal system in deep suicidal depression and mourning, having been found guilty of manslaughter for taking the lives of his fiancé and her lover, such programs provided HOPE ("Holding on to Positive Energy"). Once he was sent to Sing Sing, John's efforts to start Hudson Link began, oddly enough, with a photocopying machine:

John (Phone Interview): The ironic part about this whole thing, when I was first at Sing Sing in 1989, there were a couple guys who asked me to be a part of the Quaker Copier Project. "What's that?" "We're trying to raise money so we can become more educated. It's an educational fund." I said, "Great, what are you doing?" They said, "We had a Quaker business guy donate a copying machine for the law library and we got it OK'd, so now we can make copies for other prisoners, and we can charge them 5 cents a copy." That first machine was so old. It had already made 600,000 copies in 1990. With octopus oil, rubber bands, and paper clips, I kept that machine running for another 150,000 copies, and we bought a new machine. The first money that went to Hudson Link was $5,000 from the copy machine project over a period of ten years. Unfortunately, that history is not always talked about, but that's how it all began.

What seems like a standard piece of office equipment was for inmates akin to the Gutenberg printing press. The Quakers, who played a large role in founding the U.S. prison system (Biggs, 2009), were integral in many ways for helping Ray, John, and Angel develop the mindset of Breathing Space, and not only through the copier project, but through the Alternatives to Violence Project. Affectionately known as AVP, the project blossomed at Greenhaven Prison in 1975, where participants from the Attica uprising reached out to Quakers, like Lawrence Apsey and Civil Rights leader Bernard Lafayette, to design 20 hour weekend workshops to help inmates explore nonviolent resolutions to conflict. Ray and John became facilitators and coordinators for AVP at Sing Sing while Angel became a facilitator at Auburn Prison, the third facility to adopt the all-volunteer program that is now active in 33 states and 45 countries.[8] As Ray states, "I've been working with them for damn near 30 years. I see it as a catalyst to awakening."

As an outside facilitator for AVP, I initially met Ray, then Angel and John. AVP was one among a constellation of programs that made Sing Sing, the maximum-security prison known infamously as "The Big House" where men are sent, "up the river," into a somewhat magical place, full of hope and possibilities, because of the wealth of programs created:

Ray Rios: We came up with ideas all the time. It was like Camelot. We were making – I was working with Johnny Yuen, T. Hayward, and some other kid. I think his name was John. We came up with the Peace Initiative. Johnny Yuen went back to his cell and typed up the original proposal. He said, "Hey, read this." I'm like, "Damn, Johnny, that's all the stuff we talked about." There were ideas all over. Someone has to capture it, write it, and then a group of people own it, and then move it. So, John captured Hudson Link. A group of people got together and made it concrete, and started moving it, and other people continue to move it to this day. So much so that Warren Buffet's family funds the damn program now.

To this day, the Peace Initiative, or Peace Day, is a powerful annual event at Sing Sing, where inmates take a pledge to not engage in violence, to honor the mother whose cries resounded in the prison halls when she found that her son, whom she had come to visit, had been murdered. Later, when Ray was transferred to Otisville Penitentiary, he wrote the ideas for Breathing Space:

Ray Rios: I wrote Breathing Space myself at Otisville [Prison]. That was probably in 1997. Actually, I wrote it and then my other friend Fletcher helped me redefine some of the ideas, but then Fletcher passed away. Originally there were ideas that were all over the place. I knew what I wanted back then, but it didn't really have the idea of how the world worked. Until you're confronted with how it really happened – it's like weeds and cracks. Weeds will continue to grow, but they're going to find the path of least resistance to flourish. Then you can get beautiful flowers. Entrepreneurialism, self-sustaining communities. Community isn't just in one place. Sometimes people think Breathing Space is a place. Breathing Space is sometimes more of a mindset, like setting yourself free. And a lot of people that I've been involved with are really different kinds of thinkers, like John Mandala. He'll work for people when he needs to, but he doesn't want to have a 9–5. He figured out there's a way to sustain yourself outside of that.

The excitement, energy, and inspiration around this period was not lost, but it was challenged. Ray has been out of prison for 18 years, and John and Angel each for about ten years, and they have persevered and sustained their vision, but not without some bumps along the way.

Getting Out

From Struggles to Challenges

John Mandala, Founder of Breathing Space, Florida, during a phone call, said:

So it's been a constant struggle – challenge. I call it a challenge. Yesterday I met with someone and said it was a struggle. She said, "No, it's just a challenge." I said, "I like that." So from now on I want to use that. It's been that way and it's not going to change.

Inmates are released from New York penitentiaries with just $40 and a bus pass. Those who are fortunate are embraced by family (Scheyett & Pettus-Davis, 2013). For others, their former gang serves as a cushion but increases their risk of recidivism (Scott, 2004; Martinez & Abrams, 2012). Others go to a halfway house or the less regulated ¾ houses, which are typically over-crowded, dirty, and vermin-infested, and where the rules are often arbitrarily enforced or overlooked, which sometimes leads to a ¾ house becoming a haven for drug selling and use and Medicaid abuse by landlords (see Barker, 2015).

Ray, John, and Angel all found the support of family upon release, but were subject to extensive discrimination in the job market, even at institutions that were ostensibly intended to support ex-inmates. Below, Ray tells of one memorable experience.

Ray: In 22 [job] interviews I had one lady, I swear. I never saw a White person turn whiter. I was in the interview and I mentioned I was in prison. Then all of a sudden her whole face turned strange. And this is the realm of people that are helping people who come home from prison so you're just like, what the hell? Aren't you guys – ? But then again, it is what it is and it's always gonna be that way until there's an extremely large social movement to change that. What I believe in is, use the system as fast as you can as much as you can to become self-sufficient, because sooner or later the system's gonna bite you in the ass. Once you're independently financially secure, just be careful to maintain your money and your flow.

Here, Ray makes evident how the desire to fulfill his dreams of Breathing Space was bolstered by his negative experiences on the traditional job market. Without "an extremely large social movement," his best bet was to try to use the system to beat the system. Once he landed a job with an agency, providing outreach to ex-cons like himself, he continued to face discrimination, often in surprising ways.

Ray: At the last [job] interview I got [at a health clinic], the guy who hired me believed in helping people who came home from prison. He was instrumental in helping me feel like a [whole] person. Other people at the job were assholes. I remember being in a staff meeting where I heard, "We don't hire ex-cons." I'm sitting there going, "Wow." And this is the CEO of the company. Not even understanding that you can't even say that legally. Second of all, she didn't even understand the culture of her own home business. Even in that room, even with someone who gives you a second chance, I'm still a second-class citizen. I'm not going to contradict the CEO who says "we don't hire ex-cons," but there were like four or five people there who knew I was in prison. It's just like, wow, that person is just that –.

Like Ray, Angel Ramos landed a job at a nonprofit organization after numerous job interviews. Similar to Ray, his disenchantment spurred his motivation to work at Breathing Space.

Angel Ramos: I was at Fortune [Society: Building People, Not Prisons, nonprofit organization in New York City]. I was kind of disenchanted with the nonprofit world. Everyone starts out with a good idea and then they get the government contract, and then it becomes about the contract and about the money. Keeping people employed, stuff like that, and the client starts taking second hand. The philosophy's the same, but then it's just, people just talking about something. Talk about the mission but the mission is falling short. That tends to happen a lot with nonprofits. That's one of the reasons we decided not to go government, to try to do it with private funding, do it small.

For John, his reentry included caring for his aged mother. If he had not fought his parole board for an early release date, and had a bulging file of certificates and commendations from his time inside, he would not have been able to assist her in her final years.

John: So my reentry started in a very weird way. But you have to remember, I had a roof over my head, I had food. Someone invited me to come down to Daily Bread where you feed people that are homeless. So I volunteered. I went there and lo and behold, two weeks later, he said, "Hey, do you want a part time job here?" I said, "Yeah." So I took a job there, and I was working there for three to four months. My mother got very sick and I had to take care of her. Full time job. However, I started a handy man business. I became self-employed. It wasn't much, but it was enough to make ends meet and take care of my mom at the same time, take her the doctor, spend time with her.

John moved to Florida to be with his mother, and despite his entrepreneurial success, he continues to face discrimination. He is currently the director of a nonprofit organization and is finding that during his efforts to implement Breathing Space, Florida, he incurs people's mistrust.

John (Phone Interview): Florida is a very difficult place to do anything when it comes to criminal justice. This is the South. I have struggled 13 years here. I still struggle, even today. There are doors that don't open because I'm formerly incarcerated. "You're this, you're that," whatever. How do you overcome people's mistrust? Very, very difficult. Time sometimes does it. But when you're associated with people who are homeless, people who are prisoners, women who are strippers and prostitutes, all of that is looked upon as a negative thing.

Parole Officers

A second way that the men who imagined Breathing Space into being turned struggles into challenges was in their dealings with their parole officers (POs). John was very proactive with his PO, going so far as asking him

376 Robert Garot

to help avoid anything that might get him into trouble, even if it involved his family.

John (Phone Interview):   I had 17 different restrictions. I couldn't have a girl-friend unless I told my parole officer. I couldn't do this, I couldn't do that. But I had a great parole officer. The guy was unbelievable. To the point where I went in to him one day and he looked at my stack of papers. I brought him everything that I had done, every certificate. When he saw that, he said, "Pretty impressive." I said, "I need a favor." He said, "What's that?" I said, "If my daughter calls you and asks you if I can go to Lindale, tell her 'no.'" He said, "You know, you're a wise guy. You're a smart guy." I said, "I'm not going back to prison for any-one. Not even my own child."
Robert: If your daughter asked you what?
John: To come visit her. Because she was messing around with drugs, and I didn't want any part of it.

John so impressed his PO that he invited him to speak at a high school graduation.

Unfortunately, Ray's experience was far less positive, and had long-term traumatizing consequences.

Ray: It's your attitude. I kept a journal for almost ten years. The parole officer, when he looked at the room, he noticed there was a stack of journals. He confiscated them and read through them.
Robert: Did you get them back?
Ray: Yeah, but then he commented on one of them. Because I wrote about the parole officer that "he seems almost human." He actu-ally said, "Oh, I'm almost human." That was the last time I actually wrote in my journals. I gave that up. Why? It was the one place where I felt like I could write, debrief, process, and everything else. That was one of the greatest violations I've experienced in my life.

Giving Back

Throughout their many challenges, the men who had imagined Breath-ing Space and brought it into being were constantly looking to offer simi-lar experiences to others as had been offered to them. After having been instilled with the spirit of such programs as Rehabilitation through the Arts and Alternatives to Violence Project, such a spirit seems to come naturally to John, Ray, and Angel.

Angel discusses how his many years in prison helped him to "see things differently," an asset often underappreciated on the job market.

Angel: People are like, "Wow, you did all that time and you're not nuts?" Yeah, I'm more sane and rational than most people. I see things differently. I solve problems differently. Unlike a lot of people, I'm not a material person. I'm more into people than into things. Which is really helpful in this work – trying to teach people. Like when people are homeless, the first thing they lose are the social niceties. You become very jaded towards people, about people. We introduce you to the human family, which is very important. Try to get you attached to a spiritual side. Get up in the morning, make your bed, look after yourself, don't let yourself slide. Get rid of attitudes, it's not helpful. Getting you to go church, getting you to look at your past, your own violence.

For John Mandala, Breathing Space, Florida, has evolved into a wealth of programs and opportunities.

John: A gentleman donated to me a double-wide trailer home, with the property and everything. That has been where I have my AVP discussion group. It's not huge, but I have a 90x90 garden. I grow food to feed the homeless down at Daily Bread. I told you that was my first job, my first place to go. I try to give back to them even though I don't agree with the policy. I don't believe in giving people a handout, I believe in giving people a hand-up. I'm building a greenhouse there as we speak. That's a technological thing that I've dreamed about with heaters and different things, to try and show that we can do a lot with just what we have. I don't use any fertilizer or bug repellant. I don't grow organic, but I use compost. I have no problem living at peace with nature, especially since we're only 1000 feet from the river. So Breathing Space here in Florida is a big advocate of the river. I go to meetings, I put up signs, I call different communities.

Ray looks at what ex-inmates did on the inside to evaluate their potential as a future collaborator.

Ray: I think it depends on what level you're at. You can do 20 years in prison and hang out on the basketball court, or you can read every valuable book that was ever written. You can go to college. You can be self-taught. You can be a Malcolm X or you can be the recidivist king. You've gotta make a choice about what you want. I tend not to deal with recidivist kings. 80% of people are just going to keep going back in. If you want to choose to flush your life down the toilet, go ahead. Keep flushing. I don't have time for that. I don't mean to be mean, but there comes a point where you have to be responsible to yourself. Then hold yourself to a higher standard. So, what self-development work was that person doing? Some of it could be AVP. On what level were you doing AVP? Were you a facilitator then a coordinator? As you learned, were you doing more? There's plenty of guys that just stop at being an AVP facilitator. Again, there's nothing wrong with that. I want to see the people in life that want more. It's not just, "I'm a coordinator." It's what are you going to do when you come out? When you come home, all of that gets washed away. You come home with $40. Do you have a plan? What's your plan?

We see here once again how rehabilitation programs inside are reentry. Programs, so often contested in criminology and by criminal justice scholars (Cullen, 1994, 2013; Link & Williams, 2017; Phelps, 2011; Steen, Lacock, & McKinzey, 2012), become integral for inmates to find and follow their dreams, as well as to find partners and allies who face similar challenges. One of Ray's truest finds was Mikey, founder of the ice cream store, Mikey Likes It. Mikey had won an award with Defy Ventures, an organization that capitalizes off helping ex-inmates to become entrepreneurs. According to Ray, when Defy did not follow through on their promises, Mikey was introduced to Ray.

Ray: What happened was Mikey worked with Defy Ventures. And he went through their program and everything else. When they denied him the funding they had promised, another friend of mine, Raul Bias, said "You've gotta meet this guy Mikey." I was like, "ok." He set up a meeting with us. Me and Raul go back to Otisville [Prison] . . . Mikey's been written up by *The New York Times, The New York Post, The Daily News, Oprah Magazine,* and we still can't get a fucking bank loan. So it's amazing that in that realm of things, it's just amazingly stupid.

Without the support of individuals like Ray, Mikey would likely have never been able to open his storefront. In 2016, at the national AVP gathering in Denver, Ray was introduced to another formerly incarcerated person, Kerry Humphrey. She had just started her own candle company, called Pearl Street Lights (PSL).[9] Ray worked with her to enhance PSL so it could provide a full-time paid job for her and other disenfranchised women. By 2018, PSL has three part-time employees and one full-time employee.

Although not all efforts are initially successful, wisdom develops through hindsight. Consider Ray's discussion of Ted, a homeless man whom they helped get on his feet.

Ray: Ted moved on. Then again, it's a lesson learned. Ted got a job but he got a girlfriend. And the rent kept getting shorter and shorter. It sounded like Wimpy: "I'll be glad to pay you next week." You're not my kid. So I had to learn that lesson.

Robert: So you had to cut him loose – encourage him to fly the coop.

Ray: Mm hm. And actually, that's the best thing. At first I felt it was a failure. But then I realized that four years ago he was homeless on a street corner. Now he has a job, he has a girl, he has a house. So you're actually not a failure, you're an extreme success story. So it depends how you tell yourself the story. Just because he didn't pay rent doesn't mean that he failed. If anything, he felt so empowered he could stand up and tell me – I was like, "Damn, you got some balls on you. OK." I'm like, "Hey, I guess I did my job."

Ray uses the analogy of a lifeguard to discuss his lessons in helping others:

Ray: There comes a point where you have to think about yourself. Not in a bad way. Make yourself healthy, because you can't help people unless you're in a good place. I have to develop certain things in order to help more people. That comes from the place of being firm. It comes back to being a lifeguard. I can't save you if I can't swim. If you're pulling me under, I've got to let you go. That's lifeguard 101. So when you're in a good place you can help more people.

Conclusion

Throughout the journey of Ray Rios, John Mandala, and Angel Ramos, we find they struggle on their journey for redemption and hope. After being incarcerated and all seemed lost, rehabilitative programing literally saved these men's lives. Although Robert Martinson dismissed prison rehabilitation programs in 1974 (Cullen, 2013), volunteer projects like AVP sprung up in 1975, along with projects, such as Rehabilitation through the Arts, to guide and inspire inmates with a mindset of peace, possibility, and growth (see Fox, 2016). That mindset spawned a revolution for some of the incarcerated, to imagine the previously unimaginable, to dream.

The volunteers that worked behind prison walls led Ray, John, Angel, and others to dream big. Some of these dreams, like Hudson Link, became prominent rehabilitation programs that continue to thrive. Others, like Breathing Space, were in a long period of gestation, and took years of careful planning, saving, and risk-taking to manifest. Ray, John, and Angel, through their work, provide hope to men and women behind bars: In the words of John Mandala, "hold on to positive energy."

Notes

1. Participants in Breathing Space self-consciously refer to themselves as "returning citizens," and it is important to respect the members' term (see Pager, 2003). As noted prominently on the Breathing Space homepage, "Words have power." "Convicted," "ex-con," "offender," "prisoner," "predator," "murderer," are all words that shape the self-image and thought patterns of men and women on their reentry journey.

380 Robert Garot

Defining themselves as "Returning Citizens" embodies their thoughts and feelings on rejecting being branded by a term that voids their right to true redemption. Many returning citizens recognize that their respective prison sentence never ends, as long as discrimination against them continues (see Alexander, 2012; Middlemass, 2017). Breathing Space is built on a community of honesty, respect, and caring.

2. Mikey Likes It Ice Cream, https://mikeylikesiticecream.com/.
3. Breathing Space, www.breathingspaceny.org.
4. www.youtube.com/watch?v=RzGk9Ks9Ckw.
5. The participants asked to use their real names in this chapter.
6. Hudson Link (www.hudsonlink.org/). Ray, John, and Angel received Master's Degrees through the New York Theological Seminary (NYTS). See Halkovic and Michelle (2013) to explore challenges faced by returning citizens and the gifts they brought to higher education. See Flores and Cossyleon (2016, p. 662) on how "civil religion enables collective and political action by de-privatizing personal narratives."
7. Rehabilitation Through Arts Program, www.rta-arts.org/
8. Alternatives to Violence Project, https://avpusa.org/
9. Pearl Street Lights, www.pearlstreetlights.com

References

Alexander, M. (2012). *The new Jim Crow: Mass incarceration in the age of colorblindness.* New York: The New Press.

Barker, K. (2015). A choice for recovering addicts: Relapse or homelessness. *New York Times.* Retrieved from www.nytimes.com/2015/05/31/nyregion/three-quarter-housing-a-choice-for-recovering-addicts-or-homelessness.html?mtrref=www.google.com&gwh=E9283F1CDBF90CBC6DAD70C84209FCDD&gwt=pay

Biggs, B. S. (2009, March 3). Solitary confinement: A brief history from Quaker logic to America's first electric chair, a quick tour of prisons past. *Mother Jones.* www.motherjones.com/politics/2009/03/solitary-confinement-brief-natural-history/

Bloom, D. (2009). *Transitional jobs reentry demonstration.* Chicago, IL: The Joyce Foundation.

Charmaz, K. (2006). *Constructing grounded theory: A practical guide through qualitative analysis.* London: Sage.

Cullen, F. T. (1994). Social support as an organizing concept for criminology: Presidential address to the academy for criminal justice sciences. *Justice Quarterly, 11,* 528–559.

Cullen, F. T. (2013). Rehabilitation: Beyond nothing works. *Crime and Justice, 42*(1), 299–376.

Emerson, R. M., Fretz, R. I., & Shaw, L. (1995). *Writing ethnographic fieldnotes.* Chicago, IL: University of Chicago Press.

Flores, E. O., & Cossyleon, J. E. (2016). 'I went through it so you don't have to': Faith-based community organizing for the formerly incarcerated. *Journal for the Scientific Study of Religion, 55*(4), 662–676.

Fox, C. J. (2016). Civic commitment: Promoting desistance through community engagement. *Punishment and Society, 18*(1), 68–94.

Garot, R. (2010). *Who you claim: Performing gang identity in school and on the streets.* New York: New York University Press.

Garot, R. (2011). The use of rules in determining public housing eligibility. In P. Becker (Ed.), *Sprachvollzug im Amt Kommunikation und Verwaltung im Europa.* Bielefeld, Germany: Transcript Publishers.

Garot, R. (2013). Immigration law and discretion in contemporary Italy. In D. Brotherton, D. Stageman, & S. Leyro (Eds.), *Outside justice.* New York: Springer.

Garot, R. (2014). The psycho-affective echoes of colonialism in fieldwork relations. *FQS*, *15*(1). Retrieved from www.qualitative-research.net/index.php/fqs/article/view/2102/3624

Garrett, J. S. (2017, January–February). Road to redemption: Federal bureau of prisons inmates use CDL program to drive their success. *Corrections Today*, 32–35.

Gideon, L., & Sung, H. (2011). *Rethinking corrections: Rehabilitation, reentry, and reintegration.* Los Angeles: Sage.

Halkovic, A., & Michelle, F. (2013). *Higher education and reentry: The gifts they bring.* New York, NY: The Prisoner Reentry Institute and John Jay College of Criminal Justice.

Halsey, M. (2010). Imprisonment and prisoner re-entry in Australia. *Dialectical Anthropology, 34*, 545–554.

Halushka, J. (2017). Managing rehabilitation: Negotiated performance accountability at the frontlines of reentry service provision. *Punishment and Society, 19*(4), 482–502.

Katz, J. (1983). A theory of qualitative methodology: The social system of analytic fieldwork. In R. M. Emerson (Ed.), *Contemporary field research: A collection of readings* (pp. 109–126). Prospect Heights, IL: Waveland.

Kontos, L. (2010). The irrationality of the prison-industrial complex. *Dialectical Anthropology, 34*, 575–578.

Link, A. J., & Williams, D. J. (2017). Leisure functioning and offender rehabilitation: A correlational exploration into factors affecting successful reentry. *International Journal of Offender Therapy and Comparative Criminology, 61*(2), 150–170.

Martinez, D. J., & Abrams, L. S. (2012). Informal social support among returning young offenders: A metasynthesis of the literature. *International Journal of Offender Therapy and Comparative Criminology, 57*(2), 169–190.

Middlemass, K. (2017). *Convicted and condemned: The politics and policies of prisoner reentry.* New York: New York University Press.

Pager, D. (2003). The mark of a criminal record. *American Journal of Sociology, 108*, 937–975.

Phelps, M. S. (2011). Rehabilitation in the punitive era: The gap between rhetoric and reality in U.S. prison programs. *Law and Society Review, 45*(1), 33–68.

Reentry Policy Council. (2008). *President Bush to sign unprecedented prisoner reentry legislation.* Retrieved from http://reentrypolicy.org/announcements/bush_sign_SCA

Rutter, M. (1987). Psychosocial resilience and protective mechanisms. *American Journal of Orthopsychiatry, 57*, 316–331.

Scheyett, A. M., & Pettus-Davis, C. (2013). Let momma take 'em': Portrayals of women supporting male former prisoners. *International Journal of Offender Therapy and Comparative Criminology, 57*(5), 78–591.

Scott, G. (2004, March). 'It's a sucker's outfit': How urban gangs enable and impede the reintegration of ex-convicts. *Ethnography, 5*, 107–140.

Steen, S., Lacock, T., & McKinzey, S. (2012). Upsetting the discourse of punishment? Competing narratives of reentry and the possibilities for change. *Punishment and Society, 14*(1), 29–50.

Thompkins, D., Curtis, R., & Wendel, T. (2010). Forum: The prison reentry industry. *Dialectical Anthropology, 34*, 427–429.

Travis, J., Solomon, A. L., & Waul, M. (2001). *From prison to home: The dimensions and consequences of prisoner reentry.* Washington, DC: Urban Institute.

Chapter 30

Making Good One Semester at a Time

Formerly Incarcerated Students (and Their Professor) Consider the Redemptive Power of Inclusive Education

James M. Binnall, Irene Sotelo, Adrian Vasquez, and Joe Louis Hernandez

Preface

My name is James M. Binnall, and I am an Assistant Professor at California State University, Long Beach. Roughly 12 years ago, I walked out of a maximum-security prison in central Pennsylvania. My journey from convict to professor began behind bars, when I petitioned prison administrators to allow me to take the Law School Admission Test. Upon release, I enrolled in the only law school that would allow me to begin my legal studies while still on active state parole. Since then, I have won admission to the California State Bar, earned my Ph.D., and published numerous articles on criminal law, punishment, and the civic marginalization of convicted felons. Like many former offenders, I found self-confidence and hope in education. I poured myself into my studies, striving to excel at what I considered a second chance at life. Now, as a professor and a mentor to former offenders, I repeatedly witness the transformative power of inclusive education.

Introduction

Community involvement and immersion are necessary precursors to successful reentry (Fox, 2015). Like California State University, Long Beach, institutions of higher education that are willing to accept students with a criminal past seemingly understand this basic fact, and take a decidedly strengths-based approach to reintegration (Maruna & LeBel, 2003; Bazemore & Stinchcomb, 2004a, 2004b). The strengths-based model conceptualizes former offenders "as assets to be managed, rather than liabilities to be supervised" (Travis, 2005, p. 7). Inclusive institutions see value in the experiences of those who have been directly or indirectly impacted by the criminal justice system, and offers those shut out of many civic and social outlets a chance to thrive. Such efforts facilitate reintegration in a host of ways.

Inclusion breeds a change in a former offender's self-concept (Maruna, 2001). Notably, research suggests that to successfully reintegrate into society, former offenders must reconcile their criminal pasts with their aspirational law-abiding present and future selves (Bazemore & Maruna, 2009; Maruna, 2001). As part of that process, former offenders often build a personal desistance narrative (Giordano, Cernkovich, & Rudolph, 2002; Vaughan, 2007). As King (2013a) explains, "it is the building of a desistance narrative which underpins the development of new identities" (p. 152). To build a desistance narrative, many former offenders make use of a "redemption script" (Maruna, 2001, p. 87).

Redemption scripts typically reinterpret a criminal past, not as a negative, but as a positive. Such reinterpretation highlights the value of having been there, allowing a former offender to move past embarrassing, and sometimes tragic life events (Bazemore, 1999). As Maruna explains, "[s]ometimes the benefits of having experienced crime and drug use are literal . . . [e]x-offenders say they have learned from their past lives, and this knowledge has made them wiser people" (2001, p. 98). For many of my students, who have had contact with the criminal justice system, they have moved beyond their pasts by calling on the negative experiences in their lives and reframing those experiences in constructive ways, such as a source of wisdom. In this way, many of my students have initiated their own desistance process (King, 2013b).

Still, without external corroboration of reformation, former offenders will struggle with the label of "convicted criminal" or "convicted felon" (Middlemass, 2017; Matsueda, 1992; Matsueda & Heimer, 1997; Bontrager, Bales, & Chiricos, 2005). In order to overcome societal labels or the mark of a criminal record (Pager, 2003), delabeling must occur (Maruna, LeBel, Mitchell, & Naples, 2004).[1] This is a necessary step because "[u]ntil ex-offenders are formally and symbolically recognized as 'success stories,' their conversion may remain suspect to significant others, and most importantly to themselves" (Maruna, 2001, p. 158). The most powerful form of delabeling comes from structures and institutions that may have taken part in a former offender's initial labeling (i.e., criminal justice authorities; Maruna et al., 2004). As Maruna et al. (2004) explain:

if the delabeling [process] were to be endorsed and supported by the same social control establishment involved in the "status degradation" process of conviction and sentencing (e.g., judges or peer juries), this public redemption might carry considerable social and psychological weight for participants and observers

(p. 275).

384 James M. Binnall et al.

Accordingly, powerful affirmation can also come from official institutions and structures, like colleges and universities. Winning admission to an institution of higher education – where all the "straight-laced" students attend – demonstrates a level of acceptance that can bolster the self-esteem of a former offender, helping to shore up their "new" personal narrative, which is under construction.

Finally, acceptance into an inclusive institution of higher learning facilitates reintegration by offering former offenders the chance to engage in what Cressey (1955) termed, "reflexive reformation" (p. 119). Through reflexive reformation, offenders who are immersed in inter-offender rehabilitative efforts feel compelled to conform to pro-social group norms and behaviors (Cressey, 1955, 1965; Reissman, 1965). Studies in the substance abuse treatment context support these findings, demonstrating that the "professional ex" (Brown, 1991) or "wounded healer" (White, 2000) paradigms[2] benefit formerly addicted counselors and their clients by providing "a reference group whose moral and social standards are internalized" (Brown, 1991, p. 227).

For students impacted by the criminal justice system who counsel other former offenders on the benefits of higher education, these experiences have proven reformative. Indeed, research demonstrates that former offenders who come together for a pro-social goal derive extraordinary benefits from these types of interactions (LeBel, Richie, & Maruna, 2015; Heidemann, Cederbaum, Martinez, & LeBel, 2016; Perrin, Blagden, Winder, & Dillon, 2017). In such a setting, when former offenders share their personal stories and journeys with each other, they are encouraged to call on their experiences, however deviant, in an effort to aid others struggling to readjust to a society from which they were plucked months, years, and sometimes decades earlier.

Rising Scholars

Today, Dr. Binnall is the faculty advisor to Rising Scholars, a student organization for formerly incarcerated students and students directly impacted by the criminal justice system. Rising Scholars connects these students to resources and information that are designed to increase their success, and was made possible because California State University, Long Beach, opened its doors to formerly incarcerated students.

Rising Scholars became a reality because a particular group of former offenders doggedly pursued their own desistance narratives by reframing their criminal pasts and engaging in the selfless practice of aiding other former offenders trying to access higher education. Their stories are not unique; rather, what is unique about the men and women who founded Rising Scholars is their commitment to those who will follow their lead. What follows are the stories of the founding members of Rising Scholars at California State University, Long Beach.

Irene Sotelo (Co-Founder)

My name is Irene Sotelo. I have a son, a daughter, and two grandchildren. I am a cancer survivor, a victim of domestic violence, and a recovering addict who was formerly incarcerated in a California state prison for women. I am also currently a graduate student in the Master of Social Work program at California State University, Long Beach. I have a Bachelor of Arts degree in Sociology and a minor in Criminal Justice. My hope is to work with former offenders and to help them accomplish their goals, even in the face of a criminal past.

At age eleven, my mother, who was a victim of domestic violence, committed suicide. I was the oldest of five children. This experience was very traumatic for all of us, and this is where my life took a turn for the worse. At the time, I was just entering seventh grade, and going through puberty without my mother to teach and guide me. Instead, my grandparents raised me. They did not know how to speak English or how to read or write. As a result, I turned to the streets for guidance. Living in the heart of the gang-infested barrio of Norwalk, California, this decision was a dangerous one.

Soon, I stopped attending school, joined a gang, and was experimenting with drugs. Within a year, I was trying PCP, LSD, and whatever else that took the pain away of losing my mother. In short, I rebelled. I had no parents and wanted no guidance, I did not have anyone to tell me what to do or how to live my life. I was angry with my mother for dying and leaving me alone. In turn, I took it out on everyone who tried to help me. Each passing year, I got worse. My drug use escalated and I began to have regular contact with the criminal justice system.

Even though I was a minor, I acted like an adult. I was part of a Mexican gang, and I lived by the rules of the street. At 15, I started seeing my child's father. I got pregnant for the first time at 16, but miscarried soon after. I gave birth to my son, my first child, when I was 20-years-old, then I had my daughter when I was 23. Their father and I never married, but we were together for 25 years. I loved being a stay-at-home mother to my son and daughter. I was off drugs and did everything I was supposed to be doing, living life on life terms, which meant being the best mother for my kids and being the best domestic partner for my kids' father who provided for us and putting my past behind me. Yet I was the victim of domestic violence, a fact that I hid from family and friends. My child's father was an alcoholic and sometimes he would hit me until I ended up in the hospital.

At the age of 34, I was diagnosed with cervical cancer and was told I was not going to live. I made peace with it. But soon thereafter, I went into remission. That is when I realized that I was addicted to pain medication. My painkiller addiction ultimately led me to methamphetamine, a drug that got me out of bed in the morning and helped me have normal days and lead a mostly productive life. But the drug was so addictive that I left my home of 19 years and a 25 year relationship with my children's father to live on the streets. That was my low point. At that time, I was living in a riverbed under a freeway bridge and doing crimes to support my drug habit. I knew this lifestyle was putting my life in danger, but I didn't care; my drug habit was the only thing that was important to me. Even a brutal rape and beating did not stop me from doing drugs.

When my lifestyle finally caught up to me, I was sent to prison for almost two years. In October 2009, I was released to a drug rehabilitation program and was given six months to figure out what to do with my future. Looking to begin a new and better chapter in my life, I registered for classes at a community college. Fresh out of prison, I knew nothing about college. To start, I had no concept of a "major." I was not even sure why I wanted to pursue an education. I never thought, that with my background, I would be accepted in an academic setting or that I would be able to secure employment after I completed my degree. Yet, despite these questions and concerns, I knew that I had to learn how to succeed at life, and education seemed like a good place to start.

When I took my first administrative justice class, not only did I understand what I was being taught, I got my first "A" ever in my life! What a feeling! It was like a tall refreshing glass of cold water – sweet in its own way and invigorating. That is when I knew I wanted more of that same feeling. I felt empowered then to reach out to my professor at the time and let him know that I was an ex-felon. I did and asked him, will I be able to work in the criminal justice field with a felony? He said, "of course!" Those two words gave me more hope and a better high than all the drugs in the world. It gave me a sense of accomplishment, which was a feeling I have never felt before. Eventually, I graduated from community college with honors and an Associate's Degree. With that degree came a sense of accomplishment and a new sense of direction. I realized, for the first time in my life, that I was worth something.

Since then, other professors and students have encouraged and supported me, helping me to achieve all that I want in life, such as my professor, Dr. James M. Binnall. After transferring to California State University, Long Beach, I had the privilege of meeting Dr. Binnall, who is a formerly incarcerated person. Dr. Binnall introduced me to other students who were formerly incarcerated, and encouraged us to start an organization for those who have been impacted by the criminal justice system. Now, a year later, I am one of the founders of Rising Scholars, an organization for formerly incarcerated students in higher education. Since creating this organization, doors are opening for me. I have gotten the chance to tell my story at a number of different conferences all over the country. We are building the prison to college pipeline and helping those who are getting released to also pursue higher education.

Since graduating with my bachelor's in May 2018, I was accepted into the Social Work graduate program at California State University, Long Beach. With my master's degree, I want to help build a pathway for the formerly incarcerated that leads each of them from prison to college. I want to share with them all of the knowledge I have acquired, about how to navigate reentry obstacles. In particular, I want to connect returning citizens to resources that can help them succeed; resources I had to discover for myself. I know that getting an education is why I am succeeding in life for the first time. Today, I am happy and excited for the future. That is a new feeling for me, and one that I hope I can give to others. If I can be an example to others, and show them that it is never too late to start a new, better life, then I have accomplished my goal.

Adrian Vasquez (Co-Founder)

My name is Adrian Vasquez. I am 43 years old and live in Carson, California. I am the oldest of three brothers. I grew up in South Central Los Angeles, and at 19, I was arrested for homicide. I was convicted and sentenced to 16 years to life. In February 2014, I was released after serving 20 years in a California State Prison. Since my release, I have worked for the nonprofit organization, Anti-Recidivism Coalition, as an Intake Specialist and Job Developer. There, I help men and women who are affected by the criminal justice system by providing them support with housing, employment, mentoring, and counseling. I am also a graduate of California State University, Long Beach. My major was sociology. Through my work and my studies, I advocate for fair and just policies in the criminal justice system. My goal is to one day become a lawyer and work in the field of criminal justice.

I grew up in South Central Los Angeles in a gang-infested neighborhood during the late eighties and early nineties. My parents did their best to protect me from gang life and the negative influences exerted by my gang-affiliated friends. Along those lines, my parents enrolled me in a private Catholic school, which I attended from kindergarten to twelfth grade. Upon graduating from high school, I enrolled at California State University Long Beach, where I studied through my sophomore year. My goal was to complete a double major in Criminal Justice and Business Administration, and I was well on my way to achieving that goal.

Just when it seemed like my life was taking off, I made a decision that would change my world forever. Led to believe that another man had raped my then girlfriend, I, along with three of my friends, went to find the accused man and teach him a lesson. The situation soon became uncontrollable as my friends and I beat and ended up killing the accused rapist. Months later during my trial, I discovered that my former girlfriend was never raped and that she had had a consensual one-night stand with the man we killed. She lied about the truth to conceal her cheating. Finding out she lied, I felt anger, disappointment, but most of all shame. I realized an innocent man lost his life for a false belief which brought anguish to my heart for his death. At the age of 19, I was sentenced to serve a 16-year to life sentence. Prison was a traumatic experience that drastically altered the course of my life.

For the first ten years of my prison sentence, I struggled. I acted out and had disciplinary issues. My behavior landed me in Administrative Segregation[3] multiple times throughout those first ten years. The turning point in my life came after a visit from my mother. She told me she had been diagnosed with a malignant tumor and begged me to change my behavior so that I could be released while she was alive. "I want you to get out," she told me, "so I can hug you again before I die." The impact of her words hit home immediately. I wanted to make changes right away, and that was when I consciously decided I couldn't live like I had been anymore, but I did not know where to begin or who to ask for help.

I began searching for positive outlets available in prison, yet there were very few. I found myself struggling to find something that gave me hope and a sense of self-worth. Finally, I came across a correspondence college program called Coastline Community College in Old Folsom State Prison. In the beginning, I was very skeptical and not sure what I was undertaking. At the time, I was 28 years old and still involved in prison politics.[4] I was in a mental tug of war with wanting to grant my mother's wishes and wanting to change, yet I did not want to look weak among my peers. I finally made the decision and enrolled in Coastline Community College in spring 2005 when the prison shot-caller[5] for the Southerners[6] told me, "you're too smart for this shit, go to school and go home to your mom."

I enrolled and took Counseling 101 and Astronomy. After three months of reading and taking courses, I found a sense of self-worth and empowerment. I discovered taking college courses kept me out of trouble. I found myself studying and reading in my cell, too busy to hang out on the prison yard and get caught up in prison politics. Prison guards began viewing me as more than "just a thug" and more as an individual attempting to better himself. In this way, education became my escape from the prison environment and a pathway to a new life. In 2012, while housed at R.J. Donovan Correctional Facility, I was the first inmate to achieve two Associate's degrees from Coastline Community College. I was commended, not only by the education department at the facility, but also by the Warden of the prison. I became a role model, proving to others that change is possible and that your past does not have to define you.

Finally, on October 24, 2013, after my fourth parole hearing, I was granted a parole date from the Board of Prison Terms. I was released from prison on February 25, 2014. The education I obtained in prison became instrumental for my pathway to a four-year university and transitioning back into society. It created a layer over my criminal background, and in part, shielded me from the stigma of being viewed as another parolee up to no good. I became a student, not a parolee, and was able to grant my mother's wishes. I am now a free college student and I now use my past to help others. I am a founding member of the Rising Scholars student organization at California State University, Long Beach.

Higher education has allowed me, and others like me, to overcome the challenges of having a criminal background. No longer was I just another convicted individual with no future; instead, I am a person who can achieve success in life. The educational pathway has opened doors that were once locked. Immersed in education, I do not feel stigmatized any longer. I feel as though I have shed my criminal background and built a foundation to reach my potential. Instrumental to my success has been the mentoring I have received from those with similar life experiences.

Many formerly incarcerated people struggle in their first year of college or university. They experience what I call the "spot-light effect," which is the strong belief one will be singled out on campus or in class if others know they have been incarcerated. This is a real challenge, and I was one of those individuals. Yet, with the help of Rising Scholars and other peer mentorship networks, I no longer feel that spotlight. Who better to guide and uplift, but those who have walked – to a point – in my shoes? This is what a diverse and inclusive educational experience has given me, the opportunity to connect with people like myself who can understand my experiences and guide me. Overall, education gave me a pathway to escape the harsh realities of a criminal background, and at the same time provided me new and exciting opportunities.

Joe Louis Hernandez (Co-Founder)

I am Joe Louis Hernandez, and I am a graduate student at California State University, Long Beach, where I am working towards my Master of Science in Counseling, with an emphasis in student development in higher education. I am also a Success Coach for formerly incarcerated students at Rio Hondo Community College. In a prior life, I was a gang member, a drug addict, and an inmate.

As I sat in my first college class, these were my thoughts:

Damn, I don't belong here. How am I gonna make it in college when I didn't even go to high school. I have so much I must do before I am even able to graduate from Mt. San Antonio College, this is never happening for me, I should just give it up. Even if I do graduate, who is going to give me a good job; I have felonies and a rap sheet. Nobody is going to hire me for a good job. Why even try?

I had just begun my journey away from addiction and towards education. I was still not sure it would pay off. I doubted everything, and my professor had not even reviewed the syllabus! This wasn't the first time that I attended college. The first time I dropped out. I hoped this time would be different. Still, I was unsure. Ultimately, my fears were unfounded. That day I had no idea that this time, education would change my life.

What was different this time? This time I had direction and drive, something that I had never had before. This time I began school with a hustler's mentality, the same mentality I had back in the streets. I got on and stayed on my "grind."[7] My cousin told me to apply to all the programs on campus, and to look for help. I took her advice, and applied to Extended Opportunity Programs and Services, and to the school's Trio Program Aces. I was admitted to both. These opportunities helped me build a foundation on which I could begin to rebuild my life.

It was during this time that I met my mentor, Diana Felix. She believed in me, and what I could achieve with an education. While I was still in the remedial English classes, she was already talking to me about writing a thesis and going to graduate school. I had never considered either. To be honest, I didn't even think that I was going to make it through community college. But, because she believed in me, I followed her direction. I obeyed her like I was back in the 'hood, and whatever my big homies told me to do, I did. Before that, I took "penitentiary chances,"[8] so why would I not try to take chances that could lead to new life?

Still, some days, in the back of my mind, I had a negative voice that would say, "you're not going to make it, you don't belong here." Even though I felt this way, I pushed on and kept at it. I remember being scared and thinking, "shit, why am I scared, I have been locked up with killers, and shot at multiple times." Nonetheless, nothing scared me more than going to college and taking college algebra, or doing statistics. But, just like when I was on the streets, I looked to the homies for back up. So, I went to the tutoring centers, and I got help from the tutors for my programs. Ultimately, I passed Statistics, earning an A. During my time at Mt. San Antonio College, I grinded and put in the work and was able to finish my degree within two years. At that point, I applied to transfer with an Associate's Degree to Social and Behavioral Sciences.

Succeeding at the community college level gave me confidence. With that confidence, I moved on to California State University, Los Angeles (CSU-LA). For me, this was a surreal experience. I remember previously living just a few miles from this university. Ironically, while in high school, I visited this same university for a gang prevention program at which they told us we too could attend college. I remember thinking to myself, "who wants to go to school, I am only here 'cause I didn't have to go to school today."

Ultimately, the guy at my gang prevention program was right, I could go to college. He had planted a seed. During my time at CSU-LA, I made the decision to pursue a career as a community college counselor. I wanted to help people that had been in situations similar to my own. Specifically,

I wanted to help people who have histories of incarceration and feel like they don't belong on a college campus. I want to be there to welcome them and to help them to feel like they are accepted. So, when I was done with my degree at CSU-LA, I began to apply to graduate programs. California State University, Long Beach (CSU-LB) accepted me and helped me move one step closer to my goal.

At the start of my studies at CSU-LB, I still doubted myself. One particularly dark day, early on, I ran in to a friend – Adrian Vasquez – who told me about Professor Binnall, who had been incarcerated. He then told me of all the social movements and efforts going on in California focused on aiding former offenders reenter society. As we talked that day, Adrian and I decided that we should pursue the formation of a student organization at CSU-LB, an organization that would help formerly incarcerated students. So, with the help of other formerly incarcerated students, Professor Binnall, and other allies, we formed Rising Scholars.

Rising Scholars is now part of a movement that has taken hold in California. Across the state, a union of students who have been incarcerated has formed. It has been this work and this movement that has helped me redefine myself in the context of higher education. At one time, I thought that I was hopeless because of my criminal past, and today I see value in that past. My value, in part, lies in how I am able to utilize my past experiences to help myself and others achieve their educational goals. I do not look at those dark times in my life as periods of failure, but instead I now see them as lessons that have taught me how to stay hungry and to keep hustling for good.

My past experiences taught me valuable lessons. For instance, as a Gangster, I learned that I was willing to do anything to get ahead. I now apply that mentality to my educational pursuits and I have shared that mentality with others. I have begun to mentor and to use my voice to help create spaces for those that are afraid of being stigmatized. I feel that with my voice, I can help to change the narrative about incarceration and the formerly incarcerated. In my opinion, we need to assist one another, not just through words, but also with actions. Growing up, all I wanted to be was a "GEE," which is a Gangster. Today I am still a "GEE" – I am a college graduate and a graduate student, and I like the way my world has changed.

Conclusion

Taken together, the experiences of the Rising Scholars' Founders suggest that education initially served as a means of shedding an antisocial, criminal identity. Still, woven through each of their stories is a sense of doubt that plagued their early entry into higher learning. This doubt, while potentially detrimental to their success, seemingly fueled their desire to alter their lives in positive ways. As each of the Rising Scholar Founders progressed on their own educational journey, they began to build new identities, referring to but not essentializing their criminal pasts. In short, the Rising Scholar Founders "became" students, drawing on their own deviant, often tragic backgrounds, as tools with which to build new pro-social identities.

Though ostensibly logical and linear, the reformation of the Rising Scholar Founders at CSU-LB was anything but straightforward. As they note, setbacks were part of their journey. To overcome these setbacks, the Founders, and myself, relied on the lessons we learned as gangsters, criminals, and then convicts. As a group, we have all navigated experiences – crime, incarceration, and reentry – that require tenacity and skill. Those same qualities helped all of us excel in higher education.

As the advisor to Rising Scholars, I have seen the Rising Scholar Founders struggle. These struggles often stem from a desire to succeed now, while failing to appropriately appreciate the process. For those who have been incarcerated, who have lost years of our lives, the need for immediate gratification is understandable. We are "behind." Our life cohort moved on without us while we were addicted, deviant, or incarcerated. We must now try and catch up. My job, as faculty advisor, is to harness students' enthusiasm while tempering their expectations, and reminding them, always, that our members are exceptional students, not exceptional students who were once incarcerated.

The value of Rising Scholars is the community and the commonality of experience within that community of students. As formerly incarcerated and returning citizens, we, who are now students, faculty, and allies, speak the same language and understand the frustrations and self-doubt felt when faced with setbacks. This bond creates a collective sense of empathy and accountability. With both at the ready, the group is better positioned to confront and overcome obstacles unique to returning citizens. For our members, Rising Scholars is a resource that provides not only instrumental assistance and emotional support, but also an achievable model. We draw inspiration from one another without begrudging individual successes. In this way, Rising Scholars hold one another to a standard that is realistic and attainable, so long as we work together.

In my own experience, I returned to education to change my life story. It "worked" because I had many teachers and mentors who offered assistance. Rising Scholars does the same for students – it is a group that brings together the vast assets and skills of the returning community. For me, the collective knowledge of our group is astounding. The encyclopedic knowledge of resources and opportunities our members possess amazes. When I left prison and began my own educational journey, I had to hope that I would find help. Ultimately, I did. As the Faculty Advisor to Rising Scholars, my goal has always been to remove the uncertainty from our members' experiences; Rising Scholars has done just that.

As I noted in the introduction, the stories of the Rising Scholars founding members at CSU-LB are not unique. Every day, young men and women

Making Good One Semester at a Time   393

are sentenced to serve prison sentences that can effectively end their hopes of ever achieving their goals and dreams, and most of them return to society at some point. An inclusive educational experience offers these men and women an opportunity to excel, contribute, and alter their lives while helping other former offenders chase their own goals. Through their contributions to this chapter, the founding members of Rising Scholars have taken the brave step of sharing their pasts, presents, and future goals with the world. For that, they ought to be commended; too often, formerly incarcerated people are "data" to be analyzed and published. In this context, the formerly incarcerated, remarkable men and women, get to critically analyze their own lives and experiences, and offer a favorable direction for new types of research on a population of which I am a part.

Notes

1. Maruna (2001) and Maruna et al. (2004) note that scholars describe the "delabeling process" using a host of monikers including: "certification process" or "destigmatization process" (Meisenhelder 1977, 1982), "elevation ceremony" (Lofland, 1969), and "integration ceremony" (Braithwaite & Mugford, 1994).
2. "Professional ex" (Brown, 1991) and "wounded healer" (White, 2000) paradigms refer to situations in which someone afflicted with an infirmity (addiction, formerly incarcerated, etc.) takes on the role of helping others with that same affliction.
3. "Administrative Segregation" refers to a housing unit inside of a correctional institution where an inmate is housed in solitary confinement because of a disciplinary infraction or because of a safety concern.
4. "Prison Politics" refers to the manner in which inmates negotiate the unwritten rules of prison.
5. "Shot-Caller" refers to a high-ranking, influential member of a gang.
6. "Southerners" refers to the classification of an inmate who is geographically from southern California.
7. "Grind" refers to a person's willingness to work hard and remain dedicated to their pursuits.
8. "Penitentiary chances" is an expression which means taking risk's that could result in a prison sentence.

References

Bazemore, G. (1999). After shaming, whither reintegration: Restorative justice and relational rehabilitation. In G. Bazemore & L. Walgrave (Eds.), *Restorative Juvenile justice: Repairing the harm of youth crime* (pp. 155–194). Monsey, NY: Criminal Justice Press.
Bazemore, G., & Maruna, S. (2009). Restorative justice in the reentry context: Building new theory and expanding the evidence base. *Victims & Offenders: An International Journal of Evidence-Based Research, Policy, and Practice, 4*(4), 375–384.
Bazemore, G., & Stinchcomb, J. (2004a). A civic engagement model of reentry: Involving community through service and community justice. *Federal Probation, 68*(2), 14–24.
Bazemore, G., & Stinchcomb, J. (2004b). Civic engagement and reintegration: Toward a community focused theory and practice. *Columbia Human Rights Law Review, 36*, 241–286.

Bontrager, S., Bales, W., & Chiricos, T. (2005). Race, ethnicity, threat, and the labeling of convicted felons. *Criminology, 43*(3), 589–622.

Braithwaite, J., & Mugford, S. (1994). Conditions of successful reintegration ceremonies: Dealing with juvenile offenders. *British Journal of Criminology, 34*(2), 139–171.

Brown, D. J. (1991). The professional ex-: The alternative for exiting the deviant career. *Sociological Quarterly, 32*(2), 219–230.

Cressey, D. R. (1955). Changing criminals: The application of the theory of differential association. *American Journal of Sociology, 61*(2), 116–120.

Cressey, D. R. (1965). Social psychological foundations for using criminals in the rehabilitation of criminals. *The Journal of Research in Crime and Delinquency, 2*(2), 49–59.

Fox, K. J. (2015). Theorizing community integration as desistance-promotion. *Criminal Justice and Behavior, 42*(1), 82–94.

Giordano, P. C., Cernkovich, S. A., & Rudolph, J. L. (2002). Gender, crime and desistance: Toward a theory of cognitive transformation. *American Journal of Sociology, 107*(4), 960–1164.

Heidemann, G., Cederbaum, J. A., Martinez, S., & LeBel, T. P. (2016). Wounded healers: How formerly incarcerated women help themselves by helping others. *Punishment and Society, 18*(1), 3–26.

King, S. (2013a). Early desistance narratives: A qualitative analysis of probationers' transitions towards desistance. *Punishment and Society, 15*(2), 147–165.

King, S. (2013b). Transformative agency and desistance from crime. *Criminology and Criminal Justice, 13*(3), 317–335.

LeBel, T. P., Richie, M., & Maruna, S. (2015). Helping others as a response to reconcile a criminal past. *Criminal Justice and Behavior, 42*(1), 108–120.

Lofland, J. (1969). *Deviance and identity.* Englewood Cliffs, NJ: Prentice Hall.

Maruna, S. (2001). *Making good: How Ex-convicts reform and rebuild their lives.* Washington, DC: American Psychological Association.

Maruna, S., & LeBel, T. P. (2003). Welcome home? Examining the reentry court from a strengths-based perspective. *Western Criminology Review, 4*(2), 91–107.

Maruna, S., LeBel, T. P., Mitchell, N., & Naples, M. (2004). Pygmalion in the reintegration process: Desistance from crime through the looking glass. *Psychology, Crime, and Law, 10*(3), 271–281.

Matsueda, R. L. (1992). Reflected appraisals, parental labeling, and delinquency: Specifying a symbolic interactionist theory. *American Journal of Sociology, 97*, 1577–1611.

Matsueda, R. L., & Heimer, K. (1997). A symbolic interactionist theory of role transitions, role commitments and delinquency. In T. Thornberry (Ed.), *Developmental theories of crime and delinquency* (pp. 163–213). New Brunswick, NJ: Transaction.

Meisenhelder, T. (1977). An exploratory study of exiting from criminal careers. *Criminology, 15*(3), 319–334.

Meisenhelder, T. (1982). Becoming normal: Certification as a stage in exiting from crime. *Deviant Behavior: An Interdisciplinary Journal, 3*(2), 137–153.

Middlemass, K. (2017). *Convicted and condemned: The politics and policies of prisoner reentry.* New York: New York University Press.

Pager, D. (2003). The mark of a criminal record. *American Journal of Sociology, 108*(5), 937–975.

Perrin, C., Blagden, N., Winder, B., & Dillon, G. (2017). 'It's sort of reaffirmed to me that I am not a monster, I'm not a terrible person': Sex offender's movements towards desistance via peer-support roles in prison. *Sexual Abuse: A Journal of Research and Treatment, 30*(7), 759–780.

Reissman, F. (1965). The 'helper' therapy principle. *Social Work, 10*(2), 27–32.

Travis, J. (2005). *But they all come back: Facing the challenges of prisoner reentry.* Washington, DC: The Urban Institute Press.

Vaughan, B. (2007). The internal narrative of desistance. *British Journal of Criminology, 47,* 390–404.

White, W. L. (2000). The history of recovered people as wounded healers: The era of professionalization and specialization. *The History of Alcoholism Treatment Quarterly, 18*(2), 1–25.

Chapter 31

"I Can't Depend on No Reentry Program!"

Street-Identified Black Men's Critical Reflections on Prison Reentry

Yasser Arafat Payne, Tara Marie Brown, and Corry Wright

> We need reentry programs to be *committed* to helping you find a job. . . . If you [the state] committed, we gonna be committed. A lot of people would rather work [a legal job]. . . . Ain't nothing [money] out here no more [in the streets]. *This* [street life] *is dead!* Motherfuckers getting killed every day, over this kind of shit [trying to make money in the streets].
>
> – Jerome (age 31), Participant

Approximately 630,000 individuals are released from state and federal prisons each year in the U.S. (Carson, 2018). Given that Black men are grossly overrepresented in the prison population, the large number of returnees has prompted a proliferation of research on Black men's experiences with reentry over the last decade (Arditti & Parkman, 2011; Johnson, 2017; Middlemass, 2017; Trimbur, 2009). However, despite growing attention to reentry processes and programs, three-fourths of reentering Black men are rearrested within three years of release (Carson, 2018), indicating the lack of effectiveness of reentry programming for Black men. Studies on the perceptions and experiences of street-identified Black men, which are scant within reentry research studies, can inform reentry services and assist with housing, health, and counseling concerns, as well as job training and placement. To address this gap in the literature, we examine the attitudes towards reentry processes of street-identified Black men in two low-income neighborhoods in Wilmington, Delaware.

Sites of Resilience Theory and Reentry

According to sites of resilience (SOR) theory, street-identified Black men are, in fact, resilient (Payne, 2011). "The streets" or a "street" identity is phenomenological language that represents a worldview or value system centered on personal, social, and economic survival. The men in this study were committed to uplifting themselves, their families, and their communities, and they reentered in the best way they knew how, which required resilience and embracing legal and illegal reentry strategies. An understudied component of reentry studies is how Black men reframe their agency as a core value and a prison reentry strategy. We argue that street-identified Black men also play an active role in supporting returning citizens.

SOR theory is reinforced by structural violence theory (Galtung, 1969). The structural-violence complex is a web of racialized policies, laws, institutions, and structural systems designed to privilege the ruling elite at the expense of various marginalized populations, and especially low-income Black Americans. Reentry and reentry experiences of Black men in Wilmington, Delaware, sharply represent this nefarious complex. The criminal justice system, an integral dimension of broader society, negatively impacts returning Black men's ability to secure quality employment, stable housing, and voting privileges. In response to structural violence, some returning Black men draw on the values and activities of the streets to support their reentry needs.

Black Men's Perspectives on Reentry

Returning citizens face a multitude of obstacles to successful reintegration. Research suggests that many previously incarcerated Black men understand there are multiple structural forces intentionally working against their success (Panuccio & Christian, 2019; Payne & Brown, 2017). For example, state-sanctioned labor market discrimination legally disqualifies ex-offenders from particular jobs, and community supervision mechanisms are designed to restrict social and professional mobility and extract unlimited fees and fines from an economically vulnerable population. Despite awareness of such structural barriers, Black men still hold themselves accountable for their reentry successes and failures (Gunnison & Helfgott, 2011; John, 2016).

Examining experiences of Black men on parole, Arditti and Parkman (2011) describe the "developmental paradox" (p. 205), that while successful reentry requires dependence on others, this reality is often in conflict with Black men's expectations of themselves and their reentry responsibilities (Payne, 2016; Payne & Brown, 2016; Middlemass, 2017). In Hlavka, Wheelock, and Cossyleon's (2015) research on employment among 39 returning citizens, Black men "reported intense self-blame" (p. 222) despite their awareness of significant structural barriers. Research indicates that returning Black men feel they must be financially self-sufficient and support their families (Johnson, 2017; Panuccio & Christian, 2019; Trimbur, 2009), which conflicts with the reality of obtaining legal employment when someone is returning home after serving time in prison (Middlemass, 2017).

Returning Black men, who often depend on families for basic resources, report feeling badly because they believe that they should be the chief provider (Arditti & Parkman, 2011; Middlemass, 2017; Panuccio & Christian, 2019). Although low-income families are a vital source of support, they often lack the resources and patience needed to assist returning Black men for an extended period of time. Panuccio and Christian (2019), for instance, found family support for returning Black men, "was contingent on their eventual ability to be independent or at least make a significant contribution to the household" (p. 15). Despite family members' awareness of structural obstacles, returning Black men's inability to contribute to their family and the household often leads to conflict, which reinforces Black men's view that they are "on their own" (Panuccio & Christian, 2019, p. 14) in the reentry process. Inadequate reentry programming and services may contribute to this view.

Although research on returning Black men's perspectives on the quality of reentry programs is scant, extant studies suggest programmatic limitations. For example, returning citizens in Rossman's and Roman (2003) evaluation of the national, multi-service Opportunity to Succeed Program (OTSP) reentry program, the majority of whom where Black men, reported that they did not have timely or adequate access to OTSP's assisted job searches, and the jobs with which the program connected them were extremely low-wage. These critiques, which were corroborated by OTSP staff and program evaluators, are echoed by participants in Johnson's (2017) interview-based study on African-American men's experiences with multiple reentry programs in northern California. Additional shortcomings cited by Black men in Johnson's research include reentry programs' failures to provide: (1) marketable job skills; (2) adequate assistance in navigating health and social service systems; (3) long-term, high-quality substance abuse rehabilitation services; and (4) culturally relevant counseling and programming.

Regardless of the institutional and structural barriers faced by previously incarcerated Black men, their failure to meet the inflexible and infeasible expectations of reentry programs and personnel often leads to their re-incarceration. For instance, individuals under community supervision must pay monthly monitoring dues and other court-related fees, and employment is often a condition of release. Black male returnees report that parole officers violate them for minor infractions, hold them to unreasonable parole expectations including rigid curfews, or tell them to identify and avoid so-called "known felons" in communities where large numbers of Black men have felony convictions (Trimbur, 2009). Trimbur (2009) concludes: "Ironically, men who trust the system to help them reenter fare much worse by their own estimation than those who do not, and, in a sense, remain much more vulnerable to the social injury of unmet expectations" (p. 275). Thus, the shortcomings of reentry services and the sabotaging practices of parole officers, in addition to the limitations of family support and notions of Black

"I Can't Depend on No Reentry Program!" 399

manhood, create a context in which many returning Black men feel that, ultimately, they can only rely on themselves.

Reentry services in Wilmington, Delaware, come in many forms and were often funded with grants. Only two major nonprofits with a central mission focused on reentry existed between both the Eastside and Southbridge communities. Services offered by these organizations and supplemental programs generally included case management, cognitive behavioral therapy, housing assistance, and job training and development. Civic and political leadership's public commitment to reentry was rhetorical, at best; there was little permanent support or budget lines by the public and private sectors to assist reentry efforts. Rarely did service organizations openly challenge the structural inadequacies; instead, they were inclined to publicly blame the men's unemployment or recidivism, for instance, on their lack of discipline or poor cultural values.

Methods

Street Participatory Action Research (Street PAR)

Participatory Action Research (PAR) is an epistemological orientation or methodological framework that includes members of the target population in the research-activism process. Street PAR draws from the theoretical and methodological traditions of PAR (Baum, MacDougall, & Smith, 2006); specifically, it engages street-identified Black populations in a participatory enterprise (Payne, 2017; Payne & Bryant, 2018). To implement this project, a collaborative agreement between three universities, five nonprofit organizations, and the HOPE Commission, a nonprofit local organization founded by Mayor James Baker, was established. The partnership was asked to address Wilmington's violence, incarceration, and recidivism.

The first step was to hire and train part-time workers to be a "change agent" or "research activist" in the community. Criteria required applicants to be: city residents; living below the poverty line; experienced in the streets and/or criminal justice system; and interested in doing community research and local activism. From the 150 applications, 12 men and three women between the ages of 20 and 48 were hired to be Street PAR Associates for the Wilmington Street PAR Project; ten associates were previously incarcerated and had been released between six-months to one-year prior to Street PAR training. Street PAR Associates participated in two months of training, and upon completion of training, they worked a minimum of 20-hour weeks.[1]

Site Location

The study was conducted in the Eastside and Southbridge neighborhoods of Wilmington, Delaware. Wilmington (population 71, 000) is Delaware's biggest city, and is a city of two-tales. It has the largest concentration of Blacks (58%) in the state and accounts for 25% of all crime in Delaware. Whites, at 32% of the states' population, are better employed and wealthier than Blacks, who generally reside in low-income communities, like the Eastside and Southbridge.

At the time of the study, 5,793 people lived in the Eastside, and >90% of them were Black; 90.4% of Black families lived below the poverty line (The City of Wilmington Delaware, 2018). Black men (18 and older), who made up 29.4% of Eastside residents, had a labor force participation rate of 47.4%. The population of Southbridge was 1,918, 71.7% of whom were Black; 78.7% of Black families lived below the poverty line. Black men made up 18.3% of Southbridge residents, and 45.7% of them were in the labor force. In 2011, 1,049 individuals were released from Delaware prisons, 56.2% of whom were Black men (Kervick & MacLeish, 2015). The overall three-year recidivism rate for Black men in Delaware was 77.9% (2009–2011); Black men age 24 and younger had a staggering recidivism rate of 93% (Kervick & MacLeish, 2015).

These statistics demonstrate a need for reentry programs and services in Eastside and Southbridge; however, quality reentry services, programs, and/or nonprofit organizations were few and far between in the Eastside and Southbridge communities. Most reentry organizations and supplemental programs were severely under-resourced. However, because Wilmington is a small city, and the neighborhoods are even smaller, a relative handful of reentry initiatives could serve most returning citizens in Wilmington.

Data Collection

Community-level data was collected by Street PAR Associates from 2010 to 2011. During that time, Street PAR Associates interacted with street-identified Black men and women between the ages of 18 and 35. As part of a large multi-method Street PAR study, 520 surveys were collected; 24 individual interviews, four dual interviews (n = 8), and three group interviews (n = 15) were conducted; extensive field observations were recorded (Payne & Brown, 2016; Payne, Hitchens, & Chambers, 2017).

For this particular study, a subset of data focusing on the reentry experiences of street-identified Black men is analyzed, which includes 210 men; 65% were residents of the Eastside, 21% were residents of Southbridge, and 14% lived outside of these two neighborhoods, but reported frequenting the two neighborhoods. Neighborhood "frequenters" were participants that socialized and/or participated in illegal activity in the Eastside and/or Southbridge neighborhoods.

Trained Street PAR Associates approached residents to survey and be interviewed; if they agreed, respondents received a consent form, $5 in cash, and a resource package with recommendations for employment and educational

"I Can't Depend on No Reentry Program!" 401

and counseling services. Surveys took approximately 45 minutes to complete. Interviewees received a consent form, $10 in cash per interview, and a resource package. Interviews took one-to-two hours to complete and they were conducted in a private office space located in Southbridge. Participants signed waivers for their legal or street-identified names to be used. Study participants were not asked incriminating questions about their behavior.

In order to understand violence, incarceration, and recidivism, neighborhood-level survey data were collected, and alongside the qualitative data from street-identified Black men between the ages of 18 and 35, four public spaces in the two neighborhoods were identified and mapped: *Cool sites* were identified as having very little or no identifiable illegal activity; *warm sites* had a consistent level of legal and illegal activity; and *hot sites* had a high or frequent level of illegal street activity.

Returning to Structural Violence

Reentry services and programs should recognize how street-identified Black men are sincerely sympathetic towards and supportive of returning citizens; if anyone understood the perils of reentry, it was street-identified Black men. This often-overlooked but nurturing group is able to provide the expertise for formerly incarcerated Black men; the street-identified Black men in this study had either reentered themselves and/or supported someone else returning home, and provided emotional support and advice, temporary housing, financial assistance, and tips on reliable service providers and programs. They had no interest in observing droves of other Black men coming home to fragile support systems, especially as those returning home were also loved-ones. Their favorable attitudes reflected empathy grounded in their own reentry experiences and their understanding of how reentry impacted the wellbeing of families and friendships. About 73% (n = 210) of survey respondents noted, "People who come home from prison deserve another chance."

Economics, Family and Reentry

Returning citizens' difficulties with employment often harm family dynamics and destabilize living arrangements. Most crippling, however, was the humiliation and frustration they internalized when they were unable to provide financially. Participants were often considered a "burden" by family and a suspect by police, city leadership, and the business community, while a felony conviction stigmatized and barred them from participation in basic rights of American life. Consequently, because of the structural violence, some participants reverted to the streets to cope with the toxic combination of marginal resources and dissipating respect from friends, families, and professionals.

402 Yasser Arafat Payne et al.

According to Louis (age 31), desisting from crime actually made him more vulnerable to negative treatment by those he loved most. Given Louis family's financial desperation, their awareness of inequality experienced by returning citizens rarely mitigated their irrational frustration with Louis' inability to obtain a job. Louis was able-bodied, and they wanted, rather *needed*, him to contribute financially to the household. Louis' challenges with reentry sharply reflected a lack of dignity and structural dislocation. He further explained:

> When your stomach's touching your back [you are hungry] and you can't find a job, but you really are tryin' to find a job. And you're about to get kicked out, 'cause you don't have your rent paid on time. And your child support is due, or your baby's cryin' for diapers and milk. And you're sittin' at home lookin' stupid because you know deep down inside, you tryin' to get a job, but it ain't comin' fast enough. And if you do get a job, you gotta wait two or three weeks to get your first check. And then when you do get that check . . . it's . . . minimum wage . . . [then] people do what they gotta do [go to the streets]. It's a positive risk, sometimes. But that positive risk might . . . land you in jail or dead.

Terrel (age 27), lived in Southbridge with his wife and four sons, and was baffled by how felony convictions destabilized Southbridge by robbing Black men of economic mobility. Terrel could not comprehend how one "(poor) decision" could harm someone's life chances in perpetuity. Convinced most returning home were sincerely smart, talented, hardworking, and willing to "be productive," Terrel exclaimed in his individual interview:

> There should be more programs helping them so they *can get a job* . . . they might have made a decision when they were 16 . . . [and now] the decision that they made when they were 16, has affected them throughout their lifetime . . . it shouldn't be a felony that's stopping someone to be productive . . . you got people with felonies that got all types of brains, education, talents.

Crime was generally conceptualized as a means to an economic end and sometimes worth the risk of incarceration (Contreras, 2012; Duck, 2016; Payne, 2011). A *both/and* as opposed to *either/or* perspective was typically used to assess people's characters in the Eastside and Southbridge (Payne, 2011). Participants rarely understood illegal activity as a cultural failing. Instead, returning citizens were understood to have strengths *and* limitations, or a multilayered social identity.

Rugged Individualism and Reentry

Returning Black men employed a range of reentry strategies, which meant they maximized their opportunities in reentry programs and/or participated in crime for different kinds of support. However, they mostly went to the streets when legal opportunities were exhausted. Self-reliance was considered the most adaptive and realistic approach to legal and illegal opportunities for reentry. Giving up was not an option, even in the face of extreme structural violence. Participants learned to trust themselves as city leadership and loved-ones proved unreliable. Strategies grounded in personal responsibility were largely considered the most functional approach to coping with structural indifference and dis-opportunity.

Banks (age 27) was among the most critical participants; he criticized people coming home from prison. He believed Wilmington's high recidivism rate was the result of returning citizens "giving up;" he held himself accountable for his previous recidivation. Banks, who had two drug felony convictions, acknowledged he "made some wrong decisions." He was proud to receive a "second chance" from the Plummer Community Corrections Center (PCCC) in Wilmington. PCCC temporarily housed returning citizens, and helped them identify counseling, housing, and employment opportunities (PCCC, 2013). Although most participants complained about PCCC's services, Banks spoke glowingly about this transitional facility, even sharing how PCCC helped him to secure "full custody of [his] son."

Participants discussed both individual *and* structural aspects of reentry, but no participant challenged the role of the individual. For example, Anthony B. (age 33) reported self-reliance was his sole strategy for reentry. Unlike Banks, he refused reentry services and had not recidivated since his last incarceration, almost a decade ago. He attributed his success at reentry to his entrepreneurism; he and many others strongly encouraged returning citizens to "open up their own businesses." Anthony B.'s sharp criticism of reentry programs was anchored in the misuse of parole violations, and he insisted parole officers were monetarily incentivized to violate parolees. For Anthony B., recognizing the structural pitfalls designed for returning citizens was the first step to creating a viable strategy for successful reentry. He said:

> I really haven't seen any . . . positive things come out of most reentry programs. All I see is like reentry, to come back to jail . . . *It's not no reentry program to come back in society and be a productive citizen* . . . they want to continuously keep you on parole so they can violate you for any given reason . . . then they keep adding the time on . . . . Now a brother can start from level two probation and catch a technical violation and get bumped up to level three . . . all the way up to level four which is home confinement . . . every time you get violated, the probation officer gets a bonus on his check. . . . They want to keep you on parole . . . I don't see no reentry program helping anybody. *All I see, is harming.*

Rennie Rox (age 35) also shared his individual and structural perspectives of reentry. Rennie was aware of structural barriers but mostly focused on personal accountability as a method to successfully reenter, vis-à-vis

404 Yasser Arafat Payne et al.

preparation, endurance, and patience. Like most participants, he trusted few institutions and believed reentering Black men were forced to rely on themselves to overcome the impact of structural violence. Raised in economic poverty and around drug addiction on the Eastside, Rennie started selling drugs and committing armed robberies by age 14. At age 19, Rennie was sentenced to 10 years for a drug conviction. He was released at age 28, but recidivated after five months, and was sentenced to another four-and-a-half years. Rennie described acquiring a new perspective during his second incarceration.

> I'm laying up on [the top] bunk [in his cell] . . . after doing eight years and then getting locked back up five months later. It felt like . . . somebody had a belt around my neck and was turning it from underneath the bunk, like it was *killing me* . . . the biggest regret was me coming home and realizing that *a life could be lived*. . . . I really could have just chilled out [didn't have to revert to crime to survive]. I really could of, kept trying and pushing, and I could still be home.

Based on his experiences and disappointment with reentry services, Rennie decided his reentry strategy would be centered on the principles of rugged individualism. Rennie explained:

> You have a program that's in place and it's not doing what it's supposed to be doing . . . [people] depend on these programs to get their self together, but it's not there . . . I realized when I came home. . . . *I can't depend on no reentry program!* I can't depend on probation and parole. . . . I'm not even looking for none of these people to help me do anything because it's just going to be a disappointment and cause me to [recidivate] out of frustration. Because, I done put all my faith in that these people were going to help me. . . . *I can't wait on them to give me an opportunity!*

Wilmington's Reentry Services

Although city leadership and reentry organizations "promised," in countless ways to address the employment, housing, educational, and counseling needs of returning citizens, approximately 62% (n = 208) "disagreed" with the following statement: "There are good prison reentry programs in the City of Wilmington." Also, about 52% (n = 210) "disagreed" that, "Most people returning home from prison can find a job, if they really want to," and 58% (n = 208) of participants reported there were not, "enough educational programs available for people incarcerated in prison."

Reentry programs were characterized as narrowly focused, training-centered, referral-oriented, and culturally insensitive. Reentry initiatives rarely focused on direct *job placement*, and participants were enraged that their demands for quality employment were repeatedly ignored by city leadership. For instance, like Anthony B., Rennie agreed that a sound reentry strategy was grounded in individual accountability and entrepreneurism because, according to Rennie, who bitterly critiqued Wilmington's reentry services, the programs were not helpful; he felt the appropriate response to systemic barriers was self-determination.

Rennie responded to the institutional shortcomings of Wilmington's reentry programs by sifting through and focusing on the relative worth of their services. He and others carved out whatever opportunities they could but mostly relied on themselves to get through what they realized would be a tough reentry journey. Rennie noted, reentry services generally focused on job training or soft skills like resume building, or how to select a two-piece suit and tie. Job interviews or employment opportunities were never provided for him. From his perspective, reentry services rarely contended with the social and structural realities of reentry. Rennie had few resources, but was still expected to figure out how to use public transportation to travel between agencies (e. g., driver's license, housing, child support, etc.).

Rennie shared a disheartening story of being selected for a coveted and "specialized" reentry program. Unlike Banks and Anthony, Rennie had access to a formal reentry program while he was incarcerated. He was convinced that with the media attention the program received and the fact that he was among a few chosen for the program, he would receive adequate support. To his surprise, the reentry intervention and program yielded little benefit after he was released.

Rennie's motivation to stay out of prison was, instead, driven by his need to be present in his children's lives. Rennie feared another extended absence from his children would reproduce for them the social-structural conditions he faced during his childhood. After his second incarceration and negative experiences with reentry services, he decided to use brute will to endure low-wage employment to provide for his children and stay out of prison. A felony conviction made it nearly impossible to secure quality employment, but this did not prevent Rennie from doing whatever he had to, including working long hours to build his landscaping business in "90-degree heat." Rennie said:

> I had to get my brother's lawnmower . . . [Now] I'm handing out fliers that I cut grass. $20 front and back. I'm trying to do three, four, houses a day in 90-degree heat . . . [I'm] the same cat that would run in your house and take all your drugs, pistol whip your whole family, and shoot somebody, if they don't give it up. I was the same dude that'll stand on the corner trying to sell a thousand dimes ($10) a day of cocaine . . . I can't do that no more. I got to do what I got to do to feed my family and try to contribute to these bills. . . . *And I don't let these felonies hold*

406 Yasser Arafat Payne et al.

me back! . . . I'm all about trying to raise my children and live a beautiful, peaceful life. . . . Ain't none of that in jail.

Rennie argued, for successful reentry, returning citizens must lose their dignity by enduring periodic access to low-skill and low-wage employment. Rennie's story was emblematic of many voices in the streets of Wilmington. Resigned to low wages, Rennie insisted he was not defeated. Instead, an honorable life was achieved by cutting three-to-four lawns per day for $20 each. Ideally, Rennie would accrue $560 per week, assuming he worked seven days. It was unlikely he could maintain this pace long-term. Although Rennie expected to work arduously to demonstrate his worth as a father and productive citizen, in reality it was irrational. Rennie's lofty goal of making $560 each week, under distressing conditions, did not account for travel, gas, the maintenance of his car, and landscaping materials. Nor did he account for sick days, health insurance, retirement, or taxes. With these additional costs, Rennie actually made less than Delaware's $7.25 hourly minimum wage. Although Rennie's strategy was impracticable, he found it empowering. Sadly, Rennie taught us that negative social treatment, professional rejection, and being overworked was realistically his only legal option.

Conclusion

Largely missing from the reentry literature are ethnographic analyses of street-identified Black men's perceptions of returning citizens and formal reentry programs. Street-identified Black men have invaluable perspectives that can greatly improve services, offer insights about cultural worldviews and structural conditions surrounding the reentry process, and could help community professionals. Contrary to the reentry literature's dominant individualistic or personal accountability frameworks, we found that street-identified Black men cared deeply about people returning home from prison, and they wanted to help returning citizens reenter in a more dignified way.

It is imperative that reentry service providers and organizations recognize and explicitly incorporate in their programming how street-identified Black men sincerely desired to be legally employed. Although these men were hard workers and very willing to accept low-wage work, they were more interested in pursuing their entrepreneurial aspirations. And reentry organizations needed to figure out how to nurture their motivation to own businesses and create wealth. Reentry providers also needed to publicly express to the men and their communities that structural violence, not their personal or cultural failings, was much more of an explanation for their incarceration and harrowing experiences with reentry. Such acknowledgement, even with the structural barriers, would help to establish the trust that is often missing from the men and service providers.

"I Can't Depend on No Reentry Program!" 407

Returning Black men in Wilmington genuinely wanted to stay out of prison, but their recidivism rates did not reflect this goal. In many instances, being in the streets made more cognitive and cultural sense to them; it was better to risk the dangers of the streets (i.e., injury, prison, death) and provide for themselves and their loved-ones rather than doing nothing and draining precious family resources. Permanently boxed into a life of disenfranchisement, many participants willingly submitted themselves to an ethos of rugged individualism and willingly acquiesced to humiliation because they had no choice.

In particular, study participants conceptualized the justice system and parole as a profit-generating industry designed to perpetuate institutionalized racism. Felony convictions, parole violations, unemployment, inadequate educational opportunities, and poor housing, as well as lackluster prison reentry programs and service providers, were understood as apparatuses of a larger structural violence complex. Given the stakes, Black men repeatedly reminded us that successful reentry required firm discipline, with little material return, over a prolonged period of time. Countless narratives described how the cyclical triad of street involvement, incarceration, and reentry was filled with sadness and joys, successes and failures, and in some instances, redemption.

Note

1. Training was provided by partners in the collaborative effort. The Metropolitan Wilmington Urban League provided job training; faculty and graduate students from one university provided case management; and other partners provided media, political, infrastructural, and funding support, as well as employment and educational opportunities.

References

Arditti, J. A., & Parkman, T. (2011). Young men's reentry after incarceration: A developmental paradox. *Family Relations, 60*(2), 205–220.

Baum, F., MacDougall, C., & Smith, D. (2006). Participatory action research. *Journal of Epidemiology & Community Health, 60*(10), 854–857.

Carson, A. E. (2018). *Prisoners in 2016.* Washington, DC: U.S. Department of Justice, Office of Justice Programs. Retrieved January 18, 2019, from www.bjs.gov/content/pub/pdf/p16.pdf

The City of Wilmington Delaware. (2018). Population & demographics: City of Wilmington Census 2010 data. Retrieved September 1, 2018, from www.wilmingtonde.gov/about-us/about-the-city-of-wilmington/population-demographics

Contreras, R. (2012). *The stick-up kids: Race, drugs, violence and the American dream.* Los Angeles, CA: University of California Press.

Duck, W. (2016). *No way out: Precarious living in the shadow of poverty and drug-dealing.* Chicago, IL: University of Chicago.

Galtung, J. (1969). Violence, peace, and peace research. *Journal of Peace Research, 6*(4), 167–191.

Gunnison, E., & Helfgott, J. B. (2011). Factors that hinder offender reentry success: A view from community corrections officers. *International Journal of Offender Therapy and Comparative Criminology, 55*(2), 287–304.

Hlavka, H. R., Wheelock, D., & Cossyleon, J. E. (2015). Narratives of commitment: Looking for work with a criminal record. *The Sociological Quarterly, 56*(2), 213–236.

John, H. (2016). Work wisdom: Teaching former prisoners how to negotiate workplace interactions and perform a rehabilitated self. *Ethnography, 17*(1), 72–91.

Johnson, O. O. (2017). *The voices of survivors: The lived experiences of African American males who enter reentry or rehabilitation programs after incarceration: Culturally-informed lessons learned* (Doctoral Dissertation, Saybrook University).

Kervick, C., & MacLeish, T. F. (2015). *Recidivism in Delaware: An analysis of prisoners released in 2009 through 2011.* Dover, DE: State of Delaware Statistical Analysis Center.

Middlemass, K. M. (2017). *Convicted and condemned: The politics and policies of prisoner reentry.* New York: New York University Press.

Panuccio, E., & Christian, J. (2019). Work, family, and masculine identity: An intersectional approach to understanding young, Black men's experiences of reentry. *Race and Justice, 9*(4), 407–433.

Payne, Y. A. (2011). Site of resilience: A reconceptualization of resiliency and resilience in street life-oriented Black men. *Journal of Black Psychology, 37*(4), 426–451.

Payne, Y. A. (2016). "I am a man too!": Masculinity, economic violence and resilience in *The Streets* of Black America. In J. Sullivan & W. E. Cross (Eds.), *Meaning-making, internalized racism, and African-American identity.* Albany, NY: SUNY Press.

Payne, Y. A. (2017). Participatory action research. In B. S. Turner, C. Kyung-Sup, C. F. Epstein, P. Kivisto, & W. Outhwaite (Eds.), *The Wiley Blackwell encyclopedia of social theory* (pp. 1–15). Hoboken, NJ: Wiley-Blackwell.

Payne, Y. A., & Brown, T. M. (2016). "I'm still waiting on that golden ticket": Attitudes toward and experiences with opportunity in "The Streets" of Black America. *Journal of Social Issues, 72*(4), 789–811.

Payne, Y. A., & Brown, T. M. (2017). "It's set up for failure . . . and they know this!": How the school-to-prison pipeline impacts the educational experiences of street identified Black youth and young adults. *Villanova Law Review, 62*(2), 307–326.

Payne, Y. A., Hitchens, B. K., & Chambers, D. L. (2017, December). "Why I Can't Stand Out in Front of My House?": Street-identified Black youth and young adult's negative encounters with police. *Sociological Forum, 32*(4), 874–895.

Payne, Y. A., & Bryant, A. (2018). Street participatory action research (Street PAR) in prison: A methodology to challenge privilege and power in correctional facilities. *The Prison Journal, 98*(4), 449–469.

Plummer Community Corrections Center. (2013). *Plummer community corrections center/ department of corrections.* Retrieved September 1, 2018, from https://doc.delaware.gov/ views/plummerccc.blade.shtml

Rossman, S.B. & Roman, C.G. (2003). Case-managed reentry and employment: Lessons from the opportunity to succeed program. *Justice Research and Policy, 5*(2), 75–100.

Trimbur, L. (2009). "Me and the law is not friends": How former prisoners make sense of reentry. *Qualitative Sociology, 32*(3), 259–277.

Conclusion
What's Next for Critical Reentry

CalvinJohn Smiley and Keesha M. Middlemass

This volume set out to explore, understand, and assess reentry in the 21st century. Moreover, it lends itself to establishing a critical voice within this growing field of social science research. The various contributors offer critical and transformative ways of understanding the reentry process, and summarize some of the programs offered to returning citizens. This foray into what we call, critical reentry studies, hopes to offer greater insight into the realm of post-incarceration by bringing new paradigms, theories, and epistemologies to this important field of study.

It is important to recognize the ever-changing nature of language surrounding the topic of reentry, which is visible throughout this volume. When it comes to the field of "reentry," there are not universally accepted terms, as different words have various political connotations associated with them. For example, the term "prisoner reentry" has, in some circles, been simply shortened to "reentry" to remove the stigma and label of prison. Additionally, the terms used to describe individuals coming out of institutional settings have evolved from "ex-cons" to "former prisoners" to "former felons" to "formerly incarcerated" to "justice-affected persons" to "returning citizens." These sometimes subtle, but drastic, word changes highlight the growing understanding about what language is used to describe the shifting focus from the individual to the institution, which challenges who has the responsibility of supporting individuals' successful reentry. The conscious effort to destigmatize the reentry experience is important as it highlights the need to continue to provide more scholarship, activism, and policy analysis on this topic.

The Russian writer, Fyodor Dostoevsky, wrote, "The degree of civilization in society can be judged by entering its prisons" (Shapiro, 2006). A 21st century adaptation of this quote could read: "The degree of civilization in society can be judged by *exiting* its prisons." Hundreds of thousands of women and men leave American jails and prisons annually with extraordinary rates of recidivism, and as this volume highlights, there are many complicated and intersecting issues that make reentry hard. Hence, we can surmise that the vast majority of those exiting prison cells leave ill-prepared for their return to society and often with no more skills or education than when they went into prison. Quite literally, millions of American residents have cycled through the criminal justice system over the last 50 years since the inception of the "tough on crime" focus of the early 1970s, which has made the United States the world's leader in incarceration and by extension reentry.

The United States has primarily focused on retributive punishment that instills a culture of cruelty within jails and prisons. For example, recently, five members of MOVE, a revolutionary Black activist group founded and located in Philadelphia, Pennsylvania, have been released from prison.[1] Known as The MOVE 9, each were sentenced to a maximum of 100 years in prison. The MOVE 9 were incarcerated because of a standoff with the police in 1978; during that stand-off, James Ramp was killed; he was a Philadelphia police officer, and was shot in the back of the neck as the police attempted to enter MOVE's Powelton Village House (Pilkington, 2018). Nine MOVE members were tried and convicted of the 1978 death of Ramp, despite conflicting accounts of the shooting. The MOVE 9, as well as eyewitnesses, claim Ramp died from friendly fire because the fatal shot came from the opposite direction from where MOVE members were located (Pilkington, 2018). The MOVE 9 were charged with third-degree murder for Ramp's death and incarcerated in Pennsylvania State prison facilities. To date, two members of the MOVE 9 died while incarcerated; Merle Africa in 1998 at age 47, and Phil Africa, in 2015, at age 59. Each of the MOVE 9 were eligible for a parole hearing starting in 2008, and every year parole has been denied until 2018. After serving more than 40 years in prison, in June 2018 Debbie Sims Africa and in October 2018 Michael Africa were released. The following year, May 2019, Janine and Janet Africa were released on parole, and most recently Eddie Goodman Africa was released in June 2019. Meanwhile, Chuck and Delbert Africa remain imprisoned.

We highlight this case as a profound example of state sanctioned violence; by insisting on such lengthy sentences, the state was condemning the MOVE 9 to death; the fact that several have been released means that they must now think about reentering society in the 21st century. As discussed in the Introduction, those who were sentenced to long punitive sentences in the 1970s, 1980s, and 1990s are coming home, and it will be necessary for individuals, their remaining family members, and communities to grapple with the complicated realities of reentry, particularly as society has changed in numerous ways since the MOVE 9 were initially incarcerated. Thinking about how society has changed from 1978 to 2019, the question looms: Will individuals who have served such extremely long sentences be able to function in society or will they simply exist and survive in a society in which its institutions do not offer the proper training, tools, and preparation to come back to society? The contributors in this volume demonstrate that reentering society is often a struggle to survive.

As indicated by the individual chapters, the state is heavily involved in criminal justice, incarceration, and reentry, yet it is rare that prisons offer proper or appropriate types of educational programs (see Willingham chapter) and fail to provide parenting classes (Reviere et al. chapter). Additionally, programs to deal with physical and mental health issues rarely address the underlying issues of individuals' addiction, trauma, or circumstances of their upbringing (Section V chapters). Several chapters in this volume look at how trauma leads to imprisonment, but policies over the last 50 years have systematically curbed institutions from providing the services men and women who are incarcerated need.

The criminal justice system has poured billions of dollars into surveillance, technology, weaponry, policing, corrections, prisons, and other punitive measures, such as using restrictive long-term housing (Carson chapter). Policies under various state and federal administrations have helped inflate the prison population, yet far less has been invested in restorative justice, community reinvestment, employment, and anti-poverty legislation that would ensure housing, education, and healthcare for all residents, especially those who are reentering society. Therefore, the focus on reentry must be two-fold.

First, reentry programs need to place a greater emphasis on proactive approaches to equity prior to any form of criminal justice contact or intervention. Although this is technically not reentry, the focus is on creating communities that are safe and affordable, which protect rather than punish, and reduce the likelihood of entering the criminal justice system in the first place. Second, reentry should not begin when a person is exiting a prison setting, but when they arrive, from the first day of incarceration forward (Reentry Ready, 2019). The purpose of prison should no longer be primarily about punishment, but prison should be viewed as an opportunity to restore individuals by incorporating case management care that focuses on individual needs (e.g., mental health, trauma), providing the necessary programs to address individual deficits (e.g., educational attainment, vocational training), and creating a sequence of classes that prepares individuals to return to society (e.g., family reunification, parenting skills, resource management and access). For reentry to be successful based on this model, then families and communities harmed by prison and taking on the responsibilities of helping their loved-one reenter should also be offered services; we know that neighborhoods of disadvantaged backgrounds are struggling the most.

A moral failure is to view incarceration, and by greater extension crime, as an individual problem. The moment it was viewed as an individual's responsibility based on bad behavior and breaking the social contract, society stopped looking at the larger structural reasons about why crime occurs, as well as why only certain segments of society are overly impacted by the criminal justice system (see Bronson & Carson, 2019). Understanding how policies, racism, gender, and other structural barriers impact individual lives and therefore influence their decision-making is vital to a critical reentry studies lens so that we can move forward in changing reentry practices. Reentry does not happen in a vacuum and individuals who are not supported cannot be expected to adjust and "do better."

The American liberal notion of individualism manifests in many of the more popularized narratives of reentry, where individuals tell their stories of overcoming all obstacles. Although this is commendable, it is often not the reality; many need support, assistance, and networks to rely on, which is the responsibility of the state. Reentry will *not* get better spontaneously or organically; like many changes to policy surrounding prison and incarceration, changes in reentry will come from prison activism and grassroots approaches that highlight disparities and call for equality and from critical reentry studies. For instance, prison movements, such as the 1971 Attica Rebellion, shed light on the inhumane conditions of carceral settings (Thompson, 2017). The takeover of Walpole Prison in 1973 highlighted the many ways persons incarcerated could find common ground and work together (Bissonette, 2008). The written works by individuals who experience incarceration first hand, such as Angela Davis, Leonard Peltier, Mumia Abu-Jamal, and Assata Shakur (to name a few), emphasize the ways prison conditions impact the human spirit, mind, and body.

One important takeaway from this volume is that *prisons do not prepare individuals for release*. Prisons are solely used as places of quarantine to temporarily segregate individuals from the larger society as punishment for violation of social norms, mores, and rules. While incarcerated, contributors' chapters demonstrate that individuals experience various forms of psychological and emotion violence, such as the use of solitary confinement, withholding of basic hygienic supplies, and other forms of torment. Additionally, prisons are breeding grounds for hyper-physical violence, which can lead to bodily injury and death, as well as exacerbate mental health issues, such as depression, anxiety, mood disorders, and post-traumatic stress disorder. If our society wants to help individuals coming home, we must actively rethink our punishment system. In fact, it is imperative to do this by replacing punishment with a restorative justice system and welfare policy. The culture of our society must move from being focused on retributive justice that creates adversarial models to more compassionate models. The future of reentry is reliant on making systems whole rather than further fractured.

The criminal justice system disproportionately impacts people of color, namely Black and Latinx folks. However, there is a growing need to understand that even within these populations there are further marginalized sub-groups that need to be recognized, appreciated, and focused on, particularly recognizing their unique needs (Booth's chapter on reentry for individuals convicted of sex crimes). There are multiple glaring stories of how criminal justice institutions inflict pain on Black women (see Battle and William's chapter), and how individuals in the LGBTQ+ populations are further marginalized.

Although this volume does not address the specific needs of the LGBTQ community, we encourage future scholars to critically assess how they are treated. Studies have shown that transgender individuals experience disproportionate rates of poverty, homelessness, and unemployment compared to the general population (Transgender FAQ, 2018). One example of this occurred in June 2019, when a transgender woman, Layleen Cubilette-Polanco, who was arrested in April, was found dead in her cell at New York City's largest jail, Riker's Island. Cubilette-Polanco was being held at Riker's because she could not afford bail, which was set at $500. Her death highlights one of the biggest travesties of the current cash bail and reentry system (see Smiley's chapter on Bail Reform). The criminal justice system and current bail system have been designed as an apparatus that criminalizes low-income residents. The cash bail system delays and prevents reentry from occurring and the longer a person remains incarcerated the more difficult the reentry process becomes (Lowenkamp, VanNostrand, & Holsinger, 2013). This story, while tragic, is unfortunately not an isolated incident in America. Future research, particularly on marginalized populations within already marginalized communities, must be the focus of future reentry scholarship in order to put pressure on policy-makers to ensure human and civil rights of all people are not being violated.

Finally, there have been scholars, activists, entrepreneurs, politicians, and other community leaders who have sought to create and implement the best reentry model(s) in an effort to lower the rate of recidivism. Although the intention of this rationale is good, it is ultimately flawed because it intends to keep a system intact that will disproportionately incarcerate and release disadvantaged members of society. Therefore, the best model for reentry is to ultimately not have a need for reentry. The only way society can get to a point where reentry is no longer needed is by swapping out the need to incarcerate and use other punitive practices and replace them with alternative methods to deal with crime, social wrong doers, and trauma.

We want this edited volume to contribute to the ongoing narrative and discourse about reentry, and encourage scholars to look at reentry through a new lens of critical reentry studies. Critical reentry studies offer scholars an opportunity to challenge the norms of the system in order to think about creating and implementing a transformative understanding about reentry experiences of individuals who are actively going through the reentry process. The goal should be to push society to think beyond prison walls.

Note

1. MOVE is not an acronym; rather, it is a purposeful name chosen by one of its leaders, John Africa. The title is what members of the organization intend to do – move, act, change, progress, and advance – as it pertained to fighting for equal importance of Black lives and Black bodies. MOVE, as an organization, was modeled after the Black Panthers and green politics (i.e., animal rights advocacy).

References

Bissonette, J. (2008). *When the prisoners ran Walpole: A true story in the movement for prison abolition.* Cambridge, MA: South End Press.

Bronson, J., & Carson, E. A. (2019). *Prisoners in 2017.* NCJ 252156. Washington, DC: U.S. Department of Justice, Bureau of Justice Statistics.

Lowenkamp, C. T., VanNostrand, M., & Holsinger, A. (2013). *The hidden costs of pretrial detention.* Houston, TX: The Laura & John Arnold Foundation.

Pilkington, E. (2018, June 18). 'This is huge': Black liberationist speaks out after her 40 years in prison. *The Guardian.* Retrieved June 27, 2019, from www.theguardian.com/us-news/2018/jun/18/debbie-sims-africa-free-prison-move-nine-philadelphia-police

Reentry Ready. (2019). *Reentry ready: Improving incarceration's contribution to successful reentry.* Washington, DC: Convergence Center for Policy Resolution. Retrieved from www.convergencepolicy.org/latest-projects/successful-reintegration/

Shapiro, F. R. (2006). *The Yale book of quotations.* New Haven, CT: Yale University Press.

Thompson, H. A. (2017). *Blood in the water: The Attica prison uprising of 1971 and its legacy.* New York: Vintage.

Transgender FAQ. (2018, June 1). *GLAAD.* Retrieved from www.glaad.org/transgender/transfaq

Index

#MeToo 215, 219, 228
#SayHerName 152, 182, 184, 347
¾ houses 11, 373; *see also* halfway house
12 step Program 18, 19, 21, 23, 121, 195; *see also* Alcoholics Anonymous; drugs
8th Amendment 347
13th Amendment 290
14th Amendment 247, 249, 255, 262
15th Amendment 249, 261

Adam Walsh Act (AWA) 222
addiction 47, 55, 73, 79, 80, 87, 89, 90, 102, 120, 121, 152, 162, 204, 205, 211, 279, 296–7, 385, 389, 404, 411; alcohol 195, 205–6; recovery 16, 18, 23, 81, 120, 121, 124–5, 204, 360, 385
Addiction Severity Index (ASI) 162
administrative segregation 96, 99, 101, 296, 388; long term segregation 164; regimes 108; *see also* supermax
AIDS 207, 220; *see also* HIV
alcohol 5, 47, 67, 70–1, 73, 81, 87, 90, 162, 191, 195–6, 275, 385; abstinence 124; Alcohol Use Disorder (AUD) 120; *see also* addiction; drugs
Alcoholics Anonymous (AA) 18, 30, 121, 124, 304; *see also* alcohol programs; drugs
Amendment 4 (Florida) 217, 247, **253**, 259–60, 262–5, 266, 269–71, 272n4, 272n5; *see also* felon disenfranchisement; voting; voting rights
anti-Black: policies 255–6
Anti-Recidivism Coalition (ARC) 387
Auburn Correctional Facility 275, 372

bail 180, 219, 345–53
Balla v. Idaho State Board of Corrections (1984) 57, 59–60
Black Panther Party 172–3, 174–6, 178–81

Black radicalism 172, 177
Bland, Sandra 173, 177, 182–3, 185, 347
Browder, Kalief 345, 346, 352
Brown, Elaine 175
Building Opportunities for Self Sufficiency (BOSS) 336, 338n3
Bureau of Prisons (BOP) 43, 122
business profit model 300, 308, 318n4; *see also* Reentry, Inc.

California 35, 359–60, 385, 387, 391, 398
California Department of Corrections and Rehabilitation (CDCR) 232, 329
California maximum-security 178
California State University, Long Beach 343, 382, 384–7, 389
California State University, Los Angeles 390
California State University, San Bernardino 216, 233, 236
calisthenics 81, 129, 131
carceral space 60, 110, 131, 179, 220, 296, 315, 341, 342, 412; non-carceral sites 41, 240, **241**, 242, 240
case management 31, 39, 45, 161, 233–4, 237, 239, 241, 242, 308, 324n1; manager 212, 241, 308
children 80, 83, 86, 87–8, 89, 90, 100, 110, 112, 114, 115–16, 147, 149, 151, 160, 176, 194, 196, 198–9, 204, 217, 220, 221–2, 224, 225–6, 234–5, **238**, 242, 277, 285–6, 297–8, 300, 302, 304, 306, 307–8, 309–10, 316, 350, 361, 385, 405–6; child support 89, 217, 218, 250, **253**, 256, 278–84, 323
Circles of Support and Accountability (COSA) 227; *see also* restorative justice
civil death 224–5, 260; disabilities 215
civil rights 58, 220, 248–9, **253**, 256, 261–2, 264, 413; organizations 263
Civil Rights Act, 1964 (CRA) 48

416 Index

Civil Rights Movement 172, 341
Cleaver, Kathleen 175, 176, 178, 181, 185
cognitive behavioral therapy (CBT) 46, 57, 122–3, 233–4, 399; cognitive skills 100, 121, 162, 407; disequilibrium 111, 296
COINTELPRO 176–7, 180–1
collateral consequences 88, 215, 218, 226–7, 260–1, 275, 345, 357, 362
College Prison Education Initiative 207
Commercial Driver's License (CDL) 323
community college 30, 207, 211, 232–3, 237, 303, 386, 388, 389–91
community activism 219, 341, 342, 345, 357–64, 399
community-based facilities, organizations, services 28, 32, 33, 44, 61, 88, 89–90, 114, 123, 162, 165, 177, 191, 193, 232–3, 301, 329, 336, 337, 338, 349; corrections 191, 370; justice 181
community notification 216, 221, 223
community supervision 224–5, 234, 325; see also parole; probation
Conservation Fire Camp 291, 329, 330; CalFire 329, 331
conviction 36, 54, 59, 66, 68, 79, 85, 109, 130, 141–2, 215, 217–18, 220, 222–3, 224, 226, 248, 250, 251–2, 256, 259, 261, 263, 265, 285, 291, 307, 308–9, 341, 348, 383, 398, 402–3, 407; see also criminal record
coping 76, 87, 89, 90, 102, 134, 135–6, 141, 191, 205, 306, 316, 364, 403
corrections 411; correctional environment 109, 122, 308; correctional/prison staff and administrators 27, 33, 34, 43, 80, 102, 142–3, 161, 163, 164, 165, 192, 308, 313; correctional supervision 191, 192, 199, 247, 249, 250, 252, 255–6, 256n2, 277, 278, 281, 291; corrections officers (COs) 28, 35, 178, 276, 290, 293, 320, 321, 329, 330, 331, 332–3, 338; facilities 124, 159, 200, 290, 318, 322, 336–7; gender-responsive 165–6; New York City 351; practices 41, 60, 161; prison guards 35, 36, 152, 206, 296, 298; programming 28, 29, 57, 86, 88, 102, 242–3, 304; system 163, 165, 275, 306, 308, 311, 313, 315, 325, 327, 328
Corrections Corporation of America (CCA) 313
credible messenger 357–60, 362–5
criminal justice reform 26, 27, 42, 102, 131, 213, 216, 219–20, 342, 346, 357; 342, 346, 357; New Jersey Criminal

Justice Reform 352; revolutionary reform 108, 110, 116
criminal records 18, 23, 42, 68, 75, 89, 131, 208–9, 210, 215, 217, 239, 240, 277–8, 282, 285–6, 328, 359, 362, 383; arrest 193, 236, **239**, 250, 251, 256, 265, 275–8, 279, 282, 284, 285–6, 303, 316, 321, 328
Crist, Governor Charlie 262, 264
critical intersectional analysis 80, 83, 84, 86, 90–1, 172, 215, 255; see also intersectionality
critical penology 41, 43, 49
critical race theory 173

Davis, Angela 173, 177, 178–9, 318n1, 412
death 120, 180, 184, 205, 225, 307, 311, 314, 347, 360, 363, 388, 407, 410, 412–3; penalty 179, 295, 353; row 180, 290, 295–6
debt 66, 69, 73, 74, 278–80, 282, 283–4, 285
deficiency framework 130
Democratic Party 217, 262, 263, 265, 267, 269, 271
DeSantis, Governor Ron 263, **269**, 270
desistance 66, 67, 71, 75, 76, 159, 232, 348, 383–4, 402; alcohol 120, 121
discharge 48, 257n4, 338n1
disenfranchisement 157, 216–17, 224, 248, 251, 252, 255–6, 407; see also felony disenfranchisement; voting
Dollar Bail Brigade 350, 351
domestic violence 45, 72, 73, 86, 87, 211, 385
drugs 120, 175, 191, 194–5, 306, 336, 376, 385–6, 404–5; abstinence/desistance 70–1, 124, 385; abuse 31, 33, 47, 70, 87, 120, 121, 122–3, 236, 275, 281; addiction 30, 73, 107, 204, 205–6, 211, 279, 296, 306, 311; dealing/selling 109, 150, 181, 195, 204, 209, 325; education 122; charge/offense/possession 107, 158, 159, 195, 235, 275, 285, 325, 346, 351, 353; race 152; substance abuse 33, 55, 58, 123, 150, 157, 158, 159–60, 162, 164–5, 191, 195–6, 198, 206, 211, 235, 236, 338n3, 384; treatment 55, 56, 191, 193, 195–6, 211, 275; use 17, 19, 31, 87, 158, 162, 163, 209; violence 150; War on Drugs 79, 83, 84–5, 109, 275, 326; women 109, 150, 151–2, 158

education 23, 26, 28, 29–30, 48, 66, 68, 69, 83, 86, 90–1, 99–100, 102, 124, 130, 135, 157, 159, 160, 165, 175,

177–8, 180, 181, 190, 193, 198–9, 216, 223, 232, 234, 256, 286, 301, 302, 304, 313, 323, 343, 346, 348, 350, 351, 363, 382, 384, 386–92, 400, 402, 404, 407, 410–11; Alcohol Use Disorder (AUD) 121; higher education 143, 203–4, 216, 232, 235, 236, **241**, 296; inside out 203, 205, 211–12, 370; programs for women 205–6, 209, 212–13; reentry educational kit 336; voter education 263, 264–5, 270
employment 23, 24, 29, 30, 32, 53–4, 55, 56, 66, 68, 69, 72, 74, 75–6, 85, 89–90, 100, 102, 129–30, 157, 161, 165, 175, 190, 196, 198–9, 203, 213, 215, 216–17, 223, 232, 233–4, 236, **238**, 243n1, 256, 277, 281, 285, 291, 301, 303, 316, 346, 348, 353, 368, 386–7, 397–8, 400–1, 403–6, 411; discrimination 48; job 23, 66, 69, 70, 71, 73, 74–5, 97, 99, 100–1, 102, 190, 195, 196, 197–9, 203, 206, 208, 210, 212, 237, 243n1, 281, 285; unemployment 124, 175, 181, 203, 210; work 108, 151, 195, 198, 200, 224, 225, 237, **238**, 280, 282, 278, 279–80, 281–3, 286, 301, 323, 363, 385–7, 390–1, 396, 399, 406, 407, 413
entrepreneurialism 342, 345, 373, 403, 405–6, 413
evidence-based practices 11, 26, 27–9, 30–1, 36, 225; lack of evidence 224–5, 226

family 16, 17, 21, 28, 30, 70, 71–2, 73, 75, 88, 89–90, 97, 100, 102, 108, 112, 124, 157, 165, 180, 193, 206, 210, 234–5, **238**, 243n1, 276, 277, 284, 291, 298–9, 302, 303–4, 307–8, 311, 313, 316, 321, 323, 325–6, 327–8, 332, 333, 335, 337, 338n1, 342, 346, 347, 358, 361–3, 365, 373, 376–7, 385, 401, 405, 410; Black family 150–1, 398; counseling 193–4, 195, 199; court 278–9, 280, 282, 283–4, 286; estrangement 114, 190, 204, 312, 317, 332–3; reunification 32, 303, 313, 411; stranger danger 225–6; support 373, 398, 407; violence 109, 228n1, 235
father 15, 72, 74, 83, 87, 115–16, 147, 151, 160, 196, 199, 200, 279–81, 283, 286, 299, 306, 307, 309, 316, 326, 363, 385–6, 406
felon disenfranchisement 216–17, 248–52, **253**, 254–5, 261, 262, 270–1, 378; see also disenfranchisement; voting
felony lynching 183
feminist criminology 108, 142, 158, 186

Florida 215, 217, 220, 224, 247, **253**, 255, 256n1, 257n3, 259–60, 261–2, 263, 264–6, 267–8, **269**, 270–1, 370, 373, 375, 377
Florida Board of Executive Clemency 247, 251, **253**, 262, 264–5, 270
Fortune Society 368, 374
foster care 87, 151, 194, 233, 279

gangs 17, 60, 132, 163, 208, 342, 360–3, 369, 387, 389; Original Gangsters 357; prevention 390
gender 86, 88, 91, 133, 137n2, 141, 190, 221, 235, **238**, 296, 305, 321, 342, 347, 349, 351, 360, 411; criminality 141, 142; criminal justice system 141–2, 145–6, 153, 349; differences 46, 83, 142, 145, 153, 161, 196, 200, 213, 299–300; expectations 84, 142–3, 145–6, 150, 151, 153–4n2, 175–6, 198, 200; gender-responsive strategies 142, 161–2, 165, 190; gender-specific programs 198–9; hierarchies 145, 148, 174, 184; norms 141, 145, 148, 150, 152, 200; oppression 173, 180, 213; pathways 203, 211; politics 172; programs 141, 142, 160, 162, 190–1; reentry 165, 296; roles 146–7, 148, 153, 153–4n2, 175–6; social conditions 172, 209; stereotypes 145, 147, 149, 150–1, 152, 200; violence 148, 150, 152; see also women
General Equivalency/Education Diploma (GED) 30, 32, 99, 324n1
Gillum, Andrew 263, **269**, 271
Greenhaven Prison 372

halfway house 11, 15, 17–18, 66–7, 206, 289, 373
Hayden v. Pataki (2006) 249
Hernandez, Pedro 346
high risk offenders 29, 30–2, 226
HIV 86, 163, 164, 198, 207, 209, 210, 220, 338n3; see also AIDS
homeless 22, 54–5, 66, 80, 85, 87, 89, 90, 124, 159, 163, 209, 210, 211, **238**, 266, 275, 309, 311, 413
housing 47, 54–6, 66, 68, 71, 89, 129, 157, 164, 175, 181, 191, 215, 217, 224, 227, **238**, 256, 260, 285, 301, 302, 316, 324n1, 387; prison 110, 115, 164, 403–5, 407; projects 362, 364; restrictive 80, 96; sex crimes 215, 224–5, transitional 55–6, 301; see also administrative segregation; supermax

418 Index

Howell v. McAuliffe (2016) 251–2
Hudson Link 370–1, 379

ID13 Prison Literacy Project 305, 315, 317, 318n1
Idaho 53
Idaho Department of Corrections (IDOC) 53, 55, 56–8, 60
inside out *see* education
intersectional 141, 145, 146, 172, 233, 235–6, 237, 239, 241–2, 255; criminology 142, 172, 178, 184–6; framework 142
Iowa 251–2, **253**, 257n3, 257n4
Iowa Correctional Institution for Women (ICIW) 27–8, 32, 34, 35

Jackson College Prison Education Initiative 207, 213
jail 16, 46, 55, 58, 71, 83, 88, 108, 159, 175, 182–3, 219, 251, 256n2, 260, 275, 276–7, 279, 280–1, 283, 284, 298–9, 307, 309, 310, 312, 320–1, 325, 332, 342, 345–53, 402–3, 406, 409–10, 413; Alcoholics Anonymous inside 123–4; rural jail 61
Jay-Z 351–2
Jefferson County Correctional Facility 291
Jim Crow 83, 255
job training 27, 34, 56, 72, 74, 233–4, 323, 324n1, 387, 396, 399, 405; vocational 100, 191, **239**, 323; *see also* employment
Justice Reinvestment Initiative (JRI) 57
juvenile offenders 142–3, 190–2, 194, 196, 198, 234, 236, 276, 329

labeling 99, 112, 219–20, 228n1, 304, 327, 409; *see also* stigma
Lake Erie Correctional Institute (LaECI) 290, 318n1
LGBTQ 221, 351, 353, 412–13; *see also* transgender
life course 12, 66, 67, 74, 76, 141, 348
lifers 294, 295–6
liminality 11, 17–18, 23, 24
Louisiana 224, 225, 252

masculinity 198, 315
mass imprisonment/incarceration 12, 116, 306, 357–8, 364–5
medication-assisted treatments (MAT) 122, 225
Megan's Law 220, 221–2, 223, 224
mental health 29, 30, 32, 47, 79, 80, 81, 83, 85–6, 87, 88, 89, 90–1, 97–8, 114, 116, 130, 134–5, 158, 159–60, 162, 163,

165, 174, 207, 283, 296–7, 308, 309–10, 315, 320, 327, 358, 364–5, 411–12; diagnosis 102, 207; disorders 120, 122, 235; impairment 151; incompetent 261; mental illness 99, 107, 123, 151–2, 158, 159, 162, 163, 204, 296, 338n3, 361, 363; resources 152
Michael Hand et al vs. Rick Scott et al (2018) 247, 256n1, 262
Mill, Meek 327–8, 351
Minnesota Correctional Facility 204, 207, 209
mother 70, 73, 80, 83–4, 85, 87–8, 89–91, 107, 111, 114, 147, 149, 191, 193, 194–5, 198–9, 205, 211–12, 320, 326–7, 328, 352, 372, 375, 385, 388–9; Black 116, 147, 149, 151, 279–81, 283–4, 285–6, 298–9, 302, 350; incarcerated 115, 160, 350; pregnant 115, 151, 152, 160, 182, 191, 193, 194, 196, 198, 199, 209, 279
MOVE 410, 413n1

Narcotics Anonymous (NA) 18, 22, 30, 302; *see also* addiction; drugs; substance abuse
National Bailout 350
Nelson, U.S. Senator Bill **268**, 269
New Jersey 181–2, 290, 322, 323, 352–3, 360
New York City 179, 181, 275, 276, 277–8, 279, 280, 283, 284, 285, 320, 325, 327, 346–7, 350, 363–4, 374, 413
New York State 321, 326, 369; penitentiaries 370, 373; Theological Seminary (NYTS) 370
non-governmental organizations (NGOs) 39; not-for-profit, nonprofit organizations, service providers 130, 136, 165, 387, 399–400
nonviolent offenders 57, 85, 107, 219, **253**, 275, 285, 325

Ohio 101, 220, 290, 309, 311
Ohio Department of Rehabilitation and Correction (ODRC) 305, 318n3
Osborne Association 368
Otisville Penitentiary 372, 378

parole 12, 16, 18, 26, 27, 28, 31–2, 43, 54, 55, 57–8, 60, 68, 102, 124, 157, 159, 162, 219, 232, 234, 236, 249, 250–2, **253**, 256, 256n2, 263–4, 276–8, 281, 286, 291, 323, 325, 331, 333–4, 335, 338, 338n1, 375, 382, 388, 397–8, 403–4, 407, 410; in Germany 75; officers 370, 375–6

Index   419

Peace Initiative 372; peace builders 362; peace 363, 385
Pennsylvania 276, 277, 278, 285, 303; Department of Corrections 283, 382
political repression *see* felon disenfranchisement
politics 247, 248, 251, 263; abolition 137n2, 345, 349–53; plantation 148; prison 132, 388
post-incarceration 260; post-prison 46, 66, 67, 69, 70, 75, 76, 86, 90–1, 134, 215, 216, 217, 289, 323, 325, 333; post-punishment 260; post-release 121, 213, 220, 232; post-sentence 248–9, 250, 252, **253**, 254–5
prison design: carceral settings 81, 108, 110, 113–14, 115–16, 131, 133–4, 137n6, 315, 322; environment 122, 129; maximum-security 382; penal setting 132–3
prison programs 26, 29, 31, 36, 89, 122, 203, 205–6, 209, 212–13, 232, 341–3, 369–70
prison guards *see* correctional officers (COs)
prison industrial complex 108, 129, 219, 227, 306, 318n1, 351
prison movement 58–60, 108, 113
prisons-within-prisons *see* administrative segregation; supermax/super-maximum
probation 16, 18, 26, 27, 31, 54, 55–7, 60, 75, 183–4, 193–4, 195, 208, 209, 219, 236, 247, 250, 251–2, **253**, 256, 256n2, 257n4, 263–4, 291, 302, 321, 325, 335, 338
Project Morry 326
Project Rebound 216, 232, 233, 236–8, 240, **241**

Quakers 372

racism 39, 129, 145, 147, 177, 248, 254–5; structural 145, 180–1, 254, 363, 407
recidivism 12, 45, 57, 59, 66–7, 70, 88, 90, 100, 113, 122, 203, 212–13, 226, 232, 234–5, 236, 242, 266, 305, 308, 316, 323, 352, 373, 399–401, 403–4, 407, 409, 413; Ant-Recidivism Coalition 387
reentry 121, 129, 141, 203–4, 232, 236, 247, 256, 289–90, 293, 305, 315, 322, 331, 341–3, 345, 347–9, 353, 358–60, 368–9, 371, 382, 387, 392, 409–13; AUD programs 124, 371, 378, 396–407; barriers/challenges 107, 163, 165, 200, 215–16, 220, 296, 328, 336, 357; community 120, 121–2, 123, 124,

210, 375; critical reentry 113, 116, 129–30, 135, 136, 143; discrimination 107; education 143, 203; gender 141–2, 142, 157, 165; juvenile 192, 196–7; movement 129, 130, 135; organizations 130, 136, 233, 265, 324n1; parole 102; process 129, 134, 165, 200–1, 208, 215, 233–4, 259, 300, 303, 316–17, 322, 337–8; programs/services 28, 30, 32, 33–4, 56, 57, 60, 123, 129, 136, 141, 142, 157–8, 160, 164, 165, 190–1, 198, 200, 216, 233, 237, 239, 242, 290–1, 295, 323, 336, 368; rural 53, 60; success 116, 120, 125, 159, 160–1, 191–2, 198, 211, 213, 216, 232, 233, 235, 237, 291, 316, 318n4, 320–1, 336; transitional programs 123; women 165, 203, 210, 235
Reentry, Inc. 39; correctional industry 107, 108
rehabilitation 28, 30, 31, 33–4, 58, 66, 69, 88, 96, 102, 110, 120, 193, 194, 197, 203, 206, 212, 213, 219, 260–1, 291, 308, 309, 313, 314, 316, 317, 318n4, 329, 342, 359, 368–70, 376, 378–9, 398; *see also* reentry
religion 34, 48, 311; biblical 147; Christian 47–8, 56; ministry 44–5, 48; spiritual 120, 124, 130, 311, 312, 315, 327, 377
Republican Party 251, 262–3, **267**, 268–9, 270–1
resistance 27, 40, 42, 48–9, 54, 81, 108, 137n3, 142, 145, 172–3, 178, 180–1, 350, 373
restorative justice 103, 121–2, 227–8; practices 360, 363; restorative circles 122
Richardson vs. Ramirez (1974) 249, 255
Rikers Island 290, 320–1, 346, 348, 413
Rising Scholars 343, 384, 386, 389, 391–3
R. J. Donovan Correctional Facility 388
rural communities 53–4, 55, 100–1, 298, 325, 342

San Bernardino County 234, 236
Scott, Governor Rick 247, 262, **268**
sentencing laws, practices 109, 111, 206, 247, 248, 276, 307, 313, 325, 335, 383; determinate 109; indeterminate 211
sex crimes 209, 215–16, 219–20, 221–3, 225–6, 227, 412
sex offender registration and notification (SORN) requirements 215–16, 220–3, 224–8

420 Index

sex offenders 12, 13, 36, 66, 67, 69, 70, 71,
72, 74, 75–6, 215–16, 219, 220, 224,
225, 228, 228n1, 248, 263, 264
Shakur, Assata 173, 175–6, 178, 181–2, 328
Sing Sing Penitentiary 370–2
slavery 145, 147–9, 152, 153, 182, 255,
290, 300; post-slavery 255
social capital 55, 58, 60, 66, 71
social disorganization 360
social justice 129, 142, 175, 180, 181, 185,
247, 248, 256, 342, 358
Soledad Prison 178–9
Stack v. Boyle 347
Steinberg, Robin 349
stigma 23, 31, 41, 66, 69, 70, 72, 74, 76,
99, 107, 204–5, 207, 224, 306, 316, 365,
368, 388, 389, 391, 401, 409
Street Participatory Action Research
(Street PAR) 343, 399–400
structural violence *see* violence
substance abuse *see* drugs
super-maximum (supermax) 96–7,
99, 100–1, 102, 103n1; *see also*
administrative segregation

Temporary Assistance for Needy Families
(TANF) 151, 401; *see also* welfare
Tennessee 224, 250, **253**, 255, 257n3
T.I. 351–2
trans 220–1; transgender 142, 157, 162–4,
165–6, 413; California transgender
inmates 163; transwomen 221
transitional: community 368; facilities 192,
195, 199, 201, 301, 403; *see also* halfway
house
trauma 108, 109, 111, 143, 159, 161–2,
165, 194, 204, 205, 213, 227, 284,
291, 296, 316, 326, 327, 328, 346, 348,
360–5, 385, 411, 413; childhood abuse
55, 68, 107, 158, 194, 376; mental 85,
297, 306, 309, 312, 315, 316; pipeline to
prison 205, 232; PTSD 107, 162, 296;
prison 388; psychologically 107, 205,
327; rape 205, 306, 313; sexual abuse 46,
83, 85–6, 87, 107, 149, 158, 213, 220,
222, 228n1, 227, 275, 306; survivors/
survival 114, 165, 306, 311, 315

unemployment *see* employment
United States v. Salerno 347

violence 363–4, 372, 377, 399; domestic
385; interrupting 342, 357; physical
135, 158, 159, 300, 306, 327; partner
164, 235; prison 133–4, 137n6,
216, 348, 358; project 372, 376;
psychological 412; public health 357,
360–2; sexual abuse 148–50, 148, 150,
159, 162, 275; sexual violence 221,
224; state 109, 137n2, 142, 152, 327,
410; structural violence 150, 185, 327,
359, 397, 401, 403, 404, 406–7; violent
offender 12, 13, 57, 66, 67, 68, 69, 70–2,
73–4, 75–6, 99, 114, 216, 219, 221
Violent Crime Control and Law
Enforcement Act 96
Virginia 147, 216, 251–2, **253**, 255,
257n3, 259, 272n1
volunteers 16, 36, 41, 45, 47, 122, 227,
329, 379
Volz, Neil 263
voting *see* Amendment 4 (Florida); politics
voting rights 215–17, 247–8, 250–1,
253, 254–5, 259, 261, 263, 266,
272n1, 348, 397
Voting Rights Act of 1965 (VRA) 249

welfare: benefits 69, 70, 73–4, 75, 84–5,
215, 260, 286; policies 150; queen 151;
state 39, 40; system 165
Wetterling: Jacob Wetterling 220; the
Jacob Wetterling Crimes Against
Children and Sexually Violent
Offender Registration Act 221;
Wetterling Act 221
Wisconsin 40, 43, 48, 50
women 44–5, 46–7, 60, 72, 79, 107,
135, 157, 160, 172, 190–2, 196, 203,
210–13, 293, 298, 300, 309, 311, 324n1,
351, 353, 384, 387, 389, 393, 399, 409,
411; Black 116, 141–2, 145, 151, 172,
174, 177–8, 350, 375, 400, 412; Black
Panther Party 175–7; criminalization
of 219; disenfranchised 378; gender
identity 221; incarcerated 107, 158–9,
204–5, 208, 232, 235, 289–90, 294,
296, 299–300, 304, 349, 379, 385, 388;
offenders 80, 83, 84, 85, 107, 109, 115,
158, 161–2, 208, 296; womanhood
147–50, 151, 152–3, 153n2
work *see* employment